Science, Philosophy, and Human Behavior in the Soviet Union

SCIENCE, PHILOSOPHY,
and
HUMAN BEHAVIOR
in the SOVIET UNION

LOREN R. GRAHAM

New York
COLUMBIA UNIVERSITY PRESS
1987

An expanded, updated, and revised version of
SCIENCE AND PHILOSOPHY
IN THE SOVIET UNION

Acknowledgment is gratefully extended to the following to reprint from their works:

Academic Press, Inc.: From THE ORIGINS OF PREBIOLOGICAL SYSTEMS AND OF THEIR MOLECULAR MATRICES, edited by Sidney W. Fox. Copyright © 1965 by Academic Press, Inc. From LIFE: ITS NATURE, ORIGIN AND DEVELOPMENT, by A. I. Oparin. Copyright © 1961 by Academic Press, Inc.

Commonwealth Agricultural Bureaux, England: From THE NEW GENETICS IN THE SOVIET UNION, by P. S. Hudson and R. H. Richens.

Humanities Press Inc. and D. Reidel Publishing Company: From THE PHILOSOPHY OF QUANTUM MECHANICS, by D. J. Blokhintsev.

International Publishers Co., Inc.: From READERS IN MARXIST PHILOSOPHY, edited by Howard Selsam, *et al.* Copyright © 1963 by International Publishers Co., Inc. From DIALECTICS OF NATURE, by Friedrich Engels. Copyright 1940 by International Publishers Co., Inc.

The Macmillan Company: From THE ORIGIN OF LIFE, by A. I. Oparin (1938). From THE MYSTERY OF THE EXPANDING UNIVERSE, by William Bonnor (1964).

Pergamon Press Limited: From THE THEORY OF SPACE, TIME AND GRAVITATION, by V. A. Fock (1959). From PROCEEDINGS OF THE FIRST INTERNATIONAL SYMPOSIUM ON THE ORIGIN OF LIFE ON THE EARTH, edited by A. I. Oparin, *et al.* (1959). From PRESENT DAY RUSSIAN PSYCHOLOGY, edited by Neil O'Connor (1966).

Universe Books, Inc. and George Weidenfeld & Nicolson Ltd.: From THE ORIGIN OF LIFE, by J. B. Bernal (1967).

Book design by Laiying Chong.

Library of Congress Cataloging-in-Publication Data

Graham, Loren R.
  Science, philosophy, and human behavior in the Soviet Union.

    Bibliography: p.
    Includes index.
    1. Science—Soviet Union—History. 2. Dialectical materialism. I. Graham, Loren R. Science and philosophy in the Soviet Union. II. Title.
  Q127.S696G73 1987   509'.47   86-26357
  ISBN 0-231-06442-X

Printed in the United States of America

For
P.P.A.

CONTENTS

PREFACE

Soviet philosophy of science—dialectical materialism—is an area of intellectual endeavor that engages thousands of specialists in the Soviet Union but passes almost entirely unnoticed in the West. It is true that a few Western authors have examined Soviet discussions of individual problems in philosophy of science, such as philosophical issues of biology, or psychology; nonetheless, no one else in the last twenty-five years has tried to study in detail the relationship of dialectical materialism to Soviet science as a whole. It is an unusual experience, rewarding yet worrisome, to be the only scholar making this endeavor. The Western neglect of Soviet philosophy of science is regrettable, as the attempt to provide a synthetic view of nature in its entirety is highly intriguing. Western studies of Soviet philosophy of science that do not engage with its universalistic aspiration miss one of its important characteristics.

One reason for the lack of Western interest in Soviet dialectical materialism has been the assumption that its influence on natural science was restricted to the Stalinist period and was an unmitigated disaster. Since most educated Westerners know about the harmful effects of the form of dialectical materialism promoted by the Soviet agronomist Trofim Lysenko in the Stalinist period, such an assumption is understandable; most Westerners tend to equate the sorry episode of Lysenkoism with Soviet dialectical materialism as a whole. Over thirty years after Stalin's death and twenty years after the end of Lysenko's reign in genetics, however, Soviet dialectical materialism continues to develop.

Today, dialectical materialism is elaborated by more Soviet authors than ever before, many of them mere political ideologists, to be sure, but a few of them able and prominent natural scientists and philosophers. The desire to create a synthetic view of nature has not diminished. Furthermore, this effort touches all educated Soviet citizens. Each student in every Soviet higher educational institution is required to take a course in dialectical materialism in which a unified picture of nature based on Marxism is presented; this requirement was as prevalent in 1986 as it was in 1936, and by now has variously affected millions of Soviet citizens. In the mid-1980s the Communist Party took steps to increase the attention that was paid to Marxist philosophy in the study of natural science. No attempt to understand the mentality of the educated elite of the Soviet Union can succeed without attention to this aspect of Soviet ideology.

Despite their effort to create an integrated picture of nature, Soviet dialectical materialists of the eighties often disagree with one another; one camp, known as the "ontologists," constantly argues about the place of Marxism in science with the other camp, known as the "epistemologists" (see the discussion on pp. 58ff.). Nonetheless, dialectical materialism continues to have intellectual force. In the mid-eighties the "ontologists," the writers who insist that Soviet Marxism must explain nature as well as society, enjoyed something of a resurgence. The common Western assumption that dialectical materialism is a peculiarly Stalinist aberration that will soon disappear in the Soviet Union does not appear to be well founded.

The time will come, I believe, when the role played by natural science in the ideology of the Russian Revolution and of the regime that followed it will be seen as the most unusual characteristic of that ideology. Other great political revolutions of modern times, such as the American, French, and Chinese revolutions, have given some attention to science, but none of them resulted in a systematic, long-lived ideology concerning physical and biological nature, as has been the case with the Russian Revolution. An enormous attention to philosophy of nature has been a constant theme in Russian and Soviet Marxism for over seventy years. All of the early major Soviet leaders—Lenin, Trotsky, Bukharin, Stalin— studied science, wrote about topics as diverse as physics and psychology, and considered such issues to be intimate components of an overarching political ideology. The fourth member of this series, Stalin, converted this interest in philosophy of science into a dogmatic interpretation of natural phenomena that rivaled the scholastic system of the Catholic church in the Middle Ages. With the passing of the worst of Stalinism, the quality of Soviet philosophy of science has improved. What has not changed has been the Soviet conviction that Marxism must provide an explanation for both social and natural history.

In this book I give evidence that even now—in the 1980s—many standard science textbooks and occasional research papers in the Soviet Union have been influenced by Marxist philosophy. Sometimes the authors are aware of the influence, sometimes they are not. Occasionally the influence is a reverse one, with Soviet scientists expressing views best explained by their opposition to what they see as earlier erroneous Marxist positions. (This phenomenon is particularly clear in Soviet writings about cybernetics in the sixties and early seventies, and about human genetics today.)

I conclude that even good Soviet science bears the marks of Marxist philosophy, including "hard" sciences such as physics, a conclusion extremely difficult for most Western scientists to accept. Historians of science, more accustomed to the idea that social and political factors affect science, may find it more palatable. For the historians and sociologists of science, I would like to add that while I obviously support the "externalist" view that the social environment affects the development of science (in all nations), I do not agree with those extreme proponents of this approach who maintain that science is entirely a "social construction." The painful reentry of Soviet genetics into international biology after 1965 is evidence that a real world of nature does exist, and that social factors occasionally lead to such a marked departure from descriptions of that real world that a correction becomes necessary. But science inescapably remains under the influence of its social milieu, even after such changes in course, and cannot be accurately described as an objective mirror of nature.

Although I hope that many readers will wish to read this entire book, it is not necessary to do so in order to learn what role Marxist philosophy has played in the Soviet Union in a given scientific field. Chapters 3 through 12 are parallel chapters about different scientific disciplines, any one of which can be read separately. All readers should, however, examine chapters 1 and 2, which give necessary political and philosophical background for understanding the subsequent chapters. After reading these opening chapters, a physicist may wish to skip ahead to the chapters on quantum mechanics and relativity physics, while a psychologist, biologist, or computer scientist may go directly to the appropriate chapters for those fields.

Much of the material in this book was first published in 1972 by Alfred A. Knopf, Inc., under the title *Science and Philosophy in the Soviet Union*. In the present version I have added two entirely new chapters on human behavior, a topic omitted in the earlier book (hence the new title), and I have revised and reordered each of the other chapters, adding much new material and deleting some of the old. Soviet scientists and authors who are extensively discussed in this version who were not in the earlier volume include the philosophers I. T. Frolov, E. K.

Chernenko, K. E. Tarasov, S. A. Pastushnyi, P. V. Kopnin, V. G. Afanas'ev; the geneticists V. P. Efroimson, N. P. Dubinin, V. A Engel'gardt; the historian-ethnographer L. N. Gumilev; the psychologists A. N. Leont'ev, A. R. Luria, B. P. Nikitin; and the physicists and astrophysicists V. S. Barashenkov, V. S. Ginzburg, Ia. B. Zel'dovich and I. D. Novikov. Many other prominent Soviet scholars were discussed in the earlier book, and most of these sections have been retained in revised form. The 1972 version covered Soviet philosophy of science up to 1970; this volume includes material up to mid-1985. The most distinctive aspect of this version is the description and analysis of the most interesting development in Soviet philosophy of science in the last fifteen years: the new debate over human nature, the relative role of genetics versus environment in determining human behavior, and issues of biomedical ethics, which are covered in chapters 6 and 7.

The information presented in this book is based on repeated research trips to the Soviet Union over a period of twenty-five years, starting in 1960–61 and continuing every several years since—most recently, in December of 1985. I am indebted to a host of institutions and individuals for support during these years, including the International Research and Exchanges Board, the Department of State, the Academy of Sciences of the USSR, the National Academy of Sciences of the United States, the Institute for Advanced Study, the Guggenheim Foundation, the American Council of Learned Societies, the National Endowment for the Humanities, the Kennan Institute for Advanced Russian Studies, Columbia University, the Massachusetts Institute of Technology, and Harvard University.

As was the case with the first version, I am deeply indebted to colleagues and friends who have helped me with this volume, although no one of them has read the entire manuscript in its new form. They include: Mark Adams, Harley Balzer, Marjorie Mandelstam Balzer, Joseph Brennan, Peter Buck, Michael Cole, Sheila Cole, Paul Doty, Erich Goldhagen, Seymour Goodman, Patricia Albjerg Graham, Gregory Guroff, Thane Gustafson, Bert Hansen, Paul Josephson, Edward Keenan, Mark Kuchment, Linda Lubrano, Everett Mendelsohn, Robert Morison, Philip Pomper, David Powell, Douglas Weiner, James Wertsch, and Deborah Wilkes. I would like to pay special tribute to Carl Kaysen, Director of the Program on Science, Technology, and Society at the Massachusetts Institute of Technology, and to Adam Ulam, Director of the Russian Research Center at Harvard University, for providing such stimulating environments for conducting research.

Loren Graham
Grand Island, Lake Superior
September, 1986

CHAPTER 1

HISTORICAL OVERVIEW

> Ontological meanderings have still not been eliminated in our philosophy. On the contrary, recently they have gotten a sort of "second breath." There are plans for the conversion of Marxist philosophy into a system of ontological knowledge.
> —Two Soviet philosophers in the main
> Soviet philosophy journal, *Problems of Philosophy*, 1982.

The origin of the philosophic schools of materialism and idealism is to be found in two basic questions: What is the world made of? How do people learn about the world? These questions are among the most important ones that philosophers and scientists ask. They have been posed by thinkers for at least twenty-five hundred years, from the time of such pre-Socratic philosophers as Thales and Anaximenes.

Materialism and idealism were two of the schools of thought that developed as attempts to answer these questions. Materialists emphasized the existence of an external reality, defined as "matter," as the ultimate substance of being and the source of human knowledge; idealists emphasized the mind as the organizing source of knowledge, and often found ultimate meaning in religious values. Both schools of thought have usually been connected with political currents and often been supported by political establishments or bureaucracies. This political element has not, however, always destroyed the intellectual content of the writings of scholars addressing themselves to important philosophical questions. For example, the support of the Catholic church for the scholastic system of the Middle Ages, despite the well-known restrictions of that system, was one of the causes for the innovations in Aristotelian thought in Oxford and Paris in the fourteenth century. This new scholastic thought had an impact on subsequent scientific development, leading to a new concept of impetus, or inertia. It is the thesis of this book that despite the bureaucratic support of the Soviet state for dialectical materialism, a number of able Soviet scientists have created intellectual schemata within the framework of dialectical materialism that are sincerely held by their authors and that, furthermore, are intrinsically interesting as the most advanced developments of philosophical materialism. These natural scientists are best seen, just as in the case of the fourteenth-century scholastic thinkers, not as rebels against the prevailing philosophy, but as intellectuals who wish to refine the system, to make it more adequate as a system of explanation.

The history of materialism is to a large degree a story of exaggerations built on assumptions that in themselves have been quite valuable to science. Those assumptions have been that explanations of nature and natural events should avoid reference to spiritual elements or divine intervention,[1] should be based on belief in the sole existence of something called matter or (since relativity) matter-energy, and should to a maximum degree be verifiable by means of people's perceptions of that matter through their sense organs. The exaggerations based on these assumptions have usually been attempts to explain the unknown in terms of materialistic knowns that were quite inadequate for the task at hand. Forced to rely upon that portion of the constantly developing knowledge accepted by science at any one point in time, materialists have frequently posed hypotheses that were later properly judged to be simplistic. Examples of such simplifications—materialists' description of man as a machine in the eighteenth century, or their defense of spontaneous generation in the mid-nineteenth century—are often taken by readers of a later age as no more than amusing naivetés. But the oversimplicity of these explanations, now evident, should not cause us to forget that the accepted science of today, from which we look back upon these episodes, does not contradict the initial materialistic assumption upon which these exaggerations were constructed. It is this continuity of initial assumption that continues to sustain the materialist view.

Materialism, like its denial, is a philosophical position based on assumptions that can neither be proved nor disproved in any rigorous sense. The best that can be done for or against materialism is to make a plausible argument on the grounds of adequacy. Important scientists of modern history have included both supporters and detractors of materialism, as well as many who consider the issue irrelevant. The sophistication of a scientist's attitude toward materialism is probably more important than the actual position—for, against, or undecided—he or she chooses to take. Yet it is also probably safe to say that since the seventeenth century, supporters of materialism have forced its detractors to revise their arguments in a more fundamental way than the reverse. In that sense, the materialists have won many victories.

Within the Soviet Union in recent decades there have been a number of important discussions concerning the relation of dialectical materialism to natural science. Many outside the USSR are familiar with the genetics controversy and the part played in it by Lysenko, but few are aware of the details of other debates over human behavior, psychophysiology, origin of life, cybernetics, structural chemistry, quantum mechanics, relativity theory, and cosmology. The two editions of the present volume, which treats each of these topics at length, have been first attempts at sketching out what is the largest, most intriguing nexus of scientific-philosophical-political issues in the twentieth century. The thousands of Soviet books, articles, and pamphlets on dialectical materialism and science contain all sorts of questions deserving discussion. Historians and philosophers of science will long argue over the issues raised in these publications: Were they real issues, or were they only the artificial creations of politics? Did Marxism actually influence the thinking of scientists in the Soviet Union, or were their statements to this effect mere window dressings? Did the controversies have effects that historians and philosophers of science outside the field of Russian studies must take into account? I have posed tentative answers to these questions, based on information I have been able to obtain in the Soviet Union and elsewhere. Much of this voluminous Soviet discussion was the immediate result of political causes, but the debates have now gone far beyond the political realm into the truly intellectual sphere. The political influence is neither surprising nor unique in the history of science; it is, rather, part of that history. Marxism is taken quite seriously by some Soviet scientists, less seriously by others, and is disregarded by still others. There is even a category of Soviet philosophers and scientists who take their dialectical materialism so seriously that they refuse to accept the official statements of the Communist Party on the subject; they strive to develop their own dialectical materialist interpretations of nature, using highly technical articles as screens against the censors. Yet these authors consider themselves dialectical materialists in every sense of the term. They are criticized in the Soviet Union not only by those scientists who resist any intimation that philosophy affects their research (a category of scientist that exists everywhere), but also by the official guardians of dialectical materialism, who believe that philosophy has such effects but would leave their definition to the Party ideologues. I am convinced that dialectical materialism has influenced the work of some Soviet scientists, and that in certain cases these influences helped them to arrive at views that won them international recognition among their foreign colleagues. All of this is important to the history of science in general, and not simply to Russian studies.

One of the more specific conclusions issuing from this research is that the controversy known best outside the Soviet Union—the debate over Lysenkoism—is the least relevant to dialectical materialism in a philosophical sense. Nothing in the philosophical system of dialectical materialism lends obvious support to any of Lysenko's views. On the other hand, the controversy known least well outside the Soviet Union—that over quantum mechanics—touches dialectical materialism very closely as a philosophy of science. Not surprisingly, the terms of this particular controversy most closely approach those of discussions of quantum mechanics that have taken place in other countries.

In the genetics debate, Lysenko advanced the position that affirmed the inheritance of acquired characteristics, together with a vague theory of the "phasic development of plants." Nowhere in systematic dialectical materialism can support for these views be found.[2] The claims advanced by Lysenko were staked outside the small circle of Marxist biologists in the Soviet Union as well as outside the established groups of Soviet philosophers. Contrary to the views of a number of non-Soviet authors, there did not exist a peculiarly "Marxist" form of biology from Marx and Engels onward.[3] The concept of the inheritance of acquired characteristics was part of nineteenth-century biology, not specific to Marxism.[4] True, an assumption of the inherent plasticity of man was consonant with the desire of Soviet leaders to create a "new Soviet man," and the inheritance of characteristics acquired during one's lifetime might seem a promising function of such plasticity. Surprisingly, however, the application of Lysenkoism to human genetics was not supported in the Soviet Union; this was a common interpretation of Lysenkoism outside the Soviet Union rather than the justification for it given within that country. Close reading of Soviet sources lends no support to the view that Lysenkoism prospered because of its implications for eugenics. During the entire period of Lysenko's influence the shaping of human heredity was a subject frowned upon in the Soviet Union. The rise of Lysenkoism was the result of a long series of social, political, and economic events rather than connections with Marxist philosophy. These events, together with their results, have been well described in the works of David Joravsky and Zhores Medvedev.[5] Since the decline of Lysenkoism in the Soviet Union after 1965, however, the vestiges of that doctrine have affected discussions of other issues in the philosophy of science in a rather paradoxical way. Some Soviet biologists have been so eager to show that they disagree with Lysenko's rejection of genetics that they have elevated the role of genetics in human behavior to a level higher even than most supporters of sociobiology in the West. These Soviet geneticists have been sharply criticized by some Marxist philosophers and scientists, leading to a great debate in the seventies and eighties over nature vs. nurture (see pp. 220–244).

In the Soviet discussions over quantum mechanics an approach was made to the heart of dialectical materialism as a philosophy of science. Because of different political factors, however, the result was quite unlike that of the genetics affair. The core of dialectical materialism consists of two parts: an assumption of the independent and sole existence of matter-energy, and an assumption of a continuing process in nature in accordance with dialectical laws. Quantum mechanics, in the opinion of some scholars, undermined both parts: Its emphasis on the important role played by the observer seemed to favor philosophical idealism, while the impossibility of predicting the path of an individual particle called into question the concept of causality implicit in the assumption of a continuing process in nature. During the course of the discussions several interpretations of quantum mechanics were developed in the Soviet Union that were considered consonant with dialectical materialism. They also have interest from a scientific point of view. The Soviet theoretical physicist Fock, a frequent writer on science and dialectical materialism, debated the issue with Niels Bohr and, according to Fock, helped to shift Bohr's opinion away from emphasis on measurement to a more "realist" view (see pp. 337–338).

One of the most notable characteristics of the Soviet controversy over quantum mechanics was its similarity to the worldwide discussion on this topic. If Omel'ianovskii objected to the idea that the macrophysical system surrounding the microparticle somehow caused the particle to display the particular properties with which we describe it, so did many non-Soviet authors, such as the American philosopher Paul Feyerabend. If Blokhintsev rejected von Neumann's claim to have refuted the possibility of hidden parameters, so did some scientists elsewhere, including David Bohm. If Fock refused to accept the idea that quantum theory implied a denial of causality, so did the French scientist de Broglie and (for different reasons) the American philosopher Ernest Nagel.[6] What seems most striking in the quantum controversy is the similarity between views advanced by Soviet scientists and dialectical materialists on the one hand, and by non-Soviet scholars with rather different philosophies of science on the other. From this one might be tempted to conclude that dialectical materialism is meaningless. But one may also conclude that the concerns of dialectical materialists in the Soviet Union and those of philosophers of science in other parts of the world are in many ways similar, and that one of the reasons for this is the essential character of the problem of materialism. One should not forget the fact that the debate between materialism and idealism did not arise with the Soviet Union but is, instead, more than two thousand years old. Soviet and non-Soviet interpreters of nature frequently ask the same questions, and occasionally they give very similar answers.

Great harm was done to science in the Soviet Union, particularly to genetics, by the wedding of centralized political control to a system of philosophy with claims to universality. Observers outside the Soviet Union have frequently placed the blame for this damage on the philosophy concerned rather than on the system of political monopoly that endeavored to control it. As a philosophy of science, dialectical materialism has been significant in the Soviet Union, not in promoting or hindering fields of science as a whole, but rather in subtle areas of interpretation. Occasionally a certain formulation of Marxist philosophy of science has been converted to an official ideological statement by endorsement from Party organs. Then harmful effects have indeed occurred; the genetics controversy was the most tragic of these events.

Yet it is clear that human beings, whether in the Soviet Union or elsewhere, will never be content without asking the kinds of ultimate questions that universal systems of philosophy attempt to answer. Dialectical materialism is one of these philosophical systems. If we admit the legitimacy of asking fundamental questions about the nature of things, the approach represented by dialectical materialism—science-oriented, rational, materialistic—has some claims of superiority to available rival universal systems of thought, claims it is appropriate to receive with respect. If dialectical materialism were allowed to develop freely in the USSR, it would no doubt evolve in a direction consistent with the common assumptions of a broad nonmechanistic, nonreductionist materialism (see pp. 50ff.). Such results would be fruitful and interesting. We can hope, therefore, that the day will come when this further development of dialectical materialism can take place under conditions of free debate; such conditions would contrast both with the official protectionism found in the Soviet Union, which makes it difficult to revise dialectical materialism substantially, and the informal hostility to it existing in the United States, which makes it difficult to speak of its strengths.

HISTORICAL AND POLITICAL BACKGROUND

The revolutions of 1917 occurred in a nation that was in an extremely critical position: On a gross scale the Soviet Union was a backward and underdeveloped country in which a quick solution to the major problems of poverty and suffering was inconceivable. The USSR inherited a tradition of autocratic government that strongly influenced the new regime. The new nation was subject to overwhelming pressures of military and economic rivalries. On the European scene it was viewed jealously before the successful Bolshevik Revolution and with quite extraordinary hostility after that event. The new Soviet Union possessed an able group of intellectuals, heir to a distinguished scientific and cultural tradition, whose members were, however, forcefully opposed to the new government. The political leaders of that new government were products of a conspiratorial tradition, hardened to the use of terror by having been previously the objects of terror; they were men who possessed a world view persuasive as an explanation of their role in history and convenient as a method of discipline.

Within this troubled context it should not have been surprising that the degree of intellectual freedom that developed in Soviet Russia was substantially less than in those countries in Western Europe and North America with which the nation would be most frequently compared. The possibility of unusual controls over intellectual life was heightened soon after the revolution by the elimination of all political parties other than that of the Bolsheviks, later renamed the Communist Party of the Soviet Union. The Party soon developed a structure paralleling the government's on every level and controlling the population in almost every field of activity. The population did not object to the controls nearly so much as non-Soviet observers have proclaimed; the government enjoyed the support or toleration of a majority of the workers, a minority of the peasants, and a dedicated small group of Marxist activists. The existence of this support strengthened the freedom of action of the Party leaders in intellectual fields although the intellectuals themselves, a relatively small group, were frequently opposed to Party politics. The possibility of intervention in intellectual fields was further strengthened by the Party leaders' past expressions of strong opinions and preferences on certain issues in the arts and sciences.

Nonetheless, in the years immediately after the Revolution almost no one thought that the Communist Party's supervision of intellectuals would extend from the realm of political activity to that of scientific theory itself. Party leaders neither planned nor predicted that the Party would approve or support certain viewpoints internal to science; indeed, such endorsement was fundamentally opposed by all the important leaders of the Party. A specific Soviet Marxist philosophy of nature does not necessarily entail official pronouncements on scientific issues; indeed, a condition free of such entailment actually obtained in the early 1920s, in the late fifties and sixties for all the sciences except genetics, and for genetics as well since 1965. Besides, among Soviet scientists and philosophers there never was a single interpretation of Marxist philosophy of science.

During the early period of Soviet history known as that of the New Economic Policy (NEP), which lasted from 1921 to 1926, the intellectual scene was relatively relaxed. Usually, so long as scholars and artists refrained from political activity offensive to the Communist Party, they did not need to fear persecution by the police or interference from ideologists. Those persons whose backgrounds or previous political activities were considered particularly incriminating were exceptions to this generalization. But even people who previously had been members of non-Bolshevik political parties, as well as those with past connections to the tsarist bureaucracy, were able to maintain positions in cultural and educational institutions. The universities, the Academy of Sciences, health organizations, archives, and libraries all served as relatively secure refuges for "former people," most of whom sought no more than living out their lives uneventfully under the drastically new conditions.

In the second half of the 1920s, there emerged two developments of critical significance for the future of the Soviet Union: the struggle between the leaders of the Party culminating in the ascendance of Stalin, and a decision to embark on ambitious industrialization and collectivization programs. The story of the rise of Stalin to supreme power has been told innumerable times (although there are many aspects of it that are still unclear), and no attempt will be made to retell that history here. But Stalin's personal influence on subsequent developments in the intellectual world of the Soviet Union proved to be of tremendous importance. His intellectual predilections had impact on a number of fields, including certain areas of science. Most foreign historians of the Soviet Union have doubted that ideology played an important role in determining Stalin's actions, preferring to believe that power considerations dominated his choices. These historians have noticed how Stalin retreated from ideological positions when such shifts seemed desirable from a practical standpoint, and they cite as an example the turn in the Soviet government's attitude toward the Church. More recent study of Stalin has indicated, however, that a simple interpretation of the man in terms of power is insufficient to explain him. Leader of the Soviet Union for a quarter of a century, Stalin was governed by a complex mixture of motivations. These drives were power-oriented in many respects, but they also contained ideological elements. Important leaders often combine ideological and power factors in their decisions; the history of the popes of the Catholic church, of many crowned rulers of Europe, and of leaders of modern capitalist countries illustrates this interplay of power and idea. In Stalin the ideological and power-oriented factors combined; moreover, the actual political power he possessed was truly extraordinary, and he used it with increasing arbitrariness.

The traumatic break that occurred in the years 1927–29, the abrupt shock of an industrial, agricultural, and cultural revolution, will always be causally linked with Stalin. True, it was not only Stalin but almost all of the Soviet leaders who had declared the need to industrialize rapidly and to reform cultural institutions. But it was Stalin who in large part determined the specific forms and tempos of these campaigns, and these in the end became as important as the campaigns themselves. Of the varieties of rapid industrialization programs proposed in the second half of the twenties, Stalin supported the most strenuous course; his choice required forcible methods for enactment. Similarly, Stalin's collectivization program in agriculture was breathtaking in its tempo and staggering in its violence. Ten years after Stalin's death, Soviet historians permitted themselves to observe on occasion that Stalin's agricultural collectivization program had been premature and coercive, however much they agreed with its goal of creating large farms tilled by collective labor.[7]

Accompanying the industrial and agricultural campaigns was the cultural revolution. Personnel of educational and scientific institutions were submitted to political examinations and purges. Here purge must be taken to mean not only imprisonment or execution, but the almost equally tragic dismissal of personnel from academic positions. Functionally, the purge had begun in Soviet academic institutions as a means of personnel replacement, often supported by young Communists eager for advancement. In the late 1920s, this renovative technique was used to oust bourgeois academicians of certain institutions in order to replace them with supporters of the Communist Party. These replacements were frequently persons of inferior scholarship whose enthusiasm for social reconstruction commended them to preferment. Later, under Stalin's complete control, the purge became quite arbitrary and violent. Dismissal and exile to labor camps were more common among social scientists than among natural scientists, but even in the institutions of the natural sciences a structure of control was created. In the period 1929–1932, the Academy of Sciences was thoroughly renovated and brought under the control of the Communist Party.[8] Even at this time, however, no attempt was made to impose ideological interpretations upon the work of scientists; nonetheless, the precedent of forcing submission to specific political, social, and economic campaign pressures would later prove to be significant, especially immediately after World War II, when the ideological issues in the sciences became most aggravated.

The passing of the twenties into the thirties in the Soviet Union was marked by a growing tendency to classify science itself as "bourgeois" or "idealistic"—clearly something beyond the distinguishing of certain philosophers' interpretations of science. While this tendency is now the subject of sharp criticism on the part of several leading Soviet philosophers of science, it had a long and harmful influence on Soviet science.[9] The attribution of political character to the body of science itself eased the way for Lysenko's concept of "two biologies," as well as for ideological attacks on the substance of other branches of natural science. As early as 1926, V. P. Egorshin, writing in *Under the Banner of Marxism*, an influential philosophy journal of the time, declared that "modern natural science is just as much a class phenomenon as philosophy and art. . . . It is bourgeois in its theoretical foundations."[10] And an editorial in the journal *Natural Science and Marxism* in 1930 asserted that "philosophy and the natural and mathematical sciences are just as politically partisan as the economic and historical sciences."[11]

Not all Soviet philosophers and very few Soviet scientists accepted the assumption that the natural sciences contained political elements in themselves and the corollary that Western science was implicitly distinct from Soviet science. Many scientists and philosophers of the strongest Marxist persuasion were still capable of drawing distinctions between science and the uses made of it, whether moral or philosophical. Even those who thought, with justification, that the theoretical body of science cannot be completely separated from philosophical issues usually realized that any attempt to determine those issues by political means would be quite harmful. The prominent Marxist scientist O. Iu. Schmidt, who will appear as an important participant in the cosmology debate, declared in 1929 that:

> Western science is not monolithic. It would be a great mistake indiscriminately to label it "bourgeois" or "idealistic." Lenin distinguished uncon-

scious materialists, who included most experimenters of his time, from idealists. . . . An unconscious attraction to the dialectic is growing. . . . There are no conscious dialectical materialists in the West, but elements of the dialectic appear among very many scientific thinkers, often in idealistic or eclectic garb. Our task is to find these kernels and to refine and use them.[12]

The debates over the nature of science in the late twenties and in the thirties did not touch most practicing Soviet scientists of the period. The majority of researchers tried to remain as far from considerations of philosophy and politics as scientists elsewhere. The importance of these discussions was not their immediate impact but the precedent they provided for the much sharper ideological debates of the postwar period, when Stalin accepted Lysenko's definition of "two biologies" and intervened personally in choosing between them. Without Stalin's arbitrary action the actual suppression of genetics in the Soviet Union would not have occurred, but the discussions of the thirties helped to prepare the way for the suppression by strengthening the suspicion in which Western science was held by some Soviet critics.

Another characteristic of Soviet discussions of the thirties that re-emerged after World War II was the emphasis on utility. In a nation rapidly modernizing in the face of external threats, the priority of practical concerns was not only understandable but necessary. As is often the case with underdeveloped nations that nonetheless possess a small highly educated stratum, Russia's past scientific tradition had been excessively theoretical. The emphasis on industrial and agricultural concerns in the thirties was a needed correction to this tradition. At its root, the high priority given to practice had a positive moral content, since the ultimate results of a growing economy were a higher standard of living, greater educational opportunities, and better social welfare. So long as the value of theoretical science was also recognized, a relative shift toward applied science was a helpful temporary stage. The new priority was carried to an extreme, however, and had results that were philistine and anti-intellectual. In art and literature the stress on in-dustrial expansion buttressed "socialist realism," the art style supplanting the earlier experimental forms that sprouted immediately after the Revolution. Socialist realism commended itself to the bureaucrats who were gradually replacing the more sophisticated and cosmopolitan older revolutionaries. The situation in the arts in these years was only in-directly related to that of the sciences, but it was nonetheless a significant aspect of the general environment of the Soviet intellectual. Analogous to the desired artistic concentration on themes calculated to inspire the workers aesthetically and emotionally was the role assigned to scientists as discoverers of new means to speed industrialization. Many scientists who had been trained in highly theoretical areas found themselves in the thirties closely involved with the industrialization effort. In addition to their research duties, they began to serve as industrial consultants.

Thus, a result of the industrialization and collectivization efforts in the Soviet Union was an increase in pressure upon scientists and intellectuals to mold their interests so that their work would benefit the construction of "socialism in one country." One of the effects of this pressure was the growth of nationalism in science, as in other fields. The very possibility of constructing socialism in one country had, of course, been the subject of one of the great debates among Stalin and his fellow leaders. The original revolutionaries had believed that the Revolution in Russia would fail unless similar revolutions occurred in other more advanced countries. Stalin announced that socialism could be constructed in one country and called for reliance upon native resources, scientific and otherwise. This shift in emphasis represented a weakening of the internationalist strain in the Communist movement that historians have linked with the name of Trotsky and that resulted, among other things, in a greater isolation of Soviet scientists. Stalin called for a maximum effort by all Soviet workers, including scientists, to achieve the nearly impossible—to make the Soviet Union a great industrial and military power in ten or fifteen years. An intrinsic part of this effort, Soviet nationalism, gradually gained strength in the thirties as the possibility of a military confrontation with Nazi Germany grew.

During World War II, as a result of stress upon patriotism and heroism, the nationalist element in Soviet attitudes emerged all the more clearly. In science, this emphasis on national achievement had many effects. Into controversies over scientific interpretation it introduced an element, national pride, that was totally absent from the dialectical materialism derived from Marx, Engels, and Lenin. It resulted in claims for national priority in many fields of science and technology. Many of these claims have now been abandoned in the Soviet Union, where they are regarded as consequences of the "cult of the personality." Others have been retained. Of these, some are justified or at least arguable in light of the long years in which appreciation of Russian science and technology by non-Russians was obstructed by linguistic barriers, ethnic prejudices, and simple ignorance.

Perhaps the most important characteristic of Soviet society contributing to the peculiar situation that developed in the sciences after World

War II was the very high degree of centralization of control over public information, personnel assignment and promotion, academic research and instruction, and scientific publishing. This system of control had been completed long before Stalin decided to intervene directly in the biology dispute after the war. Indeed, any effort actively to oppose this awesome accumulation of power became unthinkable during the great purges of the thirties, when it became clear that not even the highest and most honored officials of the Party were immune to Stalin's punitive power. The atmosphere created by these events permeated all institutions of Soviet society. People on lower levels of power looked to those above for signals indicating current policy; as soon as these signals were discernible, the subordinates hurried to follow them. By the late thirties, for example, no local newspaper would have thought of contradicting or questioning a policy announced in *Pravda*, the official publication of the Central Committee of the Communist Party. Censorship was not left, however, to voluntary execution; it was officially institutionalized and extended even to scientific journals, although the limits of toleration there were usually greater and varied from time to time somewhat more than elsewhere. Appointment of officials influential in science and education—ministers of education and agriculture, presidents of the All-Union Academy of Sciences and of other specialized academies, rectors of the universities, editorial boards of journals—all were under the control of Party organs. Approval of science textbooks for use in the school system and even the awarding of scientific degrees to individual scholars were also under close political supervision. All these features of the Soviet power structure help explain the way in which Stalin was able, after the war, to give Lysenko's interpretation of biology official status despite the opposition of established geneticists, men of science who fully recognized the intellectual poverty of Lysenkoism.

The above description of the centralization of power in Soviet society is familiar to all students of Soviet history. What is much less well known, and indeed frequently entirely overlooked, is that beneath this overlay of centralized political power there existed among the Soviet population rather widespread support for the fundamental principles of the Soviet economy, and among intellectuals, increasing support for a materialist interpretation of the social and natural sciences. Studies of refugees from the Soviet Union during World War II have shown that despite a large degree of disaffection toward the political actualities of the Soviet Union, these people remained convinced, by and large, of

the superiority of a socialist economic order.[13] Similarly, there is much
evidence that Soviet intellectuals of genuine ability and achievement
found historical and dialectical materialist explanations of nature to be
persuasive on conceptual grounds. O. Iu. Schmidt, I. I. Agol, S. Iu.
Semkovskii, A. S. Serebrovskii, A. R. Luria, A. I. Oparin, L. S. Vygotsky,
and S. L. Rubinshtein are examples of distinguished Soviet scholars
who made clear their belief, in diverse ways, that Marxism was relevant
to their work before statements of the relevance of Marxism were
required of them. The views of Schmidt, Oparin, Luria, Vygotsky, and
Rubinshtein will be discussed in some detail later, since their views
continued to be influential after 1945. In the concerns of these men,
science came first, politics second. But one should not assume that the
presence of strong political motivation necessarily undermines the intellectual value of a person's views. Nikolai Bukharin, a Party leader,
was a Soviet politician to whom a materialistic, naturalistic approach
to reality was far more than rhetoric; portions of his writings are
remarkable for the degree to which they draw upon a materialist
interpretation of natural science and for the intellectual clarity with
which this view is presented.[14]

Several of the persons named above, and many more of their type,
disappeared in the purges and had their writings banned in the Soviet
Union. But unless one remembers that there existed before the forties
a category of Soviet scholars who took dialectical materialism seriously,
it will be difficult to understand why, after the passing of the worst
features of Stalinism, scientists reemerged in the Soviet Union who
combined a dialectical materialist interpretation of nature with normal
standards of scientific integrity.

Immediately after World War II many intellectuals in the Soviet Union
hoped for a relaxation of the system of controls that had developed
during the strenuous industrialization and military mobilizations. Instead, there followed the darkest period of state interference in artistic
and scientific realms. This postwar tightening of ideological controls
spread rather quickly from the fields of literature and art to philosophy,
then finally to science itself. Causal factors already mentioned include
the prewar suspicion of bourgeois science, the extremely centralized
Soviet political system, and the personal role of Stalin. But there was
another condition that exacerbated the ideological tension: the cold war
between the Soviet Union and certain Western nations, particularly the
United States. This struggle was rising to a peak in the years immediately

following the war.[15] These were years in which ideological sensitivity ran feverishly high in both the United States and the Soviet Union; the two great countries reinforced each other's fears and prejudices. The cold war involved passions of a sort reminiscent of past quarrels over religion. The Soviet suppression of genetics in 1948 has often been compared to the Catholic condemnation of Copernicus in 1616. The Catholic sensitivity to the astronomy issue at the time was in part a reaction to pressures upon the Church brought about by the Protestant Reformation.[16] Similarly (although allowing for enormous differences), in the late 1940s the Soviet Union considered itself in the midst of a global ideological struggle, and the cold war produced emotions not unlike those current during the Counter-Reformation.

"Zhdanovshchina" is the name by which the postwar ideological campaign came to be known; it was named for Andrei A. Zhdanov, Stalin's assistant in the Central Committee of the Party. Most Western historians of the Soviet Union believe that Zhdanov was in some personal way responsible for the ideological restrictions in all areas of culture, including science. There is, however, reason to doubt that Zhdanov was responsible for ideological interference in the sciences. Evidence exists that Zhdanov actually opposed the Party's intervention in Lysenko's favor, and even attempted to stop it.[17] In any event, we know that Zhdanov carried out a campaign of intimidation and proscription in literature and the arts. A series of decrees laid down ideological guides for fiction writers, theater critics, economists, philosophers, playwrights, film directors, and even musicians. Until the month of Zhdanov's death, however, natural scientists escaped the rule by decree that obtained in other cultural fields.

When Lysenko's views of biology were officially approved in August 1948—an event to be reviewed in some detail in my analysis of the genetics controversy—a shock wave ran through the entire Soviet scientific community. No longer could it be hoped that Party organs would distinguish between science and philosophical interpretations of science. Evidently Stalin had no intention of making such distinctions, and he was in control of the Party. It soon became clear that other scientific fields, such as physics and physiology, were also objects of ideological attack, and Soviet scientists were genuinely fearful that each field would produce its own particular Lysenko.

Soviet scientists now found themselves in a difficult dilemma. By this time the Party's control over scholarly institutions was almost absolute. Open resistance to the Party's supervision was possible only if the resisters were prepared to sacrifice themselves entirely; opposition to Party control usually meant professional ruin and imprisonment in labor camps. A few scientists resisted openly and met the fate of the geneticist N. I. Vavilov, who was destroyed even before the war. Another approach was taken by a relatively small but quite influential group of scientists who decided to meet the ideological onslaught by defending their respective sciences from within the framework of dialectical materialism. Their subsequent accomplishment was genuine, significant, and intellectually interesting; a good part of this book concerns their feat. What many non-Soviet observers have failed to see is that this defense of science from the position of dialectical materialism was not merely a tactic or an intellectual deceit; the leaders of this movement—whose names will be mentioned many times in this book—were sincere in their defense of materialism. As Soviet observers frequently say, "their dialectical materialism was internal." They included Soviet scientists with eminent international reputations. A few associates of this group may have been initially hypocritical in their approach, willing to use any terminology or any philosophical system that would save their science from the fate of Lysenkoism. But the majority, certainly including those who had even before the war been interested in dialectical materialism, as well as a new group now making their previous materialistic views explicit, saw no contradiction between science and a sophisticated form of materialism. In speaking of dialectical materialism and science as congenial intellectual frameworks, they did not think they were compromising their professional integrity. Indeed, they strove to increase the sophistication of both Soviet natural science and Soviet philosophy, and in both goals they eventually had genuine success. They were assisted by those professional philosophers who saw the validity of this defense of scholarship and who greeted the work of these scientists as a contribution to a philosophical understanding of science.[18]

The scientists of the immediate post-World War II period began reading Marx and Engels on philosophical materialism in order better to answer their ideological critics. They developed arguments more incisive than those of their Stalinist opponents; they constructed defenses that exposed the fallacies of their official critics yet were in accord with philosophical materialism and—most important of all—preserved the cores of their sciences. They were even willing to examine the methodological principles and terminological frameworks of their sciences, revising them if necessary. As scientists they now had a stake of self-interest in the philosophy of science. They took heart in the defeat, even while Stalin was alive, of G. V. Chelintsev, a mediocre chemist who tried to win the position of a Lysenko in chemistry at an All-Union conference that bore some resemblance to the 1948 biology conference (see pp. 298ff.). They turned back the ideological campaigns in relativity physics and quantum mechanics by developing materialist interpretations of these unsettling developments in physical theory and stoutly resisting attempts to displace them. Some eventually became personally committed to these interpretations, continuing to defend them long after Stalin's death. During these later years, younger scholars, both scientists and philosophers, joined the discussion. For them, motives of self-defense were no longer overriding in importance. The intellectual issues themselves emerged more fully. A comprehensive and cogent philosophy of science was being created.

Since the scientists were frequently people of genuine intellectual distinction and deep knowledge of their fields, and since science does contain serious and legitimate problems of philosophical interpretation, it was only natural that the entrance of the scientists into the debates would result in discussions important in their own right. Outside the field of genetics—where the issues remained on a very primitive level until the final overthrow of Lysenko—many of the discussions in the Soviet Union contained authentic issues of philosophical interpretation. These issues included, in the physical sciences, the problem of causality, the role of the observer in measurement, the concept of complementarity, the nature of space and time, the origin and structure of the universe, and the role of models in scientific explanation. In the biological sciences, relevant problems included those of the origin of life, the nature of evolution, and the problem of reductionism. In physiology and psychology, discussions arose concerning the nature of consciousness, the question of determinism and free will, the mind-body problem, and the validity of materialism as an approach to psychology. In cybernetics, problems concerned the nature of information, the universality of the cybernetics approach, and the potentiality of computers.

Occasionally the Soviet philosophers made genuine contributions to the discussions, even though Soviet scientists often directed well-deserved criticism against them. It is worth noticing that the worst threats to Soviet science in the late forties and early fifties did not come, as is often thought, from professional philosophers, but from third-rate scientists who tried to win Stalin's favor. These people included T. D. Lysenko in genetics, G. V. Chelintsev in chemistry, A. A. Maksimov and R. Ia. Shteinman in physics, and O. B. Lepeshinskaia in cytology.[19] These persons were criticized by both scientists and philosophers whenever political conditions permitted. What was going on in the worst period of the ideological invasion of science was not primarily a struggle between philosophers and scientists. It was a struggle, crossing these academic lines on both sides, between genuine scholars on the one hand and ignorant careerists and ideological zealots on the other.

As the ideological campaign of 1948–1953 receded into the past, it became less and less a determining factor in Soviet discussions of the relationship of science and philosophy. To be sure, censorship is still a universal fact in the Soviet Union. Genetics did not regain full status until 1965, and even now that science suffers the effects of its years of suppression. Anti-Semitism also continues to plague Soviet intellectual life, and grew in intensity in the seventies and eighties. Furthermore, the repression of dissident Soviet scientists showed that the regime would not tolerate independent political activities on the part of its scientists. Nonetheless, after the mid-sixties most technical disciplines regained that rather large degree of autonomy they enjoyed before World War II. Science was much more free than literature and the arts. So long as Soviet scientists stayed clear of political issues such as human rights, international relations, and the reform of the Soviet system, they could expect little interference in their professional work. With the exception of their right to travel abroad, a fairly normal intellectual life prevailed in the natural sciences, and this normality extended on many technical issues to the philosophy of science as well.

A scholar outside the Soviet Union might assume that a normal intellectual life among Soviet scientists would mean their dropping all interest in dialectical materialism. A number of Soviet scientists who were earlier involved in ideological discussions have, indeed, returned entirely to research work or scientific administration. But the most striking characteristic of the recent period has been the degree to which discussions in the philosophy of science have continued and even expanded. The professional philosophers have played a larger and wiser role than previously, but natural scientists have also continued to be involved in the discussions. In philosophy of physics, for example, important books were written in the late 1970s and early 1980s by physicists such as V. L. Ginsburg, P. L. Kapitsa, M. A. Markov and B. S. Barashenkov.[20] All these authors were known internationally for their work in physics, and the first two were eminent.

Professional philosophers have also been active in epistemological and methodological problems of physics. Leading authors in this area recently have been M. E. Omel'ianovskii, E. M. Chudinov, S. B. Krymskii, E. A. Mamchur, V. S. Stepin, L. B. Bazhenov, M. D. Akhundov, V. S. Gott, and A. I. Panchenko.[21] Several of these philosophers, including Omel'ianovkskii, Chudinov, and Bazhenov, will be discussed elsewhere in this book. A particularly interesting philosopher of science who wrote on these issues in the seventies and eighties was M. D. Akhundov, a student of Omel'ianovskii. Akhundov's first book, entitled *The Problem of the Discreteness and Indiscreteness of Space and Time*, published in 1974, was a successful effort to trace and analyze throughout the history of science descriptions of the universe in terms of either a continuum or of atomistic concepts. His second book, entitled *Concepts of Space and Time: Origins, Evolution, Prospects*, published in 1982, was an original interpretation of space and time in different cultures with a final section giving a philosophical analysis of contemporary concepts of space and time. Akhundov believed that the study of spatial and temporal concepts among children and among people with pathological disabilities is useful for understanding the way in which these concepts have changed over history in different sociocultural settings.

By placing emphasis on the problem of cognition rather than on nature philosophy, Akhundov strengthened the position of those Soviet philosophers of science who wish to stress epistemological problems and want to avoid evaluating physics itself, leaving that function to the physicists. Indeed, Akhundov and two other Soviet philosophers in 1981 wrote in an article summarizing recent Soviet philosophy of science: "A definite demarcation of sorts is occurring between purely physical and philosophical problems, and the latter are gradually gaining priority. If the majority of works of the previous decade was characterized by an intimate intertwining of physical and philosophical problems and a certain predominance of the former, then today we observe a familiar evolution toward consideration of purely philosophical issues, i.e., an increase in the quality of research."[22]

Despite the clear signs of improvement in technical areas, Soviet philosophy of science during the seventies and eighties developed in an uneven and contradictory way.[23] While the quality of specialized works in concrete areas of science continued to rise, this improvement was accompanied by growing political difficulties which threatened the gains made in the intellectual sphere. Furthermore, in recent years disturbing signs of a resurgence of a form of neo-Stalinist thought among a few philosophers of science led to the outbreak of sharp controversy in the discipline. The changes of regime marked by the deaths of Leonid Brezhnev, Iurii Andropov, and Konstantin Chernenko in, respectively, 1982, 1984, and 1985, and the resulting shifts in the leadership of philosophical institutions left the development of philosophy in the Soviet Union in a very indefinite state.

The healthiest period in Soviet philosophy of science during the last twenty years was from 1968 to 1977. During that time the editor of the main Soviet philosophy journal, *Problems of Philosophy*, was I. T. Frolov, the philosopher who made his reputation by writing a strong attack on Lysenkoist biology in 1968, which I have discussed on pp. 152–153. Taking over the editorship of the journal at the peak of his popularity following his critique of Lysenkoism, Frolov set about refreshing Soviet philosophy of science by establishing closer ties with the rest of the scientific community. Because of his reputation as a philosopher who opposed ideological interference in science, he was able to arrange meetings between philosophers and leading natural scientists who in the past had usually stayed away from the dialectical materialists. The reports of these meetings, printed in the journal in a regular feature entitled "The Round Table," changed the tone of Soviet philosophy in a marked fashion. Here was visible evidence that Soviet philosophers genuinely wished to make contact with the best natural scientists in the country in order to continue to try to overcome the legacy of Stalinism in philosophy.

Frolov was helped in his endeavor to modernize dialectical materialism by the presence in the late sixties and early seventies of a group of like-minded philosophers in the Institute of Philosophy of the Academy of Sciences, including its director, P. V. Kopnin; the historian and philosopher of science B. M. Kedrov, who had in the immediate post-World War II period made an unsuccessful similar effort; the philosopher of physics, M. E. Omel'ianovskii; and several other researchers in philosophy, including E. M. Chudinov and L. B. Bazhenov. While these scholars did not all agree with one another, they were united by the wish to avoid the infamous "dialectics of nature" approach that had, in the previous generation, often led to infringements on scientific research in the name of philosophy. The reformers of the sixties and early seventies wanted to concentrate on specifically philosophical questions, and leave the content of science to the natural scientists.

This school of thought still reigns among the professional philosophers of science centered in the Institute of Philosophy of the Academy of

Sciences of the USSR, but in recent years this viewpoint has lost several of its most influential leaders and has been challenged intellectually. The deaths of P. V. Kopnin, M. E. Omel'ianovskii, E. M. Chudinov, and B. M. Kedrov in 1971, 1979, 1980, and 1985, respectively, were serious blows to the reformers. Kopnin was replaced as director of the Institute of Philosophy by B. S. Ukraintsev, a much more orthodox thinker who once published a book jointly with G. V. Platonov, an old Lysenkoite who was a leading critic of the reformers.[24] In 1977, in turn, Frolov was replaced as editor of *Problems of Philosophy* by V. S. Semenov, who made a few half-hearted attempts to continue "The Round Table" but was never able to give the series the sort of intellectual vitality that it had under Frolov's direction.

Frolov remained a member of the editorial board, but he knew that his reformist views on the relationship of science and Marxist philosophy had suffered a setback; from this time on he shifted his interest from genetics to "global problems," i.e., the challenges to all industrialized nations in areas such as environment, energy, biomedical ethics, third world development, and technology assessment. In 1986 Frolov became editor of the leading Communist Party journal *Kommunist.* I have discussed his views on biomedical ethics on pp. 260ff.

Frolov did not, however, escape controversy by transferring his interests from philosophy of biology to global problems. The study of such problems was viewed by the old-fashioned ideologists as unorthodox; the dogmatists criticized the assumption made by most "globalists" like Frolov that the problems of industrialized nations transcend class and economic rivalries to such a degree that traditional rivals such as the United States and the Soviet Union should work together. In the mid-seventies, however, at the height of detente between these two nations, Frolov and his colleagues were able to defend such an assumption as quite reasonable. On the basis of expanding scientific and technical exchanges between the United States and the USSR dozens of study groups worked jointly on such problems as pollution of the environment, cardiovascular health, transportation, solar energy, and space research.[25] With the decline of detente in the late seventies, however, the opinions of the orthodox ideologists who maintained that ideological conflicts can never be transcended gained in influence.

Soviet philosophy of science in the seventies and eighties was increasingly divided into two schools of thought, called in the Soviet Union "the epistemologists" and "the ontologists." Although these philosophical terms give the controversy an academic sound, the underlying issue was highly political. The epistemologists were those philosophers who made a distinction between philosophical and scientific issues, and criticized the older generation of Soviet philosophers and scientists for confusing those two kinds of questions. To the epistemologists, the proper concerns for philosophers of science were such questions as cognition, logic, methodology, and theory of knowledge. They believed it quite improper for philosophers of science to discuss such issues as whether various theories of the creation of the universe were reconcilable with Marxism, believing that by taking stands on such topics the philosophers not only got involved in judging scientific theories—something they thought should be left to the natural scientists—but also risked damaging Marxism by linking it to scientific theories later judged wrong by the scientists. The ontologists, on the other hand, continued to defend the view that dialectical materialism was the "most general science of nature and society" and therefore that dialectical laws could be seen operating in the inorganic and organic matter studied by chemists, physicists, and biologists. To the ontologists it was not only proper, but essential, to find evidence of the validity of dialectical materialism in the research findings and theories of natural scientists. The ontologists were usually willing to admit that the issues studied by the epistemologists were also legitimate ones for Marxist philosophers, but their real interest lay in dialectics of nature.

This dispute is currently a major one in Soviet philosophy. It is discussed in detail in subsequent chapters. While the controversy is discounted as intellectually not interesting by some of the leading research philosophers, it is crucially important from a political standpoint. The main issue is the relationship between natural science and philosophy, one of the critical questions in Soviet intellectual life for more than half a century. The outcome is still not clear. The leadership of the Institute of Philosophy in the mid-eighties seemed to be making some effort to shift research attention away from questions of natural science toward issues in social science. The director of the Institute in 1984 and 1985, G. L. Smirnov, was an expert on political philosophy, not philosophy of science. In late 1985 Smirnov was promoted by Party head Mikhail Gorbachev to a new position as advisor to the Central Committee. In 1986 N. I. Lapin, a specialist on Karl Marx and systems analysis, succeeded Smirnov as director of the Institute of Philosophy. These shifts toward political and social concerns and away from traditional Soviet philosophy of science indicate that the significance of the dispute between the ontologists and the epistemologists may diminish. However, the habit of debating dialectics of nature is so well established in the Soviet Union that dramatic changes are not likely to happen soon. Recent Soviet publications illustrate that the debate between the ontologists and the epistemologists is continuing.

CHAPTER 2

DIALECTICAL MATERIALISM IN THE SOVIET UNION: ITS DEVELOPMENT AS A PHILOSOPHY OF SCIENCE

Marxist dialectic is not a collection of rules: You don't just directly apply it to a specific problem and receive a direct answer. No, the Marxist dialectic is something else; it is a general orientation and culture of thought that helps each person to pose a problem with greater clarity and purpose and thereby helps him to solve the riddles of nature.

—N. N. Semenov
Soviet Nobel-laureate chemist, 1968.

DIALECTICAL MATERIALISM: SOVIET OR MARXIST?

Contemporary Soviet dialectical materialism as a philosophy of science is an effort to explain the world by combining these principles: All that exists is real; this real world consists of matter-energy; and this matter-energy develops in accordance with universal regularities or laws. A professional philosopher would say, therefore, that dialectical materialism combines a realist epistemology, an ontology based on matter-energy, and a process philosophy stated in terms of dialectical laws.

Dialectical materialism incorporates features of both absoluteness and relativity, of both an Aristotelian commitment to the immutable and independent and a Heraclitean belief in flux. To its defenders, this combination of opposite tendencies is a source of flexibility, strength, and truth; to its detractors, it is evidence of ambiguity, vagueness, and falseness.

Dialectical materialism has usually been discussed as if it were a uniquely Soviet creation, far from the traditions of Western philosophy. It is true that the term "dialectical materialism" comes from a Russian and not from Marx, Engels, or their Western European followers. It is also true, of course, that Soviet dialectical materialism has acquired characteristics that are only explicable in terms of, first, its revolutionary, and later, its institutional setting. But the roots of dialectical materialism extend back to the beginning of the history of thought, at least to the Milesian philosophers, and continue forward as subdued, changing, but reappearing strands in the history of philosophy. It is not possible to present here a discussion of the origins of dialectical materialism, which would constitute a large book in itself; nonetheless, many similarities between dialectical materialism and previous currents of European philosophy will appear in the following pages.

The term "dialectical materialism" was first used in 1891 by G. V. Plekhanov, a man frequently called the father of Russian Marxism.[1] Marx and Engels utilized terms such as "modern materialism" or "the new materialism" to distinguish their philosophical orientation from that of classical materialists such as Democritus or thinkers of the French Enlightenment such as La Mettrie or Holbach. Engels did speak, however, of the dialectical nature of modern materialism.[2] Lenin adopted the phrase used by Plekhanov, "dialectical materialism."

The basic writings of Marx, Engels, and Lenin on the philosophic and social aspects of science are Engels' *Anti-Dühring*, printed first as a series of articles in 1877; his *Dialectics of Nature*, written in 1873–1883 but not printed until 1925; his *Ludwig Feuerbach and the End of Classical German Philosophy*, published as a series of articles in 1886 and as a pamphlet in 1888; Marx's doctoral dissertation, written in 1839–1841 and first published in 1902; pieces of the correspondence of Marx and Engels; a few sections of Marx's *Capital*; Lenin's *Materialism and Empirio-Criticism*, published in 1908; his *Philosophical Notebooks*, published in 1925–29 and later, in a complete form, in 1933; and fragments from his correspondence and speeches.[3] Marx also left a number of unpublished manuscripts concerning science, technology, and mathematics, most of which are now in the Institute of Marxism-Leninism in Moscow. Some of these appeared in print only in the late 1960s.[4] Together all these writings establish the basis of dialectical materialism as it is usually discussed in the Soviet Union, with the older writings obviously playing a more formative role than the newer ones. In this rather large body of material written over a period of many decades by different authors for different purposes one can find a considerable diversity of viewpoints and even contradictions on fairly important questions. The dates of publication of the various works and the context in which each was composed are quite important in gaining an understanding of the evolution, modification, and structure of Soviet Marxist thought on the nature of science.

Although the primary interests of Marx and Engels were always in economics, politics, and history, they both devoted a surprisingly large segment of their time to the scrutiny of scientific theory, and cooperated in publishing their views on science. Engels described their background in the sciences:

> Marx and I were pretty well the only people to rescue conscious dialectics from German idealist philosophy and apply it in the materialist conception of nature and history. . . . But a knowledge of mathematics and natural science is essential to a conception of nature which is dialectical and at the same time materialist. Marx was well versed in mathematics, but we could only partially, intermittently and sporadically keep up with the natural sciences. For this reason, when I retired from business and transferred my home to London, thus enabling myself to give the necessary time to it, I went through as complete as possible a "moulting" as Liebig calls it, in mathematics and natural sciences, and spent the best part of eight years on it.[5]

Engels was much more important in elaborating the Marxist philosophy of nature than was Marx. This commitment to the study of the natural sciences as well as the social sciences was, in Engels' mind, a necessary consequence of the fact that man is, in the final analysis, a part of nature; the most general principles of nature must, therefore, be applicable to man. The search for these most general principles, based on knowledge of science itself, was a philosophic enterprise. Engels believed that by means of a knowledge of a philosophy that was materialistic, dialectical, and grounded in the sciences, both natural scientists and social scientists would be aided in their work. Those natural scientists who maintained that they worked without relying on philosophical principles were deluded; better to form consciously a philosophy of science, Engels thought, than to pretend to avoid one:

> Natural scientists may adopt whatever attitude they please, they will still be under the domination of philosophy. It is only a question whether they want to be dominated by a bad, fashionable philosophy or by a form of theoretical thought which rests on acquaintance with the history of thought and its achievements.[6]

Engels' interest in the philosophy of science was so much more evident than Marx's that many scholars have maintained that it was Engels, not Marx, who was responsible for the concept of dialectical materialism; and that in bringing the natural sciences into the Marxist system, Engels violated original Marxism. Among the scholars holding this view are those who emphasize the young Marx as a theorist interested, not in universal systems, but specifically in man and his sufferings, a person whose first achievement was to present an explanation of the role of the proletariat in the modern world through the concept of alienated labor. Examples of exponents of this view are George Lichtheim, who wrote that dialectical materialism is a "concept not present in the original Marxian version, and indeed essentially foreign to it, since for the early Marx the only nature relevant to the understanding of history is human nature,"[7] and Z. A. Jordan, who maintained that dialectical materialism was a "conception essentially alien to the philosophy of Marx."[8]

Scholars such as Lichtheim and Jordan have correctly emphasized the humanitarian ethic of the young Marx and the anthropological nature of his analysis, but they have erred in saying or implying that the idealistic young Marx was interested only in human nature, not physical nature. Marx's doctoral dissertation, written in 1839–1841, several years before the now noted "Economic and Philosophical Manuscripts," was suffused with the realization that an understanding of man must begin with an understanding of nature.[9] Entitled "The Difference Between the Nature Philosophy of Democritus and the Nature Philosophy of Epicurus," the dissertation was a long discussion of the physics of the ancients, of the deviations from straight line descent in the atomic theory of Epicurus, of the nature of elementary substances, and of elementary concepts such as time. Marx's attention to physical nature for an understanding of philosophy as a whole was entirely within the context of much of European thought; it was, further, an advantage rather than a disadvantage of his approach. Those recent writers who have tried to divest Marxism of all remnants of inquiry into physical nature have not only misrepresented Marx but have also deprived Marxism of one of its intellectual strengths. It is not necessary to restrict Marx's interests to ethics and economics to free him from vulgar materialism of the type of Vogt or Moleschott. Indeed, one of the points of Marx's dissertation was to show that Epicurus, although like Democritus a believer in atoms and the void, was not a strict determinist. The twenty-three-year-old Marx saw the atom as an abstract concept containing a Hegelian contradiction between essence and existence.[10] Marx would later discard the philosophic idealism underlying this formulation, but there is no evidence that he ever abandoned his interest in physical nature itself.

As a young student of philosophy, Marx was affected by the metaphysical aspirations of almost all great philosophical systems prior to his time and accepted the necessity of making certain epistemological and ontological assumptions. In later years, he attempted to move away from metaphysics, a tendency of some significance since materialism (like all other philosophical systems, including pragmatism) is in the final analysis founded on metaphysical assumptions. At no known point, however, did he resist Engels' effort to bring nature explicitly into their intellectual system. Engels read the entire manuscript of his *Anti-Dühring* to Marx, who presented no objections and even contributed a chapter himself (not on natural philosophy, however) for inclusion in the book. At least as early as 1873, ten years before Marx's death, Engels began work on what became many years later *Dialectics of Nature;* their correspondence illustrated that the mature Marx shared Engels' interest in "modern materialism" in nature notwithstanding the fact that he usually yielded to Engels on issues concerning science. Another spot where Marx indicated his agreement with Engels' effort occurred in *Capital;* Marx observed that the dialectical law of the transition of quantity into quality, applicable to economics, also applied to the molecular theory of modern chemistry.[11]

The point here is not that Marx's and Engels' views were identical, which has been maintained in the past both by Soviet scholars who wished to preserve the unity of dialectical materialism and by anti-Soviet scholars who wished to condemn Marx with the albatross of Engels; rather, the main point is that to emphasize primarily the differences of two men whose views have a great many affinities and who did both consider themselves modern materialists is as much, if not more, of an inaccuracy as crudely to lump them together. It is one thing to say that Marx never committed himself to finding dialectical laws in nature to the extent to which Engels did; it is quite another to say that such an effort contradicted Marx's thought, particularly when Marx is known to have supported the effort on several occasions. Jordan called Marx a "naturalist" rather than a "materialist," meaning that Marx wished to avoid a metaphysical commitment to matter as the sole source of knowledge, but acknowledged elsewhere:

> The materialist presuppositions which were shared by Marx might have included the principle of the sole reality of matter ("matter" being the term used to denote the totality of material objects, and not the substratum of all changes which occur in the world), the denial of the independent existence of mind without matter, the rule of the laws of nature, the independent existence of the external world, and other similar assumptions traditionally associated with materialism.[12]

Jordan pointed out that Marx did not regard knowledge as the mere passive reflection of external matter in the human brain; rather, Marx saw knowledge as a result of a complex interaction between man and the external world. This epistemology does not deny materialism if one assumes that man is a part of the material world, but neither does it absolutely require it. There is a certain leeway in Marx's thought, permitting the supposition of naturalism instead of materialism, just as there is room in the Lenin of the *Philosophical Notebooks* (but not in the Lenin of *Materialism and Empirio-Criticism*) for several epistemologies. But despite these elements of latitude in Marx's thought, he never disclaimed "modern materialism," frequently accepted or used the term, supported Engels' elaboration of it, and in consequence is, I believe, more accurately described as a materialist than as a naturalist.

The recent effort by many non-Soviet scholars to eliminate from Marxism an interest in physical nature can be explained, on the one hand, by their distaste for the ideological restrictions on science that were imposed in the Soviet Union, and on the other, by the general trend of philosophical thought in Western Europe and North America. The interface of ideology with science in the Soviet Union, culminating in most people's minds in the Lysenko episode, led to a discrediting of the claims of Marxist philosophy in the natural sciences. Meanwhile, in the countries of Western Europe and North America, metaphysical and ontological studies were out of fashion; dialectical materialism as an approach to nature was often seen as a vestige of archaic *Naturphilosophie*, an attempt to invade a realm that now belonged exclusively to the specific sciences.

Scholars still committed to Marxism often attempted to save it from *Naturphilosophie* by trying to separate the writings of Engels on science from those of Marx, an operation that is technically possible but that, as we have already seen, usually resulted in conclusions incorrectly restricting the breadth of Marx's interests. On the other hand, those scholars who were opposed to Marxism used the ideological incursions on science in the Soviet Union as important supports in their effort to prove that Marxism was essentially a perversion of science, antirational and even anti-Western, ignoring the deeply Western origins of Marxism and the fact that the Lysenko affair had little to do with Marxism as a philosophy of science.

In the Soviet Union philosophers have not attempted to divest Marx of his interest in all of reality, including physical as well as human nature; they have not followed the trend elsewhere in abandoning the effort to construct comprehensive explanations of reality based on studies of nature itself. They have recognized that one of the most intellectually attractive aspects of Marxism is its explanation of the organic unity of reality; according to Marxism, man and nature are not two, but one. Any attempt to explain either will inevitably have implications for the other. But Soviet philosophers have frequently squandered this intellectual advantage by supporting a dogmatic philosophy, by raising it to a status of a political ideology used for the rationalization of the existing governmental bureaucracy. Instead of being independent philosophers, they have usually been servitors of an oppressive government. They have failed to recognize the essential intellectual revisionism contained within Marxism's claim to a scientific approach. As a result they have not been adept in connecting dialectical materialism with new interests arising in non-Soviet philosophy with which it is potentially compatible, such as process philosophy.

ENGELS AND LENIN ON SCIENCE

Although both Marx and Engels were interested in science from early ages, it is nonetheless true that Engels turned most seriously to science only after the Marxist philosophy of history had been fully developed. By 1848 their political and economic views were well formed, but Engels did not begin systematic study of the sciences, nor did Marx initiate his most detailed studies of mathematics, until some time later. Engels remarked that he took up the study of science "to convince myself in detail—of what in general I was not in doubt—that amid the welter of innumerable changes taking place in Nature, the same dialectical laws are in motion as those which in history govern the apparent fortuitousness of events."[13]

Just what the term "law" (Gesetz) meant to Engels is not altogether clear. He did not attempt a philosophical analysis of the many different meanings that have been given to such terms as "law of nature," "natural law," and "causal law," and he did not clearly indicate what he meant by "dialectical law." Engels' dialectical laws were considerably different from those laws of physics that, within the limits of measurement, permit empirical verification. Engels saw, for example, the dialectical law of the transition of quantity into quality in the observed phenomenon that water, being heated, exhibits a quantitative rise in temperature until it comes to a boil at 100 degrees Celsius (at atmospheric pressure), and then experiences qualitative change from liquid to gas. Such a change can, indeed, be empirically verified by heating many samples of water to 100 degrees. But Engels believed (and Marx agreed in *Capital*) that the same law describes the fact that "not every sum of money, or of value, is at pleasure transformable into capital. To effect this transformation, in fact, a certain minimum of money or of exchange-value must be presupposed in the hands of the individual possessor of money or commodities."[14] The latter case of the dialectical law of the transition of quantity into quality is rather different from the former, even though both are described as instances of the same law. In the case of economics, there is no way in which the law can be verified in every instance; if a certain accumulation of money occurred without its being able to be converted into capital, one could merely say that the correct point had not yet been reached. In the case of the water, one not only possesses the description of *what* change is to occur, but information about *when* it is to occur.

Engels believed that nothing existed but matter and that all matter obeys the dialectical laws. But since there is no way of deciding, at any point in time, that this statement is true, the laws that he presupposed are not the same as usual scientific laws. It should be admitted that even in the case of "usual" laws in natural science the stated relationship, as a universal statement, is not subject to absolute proof. One cannot say, for example, that there will *never* be a case in which a standard sample of water heated to 100 degrees Celsius fails to boil. But when the violation of such laws does occur, it is, within the limits of measurement, apparent that something remarkable has happened.

The definition of "law" is a very controversial and difficult topic within the philosophy of science,[15] and I shall not pursue it beyond noting that Engels' concept of dialectical laws was quite broad, embracing very different kinds of explanations. Indeed, he referred to the dialectical relationships not only as "laws," but also as "tendencies," "forms of motion," "regularities," and "principles."

Engels is known for two major works on the philosophy of science, *Anti-Dühring* and *Dialectics of Nature*. Since only the first of these was a finished book and appeared almost fifty years earlier than the second, it exercised the greater influence on the formation of the Marxist view of nature. In *Anti-Dühring* Engels criticized the philosophic system advanced by Eugen Karl Dühring in his *Course of Philosophy*.[16] Dühring was a radical lecturer on philosophy and political science at the University of Berlin, a critic of capitalism who was gaining influence among

German social democrats. Engels disagreed with Dühring's claim to "a final and ultimate truth" based on what Dühring called "the principles of all knowledge and volition." Engels did not object to Dühring's goal of a universal philosophic system, but rather the method by which he derived it and his claims for its perfection. Dühring's "principles" were to Engels a product of idealistic philosophy: "What he is dealing with are *principles*, formal tenets derived from *thought* and not from the external world, which are to be applied to nature and the realm of man and to which therefore nature and man have to conform. . . ."[17] Engels believed, contrary to Dühring, that a truly materialistic philosophy is based on principles derived from matter itself, not thought. The principles of materialism, said Engels, are:

> not the starting-point of the investigation, but its final result; they are not applied to nature and human history, but abstracted from them; it is not nature and the realm of humanity which conform to these principles, but the principles are valid in so far as they are in conformity with nature and history. That is the only materialistic conception of matter, and Herr Dühring's contrary conception is idealistic, makes things stand completely on their heads, and fashions the real world out of ideas, out of schemata, schemes or categories existing somewhere before the world, from eternity— just like *a Hegel.*[18]

A number of writers have commented that this desire to counteract Dühring's idealistic philosophy pushed Engels' first philosophical work toward the positivistic position of maintaining that all knowledge must be composed of verifiable data derived from nature.[19] They have frequently cited *Dialectics of Nature*, the later work, as containing an opposite metaphysical tendency, and have observed that the tension between these two strains in Marxist thought—positivistic materialism and metaphysical dialectics—has been present throughout its history. A tension between materialism and the dialectic has indeed existed within Marxism, and will be commented upon later, but the extent to which *Anti-Dühring* is positivistic and *Dialectics of Nature* metaphysical has been overdrawn. True, Engels in *Anti-Dühring* directed his chief criticism against a philosopher (Dühring) for not being materialist, while in *Dialectics of Nature*, more in passing, he chastised scientists (such as Karl Vogt, Ludwig Büchner, and Jacob Moleschott) for not being dialectical. But in both works Engels attempted to locate a balance point between reliance on the empirical findings of science, on the one hand, and the dialectical structure inherited from Hegel on the other. In *Anti-Dühring,* the reputedly positivistic work, Engels also presented some of his best-known discussions of the dialectic in nature; while in *Dialectics of Nature*, the work supposedly heavily Hegelian in inspiration, he stoutly defended the concept of the materiality of the universe.[20]

If one turns from Engels' works on the philosophy of science to a consideration of his knowledge of science itself, one is likely to conclude that although essentially a dilettante, he was a dilettante in the best sense. For a person of his background he possessed a remarkable knowledge of the natural sciences. Engels' formal education never went beyond the *gymnasium*, but he immersed himself in the study of science at certain periods of his life; he was able, for example, to write a long chapter on the electrolysis of chemical solutions, including computations of energy transformations.[21] He was familiar with the research of Darwin, Haeckel, Liebig, Lyell, Helmholtz, and many other prominent nineteenth-century scientists. In retrospect his errors do not draw so much attention as his unlimited energy and audacity in approaching any subject and the high degree of understanding that he usually achieved. Even if one is not willing to accept J. B. S. Haldane's observation that Engels was "probably the most widely educated man of his day," he was, indeed, a man of impressive knowledge.[22] Elements of naivete and literalness are easily found, but they are less significant than his conviction that an approach to all of knowledge, and not just one portion, was necessary for a new understanding of man.

Indeed, a reevaluation of Engels by historians of science is overdue. Engels' "errors" in science, as seen from the vantage of today—his quaint descriptions of electricity, his discussions of cosmogony, his descriptions of the structure of the earth, and his assertion that mental habits can be inherited—were usually the "errors" of the science of Engels' time. Engels was a materialist, and suffered from the tendency toward simplification that has plagued many materialists, but he was far more sophisticated than the popularizers of materialism of his day, who were usually scientists, such as Büchner and Moleschott. Those recent writers who have dismissed Engels' writings on science have usually forgotten the context of nineteenth-century materialism in which they were written. Against the background of this materialism Engels appears as a thinker with a genuine appreciation of complexity and an awareness of the dangers of enthusiastic reductionism. He was, for example, convinced that life arose from inorganic matter, but he ridiculed the simple approach of the supporters of spontaneous generation who had in the 1860s suffered defeat at the hands of Pasteur. Engels' attitude toward the origin of life has been praised by biologists even recently.[23]

Lenin's writings on science are similar to Engels' not only in terms of philosophical commitment, but also in several other secondary respects: he came to science after formulating his political and economic views; he first entered the field of philosophy of science for polemical reasons; he was responsible for two major works with somewhat different emphases; and his later, more sophisticated period is much less well known than his earlier, relatively untutored phase.

The particular viewpoints of Lenin on the philosophy of science, as expressed in *Materialism and Empirio-Criticism* and in the *Philosophical Notebooks* will be discussed in the following sections on epistemology and dialectics, but at this point it is necessary to mention the fact that most non-Soviet discussions of Lenin's philosophic views are based on *Materialism and Empirio-Criticism*. The *Philosophical Notebooks*, which consist of abstracts, fragments, and marginal notes, were not published until the end of the twenties, and did not appear in English until 1961. Consequently, they have been neglected by Anglo-American students of Leninism. Yet to the extent that Lenin achieved sophistication in philosophy, that stage is revealed in the *Philosophical Notebooks*, where we have his comments on Hegel, Aristotle, Feuerbach, and other writers. As two editors of Marxist philosophy commented:

> His main concern was to reconstruct the Hegelian dialectics on a thoroughly materialist foundation. . . . While Lenin was always the enemy of idealism, he opposed the offhand dismissal of this type of philosophy. As against vulgar materialism, he insisted that philosophical idealism has its sources in the very process of cognition itself. His conclusion was that "intelligent idealism is closer to intelligent materialism than stupid materialism." Thus, these *Philosophical Notebooks* are an indispensable supplement to Lenin's previous philosphical works and observations. Indeed, they constitute a plea for a richer and fuller development of dialectical materialism.[24]

The interpretaion of the *Philosophical Notebooks* and their integration into Lenin's thought present particular problems for the historian. Lenin composed these fragments for himself alone, jotting down what first came to mind, and did not rewrite or rethink them. Obviously such materials must be treated more carefully than his published *Materialism and Empirio-Criticism*. Yet to rely upon the published work entirely would mean underestimating the full development of Lenin's thought. Lenin was quite aware of his shortcomings in philosophy in the earlier years; his efforts to overcome these deficiencies and his subsequent viewpoints emerge impressively in the *Philosophical Notebooks*.

The *Philosophical Notebooks* have exercised increasing influence in Soviet dialectical materialism since their publication, although they are still considered secondary to *Materialism and Empirio-Criticism*. As we shall see, this influence was usually in the direction of a greater appreciation of the subtleties of epistemology and the dangers of reductionism. When the *Philosophical Notebooks* first appeared in the Soviet Union, they became elements in the debates between the dialecticians and the mechanists. In later years, they were frequently considered to be particularly suited for advanced students of dialectical materialism, partly because of their fragmentary and unsystematized nature, but even more, no doubt, because of the greater awareness that Lenin displayed there of the alternatives of epistemology.

MATERIALISM AND EPISTEMOLOGY[25]

In the Marxist philosophy of science as presented by Engels, there is nothing in the objective world other than matter and its emergent qualities. This matter has extension and exists in time; as Engels remarked, "The basic forms of all being are space and time, and being out of time is just as gross an absurdity as being out of space."[26] (This view was somewhat modified in the Soviet Union after the advent of relativity, as will be shown.) The material world is always in the process of change, and all parts of it are inextricably connected. All matter is in motion. Furthermore, Engels agreed with Descartes' assertion that the quantity of motion in the world is constant. Both motion and matter are uncreatable, indestructible, and mutually dependent: "Matter without motion is just as inconceivable as motion without matter."[27]

It is important to note that Engels did not think of matter as a substratum, a *materia prima*. Matter is not something that can be identified or defined as a unique and most primitive substance that enters into an infinite number of combinations resulting in the diversity of nature. Rather, matter is an abstraction, a product of a material mind referring to the "totality of things." Engels commented:

Matter as such is a pure creation of thought and an abstraction. We leave out of account the qualitative difference of things in comprehending them as corporeally existing things under the concept matter. Hence matter as such, as distinct from definite existing pieces of matter, is not anything sensuously existing. If natural science directs its efforts to seeking out uniform matter as such, to reducing qualitative differences to merely

quantitative differences in combining identical smallest particles, it would
be doing the same thing as demanding to see fruit as such instead of
cherries, pears, apples, or the mammal as such instead of cats, dogs,
sheep, etc., . . .[28]

According to Engels, abstractions such as matter are parts of thought
and consciousness, the emergent products of a material brain. In discussing the materiality of the brain, Engels carefully dissociated himself
from simple materialists such as Büchner, Vogt, and Moleschott. He
agreed with them that thought and consciousness are products of a
material brain, but he disagreed with simple analogies such as "the
brain produces thought as the liver produces bile." On the contrary,
on the basis of Hegelian quantitative-qualitative relationships Engels
believed that each level of being has its own qualitative distinctiveness;
to compare in a reductionist manner thought produced by the brain to
bile produced by the liver or motion produced by a steam engine
conceals more than it reveals. Yet for all the distinctiveness of motion
on each level of being, the carrier of that motion is matter: "One day
we shall certainly 'reduce' thought experimentally to molecular and
chemical motions in the brain; but does that exhaust the essence of
thought?"[29] These views of Engels on thought would one day have
impact on Soviet discussions of the possibility of computers reproducing
human thought, as we shall see later.

According to Engels, man's knowledge flows from nature, the objective, material world. He saw two different epistemological schools
in the history of philosophy; the materialists, who believe knowledge
to derive from objective nature, and the idealists, who attribute primacy
in cognition to the mind itself. As Engels said, "The great basic question
of all philosophy, especially of more recent philosophy, is that of the
relation of thinking and being."[30] At this point in *Ludwig Feuerbach*
Engels proceeded to link the epistemological problem of knowledge to
the ontological one of the existence of God:

The question of the relation of thinking to being, the relation of spirit to
nature—the paramount question of the whole of philosophy—has, no
less than all religion, its roots in the narrow-minded and ignorant notions
of savagery. . . . The question: which is primary, spirit or nature—that
question, in relation to the Church was sharpened into this: Did God
create the world or has the world been in existence eternally?[31]

A number of Engels' critics have pointed to what they call a "fatal
flaw" in his reasoning at this point: his confusion of epistemology and

ontology.[32] There is no reason, they have said, for identifying idealism with a belief in God, or realism with atheism. A person could believe in objective reality and withhold judgment on the question of God or even consider God to be "objectively real." Within the framework of the problem of epistemology alone the critics are correct; there are more than two camps on the issue of cognition. In describing how man comes to know, one can emphasize the role of objective reality (realism); the role of matter (materialism); the role of the mind (idealism); or one can maintain that it is impossible to know how man comes to know (agnosticism). Furthermore, one's religious views are not determined by one's epistemology. But for Engels the ontological principle that all that exists is matter came before all others. Therefore, for him a God who could be objectively real to a person in terms of epistemology but nonmaterial in terms of ontology was nonsense.

The key to the Marxist philosophy of science is not its position on cognition, which contains considerable flexibility, as evidenced not only by Lenin's writings in the *Philosophical Notebooks* but even more so by subsequent developments (particularly in countries such as Yugoslavia in the 1960s), but its position on matter itself. What justification do we have for assuming that an ill-defined "matter" (later "matter" was equated with "energy") alone exists? The more thoughtful Russian Marxists such as Plekhanov (and perhaps Lenin at moments) have veered toward the position that the principle of the sole existence of matter is a simplifying assumption necessary for subsequent scientific analysis. Other Marxists, such as Engels, the Lenin of *Materialism and Empirio-Criticism*, and many Soviet philosophers, have maintained that the principle of materialism is a fact presented by scientific investigation. But as a result of the sensitivity of the subject, the issue of the justification for the belief in materialism has not been thoroughly investigated by philosophers in the Soviet Union.

To return to Engels' treatment of the opposition of idealism and materialism, we can see his merging of the problems of existence and cognition in the following quotation:

> Contrary to idealism, which asserts that only our mind really exists, and that the material world, being, Nature, exists only in our mind, in our sensations, ideas and perceptions, the Marxist materialist philosophy holds that matter, Nature, being, is an objective reality existing outside and independent of our mind; that matter is primary, since it is the source of sensation, ideas, mind, and that mind is secondary, derivative, since it is a reflection of matter, a reflection of being. . . .[33]

Engels' last phrase, "mind . . . is a reflection of matter," strikes to the heart of the mind-matter relationship. In Russian Marxist philosophy the description of this relationship has been a major issue. Engels' term "reflection" was followed by Plekhanov's "hieroglyphs," Bogdanov's "socially-organized experience," and Lenin's "copy-theory." The copy-theory of Lenin, to be subsequently discussed, became the most influential model for Soviet philosophy. Its importance will also be seen in the discussion of physiology and psychology in this volume.

Connected with Engels' view of the nature of the material world was his opinion on the attainability of truth about that world. Parallel to the existence of matter apart from mind was the existence, potentially, of truth about that matter. Scientists strive toward complete explanations of matter even though these explanations are never reached. The relationship between man's knowledge and truth, according to Engels, is asymptotic (knowledge approaches truth ever more closely, but will never reach its goal).[34] It is not correct to say that Engels believed in the attainability of absolute truth. Only at the unattainable point of infinity in the relationship between man's knowledge and truth does an intersection obtain. Nonetheless, Engels believed in a cumulative, almost linear, relationship of knowledge to truth. Lenin, on the contrary, saw many more temporary aberrations in the upward march, and used the image of a "spiral movement" to describe the process.

REINTERPRETATION OF RUSSIAN MARXIST VIEWS ON MATERIALISM AND EPISTEMOLOGY

Among Russian Marxists the problems of epistemology and the philosophy of nature attracted considerably more attention than among Western European Marxists. G. V. Plekhanov, Lenin's tutor in Marxism and later an opponent of the Bolsheviks, developed his "hieroglyphic" theory of knowledge in 1892 in his notes to his translation of Engels' *Ludwig Feuerbach*. Plekhanov wrote:

> Our sensations are sorts of hieroglyphs informing us what is happening in reality. These hieroglyphs are not similar to those events conveyed by them. But they can completely truthfully convey both the events themselves and—and this is important—also those relationships existing between them.[35]

The analysis presented by Plekhanov was an attempt to go beyond the common-sense realism implied by Engels' writings to a recognition of the difference between objects-in-themselves and our sensations of them. In Plekhanov's view there was a distinct difference—so much so that he felt that these sensations "are not similar to those events conveyed by them." Nonetheless, he said, there is a correspondence between these events and our sensations. Thus, Plekhanov went from a "presentational" theory of perception to a "representational" one.[36] His epistemology was still materialistic since it assumed the existence of material objects outside the mind that reveal themselves in an indirect but trustworthy fashion by means of man's sensations.

It was important to Plekhanov that to each of man's sensations in the process of perceiving an object there be a materialistic correlate, and to each of the changes in a material object there be a sensational correlate. He said that one should imagine a situation in which a cube is casting a shadow on the surface of a cylinder:

> This shadow is not at all similar to the cube: The straight lines of the cube are broken; its flat surfaces are bulged. Nevertheless for each change of the cube there will be a corresponding change of the shadow. We may assume that something similar occurs in the process of the formation of ideas.[37]

Plekhanov was aware that his epistemology was not scientifically provable, as the above words "we may assume" indicate. He discussed respectfully Hume's view that there was no way of proving that physical objects are anything more than mental images.[38] Plekhanov's writings implied that by assuming the primacy of matter in cognition, he considered himself to be making a plausible and useful philosophic choice rather than coming to a scientific conclusion.

In the early twentieth century a controversy arose among Russian Marxists that ultimately led to the entry of Lenin into the field of epistemology. In the resulting *Materialism and Empirio-Criticism* Lenin criticized not only his immediate disputants, the "Russian Machists," but also Plekhanov. In order to introduce the controversy, some mention must be made of Ernst Mach (1830–1916).

The late nineteenth century's most formidable criticism of the philosophic belief in a material world independent of man's mind was contained in Mach's sensationalism. Mach was an Austrian physicist and philosopher who provided much of the impetus to the development of logical positivism and who prepared the way for the acceptance of relativity and quantum theory. His antimetaphysical views were equalled by those of his contemporary, the German philosopher Richard Avenarius, the proponent of the theory of knowledge known as empiro-criticism. Mach and Avenarius occupy a special place in Soviet Marxist philosophy, since they are the objects of copious criticism in Lenin's *Materialism and Empirio-Criticism.*

In *Analysis of Sensations* Mach defended the view, already ancient among philosophers but now made particularly relevant to modern science, that the "world consists only of our sensations."[39] According to Mach, space and time were as much sensations as color or sound.[40] A physical object was merely a constant sensation (or "perception," taken as a group of sensations). Mach followed Berkeley, then, in denying the dualism of sense perceptions and physical objects. But while Berkeley was a realist in the sense of assuming the reality of mental images and of an external God, Mach endeavored to introduce no elements into his system that were not scientifically verifiable. Therefore, he made no pronouncements about ultimate reality. According to his "principle of economy," scientists should select the simplest means of arriving at results and should exclude all elements except empirical data.[41] Mach's approach employed on the practical scientific level, where he intended it to be utilized, would mean that a scientist would cease worrying about the "real" or "actual" nature of matter and would merely accept his sense-perceptions, working as carefully and thoroughly as he could. A theory that found a pattern in the data would be judged entirely on the basis of its usefulness rather than its plausibility in terms of other existing considerations. There might even be more than one "correct" way of describing matter (a concept that would have influence later in discussions of quantum mechanics). Two explanations, working from opposite directions, could both be useful and could supplement each other, even if there seemed to be a contradiction between the two approaches.[42]

Mach had shifted the emphasis from matter *reflecting* in the mind to the mind *organizing* the perceptions of matter. A group of Marxist philosophers soon followed Mach's lead. This school of Russian empirio-critics included A. Bogdanov (pseudonym of A. A. Malinovskii); A. V. Lunacharskii, the future commissar of education; V. Bazarov (V. A. Rudnev); and N. Valentinov (N. V. Vol'skii). Bogdanov, a medical doctor, was swayed by the lucidity and scientific nature of Mach's arguments, but dissatisfied with what he saw as their inconsistencies. If, as Mach maintained, sensations and objects are the same, why do two different realms of experience—the subjective and the objective—continue to exist?[43] Why are there two different sets of principles or "regularities" (zakonomernosti) in these different realms? Thus, in the objective world, there are such sensations as sight, sound, and smell. In the subjective realm are emotions and impulses: anger, desire, and so forth. Bogdanov defined objective sensations as those that are universally perceived,[44] and subjective sensations as those that may be apparent to only one person or a small group of persons. Bogdanov then attempted to find the roots of this dualistic system and thereby unite them in a philosophical system called empiriomonism. The key to this development is the concept of the "organization of experience." To Bogdanov, the physical world equals "socially organized experience," while the mental world is "individually organized experience." Therefore, "if in the single stream of human experience we find two principally different conformities of law (zakonomernosti), then nevertheless, both of them arise in equal measure from our own organization: they convey two biological-organizational tendencies. . . ."[45] Parenthetically, it is worthwhile to note that Bogdanov's emphasis upon organizational structure and the means of transmitting information would cause a new surge of interest in his work in the Soviet Union many years later when cybernetics and information theory were applied to psychology and epistemology.

Lenin's original entry into the field of philosophy was the result of his being disturbed by the views of Russian Marxist writers such as Bogdanov and Plekhanov. His first motivation was a tactical one; he wished to protect the Bolsheviks' claim to a materialistic view of nature and history. Only many years later did he become genuinely interested in problems of philosophy.

In 1908 Lenin set himself the task of writing a major work on philosophy in order, as he put it, "to find out what was the stumbling block to these people who under the guise of Marxism are offering something incredibly muddled, confused, and reactionary."[46] The stumbling block, he found, was the influence of the latest developments of science upon philosophers, including Marxist philosophers such as Bogdanov.

By the early twentieth century many people believed that the foundations of materialism were being undermined by scientists themselves.[47] The relative confidence of scientists of Marx's and Engels' time in their knowledge of nature had been replaced by perplexity. The investigation of the radiations of radium and uranium, resulting in the identification of alpha rays (helium nuclei) and beta rays (high-speed electrons), had discredited the concept of nondivisible atoms. Such scientists as L. Houllevigue remarded that "the atom dematerialises, matter disappears."[48] Henri Poincaré observed that physics was faced with "a debacle of principles."[49]

The rise of philosophical schools such as empirio-criticism on the continent and phenomenalism in England was largely a response to these and other developments in science. In Lenin's opinion, the philosophers following these trends were subordinating the search for truth about matter to attempts to provide convenient explanations of isolated perceptions. Idealism was again a threat, and Bishop Berkeley's theories were reborn, in the name of science rather than God.

In countering these new movements, Lenin stressed two tenets of his interpretation of dialectical materialism: the copy-theory of the mind-matter relationship and the principle that nature is infinite. It seems clear that Lenin regarded these principles as minimum requirements in order for dialectical materialism to have philosophical consistency or significance. He was not attempting to impose philosophy upon science, but to locate the bedrock of the materialist philosophy of science; he believed it impossible for science to contradict these principles.

By the "copy-theory" of matter Lenin meant that materialism is based on recognition of "objects-in-themselves" or "without the mind." According to him, "ideas and sensations are copies or images of these objects." Just how similar these ideas are to the objects themselves was left unsaid. There is good reason to believe that at the time of the writing of *Materialism and Empirio-Criticism* Lenin considered man's mental images to be quite similar to the corresponding objects. His epistemology was at this time close to that of common-sense realism; he criticized the "vagueness" of Plekhanov's hieroglyphic epistemology. Yet even in some of his remarks in *Materialism and Empirio-Criticism* Lenin indicated that the essential aspect of dialectical materialism was the principle of objectively existing matter, not the degree of correspondence between man's images and the objects of the material world. Indeed, he approached reducing the fundamentals of materialist epistemology to one principle: "Only one thing is from Engels' viewpoint immutable—the reflection by the human mind (when the human mind exists) of a world existing and developing independently of the mind."[50] Lenin added that this independent objective world can be known by man; "To be a materialist is to acknowledge objective truth, which is revealed to us by our sense organs."[51]

It should be noticed that if a person accepted literally the last sentence in the above paragraph as Lenin's definition of materialism, he or she would be fully justified in saying that Lenin confused realism ("all that exists is real") with materialism ("all that exists is material") and that Lenin was, in fact, not a materialist, but a realist. For one could take Lenin's statement "To be a materialist is to acknowledge objective truth, which is revealed to us by our sense organs" and with complete justification change it to read "To be a realist is to acknowledge objective truth, which is revealed to us by our sense organs." Was Lenin, then, a realist rather than a materialist? An accurate answer to this question, one which takes into consideration all of Lenin's writings, would have to be negative. Lenin always spoke of materialism, not realism, and he saw the difference, particularly in his later works; he supplemented his realist epistemology with an assumption of ontological materialism resulting from his belief in the conceptual value of such an assumption. The fact that Lenin's materialism was founded on an assumption has not been openly discussed in the Soviet Union, where dialectical materialism is usually portrayed as a provable doctrine, even an inevitable conclusion of modern science. Yet the best argument for materialism starts out with a recognition of its assumptive or judgmental character and a defense of such a minimal assumption or judgment as being consonant with all available evidence and persuasive to many scientists. This argument must, of course, leave room for the person who wishes to make a different initial assumption. Individual scientists are likely to have preferences for one or the other. The noted American biologist Hermann J. Muller recognized and approved the assumptive origin of Lenin's materialism in an article that he wrote in 1934. To Muller, Lenin's assumption could be defended, further, on the basis of inductive judgment:

> To those scientists who would protest that we should not make such pre-judgements regarding scientific possibilities, on the basis of a prior "philosophical" assumption of materialism, but should rather follow in any direction in which empirical facts of the case seem to be leading, we may retort, with Lenin, that all the facts of daily life, as well as those of science, together form an overwhelming body of evidence for the materialistic point of view . . . and that therefore we are justified, in our further scientific work, in taking this principle as our foundation for our higher constructions. It too is ultimately empirical, in the better sense of the word, and it has the overwhelming advantage of being founded upon the evidence of the whole, rather than upon just some restricted portion of the latter.[52]

But Lenin in 1908 was not yet able to recognize the judgmental or preferential bases of materialism, although he would approach them later in his *Philosophical Notebooks*. In 1908 he was, instead, concentrating on a criticism of the Russian followers of Mach, and he naturally was more interested in revealing the vulnerable points in their analysis than in his own. He asserted that Bogdanov's idealistic philosophy actually concealed a belief in God, in spite of his repudiation of all religion. If, said Lenin, the physical world equals merely "socially organized experience," then the door is opened to God, "for God is undoubtedly a product of the socially organized experience of living beings."[53]

In Lenin's opinion, the epistemological problem was not separate from the question of the nature of matter itself. The mental realm of experience is not distinct from the material realm, but is a result of it on a higher level. Matter itself is not at all threatened by Rutherford's dismantling of the atom because "the electron is as inexhaustible as the atom, nature is infinite, but it infinitely exists."[54] Lenin believed that the expression "matter disappears" was an indication of philosophical immaturity by scientists and philosophers who did not understand that science will constantly discover new forms of matter and new principles of motion.

Lenin believed that philosophies opposing science were based either on idealism or simple materialism, not dialectical materialism. He attempted to make dialectical materialism less vulnerable to criticism and less likely to retard science by drawing a line between it and simple materialism. Yet, if one judges by *Materialism and Empirio-Criticism*, one must conclude that this line was not drawn with any degree of clarity. Lenin did not even discuss in this work the laws of the dialectic, the principles that distinguish dialectical materialism from simple materialism. He merely maintained that dialectical materialism, a philosophical viewpoint, cannot be affected by the vacillations of scientific theory. Lenin labored to reforge the bond between the theory of dialectical materialism and the practice of science. While insisting on the materialist copy-theory, he also affirmed that nature is infinite. The division of particles into smaller particles could go on forever, he believed, but matter would never disappear.

In the notations that Lenin made six or seven years later during his further study of philosophy, he revealed a greater appreciation of the alternatives of epistemology. Although he did not repudiate his earlier copy-theory, he now saw the link between the material objects of the world and man's images as much more indirect. Indeed, he seemed to believe that in the highest forms of their development, materialist and idealist theories of cognition were linked in a unity of contradiction; they tended to pass into one another. Thus Hegel, whom he believed to be the greatest idealist in philosophy, arrived unwittingly at the threshold of dialectical materialism. Lenin's evolution was from another direction, from the side of materialism, but he approached the same spot as Hegel, the moment of unity between two philosophies. As Lenin observed, "the difference of the ideal from the material is not unconditional."[55] The area where the distinction between idealism and materialism became nearly imperceptible was that of mental abstraction; in order to understand nature it is necessary for man not only to perceive matter but to construct a series of concepts that "embrace conditionally" eternally moving and developing nature. And these abstractions may include elements of fantasy:

> The approach of the (human) mind to a particular thing, the taking of a copy (= concept) of it is *not* a simple, immediate act, a dead mirroring, but one which is complex, split in two, zigzag like, which *includes in it* the possibility of the flight of fantasy from life; more than that: The possibility of the *transformation* (moreover, an unnoticeable transformation, of which man is unaware) of the abstract concept, idea, into a *fantasy* (in the final analysis = God). For even in the simplest generalization, in the most elementary general idea ("table" in general), *there* is a certain bit of *fantasy*. (Vice versa, it would be stupid to deny the role of fantasy, even in the strictest science. . . .)"[56]

The Lenin who is revealed in the above passage is not the one who is known to most students of Leninism; this Lenin recognizes the painful, halting, indirect path of knowledge, a path that includes clear reversals. He grants the useful role of fantasy "even in the strictest science." He sees this fantasy as an inherent possibility in scientific thought and is aware that in the final analysis it can lead to a belief in God. In his statement that the possibility of fantasy is included in the approach of the human mind to nature, he, like Plekhanov before, seemed to recognize that the rejection of idealism is not a matter of scientific proof but philosophic choice. And Lenin continued, of course, to choose materialism.

This more flexible view of materialism, which sees it as a result of choice and not of proof, opened up room for its potential accommodation with some other philosophic currents, a development that, however, still has not occurred. If one considers, for example, some of the writings of W. V. O. Quine, it becomes apparent that there are similarities of argument. Quine wrote in his "Two Dogmas of Empiricism":

As an empiricist I continue to think of the conceptual scheme of science as a tool, ultimately, for predicting future experience in the light of past experience. Physical objects are conceptually imported into the situation as convenient intermediaries—not by definition in terms of experience, but simply as irreducible posits comparable, epistemologically, to the gods of Homer. For my part I do, *qua* lay physicist, believe in physical objects and not in Homer's gods; and I consider it a scientific error to believe otherwise. But in point of epistemological footing the physical objects and the gods differ only in degree and not in kind. Both sorts of entities enter our conception only as cultural posits. The myth of physical objects is epistemologically superior to most in that it has proved more efficacious than other myths as a device for working a manageable structure into the flux of experience.[57]

The possibility for the convergence of the epistemological view represented by the quotation from Quine above and the epistemology of dialectical materialism is considerable. Holders of both views prefer a concept of "physical objects," and both find justification for this concept in pragmatic success. To be sure, what Quine calls "superior myth," the dialectical materialist has called "truth." But does the word "myth" here mean "that which is false" or "that which can not be proved"? And does the dialectical materialist really believe that the "truth" of his position can be illustrated, or is his position one that he assumes to be true for reasons similar to those for which Quine assumes his myth to be "superior"? And if the dialectical materialist may have some difficulty in defining "matter-energy," falling back eventually to Engels' reference to the "totality of things," Quine says with equal indefiniteness that "physical objects are postulated entities which round out and simplify our account of the flux of experience."[58] In the final analysis there are differences between the positions, to be sure, but hardly of the type that would place dialectical materialism outside the realm of philosophy while leaving Quine's epistemology within.

THE LAWS OF THE DIALECTIC

The discussion of dialectical materilaism has so far centered on the latter half of the term: materialism. The other half, the dialectic, concerns the characteristics of the development and movement of matter.

There are two rather different views of the dialectic that Soviet thinkers have, at different moments, taken; one is the belief not only that matter-energy obeys laws of a very general type, but that these laws have been identified in the three laws of the dialectic to be discussed below. This view has numerous adherents and has also been officially expressed in Soviet textbooks on dialectical materialism. The other view is that matter-energy does indeed obey general laws, but that the three laws of the dialectic are provisional statements to be modified or replaced, if necessary, as science provides more evidence. This unofficial view has appeared in the Soviet Union from time to time, particularly among professional philosophers and younger scientists.[59]

The dialectic as applied by Engels to the natural sciences was based on his interpretation of Hegelian philosophy. This interpretation involved not only the well-known conversion of Hegelian philosophy from idealism to materialism, but also the reduction of Hegel's thought to a simple scheme of dialectical laws and triads.

In his *Science of Logic* Hegel spoke of "dialectic" as "one of those ancient sciences which have become most misjudged in modern metaphysics and in popular philosophy of ancients and moderns alike."[60] Hegel believed that the way in which dialectic had previously been used had involved only two terms (dualisms, antinomies, opposites); he referred to Kant's discussion of "Transcendental Dialectic" in his *Critique of Pure Reason*, in which Kant advanced the view that human reason is essentially dialectical in that every metaphysical argument can be opposed by an equally persuasive counter argument. Hegel saw a means of transcending this contradiction in a third position, "the second negative," which is "the innermost and most objective moment of Life and Spirit, by virtue of which a subject is personal and free."[61]

Contrary to much opinion, Hegel never used the terms "thesis-antithesis-synthesis" in the neat fashion so often attributed to him; he recognized, however, the importance of the thesis-antithesis contradiction in the writings of Kant, Fichte, and Jacobi, and he did sparingly use the term "synthesis" to indicate the moment of transcendence of such a polarity.[62] But Hegel opposed reducing his analysis to a triadic formula, and warned that such a scheme was "a mere pedagogical device," a "formula for memory and reason."[63]

Hegel did not provide a straightforward method of analysis that merely had to be "turned on its head" in order to become dialectical materialism. Engels' use of Hegel involved not only inversion, but also codification, a dubious reduction of rather obscure complexity. Nonetheless, many of the elements of Engels' dialectical materialism were indeed present in Hegel's thought. The very fact that Engels sought to simplify Hegel is not surprising—many men, including Goethe, have condemned the great Prussian philosopher for being unnecessarily complex—but Engels' centering of attention upon the laws of the dialectic had the unfortunate effect of tying Marxism to three codified laws of nature rather than simply to the principle that nature does conform to laws more general than those of any one science, laws that may, with varying degrees of success, be identified.

To Engels the material world was an interconnected whole governed by certain general principles. The great march of science in the last several centuries had, as a regrettable by-product, so compartmentalized knowledge that the important general principles were being overlooked. As he observed, the scientific "method of work has also left us as legacy the habit of observing natural objects and processes in isolation, apart from their connection with the vast whole; of observing them in repose, not in motion; as constants, not as essentially variables; in their death, not in their life."[64]

By "dialectics" Engels said that he meant the laws of all motion, in nature, history, and thought. He named three such laws: the Law of the Transformation of Quantity into Quality, the Law of the Mutual Interpenetration of Opposites, and the Law of the Negation of the Negation. These dialectical principles or laws were supposed to represent the most general patterns of matter in motion. Like Heraclitus, dialectical materialists believe that nothing in nature is totally static; the dialectical laws are efforts to describe the most general uniformities in the processes of change that occur in nature. The concept of the evolution or development of nature is, therefore, basic to dialectical materialism. The dialectical laws are the principles by which complex substances and concepts evolve from simple ones.

According to Engels, the laws were equally valid in science and human history. This universal applicability of the laws has served both as a source of strength and of weakness for dialectical materialism. On the one hand, the possession of the dialectic has given Marxists a conceptual tool of considerable power; many thinkers have been attracted by the Hegelian framework of dialectical materialism. The urge to possess a key to knowledge has been perhaps the strongest motivation in the history of philosophy.

On the other hand, the universality of dialectical materialism has been frequently a disadvantage for its adherents. Many non-Soviet philosophers have turned away from it in the belief that it contains precisely those elements of Western philosophy that should have been abandoned before they were; dialectical materialism is a vestige, they say, of scholasticism. Rather than describing *how* matter moves, in the post-Newtonian sense, it attempts, in the Aristotelian sense, to explain *why* matter moves. Furthermore, the generality of the dialectic is achieved at the price of such diffuseness that to many critics its usefulness seems negligible. As one critic of the dialectic, H. B. Acton, remarked, the Law of the Negation of the Negation is "already general almost to the point of evanescence" when it is applied to such very different things as mathematics and the growing of barley; when the law is then extended to the transition from capitalist to communist society, "the only point of likeness appears to be the words employed."[65] To this criticism dialectical materialists would reply that if one accepts the existence of one real world of which all aspects of man's knowledge are derivative parts, one should expect there to be at least a few general principles that are applicable to all those parts. Some of the more sophisticated dialectical materialists of the post-Stalin period would add that they are in principle prepared to reject the three laws of the dialectic enunciated by Engels if superior substitutes can be found, and there have been a few attempts to achieve this through the application of information and systems theory.

The principle of the Transformation of Quantity into Quality derived from Hegel's view that "quality is implicitly quantity, and conversely quantity is implicitly quality. In the process of measure, therefore, these two pass into each other: each of them becomes what it already was implicitly. . . ."[66]

Engels pointed to what he considered numerous examples of the operation of this law in nature. These were the cases when quantitative succession in a natural phenomenon is suddenly interrupted by a marked qualitative change. One example given by Engels was the homologous series of carbon compounds. The formulas for these compounds (CH_4, C_2H_6, C_3H_8, and so on) follow the progression C_nH_{2n+2}. The only difference among members of the progression, Engels observed, is the quantity of carbon and hydrogen. Nevertheless, the compounds have greatly differing chemical properties. In these diverse properties Engels saw the Law of the Transformation of Quantity into Quality at work.[67]

Perhaps the most unusual case that Engels cited as an example of the transformation of quantity into quality concerned Napoleon's cavalry during the Egyptian campaign. During the conflicts between French and Mameluke horsemen a curious relationship became apparent. Whenever a small group of Mamelukes would come upon a small group of Frenchmen in the desert, the Mamelukes would always win, even if somewhat outnumbered. On the other hand, whenever a large group of Mamelukes would come upon a large group of Frenchmen, the Frenchmen would always win, even if somewhat outnumbered. Engels' description can be represented in the following table:

Number of Mamelukes	Number of Frenchmen	Victors
2	3	Mamelukes
100	100	Even match
1500	1000	Frenchmen

The reason for the apparently paradoxical results was that the Frenchmen were highly disciplined and trained for large-scale maneuvers, but were not veteran horsemen. The Mamelukes had been on horses from the earliest age, but knew very little about discipline and tactics. Hence, a qualitative-quantitative relationship existed that yielded contrasting results at different quantitative levels.[68]

To Marx and Engels, Darwin's theory of evolution was an important illustration of the principle of the transition of quantity into quality. This tenet as a part of the Hegelian dialectic preceded Darwin, of course, but Marx and Engels considered Darwinism a vindication of the dialectical process. In the course of natural selection, different species developed from common ancestors; this transition could be considered an example of accumulated quantitative changes resulting in a qualitative change, the latter change being marked by the moment when the diverging groups could no longer interbreed.[69]

In the interpretation of science, the principle of the transition of quantity into quality has been important in the Soviet Union as a warning against reductionism. Reductionism here means the belief that all complex phenomena can be explained in terms of combinations of simple or elemental ones. A reductionist would maintain that if a scientist wishes to understand a complex process (growth of crystals, stellar evolution, life, thought), he must build up from the most elemental level. Reductionism tends to emphasize physics at the expense of all other sciences. It is a view that was often supported by nineteenth-century materialists and today continues to have much strength among "hard" scientists around the world. Reductionism is highly criticized by Soviet dialectical materialists, who carefully distinguish themselves from earlier materialists. In the biological sciences in particular, the quantity-quality relationship has been interpreted in the Soviet Union as foreclosing the possibility of explaining life processes—most of all, thought—in elementary physico-chemical terms. Soviet philosophers see the development of matter from the simplest nonliving forms up through life and eventually to human beings and their social organizations as a series of quantitative transitions involving correlative qualitative changes. Thus, there are "dialectical levels" of natural laws.[70] Social laws cannot be reduced to biological laws, and biological laws cannot be reduced to physico-chemical laws. In dialectical materialism the whole is greater than the sum of its parts. This principle has been a valuable guard against simplistic explanations in materialistic terms, but it has also, on occasion, skirted the opposite danger of organicism or even vitalism.

The principle of the transition of quantity into quality distinguishes dialectical materialism from mechanistic materialism. A materialist, similar to Democritus, would say, for example, that the human brain is essentially the same as an animal's brain but is organized in a more efficient manner. According to this line of thinking, then, the difference is merely quantitative. The Marxist materialist, however, would say that the human brain is distinctly different from that of an animal and that this difference is a qualitative change resulting from accumulated quantitative changes during the course of the evolution of man from lower primates. Therefore, human mental processes cannot be reduced to those of other animals. Indeed, life processes in general cannot be totally reduced to physical and chemical processes if the latter are defined in contemporary terms. This emphasis on the qualitative distinctiveness of complex entities from simple ones has led dialectical materialists in recent years to become interested—although cautiously—in such concepts as "integrative levels" and "organismic biology," approaches widely discussed in Europe and America in the thirties and forties and displaying new vigor with the advent of cybernetics. The views of Soviet scholars regarding these concepts will be discussed more fully in a subsequent chapter (see, in particular, pp. 152ff.).

The attitudes of Soviet philosophers toward explanation of organic processes illustrate the complex and perhaps even contradictory nature of dialectical materialism. The dialectical materialist says, in effect, "There is nothing but matter, but all matter is not the same." Some critics have seen this expression as a paradox existing at the very root of dialectical materialism. Berdyaev wrote, for example, "Dialectic, which stands for complexity, and materialism, which results in a narrow one-sidedness of view, are as mutually repellent as water and oil."[71] Of course, one can easily note that almost every philosophical or ethical system contains tensions: The strain existing between the ideals of individual freedom and social good has existed in much of Western thought without destroying the value of that body of thought. Similarly, the tension between complexity and simplicity in dialectical materialism is by itself of small consequence in judging the adequacy of the system for the problems which face it. For the practicing scientist this tension has the merit of providing confidence that nature can be fruitfully approached, while warning against assuming that success in one area or at one level will answer ultimate questions.

Thus, the tension between complexity and simplicity that inheres in the principle of the transition of quantity into quality is simply a permanent feature of dialectical materialism that, operating at different times in different ways, both strengthens and weakens it. This tension was an important source of the disputes that rose in Soviet philosophy in the 1920s.

A partial rationalization of this dichotomy is offered by the second principle of the dialectic, the Law of the Mutual Interpenetration of Opposites, sometimes called the Law of the Unity and Struggle of Opposites. Hegel gave his views on this principle in terms of "positive" and "negative":

> Positive and negative are supposed to express an absolute difference. The two however are at bottom the same: the name of either might be transferred to the other. Thus, for example, debts and assets are not two particular self-subsisting species of property. What is negative to the debtor, is positive to the creditor. A way to the east is also a way to the west. Positive and negative are therefore intrinsically conditioned by one another, and are only in relation to each other. The north pole of the magnet cannot be without the south pole, and *vice versa*. If we cut a magnet in two, we have not a north pole in one piece and a south pole in the other. Similarly, in electricity the positive and the negative are not two diverse and independent fluids. In opposition, the difference is not confronted by any other, but by its other.[72]

By the principle of the unity of opposites Engels meant that harmony and order are found in the resulting synthesis of two opposing forces.[73] Engels saw the operation of this law in the rotation of the earth around the sun, which resulted from the opposing influences of gravitational and centrifugal forces. The same law governed the formation of a salt by the chemical interaction of an acid and a base. Other examples of the unity of opposites cited by Engels were the atom as a unity of positive and negative particles, life as a process of birth and death, and magnetic attraction and repulsion.[74]

The Law of the Unity and Struggle of Opposites is cited by dialectical materialists as an explanation for the energy inherent in nature. To the question, How did the matter in the world acquire its motion? dialectical materialism answers that matter possesses the property of self-movement as a result of the contradictions or opposites present in it. Thus, it is not necessary for dialectical materialists to postulate the existence of a First Mover who set the planets, molecules, and all other material objects in motion. This concept of self-movement derived from internal contradictions was also present in the thought of Hegel, who commented in his *Science of Logic*, "contradiction is the root of all movement and life, and it is only in so far as it contains a contradiction that anything moves and has impulse and activity."[75]

The Law of the Negation of the Negation is closely connected with the second law, since negation is supposedly the process by which synthesis occurs. Negation, according to Hegel, is a positive concept, an affirmation. The constant struggle between the old and the new leads to superior syntheses. In its most general sense, the principle of the negation is merely a formal statement of the belief that nothing in nature remains constant. Everything changes; each entity is eventually negated by another. Engels considered the principle of the negation of the negation extremely important to dialectical and historical materialism; he wrote that it is a law of development of "Nature, history and thought," and a law that "holds good in the animal and plant kingdoms, in geology, in mathematics, in history and in philosophy."[76] He gave a number of examples of the law: the negation of capitalism (which was a negation of feudalism) by socialism; the negation of plants such as orchids by artificially altering them through cultivation, yielding better seeds and more beautiful blooms; the negation of butterfly eggs by the birth of butterflies, which then lay more eggs; the negation of barley seed by the growth of the plant, which then yields more barley grains; differentiation and integration in calculus; and the mathematical process of squaring negative numbers.[77]

It is clear that "negation" meant a number of different things to Engels: replacement, succession, modification, and so forth. The last example above deserves more comment. Engels proposed taking the algebraic symbol a and negating this quantity by making it $-a$, then "negating the negation" by multiplying by $-a$, obtaining a^2. He said that a^2 represented a "synthesis of a higher level" since it was a positive number of the second power.[78] One might ask, Why did Engels multiply in order to negate the negation, instead of adding, subtracting, or dividing? Why did he multiply by $-a$ instead of some other figure? The obvious reply is that Engels picked a particular example that suited his purpose from the myriad of examples available. One of his discussions of the square root of -1 (evidently to prove the Law of the Mutual Interpenetration of Opposites) caused one anguished mathematician to write to Marx complaining about Engels' "wanton attack on the honor of -1."[79]

The dialectical laws in Marxist philosophy remained virtually as Engels elaborated them for many years. In the period immediately after the Russian Revolution, Soviet philosophers neglected the dialectical laws. At that time neither Engels' *Dialectics of Nature* nor Lenin's *Philosophical Notebooks* was known to them. The latter work, published separately in 1933, introduced one change in the Soviet treatment of the dialectical laws: Lenin considered the Law of the Unity of Opposites the most important of the three. Lenin even hinted that the transformation of quantity into quality was really only another description of the unity of opposites; if the two were truly synonymous, only two of the three primary laws would remain.[80]

While most Soviet philosophers today maintain that the actions of the three dialectical laws are observable everywhere (in nature, society, and thought) some of them believe that the laws operate only in human thought, not in inorganic or organic nature. This minority belongs to the camp of the "epistemologists," who are opposed by the "ontologists." Such an epistemologist was V. L. Obukhov, who in a book published in 1983 criticized his Soviet colleagues for their eagerness to see signs of the dialectical laws at work on every hand. But Obukhov's viewpoint was rejected by three reviewers in the main Soviet philosophy journal who wrote in 1985 that Obukhov's ideas "lead nowhere except to confusion."[81]

Before this discussion leaves the subject of the dialectic, a few words must be said about the "categories." In dialectical materialism the term "categories" is employed to refer to those basic concepts that are necessary in order to express the forms of interconnection of nature. In other words, while the laws of the dialectic just discussed are attempts to identify the most general uniformities of nature, the categories are those concepts that must be employed in expressing these uniformities. Examples of categories given in the past in Soviet discussions of the dialectic have been concepts such as matter, motion, space, time, quantity, and quality.

Nowhere does dialectical materialism reveal its affinities with traditional philosophy more clearly than in its emphasis on categories, although dialectical materialists have given the classical categories a new formation and meaning. The word "category" was first used as a part of a philosophical system by Aristotle. In his treatise *Categories* Aristotle divided all entities into the following ten classes: substance, quantity, quality, relation, place, time, posture, state, action, and passion. Objects or phenomena that belonged to different categories were considered to have nothing in common and, therefore, could not be compared. In his writings Aristotle frequently listed only some of the above ten categories, with no indication that others had been omitted. Aristotle apparently considered the exact number of categories and the terminology best suited for describing them open questions. Following Aristotle, many thinkers relied on a system of a priori categories of varying number and nature as a base for their philosophical systems. Medieval philosophers usually considered the original ten categories of Aristotle complete, ignoring Aristotle's latitude on the issue.

The two greatest modifiers of the Aristotelian concept of categories were Kant and Hegel. Kant based his categories not on particular subjects or entities, but on different types of judgments or propositions. To him, categories applied to logical forms, and not to things in themselves. "Quality" to Kant meant not "bitter" or "red," as it did to Aristotle, but logical relationships such as "negative" or "affirmative." "Quantity" meant to him not "five inches long" but "universal," "particular," and "singular." Thus, Kant carried out a radical reform of the Aristotelian categories.

Soviet philosophers have borrowed heavily from the approaches of Aristotle and Kant, adding to them Hegel's belief that the categories are not absolute. They consider Aristotle's writing amenable to the interpretation that the categories are reflections of the general properties of objectively existing objects and phenomena, although, as one Soviet text comments, "he did not always hold to this view, and, moreover, he did not succeed in revealing the inner dialectical connection of the categories."[82] Kant's major contribution to an understanding of the categories, in the opinion of Soviet philosophers, was his research into the logical functions of the categories and into the role of thought in refining sense perceptions. But Kant, they continue, made the great error of eliminating all connection between the categories and the objective world, looking upon them as the product of reason. Hegel's achievement in understanding the categories, according to Soviet dialectical materialists, was his realization that the categories are not static, but are in the process of development and are connected with each other. Thus, for example, the category "quantity" can grow into "quality."

The major distinction of the dialectical materialist approach to the categories is its heavy emphasis on natural science. Since, according to Marxism, being determines consciousness and not consciousness being, the material world, as reflected in human consciousness, determines the very concepts by which people think—that is, the categories. Thus, "in order for the materialist dialectic to be a method of scientific cognition, to direct human thought in search of new results, its categories must always be located at a level with modern science, with its sum total of achievements and needs" (p. 120).

Since man's knowledge of the material world changes with time, so then will his definition of the categories. *The Short Philosophical Dictionary*, published in Moscow in 1966, defined the categories as "the most general concepts, reflecting the basic properties and regularities of the phenomena of objective reality and defining the character of the scientific-theoretical thought of the epoch" (p. 119). The same source listed as examples of the categories matter, motion, consciousness, quality and quantity, cause and effect, and so on (p. 119).

The inclusion of the "and so on" at the end of the list of categories is an important indication of the flexibility of the categories within dialectical materialism. As with Aristotle, the list is purposely kept open and subject to revision. Lenin remarked that "if *everything* develops, then doesn't this refer to the most general *concepts* and *categories* of thought as well? If it doesn't, then that means thinking is not connected with being. If it does, then it means that there is a dialectic of concepts and a dialectic of knowledge having an objective significance."[83] The same approach is reflected in the following description in the *Short Philosophical Dictionary*: "The categories are regarded as flexible and changing because the very properties of objective phenomena are also mobile and changing. The categories do not appear at once in a completed form. They are formed during the long historical process of the development of knowledge" (p. 120). Thus, the categories develop with science itself.

The avowed elasticity of the categories gives, indirectly, room for interpretation of the dialectical laws themselves, since the categories are the terms in which the laws are expressed. In this study the possibility of revising the categories will be particularly relevant in the discussion of cosmology, where certain authors reinterpreted the term "infinity" after 1956 by examining the categories. "Time" and "space" had been listed as categories in the texts of the fifties, and these concepts were reexamined.[84] Another area where the categories were scrutinized was quantum mechanics. Here the concept of causality, or the category of "cause and effect," was actually modified.

THE UNITY OF THEORY AND PRACTICE

Another aspect of dialectical materialism that has relevance for science is not so much an integral part of the intellectual structure of the system as it is a methodological principle; this aspect is the unity of theory and practice. During a considerable portion of Soviet history the unity of theory and practice meant for scientists that they should give their research a clear social purpose by tying it to the needs of Soviet society. The strength of this recommendation has varied greatly in different fields and at different times. The unity of theory and practice can be traced back to Marx's opposition to speculative philosophy; he hoped to transcend philosophy by "actualizing" it. One of his best-known sentences referred to this effort to build a conceptual theory that would result in concrete achievements: "The philosophers have only *interpreted* the world in various ways; the point however is to *change* it."[85]

Engels believed that the unity of theory and practice was connected with the problem of cognition. The most telling evidence, he believed, against idealistic epistemologies was that man's knowledge of nature resulted in practical benefits; man's theories of matter "worked" in the sense that they yielded products for his use. As Engels commented, "If we are able to prove the correctness of our conception of a natural process by making it ourselves, bringing it into being out of its conditions and using it for our own purposes into the bargain, then there is an end of the Kantian incomprehensible 'thing-in-itself.' "[86] Thus, practice becomes the criterion of truth. Of course, Engels admitted that many theories or explanations "worked" while being incomplete or based on false assumptions. The Babylonians were able to predict certain celestial phenomena through the use of tables, with almost no knowledge of the location and movement of the bodies themselves. Every scientific theory at any point in time contains false assumptions and lacks important evidence; many useful theories, such as Ptolemaic astronomy, are "overthrown." But Engels maintained that the successful application of a theory about nature indicated that it contained somewhere within it a kernel of truth.[87]

THE DISPUTE BETWEEN THE EPISTEMOLOGISTS
AND THE ONTOLOGISTS

As mentioned several times previously, a major recent controversy among Soviet dialectical materialists has been between those people who believe that the laws of dialectic are inherent in nature and that Marxist philosophy can even help a scientist predict research results (the ontologists' position), and those who assign dialectical materialism the more restricted role of the study of uniquely philosophical issues such as cognition, logic, and methodology (the epistemologists' position). A leading member of the epistemologists was Engels' Matveevich Chudinov. Named after Friedrich Engels, Chudinov was a dedicated Marxist who wanted to help Soviet dialectical materialism become a much more sophisticated form of philosophy than it had so far been able to be. In the 1970s Chudinov published a number of works that demonstrated his deep knowledge of philosophy of science in both the Soviet Union and Western countries. Perhaps his best work (he died in 1980) was *The Nature of Scientific Truth*, published in 1977, in which he tried to work out a sophisticated Marxist epistemology.[88] In the book he discussed intelligently a whole array of Western authors, including O'Connor, Rescher, Popper, Kuhn, Lakatos, Russell, Feyerabend, Bunge, Hempel, Carnap, Musgrave, Quine, Grünbaum, and Gödel.

Chudinov described dialectical materialism as a further and superior development of the classical conception, originally undertaken by Plato and Aristotle, in which "truth" is seen as correspondence between ideas and reality. But dialectical materialism differs from this traditional view, he continued, by introducing such concepts as "relative truth," and by emphasizing that the major criterion of truth is practice. Thus, the dialectical materialist knows that he or she will never possess absolute truth, but only increasingly accurate approximations asymptotically approaching objective reality.

With his commitment to objective reality, Chudinov disagreed with Thomas Kuhn's conception of successive paradigms in the history of science on the grounds that it did not give enough place to the idea of progress through increasingly accurate approximations of truth; he similarly rejected Karl Popper's criticism of Kuhn because Popper's concept of "refutation" did not emphasize practice, which to Chudinov was the positive criterion of truth.

While it is possible to criticize Chudinov's position from several different viewpoints, his effort to work on truly philosophical questions rather than try to comment on the validity of developments in specific sciences in the manner of the previous generation was a positive development in Soviet philosophy. In that sense he was a true "epistemologist," a representative of the reforming generation of Soviet philosophers of science who came to academic maturity in the sixties and seventies.

Until the mid-seventies it seemed that the epistemologists would gain the upper hand over the ontologists. After all, many of the ontologists were educated in the time of Stalin, when philosophy's role in science had been much stronger. The weakening of the grip of Stalinism went in step with the diminishing of the role of ontologists. B. M. Kedrov even wrote that much of the inspiration for the ontological approach came from the fourth chapter of Stalin's famous *Short Course of the History of the Communist Party*, where dialectics had been crudely applied to nature. As Kedrov aptly observed, "Such an approach later received the name 'ontological.' "[89]

Most of the ontologists were either older philosophers or philosophers and natural scientists of various ages located in institutions outside the prestigious Academy of Sciences. However, by the end of the seventies the ontologists began to make inroads on the establishment, finding new strength. The most surprising development was that in the seventies and eighties the ontologists produced a number of younger scholars who were committed to the old form of dialectics of nature. One of the reasons for this success was the didactic ease with which that form of philosophy could be taught in the universities, where every Soviet student was required to take a course in dialectical materialism.

An important influence in strengthening the ontologists' position was M. N. Rutkevich's book *Dialectical Materialism*, published in 1973, and adopted by the Ministry of Education as a textbook for philosophy departments in universities of the USSR. The book contained statements indicating that Marxism is not only a philosophy describing the future of social and political history, but also that it can evaluate theories of natural science. This sort of arrogance by a philosopher offended many research scientists, who frequently criticized the Rutkevich text. Nonetheless, it continued to have influence, especially among undergraduates and secondary school teachers.

Perhaps the most disturbing aspect of the Rutkevich text was its lack of clarity on cardinal questions of heredity. Rutkevich described Lamarckian and Mendelian views as having equal intellectual standing at the present time, and predicted future victories for the Lamarckian

approach.[90] Many Soviet geneticists found this description grossly mis-
leading; they were further irritated by what they saw as Rutkevich's
assumption that a philosopher could assess the validity of theories of
heredity more accurately than biologists. And they objected most of all
to Rutkevich's failure to inform his readers that such arguments about
Marxism and biology in previous decades had disastrous effects on
Soviet science. Rutkevich seemed to have learned little from the past.

   In 1974 a sharp conflict between the ontologists and the epistemologists broke out in the journal *Philosophical Sciences*.[91] The discussions
revealed more clearly the institutional and professional bases of the
various factions. *Philosophical Sciences* is a journal published by the
Ministry of Higher and Secondary Specialized Education of the USSR,
in charge of Soviet universities. The editorial board of the journal in
1974 included faculty members from universities in Sverdlovsk, Erevan,
Rostov-on-the-Don, Kiev, Leningrad, Moscow, Minsk, Odessa, and Stu-
pino. University philosophy faculties, especially those from provincial
cities, have in recent years contained far more "ontologists" than the
institutes of the Academy of Sciences, where the "epistemologists" have
been stronger. The reason for this difference is not difficult to identify:
university faculties in the USSR are more responsible for teaching than
for research, and the ontological view that dialectical laws are found
in nature is very easy to teach, using standard textbooks and a few
selections from the classical writings of Engels. The Academy of Sciences,
however, contains more professional research philosophers who are
studying problems of cognition, logic, and semantic meaning. These
professional research philosophers are eager to demarcate philosophy
from natural science so that both the philosophers and natural scientists
have autonomous professional realms.

   This split occurred graphically in the exchange of views between
V. V. Orlov, a university teacher from Perm, and L. B. Bazhenov, a
research philosopher from the Institute of Philosophy of the Academy
of Sciences of the USSR. Orlov maintained that philosophy must "explain" the origin of life and of consciousness, but Bazhenov disagreed,
saying that providing such explanation is the role of natural science,
not philosophy. Philosophy, said Bazhenov, can only produce methodological principles of thought. The concrete sciences must do the
actual explaining.

   Orlov considered Bazhenov's position an abdication of the heuristic
and pedagogical function of dialectical materialism. The very definition
of "matter," he continued, must be in terms of philosophical categories

taken from Marxism; furthermore, this "matter" which lies at the basis of nature develops according to dialectical laws in a certain direction, leading successively toward the origin of life, the origin of consciousness, and, finally, the origin of man. Orlov was known as the leader of a group of Marxist philosophers at Perm University who insisted that dialectical materialism includes a goal-oriented evolution of matter culminating in human beings. "Man," said Orlov, "is the summit of the development of matter, its crown, and the master of nature."[92]

Bazhenov critically responded that Orlov's view was "frankly teleological." He further said that by demanding that matter be defined in Marxist terms Orlov was condemning Marxism to obsolescence as the physicists' definition of matter changes, as scientists discard even more such traditional characteristics of matter as spatial and temporal dimensions.

By the late seventies and early eighties the ontologists were regaining strength impressively, in step with the resurgence of ideological conservatism in the Soviet Union in many fields. In 1980 another textbook on philosophy was published that emphasized dialectics in nature just as Rutkevich had done seven years earlier.[93] Much of the strength of the ontologists centered in courses "For the Raising of the Qualifications of Teachers of the Social Sciences." These courses were a form of adult education offered in universities, especially provincial ones, technical institutes, correspondence schools, and the equivalent of junior colleges. The quality of instruction was low, but the quantity of students taking such courses was very great. By sheer weight of numbers, the form of simplistic dialectical materialism taught so readily by the ontologists was beginning to gain the upper hand as an influence in Soviet education. The year 1982 saw a new outbreak of the controversy, with over seventy different authors speaking out on the subject in philosophical journals. As two Soviet philosophers lamented at the end of that year, "ontological meanderings have still not been eliminated in our philosophy. On the contrary, recently they have gotten a sort of 'second breath.' There are plans for the conversion of Marxist philosophy into a system of ontological knowledge. The 'unharnessing' of the ontological element in Marxist philosophy will lead objectively to prescientific philosophical conceptions."[94]

NURTURISM

Although it is much more pronounced in Soviet philosophy than it was in the thought of Marx and Engels, another characteristic of dialectical materialism is its belief that human thought is primarily influenced by the social environment. A corollary of this principle is that people raised in different social and cultural environments will differ not only in the content of their thought, but in their very modes of thought. This nurturist principle derived from Marx's observation that "being determines consciousness," and was emphasized by Soviet leaders because of its potential for transforming society. In the Soviet Union this principle has been an important aspect of Soviet educational doctrine since the 1920s, when the Soviet pedagogue A. S. Makarenko (1888–1939) established camps for delinquent children where he claimed he rehabilitated them by using "socially useful labor" as a formative influence.[95] The prominent Soviet Marxist psychologists L. S. Vygotsky, A. R. Luria, and A. N. Leont'ev also emphasized the effect of the social environment on the formation of the human psyche, as will be discussed in this volume in the chapter on psychology. During both the Stalinist and post-Stalinist periods a major goal of the Soviet government has been the development of a "new Soviet man" by surrounding Soviet citiz ns with a social environment favoring those forms of behavior deei ied appropriate in "Soviet socialist society."

Soviet Marxists have therefore generally favored "nurturism" over "naturism" as an explanation of human behavior, but considerable vacillation on this issue has occurred. As we will see in later chapters, both in the 1920s and in the 1970s and 1980s, certain Soviet Marxists have argued that nothing in dialectical materialism forbids attributing some influence to genetics in explaining human behavior. This issue has in recent years led to a great debate in the Soviet Union over the sources of human behavior, one that is still going on. This controversy will be discussed in detail in chapters 6 and 7.

Looking back over the system of Soviet dialectical materialism, we see, on the most general level, that it represents a natural philosophy based on the following quite reasonable principles and opinions:

The world is material, and is made up of what current science would describe as matter-energy.

The material world forms an interconnected whole.

Man's knowledge is derived from objectively existing reality, both natural and social; being determines consciousness.

The world is constantly changing, and, indeed, there are no truly static entities in the world.

The changes in matter occur in accordance with certain overall regularities or laws.

The laws of the development of matter exist on different levels corresponding to the different subject matters of the sciences, and therefore one should not expect in every case to be able to explain such complex entities as biological organisms in terms of the most elementary physicochemical laws.

Matter is infinite in its properties, and therefore man's knowledge will never be complete.

The motion present in the world is explained by internal factors, and therefore no external mover is needed.

Man's knowledge grows with time, as is illustrated by his increasing success in applying it to practice, but this growth occurs through the accumulation of relative—not absolute—truths.

The history of thought clearly shows that no one of the above principles or opinions is original to dialectical materialism, although the total is. Many of the above opinions date from the classical period and have been held by various thinkers over a period of more than two thousand years. Today many working scientists operate, implicitly or explicitly, on the basis of assumptions similar to the above principles (hence the Soviet view that outstanding non-Marxist scientists are often at least implicit dialectical materialists). Yet the common currency of many of the most general principles of dialectical materialism does not devalue it. First, these principles have been more fully developed and more closely linked to science in the writings of dialectical materialists than in any other corpus of literature. Furthermore, unexceptional as some of these opinions may at first glance seem, dialectical materialists have their opponents even on these broadest principles. Their commitment to the primacy of matter is rejected by many, probably most, philosophers. Materialism has never been a philosophy of the majority of philosophers at any point in the history of Western philosophy; its most ardent advocates have not usually been professional philosophers. In addition, dialectical materialists disagree not only with their most obvious opponents—theists and idealists—but also with materialists of the old type, the thoroughgoing reductionists who believe that all science will eventually be absorbed by physics. In sum, dialectical materialism— despite what some observers regard as the unobjectionable character of its most general principles—is still a controversial world view, one that enjoys the explicit support of only a small minority of philosophers and scientists in the world. When one adds to these intellectual obstacles the political liability deriving from dialectical materialism's support by the bureaucracy of an authoritarian and repressive state, it is not surprising that dialectical materialism has won relatively few supporters outside the Soviet Union. Yet it should be noticed that in intellectual terms dialectical materialism is a legitimate and valuable point of view, far more interesting than non-Soviet scientists and philosophers have usually assumed.

Soviet dialectical materialism as a philosophy of science draws upon both Russian sources and traditional European philosophy. The Soviet contribution has been primarily one of emphasis on the natural sciences as determining elements of philosophy. In the opinion of Soviet philosophers, dialectical materialism both helps scientists in their research and, in turn, is ultimately affected by the results of that research. Their critics have occasionally maintained that such a description of the relation of science and philosophy is no description at all. Exactly what meaning is carried in the statement "Philosophy influences science and is, in turn, influenced by it"?

An answer that accurately weighs the mutual influence of philosophy and science is difficult, but it is clearly true that such a mutual influence exists. Furthermore, that interaction is an important element in the genesis and elaboration of scientific schemes. Questions may revolve around the degree of influence of philosophy upon science, or the mechanisms by which such influence is transmitted, but the existence of the interaction can not be questioned. Throughout the history of science, philosophy has significantly affected the development of scientific explanations of nature, and, in turn, science has influenced philosophy. Scientists inevitably go beyond empirical data and proceed, implicitly or explicitly, on the basis of one or another philosophy. Philosophers, on the other hand, have been forced by the evolution of science to revise basic concepts underlying their philosophic systems, such as the concepts of matter, space, time, and causality.

Moments when philosophy has importantly influenced science can be found from the earliest points in the history of science, and similar influences continue today in all countries. The early teachings of the Ionian natural philosophers, based on a naturalistic or nonreligious approach to nature, were heavily modified by the post-Socratic Greeks in the name of philosophic viewpoints that assumed the necessity of a divine being for an understanding of the cosmos. Benjamin Farrington commented that astronomy was "Pythagoreanized and Platonized within a few generations of the Ionian dawn." He also observed that "astronomy did not really make its way with the Greek public until it had been rescued from atheism."[96] Here was an example in which a philosophic world view influenced a scheme of scientific explanation.

Many others have followed. The historian of science Alexandre Koyré maintained that Galileo was a Platonist in his understanding of nature, and that this view had important influences on his scientific development. Koyré's view has been criticized, but not from the standpoint of a denial of philosophic influence on Galileo.[97] Newton's explanation of nature was presented within a religious framework that made it more acceptable to the society of his time and yet also revealed something important about Newton's internal convictions and presuppositions. Descartes actually postponed publication of his *Principia Philosophiae* in an effort to fit an orthodox and religious interpretation to his view of nature; this orthodoxy accorded with his views, but the fitting process was not obvious. The impact of German nature philosophy upon European scientists in the early decades of the nineteenth century is well known, and such historians of science as L. Pearce Williams would even see nature philosophy as an important ingredient in the origin of field theory, maintaining that convertibility of forces "was an idea that was derived from nature philosophy and one to which the Newtonian system of physics was, if not hostile, at least indifferent."[98] In each of these cases interaction between science and philosophy is one of the prime topics of study for the historian of science.

The impact of philosophy upon science has continued through the present day; it should not be regarded as a vestige of the past that will hopefully soon be overcome if it has not already been vanquished. Einstein even wrote, "In our time physicists are forced to concern themselves with philosophical questions to a greater degree than physicists of previous generations."[99] Einstein frequently acknowledged his personal debt to philosophical criticisms of science; out of such criticisms arose a revolution in twentieth-century science.

We stand so close to the development of contemporary science that we may not at first discern the interaction of philosophy and science, but it is certainly there. As an example, the new concepts in quantum mechanics and relativity physics of this century not only had a philosophic background, but in turn exerted a considerable influence on subsequent philosophy in Western countries in the first half of this century. These were countries in which many different philosophic viewpoints were expressed but the most popular ones favored religion over atheism and idealism over materialism. Consequently, it is not surprising that a number of influential scientists and philosophers in these countries seized upon the new physics and attempted to build philosophical systems justifying their religious and epistemological points of view. The uncertainty principle was to some of them an opportunity for the defense of freedom of will, while the rise of relativity physics signaled to many of them the end of materialism. In the Soviet Union the defenders of materialism answered back in full measure—indeed, in more than full measure—criticizing idealistic and religious points of view. Each side went far beyond conclusions that were intellectually justified, treating the opposition as if its position were groundless. The outcome of this debate was to illustrate that neither side possessed the clear superiority of argument that it claimed. This gradually became apparent to many writers, and the quality of their arguments began to improve. The Soviet authors, the main concern of this study, were able to develop a dialectical materialist interpretation of the universe based on the very principles of contemporary science that their opponents attempted to use against them.

The fact that emerges from these considerations is that science and philosophy have interacted at all times and places, not merely in the ancient past or in the contemporary Soviet Union. Soviet science is a part of world science, and the type of interaction of philosophy and science that can be found in Soviet scholarly writings (those of intellectuals, not of Party activists) is not essentially different from the interaction of science and philosophy elsewhere. But since the philosophical tradition in the Soviet Union is different from the tradition in Western Europe and the United States, the results of that interaction have not been identical with the results of similar interactions in other geographical areas.

Thus, the significance of dialectical materialism is not so much its insistence on this mutual interaction of philosophy and science—many of its critics would readily grant such a relation—but the way in which this interaction has actually occurred in the Soviet setting. Dialectical materialism in the Soviet Union today is not the same as dialectical materialism there fifty years ago, and the impact of developments in science is one of the reasons for its change. But then neither is science itself in the Soviet Union the same as it was fifty years ago, and one of the many influences upon it has been dialectical materialism. Although the Communist Party has attempted at times to control this interaction—much more so a generation ago than now—it quite obviously was not able to do so. An independent intellectual process of significance and interest to historians and philosophers of science was also at work. The following chapters contain discussions in detail of the mutual influence of science and dialectical materialism in the Soviet Union. The most helpful sources for these discussions were the writings of individual Soviet scientists.

CHAPTER **3**

ORIGIN OF LIFE

In the late Twenties and early Thirties the basic thinking was done which led to the view that saw life as a natural and perhaps inevitable development from the non-living world. Future students of the history of ideas are likely to take note that this view, which amounts to nothing less than a great revolution in man's philosophical outlook on his own position in the natural world, was first developed by Communists. Oparin of Moscow, in 1924, and J. B. S. Haldane, of Cambridge, England, in 1929, independently argued that recent advances in geochemistry . . . made it possible to imagine the origin of systems that might be called "living."
—C. H. Waddington, British geneticist, 1968[1]

The topic of the origin of life is one of the most interesting and least understood of the areas of the interaction between science and Marxist philosophy. Much essential information on this issue is still missing and will be uncovered only by careful monographic studies of the original workers in this field in the 1920s and 1930s, particularly in Russia and Britain. Already, however, important interpretive issues have emerged, as indicated in the statement by C. H. Waddington that heads this chapter.

Most scientists and historians of science are very skeptical of easy associations of science and political ideology, and no doubt Waddington did not intend to imply a direct causal link here. In this rather casual comment in a book review he was opening the question of the possible influence of Marxism on the significant theories of life of the first half of the twentieth century, not attempting to answer it. There are many opportunities in the history of science for linking science and politics, but frequently upon close examination the links either dissolve or turn out to be much more complex than was thought earlier. As we will see, there are very weighty pieces of evidence against the belief that Oparin and Haldane were applying Marxism in 1924 and 1929. Nonetheless, the question of the interaction of Marxism and biology in the twentieth century is a legitimate and important one.

At the outset it will be useful to compare what Western observers have done with two different developments in the history of science: The Lysenko affair and discussions of the origin of life. In neither case is it self-evident that Marxism as a system of thought was significant in the formulation of the interpretations of biological phenomena known, respectively, as the Oparin-Haldane hypothesis and Lysenko's theory of inheritance. However, all three scientists—Oparin, Haldane, Ly-senko—explicitly declared at times subsequent to the original development of their respective and differing hypotheses that Marxism was an important influence in their biological thought. All three became vocal dialectical materialists. Yet if one mentions "Marxism and biology" to the average educated citizen of Western Europe or America, he or she will think only of Lysenko. This tendency to explain an acknowledged calamity in science as a result of Marxist philosophy while assuming that a brilliant page in the history of biology had nothing to do with Marxism is a reflection, at least in part, of the biases and historical selectivity of Western journalists and historians.

The important question still remains: Did Marxism have anything to do with the Oparin-Haldane hypothesis? Although this question cannot be definitively answered at this time, and no doubt will long remain controversial, certain clarifications can be made. Before attempting these clarifications, I would like to make some general comments about A. I. Oparin and the issue of the origin of life. As a Russian, with an active life extending through almost all of Soviet history, Oparin is central to this study, while Haldane falls outside of it. Oparin's initial work on this issue was prior to Haldane's entirely independent but similar approach; the British scientist graciously declared in 1963, "I have very little doubt that Professor Oparin has priority over me."[2]

The question of the origin of life is one of the oldest in the history of thought. At almost all periods of time a belief in spontaneous generation was commonly held. This belief was by no means the property of one school of thought; Democritus, Aristotle, St. Augustine, Paracelsus, Francis Bacon, Descartes, Buffon, and Lamarck are only a few of those who expressed support for the concept, but within the frameworks of quite different interpretations of nature. With the development of microscopy the center of attention in discussions of the origin of life shifted to the level of the invisibly small. A famous debate in the late 1860s between the French scientists Felix Pouchet and Louis Pasteur over the possibility of the spontaneous origin of microorganisms ended with a negative result that left the subject of spontaneous generation in disrepute for the remainder of the century. To be sure, a few writers such as H. Charlton Bastian continued to consider spontaneous generation possible.[3] Friedrich Engels observed ironically that it would be foolish to expect men with the help of "a little stinking water to force nature to accomplish in twenty-four hours what it has cost her thousands of years to bring about."[4] And most people did not notice that Pasteur himself commented in 1878, "Spontaneous generation? I have been looking for it for 20 years, but I have yet to find it, although I do not think it is an impossibility."[5]

Much of the foregoing would seem to serve as an introduction to A. I. Oparin as a twentieth-century exponent of spontaneous generation. Yet if one understands spontaneous generation to mean the sudden arising of a relatively complicated living entity—whether an organism, a cell, or a molecule of DNA—from nonliving matter, Oparin was actually an opponent of spontaneous generation. In his opinion, the belief that such an orderly entity as a cell or even a "living" molecule of nucleic acid could arise spontaneously is based upon "metaphysical materialism" and suffers from the same improbabilities (to be discussed below) as Pouchet's arguments.

Aleksandr Ivanovich Oparin (1894–1980) was a prominent biochemist who graduated from Moscow University in 1917 and subsequently became a professor there.[6] He was closely associated with the Institute of Biochemistry of the USSR Academy of Sciences, which he helped to organize in 1935 and of which he became director in 1946. In the same year he became a full member of the Academy of Sciences. In 1950 he received the A. N. Bakh and I. I. Mechnikov prizes. He worked on several different topics, including such practical ones as the biochemistry of sugar, bread, and tea production, but he was best known both in the Soviet Union and abroad for his theory of the origin of life. Over a period of almost sixty years he published numerous books, revised editions, and journal articles on this topic. As early as 1922 he delivered a talk on the origin of life to the Moscow Botanical Society; he subsequently published these views in a small booklet in 1924.[7] Although frequently cited in the scientific literature, the 1924 publication was an exceedingly rare one and was not translated into English until 1967.[8] Most references by English readers to Oparin' s work have been to the 1938 and subsequent editions, which differed from his earliest publications in several ways that are interesting to the historian. These differences will be discussed later. With the growing interest in Soviet science prompted by Soviet achievements in space in the late fifties, Oparin's work received international attention more rapidly; his 1966 *The Origin and Initial Development of Life* was translated into English by the U.S. National Aeronautics and Space Administration in 1968.[9]

The most prominent contribution by Oparin to the study of the origin of life was his reawakening of interest in the issue. The American biologist John Keosian wrote in his popular text *The Origin of Life*, "Oparin's unique contribution is his revival of the materialistic approach to the question of how life originated, as well as his detailed development of this concept."[10] The British scientist J. D. Bernal commented in 1967 that Oparin's 1924 essay

> contains in itself the germs of a new programme in chemical and biological research. It was a programme that he largely carried out himself in the ensuing years, but it also inspired the work of many other people. . . . Oparin's programme does not answer all the questions, in fact, he hardly answers any, but the questions he asks are very effective and pregnant ones and have given rise to an enormous amount of research in the four decades since it was written. The essential thing in the first place is not to solve the problems, but to see them. This is true of the greatest of all scientists. . . This paper is important because it is a starting point for all the others and, though it is clearly defective and inaccurate, it can be, and has been, corrected in the sequel. (pp. 240–41)

Turning now to the question of intellectual and social influences on Oparin, it can be clearly established that from the early 1930s onward Oparin was influenced by dialectical materialism. The evidence is not only his frequent statements favoring dialectical materialism, but, much more importantly, the very method of analysis of his later publications, which are permeated with an assumption of a process philosophy and a concept of differing dialectical levels of regularities in nature. All of this was described in his works in the language of dialectical materialism. Oparin spoke out so frequently on the relevance of dialectical materialism to theories of biological development that almost all of his publications of substantial length contained such statements. To be sure, there is the possibility that these sections of his writings were merely responses to political pressures, but if one reads in chronological order through Oparin's works published over many years at times of greatly varying political atmospheres one can not avoid the conclusion, it seems to me, that dialectical materialism became an ever-increasing and substantial influence on his work. In 1953 Oparin wrote, "Only dialectical materialism has found the correct routes to an understanding of life. According to dialectical materialism, life is a special form of the movement of matter which arises as a new quality at a definite stage in the historical movement of matter. Therefore, it possesses properties that distinguish it from the inorganic world, and is characterized by special, specific regularities that are not reducible merely to the regularities of physics and chemistry."[11]

And in 1966 in the book translated by NASA Oparin commented:

Regarding life as a qualitatively special form of the motion of matter, dialectical materialism formulates even the very problem of understanding life in a different way than does mechanism. For the mechanist, it consists of the most comprehensive reduction of living phenomena to physical and chemical processes. On the other hand, from the dialectical materialist point of view, the main point in understanding life is to establish its qualitative difference from other forms of motion in matter.[12]

As I discuss in chronological order a number of Oparin's other publications on the origin of life, more specific effects of his dialectical materialist approach will come to light. This discussion should not be confused with a general history of Oparin's theories, which remains to be written and would take into account in a much fuller way the development of biochemistry as a whole. In such a history dialectical materialism would play a less prominent role than in this discussion. Nonetheless, it will always be seen, I think, as one of the important influences upon Oparin.

If we turn to Oparin's 1924 booklet, however, we will find no mention of Marxism. Even more significantly, Oparin's analysis in this small book differed from almost all of his later works in containing no concept of "different levels of regularities," no statement that qualitatively distinct principles govern the movement of matter on different onto-logical levels. The Oparin of 1924 was a materialist (and here the influences of his political and social milieu no doubt enter in), but he seems to have been an old-fashioned materialist, one who believed that life can be entirely explained in terms of physics and chemistry. Com-pare, for example, his 1953 statement quoted above, in which he said that life is characterized by special regularities that are not reducible to those of chemistry and physics, to the following statement, which was contained in the 1924 booklet:

The more closely and accurately we get to know the essential features of the processes which are carried out in the living cell, the more strongly we become convinced that there is nothing peculiar or mysterious about them, nothing that cannot be explained in terms of the general laws of physics and chemistry. (p. 214)

And in another place in the same work he commented, "Life is not characterized by any special properties but by a definite specific com-bination of these properties" (p. 217). Here again, the assumption is a reductionist one, although the "definite specific combination" allowed a bit of room for the later development of the concept of "special biological regularities" distinct from those of physics and chemistry, a concept that later became fundamentally important to his work. Ironically, the Oparin who in 1924 campaigned against vitalism in the name of purely physicochemical explanations of life would in the fifties and sixties defend the uniqueness of biological regularities against those molecular biologists who would try to explain life entirely in terms of the structure of a molecule of nucleic acid—that is, in terms of purely physicochemical explanation.

The fact that Oparin did not possess a knowledge of systematic dialectical materialism in 1924 does not prove that Marxism had nothing to do with the timing of his expression. Russia in the early twenties was the home of a victorious revolution carried out in the name of Marxism. "Materialism" was one of the most popular slogans of the day, and most of it was of the rather elementary, mechanistic sort espoused by Oparin, not the more subtle dialectical materialism developed later. Neither Engels' *Dialectics of Nature* nor Lenin's *Philosophical Notebooks* had yet appeared in print; these are the two books that more than any others have counteracted the severe reductionism of earlier materialism with the concept of qualitatively distinct realms of operation of natural laws. Oparin's materialism developed parallel to the predominant philosophical views of his society. Communism probably had something to do with Oparin's 1924 statement, but not in the sense of a relationship between dialectics and theories about the origin of life; rather, communism in Russia in the twenties provided the kind of atmosphere in which the posing of a materialistic answer to the question "What is life?" seemed natural. The Soviet Union of the twenties was an environment in which speculation about nature on the basis of materialist assumptions was not only welcome but very nearly inevitable. Oparin certainly had nothing to fear from his political and social milieu in expressing such views, and he made no effort to soften their impact. Similar viewpoints were still capable of causing quite an adverse reaction in Britain, as the reception of Haldane's similar views five years later showed; Bernal commented, "Haldane's ideas were dismissed as wild speculation" (p. 251). Haldane assured his readers in 1929 that his opinions (not entirely identical with Oparin's, but similar) were also compatible with "the view that pre-existent mind or spirit can associate itself with certain kinds of matter."[13] Yet it was clear that Haldane did not share this vitalistic view, and his inclusion of it came from his hope that his scientific conception would not be rejected simply because "some people will consider it a sufficient refutation of the above theories to say that they are materialistic."[14]

How close Oparin personally was to Marxist ideas at this early period is still unknown. From 1921 onward he was closely associated with the older Soviet biochemist A. N. Bakh, who was a political revolutionary and former emigré, and who published on Marxism as early as the 1880s.[15] But until we know more about Oparin's philosophical orientation in the period 1917–1924, not much more can be said about the influence of Marxist materialism on his 1924 publication.

It might be added parenthetically that a similar problem of interpretation exists in the case of Haldane. Like Oparin, he seems to have been most influenced by Marxist thought *after* he published his first fundamental work on the origin of life. Haldane's first article on the subject appeared in 1929, as already noted. As late as 1938 Haldane wrote, "I have only been a Marxist for about a year. I have not yet read all the relevant literature, although I had of course read much of it before I became a Marxist."[16] Yet this does not prove, of course, that Haldane had not learned of Marxist ideas of development by 1929. Since the late twenties Haldane had been a leader of a group of Cambridge intellectuals who were very interested in Marxism. But there were other influences in the air, too, that were interesting to men like Haldane and relevant to the biological issue, such as the early process philosophy of A. N. Whitehead. Some writers have argued that Haldane's view of science grew out of a complicated interaction of reductionist biochemistry, the process philosophy of Whitehead, and Marxism. Whatever the ingredients and the proportions of the early intellectual influences on Haldane, a hand-in-hand evolution based on interaction seems to have occurred.[17] It eventually resulted in his writing a volume entitled *The Marxist Philosophy and the Sciences*. A similar long-term intellectual development will be seen in Oparin, with the difference that his interests in Marxism continued to deepen throughout his career.

The task that faced Oparin in 1924 in biology was as much one of changing the psychological orientation of scientists as it was altering their research itself. He had to convince his readers that despite Pasteur's victory over Pouchet years before and the complete inability of scientists to produce even the most elementary living organisms in a laboratory, a materialist explanation of the origin of life was still worth the effort.

In restrospect, Oparin observed, we should not be surprised or fundamentally affected by the outcome of the Pasteur-Pouchet debate.

Pouchet was indeed incorrect, but not because of his materialist assumptions. Even the simplest microorganisms, and certainly those that Pasteur and Pouchet observed, are extremely complex bits of matter; they possess an "extraordinarily complicated" protoplasm. How could Pouchet even suppose that such a highly differentiated form of matter could "accidentally" have arisen in a few hours or even days from a relatively formless mixture? To assume such an incredibly improbable occurrence was unscientific in the deepest sense, a violation of the principle of explaining nature in the simplest and most plausible fashion available. As Oparin observed,

> Even the simplest creatures, consisting of only one cell, are extremely complicated structures. . . . The idea that such a complicated structure with a completely determinate fine organization could arise spontaneously in the course of a few hours in structureless solutions such as broths or infusions is as wild as the idea that frogs could be formed from the May dew or mice from corn. (p. 203)

How then could one begin to explain an origin of life on the basis of materialist assumptions? Only, said Oparin, by going back to the very simplest forms of matter and by extending the Darwinian principles of evolution to inanimate matter as well as animate matter. The "world of the living" and the "world of the dead" can be tied together by attempting to look at them both in terms of their historical development. Any finely structured entity, alive or dead—whether a one-celled organism, a piece of inorganic crystal,[18] or an eagle's eye—seems inexplicable unless it is examined in historical, evolutionary terms. Pouchet failed because the specimens he thought would arise spontaneously— microorganisms— were already the ultimate products of an extremely long evolutionary history and can be brought into existence only through that chain of material development, not by side-stepping it.

In the section of his 1924 work subtitled "From Uncombined Elements to Organic Compounds," Oparin attempted to reconstruct the historic process that might have led to the origin of life, with the simple always preceding the complex. In order to follow this sequence, it was necessary for him to reject the customary thesis that all organic compounds had been produced by living organisms, a belief still widely held at that time despite the supposed synthesis of urea by Wöhler as long ago as 1828.[19] To postulate that all organic compounds had been produced by living organisms was methodologically faulty, thought Oparin, since organisms themselves were obviously composed of organic compounds, and many of them far more complex than some of the products supposedly produced. Far better, he thought, to assume that at least some organic compounds antedated complete organisms and had been important to the origin of these organisms. An important stimulus to Oparin's thought on this subject was the theory of the carbide origin of petroleum advanced by the great Russian chemist D. I. Mendeleev many years before. Mendeleev had posed the possibility of the origin of the hydrocarbon methane by the action of steam on metallic carbides under conditions of high temperature and pressure, for example:

$$C_3Al_4 + 12H_2O \rightarrow 3CH_4 + 4Al(OH)_3$$

This inorganic source of methane would then have been followed by further transformations leading ultimately to petroleum. Oparin did not accept Mendeleev's hypothesis about the origin of petroleum (and it has not been accepted by geologists generally, although there have been a few attempts to revive it),[20] but the idea provoked him to further thought about the inorganic origin of organic compounds. As late as 1963 Oparin continued to emphasize the importance of Mendeleev's idea to his original conception of the origin of life.[21]

In order to provide the necessary temperatures and pressure and a source of energy, Oparin referred to the theory of origin of the earth that begins with the earth as an envelope of incandescent gas. Oparin maintained, "Only in fire, only in incandescent heat could the substances which later gave rise to life have formed. Whether it was cyan (nitrogen carbide) or whether it was hydrocarbons is not, in the final analysis, very important. What is important is that these substances had a colossal reserve of chemical energy which gave them the possibility of developing further and increasing their complexity" (p. 226). In the 1936 edition of his book, Oparin would tie this view of the origin of the earth to James Jeans' theory of planetary cosmogony, in which a star approaches the sun in such a way as to pull out by gravitational attraction a tidal wave of incandescent solar atmosphere. As described in the chapter on cosmology and cosmogony in this volume (see pp. 380–427), this theory came under heavy philosophical criticism in the Soviet Union in later years as "miraculous and improbable." Oparin later abandoned the Jeans theory of planetary cosmogony, finding other available sources of energy for the formation of complex hydrocarbons.

In the last section of his original work Oparin discussed how some of the simple organic compounds could evolve into living organisms.

And here he presented one of the paradoxical but now quite believable elements of his theory that continued to characterize it to the end of Oparin's life: The prior nonexistence of life was one of the necessary conditions for the origin of life, and consequently, now that life exists on earth it cannot originate again, or at least not in the same way in which it first did. Oparin explained this conclusion quite graphically:

> Even if such substances were formed now in some place on the Earth, they would not proceed far in their development. At a certain stage of that development they would be eaten, one after the other. Destroyed by the ubiquitous bacteria which inhabit our soil, water and air.
> Matters were different in that distant period of the existence of the Earth when organic substances first arose, when, as we believe, the Earth was barren and sterile. There were no bacteria nor any other micro-organisms on it, and the organic substances were perfectly free to indulge their tendency to undergo transformations for many, many thousands of years. (p. 228)

The posing of prior nonexistence of life as a necessary condition for the origin of life seemed somewhat more original in 1924 than it does today, since in the interim there has come to light a letter of Charles Darwin's in 1871 mentioning the same hypotheses.[22] Several other scientists also seem to have mentioned this hypotheses in the late nineteenth and early twentieth centuries.[23] In Oparin's later editions this seeming paradox was explained within the framework of dialectical concepts of natural law: On each level of being different principles obtain; therefore, the laws of chemistry and physics that operated on the earth in the absence of life were different from, and superseded by, the biological laws that qualitatively emerged with the appearance of life. In the case of man, the biological laws were transcended, in turn, by social ones.

Oparin continued his hypothetical scenario of the origin of life with a description of the way in which substances with complicated molecules form colloidal solutions in water (p. 229). This emphasis on the arising of life in a liquid medium by means of the separating out of gels became one of the hallmarks of Oparin's views; once his general materialistic approach to the origin of life had been widely accepted, the gel theory or "coacervate theory" was often considered to be that part of his work that was unique to him. Consequently many later discussions of the validity of Oparin's views revolved entirely around the tenability of the coacervate theory.

The idea of life's arising in a sea jelly of some sort was not new, of course, having been a part of T. H. Huxley's bathybius hypothesis, but

Oparin was to present it in a particularly plausible way. In 1924, however, Oparin did not even use the term "coacervate." All that was to come in later editions, after Oparin could make use of the research on coacervation carried out in the early thirties by Bungenburg de Jong. But both in the original 1924 work and in his subsequent publications, Oparin remained steadfast on the principle that life arose on a level of fairly large dimensions: the coagula, the gels, the coacervates, were all definitely multimolecular, and they all possessed a rather complex structure before they could be called "alive." After they became alive, a natural selection began that through the costs of survival resulted in increasingly viable and complex organisms.

From the philosophic or methodological point of view the transition from the "nonliving" to the "living" is the crucial moment. Oparin was not one to attempt rigorous definitions of "life," preferring to speak in metaphors or in terms of varying combinations of characteristics necessary for life, but it is clear that his opinion about the moment when life appeared changed somewhat with time. In 1924 he described the moment when "the gel was precipitated or the first coagulum formed" and then observed, "With certain reservations we can even consider that first piece of organic slime which came into being on Earth as being the first organism. In fact it must have had many of those features which we now consider characteristic of life" (p. 229). This observation accorded with the reductionist, mechanist approach of the young Oparin, in which a simple physical process—coagulation—could herald a major transition. In later years, he would maintain that the first coacervate droplets were definitely not alive and that a "primitive natural selection" (a concept for which he was much criticized; see pp. 93ff.) occurred among these nonliving forms. The transition to life occurred after not only the more commonly named characteristics of life had appeared (metabolism, self-reproduction), but in addition, after a certain "purposiveness" of organization had been achieved.[24] This controversial aspect of his scheme, linked to Aristotelian entelechy by his more aggressive critics, will be discussed in subsequent sections.

One metaphor that Oparin used in his early statement remained constant throughout his works; this was his comparison of life to a flow of liquid. In 1924, he wrote that "an organism may be compared with a waterfall which keeps its general shape constant although its composition is changing all the time and new particles of water are continually passing through it" (p. 211); in 1960, he commented, "Our bodies flow like rivulets, their material is renewed like water in a stream.

This is what the ancient Greek dialectician Heraclitus taught. Certainly the flow, or simply the stream of water emerging from a tap, enables us to understand in their simplest form many of the essential features of such flowing, or open systems as are represented by the particular case of the living body."[25] These metaphors, all based on the concept of the constant flow of matter in living organisms, involved Oparin in many discussions about whether relatively static entities sometimes considered alive (crystallized viruses, dried seeds) could be accommodated to his understanding of life.

If one shifts from Oparin's 1924 booklet to his 1936 major work (the first was approximately 35 pages in length, the latter, 270), a number of changes become apparent. The biochemist would notice the much fuller description of the initial colloidal phase and a subsequent section on the development of photosynthesis by the ancestors of vegetative organisms. The historian and philosopher would remark on Oparin's growing philosophic awareness, his refinement of his definitions and his stated shift toward Marxist interpretations.

By 1936 Oparin could take advantage of the recent work by Bungenburg de Jong on "coacervation," a term used by de Jong to distinguish the phenomenon from ordinary coagulation. In solutions of hydrophilic colloids it is known that frequently there occurs a separation into two layers in equilibrium with each other; one layer is a fluid sediment with much colloidal substance, while the other is relatively free of colloids. The fluid sediment containing the colloids, de Jong called the coacervate, while the noncolloidal solution was the equilibrium liquid. Oparin emphasized the interface or surface phenomena that occur in coacervation; various substances dissolved in the equilibrium liquid are absorbed by the coacervate. Consequently, coacervates may grow in size, undergo stress with increasing size, split, and be chemically transformed. In discussing the active role of coacervates, Oparin was attempting to establish them as models for protocells. A "primitive exchange of matter" occurs between the coacervate and the equilibrium liquid, the beginning of that metabolic flow necessary for life, according to Oparin. To initiate life, however, Oparin said that it was necessary for coacervates to acquire "properties of a yet higher order, properties subject to biological laws."[26] He had higher requirements for life in 1936 than in 1924, and his scheme now contained a phase of evolution of the lifeless coacervates.[27]

In Oparin's 1936 scheme the transition from the nonliving to the living was still not defined clearly. It occurred, he thought, when the "competition in growth velocity" was replaced by a "struggle for ex-istence." This sharpening struggle resulted from the fact that the pre-biological organic material on which the coacervates were "feeding" was being consumed. Ultimately, this shortage would lead to an im-portant split in the ways in which organisms gained nourishment—resulting in the distinction between heterotrophs and autotrophs—but before that division occurred, the all-important transition to the bio-logical level was reached. As the amount of organic material outside the coacervates lessened, the first true organism appeared. As Oparin described this moment:

> The further the growth process of organic matter advances and the less free organic material remains dissolved in the Earth's hydrosphere, the more exacting "natural selection" tends to become. A straight struggle for existence displaces more and more the competition in growth velocity. A strictly biological factor now comes into play. (pp. 194–95)

It should be obvious from Oparin's scheme of development that he thought that heterotrophic organisms (organisms that are nourished by organic materials) preceded in time autotrophic organisms (those nour-ished by inorganic materials). Many scientists had earlier thought that the sequence was the opposite and assumed that carbon dioxide—necessary for photosynthesis by autotrophic green plants—was the primary material used in building up living things. Oparin found this thesis dubious. As evidence against it he cited the fact that heterotrophic organisms are generally capable of using only organic compounds for nourishment, while many autotrophic green plants "have retained to a considerable degree" the ability to use preformed organic substances for their nourishment (p. 203). The significance here of the word "retain" is obviously one of time sequence; Oparin thought that all organisms had originally been heterotrophic, but that as the supply of organic food diminished, they split along two different paths of development. (This division is not, strictly speaking, the same as that between the plant and animal worlds, but is close to it, since green plants are largely autotrophic while all the highest and lowest animals and most bacteria and all fungi are heterotrophs.)

Oparin explained this scheme in a much fuller philosophic framework than previously. By 1936 he had read Engels' *Dialectics of Nature*, and cited it in his footnotes, as well as the earlier-published *Anti-Dühring*. He commented that Engels had "subjected both the theory of spon-taneous generation and the theory of eternity of life to a withering criticism (p. 31). (In his 1924 work, "spontaneous generation" had still been a positive term, although he had thought the efforts to find it crude.) Oparin now thought that any effort to explain "the sudden generation of organisms" could rely only on either an act of "divine will" or "some special vital force." Such a view, Oparin observed, is "entirely incompatible with the materialistic world conception" (p. 32). On the contrary, "Life has neither arisen spontaneously nor has it existed eternally. It must have, therefore, resulted from a long evolution of matter, its origin being merely one step in the course of its historical development." (p.33).

More indicative of essential changes in Oparin's thought was his shift away from mechanism. Crude materialism, the belief that all phenomena could be explained in terms of the elemental, was now one of the objects of his criticism:

> Attempts to deduce the specific properties of life from the manner of atomic configuration in the molecules of organic substance could be regarded as predestined to failure. The laws of organic chemistry cannot account for those phenomena of a higher order which are encountered in the study of living cells. (p. 137)

Although Oparin now frequently cited Engels and thought that he had been remarkably prescient in his discussions of life, Oparin was also willing to interpret and modify Engels' formulations. When Engels said that "life is a form of the existence of protein bodies," he did not intend to say, maintained Oparin, that "protein is living matter." Instead he meant that protein has hidden in its chemical structure "the capacity for further organic evolution which, under certain conditions, may lead to the origin of living things" (p. 136). This interpretation by Oparin fits well with his belief that life is not inherent in a structure, but instead is a "flow of matter," a process. Structure has a great deal to do with life, he thought, but to confuse it with life itself would be roughly like confusing a frozen stream of water with a flowing one. This emphasis on process, on "coordinated chemical reactions" rather than on determinate structure, would eventually involve Oparin in controversies with spokesmen from two quite different camps: the ultraorthodox dialectical materialists who wished to stick to Engels' literal word—"protein"—as the essence of life, and the new molecular biologists, who saw the essential features of life in the structure of nucleic acid and whose very terms of description—"template," "code"— carried the sense of the static.

It was the 1936 book, translated into English in 1938, that brought Oparin international stature. At this moment of first impact his primary message was still seen as the legitimacy of a materialistic approach to the study of the origin of life. Consequently, a number of writers who actually differed considerably with Oparin on details considered themselves in agreement. Haldane in his 1929 article, for example, hypothesized—in contrast to Oparin—a primitive earth atmosphere rich in carbon dioxide, described the first "living or half-living things" as "probably large molecules," and did not mention coacervates, coagula, or gels. These are important points of difference. Yet the hypothesis became known as the Haldane-Oparin (or Oparin-Haldane) one and even now is frequently referred to in that way.

Oparin's 1936 work remained substantially unchanged for twenty years. The 1941 edition contained few modifications; not until 1957 was a third, revised edition published, almost simultaneously appearing in Russian and in English. In the meantime the science of biochemistry was developing extremely rapidly. The new knowledge of molecular biology led to a union of biochemistry and genetics culminating in the 1953 publication of the Watson-Crick model of the DNA molecule. The relevance of molecular biology to theories of the origin of life was obvious to most observers in all countries, although just where the developments would lead was a subject of genuine debate.

The topic of viruses was particularly close to the question of the nature of life when viewed from the molecular level; viruses consist of nucleic acid (DNA or RNA) with a protein coat. The relevance of molecular biology to Oparin's work was to center, in part, on discussions of viruses. The most urgent questions could be stated in simple forms: Are viruses alive? If they are alive, in view of the fact that the simplest of them are essentially nucleic-acid molecules, was not Oparin incorrect in stating that life arose on the multimolecular level? Was not the first form of life a molecule of nucleic acid?

In the Soviet Union such issues were discussed in rather difficult circumstances, since the new union of biochemistry and genetics in world science had occurred at approximately the same time that Lysenko and his followers won control over Soviet genetics. Politically, Oparin and Lysenko were linked, however far apart they may have been in intellectual sophistication. Both had won favor from the Stalinist regime, both had built their careers within it, and around both there had arisen schools of biology that were officially described as "Marxist-Leninist" or "Michurinist." They benefited from the government, and they repaid the government in political praise and cooperation. Oparin was active in Soviet political causes in international organizations. As a high administrator in the biological sciences in the Soviet Union during these years he was important in perpetuating the Lysenko school. From 1949 to 1956 he was academician-secretary of the Department of Biological Sciences of the USSR Academy of Sciences, a position that meant that he exercised great influence over appointments and promotions at a time when these were keys to Lysenko's continuing power. The Soviet biologist Medvedev wrote in his history of Lysenkoism that in 1955 a petition directed against the administrative abuses of both Lysenko and Oparin was circulated among Soviet scientists.[28] Oparin was for many years a supporter of Lysenko, praising him in print on numerous occasions.[29] Nonetheless, as will be seen, Oparin struggled against several attempts by sympathizers with Lysenko to invade Oparin's field. Medvedev reported that in the final struggle with Lysenko, Oparin took a neutral position.[30]

One of the low points of Oparin's intellectual career came in his praise in 1951 of the new cell theory of Olga Lepeshinskaia. Lepeshinskaia was a mediocre biologist of impressive political stature as a result of her membership in the Communist Party from the very date of its founding and of her personal association with Lenin and many other political leaders. In 1950, a year of great political pressure in the Soviet Union, Lepeshinskaia claimed that she had obtained cells from living noncellular matter. Lepeshinskaia even maintained that she had obtained cells from noncellular nutrient mediums in as short a time as twenty-four hours.[31] Her work won praise from Lysenko himself.[32] It should be obvious from the past discussion of Oparin's views that he was skeptical in the extreme of all hypotheses that supposed the sudden appearance of a finely articulated entity from a less organized medium. Such an error had been made in the past, he thought, by all crude supporters of spontaneous generation. But in 1951, Oparin succumbed to the political pressures of Stalinist Russia and praised the "great service" of Professor Lepeshinskaia in "demonstrating" the emergence of cells from living noncellular matter even though Lepeshinskaia's evidence was rejected everywhere outside the Soviet bloc. He even agreed that this emergence of cells from living noncellular matter was occurring "at the present time," although he had opposed such a view many times in the past.[33] As we will see, not until 1953 did Oparin begin to resist these views in print. By 1957, however, he had returned to his flat opposition to spontaneous generation and to the sudden emergence of cellular forms in the manner described by Lepeshinskaia. Between 1953 and 1958 the supporters of Lepeshinskaia, and Lepeshinskaia herself, responded to Oparin's emerging remonstrances by, in turn, increasing their criticism of Oparin.

Oparin was criticized by ideologists who were close to Lysenko in their viewpoints. One of their objects of criticism was his opinion that although life had once arisen on earth, such an event would never again be repeated. Several militant ideologists felt that Oparin's view attributed to life a uniqueness that contradicted uniformitarian and materialist doctrines. These writers were somewhat similar to the materialists of the nineteenth century who felt that the doctrine of spontaneous generation was logically required by materialism. They called themselves dialectical materialists, but they ignored Engels' perceptive criticism of that form of spontaneous generation; the fact that Oparin also opposed spontaneous generation was evidence to them of his philosophical waverings.[34]

In early 1953 Oparin commented on some of these criticisms.[35] "Does life arise now, at the present time?" he asked. No doubt it does, he replied, because matter never stays at rest, but constantly develops ever new forms of movement. But life is not arising now on the earth— that stage of the development of matter has already been passed through here—but instead on other planets in the universe. He admitted that his critics had made a legitimate point in noting that his books were entitled *The Origin of Life*, as if what happened on earth were the whole story. (The following edition of his book would be entitled *The Origin of Life on the Earth* in recognition of this correction.) But he defended stoutly his belief that the prior nonexistence of life was a necessary condition for its origin.

In 1956 Oparin and the noted Soviet astrophysicist and astronomer V. Fesenkov (whose cosmological views are mentioned in chapter 12) cooperated in publishing a small volume entitled *Life in the Universe*.[36] Oparin had been criticized in the Soviet Union on grounds similar to those involved in discussions of James Jeans, upon whose hypothesis of the incandescent origin of the planetary system Oparin had relied in his earlier works. Now, in 1956, Oparin and Fesenkov acknowledged that Jeans' view "inevitably leads to the ideologically erroneous conclusion about the exceptionalism of the solar system in the Universe. Besides, Jeans' hypothesis is unable to explain the basic peculiarities of the solar system" (p. 121). Both Oparin and Fesenkov now agreed that O. Iu. Schmidt's idea that the sun had seized part of a dust cloud was a superior approach (see pp. 389ff.).

Oparin's critics tried to find other similarities between his views and those of Jeans. Just as Jeans' "near-collision" of stars seemed to them to bestow an exceptional or miraculous character on the origin of the earth, so Oparin's establishing of very special conditions for the origin of life and his insistence that this event could never be repeated on earth seemed to attribute exclusive properties to the origin of life and, ultimately, to man. Oparin attempted to answer this criticism in his joint book with Fesenkov. The origin of life, the two writers said, was a perfectly normal development in the evolution of matter:

> In its constant development matter pursues various courses and may acquire different forms of motion. Life, as one of these forms, results each time the requisite conditions for it are on hand anywhere in the Universe. (p. 239)

But just because life is a lawful and normal development does not mean, they observed, that it should be seen everywhere. Those materialists who constantly seek to find evidence of the arising of life around them in order to illustrate the unexceptional character of life are ignoring the very genuine qualitative distinctions that exist in matter, and if carried to extremes, such views will lead to a form of hylozoism. Life must not be seen as an inherent property of matter, they thought, but as a special—yes, exceptional—form of motion of matter (p. 16).

Just how rare is life in the universe? After a very long and detailed discussion of the physical requirements of life and the known characteristics of the universe, Oparin and Fesenkov came to the tentative conclusion that "only one star out of a million taken at random can possibly have a planet with life on it at some particular stage of development" (p. 245). But such a ratio should not be seen as bestowing anything approaching uniqueness upon life; indeed, the two distinguished scientists continued, in our galaxy there may be thousands of planets on which life is likely and "our infinite Universe must also contain an infinite number of inhabited planets." (p. 245)

In 1957 Oparin published the third revised and enlarged edition of his major work, with a more restricted title, *The Origin of Life on the Earth*. In this volume he attempted to answer a number of recent criticisms advanced against his system, and he incorporated much recent scientific evidence. His original 1924 booklet had now grown, thirty-four years later, to almost five hundred pages.

As in the past, one of Oparin's major points concerned his belief in the erroneousness of the concept of spontaneous generation. The book by Olga Lepeshinskaia, *The Development of Cells from Living Matter*, was in his opinion "an attempt to rehabilitate Pouchet's experiments and thus to resuscitate the theory of spontaneous generation."[37] Pouchet had expected microorganisms to be spontaneously generated; Lepeshinskaia also looked for spontaneous generation, but of cells from non-cellular matter instead of complete organisms. Both had therefore sought the sudden appearance of order out of chaos, and such attempts are "foredoomed to failure."[38]

Oparin applied a similar sort of criticism to those scientists who would propose the gene, a molecule, or a bit of DNA as the primordial speck of life. Each of these theories is materialistic and therefore commendable, said Oparin, in that they seek a material basis for life, but they are also mechanistic in the sense of all theories of spontaneous generation: they take as a starting point a bit of matter that is actually the end point of a long evolution and assume that the story of life began there. Since no explanation for the origin of this coherent bit of matter is attempted, the whole interpretation, intentionally or unintentionally, acquires a mysterious aura.

By this time J. D. Watson and F. H. C. Crick had suggested the noted double-helix model of the macromolecule of deoxyribonucleic acid (DNA). It was also clear by 1957 that DNA is the hereditary material of almost all organisms. The different sequences of the bases (adenine, guanine, thymine, and cytosine) in the nucleotides linking the helixes, and the varying amounts of bases in each organism, led to an almost astronomical number of possibilities of structural combinations. Thus, the DNA macromolecule appeared to be a code of life, varying for each species and indeed for each member of that species. Investigators were now beginning to speak of genes as "sections of DNA," and specialists in the origin of life began to suspect that the first bit of life was a DNA molecule.

Oparin considered the establishing of the structure of DNA to be an event of great importance, and described in detail, with the inclusion of diagrams, the achievement of Watson and Crick. But he was definitely opposed to the talk resulting from the work of molecular biologists about the "first living molecule of DNA." His argument was, at bottom, the same one he had used against spontaneous generation of organisms many years before. Referring to hopes for the appearance of complete microorganisms in infusions, Oparin had written then:

> If the reader were asked to consider the probability that in the midst of inorganic matter a large factory with smoke stacks, pipes, boilers, machines,

ventilators, etc., suddenly sprang into existence by some natural process, let us say a volcanic eruption, this would be taken at best for a silly joke.[39]

No longer, he acknowledged, did anyone expect the spontaneous generation of complete organisms, or even of complete cells; to stick to the metaphor, no longer did they look for the sudden appearance of the whole factory. But Oparin believed that those people who thought the story of life began with the fortuitous synthesis of DNA were making the same error; they did not pretend that a factory could suddenly spring into existence, but they acted as if they believed it possible for the blueprint of that factory to appear accidentally. Yet that blueprint (the molecule of DNA) contained all the information necessary for the construction of the factory; for such a body of coded information to suddenly appear was as wild as to assume the sudden materialization of the factory itself. In their emphasis on a molecule as the starting point of life, many scientists were ignoring the question that to Oparin was the most important of all: "How did the rigidly determinate arrangement of nucleotides in the DNA come into being?"[40]

Oparin saw a similarity between the current concentration upon the molecule of DNA as the primordial bit of life and the earlier concentration upon the gene. Furthermore, the view that the gene is a section of DNA molecule allowed room for the coalescence of the two approaches. In each case, however, valid research was being given what Oparin thought was an improper interpretation. "Life" to him was still a process, a flow, an interchange of matter, and could not be identified with any static form. Oparin thought that the new emphasis on DNA was the lineal descendant of earlier erroneous views such as: H. J. Muller's conception of the "random emergence of one successful gene among myriads of types of molecules"; T. H. Morgan's original "gene molecule"; C. B. Lipman's idea of the formation of a "living molecule"; R. Beutner's proposed "self-generating enzymes"; and A. Dauvillier's organic molecules with a "living configuration."[41]

Many molecular biologists were willing to grant that Oparin's evolutionary approach to DNA had its merits, but they felt that his commitment to a definition of life as a multimolecular phenomenon led him to strained, if not absurd, positions on the issue of viruses. Viruses were discussed several times in Oparin's 1965 book and also at an international symposium on the origin of life that he attended in Moscow in August 1957. The topic also appeared in an important book published by Oparin in 1960.[42]

With the discovery of viruses, researchers seemed to have come upon a form of "life" that could, at least in some cases, be crystallized and held static indefinitely, that in terms of size was smaller than certain molecules, that could grow and reproduce, and that had the ability to mutate during reproduction.[43] Why not recognize them as fully "living" organisms? Some researchers did. W. M. Stanley said of viruses in 1957 that "they are all, in short, by definition, alive."[44] Others, including Oparin, believed that there were serious reasons for excluding viruses from the realm of the truly living. And Oparin was particularly firm in his opinion that neither viruses nor any other "living" form on the molecular level should be considered antecedent to all other living organisms. Such molecular forms were to him the products of life, not the producers. He felt that to regard them as the starting point of life would be to begin with the unexplainable and eventually to fall prey to metaphysical, mysterious interpretations of nature. His arguments will be considered in more detail below, after a few additional comments on the nature of viruses.

A clearer view of the action of viruses, and of the central role of molecules of nucleic acid in this function, can be gained by considering bacteriophages, those viruses that prey on bacteria. A particularly suitable example of a bacteriophage is the virus that attacks colon bacilli. These viruses first attach themselves to bacilli and then literally inject their interior nucleic acid molecules inside their hosts, leaving the protein coats outside. Once inside the cell walls of the bacteria, the viruses multiply until the bacteria burst, freeing the viruses for further conquests.

It is important to see that this phenomenon is not identical with the familiar forms of parasitic action in the biological world by which the parasitic organism gains sustenance from a host; there is a much more elemental and striking mechanism at work here. The virus is incapable of metabolic action by itself and, indeed, possesses none of the physiological mechanisms necessary for such action. It uses, instead, the mechanisms of the host to the ultimate degree, bringing to it only information suitable for gaining its goals. One might say that the nucleic acid is no more than a program for using an existing process for a different goal; it is as if an impostor came into an operating chemical plant with only a coded computer tape under his arm and, by inserting that tape into a central computer, redirected the flow of chemicals to yield a different product, one valued by him. Of course, this analogy, with its inclusion of man's intelligence and its somewhat mechanistic reference to a factory, has its weaknesses, but it may convey some of the strangeness of the situation.

Of Oparin's fairly extensive discussion of viruses, the aspect that most concerns us is his opinion on whether they are alive. He did not flatly declare in his 1957 book that viruses are not alive, but his argument certainly pointed toward that conclusion. It is indeed true, he remarked, that they can replicate themselves quite readily. But replication is not the same as life, he continued, since even inorganic crystals can replicate and grow. Furthermore, viruses cannot even replicate unless they are placed "inside" an existing life process. Oparin commented:

> Nobody has succeeded in producing this so-called "multiplication" of virus particles under any other conditions or on any artificial medium. Outside the host organism the virus remains just as inert in this respect as any other nucleoprotein. Not only does it show no sign of metabolism but nobody has yet succeeded in establishing that it has even a simple enzymic effect. It is clear that the biosynthesis of virus nucleoproteins, like that of other proteins, is brought about by a complex of energic, catalytic and structural systems of the living cell of the host plant, and that the virus only alters the course of the process in some way so as to give specific properties to the final product of the synthesis.[45]

Although Oparin doubted that viruses were alive, he seemed to press that point of view less insistently in later publications. There were several potential avenues of compromise between the opposing points of view. Wendell Stanley, the man who crystallized tobacco mosaic virus (TMV), even suggested at the 1957 conference that "some may prefer to regard a virus molecule in a crystal in a test tube as a potentially living structure and to restrict the term 'living' to a virus during the time that it is actually reproducing. I would have no serious objection to this. . . ."[46] But Stanley then went on to repeat his belief that viruses are alive, without stipulating the moment in time when they became so. It was unclear what position Oparin would take on the suggestion that viruses are intermittently "alive" and "dead."

Oparin's interest in viruses centered on whether they were in the main path of the development in which life appeared or in a branch. And he believed that the answer to the question was that they were in a branch; whether or not viruses are ever alive, they were not the primordial forms of life from which all the others developed. As he commented at the 1957 symposium:

> Today I should like to formulate, in a couple of words, my own viewpoint which I have expounded and substantiated in my book. I assumed that what had arisen primarily, by abiogenetic means, was not

the functionally extremely efficiently constructed nucleic acids or proteins which we can now isolate from organisms, but only polynucleotides or polypeptides of a relatively disorderly structure, from which were formed the original systems. It was only on the basis of the evolution of these systems that there developed the functionally efficient forms of structure of molecules, not vice versa.[47]

And in 1960 he came back to the topic by discussing the tobacco mosaic virus. He emphasized what happens when this virus attacks the cells of a tobacco leaf:

All that takes place is the constant new formation of a specific nucleo-protein with the help of the biological systems of the tobacco leaf. This means that the new formation is only possible in the presence of an organization which is peculiar to life and consequently the first living thing was not a virus; on the contrary, viruses, like other modern specific proteins and nucleic acids, could have only arisen as products of the biological form of organization.[48]

Oparin cited the well-known fact that parasites frequently become simpler in organization as they become more and more dependent on their hosts and adapted to that ecological niche. All viruses are parasites. Oparin therefore suggested that although the coded nucleic acid in viruses is the evolutionary product of more sophisticated organisms, the viruses themselves are the ultimate results of parasitic "devolution." They have lost all but their genetic material itself; they are, so to speak, "escaped" bits of the genetic code, which reproduce themselves by using the metabolic processes of more sophisticated organisms. But, according to Oparin, they could never have arisen without the prior evolution of organisms with a metabolic capability.

The publication by Oparin that most clearly illustrated the refinement of his philosophic views was his *Life: Its Nature, Origin and Development*, published in Russian in 1960 and in English in 1961. In this book the form of dialectical materialism that Oparin had developed over the years permeated his scientific views to a greater degree than in any other of his major publications; dialectical materialism heavily influenced the very structure of his analysis. The careful reader of this volume cannot seriously maintain, it seems to me, that dialectical materialism was merely something to which Oparin paid lip service in prefaces and conclusions as a result of political pressure. Instead, a dialectical and materialist process philosophy, one that he had helped to elaborate, had, in turn, a systemic effect upon his scientific arguments.

The point to which Oparin returned again and again in the writing of this book is that dialectical materialism is a *via media* between the positions of frank idealists and vitalists on the one hand, and mechanistic materialists, exuberant cyberneticists, and supporters of spontaneous generation on the other. Dialectical materialism was indeed a form of materialism and therefore opposed to the idealistic view that the essence of life was "some sort of supramaterial origin which is inaccessible to experiment" (p. 4). But dialectical materialism was equally opposed to the view that all living phenomena could be explained as physical and chemical processes. To take the latter position would mean, said Oparin, "to deny that there is any qualitative difference between organisms and inorganic objects. We thus reach a position where we must say either that inorganic objects are alive or that life does not really exist" (p. 5). Dialectical materialism provides a means, Oparin continued, of accepting the principle of the material nature of life without regarding "everything which is not included in physics and chemistry as being vitalistic or supernatural" (p. 5). To dialectical materialists, life is a "special form of the motion of matter," one with its own distinct regularities and principles.

Oparin believed that a living organism must possess the characteristic of "purposiveness." This characteristic figured more prominently in this later work of Oparin's than it had in his earlier writings. He believed that purposiveness pervades the whole living world "from top to bottom, right down to the most elementary form of life" (p. 13). He recognized that his insistence on purposiveness as an essential feature of life had its dangers, since "in one form or another Aristotle's teaching about 'entelechy' had left its mark on all idealistic definitions of life (p. 11)." But Oparin believed that the purposiveness of the organization of life was "an objective and self-evident fact which cannot be ignored by any thoughtful student of nature. The rightness or wrongness of the definition of life advanced by us, and also of many others, depends on what interpretation one gives to the word 'purposiveness' and what one believes to be its essential nature and origin" (p. 13). He thought that dialectical materialists could avoid idealism by always studying this purposiveness in terms of its development, its origins. So long as purposiveness can be understood as a result of an historical interaction between the material organism being studied and its material environment, one need not fear idealism. It is only, Oparin said, when purposiveness is brought in from outside the boundaries of the material world, or is left so unexplained that such an origin seems implied, that biological explanations become idealistic. Hence, Oparin believed that the essential methodological guide through these dangers could be found in the writings of Heraclitus of Ephesus: "One can only understand the essence of things when one knows their origin and development" (p. 37). In this principle Oparin believed that dialectical materialism and Darwinism drew upon a common inspiration, one found in ancient philosophy.

A fundamental difference between man and machine, said Oparin, is the origin of purposiveness. Machines have purposiveness, just as living organisms do, but it is placed in them by man. They will therefore always differ from the "truly living." In order to understand this interesting and debatable insistence by Oparin that life can only be understood in its origin, the following quotation from a science fantasy that Oparin related is helpful. In this quotation not only will Oparin's emphasis on historical development as a key to understanding emerge more fully, but one will also see his concept of dialectical levels of regularities; for Oparin there exist distinct "physicochemical regularities," "biological regularities," and "social regularities." Only human beings display all three:

> Let us imagine that people have succeeded in making automatic machines or robots which can not only carry out a lot of work for mankind but can even independently create the energetic conditions necessary for their work, obtain metals and use them to construct components, and from these build new robots like themselves. Then some terrible disaster happened on the Earth, and it destroyed not only all the people but all living things on our planet. The metallic robots, however, remained. They continued to build others like themselves and so, although the old mechanisms gradually wore out, new ones arose and the "race" of robots continued and even, perhaps, increased within limits.
>
> Let us further imagine that all this has already happened on one of the planets of our solar system, on Mars, for example, and that we have landed on that planet. On its waterless and lifeless expanses we suddenly meet with the robots. Do we have to regard them as living inhabitants of the planet? Of course not. The robots will not represent life but something else. Maybe a very complicated and efficient form of the organization and movement of matter, but still different from life. . . . It is impossible to grasp the nature of the "Martian robot" without a sufficient acquaintance with the social form of the motion of matter which gave rise to it. This would be true even if one were able to take down the robot into its individual components and reassemble it correctly. Even then there would remain hidden from our understanding those features of the organization of the robot which were purposefully constructed for the solution of problems which those who built them envisioned at some time, but which are completely unknown to us. (pp. 33–35)

In this passage, Oparin's view of life emerges in a particularly colorful way. It is obvious that he would not accept a purely functional definition of "life." Less obvious is how he would meet the arguments of a functionalist. How, for example, would a man who meets such robots on Mars know that they are, indeed, robots? How would he know that he does not "have to regard them as living inhabitants of the planet," as Oparin put it? Surely such an explorer would expect extraterrestrial life, existing in conditions quite different from those of the earth, to have a quite different appearance from life he had already witnessed. How would he know to be suspicious even if what he saw displayed baffling characteristics? Evidently Oparin would answer that man might indeed make such a mistake, but upon further study he would probably begin to realize that the robots had a social origin, even if he never learned very much about that disappeared society.

In October 1963 Oparin attended a conference on "The Origins of Prebiological Systems" at Wakulla Springs, Florida, sponsored jointly by Florida State University, the University of Miami, and NASA.[49] At this meeting P. T. Mora of the National Institutes of Health submitted current theories of the origin of life, including Oparin's, to a methodological critique.[50] He showed what has frequently been noted by philosophers of science, namely, that questions of singularity, of origin, are not in principle resolvable by experimental science. Thus, from the standpoint of strict logic and the methods of empirical science the question to which Oparin had devoted his life was not answerable. Mora was particularly critical of the application of the term "natural selection" (in the manner of Oparin) to nonliving systems.[51]

Indeed, Mora said that the gap between physical science and biology is "too big to bridge."[52] Consequently, Mora was extremely skeptical of attempts such as Oparin's to throw a bridge across the gap, and believed that it would be achieved only by committing methodological errors:

> I believe that this accounting for the appearance of the first persistently self-reproducing unit in a prebiotic system is an unwarranted extension of the meaning of the word selection, used by Darwin in a valid, but different operational sense. Remember, the Darwinian selection and evolution concept was arrived at empirically, by observing the spectrum of living species.[53]

Mora's presentation aroused considerable controversy at the Florida conference.[54] He posed a very old and very important problem in the history of science. This issue is one of the fundamental problems of explanations of development, which can be simply stated in terms of Mora's thesis: We cannot obtain a higher degree of order or organization than that present in the interacting elements and the environment.

It was not Oparin but Bernal who took the responsibility for answering Mora at the Florida conference. (Oparin would reply in a later publication.) Like Oparin, Bernal favored a materialistic, developmental explanation of the origin of life. He differed with Oparin by doubting the fundamental role of coacervation, favoring instead a process of clay mineral absorption, but their two approaches both assumed the fruitfulness of trying to bridge the gap between the nonliving and the living. Bernal agreed with the validity of much of Mora's argument, and specifically, that questions of origin cannot be explained on the basis of logic. They have instead, Bernal said, "a logic of their own." But, said Bernal, Mora

> draws a conclusion which is the opposite to the one which I would draw. The present laws of physics, I would agree with him, are insufficient to describe the origin of life. To him this opens the way to teleology, even, by implication to creation by an intelligent agent. Now both of these hypotheses were eminently reasonable before the fifteenth or possibly even before the nineteenth century. Nowadays they carry a higher degree of improbability than any of the hypotheses questioned by Dr. Mora.
> . . .
> I do not agree with the criticisms of the limitations of scientific method which Dr. Mora puts forward, but I think he has done a very valuable service in stating them. The contrast between a Cartesian physics with material causes and a teleological biology with final causes which he poses, I think is false. Nevertheless, it contains the truth of the different laws for different levels, an essentially Marxist idea.[55]

But the real difference between Mora and Oparin-Bernal was not whether different laws exist on different levels. In fact, Mora believed in the existence of such different levels even more strongly than Oparin and Bernal, for he thought that the gap between physics and biology was unbridgeable, and therefore, the distinction between the two levels was absolute. Oparin and Bernal, on the other hand, saw the distinction as a relative one.

Oparin took up the question of the way in which the transition from one level to the next higher one occurs in his 1966 book *The Origin and Initial Development of Life*, translated by NASA in 1968.[56]

In this work, Oparin sketched out the "prebiological" state in greater detail, incorporating more of the recent evidence. He allowed more room for noncoacervate prebiological systems, pointing toward compromise with views such as Bernal's. The "coacervatelike" droplets, which had a complex and advanced organization but which are still simpler than "the most primitive living beings," Oparin now called protobions. The protobions went through a further evolution promoted by a process to which Oparin still insisted on giving the name "primitive natural selection." And in this section of his book Oparin cited Mora's criticism of his scheme at the 1963 Florida conference and attempted to answer it. He maintained that the "logic of its own" by which Bernal said the origin of life must be explained was, in fact, the logic of dialectics. As Oparin observed:

> At present, a number of opinions have been expressed in the scientific literature on the competency of the use of the term "natural selection" only in respect to living beings. It is an opinion widely held among biologists that natural selection cannot be extended to objects which are not yet alive, and particularly not to our protobions.
>
> It is, however, erroneous to think that living bodies first originated and then biological laws or vice versa, that in the beginning biological laws were formulated and the living bodies arose. . . .
>
> Dialectics obliges us to consider the formation of living bodies and the formulation of biological laws as proceeding in indissoluble unity. It is therefore quite permissible to assume that protobions—those initial systems for the formation of life—evolved by submitting to the action not only of intrinsically physical and chemical laws, but also of incipient biological laws including also prebiological natural selection. Here we may cite an analogy with the formation of man, i.e., with the rise of a social form of the motion of matter which is even higher than life. As is known, this form took shape under the influence not so much of biological as of social factors, chiefly the labor of our ancestors, coming into being at a very early state of homogenesis, and improving more and more. Therefore, just as the rise of man is not the result of the operation of biological laws alone, so the rise of living bodies cannot be reduced to the action of only a few laws of inorganic nature.[57]

In the above quotation Oparin's belief in a hierarchy of laws in nature is revealed particularly clearly; social, biological, and physicochemical laws all operate on different levels. The most difficult conceptual problem within the framework of Oparin's scheme is the transition from one realm of law to another. If one assumes, as Oparin did, that living matter evolved from nonliving matter and human beings with their social life evolved from lower orders of animals, some method of explaining these transitions must be found. Oparin relied on a dialectical concept of the emergence of qualitative distinctions; he believed that "incipient forms" of laws of a higher realm could be found in the realm immediately below it. It is the sort of concept that has appealed to many thinkers in the past—C. Lloyd Morgan's concept of "emergent evolution" was somewhat similar, but supplemented with the presupposition of God—and it has a certain persuasiveness. Nonetheless, it should be admitted that Oparin's philosophy of biology suffered from a lack of precision in definition, on which critics such as Mora correctly centered their attention; furthermore, Oparin's emphasis on the irreducibility of biology to physics and chemistry and his increasing attention to "purposiveness" circled ever more closely the very real dangers of vitalism.

The Soviet philosopher I. T. Frolov recognized these pitfalls in his 1968 book on genetics and dialectics (discussed on pp. 152ff.) when he described the irreducibility of biology as more a result of man's incomplete knowledge than a characteristic of living matter itself. In Oparin's approach, living matter is inherently distinct from nonliving matter and cannot, in principle, be reduced to physics and chemistry. Frolov was less adamant.

It should be noticed that nothing in the philosophic system of a materialist absolutely required him to believe that living matter on earth evolved from nonliving matter. Materialists have usually supported this view since it seemed the best explanation for the origin of life on earth without reliance on a divine agent. But strictly speaking, there is another alternative available to the materialist; he can maintain that matter has existed eternally in the universe in both its living and nonliving forms. Whether nonliving matter actually evolves into living matter can then be left an open question without violating any assumptions of philosophic materialism. The life that exists on earth can be explained by saying that it resulted from the depositing of primitive organisms on the surface of the globe from elsewhere at some past moment in its history. Such a hypothesis is frequently called panspermia and has been posed in the past in various forms by such well-known scientists as Liebig, Helmholtz, and Kelvin.

A few Soviet scientists began to reexamine panspermia in the late sixties. A geologist, B. I. Chuvashov, wrote in 1966 in *Problems of Philosophy* that in his opinion life had existed in the universe eternally.[58] He cited the recent criticisms of Oparin's application of the term "natural selection" to prebiological systems as one of the reasons for his dissatisfaction with Oparin's theory and his consequent interest in panspermia. Nonetheless, Chuvashov thought that nonliving matter may also occasionally develop into living matter, but perhaps only once in each planetary system or galaxy. Life was then spread throughout the neighboring area in the form of spores by meteorites and dust.

This view has been held by no more than a small minority of scientists in the Soviet Union; it enjoys similarly modest support elsewhere. Some of the scientists interested in panspermia cited the presence of carbonaceous chondrites in the lunar soil samples brought back to the earth by the Apollo II expedition as support for their hypothesis.[59] This evidence, however, is subject to differing interpretations and does not yet warrant conclusions.[60]

The emergence of life from nonliving matter remains the favored view of Marxist philosophers and biologists. Dialectical materialism has been deeply penetrated by the concept of an overall development of matter, with no impassable barriers.

In Soviet philosophical discussions of the origin of life during the 1970s and 1980s the biggest change over the previous period was the greater variety of points of view. Although the Oparin school continued to have great influence, it was no longer in the monopolistic position it had enjoyed in earlier years.[61] Indeed, critics of Oparin emerged who increasingly described him as a great pioneer who should be credited with opening up the field, but whose concrete suggestions about the origin of life were no longer in step with the latest research. The problem of the origin of life was now being studied from a variety of standpoints, many of which Oparin had not used: molecular biology, biophysics, information theory, thermodynamic analysis.

Much controversy continued to swirl around the question of the definition of life. This issue was central to the defenders of dialectical materialism, since one of the hallmarks of this doctrine was the principle that matter exists on different, nonreducible levels of being. "Life," then, needed to be defined in a way that distinguished it from mere physical and chemical processes.

In specifying criteria of "life," two basic approaches existed among Soviet writers in the seventies and eighties: the functional approach, and the substratum approach. Adherents of the first view were not particularly concerned with the actual material components of living organisms but instead concentrated on the study of processes of the preservation, transmission, and processing of information.[62] Organisms were viewed as "black boxes" whose inner structures were either unknown or considered unnecessary for analysis. Leading exponents of the functional approach were A. A. Liapunov and A. N. Kolmogorov, both of whom used highly mathematical approaches to life that were foreign to Oparin. Both were interested in processes that would result in highly stable homeostatic states. They saw the most characteristic criterion of a living organism in the presence of a "directed process" based on coded information.

The defenders of the functionalist approach differed most strikingly with the supporters of the substratum approach on the question of the possibility of varieties of living forms. Since the functionalists were interested primarily in directed processes, they believed that life might arise wherever the required form of direction arose, regardless of the chemical elements, compounds, or structures involved. They even countenanced the possibility of life without protein.

Followers of the substratum approach believed that particular substances and structures were the key to the origin of life. Most of them saw nucleic acids and proteins as the basis of life. Members of this school included Oparin himself, who emphasized particular organic substances and the coacervate structure, and another of the Soviet Union's senior biologists, V. A. Engel'gardt, who similarly believed that a proper study of life must stress chemistry, and not merely mathematics.[63]

Both the functional and the substratum approaches were reconcilable with dialectical materialism, but the substratum approach had particularly appealing characteristics to Marxists. After all, Marxist philosophers often referred to life as a "special, qualitatively distinct form of the movement of matter," and by emphasizing matter they gave priority to the substratum. Still, the functionalist approach could be accepted so long as the mathematical analyses which were its core were not taken to be the whole story of life; the material carriers of life and inheritance eventually must be identified, although that moment could await further research.

The division between the functionalists and the substantialists was only one difference among the Soviet writers on the origin of life. Another important controversy concerned the number of criteria that must be listed in order to describe the essential characteristics of life. The two camps here were often described as the "mono-attributive" approach and the "poly-attributive approach." While this distinction may seem abstruse and far from politics, one cannot understand the nature of contemporary Soviet Marxism unless one appreciates that knowledge of such topics in science is still considered to be appropriate, even necessary, for Party ideologists. Analyses of the differences between these various approaches to understanding life are published in leading political journals such as *Kommunist*, read primarily by Party activists, not by natural scientists.[64]

Much discussion revolves around the degree to which the definition of life given by Engels in the nineteenth century ("life is a mode of existence of protein substances") must be updated. The general conclusion usually drawn in such analyses is that while Engels' specific emphasis on protein must be modified, his more general positions are still valid. These general viewpoints are summarized as: (1) Life is material by its nature; (2) Life has a specific material carrier; (3) Life is a qualitatively distinct form of the movement of matter.[65] Thus, what is achieved by these analyses is the retention of a specifically Marxist philosophy of nature by means of the gradual modification of classical texts while insisting on the continuing validity of underlying principles. This intellectual operation is highly similar to that performed by intelligent theologians wishing to modernize their faiths while remaining loyal to basic doctrines.

From the standpoint of preservation of ideological principles, the difference between the mono-attributive and the poly-attributive approaches has some significance. The supporters of the poly-attributive approach, such as N. T. Kostiuk,[66] wish to broaden definitions of life far beyond what Engels had said or assumed; they would define life in terms of a whole host of characteristics, such as self-regulation, self-renewal, exchange of matter, plasticity, relative stability, and reproduction. According to one Marxist ideologist, M. Chepikov, this sort of discussion of life has both advantages and disadvantages. On the one hand, it enriches Engels' rather simple discussions of life with concepts based on recent research; on the other hand, it so broadens the definition of life that philosophical clarity has been lost. Such a definition tries to embrace all facets of complex reality, Chepikov noted, a task that is inherently impossible. Therefore, the mono-attributive approach still has value, he continued, for it is an attempt to single out the one characteristic of life that is "most essential."

But the supporters of the mono-attributive approach could not agree on what is most essential. To Oparin, it was metabolism, or the "exchange of matter"; to A. A. Liapunov, it was "directed processes or systems"; to V. N. Veselovskii, it was "dynamic self-preservation"; to A. P. Rudenko, it was "evolutionary catalysis." Other writers emphasized reproduction and development.[67]

Chepikov tried to come up with a new definition of life that would avoid the diffuseness of the poly-attributive approach while being loyal both to the results of modern science and the original position of Engels. His definition was the following: "Life is the mode of existence of a specifically heterogeneous material substratum, the universality and uniqueness of which brings about an expedient reproduction of all forms of the organic world in their unity and diversity."[68]

Until his death in 1980, Oparin continued to talk about life in very general terms such as a "flow," or a "qualitatively distinct process." On the other hand, Engel'gardt—who, like Oparin, was interested in dialectical materialism—believed that one should try to be more specific about the nature of life. In particular, Engel'gardt thought that scientific knowledge of how bits of DNA "recognize" each other permits us to emphasize "recognition" as an essential feature of life. Engel'gardt until his own death in 1984 followed a poly-attributive approach in which the essential characteristics were reproduction, metabolism, development, hierarchical structure, integration, and recognition.[69]

One of the most heated Soviet controversies over the origin of life in the seventies and eighties was whether the development of matter has a predetermined direction. Is the origin of life inevitable, or is it a result of chance? This controversy was given new impetus in the early seventies when the Nobel laureate West German physicist Manfred Eigen published several articles in which he maintained that the origin of life "must have started from random events."[70] The more orthodox dialectical materialists considered this viewpoint unacceptable. To them, such events as the origin of life and the origin of consciousness were not accidents, but the result of the inevitable development of matter. Life was to these Marxists simply one of the forms of existence of matter, needing no special events, miraculous occurrences, or happy coincidences to arise.

Oparin himself attacked Eigen's viewpoint in 1979, maintaining that life "lawfully" (not accidentally) arose at a definite stage of the history of the earth and perhaps other planets. This event is an integral part of the overall development of matter, he observed, and should not be regarded as fortuitous.[71]

Oparin s position was supported by V. V. Orlov, one of the "ontologists" in the debates among philosophers over the breadth of claims legitimately made by dialectical materialism. Orlov wrote that in accordance with Marxism "the possibility and the necessity of the origin of biological and social life is laid in the foundation of matter itself."[72] In Oparin's and Orlov's views we see more than a hint of the teleological cast of thought that has haunted some versions of Soviet dialectical materialism in the past, making it somewhat similar to Teilhard de Chardin's nature philosophy, with its striving toward an Omega point.

Several Soviet biologists and philosophers considered Oparin's and Orlov's ideas to be dangerous revivals of claims of philosophy's supremacy over science. Nikolai Dubinin, in the seventies and eighties one of the best known dialectical materialists in the Soviet Union (see pp. 230ff.), did not agree with Oparin and Orlov on this issue. He wrote that "life is not a fatalistic consequence of chemical evolution. It was possible for life not even to arise on Earth. . . ." Dubinin continued that the "uniqueness of the transition from one form of movement of matter (inorganic) to another (organic) clearly points to the role of chance."[73] A. P. Rudenko was even more critical of what he called "teleological ideas of directed evolution." Oparin's hypothesis of the lawful origin of life from coacervates, said Rudenko, is "in principle, impossible."[74]

We see, then, that on the topic of the origin of life considerable diversity of opinion existed among Soviet biologists and philosophers of biology. All writers on the subject who went beyond strictly technical reports to general philosophical questions, however, continued to support dialectical materialist interpretations of one sort or another. It is possible that some of these attempts to discuss biology in Marxist terms were insincere, merely efforts to accommodate the prevailing political atmosphere. Nonetheless, a nonreductionist approach to biology has deep roots in Russian and Soviet thought, and many of the writings on the origin of life were sustained by these authentic roots. On this topic, a close kinship existed between biologists who opposed reductionism for internal reasons and Marxists who took the same position for ideological ones. Indeed, in people like Oparin and Dubinin these two motivations could not be separated, for they united the beliefs of nonreductionist biologists and convinced Marxists.

GENETICS

If one is to judge a man by first impression, Lysenko gives one the feeling of a toothache; God give him health, he has a dejected mien. Stingy of words and insignificant of face is he; all one remembers is his sullen look creeping along the earth as if, at very least, he were ready to do someone in.
—Soviet journalist describing the young Lysenko, 1927

To many persons the phrase "Marxist ideology and science" will bring to mind one word—"Lysenko." Of all the issues discussed in the volume, the "Lysenko affair" is best known outside the Soviet Union. It is frequently considered the most important of the various controversies concerning dialectical materialism and the natural sciences. It has been discussed in hundreds of articles and dozens of books.

How ironic it is, then, that the Lysenko affair had less to do with dialectical materialism as Marx, Engels, Plekhanov, and Lenin knew it than any of the other controversies considered in this study. The interpretations advanced by Lysenko originally arose neither among Marxist biologists nor established Marxist philosophers.[1]

Compared with the other scientific issues involving dialectical materialism, the Lysenko controversy was unique in still other ways. Intellectually it is far less interesting than the other discussions. A person may experience at moments a certain fascination in watching in detail through historical sources the suppression of a science, but this reaction surely issues only from either a dramatic sense of tragedy or a desire to know how to avoid such occurrences in the future. Lysenko's views on genetics were a chapter in the history of pseudoscience rather than the history of science.

A number of authors have maintained that one of the most important reasons for the rise of Lysenko was the existence in prerevolutionary Russia of an unusual school in biology.[2] Some would tie the birth of this movement to Marx and Engels, while others would look to the populist writers such as Pisarev and Chernyshevskii.[3] It is quite true that frequent support for the concept of the inheritance of acquired characters or criticism of the early ideas of genetics can be found in the works of prerevolutionary Russian writers, often of leftist persuasion.

But such writings can be found in other countries as well. The last half of the nineteenth century was the great age of biological controversy in Western Europe, and those discussions found their reflections in Russia. Leftist writers everywhere objected to the "heartlessness" of biological theories from Darwin onward. The views on biology of populist writers in Russia such as Pisarev, Nozhin, and Chernyshevskii were rather diverse; the belief in the inheritance of acquired characters was a part of nineteenth-century biology, not a special characteristic of Marxism or populism.[4] When Marxism was introduced in Russia, its early leaders, such as Plekhanov and Lenin, did not select biology for special attention; indeed, if any field of science was proposed as a candidate for ideological concerns by the founders of Russian Marxism, it was physics.

In Russia at the time of the Revolution there were some older biologists, such as K. A. Timiriazev, who were not able to accept the new field of genetics, but such biologists also existed in other countries. As we will see, some of the greatest men in the history of genetics also wrestled in the first decades of the century with what seemed to them the troublesome implications of genetics. Russia was not unique in this respect; by the late twenties it was distinguished, on the contrary, by the degree to which the new genetics was flourishing.[5] Soviet Russia by the end of the twenties was a center of outstanding genetics research, entirely in step with the new trends and in some respects leading the way.

More interesting from the standpoint of later events is the person of I. V. Michurin (1855–1935), a horticulturist whose name was to become the label for Lysenko's particular type of biology.[6] Michurin has often been described as a Russian Luther Burbank, and there is much to be said for that description, despite Michurin's occasional criticism of Burbank.[7] Like Burbank, Michurin was a practical plant breeder and an exceptionally gifted selectionist and creator of hybrids. Also like Burbank—and most selectionists before the proliferation of modern genetic concepts—Michurin believed the environment exercised an important hereditary influence on organisms. This influence was particularly strong, he thought, at certain moments in the organism's life cycle or on certain types of organisms, such as hybrid seedlings. Furthermore, Michurin disputed, at least at one period of his life, the Mendelian laws of inheritance, which he felt were valid only under certain environmental conditions. Another of his beliefs was in graft hybridization; according to his "mentor" theory, the genetic constitution of the stock of a grafted plant could be influenced by the scion. And yet another of his theories concerned the phenomenon of dominance in inheritance; he thought that dominant characters were those that gave its organism advantages in local conditions.[8]

In all of the above theories Michurin prefigured in important ways the views of Lysenko. Despite this marked degree of resemblance, however, the fact remains that Lysenko manipulated Michurin more than he drew sustenance from him. Determining the exact correspondence of Lysenko's views with Michurin's has been complicated by the fact that for thirty years most books and articles published in the Soviet Union portrayed the positions of the men as identical. It was only after 1965, and primarily in the late sixties and early seventies, that Soviet articles and books distinguishing the two men appeared.[9]

Michurin never made a claim to a great biological system—as Lysenko did in his name. He also did not emphasize the influence of environment in inheritance to the exclusion of the internal hereditary constitution of the organism. And in the final part of his life he began to recognize the validity of Mendelism, stating that several of his experiments designed to disprove Mendel's laws had actually affirmed them.[10]

Rather than looking primarily to prerevolutionary ideology or to Russian selectionists for the most important reason for the rise of Lysenko, it is necessary to consider the history of Lysenko's early activities against the background of the economic and political events in the Soviet Union in the late twenties and early thirties.

Trofim Denisovich Lysenko was born in 1898 in the Ukraine near the city of Poltava, where he grew up in a peasant family. He received an education as a practical agronomist at the Horticultural Institute of Poltava, later continued his studies and research at several different locations in the Ukraine, and after 1925 began to investigate the vegetative periods of agricultural plants at the Gandzha (now Kirovabad) Plant-Breeding Station in Azerbaidzhan.[11]

Between 1923 and 1951 Lysenko published approximately three hundred and fifty different items, although a great many of these were repetitions.[12] The first publication in 1923 concerned sugar-beet grafting; this was followed by another 1923 article on tomato breeding. Then for five years he published nothing. It was during this time that he began to work on the effects of temperature on plants at different points in their life cycles, a topic that led him to his well-known concepts of vernalization and the phasic development of plants.

In Azerbaidzhan Lysenko was confronted with the very practical problem that the leguminous plants, needed for fodder and for plowing under as green manure, require considerable amounts of water for growth. Azerbaidzhan is an area of marginal rainfall for many crops, but irrigation provides additional water in moderate amounts. However, the main crop of the area, cotton, requires all the water in the summer. Therefore, unless a way could be found to grow the legumes in the period from late fall to early spring, when sufficient water was present, a solution to the problem did not seem apparent. The possibility of growing the legumes in the winter was worth considering since Azerbaidzhan, located in the Southern Caucasus, enjoys a mild climate. Nonetheless, temperatures below freezing are encountered in the winter, although usually only for a few days.

Lysenko decided to grow hardy legumes during the winter season. By choosing early ripeners and planting in the fall, he hoped the plants would reach maturity before the coldest days arrived. Although this goal was fulfilled "not badly" according to Lysenko, the phenomenon that he now centered on was a side effect, drawn to his attention by his knowledge of the performance of the same plants in his native Ukraine.[13] Lysenko maintained that some of the peas that in the Ukraine were early ripeners became late ripeners in Azerbaidzhan. He decided that the reason for this change in vegetative period was the "unsuitability of the environment" for the development of the pea. The whole process of the growth of the pea was, as it were, "slowed down" in these unfamiliar conditions; therefore, the peas either did not reach maturity or did so very late. The same "slowing down" concept seemed to Lysenko also to be a good explanation of the difference between winter and spring varieties of certain cereals, such as wheat. A winter variety of wheat that is—contrary to normal practice—planted in the spring finds itself in "unfamiliar conditions," its growth is slow, and it fails to reach maturity.

On the basis of this kind of analysis Lysenko came to the conclusion that the most important factor in determining the length of time between seed germination and maturity in a plant is not the genetic constitution of the plant, but the conditions under which that plant is cultivated. The underlying theme here is, of course, that of plasticity of the life cycle, although still only with reference to the limited character of length of vegetative period.[14]

Lysenko and his co-workers in Kirovabad then attempted to determine the cause of this variability of length of the vegetative period. They decided that the critical factor was the temperature immediately after sowing. The reason winter wheat could not reach maturity if sown in the spring, they decided, was that the temperature immediately after sowing was too high. This excessive heat, said Lysenko, prevented the plant from passing through the first stage of its development.

Could anything be done about this? The prospect of shortening the period of growth of cereals was a very attractive one, particularly in those parts of Russia where the winter was so severe that wheat frequently died then. But one could hardly hope to control, on a practical basis, the temperature on the field once the plants had sprouted. Fortunately from the standpoint of manipulation of the growing period, it was found, as Lysenko stated it, that "plants may pass through this phase of development even when still in the seed state, i.e., when the embryo had just begun to grow and has not yet broken through the seed integument."[15]

Therefore, Lysenko thought it was possible to influence the length of the vegetative periods of plants by controlling the temperature of seeds before planting. Lysenko tried to work out an algebraic law to express this relationship. In an article that he published in 1928 entitled "The Influence of the Thermal Factor on the Duration of the Phases of Development of Plants,"[16] Lysenko presented the formula

$$n = \frac{A_1}{B_1 - t_0}$$

by which n number of days of cooking could be computed to achieve the necessary preconditioning of seeds (B_1 equals the maximum temperature that can occur "without the preconditioning," A_1 equals the sum of degree-days necessary for completion of the phase; and t_0 equals the average daily temperature).

This 1928 article is the only one I know in which Lysenko attempted to use mathematical methods—however simple—in his research. And this venture was soon severely criticized. A. L. Shatskii chastised Lysenko in a subsequent article for his "gross error" in trying to reduce relationships to a "physical truth" that can at best be described statistically. Shatskii also criticized Lysenko for believing that he could isolate the influence of the thermal factor alone when there were so many other factors that were also pertinent, such as light, humidity, soil moisture, and so forth.[17]

In later years Lysenko was extremely antipathetic to all attempts to describe biological laws mathematically. It seems likely that part of the explanation for Lysenko's dislike of mathematics is that while a young man, he was submitted to embarrassing criticism in this area where he felt, at best, insecure. His frustration in the face of mathematics was commented upon at later times by a number of writers.[18] The 1928 article represented an attempt by Lysenko to join academic biology; it was followed by a rebuff.

Lysenko continued, however, to expound his views on the importance of temperature in determining the development of plants. In January 1929 he reported on the Azerbaidzhan researches at the All-Union Genetics Congress in Leningrad. The paper was only one of more than three hundred presented and attracted no particular attention. At this time the exciting developments in the field of biology and genetics in the USSR were coming from such scientists as Iu. A. Filipchenko, director of the Bureau of Eugenics of the Academy of Sciences, and Nikolai Vavilov, who in the same year became president of the new All-Union Academy of Agricultural Sciences. Filipchenko and Vavilov were in a completely different circle than Lysenko, that of the academicians thoroughly trained in the neo-Mendelian genetics that emerged in the first decades of this century. Much more will be heard of Vavilov, who at first supported Lysenko's work on the restricted topic of vernalization, but became Lysenko's most talented opponent when Lysenko attempted to overthrow the whole science of genetics.

After the Leningrad congress Lysenko decided to apply his new theory concerning the importance of temperature in plant growth to practical problems of agriculture. The term "vernalization" was utilized in 1929 in connection with an experiment in the Ukraine on the farm of Lysenko's father, D. N. Lysenko. In order successfully to sow a winter wheat in the spring, the workers buried sacks of germinating grain in the snowbanks for a number of days before planting. This process of applying moisture and coolness to the grain became known as vernalization. In later years the mechanics were modified, but the principle remained the same. The grain was then planted, and later in 1929 the announcement was made in the press "of the full and uniform earing of winter wheat sown in the spring under practical farming conditions in the Ukraine."[19] This was only the first of the public claims made by Lysenko that I will evaluate in the following pages.

Within a few years, and for reasons shortly to be more carefully explained, the term "vernalization" became one of the best known in Russia. Lysenko became a hero of socialist agriculture and a mighty spokesman of agronomic science. He was transferred to the Ukrainian Institute of Selection and Genetics at Odessa, where the government established a special laboratory for the study of vernalization. Between 1930 and 1936 Lysenko published dozens of articles and pamphlets detailing the methods of vernalization, which was soon extended to include specific treatments of cotton, corn, millet, sugar beets, sorghum, barley, soya, potatoes, vetch, and various other grains, tubers, and fruits. On July 9, 1931, the USSR Commissariat of Agriculture issued a resolution establishing a journal, the *Vernalization Bulletin*, for the purpose of popularizing the researches of Lysenko's Odessa laboratory and for issuing instructions for the vernalization of crops. The thirty-four-year-old Lysenko now had a journal; in different forms, it would be one of his main sources of strength for the next thirty-five years.[20] In 1935, after a hiatus, it was revived under the name *Vernalization*, and in 1946 it became *Agrobiology*, the increasingly general title growing in step with Lysenko's increasingly general biological conceptions and ambitions. The first issue gave pathetically simple directions to the peasants concerning the means of accomplishing vernalization, carefully citing inventories of all necessary equipment: buckets, shovels, barrels, scales, thermometers.[21] Here was a novel method of agriculture that could be applied with only the simplest tools and yet that in its scale of operation seemed suited for large collective farms. Its primary requirement was labor. But that was one commodity the predominantly rural Soviet Union could supply, provided the peasants would cooperate. By 1935 Lysenko announced that the vernalization of spring cereals alone in the Soviet Union had been carried out on forty thousand collective and state farms and on a total area of 2,100,000 hectares (5,187,000 acres).

The historian of this process is immediately confronted with two basic questions: (1) How valuable was vernalization? (2) If its value was slight—as will be maintained—why did the government and Party support it?

A truly definitive answer to the first question will probably never be given, as a result of the extremely inaccurate records kept of the vernalization trials and the methodological errors involved. The most obvious methodological error in these trials was the almost total absence of control groups. But an attempt to judge the value of vernalization, based both on non-Soviet and Soviet accounts, can be made.

First, it should be readily granted that the treatment of seeds before or after germination does permit, under some conditions, the shortening of the vegetative period and the growing of winter varieties of grains during the summer. This technique was known in the United States as early as 1854 and was also the subject of research in Germany by

G. Gassner shortly before the end of World War I. (Lysenko was aware of Gassner's work and credited him in his writings.) And the fact that seeds of various kinds of plants require certain conditioning periods, during which temperature and moisture are critical factors, has been a commonplace in the field of plant propagation for decades. The actual processes that take place within seeds before germination are extremely complex and are even now far from being fully understood, not to speak of the state of knowledge in the twenties. These processes involve complex biochemical and physical changes, including natural inhibitors and hormone balances. In an effort to manipulate these processes, researchers have not only controlled the temperature and humidity of the seeds, but have alternated such changes in complex patterns, scraped the seeds with sandpaper, and even treated them with acid solutions in order to render the seed coat (testa) more permeable. The refrigeration and moistening of seeds preparatory to planting is generally known as cold stratification, and the term "afterripening" is used to describe the complex processes that occur in the testa or endosperm before the plant develops normally.[22]

But not every potentially useful technique that works under laboratory conditions can be economically employed; the opinion of researchers outside the Soviet Union generally was that such techniques as vernalization involve greater losses than gains. There were a formidable number of reasons for remaining skeptical of most mass pretreatments of seeds, particularly in primitive areas. First of all, in the unmechanized conditions of Soviet agriculture in the early thirties it was an extremely labor-intensive operation. The spreading of such seeds on the ground or in trays, the application of water at controlled temperatures for what amounted in many cases to weeks, the necessity to provide huts and buildings for the protection of the seeds during soaking—all require the expenditure of enormous amounts of labor. Furthermore, the process of vernalization was an ideal situation for the spread of certain fungi and plant diseases. The losses from such diseases must have been considerable. And lastly, in the conditions of Soviet farms, where there was often no electricity and no refrigerating equipment, it must have been nearly impossible to keep the seeds in uniform conditions over long periods of time. Sometimes the seeds became too hot, too cold, too wet, too dry. Some seeds germinated too rapidly, some too slowly, some not at all. But perhaps these very losses also provided excuses for Lysenko and his helpers: if vernalization was not a success on a particular farm, the failure could easily be blamed on the conditions, not the process of vernalization.

Another fact to consider in judging the vernalization program is that Lysenko used the term in an exceedingly loose way; it covered almost anything that was done to seeds or tubers before planting. Non-Soviet scholars who have written about Lysenko's vernalization have usually concentrated on the more spectacular attempts, such as the "conversion" of winter into spring wheat. The "vernalization" of potatoes promoted by Lysenko included the sprouting of the tubers before planting—a practice that practically every gardener in potato regions is aware of. Eric Ashby commented that some of the methods advocated under the rubric of vernalization were nothing more than ordinary germination tests (although these tests may have been urged as a face-saving device after the more radical vernalization measures failed).[23] And many of the crops that were grown with vernalization techniques might well have succeeded without them. In the absence of control plots it was absolutely impossible to determine to what degree vernalization contributed to the harvest.

The last point needs some elaboration. Many experiments with vernalization worked both ways. Lysenko frequently presented his evidence in terms of yields in a certain season with both vernalized and unvernalized plantings of the same crops. While the comparisons were not rigorous enough to serve as controlled samples, they do point out one significant fact: Vernalization was only very rarely used as an attempt to make possible the previously impossible—growing crops that had never been grown before in the region because of the climate. Rather, it was usually directed toward making traditional crops ripen earlier or growing a grain that because of the length of its growing season could only occasionally be successfully harvested by traditional methods in a certain region before frost. These are the kinds of experiments in which the evidence can be manipulated very easily, or where sloppiness in record-keeping can conceal results from even an honest researcher. A two- or three-day difference in date of ripening of a grain is a very inconsiderable period, subject to many different kinds of interpretation. A little enthusiasm in claiming victories for vernalization would go a long way in conditions of inaccurate records, uneven controls, variable agronomic conditions, impatience about verification, willingness to discount contradictory evidence on the basis of peasant methods, and impure plant varieties.

The more spectacular of Lysenko's vernalization claims can probably be accounted for by the impurity of Russian plant varieties and by Lysenko's extremely small samples. The best known of his examples of the conversion of winter wheat into spring wheat is the case of the *Kooperatorka* winter wheat.[24] Lysenko himself called it in 1937 "our most prolonged experiment at the present time." (This was at a time when vernalization had already become the subject of an enormous publicity campaign.) On March 3, 1935, Lysenko sowed this variety of winter wheat in a greenhouse that was kept until the end of April at a very cool temperature, 10 to 15 degrees Celsius. After the vernalization treatment the temperature was raised. Originally there were two (!) *Kooperatorka* plants, but one perished, Lysenko said, as a result of pests. The sole surviving plant matured on September 9, proving to Lysenko that vernalization had worked, since *Kooperatorka* normally matures in the spring. Grain was then taken from the plant and immediately sown, again in a greenhouse, where it eared as an F_2 generation at the end of January. Then on March 28, 1936, the third generation was sown, producing seed in August 1936. Hereafter the grain acted as a spring variety, and Lysenko maintained that its habit had been converted.

All that can be concluded from such an experiment is that Lysenko's methods were incredibly lacking in rigor. The ridiculousness of basing scientific conclusions on a sample of two need not be emphasized. The *Kooperatorka* was probably heterozygous; the one plant that survived could well have been an aberrant form. Even had several plants survived, a selection out of the variations would naturally occur. If one is attempting to convert a winter wheat into a spring wheat, and one sows in the spring, one will be likely to gather in the fall only the grains from those plants that did in fact mature. The effects of selection could be avoided, or rather determined, only by using a variety of known purity, coupled with careful statistical studies of many plants over a number of generations, including statistics for those plants that did not mature, and including large control groups of nonvernalized plants. (Such attempts to duplicate Lysenko's results were soon made outside the Soviet Union and did not succeed.)[25]

Despite the inaccuracy of Lysenko's methods as so far described, he still has not emerged as the dictator in biology that he later became. Vernalization is a perfectly respectable field in agronomy, and despite all the inaccuracy of his methods, some genuine contribution should be granted Lysenko in this area. He may not have been the original developer of the field, but he organized greater efforts in this sort of activity and attracted more attention to it than any predecessor. Many farmers and selectionists around the world have performed experiments without proper controls and have claimed results that other people could not duplicate. Why did not Lysenko remain a somewhat eccentric agronomist or selectionist, vainly hoping for recognition by the academic biologists, working feverishly within the narrow confines of his non-scientific methods? And how did the cause of Lysenko become connected with that of dialectical materialism? In his early publications Lysenko made no effort to bring dialectical materialism into his schemes. And why, if the value of vernalization was at best dubious, did the government support him?

In order to attempt to answer these questions, it is necessary to turn from agronomy to politics. The essential clues to the Lysenko affair lie not in theoretical biology, not in Marxist philosophy, nor even in practical agronomy, but in the political, economic, and cultural environment of the Soviet Union in the late 1920s and early 1930s.

During most of the 1920s political and economic controls were rather lax, at least compared with what occurred later. The Communist Party would not, it is true, tolerate competing organized political groups; the Soviet Union was even then an authoritarian state, and the state security organs dealt summarily with persons suspected of active political opposition to Soviet power. But for the average Soviet citizen who accepted or was resigned to Bolshevik rule, the state was not seen as a threat. The workers had lost the possibility of actually controlling the factories, as some in the early twenties had wished to do, but the regime was partial to the workers as a class, and the industrialization program had not yet attained the strained tempo of the later five-year plans. The peasants were more prosperous than either before the Revolution of 1917 or after the collectivization program beginning in 1929. They had occupied most of the arable land which had belonged before the Revolution to the church, nobility, or crown, and the loose regulations on trade permitted them to profit from the sales of their produce. The academic intelligentsia, still overwhelmingly prerevolutionary in educational background and attitudes, was more uneasy than either the proletariat or the peasantry, but still tried to maintain something of its prerevolutionary mode of life.

All of this was changing by 1929, the year that Stalin called the Great Break.[26] The first five-year plan, launched in 1928, was marked by the nationalization of virtually all industry and the beginning of a frenetic pace of industrialization. The wrench of rapid industrialization was felt by every Soviet citizen. In late 1929 the peasants were swept into a collectivization program that within a few months reorganized the entire countryside into massive state or collective farms. Many of the peasants resisted this program bitterly, destroying their crops and animals when all other opposition failed. Stalin is supposed to have told Winston Churchill at Yalta that the collectivization program was more difficult for the Soviet Union than the later battle of Stalingrad. The academic profession also suffered the trauma of those years; re-elections of the members of the faculties of the universities resulted in the forcible installation of Communist professors. Members of the intelligentsia were exhorted to work for the success of the industrialization and collectivization programs.

Such, in the briefest scope, was the political and economic background impinging on intellectual life in the 1930s. The "second revolution" of those years was intended to construct socialism. Soviet socialism would involve new forms of the organization of industry and agriculture that were assumed to be superior to previous modes of economic activity. The new form in industry was based on state ownership and control of the means of production, a principle that involved a loss primarily by the previous owners or managers of industry, not the workers themselves. The new form in agriculture, however, was very different in its effects. All but the poorest peasants were deprived of their possessions and of control over land that they considered their own. The result of this deprivation was opposition by the peasantry to the government and a consequent agricultural crisis. Many peasants were deliberately withholding or destroying their produce. The survival of the Soviet regime in the early thirties was directly connected with its success in dealing with this agricultural crisis.

One of the many desperate needs of the Soviet government at this time was for politically committed agricultural specialists. The professional biologists in the universities and research institutes were ill suited for this role, both in terms of their politics and of their interests. The best of them were involved in theoretical questions that only later would have great economic benefit;[27] the twenties were the years of the fruit fly *Drosophila melanogaster*, not the years of hybrid corn, although a direct connection between the two types of genetic research showed itself dramatically in later years. Hybrid corn's day came primarily in the forties, and it would be only one of the practical triumphs issuing from the science of genetics.[28] But these achievements were not yet visible in Russia in the early thirties. Furthermore, the professional biologists, like many leading Soviet scientists of this time, were frequently from bourgeois families. Often educated abroad and almost always aware of foreign developments, at least in their fields, they were members of that class falling under suspicion in the early thirties. It would require only a little imagination to convert their disinterest in the practical side of agriculture into purposeful "wrecking" of the socialist economy, or their interest in eugenics into sympathy with fascist theories of racism, or their emphasis on the relative immutability of the gene into an attempted rescue of the biological fixity favored in earlier times by the Church.

Lysenko, on the other hand, was seen by many Soviet bureaucrats as a precious commodity.[29] Of peasant family background, he was committed to the cause of the Soviet regime, and instead of trying to avoid the tasks of practical agriculture, he placed all his limited talents at its disposal. Whatever the Party and government officials urged in the way of agricultural programs, Lysenko supported. In later years his shift of attention to support whatever the Party called for became a studied maneuver. After World War II Stalin said he would "transform nature" through the planting of shelter belts, and Lysenko came up with a plan for the nest planting of trees; after Stalin's death his successor, Malenkov, called for an increase of crops in the nonblack earth belt, and Lysenko produced a suggested method for fertilizing this kind of land; Khrushchev in turn became entranced with growing corn after visiting the United States, and Lysenko, swallowing his pride as he accepted this product of modern genetics, promoted the square-cluster method of planting it; later, Khrushchev called for the USSR to overtake the United States in milk and butter production, and Lysenko shifted his attentions to the breeding of cows with high-butterfat milk.

In the early and mid-thirties Lysenko built up his strength by urging vernalization on the collectivized farms. Completely aside from its dubious practical value, vernalization had a significant psychological value. The primary question of the times was not so much whether vernalization would work as whether the peasants would work. Still alienated by the collectivization program, the peasants at first found difficulty seeing very much "new" about "socialist agriculture" except the fact of dispossession. Lysenko and his followers introduced a great deal that was new. They organized the peasants weeks before spring plowing and planting normally began, in the historically "slack period" for the countryside, and had them preparing seed. Lysenko and his assistants not only saw to it that the seed was prepared, but that it was, in fact, planted, no mean feat at that time. They soon developed other plans that involved the peasants in projects they had never before witnessed; if they were not soaking seeds in cold water, they were planting potatoes in the middle of the summer, or plucking leaves from cotton plants, or removing the anthers from spikes of wheat, or artificially pollinating corn.[30] These are only a few of Lysenko's projects. The intrinsic value of them is doubtful—today the Soviet government does not promote a single one, at least not in the form favored by Lysenko.[31] Yet in their time they were genuinely valuable to the Soviet regime, though for reasons that have very little to do with principles of agronomy. Every peasant who participated in these projects was enrolling in the great Soviet experiment; a peasant who vernalized wheat had already clearly graduated from the stage when he destroyed his wheat so that the Soviet government would not receive it.[32] Every one of Lysenko's projects was surrounded with the rhetoric of socialist agriculture, and those who liked his projects committed themselves to that cause. A novel action in the service of a cause represents an important psychological transition. One is tempted to say that the important thing about Lysenko's proposals was that they did not do too much harm, rather than that they did a great deal of good.[33] Some of the later ones did cause much damage, but only after his strength was already very great.

After Lysenko moved from Azerbaidzhan to Odessa in 1930, he met I. I. Prezent—in contrast to Lysenko, a member of the Communist Party and a graduate of Leningrad University. Prezent had once thought that Mendelian genetics was a confirmation of dialectical materialism, but he later "diverged from the formal geneticists on the most cardinal questions."[34] Unfortunately, very little is known about the causes of that change of opinion, so fateful to Soviet genetics. The economic and social issues already referred to must have played a role. Research by Douglas Weiner in the 1980s shows that Prezent came to see contradictions between Mendelian genetics and the Soviet regime's desire to acclimatize exotic plants and animals in the interests of agricultural productivity. The combination of this realization with his ambition to become politically influential in Soviet biology led him to become increasingly critical of classical genetics.[35] Prezent is frequently described, both in and out of the Soviet Union, as the ideologue who was primarily responsible for systematically formulating Lysenko's views and for attempting to integrate them with dialectical materialism.[36] To ascertain the relative contributions of Lysenko and Prezent to the full system of Michurinist biology is an impossible task since they worked closely together and published several important works as co-authors. It is quite possible that once alerted by Prezent to the ideological possibilities of his biological views, Lysenko was as active as Prezent in expanding the system. But the fact remains that not until Prezent became his collaborator did Lysenko make an attempt either to connect his biological views with Marxism or to oppose classical genetics.

The joint publication in 1935 by Lysenko and Prezent of "Plant Breeding and the Theory of Phasic Development of Plants" marks an entirely new stage in the development of Lysenko's career. It was his first publication in which he reached beyond agronomic techniques to a theoretical conception of plant breeding science, and it was also his first publication in which he subjected classical genetics to substantial criticism. The theoretical tenets of this publication will be considered in some detail in the section of this chapter that concerns Lysenko's biological system. At this point it is necessary only to notice several alterations in Lysenko's approach. Now Lysenko was beginning to think in terms of a polarity between socialist science and bourgeois science:

> The Party and the government have set our plant-breeding science the task of creating new varieties of plants at the shortest date. . . . Nevertheless, the science of plant breeding continues to lag behind and there is no guarantee that this socialist task will be carried out within the appointed time.
>
> We are convinced that the root of this evil lies in the critical state of plant biology that we inherited from methodologically bourgeois science.[37]

The tone of this publication differed sharply from Lysenko's earlier, pedestrian publications on vernalization. His ambitions had grown enormously: "We must fight uncompromisingly for the reconstruction of genetic plant-breeding theory, for the building of our own genetic plant-breeding theory on the basis of the materialist principles of *development*, which actually reflect the dialectics of heredity."[38] Here we see that Lysenko had found a new vocabulary, based on "materialism" and "dialectics." How meaningful these references could be made remained to be seen.

Criticism of academic biologists in the Soviet Union was not totally new in 1935; it actually began at the end of the twenties, but these earlier censures should probably be seen as a part of the general suspicion of the bourgeois specialists, whatever their fields, rather than a specific attempt to displace classical genetics with a rival theory. Sometime before 1935 the various critical tendencies began to come together. Other rivulets of criticism joined the growing stream of disapproval of classical genetics in those years; the sources of these negative judgments were quite diverse. The relatively uneducated selectionists and a few of the older biologists had their own reasons for opposing modern genetic theories—reasons that had effects in other countries as well, including the United States. And the rise of fascism in Germany, supported by several prominent geneticists in Germany (and, of course, opposed by some), added a certain urgency to the growing controversy.[39]

Genetics had been seen by a number of its notable proponents as a key to radical social reform, a natural ally of Soviet socialism, rather than its opponent. A prominent geneticist in the twenties was Iurii A. Filipchenko, director of the Bureau of Eugenics of the Academy of Sciences. Filipchenko was concerned for the fate of the Russian intellectual elite, which he thought was not reproducing itself; he considered the dissemination of marriage advice to be one of the responsibilities of his bureau, and he hoped thereby to strengthen the genetic position of Russian scholars.[40]

The possibility of a Soviet sponsorship of eugenics for the cultivation of talent may seen remote in view of the later opposition to genetics as a whole, but the twenties were a period when many things seemed possible. Although Filipchenko backed away from radical eugenic proposals, other writers in this period spoke of how the dissolution of bourgeois family relations would permit couples to choose sperm donors of great intellectual ability who would provide for "1,000 or even 10,000 children."[41]

Nikolai Vavilov, the most prominent of Soviet geneticists, was also clearly attracted by the possibility of a union between the Soviet state and genetics, although on different grounds. Vavilov's commitment to an alliance of socialism and science is frequently forgotten by non-Soviet observers who know only of his subsequent martyrdom. Born in a wealthy merchant family in 1887, educated in England under William Bateson, one of the leaders of neo-Mendelism, Vavilov returned to Russia at the beginning of World War I. After the Revolution he became a leading administrator of Soviet science.[42] His most important work, *The Centers of Origin of Cultivated Plants*, published in 1926, developed the theory that the greatest genetic divergence in cultivated plant species could be found near the origins of these species. This conclusion led him to expeditions to many remote places. His other major theoretical work, "The Law of Homologous Series in Variation," first published in 1920, was based on the belief that related species tend to vary genetically in similar ways. He later criticized this work for regarding the gene as too stable.[43]

Vavilov's real importance lay, not in this theoretical work, but in his collection of plant specimens from all over the world and his administration of a network of research institutions devoted both to theoretical genetics and the improvement of agriculture. He believed that the two goals could be reached best in Russia, under a socialist government. Vavilov's commitment to socialism and his respect for Lysenko's practical abilities as a farmer were probably the reasons for his early support for Lysenko, a support that has been emphasized by Mark Popovsky.[44] After seeing how Lysenko intended to overthrow theoretical genetics, however, Vavilov moved into strong opposition to the peasant agronomist.

Among the foreign geneticists attracted to Moscow by the prospect of a union of socialism and genetics was the American future Nobelist H. J. Muller, who came in 1933 expecting to find a place where he would not suffer for his communist sympathies. An earlier visit to the USSR had had a great impact on Muller and on Soviet genetics.[45] Muller had from his early youth been committed to socialism and to the control by man of his own genetic future. In his unpublished autobiographical notes, written about 1936, he commented that after being shown fossil horses' feet at the age of eight, "the idea never left the back of my head, that if this could happen in nature, men should eventually be able to control the process, even in themselves, so as greatly to improve upon their own natures. In 1906 I began a lasting friendship with Edgar Altenburg, then a classmate. . . . He and I argued out vehemently and to the bitter end all questions of principle on which we differed, and thus he succeeded in converting me both to atheism . . . and to the cause of social revolution."[46]

In 1935 Muller published a book, *Out of the Night*, in which he stated that only in a society where class differences had been abolished could eugenics be properly implemented. In the Soviet Union Muller tried to promote his book, but was rebuffed.[47] As Lysenkoism grew in strength, Muller became a firm anti-Stalinist; he made the struggle against Lysenkoism one of the two major campaigns of his life, the other being his fight against radiation hazards. But there is no evidence that Muller's opposition to Stalinism resulted in a change of heart toward socialism. His colleague T. M. Sonneborn of Indiana University wrote of him that "his disillusionment with Stalinism left completely unchanged his conviction that a socialist economy was necessary for effective and wise control of human evolution."[48]

The first known attack upon Vavilov and his Institute of Plant Industry came in an article in 1931 by A. Kol', who called the institute "alien" and "hostile"; he criticized it for devoting its attention to the morphology and classification of plants rather than their economic significance.[49] This attack, though serious, was typical of criticisms leveled at theoretical institutes in those days, including many in fields outside biology. Vavilov attempted to answer the charges by pointing to the many varieties of plants (potatoes, corn, wheat) found by his institute around the world which might eventually help the Soviet economy.[50] He stressed how deeply his institute felt its responsibility to socialist construction. But the disadvantage of the theorist in defending his science was clearly revealed by the editor's note to the exchange between Kol' and Vavilov, which commented that despite Vavilov's reply, Kol' was correct in noting many deficiencies in Vavilov's institute. The source of these shortcomings, said the editor, was that the

> orientation toward the "needs of tomorrow" about which Academician Vavilov writes turns out to be for many partisans of "pure science" a convenient cloak for ignoring the needs of today in bringing about a socialist reconstruction of agriculture.[51]

No attempt will be made here to follow the entire sorry story of the growing campaign in the thirties against Vavilov and the classical geneticists, a campaign that Lysenko had clearly joined by 1935. That series of episodes can be best followed in the careful studies of David Joravsky. The important fact is that although Lysenko may have been the architect of a great deal that was done in his name, no aspiring promoter of a peculiar scientific system ever fell into a more personally fortunate (and historically tragic) situation. The relationship between Lysenko and his environment was one of mutual corruption. As C. D. Darlington commented:

> His modest proposals were received with such willing faith that he found himself carried along on the crest of a wave of disciplined enthusiasm, a wave of such magnitude as only totalitarian machinery can propagate. The whole world was overwhelmed by its success. Even Lysenko must have been surprised at an achievement which gave him an eminence shared only by the Dnieper dam. . . .[52]

Just who the early promoters of Lysenko within the official bureaucracy were is difficult to determine. Lysenko himself gave a great deal of credit to Ia. A. Iakovlev, who after December 1929 was people's commissar of agriculture for the USSR. Professor Joravsky has also added P. P. Postyshev, M. A. Chernov, and K. Ia. Bauman as early important supporters of Lysenko. But since all three men disappeared in the purges in the late thirties, as Joravsky notes, they were obviously not indispensable to the agronomist. Most important of all, of course, was the intermittent support of Stalin after 1935. In February of that year at the Second All-Union Congress of Collective Farmers and Shock-Workers, Lysenko presented a speech entitled "Vernalization Means Millions of Pounds of Additional Harvest," in which he called for the mobilization of the peasant masses in the vernalization campaign. At the same time, Lysenko apologized for his lack of ability as a speaker, saying he was only a "vernalizer," not an orator or a writer. At this point Stalin broke into the speech crying, "Bravo, Comrade Lysenko, bravo!"[53]

It is difficult to find the reason for this sympathy in Stalin's theoretical writings. Some authors have maintained that Stalin was from a very early date committed to neo-Lamarckism; in support of this, frequent references are made to Stalin's "Anarchism or Socialism?" published in 1906. This argument becomes less convincing upon examination; only one phrase of "Anarchism or Socialism?" refers to biology, and it may not be significant.[54] Stalin's occasional praise of Lysenko was no guarantee of permanent favor; his praise for other prominent Soviet citizens was sometimes followed by their imprisonment. Rather than enjoying an assured place, it appears that Lysenko struggled constantly, along with many others, to maintain himself under Stalin.

In 1935 a steady stream of pro-Lysenko propaganda flowed in the meetings of agriculturists, in the popular press, and, increasingly, in journals. Lysenko was by this time receiving significant support from the official bureaucracy. Vavilov was replaced as president of the Lenin Academy of Agricultural Sciences by A. I. Muralov, who tried to compromise between classical genetics and Lysenkoism. In 1936 a "socialist competition" was conducted between Vavilov's Institute of Plant Industry and Lysenko's Odessa Selection-Genetics Institute. The results are unknown, but with the emphasis placed on quick results and declarations of plan fulfillment, it is not difficult to guess what the results were.[55]

In December 1936 a great conference was held to discuss the issue of what Lysenko now called "the two trends in genetics." The conference came as a replacement for the Seventh International Congress of Genetics, scheduled to be held in Moscow, but cancelled by the Soviet authorities. The edited record of this conference, later withdrawn from circulation by the Soviet government, is one of the most interesting sources for the history of the Lysenko affair. Appropriately entitled "Controversial Questions of Genetics and Selection," it is, despite the editing, by no means a document of pro-Lysenko propaganda.[56] The speeches are so diverse in view that no classification system would be accurate. In order to give some sort of idea of the alignment of forces, however, I have categorized (somewhat arbitrarily, since a spectrum of opinion is involved) the forty-six speakers as seventeen anti-Lysenko, nineteen pro-Lysenko, and ten unclear in their stated opinions (which, of course, may not reflect their inner opinions). The roster of speakers included many of the major participants in the long struggle over Lysenko, including Vavilov, Lysenko, Dubinin, Ol'shanskii, and Prezent. Many of the opinions expressed were sharp. The theoretical aspects of the discussion will be taken up in the second section of this chapter, but some comments are appropriate at this point.

One of the most outspoken of the speakers was A. S. Serebrovskii, who said that although he agreed with the need to establish scientific research on a new socialist basis, he was horrified by the monstrous form this campaign was taking:

> Under the supposedly revolutionary slogans "For a truly Soviet genetics," "Against bourgeois genetics," "For an undistorted Darwin," and so forth, we have a fierce attack on the greatest achievements of the twentieth century, we have an attempt to throw us backward a half-century.[57]

A similar portrayal of possible disaster was made by N. P. Dubinin, who three decades later would be one of the leaders in the reconstruction of Soviet genetics:

> It is not necessary to play hide-and-seek; it is essential to say outright that if the view triumphs in theoretical genetics that Academician T. D. Lysenko says is best represented by I. I. Prezent, that will mean that modern genetics will be completely destroyed. (Voice from the hall: How's that for pessimism!)
>
> No, this is not pessimism. I wish to pose the question sharply only because the topic of discussion concerns the most cardinal issues of our science.[58]

One of the most poignant moments of the conference came when the American H. J. Muller began his rebuttal to the followers of Lysenko by quoting from a letter he had just received from the English geneticist J. B. S. Haldane, who wrote that he had dropped his laboratory work in order to go to Madrid to participate in the defense of that city against

Franco's forces. Muller said that by encouraging Lysenkoism, the Soviet Union, which had long represented to him the march of progress, was turning its back on its own ideals. Lysenkoism was not Marxism, he suggested, but its opposite. He criticized the supporters of Lysenkoism from within the framework of Marxism.[59] The Lysenkoites, not the geneticists, were guilty of "idealism" and "Machism":

> Only three kinds of people can at the present time speak of the gene as something unreal, as only a kind of "notion." These are, first, confirmed idealists; second, "Machist" biologists for whom exist only sensations about an organism, i.e., its external appearance or phenotype; some of these biologists at the present time are hiding behind the screen of a falsely interpreted dialectical materialism. And finally, the third category of such people is those simple minds who do not understand the subject of discussion.
>
> The gene is a conception of the same type as man, earth, stone, molecule, or atom.[60]

But Muller came under considerable criticism at the conference for his comment that the gene was so stable that the "period between two successive mutations is on the order of several hundred or even thousands of years." The problem of the mutability of the gene was one of the three major controversies of the meeting; the others were the mechanism of change of heredity (influence of environment; role of chance) and the practical usefulness of the two main trends in Soviet biology.

Another great conference on Soviet biology was held October 7–14, 1939. A significant difference of this conference from previous ones was that it was organized and controlled by philosophers, the members of the editorial board of the theoretical journal *Under the Banner of Marxism*.[61] Many of the philosophers had by this time begun to grant Lysenko's claims that he represented the ideologically correct attitude toward genetics, although earlier they had resisted this conclusion. The incomplete record of the conference published in *Under the Banner of Marxism* indicated that there were fifty-three speakers, a number of whom were participants at the 1936 meeting. By the same simplified classification scheme used for the earlier meeting, I would term twenty-nine as "favoring" Lysenko, twenty-three as "opposing" him in terms of their public statements. Thus, although the result of the conference was again something of a victory for Lysenko, the opposition was at this date still strong. A crude sort of compromise that granted the continued right of the classical geneticists to express their opinions was being observed. Vavilov pointed to the growing use of hybrid corn in the United States as a direct result of genetics research.[62]

By this time the tone of the Lysenkoites had become blatantly aggressive;[63] they demanded changes in school curricula and research programs. V. K. Milovanov commented, "Until the present time departments of genetics have continued to exist: we should have liquidated them long ago."[64] Lysenko had earlier said that Mendelism should be expelled from the universities.[65] Prezent was now working with the Commissariat of Education in order to revise the biology courses of the grade schools; as a result, the teachers and pupils were "completely disoriented on biological questions."[66] The belligerence was apparent in the way in which Lysenko described himself and his opponents. He appropriated the word "genetics" for his followers; his opponents were "Mendelists." Only the Mendelists were grouping together; Lysenko refused even to admit that he had a "school." Instead, he stood for the broad science of biology, loyal to Darwin and Marx, while his opponents succumbed to antiscientific and clerical views. The rapporteur of the conference, V. Kolbanovskii, hardly neutral, called Lysenko's theories "progressive" and "innovative." P. F. Iudin, the philosopher who closed the conference, called upon the academic geneticists to reject that "rubbish and slag that have accumulated in your science."[67]

In 1940 Nikolai Vavilov was arrested and subsequently died in prison.[68] The disappearance of the leader of the academic geneticists, a man whose talents were recognized even by his opponents, meant that no scientist was immune. With Vavilov gone, many of the neo-Mendelian geneticists became silent. Some sought work elsewhere, in less controversial fields. Others continued research in genetics, but on a more limited scale than previously.

The culmination of the genetics controversy in the Soviet Union came at the 1948 session of the Lenin Academy of Agricultural Sciences, when genetics as known in the rest of the world was prohibited. The background of this conference is still not clear; it seems to have been preceded not by growing support for Lysenko, as one would imagine, but by growing criticism. A Soviet biologist who wrote a history of the Lysenko affair commented that by late 1947 Lysenko's political standing was much lower than before the war.[69] Andrei Zhdanov, one of Stalin's assistants, and his son Iurii were among the most influential critics of Lysenko.[70]

The sad story of the 1948 genetics conference has been told outside the Soviet Union many times; the proceedings of the conference are available in English, unlike the records of the earlier meetings.[71] Of the fifty-six speakers, only six or seven defended genetics as it was known elsewhere, and of these the most important were later forced publicly to recant. Lysenko revealed in his final remarks that the Central Committee of the Communist Party had examined and approved his report. Evidently, he knew of this all through the conference while some of his opponents, ignorant of the prior Party decision, seriously implicated themselves by resisting Lysenko. At the moment the Party decision was announced, the entire conference arose to give an ovation in honor of Stalin. The participants sent the Soviet leader a letter of gratitude for his support of "progressive Michurinist biological science," the "most advanced agricultural science in the world."

In the months following the 1948 conference, research and teaching in standard genetics were suppressed in the Soviet Union. The ban remained until after Stalin's death in 1953. The recovery that occurred during the years after Stalin's passing was painful and fitful, and did not fully blossom until after Lysenko's downfall in 1965.

LYSENKO'S BIOLOGICAL SYSTEM

By 1948 all the major components of Lysenko's biological system had been developed. Lysenko's views on biological development were contained in a vague doctrine, the Theory of Nutrients. The word "nutrient" (*pishcha*) used in a very broad sense, seemed to include for him such environmental conditions as sunlight, temperature, and humidity as well as chemical elements in the soil, or organic food, or gases present in the atmosphere.[72] The Theory of Nutrients was, then, a putative general theory of ecology. To Lysenko any approach to the problem of heredity must start with a consideration of the relationship between an organism and its environment, and the environment in the final analysis determines heredity, although through intermediate mechanisms in such a way that each organism possesses a certain hereditary stability at any point in time.

The most important influence on Lysenko in the development of his Theory of Nutrients was his work at the end of the twenties and the beginning of the thirties on the effects of temperature on plants. Lysenko came to the conclusion that the ecological relationship between an organism and its environment could be divided into separate phases or periods during which the requirements of the organism differ sharply.

Hence, his views were sometimes broadly labeled the Theory of Phasic Development of Plants, although the Theory of Nutrients is a more comprehensive title, describing both plants and animals, both the phasic development and other ramifications of his views.

Lysenko did not see the vernalization phase as necessary for cereals only; all plants pass through different stages, he thought, and for many of them the vernalization phase is the first.[73] But Lysenko never gave a coherent description of just what these other stages were. He did maintain that for many cereals the stage immediately succeeding vernalization—in which temperature is so important—is the photo phase, during which duration of daylight becomes critical. But while in each of the two phases described Lysenko indicated that one factor becomes critical to the development of the organism, he also emphasized that these factors alone are not sufficient to guarantee correct development. Each phase should be seen as a complex of factors necessary for the organism. Here, as in many other cases, Lysenko was unclear on just how one differentiates between the phases, since in every phase both temperature and light are among the complex of factors affecting growth.

As already noted, vernalization itself is a legitimate topic of investigation in plant science; Lysenko's major errors were not in the subject of study he undertook but the methods he used and conclusions he reached. A perusal of the scientific literature reveals a vast amount of evidence on vernalization, some of it obtained in the same years during which Lysenko was working.[74]

In his "Plant Breeding and the Theory of Phasic Development of Plants," published in 1935 in collaboration with Prezent, Lysenko began reaching beyond simple studies of vernalization to a general theory of heredity.[75] His primary complaint in 1935 against classical genetics seems to have been that the geneticists could not predict which characters would be dominant in hybridization and worked primarily by means of making many thousands of combinations. Lysenko's impatience—linked with the impatience of the government in its hopes for rapid economic expansion—drove him to the hope for short cuts.[76] He believed that dominance was dependent on environmental conditions: "We maintain that in all cases when a hybrid plant is given really different conditions of existence for its development this causes corresponding changes in dominance: *the dominant character will be the one that has more favorable conditions for adapting itself to its development.*"[77]

These views were ramified in succeeding years. The most complete statement of Lysenko's theoretical views was contained in his "Heredity and its Variability," first published in 1943. It is to this source that we must turn in an effort to give a fuller statement of Lysenko's system.

Lysenko denied the distinction between phenotype and genotype[78] even over the distance of one generation. He observed that "*all the properties, including heredity, the nature, of an organism, arise de novo to the same degree to which the body of that organism (for example, a plant) is built de novo in the new generation.*"[79] The obliteration of this separation lay at the bottom of much of Lysenko's writings.

Heredity was defined by Lysenko as "*the property of a living body to require definite conditions for its life, its development and to react definitely to various conditions.*"[80] Lysenko, then, described heredity in terms of the relationship of an organism to its environment rather than in the traditional sense of the transmission of characters from ancestor to descendant. But he confused his definition by adding that "the nature of the living body" and "the heredity of the living body" are nearly alike. Just what the "nature of the living body" consisted of was left unsaid beyond returning to the already cited statement concerning the requirements for "definite conditions of life."

The heredity of a living body, according to Lysenko, was built up from the conditions of the external environment over many generations, and each alteration of these conditions led to a change in heredity. This process he called the "assimilation of external conditions." Once assimilated, these conditions become internal—that is, a part of the nature, or heredity, of the organism: "The external conditions, being included within, assimilated by the living body . . . become particles (*chastitsami*) of the living body, and for their growth and development they in turn demand that food and those conditions of the external environment, such as they were themselves in the past."[81] In the last part of this sentence Lysenko referred to the part of his biological system that avoided a totally arbitrary plasticity of organisms. The mechanics of the transition from "external conditions" (temperature, moisture, nutriments, and so on) to "internal particles" was, to say the least, unclear, but Lysenko did achieve in this way a concept of material carriers of heredity. These "internal particles" may seem at first glance the same as genes, but it is clear from Lysenko's description and later comments that they are not. Rather than being unchanging, or relatively unchanging, hereditary factors passed from ancestors to progeny, they are internalized environmental conditions.[82]

Despite this crucial distinction, Lysenko's particles did perform the function of providing—under certain conditions—fairly stable heredity.

This heredity he described as the conservative tendency of any organism in its relationship to its environment. If an organism exists in external surroundings similar to those of its parents, then it will display characters similar to its parents'. If, however, the organism is placed in an environment different from that of its ancestors, its course of development will be different. Assuming that the organism manages to survive, it will be forced, Lysenko thought, to assimilate the different external conditions of its new environment. This assimilation leads to a different heredity, which in several generations may become "fixed" in the same way in which a different heredity had been fixed in the earlier environment. In the intermediate, or transition, period, the heredity of the organism is "shattered," and therefore unusually plastic.

Lysenko believed that there existed three different ways in which one could "shatter," or remove the hereditary stability of, an organism. One could place the organism in different external environments, as already described. This method was much more effective at certain stages (for instance, vernalization) of the development process than others, he thought. One could graft a variety of a plant onto another, thereby "liquidating the conservatism" of both stock and scion. Or finally, one could cross forms differing markedly in habitat or origin. Each of these methods was attempted in Lysenko's experiments.

Organisms that were in the shattered, or destabilized, state were, Lysenko thought, particularly useful from the standpoint of manipulation. One could, within certain limits, give them new heredities by placing them in environments of carefully specified (and desired) conditions.[83] In several generations the organism's heredity would stabilize to the point that the organism would henceforth "demand," or as a minimum, "prefer," that environment.

Although Lysenko referred to hereditary particles, he was extremely indefinite about the location and function of these particles. His concept of them certainly did not involve "particulate heredity" in the usual sense of nonblending hereditary factors, nor did it permit a conceivable separation of the particles from the rest of the organism. He observed that *any living body part, and even a droplet (if the body is liquid) possesses the property of heredity, i.e., the property of demanding relatively determined conditions for its life, growth, and development.*[84] This view reminds one of Darwin's theory of pangenesis, with Lysenko's "particles" being Darwin's "gemmules," which were supposedly given off by every cell or unit of body. This theory of Darwin's has, of course, been discarded in the light of modern genetics. One might add that in

Darwin's time, the theory explained phenomena that otherwise could not be explained; Darwin was, further, aware of its speculative character, and labeled it "provisional." Lysenko's theory, on the other hand, inadequately and incorrectly accounted for phenomena that were better explained by another existing theory. Thus, even though Darwin's and Lysenko's theories in this particular instance were very similar, the historian of science would easily conclude that Darwin's effort was innovative and useful, even if tenuous, while Lysenko's was essentially retrogressive.[85]

Lysenko's view of the possible types of inheritance included the case of particulate, or mutually exclusive, inheritance, but went far beyond it. His system was borrowed largely from Timiriazev, who in turn had been influenced by earlier biologists. Here again, Timiriazev's scheme was, at the turn of the century, fairly plausible. By the time Lysenko espoused it, genetics had created a far superior scheme, which Lysenko never mastered. Timiriazev's and Lysenko's categories of inheritance can best be described in terms of a diagram given in Hudson and Richens' careful study; the same scheme was described by Lysenko in his *Heredity and its Variability:*[86]

Simple inheritance (one parent involved)	*Mixed inheritance* (mosaics of parental characters)	
Complex inheritance (two parents involved)	*Blending inheritance* (blends of parental characters)	
	Mutually exclusive inheritance (complete dominance of one or the other parent)	*Millardetism* (F_2 generation not segregating)
		Mendelism (F_2 generation segregating)

Examples of simple inheritance, in which only one parent is involved, would include all types of asexual and vegetative reproduction (self-pollination in plants such as wheat, propagation from tubers or cuttings), and parthenogenesis.

Complex inheritance involves two parents, and according to Lysenko, this *"double heredity gives rise to a greater viability of the organisms, and to their greater adaptation to varying living conditions."*[87] Lysenko, therefore, felt that the offspring of two parents possessed, in potential, all the characters of both parents, and he looked with disfavor upon inbreeding, or self-fertilization, which led, he thought, to a narrowing of the potentialities of the organism.[88] In the case of double heredity with unrelated parents, the characters that would actually be displayed depended on, first, the environment in which the organism was placed, and second, the unique properties of the particular organism involved. The interaction of the environment and these unique properties led to the "types" of complex inheritance: mixed, blending, and mutually exclusive.

Mixed heredity was, to Lysenko, represented by progeny that displayed clear (unblended) characters of both parents in different parts of their bodies; examples would be variegated flowers, piebald animals, and grafts of the type known to geneticists as chimeras (mosaic patterns of genetically distinct cells formed by artificial grafting of two different plants). Lysenko gave a number of examples of mixed heredity, the best known of which was the supposed graft hybridization of tomato plants by Avakian and Iastreb, in which the coloration of the fruit of the scion was reportedly influenced by the stock. This experiment was investigated by Hudson and Richens, who concluded that it was of doubtful validity.[89] If the tomato plants were heterozygous and if stray cross-pollination occurred, the results could be explained in terms of standard genetics. Whether graft hybridization ever occurs was a hotly disputed question in biology, but Lysenko's failure to use proper experimental controls eliminated him as a reliable participant in the debate.[90]

Blending inheritance was, to Lysenko, the merging of characters in the hybrid in such a way that they were intermediate between those of the parents. Many cases of such inheritance are known. It is obvious, for example, that the progeny of marriages between humans of distinctly different skin color are frequently intermediate in color, and a whole spectrum of intermediate forms may occur with no clear relationship to the Mendelian ratios. The major difference between Lysenko's interpretation of this continuous variation and that of modern geneticists is that the latter see continuous variation as the result of a series of independent genes that are cumulative in effect, but each of which still functions discretely, while Lysenko spoke simply in terms of blending.[91]

"Mutually exclusive inheritance" was the term used by Lysenko to cover the phenomenon of complete dominance. Lysenko did not see dominance in the customary terms of the mechanism of allelic pairs, only one of which in the hybrid form is expressed in the phenotype, but instead in terms of the relationship of the organism to the environment. There were no dominant and recessive genes, he thought, but only "concealed internal potentialities" that may or may not "find the conditions necessary for their development."

Lysenko saw two different types of mutually exclusive inheritance, which he called "Millardetism" and "Mendelism," or "so-called Mendelism." Millardetism, named after the French botanist, was used to describe hybrids that in subsequent generations supposedly never display segregation. The dominance that was displayed in the F_1 generation continues, Lysenko reported, in all other generations. Lysenko maintained that there was nothing surprising in this, since his general theory of the expression of characters rested on the relationship of the organism to the environment; therefore, the correct environment would always cause the appearance of the appropriate character. Lysenko's followers cited a number of experiments that allegedly supported this conclusion. There is nothing in classical genetics to explain these particular cases, although it is not difficult to imagine errors that might lead one to such a conclusion.[92] Lysenko's results were not verified abroad.

"So-called Mendelism," the last of Lysenko's types of inheritance, refers to hybrids that do segregate in F_2 and subsequent generations. Lysenko considered them isolated cases and insisted, like Timiriazev, that Mendel did not actually discover this type of inheritance. According to Lysenko, the Mendelian laws themselves were "scholastic" and "barren," did not reflect the importance of the environment, and did not permit the prediction of the appearance of characters before making empirical tests for each type of organism.

So far nothing has been said concerning Lamarckism or the inheritance of acquired characters, two topics that are usually mentioned early in any discussion of Lysenko. It should be clear by now that Lysenko believed in the inheritance of acquired characters. The "internalizing" of environmental conditions, which he considered the means by which the heredity of any type of organism is acquired, is obviously a type of such inheritance. And Lysenko himself stated his position unequivocally:

A materialistic theory of the development of living nature is unthinkable without a recognition of the necessity of the inheritance of individual differences by the organism in definite conditions of its life; it is unthinkable without a recognition of the inheritance of acquired characters.[93]

This is a clear case of Lysenko's appropriating Marxist philosophy to serve his own dated biological theories. There is nothing in systematic dialectical materialism that requires belief in inheritance of acquired characters. Materialism as a theory of knowledge and a view of nature does not even come close to including such a principle. Soviet dialectical materialism in Stalin's time, however, came to be associated with the inheritance of acquired characters. Since Lysenko's mentors were all representatives of old biology, it is not surprising that he subscribed to the theory. Belief in the inheritance of acquired characters "solaced most of the biologists of the nineteenth century," as a prominent geneticist of the twentieth century observed.[94] Thus Lysenko could cite Darwin as well as Timiriazev and Michurin in support of the view.[95] One might note parenthetically that the surprising aspect of Darwin's attitude toward the inheritance of acquired characters was not that he believed in it (which he did), but that he relied so little on it for his great theory. That Marx and Engels also accepted it illustrates only that they were aware of the biology of their time.

Whether Lysenko was a Lamarckist in a strict historical sense is a difficult question. The very term "Lamarckism" has been so devalued through wide currency that it probably should be discarded.[96] Lamarck believed that only use and disuse and the effort of organisms to improve themselves had effects on heredity, not the "conditions of the environment" that Lysenko emphasized. Lysenko never seemed to consider use and disuse or self-improvement important, although a few of his enthusiastic followers did.[97] Lamarck was a typical eighteenth-century materialist, Lysenko maintained, incapable of thinking "dialectically." There also seem to be no equivalents in Lamarckism to Lysenko's theory of shattering heredity, or his theory that heredity is a metabolic process. Therefore, genuine distinctions between Lamarckism and Lysenkoism do exist. Nonetheless, the two systems are similar in that both contain the principle of the inheritance of acquired characters. Soviet geneticists who later displaced Lysenko often described his system as a "naive Lamarckist view."[98]

There are other aspects of Lamarck's thought that resemble Lysenko's, but an evaluation of these similarities involves one in the very difficult problem of interpreting Lamarck. There is much debate among historians of science over whether Lamarck should be seen as one of the first of the evolutionists or the last of an earlier breed, the romantic scientist. Usually Lamarck is described as an eccentric, perverse, frequently wrong, but nonetheless brilliant precursor of Darwin. But there are some exceptions to this view. Professor Charles Gillispie of Princeton wrote:

. . . Lamarck's theory of evolution was the last attempt to make a science out of the instinct, as old as Heraclitus and deeply hostile to Aristotelian formalization, that the world is flux and process, and that science is to study, not the configuration of matter, not the categories of form, but the manifestations of that activity which is ontologically fundamental, as bodies in motion and species of being are not.[99]

According to Gillispie, it was not an accident that Lamarck achieved his position in the wake of the French Revolution. Gillispie believes that Lamarck belonged to the same radical, democratic, antirational camp as Diderot and Marat. These people, says Gillispie, were rebelling against the cold rationalism of Newtonian science, with its explanations of the "how" of things, with its emphasis on cold mathematics. They believed, says Gillispie, that "to describe is not the same thing as to explain. . . . To analyze and to quantify is to denature."

It would not take very much work of the imagination to put Lysenko in this same romantic camp, responding to the same stimuli as Lamarck, if not to his ideas. Lysenko's hostility to mathematics has already been noted. He was also in a postrevolutionary society. Gillispie observed, "It is no accident that the *Jardin des Plantes* was the one scientific institution to flourish in the radical democratic phase of the French Revolution, which struck down all others."[100] One might stress that Lysenko similarly flourished after the Russian Revolution. Lysenko believed in the inheritance of acquired characters, and after being philosophically educated by Prezent, subscribed to the view that all the world is in flux, as did Lamarck. But tempting as such a correspondence between Lamarck and Lysenko is in a number of ways, one should notice that it conceals as well as reveals. First of all, Lamarck himself is not entirely explained in this interpretation. We know that he was critical of the excesses of the French Revolution.[101] Although there were aspects of Lamarck's thought that were anachronistic, other aspects, particularly those relating to evolution, were based at least partially on the scientific evidence of his day. Lamarck was both a predecessor of Darwin and one of the last of the romantic scientists; he was much more of an intellectual than Lysenko ever thought of being. It seems quite certain that Lysenko will never be regarded as a predecessor of a geneticist of scientific importance, even if accepted views on the inheritance of acquired characters should greatly change. Lysenko's knowledge of the biology of his own day was primitive, but Lamarck's knowledge of what was known at his time was fairly sophisticated. Furthermore, if one is to tie Lysenko to Lamarck because of his similar commitment to a philosophy of flux, in Heraclitus' sense, what is one to do with the classical geneticist H. J. Muller, Lysenko's opponent, who subscribed to philosophical Marxism on much more genuine grounds? And lastly, Lysenko based his interpretation of nature on Darwinism, which romantics of the late nineteenth century found heartless. Therefore, one is left with the impression that although there are genuine similarities between Lamarck and Lysenko—both in terms of their systems and their historical situations—there are also very real differences.

The discussion above has included mention of Lysenko's Theory of Nutrients, his concept of heredity, and his view of the mechanism of heredity. Many of the issues over which Lysenko quarreled with classical geneticists, such as the genetics of earliness, pollen fertilization,[102] the deterioration of pure lines, rejuvenation, and graft hybridization can be understood within the framework of the system so far described. The missing element in the discussion so far is the philosophical ingredient. In what way was this system connected with Marxist philosophy, particularly in view of its clear basis in the thought of people unschooled in Marxism, such as Darwin, Timiriazev, Michurin, and the pre-1930 Lysenko? We have noted that the genetics controversy seems farther from dialectical materialism than any of the other issues in this study. Nevertheless, manfully struggling and aided by a few eager ideologists, Lysenko was able to drag several of the issues of genetics into the realm of philosophy. The most important of these were: (1) the question of the mutability of the gene; (2) the question of the isolation of the genotype; (3) the question of the union of theory and practice in genetics; (4) the question of probability and causation.

The question of the mutability of the gene was a serious one, and one that occupied the attention of many of the best biologists of the early twentieth century. One is tempted to say that the closest the Lysenko affair came to a legitimate intellectual issue was its concern with the integrity of the gene—tempted, but not compelled, for the questions Lysenko asked had been rather fully answered a decade or two earlier. But in the first years of the century the problem worried many geneticists.

The issue had definite philosophic and religious implications, indirect perhaps, but real enough to many thinkers, including the geneticists. At the bottom of the discussion there existed a tension between two opposite, but not necessarily incompatible, tendencies, that of heredity and that of evolution. Heredity is a conservative force that tends to preserve similarities. Evolution is a process that depends upon differences. If heredity conserved perfectly, there could be no evolution.[103] The striking characteristic of the gene (named in 1909 by Johannsen), as it seemed to the early geneticists, was its stability over many generations. It seemed a threat to the common-sense (and dialectical materialist) notion that everything changes, and to the scientific concept of evolution.

It is often forgotten by people outside the Soviet Union interested in the Lysenko affair—and it was totally ignored in the Soviet Union— that several of the men who created the science of genetics had great difficulty in accepting the concept of the extremely stable and constant gene. It seemed reminiscent of the fixity of the species favored in past centuries by the Church. T. H. Morgan was openly anticlerical in his views, and Muller accepted, as did most men of scientific bent (including the Marxists), the inevitability of change.[104] A. H. Sturtevant, another of Morgan's students, commented:

> Do new genes in fact arise, or is all genetic variability due to recombination of preexisting genes? This question was seriously discussed—though the alternative to mutation seems to be an initial divine creation of all existing genes.[105]

But more important than religious or philosophical considerations in causing some early geneticists to be skeptical of the concept of a stable gene was the impact of evolutionary theory. As L. C. Dunn remarked:

> The idea that the elements of heredity are highly stable and not subject to fluctuating variability was repugnant to many biologists. These included for a time William Bateson, W. E. Castle, T. H. Morgan, and others who helped to build the new science. There had been a natural growth in nineteenth-century biology of faith in the opposite assumption: namely, that biological forms and properties were inevitably subject to variation. The closer the biologist had been to Darwin's ideas and evidence on variation as the condition of evolutionary change, the more firmly did he hold this faith.
>   W. E. Castle was a conspicuous example of those who held the view that genes must be modifiable by selection. It was shared by many others to whom the inviolability of the gene to change from its genotypic environment in the heterozygous state seemed like arbitrary dogma. Castle cured himself of disbelief in the integrity of the gene the hard way—by fifteen years of arduous experimentation.[106]

Lysenko and his followers did not have the benefit of those fifteen years, nor would they consider seriously the published reports of the classical geneticists that had led them to change their opinions. Instead, the Lysenkoites raised the issue of mutability as evidence of the "idealism" of formal genetics. And here they were able to find support in dialectical materialism, which, like the philosophy of Heraclitus, includes the principle of universal change. At the 1937 conference Prezent attacked H. J. Muller for his remark that "the gene is so stable that the period between two successive mutations is on the order of several hundreds or even thousands of years."[107] But by this time Prezent was already striking out against a straw man; the nature of mutations had been investigated rather thoroughly, and the importance of the cumulative effects of mutations to evolution was well known. When a person considers that one organism contains thousands of genes, one change even several hundred years in each gene could result in an appreciable rate of change. Biological evolution is built on the concept of great changes resulting from minute variations occurring over vast periods of time. As Vavilov commented at the same conference, "None of the modern geneticists and selectionists believes in the immutability of genes. Essentially, genetics has the right to existence as a science and is attractive to us precisely because it is the science of the change of the hereditary nature of organisms. . . ."[108]

It becomes clear that the relative stability of the gene is not a serious obstacle to dialectical materialism. The rates of change in nature vary enormously; the rate of change of the genotype may seem very slow to the person eager for such change, but it is obviously rather rapid when seen on an epochal time scale. Both the Lysenkoites and the formal geneticists took evolution for granted, and evolution is based on truly striking changes in heredity. Furthermore, dialectical materialists were quite willing to accept the existence in nature of matter that changes much more slowly than even the most conservative estimates of the changes in the genotype. The modifications in the interior structure of many rocks are much slower than the biological ones. No one has suggested for this reason that geology is undialectical. The commitment of dialectical materialism is that there be change, not that the change occur at a certain rate.

The question of the isolation of the genotype is similar in some ways to the issue of the mutability of the gene. The separation of the genotype from the phenotype was exaggerated by Weismann, but this exaggeration was probably a necessary, or at least an understandable, step in order to throw off nineteenth-century concepts that attributed the property of heredity to all parts of the body instead of to discrete units within the body. When the full meaning of the germ plasm theory had permeated biological thought, a great change in the concept of heredity resulted. While earlier the body, or soma, had been considered the carrier of heredity, the body was now seen as a temporal husk containing within it an unbroken series of germ cells. In this view the soma was drastically demoted in status.

Early discussions of the germ plasm put great emphasis upon its isolation from the soma (the body of the orgnism, excluding the germ cells). Not until 1927, when Muller showed that mutations could be induced by radiation, did it seem possible to affect the genes by any environmental action. Before that time the gene seemed to be unapproachable by external stimuli. This question of the penetrability of the boundary between the gene and the soma became ideologically charged in the Soviet Union. According to the Stalinist version of dialectical materialism, there were no impassable barriers in nature; the short history of the Communist Party (not published until 1938, but indicative of official thought), which Stalin himself supervised, stated that "not a single phenomenon in nature can be understood if it is considered in isolation, disconnected from the surrounding phenomena."[109]

The statement of Lysenko and his followers that formal genetics postulated an entirely isolated genotype was a false one, based on obsolescent theories. Muller himself, known among geneticists precisely because he had disproved this isolation, was not able to establish his point among ideologists who did not wish to listen. Lysenko continued to insist that Mendelism was based on "an immortal hereditary substance, independent of the qualitative features attending the development of the living body, directing the mortal body, but not produced by the latter." To Lysenko, this was "Weismann's frankly idealistic, essentially mystical conception, which he disguised as 'Neo-Darwinism,' " and which still governed modern genetics.[110]

While geneticists had proved by 1927 that genes could be influenced by external stimuli, they could not obtain specifically desired changes in this way.[111] This uncontrollability of induced mutations was a major issue in the third ideological issue of the Lysenko affair, the question of the union of theory and practice. Michurin and his followers emphasized that every experimenter with plants should be a conscious transformer of nature. The formal geneticists, however, emphasized not only the extreme stability of the gene, but also the undirected character of those mutations that did occur. Thus, the Lysenkoites were able to portray the formal geneticists as having nothing of immediate value to the Soviet economy, while the followers of Lysenko, with their close ties to the soil and their commitments to socialized agriculture, were working constantly to strengthen the Soviet state. Lysenko was, in effect, constantly turning to the theoretical biologists with the query, "What have you done lately for Soviet agriculture?"[112] Michurin, Williams, Lysenko, and their disciples were among the few agricultural specialists who tried to do something immediately for Soviet agriculture. Speaking the same language as the peasants, they built up a strong set of supporters. Vavilov, it is true, was also deeply committed to the improvement of practical agriculture, but he suffered from the disadvantages of his bourgeois background and from his unwillingness to promise more than he could reasonably expect to produce. Vavilov knew well how many difficulties still faced geneticists who were seeking to control heredity. He was forced, therefore, into the position of being less optimistic than the exuberant Lysenko, who recited Michurin's words to the Soviet public: "It is possible, with man's intervention, to force any form of animal or plant to change more quickly and in a direction desirable to man. There opens before man a broad field of activity of the greatest value to him."[113]

The last ideological issue in the Lysenko affair was the question of probability and causation. A certain similarity existed here between the genetics controversy and the one over quantum mechanics. Certain writers outside the Soviet Union, such as Erwin Schrödinger, maintained that the undirected character of induced mutations obtained by radiation is connected with the indeterminism of quantum mechanics.[114] Some advanced the theory that a mutation is similar to a molecular quantum jump.[115] The reason for the necessity of approaching genetics from the standpoint of probability, said these analysts, is essentially the same as the reason for using probability statistics in quantum mechanics. Thus, all the issues involving "denial of causality" that arose in quantum mechanics also arose in genetics—coupled, moreover, with the deep resentment of mathematics long evident in Lysenkoism.

Lysenko commented on this issue in his speech at the 1948 biological conference:

> In general, living nature appears to the Morganists as a medley of fortuitous, isolated phenomena, without any necessary connections and subject to no laws. Chance reigns supreme.
>
> Unable to reveal the laws of living nature, the Morganists have to resort to the theory of probabilities, and, since they fail to grasp the concrete content of biological processes, they reduce biological science to

mere statistics. . . . With such a science it is impossible to plan, to work toward a definite goal; it rules out scientific prediction. . . .

. . . .

We must firmly remember that *science is the enemy of chance.*[116]

It is not necessary to review here the various interpretations that have been given to probability and causality by Soviet dialectical materialists; the main issues are described in this book in the chapter on quantum mechanics.[117] While the problem of determinism in quantum mechanics still has its philosophically controversial aspects in the Soviet Union (as elsewhere), since the downfall of Lysenko it is no longer significant in biology.[118]

Contrary to many non-Soviet speculations, the inheritance of acquired characters was not upheld in the Soviet Union because of its implications for man. A number of observers of the Soviet Union have assumed that this theory held sway there because of its relevance to the desire to "build a new Soviet man." If Soviet leaders believed that characters acquired in a man's lifetime can be inherited, so the analysis went, then they would believe that a unique Soviet individual would emerge all the more quickly.[119] That this interpretation should play an important role in the USSR seems almost predictable in view of Lysenko's belief that one of the advantages of Michurinism was that through knowledge of its principles scientists could control heredity, while the Mendelian approach to genetics was allegedly sterile. The logical extension of Lysenko's views would have been the employment of a "Michurinist eugenics" far more industriously than the Germans applied formal genetics. But this extension never occurred during Lysenko's lifetime, although a controversy over eugenics did erupt in the Soviet Union in the seventies (see chapters 6 and 7). Discussion of eugenics in the Soviet Union became impossible in the early thirties, because of the international situation, and remained impossible until the early seventies. The eugenicist views of Nazi Germany undoubtedly played a large role in discrediting efforts in the Soviet Union to explain the emergence of superior individuals on the basis of biological theories.[120]

LYSENKOISM AFTER 1948

The story of Lysenkoism after the historic 1948 session on biology is largely one of attempts by the biologists to displace Lysenko as the tyrant of their profession while Lysenko skillfully shifted his emphasis from one nostrum to another—from the cluster planting of trees, to the use of specified fertilizer mixes, to the square cluster planting of corn, to his methods of breeding cows for milk with a high butterfat content. At several moments in the 1950s criticism of Lysenko reached crescendos that seemed to indicate his inevitable demise, but each time he appears to have been rescued by highly placed individuals. Lysenko's resilience, his ability to take advantage of political situations and to curry favor, stood him in good stead. By this time, he was supported by an array of followers in the educational and agricultural establishments, men whose careers were intimately connected with Lysenko's school.

The first new endeavor for Lysenko after 1948 concerned Stalin's grandiose plan for the planting of forest shelter belts to control erosion and combat dry winds in the steppe regions of the Soviet Union. This plan, heralded as "the transformation of nature," was adopted in October 1948 and expanded during late 1948 and 1949 to encompass eight large shelter belts with a total length of 5,320 kilometers and an area of 117,900 hectares.[121] The area where the belts were planned was extremely dry and unsuited for trees; as the minister of forestry commented, "The history of forestry does not know any examples of forest planting in such an environment."[122]

Lysenko suggested planting the trees in clusters or nests, on the theory that competition exists only between different species in the organic world, not within species.[123] He had suggested cluster planting before for other plants.[124] Lysenko believed that in nature the life of every individual is subordinate to the welfare of its species. He maintained that while there is no intraspecies competition, there is intense competition between different species of the same botanical or zoological genus. Thus, giving the members of one species a numerical advantage helped them in their struggle with others. This position was similar to the "mutual aid" of Kropotkin, Chernyshevskii, and other nineteenth-century thinkers who found the principle of the survival of the fittest repugnant and hoped to replace it with the principle of cooperation.[125]

From all available evidence the shelter belt plan was a failure. Shortly after Stalin's death in 1953 discussion of the project disappeared from Soviet publications. The viewpoint that intraspecies competition does not exist is so obviously false that it hardly needs to be considered. Any person who has witnessed the thinning out of forests or plants in congested clumps can give graphic evidence of the competition for food, water, and light that occurs within a species. The word "competition" here should not be understood in an anthropomorphic sense, but this cautionary note is equally valid, of course, with reference to interspecific competition. Lysenko himself recognized the phenomenon of thinning, but he refused to call it competition.[126] The fact that competition exists within species does not deny the numerous examples of cooperation that can also be found.

The eventual fate of the afforestation project was clarified by an announcement that appeared in 1955 in a Soviet biological journal:

> T. D. Lysenko, contending that intraspecific competition does not exist in the organic world, proposed a method of planting trees in clusters. V. Ia. Koldanov has summed up the results of five years of using this method and has shown that it was erroneous in its very basis. Cluster plantings of trees have caused tremendous losses to the state and have threatened to discredit the idea of erosion-control forestation. T. D. Lysenko's method was refuted by the All-Union Conference on Erosion-Control Forestation held in Moscow in November 1954.[127]

Although it is frequently said that the possibility of mounting a serious attack on Lysenko after 1948 became possible only subsequent to Stalin's death, significant published criticism appeared shortly before the Soviet leader's demise on March 5, 1953. Beginning late in 1952, the publications *Botanical Journal* and the *Bulletin of the Moscow Society of Experimenters of Nature*, both under the editorship of V. N. Sukhachev, carried a long discussion of Lysenko's views, including both support and criticism.[128] The controversy eventually spilled over into other journals and even the popular press. It may not be merely coincidental that both publications that initiated the criticism were the organs of scientific societies, which, as descendants of private, voluntary associations, still preserve a greater sense of independence than the official scientific organizations of the Soviet Union.[129]

The *Botanical Journal*, in particular, organized a rather thorough discussion of Lysenko's opinions on species formation and examined in detail a number of claims promoted by followers of Lysenko concerning species transformation. In an article[130] that appeared in the November-December 1953 issue, A. A. Rukhkian revealed as a fraud the case of a hornbeam tree changing into a hazelnut, which had been reported by S. K. Karapetian in Lysenko's journal *Agrobiology* in 1952 and also in a publication of the Armenian Academy of Sciences. The branch of the hornbeam that had supposedly changed into a hazelnut was actually grafted into the fork of the hornbeam; Rukhkian even turned up a man who admitted making the graft in 1923. The article included photographs showing clear evidence of a graft. The result was the elimination of one of Lysenko's important pieces of evidence, and a severe blow to his standing. His integrity was now definitely in question. The editors also indicated their belief that the other cases of species transformation reported by Lysenko and his followers were easily explained on the basis of selection, grafting, or damage due to fungus (teratological changes).

This was only the beginning of a wave of criticism against Lysenko. In the next two years *Botanical Journal* received over fifty manuscripts analyzing some of Lysenko's claims, most of which could not be printed because of lack of space.[131] V. N. Sukhachev and N. D. Ivanov ridiculed Lysenko and his philosopher-defender A. A. Rubashevskii for the belief that intraspecific competition does not exist.[132] A detailed study by a special commission of the Latvian Republic's Academy of Sciences of an alleged pine tree with fir branches growing near Riga concluded, as in the case of the hornbeam, that the phenomenon was a graft.[133] S. S. Khokhlov and V. V. Skripchinskii examined Lysenko's claims concerning the conversion of spring wheats into winter forms, and of soft wheats into hard ones. Khokhlov concluded that the "engendering" of soft wheats from hard ones was the result of hybridization and selection.[134] Skripchinskii's conclusions were similar, and he went on to question the concept of the inheritance of acquired characters.[135] I. I. Puzanov charged that Lysenko was not so much promoting the views of late nineteenth-century biologists as he was the "naive transformist beliefs that were widespread in the biology of antiquity and the Middle Ages and that survived to some extent up to the first half of the nineteenth century."[136] S. S. Shelkovnikov maintained that Lysenko's arguments against Malthusianism and intraspecific competition were "based on equating the laws of development of nature and society, an equation that Marxism long ago condemned."[137] V. Sokolov, reporting in *Izvestiia* on his visit to the United States and Canada as a member of a Soviet farm delegation, praised hybrid corn, based on inbreeding and heterosis, two techniques condemned in past years by Lysenko.[138]

Running through all the criticism was the hope and demand for more freedom in the sciences. Two authors writing in the *Literary Gazette* observed that "the situation that has arisen in areas of such sciences as genetics and agronomy must be recognized as abnormal."[139] They called for the coexistence of differing schools in science. Two other authors, writing in the *Journal of General Biology*, observed, "The time of suppression of criticism in biology has passed. . . ."[140] In its summary of the long debate on Lysenko's view of species formation the editors of the *Botanical Journal* observed, "It has now been conclusively demonstrated that the entire concept is factually unsound, theoretically and methodically erroneous, and devoid of practical value." Furthermore, they observed, "not a single halfway convincing argument was conducted in 1954 or a single strictly scientific argument advanced in support of T. D. Lysenko's views. . . ."[141] A fairly harmless replacement for Lysenko as an idol of Soviet agriculture seemed to emerge in T. S. Maltsev, an experienced soil cultivator.[142]

The Soviet biologist Medvedev later wrote that by the end of 1955 more than three hundred persons had signed a petition requesting Lysenko's removal from the post of the president of the Lenin Academy of Agricultural Sciences.[143] In later months, during 1956 and 1957, the stream of criticism grew and seemed to many people to be irreversible. When Lysenko stepped down from the presidency of the Academy in April 1956, newspapers in countries throughout the world greeted the overdue downfall of the charlatan of biology.

Astoundingly and seemingly inexplicably, this phoenix rose to blight Soviet biology for yet another eight years. This phenomenon is even more striking than Lysenko's original ascent. By the 1950s the Soviet Union was already a modern state, dependent on sophisticated scientists and specialists of almost infinite variety, not the striving nation of the thirties, concentrating on coal, iron, and grain. In the same year in which Lysenko's new strength became discernible, the Soviet Union launched the world's first artificial satellite.

The rebirth of Lysenko in the late fifties seems to be most closely connected with the personal favor of Nikita Khrushchev, curried assiduously by the agronomist. Skillfully Lysenko maneuvered to stay a step ahead of his critics. At the time his views of species formation were being demolished in the biology journals, he was elsewhere pushing the use of organic-mineral fertilizer mixtures.[144] The Soviet fertilizer industry was not sufficiently developed to provide the large quantities of mineral fertilizers needed by agriculture. In the 1950s a desperate effort was being made to expand the fertilizer industry, but output remained insufficient. Lysenko came forward with a plan for mixing artificial and natural fertilizers, thus stretching the available supplies. His fertilizers were manure-earth composts enriched with various mineral fertilizers. This plan, of no theoretical significance to biology, had considerable appeal to the practical Khrushchev. Lysenko applied his method on his experimental farm on Lenin Hills near the city of Moscow. We know now, from a thorough investigation carried out by the Academy of Sciences in 1965, that a large part of Lysenko's considerable success with this method came not from any genuine innovation in fertilizer techniques, but simply from his farm's very privileged position relative to other farms. Located near the capital city, in constant touch with the agricultural bureaucracy that was controlled by his followers, Lysenko received the best and fullest support in various kinds of agricultural machinery, fertilizers, and other supplies. This extraordinary position, coupled with Lysenko's undisputed talents as a practical agronomist, resulted in his farm being among the several outstanding ones of the region in terms of crop production.

In 1954 Khrushchev paid a visit to Lysenko at his experimental farm; in a later speech the Soviet Premier described the visit in his typically colorful fashion:

> Three years ago I visited Lenin Hills. Comrade Lysenko showed me the fields on which he conducted experiments with organic-mineral fertilizer mixtures. We walked around the fields a great deal. I saw the striking results, and I saw how the organic-mineral mixtures influenced the crops. Right at that moment I asked Trofim Denisovich (Lysenko) and Comrade Kapitonov, secretary of the Moscow Province Party Committee, to call in the agronomists of the Moscow area and advise them to try this new method of fertilizing fields. I did not hear that they objected to this in the Moscow area. All the collective farms of the Moscow area who fertilized their fields by this method achieved good results. . . . Just why, then, do some scientists object to the method proposed by T. D. Lysenko? I don't know what's going on here. I believe theoretical and scientific arguments should be decided in the fields.[145]

Lysenko had found a new protector at the highest level of government and the Party, and he moved to support Khrushchev's agricultural policies. Lysenko's campaign to ingratiate himself with the leader of the Party received new impetus in May 1957, when Khrushchev called for the USSR to overtake the United States in per capita milk output; in July, Lysenko announced a grand plan for raising milk yields, which he had developed in his Lenin Hills farm.[146] This was to be his last ploy, and one that would end calamitously, not only for his personal standing, but for a portion of the Soviet dairy industry.

As a result of Lysenko's success in gaining Khrushchev's favor, by late 1958 he was coming back strongly. On September 29 *Pravda* announced the awarding of the Order of Lenin to Lysenko on his sixtieth birthday for his great services to the development of agricultural science and his practical assistance to production.[147] On December 14 *Pravda* carried a laudation of Lysenko and an attack on the *Botanical Journal* and the *Bulletin of the Moscow Society of Experimenters of Nature* for their articles criticizing Lysenko. In 1961 Lysenko returned to his post as president of the Lenin Academy of Agricultural Sciences.[148] Another struggle against Lysenko had ended unsuccessfully. The stamina of Lysenkoism seemed incredible, not only to non-Soviet observers, but also to many discouraged Soviet biologists.

In the 1950s and early 1960s genetics research was conducted in the USSR under various subterfuges. Such work was protected, particularly, by certain influential physicists such as I. V. Kurchatov (1903–1960), who were able to promote genetics research because of the link between mutations and the use of radioactive materials. Later these centers, such as the Institute of Theoretical Physics and the Institute of Biophysics, were to play a significant role in the resuscitation of full-scale genetics research.

Just as genetics could hide behind prestigious individuals such as the leading theoretical physicists, so also could it seek shelter under the cover of new and glamorous fields. Perhaps the most striking example of this combination of genuine scholarship and artifice was the link between cybernetics and genetics in the years between 1958 and 1965.[149] In the separate chapter on cybernetics in this book, I have discussed in some detail the way in which after 1958 cybernetics was enthusiastically promoted in the Soviet Union. The possibility of linking genetics to this new field was translated into a reality by Soviet scientists eager to overcome the effects of Lysenkoism. By assuming the label of cybernetics, genetics was able to gain access to publications, institutions, and scholarly discussions.

A link between the genetic code and information theory had been seen since early days, both in the Soviet Union and abroad. In his prescient essay of 1944 entitled *What Is Life?* Erwin Schrödinger described life as a struggle by an organism against decay (maximum entropy) by means of feeding on information (negative entropy) from its environment.[150] The genes (which Schrödinger described as a periodic crystals) were described as centers of information acting as reservoirs of negative entropy.[151] In such a description the analysis of genetics seemed quite possible from the standpoint of information theory and cybernetics.

After the outburst of cybernetics research in the Soviet Union in 1958, articles and books on genetics phrased in cybernetics terminology began to appear. Among the authors were I. I. Shmal'gauzen (Schmal-hausen) and N. V. Timofeev-Ressovskii, prominent geneticists who suffered much from Lysenkoism, A. A. Liapunov, Zh. A. Medvedev, and K. S. Trincher.[152] Liapunov criticized Michurinist biology from the standpoint of cybernetics and in cooperation with another author termed a gene "the portion of hereditary information and also its encoded material carrier." In the very first issue of the theoretical journal *Problems of Cybernetics* the editor, Liapunov, observed that genetics furnished "another example of a biological science touching on the study of control systems."

During the early 1960s Lysenko's primary claim for continued preem-inence in agricultural biology came from his attempt to raise milk production in the Soviet Union both in terms of over-all production and butterfat content. The method that Lysenko utilized was the cross-breeding of purebred Jersey bulls, obtained at high cost from Western Europe, and other breeds such as East Frisian, Kostroma, and Khol-mogory.

Crossbreeding for the purposes of dairy farming is a very old method, but one that carries considerable risks. The goal, of course, is to obtain progeny with the best characteristics of both parent breeds. Jersey cows are known for the remarkably high butterfat content of their milk (often 5 to 6 percent), the result in large part of over two hundred fifty years of careful breeding; the total yield of Jersey cows, however, is signif-icantly lower than that of many other breeds. Therefore, a logical crossbreeding would be between the Jersey breed and another, such as Holstein-Frisian, that is distinguished by its quantitative milk producing ability but that gives milk with a rather low butterfat content (usually 3 to 4 percent). The dangers or disadvantages of crossbreeding are potential loss of controls and decline of desirable characteristics. In the hands of skillful and educated specialists in genetics and animal hus-bandry such breeding can have very useful and profitable effects. Artificial insemination has greatly increased crossbreeding possibilities. Careful controls are the key to success in this field. If a mating between a member of a purebred line and one of unknown heredity occurs, the progeny may be valuable in terms of individual qualities, such as milk yield, but their value in terms of breeding is low; if such progeny are used for breeding purposes, the value of pedigreed herds can be quickly destroyed. Furthermore, several of the most important characteristics of dairy cows seem to be cases of blending inheritance—that is, tied to multiple genes: therefore, a mating between a bull from a breed that has cows with high-butterfat milk and a cow from one with low-butterfat milk usually results in progeny of intermediate butterfat capabilities. Matings in subsequent generations with low-butterfat lines will result in a gradual decline in butterfat content until the contribution of the ancestor of high-butterfat capabilities will be negligible. This absence of dominance in certain valued characters greatly complicates the task of cattle breeders.

Lysenko announced that he had found a method of providing bulls for breeding purposes whose progeny would have high-butterfat capabilities, and whose descendants in subsequent generations would continue to possess this character in an undiluted fashion. Starting with purebred Jersey bulls, he produced crossbreeds, sometimes with pedigrees as low as one one-eighth Jersey, that supposedly would sire cows with the simultaneous capabilities of high butterfat and high yield. Furthermore, these qualities, said Lysenko, would not decline in subsequent generations.

The method that Lysenko used was based on his Law of the Life of Biological Species, a very vague concept with connections to his earlier views on shattered and stabilized heredity.[153] By crossbreeding purebred Jersey bulls with cows of regular farm herds that possessed the quality of large milk yield, Lysenko knew that he could produce a first generation with reasonably high merits in both quantity and quality. Lysenko departed from the normal doctrines of cattle breeding, however, in advancing the view that the hereditary qualities of this generation could be "fixed" if certain precautions were taken; these included insuring that the cows were of large stature and that they were fed copiously during gestation. This procedure, said Lysenko, would force the embryo to develop with the butterfat capabilities of the "small breed." If the cow during gestation were poorly fed, the calves would supposedly take after the larger parent.[154] If this stabilization process were followed, subsequent generations would not need to be given special care in feeding. The bulls in this line could be used freely without fear of decline in milk yield or quality.

The bulls from Lysenko's farm were widely sold to collective and state farms in the Soviet Union; the Ministry of Agriculture issued directives recommending such purchases and giving the Lenin Hills farm enviable financial advantages in cattle breeding.[155]

But even before Khrushchev's ouster, there were many signs that Lysenko's situation was becoming increasingly desperate. The science of biology continued to advance in other countries, and even an unlimited number of agricultural stratagems by Lysenko could not have offset the publicity that genetics was attracting.[156] Lysenko seems to have tried to meet the challenge of genetics in the raising of chickens, a field revolutionized outside the Soviet Union in the years after World War II; his farm attempted to improve egg production, but silently abandoned the attempt after a few years.[157] Rumors that all was not well on the Lenin Hills farm began to circulate among agronomists and even government officials. The biologists, meanwhile, continued quietly to revive their discipline, waiting for the final discrediting of Lysenko.

The word that Lysenko's farm was experiencing difficulties opened a new avenue of criticism. In the past Lysenko had usually been attacked for the poverty of his theoretical views. Almost all his academic critics, from Vavilov onward, had granted his talents as a practical farmer. They had hoped for a *modus vivendi* that would allow them to determine theory and, if need be, permit Lysenko to have his experimental plots so long as he did not try to compete in the area of theory.[158] Now, however, the possibility of destroying the real base of his power—his reputation as a servant of practical agriculture—became apparent.

The transfer in 1956 of Lysenko's farm from the jurisdiction of the Lenin Academy of Agricultural Sciences to the All-Union Academy of Sciences was a helpful step in bringing Lysenko under the scrutiny of his critics. His farm was brought even closer to the academic strongholds by the reforms of the All-Union Academy in 1961 and 1963, which were promoted vigorously by N. N. Semenov, the Nobel Prize-winning chemist who was an opponent of the agronomist.[159] The outspoken Soviet physicist A. D. Sakharov, later to become the famous dissident, called on Soviet scientists to vote against the Lysenkoite N. Nuzhdin at Academy of Sciences elections, and Nuzhdin was overwhelmingly defeated.[160] But Lysenko continued to resist inspection; he attempted to approve all information issuing from his farm, confident of political support for his general conduct. And indeed, a Soviet biologist even reported in July 1962 an investigative committee of the Academy of Sciences had voted a censure of Lysenko's Institute of Genetics only to be overruled by political authority.[161]

Nikita Khrushchev's downfall on October 15, 1964, removed the most important obstacle in the way of a restitution of normal biology in the Soviet Union. In the following weeks articles critical of Lysenko and his views appeared in the popular press.[162] One author revealed the disastrous effect the Lysenko affair had had on high-school textbooks on biology; in the standard text for the ninth year "you would seek in vain a summary of the laws of heredity or a description of the role of the cell nucleus and the chromosome in heredity."[163] An article that was later cited by officials of the Academy of Sciences as being very important in bringing a full-scale investigation of Lysenko appeared in the *Literary Gazette* on January 23, 1965.[164] The author disputed with figures and specific cases the claims of the managers of the Lenin Hills farm to be producing bulls with the property of propagating indefinite numbers of generations of cows with high-butterfat milk. A few days later the Presidium of the Academy of Sciences of the USSR created an eight-man committee headed by A. I. Tulupnikov to conduct a thorough investigation of Lysenko's farm. The committee spent over five weeks going over the records of the farm, examining crops and cattle, and checking on the breeding success of bulls sold to other farms. The detailed data, in the form of budgetary balances, crop yields, fertilizer usage, milk and egg output, purchase and sale data on cattle, and breeding records, permitted for the first time in the history of the Lysenko affair an objective and authentic analysis of the agronomist's claims. On September 2, 1965, the reports were presented to a joint meeting of the Presidium of the All-Union Academy of Sciences, the Collegium of the Ministry of Agriculture, and the Presidium of the Lenin Academy of Agricultural Sciences. The importance of this meeting was indicated by the fact that it was chaired by M. V. Keldysh, president of the Academy of Sciences, and a whole issue of the major journal of the Academy was devoted to the final report.[165]

The committee concluded that although the farm did produce a profit and gave high yields, these characteristics could be explained by its extremely favorable position compared with other farms. With approximately 1,260 acres of arable land, the farm possessed, for example, ten to fifteen tractors, eleven automobiles, two bulldozers, two excavators, and two combines. It was practically freed from the obligation to provide grain to the government. On a proportional basis it received several times more investment funds and electrical energy than neighboring farms. The fact that the farm stood out in comparison with many of its competitors was, in the opinion of the investigators, entirely unremarkable.

The heart of the report, however, referred to Lysenko's vaunted breeding methods. During the previous ten years the average yield of milk per cow had dropped from 6,785 to 4,453 kilograms. No evidence was found to support Lysenko's contention that the descendants of his bulls would have high-butterfat milk through indefinite numbers of generations. On the contrary, a nearly direct relationship was found between the percent of butterfat and the degree of kinship to the original Jersey bulls:[166]

Degree of Jersey stock	Butterfat content of milk
Pure	5.87
3/4	5.46
1/2	5.01
3/8	4.66
9/16 (5/16?)	4.74
1/4	4.53
3/16	4.50

Furthermore, Lysenko had indiscriminately sold his low-pedigree bulls around the country, where they had ruined herds of higher purity. Some of these bulls and their offspring had to be dispatched to slaughterhouses while still in their prime. Repairing the damage to pedigreed herds in Moldavia alone, said one speaker, would require decades.[167] If Lysenko's methods were carried out fully, the result for the country would be, said one of the inspectors, equal to a "natural calamity." "How much milk, meat, leather, and livestock we would lose!" he exclaimed.[168]

How had Lysenko maintained fairly high standards of milk production on his farm if his methods were so inadequate? He had started with the finest purebred cattle and still enjoyed, several generations later, the effects of that original stock. But a hidden reason for his relative success was—despite his denials—the fact that he was eliminating the poor milk producers through selection. Lysenko had told the Central Committee of the Party that he did not eliminate a single cow because of low butterfat content during the decade of his farm's dairy experiments. The investigatory committee concluded, however, that Lysenko was simply incorrect in this assertion.[169] Over the years many members of the herd had departed through sale or slaughter, and those that had remained were "first of all those that gave the most butterfat and also the daughters of those cows with a large butterfat production."[170] Thus, the key to many of Lysenko's claims in dairying remained selection out of heterozygous populations, just as it had been years earlier in his experiments aimed at converting spring into winter wheat.

Lysenko seemed to have learned nothing concerning scientific technique since the early thirties. As one of the investigators described his farm:

There is a complete absence of a methodology of scientific research. There is no selection-pedigree plan. . . . Biometric data are not processed. Reliability is not computed. There is no account of feeding. And not only is there no weighing of food and remainders, which is done even at experiment stations, but even the records of rations that did exist have not been saved.[171]

Following the report on Lysenko's farm, the science of genetics revived in the Soviet Union. It had, of course, never completely disappeared, but had been forced to hide behind various camouflages, with the result that progress had been very difficult.[172] After 1965 all this changed rapidly. N. P. Dubinin, one of the leaders of the geneticists and a participant in the struggles of the late thirties, became the head of a new Institute of General Genetics. A Soviet journal, *Genetics*, became the theoretical organ of the reborn science. According to Dubinin, in the first two years after the discrediting of Lysenko ten new laboratories were organized in the Institute of Biological Problems.[173] N. V. Timofeev-Ressovskii, the renowned geneticist, became the head of the department of genetics radiation in the new Institute of Radiobiology. American scientists who visited the Soviet Union returned convinced that the Lysenko affair was over and that no longer could one speak of a "Soviet" genetics. Lysenko himself was described as being in semiretirement and refused to grant interviews to visiting delegations and reporters.[174]

BIOLOGY AND DIALECTICAL MATERIALISM AFTER LYSENKO

As far as theoretical biology is concerned, it seems clear that Lysenko's downfall in 1965 was permanent. His demise, however, was not accompanied by a cessation of Soviet writing on the relation of genetics and dialectical materialism. Indeed, some of the very same scholars who fought against Lysenko began interpreting molecular biology from the standpoint of dialectical materialism. Academician Dubinin, the leading Soviet geneticist who as a result of Lysenkoism lost his academic position, had his manuscripts rejected, and saw some of his closest friends imprisoned, wrote an article in 1969 entitled "Modern Genetics in the Light of Marxist-Leninist Philosophy."[175] In this and many subsequent articles he defended Marxism strongly and described mutations in terms of dialectical principles.

People with long memories will recall that certain European, Russian, and American geneticists of the 1920s and 1930s saw their science as a brilliant confirmation of the principles of dialectical materialism. Statements by such people as Haldane, Muller, Zhebrak, Agol, Serebrovskii, and Dubinin revealed their basic sympathy, at least, in certain respects, with these principles. Indeed, if one reflects on the goals and methods of modern genetics, the feeling grows that it is a major irony that so fundamentally materialist a theory as that of genetics should have been rejected in the name of materialism. The search for the material carriers of heredity, first centered on the gene, now on DNA, is in many ways a lesson in the importance of materialism rather than its irrelevance. To refuse to look for the mechanism of heredity is far more akin to religious mysticism or to naive romantic organicism than it is to materialism.[176]

The philosophers and biologists in the Soviet Union who continued to interpret biology in the light of dialectical materialism after Lysenko's demise were divided into "conservative" and "liberal" groups. Both of these groups were critical of Lysenko, but the conservatives continued to look back nostalgically to the days when there was such a thing as a "Michurinist genetics." Some of these authors called for, in effect, "Michurinism without Lysenkoism." An example was the 1965 article of G. V. Platonov in the conservative journal *October.*[177] Platonov was very upset about the "complete" rejection of Michurinism and the "complete" acceptance of formal genetics that he saw coming back to the Soviet Union. A similar view was expressed in 1965 by the author of a candidate's dissertation at Moscow University.[178] Pinter's thesis was an attempt to save Michurinist biology from Lysenko's naive views, which he saw against the background of the "cult of personality" period. The tragedy of Soviet genetics, according to Pinter, was that after 1948 Michurinist biology in the USSR did not have any representatives other than Lysenko.

Underneath the views of people such as Platonov and Pinter lurked the danger of continuing to tie a science to one man—if not Lysenko, then Michurin.[179] Dubinin tried to answer this challenge by showing that Michurin never thought of himself as the founder of a great school in theoretical biology and that significant as Michurin's practical achievements were, genetics had now gone far beyond them.[180] Furthermore, Dubinin noted, in the last part of his life Michurin moved toward Mendelism.

The more liberal camp, to which Dubinin belonged originally (we will see that he later became quite conservative himself) abandoned the term "Michurinist genetics." To them, there was only one science of genetics, the one known throughout the world. They continued, however, to defend dialectical materialism as a philosophy of science, and believed that it could provide helpful interpretations of biology. They, therefore, were making a careful distinction between "science" and "interpretations of science," as Lenin himself had done.

One of the most influential of the more sophisticated dialectical materialists writing on biology was I. T. Frolov, who in 1968 published a book entitled *Genetics and Dialectics*.[181] Frolov criticized the whole concept of "Party science," firmly stating his opinion that politics concerns only the philosophical interpretation of science, not the evaluation of science itself (p. 13). He criticized those conservatives such as Platonov who had not, in his opinion, yet seen this distinction (p. 16 and *passim*). Second, Frolov tried to begin the process of reconstructing an intellectually tenable Marxist philosophy of biology out of the shambles left by Lysenkoism. He drew attention to legitimate philosophical problems of interpretation in genetics: the problem of reductionism, the problem of determinism, and the nature of heredity. He referred to the works of E. S. Bauer and Ludwig von Bertalanffy as examples of interpretations of biology that had similarities to dialectical materialism and that, therefore, should be further explored. And third, Frolov became in the same year that his book appeared the chief editor of the Soviet journal *Problems of Philosophy*. As the editor of the most influential philosophy journal in the Soviet Union, Frolov was able to exert an important influence in the philosophy of science.

Frolov believed that the most important philosophical question in biology was that of reductionism, or the relation of the part to the whole. According to a strict reductionist, the characteristics of an organism can be entirely explained in terms of its parts. Thus, a reductionist would explain life in physicochemical terms. It was around this question that Soviet discussions of dialectical materialism and biology in the late sixties and seventies turned.

In Frolov's opinion, dialectical materialism allowed one to have the advantage of studying both the part and the whole, of approaching biology both on the level of physicochemical laws and also on the more general biological or "systems theory" level. Frolov wrote that dialectics "defines a dual responsibility: On the one hand, it opens the way for complete freedom for the intensive use of the methods of physics and chemistry in studying living systems; on the other hand, it recognizes that biological phenomena will never, at any point in time, be fully explained in physiocochemical terms" (p. 253). The quantity-quality dialectical relationship had traditionally been interpreted by Soviet Marxists as a warning against reductionism, and Frolov continued to emphasize that warning.

By the seventies Soviet genetics as a science was well on its way to recovery, but not without continuing problems. In some areas where team research in large institutions is necessary for advancement, such as DNA mapping, Soviet biologists became once again internationally prominent. The underlying issues of the Lysenko affair did not entirely disappear, however, especially in publications about philosophy and politics. Indeed, the seventies witnessed a regression, compared to the late sixties, in the degree to which science was free from political and philosophical fetters. Dubinin became increasingly authoritarian toward his fellow geneticists, evidently forgetting how he had suffered under Lysenko. Because of his stern control and because of his continuing interest in dialectical materialism, some of his colleagues began to refer to him behind his back as "Trofim Denisovich Dubinin." Even Dubinin's dismissal as director of the Institute of General Genetics in 1981 did not bring complete normalcy to Soviet genetics. These events are discussed on pp. 230ff., since they are a part of the great Soviet debate over nature versus nurture and human biology featured in chapters 6 and 7.

Among philosophers of science, the anti-Lysenkoites were the epistemologists, the scholars who maintained that Marxism could not evaluate science itself, only the methodology of knowledge. As we have seen in chapter 2, these philosophers began to lose some ground in the late seventies as the ontologists built up their strength in the universities and technical institutes. Thus, while there was little danger that neo-Lysenkoites would again gain control over scientific research itself, some of them continued to hope to have their views given more prominence in philosophical publications and in sociopolitical journals.

In 1978 one of the most surprising books in the recent history of Soviet genetics appeared: G. V. Platonov's *Life, Inheritance, Variability,* published by the Moscow University Press.[182] The publication of this volume by a university press, rather than the Academy of Sciences' publishing house *Nauka* (Science), can be explained by the fact that the universities harbored many more ontologists than the Academy. Platonov's book was a thoroughly Lysenkoite tract, appearing thirteen years after everyone in the West had assumed that Lysenkoism was dead. True, Platonov did not use the term "Lysenkoism" or praise Lysenko by name. Instead, he referred to Lysenkoist doctrines by the term "Michurinism." But Platonov revived a host of Lysenko's claims, including the hoary assertion that his followers had changed spring wheat into winter wheat.[183] As documentation for the claim about wheat he referred to Avakian's notorious article entitled "The Inheritance of Acquired Characteristics by Organisms" that appeared in Lysenko's journal *Agrobiology* in 1948, the year of Lysenko's political triumph over the geneticists. This article has long been rejected by world science. Platonov praised the doctrine of inheritance of acquired characteristics, echoed Lysenko's famous slogan "science is the enemy of chance" by rephrasing it into the statement "to deny causation is to disarm science," denigrated the role of DNA in inheritance, and called for the overthrow of the basic principles of modern genetics. And all of this was embedded in the phraseology of dialectical materialism and Marxism.[184]

Platonov attacked V. P. Efroimson, I. T. Frolov and B. L. Astaurov (after Astaurov's death) for "eliminating the qualitative differences between social and biotic forms of life." He praised A. I. Oparin, N. P. Dubinin, and L. Sh. Davitashvili for standing firm against the "cult of reductionism" and the "monopolism" and "absolutism" of DNA. (All these authors, a rather mixed lot, are discussed elsewhere in this volume, with the exception of Davitashvili.) Environmental factors could definitely become hereditary, in his opinion, and he named several mechanisms by which he thought such inheritance could occur, relying heavily on the "nutrition" (*pishcha*) and "temperature" factors that had been favorites of Lysenko (see pp. 124ff.).[185]

The academic world of Soviet geneticists ignored Platonov's book, hoping it would die quietly, which it apparently did. The only review of the book listed in the standard indexes was one which appeared in 1980 in the Party journal *Communist of the Ukraine* in which the reviewers praised Platonov's book but ludicrously chastised him for being too charitable toward Gregor Mendel and T. H. Morgan, two of the giants of modern genetics.[186] This intellectually insignificant review was politically troubling in that it revealed that in some Party circles the words "Mendelism-Morganism" were still remembered as an appropriate term of opprobrium about genetics. The nightmare of Soviet genetics was, even in 1980, not quite over.

The existence of such vestigial Lysenkoites may partially explain the phraseology and interpretations advanced by some of the defenders of genetics. If critics of genetics like Platonov advanced their arguments in the name of Marxism, it was necessary for the defenders of the science to show that their views were even more authentic ideologically. Thus, S. A. Pastushnyi in a 1981 book entitled *Genetics as an Object of Philosophical Analysis* rewrote the history of genetics so that Mendel and Morgan became unwitting dialectical materialists; furthermore, modern-day genetics, based on DNA and molecular biology, was, in Pastushnyi's hands, an illustration of dialectical materialism.[187] According to Pashtushnyi, Mendel became a monk not because of religious belief, but because he was poor.[188] Furthermore, Mendel supported Darwin, but was prevented from confessing this belief because of clerical pressure. Pastushnyi then went on to reconstruct the history of genetics according to dialectical materialism, showing who was "right" and who was "wrong" in ideological terms, and putting the Marxists on the road to modern genetics. Pastushnyi even maintained that if early geneticists like Johannsen and Morgan had been conscious dialectical materialists they would have been able to overcome some of the limitations of their views and "dialectically combine" genetics with evolutionary Darwinism.[189] In his long analysis of the history of genetics Pastushnyi attributed all the social and political causes of intellectual difficulties in modern genetics to Western society, conveniently overlooking the social and political roots of the twentieth century's greatest disaster in genetics, the rise of Lysenkoism. Yet, in the final analysis, Pastushnyi was an opponent of Lysenko, and was fashioning an argument against Lysenko's latter-day supporters that he thought would have the greatest effect in the Soviet Union.

The participants on both sides of this debate—the modern geneticists as well as the neo-Lysenkoites—were raising once again the fateful question of whether Marxism ought to be used to judge the correctness of scientific viewpoints. Frolov in the late sixties had tried to settle this issue once and for all by warning that politics concerns only the philosophical interpretation of science, not the evaluation of science itself.[190] Frolov had rebuked Platonov at that time for failing to make this distinction when he tried to show that Michurinist biology *was* Marxist biology.[191] But now, in the heat of the debates of the late seventies and early eighties, even Frolov seemed to be weakening on this point, joining scholars like Pastushnyi in portraying modern genetics (i.e., anti-Lysenkoite biology) as Marxist biology.[192] Frolov and Pastushnyi were on the right side in this controversy, but for the wrong reasons. (One can not help but wonder what will happen when and if the principles of modern genetics are overthrown.) The conditions of Soviet politics do not seem to permit biology as a science to be validated without reliance on Marxist philosophy. This is a great shame, since biology is full of philosophical issues that deserve careful discussion without the question of philosophy's validating science ever arising. The interpretation of philosophy and the validation of science are different activities, but Soviet writers often conflate them.

CHAPTER **5**

PHYSIOLOGY AND PSYCHOLOGY

In the modern world psychology fulfills an ideological function and serves class interests; it is impossible not to reckon with this.

A. N. Leont'ev, Soviet psychologist, 1975

In no other scientific field discussed in this volume does there exist an identifiably Russian tradition of interpretation to the degree that there does in physiology and psychology. Long before the Revolution the study of physiology and psychology in Russia was known for its materialism. To be sure, there were many supporters of idealistic psychology in prerevolutionary Russia, but materialism in psychology received unusual support there at a fairly early date. In 1863 Ivan Sechenov (1829–1905) published his *Reflexes of the Brain,* a book the true purpose of which is better revealed by the title that Sechenov originally gave it, but that was disapproved by the tsarist censor: *An Attempt to Establish the Physiological Basis of Psychological Processes.*[1] Sechenov wrote in this work that "all acts of conscious or unconscious life are reflexes."

Surrounding Sechenov's views there soon grew up a controversy among the St. Petersburg educated public. The particular political and ideological scene of late nineteenth-century Russia influenced the course of the debate, with the radical intelligentsia usually, but not always, responding favorably to Sechenov's opinions and the government bureaucracy usually disapproving. In 1866 the book was prohibited for sale by the St. Petersburg censors, and Sechenov himself was threatened with court action for allegedly undermining public morals. Eventually Sechenov escaped trial, but the already existing link between materialism in science and radical politics was strengthened and made more apparent.

Although materialism was strong in Russian psychology before the Revolution, it by no means monopolized the field. Sechenov was thought of primarily as a physiologist, not a psychologist. Opposing the views of Sechenov and some of his pupils were not only the censors of St. Petersburg and representatives of the Church, but also many university professors of philosophy and psychology. Indeed, Sechenov was outside the mainstream of academic psychology in Russia. Nonetheless, the essential issues that he raised concerning the nature of the psyche and the relationship of the physiological to the psychological were hotly debated among Russian psychologists, physiologists, philosophers, and political activists in the last decades of the nineteenth century.[2] The history of these debates is still insufficiently explored, but even a cursory examination reveals that some of the features of these polemics—not only between materialists and idealists, but among members of each camp and of other groups as well—resemble discussions that have continued throughout the Soviet period.[3]

The most important influence on Russian physiology and psychology was Ivan Pavlov (1849-1936), a great figure in world science. Although it is impossible and inappropriate to summarize Pavlov's views here, some aspects of his work must briefly be discussed, particularly those that would later become the subject of philosophical and methodological discussion in the Soviet Union. From the standpoint of the history and philosophy of science the greatest significance of Pavlov derives from his success in bringing psychic activity within the realm of phenomena to be studied and explained by the normal objective methods of natural science. In contrast to the introspective approach of many investigators of mental activity at the turn of the century, Pavlov's method was based on the assumption that psychic phenomena can be understood on the basis of evidence gathered entirely externally to the subject. He was not entirely original in his intention to proceed in this manner, but as a great experimentalist he was able brilliantly to combine this methodological assumption with unusual skill in devising and con-ducting experiments with animals. On the basis of these experiments he erected a theory of nervous activity that presented general principles aimed toward the eventual explanation of man's psychic activity on a physiological foundation.

Pavlov is, of course, best known for his theory of conditioned and unconditioned reflexes. Unconditioned reflexes, he said, are inborn forms of nervous activity and are transmitted by inheritance. Conditioned reflexes are acquired during the life of an organism and are based on a specific unconditioned reflex; conditioned reflexes are not normally inherited, although Pavlov believed that in some cases they could become hereditable.

In the classic case of the dog and the bell, the unconditioned reflex is the natural, inborn salivation of a dog in response to the stimulus of food. The conditioned reflex, salivation in response to a bell alone, is created by the prior repeated juxtaposition of the bell and the food.

Pavlov further illustrated that "conditioned reflexes of the second order" could be created by using the conditioned response to the bell as a basis for the formation of yet another conditioned reflex to a third stimulus, such as a light. In the latter case, it must be emphasized that at no time was the original stimulus (food) combined with the stimulus triggering the second-order reflex (the light). In this fashion Pavlov was able to point to the quite indirect ways through association by which reflexes could be created. He believed that the psychic activity of man could be interpreted in this way, or at least on this foundation. This theory of the broad significance of conditioned reflexes Pavlov called the Theory of Higher Nervous Activity, and this phrase is a part of the standard terminology of Soviet physiologists and psychologists.

The inner structure of reflex action was described by Pavlov in terms of a "reflex arc," a term that would be the subject of much later discussion. The reflex arc had three links: the *affector* neurons, the *nervous centers*, and the *effector* neurons. The original excitation caused in the sense organs by an external stimulus travels inward along a chain of affector neurons to the nervous centers; then another stimulus travels outward along the effector neurons to specific muscles or glands, causing a response to the original stimulus. The three links in this arc are sometimes described as sensor-connector-motor.

In the case of the formation of conditioned reflexes in man Pavlov believed that the nervous centers are located on the cortex of the cerebral hemispheres. "Temporary connections," an inclusive term embracing conditioned reflexes and other more rudimentary or fleeting linkages, are formed as a result of "irradiation" of stimuli reaching the hemispheres. In other words, stimulation is "generalized" in the hemispheres in such a way that other areas of the cortical region now react in the same way as that concerned in the original stimulus. Thus, the area of the cortex receiving nervous responses to light signals may be incorporated into reflex action originally based only on sound signals. As Pavlov wrote, "The fundamental mechanism for the formation of a conditioned reflex is the meeting, the coincidence of the stimulation of a definite center in the *cerebral cortex* with the stronger stimulation of another center, probably also in the cortex, as a result of which, sooner or later, an easier path is formed between the two paths, i.e., a connection is made."[4]

By a process of training, inhibition, the reverse of irradiation, can also be illustrated. Physiologically, the area of the cortical region that has been irradiated is reduced by teaching the subject to discriminate not only between very different signals, such as sound and light, but between sounds of different vibrations. Thus, Pavlov was able to teach a dog to respond to a tempo of one hundred beats a minute but not to ninety-six, as a result of producing food only after the more rapid signal. After this process of inducing inhibition, Pavlov concluded that "the nervous influx produced by the stimulus is now communicated to only a very limited area of the cortical zone under consideration."

One of the most flexible concepts that Pavlov advanced, and one still exploited only to a rather small degree, was that of the "second-signal system," a feature unique to the psychic activity of man. Most of Pavlov's research was based on experiments with dogs, but in the latter part of his life he worked with monkeys and gorillas, and his interests were shifting more and more to what he considered the ultimate goal of neurophysiology—the study of man. Man has fewer instincts than animals; Pavlov believed, therefore, that his behavior would be governed by conditioned reflexes to a much higher degree. Both animals and man can be conditioned in similar ways, but man, in addition, possesses the almost infinitely rich instrument of language. While animals respond to simple ("primary") signals or symbols (even a dog responding to a word command reacts to it in a fashion not dissimilar to the response to a bell or light), man responds to the meanings and incredibly rich associations conveyed by speech and writing ("secondary signals"). The language message that any one human subject receives will contain meanings and associations unique for him, given a message of even minimal complexity. And Pavlov saw the second-signal system as infinitely more complex than the primary one: "There is no comparison, qualitative or quantitative, between speech and the conditional stimuli of animals." Thus, Pavlov cannot be described fairly as a person who believed that human behavior can be reduced to the simple stimulus-response action of the noted experiments with dogs. He fully recognized that human beings were qualitatively quite distinct from other animals. But he believed, nevertheless, that human behavior is amenable to investigation on the basis of physiology, an assumption sensible and necessary in order for physiologists to investigate the human nervous system.

Pavlov's attitude toward psychology has been the subject of numerous inaccurate statements, many of which imply that Pavlov was opposed to the very existence of psychology. Pavlov did object to the concept of animal psychology, since he felt that there was no way for man to gain access to the inner world of animals. He was, further, deeply critical of what he considered metaphysical concepts presented in psychological terms. In his early years he was doubtful of the scientific validity of much that was presented as psychological research. As he grew older, and as experimental psychology steadily developed as a discipline, Pavlov became more and more disposed toward psychology. In a speech given in 1909 Pavlov said:

> I should like to elucidate that which might be misunderstood in these statements concerning my views. I do not deny psychology to be a body of knowledge concerning the internal world of man. Even less am I inclined to negate anything which relates to the innermost and deepest strivings of the human spirit. Here and now I only defend and affirm the absolute and unquestionable rights of natural scientific thought everywhere and until the time when and where it is able to manifest its own strength, and who knows where its possibilities will end![5]

But even in this statement affirming the right of psychology to exist, one can detect Pavlov's skeptical view of psychology. The last sentence implies a distinction between psychology and "natural scientific thought," which most psychologists would reject. And when Pavlov spoke of a fusing in the future of physiology and psychology, many psychologists thought that he was actually referring to an absorbing of psychology by physiology after the necessary progress in physiology had occurred. One must admit that Pavlov remained somewhat dubious about psychology as a science, although he was by no means so hostile as many later commentators have implied. Despite his frequent warnings against reductionism, his call for the study of the "whole organism," and his belief in the "qualitative and quantitative uniqueness" of man, Pavlov tended to see psychic phenomena, and especially the reflex arc, in somewhat mechanistic and elementary terms. This tendency was probably inevitable in the period when psychology was, indeed, heavily influenced by idealistic concepts and Pavlov had to struggle to establish his teaching on conditioned reflexes, now recognized as one of the great achievements of both physiology and psychology.

Pavlov was not a Marxist and did not defend his system in terms of dialectical materialism. For many years after the Revolution he stoutly resisted Marxist influences in educational and scientific institutions and even criticized Marxist philosophy.[6] In the last years of his life, however, his views changed; he praised the Soviet government for its support of science, and he was impressed by the intelligence of individual Bolshevik leaders, such as Nikolai Bukharin. One of his pupils, P. K.

Anokhin, a man whose views will be discussed separately, maintained that once in a conversation he tried to show Pavlov that his teaching about the contradictory but necessary effects of irradiation and inhibition was deeply dialectical and revealed the struggle and unity of opposites. To this observation Anokhin said that Pavlov responded, "There you are, it turns out that I am a dialectician!"[7]

There are many aspects of Pavlov's thought that appeal to dialectical materialists. First of all, his primary goal, the explanation of psychic phenomena on the basis of physiological processes, is one that materialists have traditionally and understandably supported. His emphasis on the necessity to study organisms as a whole, "in all their interactions," rather than by isolating out one portion or one phenomenon has been praised by Soviet writers for being in agreement with the dialectical principle of the interconnectedness of the material world. His emphasis on the unique qualities of man, with his second-signal system, has been termed an understanding of the qualitative differences of organisms at different levels of complexity, based on the principle of the transformation of quantity into quality. His description of the human body as a system "unique in the degree of its self-regulation" has been seen both as a prefiguring of cybernetic concepts of feedback and as an understanding of the dialectical process of development.

Scholars in the Soviet Union, on the one hand, and those outside that country, on the other, frequently look upon Pavlovianism in different ways and almost as different things. Non-Soviet scientists often consider it a rather restricted body of experimental data and hypotheses concerning conditioned and unconditioned reflexes. To some of them his name is nearly synonymous with the mental picture of salivating dogs. Soviet scholars, on the other hand, see Pavlovian theory not only as this body of facts and conclusions, but also as an approach to nature in general and to biology in particular. Pavlov himself contributed to this latter understanding in a conversation with the American psychologist K. S. Lashley; when Lashley asked Pavlov to define the concept of "reflex," Pavlov replied:

> The theory of reflex activity operates on three basic principles of exact scientific research: first, the principle of determinism, i.e., of a stimulus, a cause, a reason for every given action or effect; second, the principle of analysis and synthesis, i.e., of an initial decomposition of the whole into parts or units and then the gradual building up anew of the whole from its units or elements; finally, the principle of structure, i.e., the distribution of the actions of force in space, the timing of dynamics to structure.[8]

In reply to this statement by Pavlov, Lashley observed that this definition of reflex was so general that it could be taken as the general principle of all science. But Pavlov stuck to his formulation, which is often quoted in Soviet discussions on the significance of reflex theory.[9]

Some Soviet authors distinguish between the reflex principle in a philosophic sense and the reflex principle in a concrete, psychological sense, thus opening up considerable possibilities for recognizing certain limitations in Pavlov's teaching while retaining its methodological content. In 1963 F. V. Bassin, a Soviet scholar who called for much greater attention to the subconscious realm and pointed to certain elements of value in Freud's work at a time when this was rare among Soviet scholars, made this distinction; in his opinion, the most valuable aspect of Pavlov's work was the underlying idea of the essential dependence of biological factors on the environment. Bassin wrote:

> That person who abandons the reflex theory in its philosophic sense abandons more than Pavlov's teaching. He abandons the dialectical materialist interpretation of biological processes in general. This is undoubtedly so, since the primacy of the reflex principle in its philosophic sense (i.e., the idea of the dependency in principle of biological processes on factors of the environment) is that basic, that most profound element that distinguishes us from the supporters of idealistic biology, with its emphasis on immanence, spontaneity, and consequently, the absence of the reflex principle in life processes. . . . I mention this because it is necessary to see the difference between the reflex principle in its general philosophic meaning and as a concrete understanding of physiological structure. . . .[10]

The history of psychology in Russia in the years after the Revolution is a very rich and contradictory story: since our center of attention in this volume falls on the years after World War II, it will be impossible to discuss the earlier period in detail. However, some of the features of the work of L. S. Vygotsky, A. R. Luria, and A. N. Leont'ev, who continue to be influential, will be considered below. More detailed discussions can be found in A. V. Petrovskii's *History of Soviet Psychology* (in Russian) or in Raymond Bauer's *The New Man in Soviet Psychology*.[11]

Immediately after the Revolution members of several different schools of psychology could still be found in Russia. Those with the closest links to introspection and idealistic psychology were N. Lossky and S. Frank, both of whom lost their positions shortly after the Revolution. Another group was made up of experimental psychologists who had been heavily influenced by subjective psychology, but who moved after the Revolution to a position of neutral empirical psychology, hoping in that way to remain clear of the controversies. They included G. I. Chelpanov and A. P. Nechaev. A third group was made up predominantly of physiologists, such as V. M. Bekhterev, and hoped to reconstruct psychology on an objective, scientific basis. They usually doubted the validity of the term "psychology."

The first psychologist to call for an application of Marxism to psychology was K. N. Kornilov, a scholar with an interesting history in the discussions of the twenties and thirties. At congresses of psychoneurologists in 1923 and 1924 Kornilov attempted to discern the operation of the materialist dialectic in his psychological research. He maintained that the dialectical principle of universal change could be seen in psychology "where there are no objects, but only processes, where everything is dynamic and timely, where there is nothing that is static."[12] The dialectical principle of interconnectedness is illustrated, he continued, by the tendency toward "extreme determinism" in psychology including the determinism of the Freudian school. The principle accorded well, further, with the views of Gestalt psychologists and with the emphasis on the importance of total patterns rather than discrete bits of experience. And a third principle—the transition from quantity to quality by leaps—is illustrated in many ways: color discernment, in which quantitative differences in frequency of light waves result in qualitatively distinct perception of colors; the concept of thresholds of perception, in which one senses change only after a considerable amount of quantitative stimulation of sense organs; and the Weber-Fechner law of weight and auditory discrimination.

Like Engels in his more enthusiastic moments, Kornilov seemed to see the operation of the principles of the dialectic on every hand. Not surprisingly, Kornilov was soon criticized for applying the dialectic in a "purely formal" fashion, using it simply as a means of justifying research on which he was already embarked rather than as a methodology basically affecting the course of his work. He was particularly criticized for maintaining that "reactology"—his term for his approach to psychology—was a dialectical synthesis of the subjective and objective trends in Soviet psychology, one that would preserve a concept of consciousness, of the psyche, while at the same time utilizing the rich findings of the physiologists in the study of reflexes.[13]

Despite Kornilov's attempt to identify the dialectic in his research, Marxism was not a major influence on his work. His effort to combine elements of subjective psychology and the newer physiological study of reflexes stemmed from his opinion that both possessed advantages.

He thought that the physiologists and behaviorists were abdicating the responsibility of psychologists by occupying themselves exclusively with muscular responses. The traditional psychologists, on the other hand, were just as blindly ignoring the significant work of Pavlov, Bekhterev, and their followers. After 1923 Kornilov headed the Moscow Psychological Institute, where he worked with other scholars of later prominence, such as N. F. Dobrynin, A. N. Leont'ev and A. R. Luria. They were also in close communication with groups led by P. P. Blonskii and M. A. Reisner. All of these men at this time were experimenting eclectically with various currents in psychology in a manner that later became impossible because of ideological pressures.

In addition to reactology, the other major tendency in Soviet psychology and physiology at this time was the "reflexology" of M. Bekhterev. It contrasted sharply with reactology in its refusal to use subjective reports and such traditional terms as "psyche," "attention," and "memory." This school drew heavily on two different sources: the materialist tradition in Russian physiology stemming from Sechenov through Pavlov and Bekhterev himself, and American behaviorism. Bekhterev (1858–1927) had long before the Revolution maintained that every thought process, conscious or unconscious, expresses itself sooner or later in objectively observable behavior. On this basis he and his followers hoped to create a science of behavior. In the twenties their approach was so popular that the existence of psychology as a discipline was threatened. In the Ukraine in 1927 higher educational institutions replaced the term "psychology" with "reflexology" as a description of courses of study.

There was also in the twenties a genuine interest in Freudian psychology and much controversy over how well it fit with Marxist interpretations. It was by no means clear in this early period that Freudianism would become a pejorative term to Soviet Marxists. Part of the interest in Freud was simple curiosity; many of the articles in political and literary journals contained elementary descriptions of his work. Freud had not yet published his later, more speculative, works such as *Civilization and Its Discontents*, in which, in addition to some dubious psychological theorizing, there appeared a criticism of communism.[14] To some Soviet writers Freud's teachings appeared as a victory of determinism, an end to free will. Writing in the major Marxist theoretical journal in 1923, the Soviet author B. Bykhovskii commented, "We conclude that despite the subjective casing in which it appears, psychoanalysis is at its foundation inbued with monism, with materialism

. . . and with the dialectic, i.e., with the methodological principles of dialectical materialism."[15] Similar comments were made by such intellectual and political leaders as M. A. Reisner, A. P. Pinkevich, and Trotsky himself.[16] But by the latter years of the twenties, discussion of Freud had shifted to open criticism.

Aside from the question of Freudianism, a new trend in Soviet psychology became discernible by the end of the 1920s.[17] This trend stemmed from the rather widely held realization that with the defeat of the supporters of subjectivism and introspection in Soviet psychology, the greatest danger was now from the left—from those militant materialists who hoped to swallow up psychology in a purely physiological understanding of mental activity. The defenders of psychology rallied around the concept of *psikhika* (psyche) and *soznanie* (consciousness) in what has been called a "great struggle for consciousness." This controversy, which ended in victory for the defenders of psychology and consciousness, bore many characteristics peculiar to the Soviet environment. It is well, however, to guard against the tendency of non-Soviet historians to look upon all events in the Soviet Union as *sui generis*, as irrelevant to intellectual history as a whole. These were years in which the validity of the concept of consciousness was being discussed in many countries. According to Boring:

> The attack on old-fashioned analytical introspectionism was successful, and in the late 1920's Gestalt psychology and behaviorism found themselves practically in possession of the field. With their missions thus more or less accomplished, both these schools tended to die out or at least to lose their aggressiveness during the 1930's. Psychological operationism came in at this time to supplant behaviorism as a more sophisticated view of psychology, and the outstanding systematic issue in the early 1940's seemed to be whether the Gestalt psychologist could save consciousness, as observed in direct experience, for psychology, or whether the operationists would succeed in having it reduced to the behavioral terms which define the manner of its observation.[18]

Echoes of these changes in psychology internationally were reverberating within the Soviet Union. There, too, the criticism of introspectionism had been successful—indeed, to the point of overkill resulting from the peculiar political instruments at the disposal of the Communist Party, such as increasing control of faculties and editorial boards. In the Soviet Union, as abroad, the crude mechanism of early behaviorism was being succeeded by a more sophisticated approach that, nonetheless, did not deny the achievements of the behaviorists.

In the Soviet Union there were other unique elements as well. The debates were increasingly cast in the terms of theoretical Marxism. Furthermore, the policy decisions of the Communist Party were beginning to have a direct influence on the course of the psychological discussions. The decision to embark upon a rapid industrialization program required great effort on the part of Soviet citizens and enormous will power. A psychology that left more room for voluntarism, for personal resolve and dedication, was welcome on this scene. This shift in Soviet psychology has been frequently discussed by previous authors, such as Raymond Bauer, who entitled his chapter describing these events "Consciousness Comes to Man."[19] In terms of Marxist theory the shift was explained on the basis of the Leninist "theory of reflection," which maintains that the mind, or consciousness, plays an active role in the process of cognition.

In the early 1930s the place of psychology in the Soviet Union became more secure, while Bekhterev's reflexology gradually lost its popularity. As we shall see in the cases of Vygotsky, Luria, Leont'ev, and Rubinshtein, Marxism was incorporated into psychological theory in a more sophisticated way. The increase in the subtlety of psychological theory was accompanied, perhaps surprisingly, by an increasing concern with such practical activities as industry and education. Industrial psychology, the scientific organization of labor movement (NOT), and psychotechnics all grew impressively. Educational psychology was also very important in the early thirties.

The issue lying immediately behind the famous decree of the Central Committee of the Communist Party of July 4, 1936, "On Pedological Perversions in the System of the People's Commissariat of Education," seems to have been one of social class. The decree accused pedologists of attempting "to prove from the would-be 'scientific,' 'biosocial' point of view of modern pedology that the pupil's deficiency or the individual defects of his behavior are due to hereditary and social conditioning."[20] It was the perennial issue of environment versus heredity and the practical question of how an educational system can overcome the deleterious effects of both. In the thirties in the Soviet Union a great effort was being made to achieve literacy among a backward population. From the standpoint of performing this monumental educational task, what was most needed were concrete suggestions in the field of elementary pedagogy, not theoretical and inconclusive discussions of the determining elements of intelligence. The American scholar Bauer seems quite correct in his observation that much of the criticism of the educational psychologists stemmed from the fact that they appeared, at least to their critics, to be "professionally more oriented toward finding an excuse than toward the development of a cure."[21] From the standpoint of social reform, this was no inconsequential issue; similar controversies of great implication over the need to link theoretical analysis with practical reform could be found in other countries. Academic social science sometimes does become aloof to social needs, occasionally to an immoral degree. In the Soviet Union in 1936 the issue was resolved not so much by discussion from below as by political orders from above.

The political atmosphere of the Soviet Union in the late thirties was grim, and the situation would be even worse immediately after World War II. The Stalinist system of control became firmly established. The great purges within the Communist Party eliminated several early defenders of innovative psychology. Soviet historians later admitted that political controls did serious damage to many fields, including psychology. As M. G. Iaroshevskii, a Soviet historian of psychology, wrote in 1966: "The criticism of pedology occurred in the complicated environment of the second half of the thirties and frequently was accompanied by a denial of all that was good in the work of Soviet scholars in pedology, and even in pedagogy and psychology, which had been developing in a very creative fashion."[22]

Fortunately, important work had been done in the Soviet Union before these controls were imposed. A case is the achievement of L. S. Vygotsky, who did his research in the late twenties and early thirties, and was a significant Soviet psychologist.

LEV SEMENOVICH VYGOTSKY (1896–1934)

L. S. Vygotsky is one of the most important influences in Soviet psychology; in recent decades his ideas have spread widely outside the Soviet Union, particularly with the publication in English in 1962 of his *Thought and Language*. His influence is particularly remarkable in view of the fact that Vygotsky died of tuberculosis in 1934 at the age of thirty-eight; he rushed to completion some of his most important writings in his final illness. One of Vygotsky's best-known pupils, A. R. Luria, is supposed to have remarked many years later, "All that is good in Russian psychology today comes from Vygotsky."[23] Luria dedicated his important monograph *Higher Cortical Functions in Man*, published in Moscow in 1962, to Vygotsky's memory, and remarked that his own work could in many ways "be looked upon as a continuation of Vygotsky's ideas."[24]

Vygotsky did not always enjoy the esteem of official circles in the Soviet Union, however. From 1936 to 1956 his writings were in disfavor. In 1950 Vygotsky's theories on the relationship of language and thought were contradicted by Stalin himself, as will be related below. Even in the sixties and later, when Vygotsky regained his earlier popularity in the Soviet Union, he has frequently received a mixture of praise and criticism from Soviet historians of psychology. In 1966 A. V. Brushlinskii commented that Vygotsky underestimated the epistemological aspect of mental activity, but that nonetheless Soviet psychology was heavily in debt to him for his being the first to discuss in a detailed fashion the influence of sociohistorical factors on the human psyche.[25] Vygotsky is now widely praised in the Soviet Union for this service, described as an important introduction of the Marxist approach to psychology. His works have been published and circulated widely.

There seems little question that Vygotsky was influenced by Marxist philosophy, as he interpreted it. Non-Russian readers of his works may not believe that the influence of Marxism on Vygotsky was genuine, and for a very understandable reason: when Vygotsky's works were translated from Russian to English for publication in an abridged version in the United States, most of the references to Marx, Engels, and Lenin were omitted. Lenin disappeared completely. The translators believed, evidently, that the references to Marxism were extraneous to the scientific content of Vygotsky's writings and could be dropped without damage.[26] As a result it is almost impossible for the historian of psychology without knowledge of the Russian language to understand the initial assumptions of Vygotsky's approach. In the original Russian, however, it is clear that Vygotsky attempted to show a relationship between his views on children's thought and Lenin's epistemology. He spoke of the "unity and struggle of the opposites of thought and fantasy" in cognition.[27] He was, as we will see, critical of the epistemological dualism that he saw in Jean Piaget's theories of language, and in particular, Piaget's description of child's "autistic" use of language. Vygotsky emphasized that a Marxist approach to language revealed its "external" or "social" origins.

One of the main problems to which Vygotsky addressed himself was the interrelation of thought and speech. His work on this topic has frequently been compared to that of Piaget. Vygotsky praised Piaget's work, calling it "revolutionary," but commented that it "suffers from the duality common to all trailblazing contemporary works in psychology. This cleavage is a concomitant of the crisis that psychology is undergoing as it develops into a science in the true sense of the word. The crisis stems from the sharp contradiction between the factual material of science and its methodological and theoretical premises, which have long been a subject of dispute between materialistic and idealistic conceptions" (p. 10).

Piaget in his early work postulated three stages in the development of the modes of thought of a child: first, autism, second, egocentrism, and last, socialized thought. In the first, or autistic, stage the child's thought is subconscious and is directed toward self-gratification. The child does not yet use language and has not yet adjusted to the existence of other persons, with their desires and needs. He is not susceptible to the concept of truth and error. In the last stage, socialized thought, the child has adapted to reality, tries to influence it, and can be communicated with through language. He has recognized laws of experience and of logic. In the intermediate stage, egocentrism, the child "stands midway between autism in the strict sense of the word and socialized thought."[28] He uses language, but only to himself; he is thinking aloud. Thus, all three stages constitute a scheme of the development of the thought of a child based on the assumption that "child thought is originally and naturally autistic and changes to realistic thought only under long and sustained social pressure" (p. 13).

Vygotsky accepted much of this description by Piaget of the individual stages of child development, but he rejected the direction of flow of the underlying genetic sequence. As Vygotsky described it:

> The development of thought is, to Piaget, a story of the gradual socialization of deeply intimate, personal, autistic mental states. Even social speech is represented as following, not preceding, egocentric speech.
>
> The hypothesis we propose reverses this course. . . . We consider that the total development runs as follows: The primary function of speech, in both children and adults, is communication, social contact. The earliest speech of the child is therefore essentially social. At first it is global and multifunctional; later its functions become differentiated. At a certain age the social speech of the child is quite sharply divided into egocentric and communicative speech. (We prefer to use the term communicative for the form of speech that Piaget calls socialized as though it had been something else before becoming social. From our point of view, the two forms, communicative and egocentric, are both social, though their functions differ.) Egocentric speech emerges when the child transfers social collab-

orative forms of behavior to the sphere of inner-personal psychic functions. . . . In our conception, the true direction of the development of thinking is not from the individual to the socialized, but from the social to the individual. (pp. 18–20)

And thus Vygotsky arrived at the concept for which he is best known, the "internalization of speech":

Piaget believes that egocentric speech stems from the insufficient socialization of speech and that its only development is decrease and eventual death. Its culmination lies in the past. Inner speech is something new brought in from the outside along with socialization. We believe that egocentric speech stems from the insufficient individualization of primary social speech. Its culmination lies in the future. It develops into inner speech. (pp. 135–36)

Since Vygotsky believed that egocentric, and ultimately, inner speech stemmed from primary social speech, occurring through a process of internalization, it was necessary for him to explain the source of the mental states in the earliest stage, the autistic stage of Piaget. What about this child who has not yet "internalized" any part of primary social speech, who has not yet learned to speak at all? Can he think? It becomes obvious that if Vygotsky were to grant that such a child thinks, then he must find quite different roots for thought and speech. And this he did. According to Vygotsky, thought and speech have different genetic roots and develop according to different growth curves that "cross and recross," but "always diverge again." There is a "prelinguistic phase in the development of thought and a preintellectual phase in the development of speech" (pp. 33, 41). A crucial moment, explored by William Stern, occurs when the curves of development of thought and speech meet for the first time; from this time forward "speech begins to serve intellect, and thoughts begin to be spoken" (p. 43). Vygotsky believed that Stern exaggerated the role of the intellect as a "first cause of meaningful speech," but he did agree that "Stern's basic observation was correct, that there is indeed a moment of discovery" when the child sees the link between word and object. From this point on, thought becomes verbal and speech rational (pp. 28, 29, 44).

The source of prelinguistic thought is, thus, separate from the source of speech. Prelinguistic thought has a source that is similar to the embryonic thought of some species of animals, while speech always has a social origin. Vygotsky saw a clear tie here with Marxist analysis:

The thesis that the roots of human intellect reach down into the animal realm has long been admitted by Marxism; we find its elaboration in Plekhanov. Engels wrote that man and animals have all forms of intellectual activity in common; only the developmental level differs: Animals are able to reason on an elementary level, to analyze (cracking a nut is a beginning of analysis), to experiment when confronted with problems or caught in a difficult situation. . . . It goes without saying that Engels does not credit animals with the ability to think and to speak on the human level. . . . (p.49)

At this point in Vygotsky's analysis, his critic is likely to chastise him for reductionism, for drawing too crude a similarity between man and animals. But Vygotsky felt that the answer to such criticism lay in emphasizing the qualitatively new characteristics that emerged after the lines of thought and speech crossed, after the child's great discovery referred to by Stern had occurred. According to Vygotsky, the stage that followed this intersection was not a simple continuation of the earlier:

The nature of the development itself changes, from biological to sociohistorical. Verbal thought is not an innate natural form of behavior but is determined by a historical-cultural process and has specific properties and laws that cannot be found in the natural forms of thought and speech. Once we acknowledge the historical character of verbal thought, we must consider it subject to all the premises of historical materialism, which are valid for any historical phenomenon in human society. It is only to be expected that on this level the development of behavior will be governed essentially by the general laws of the historical development of human society. (p. 51)

Thus, Vygotsky developed for the explanation of the interrelation of thought and language a scheme that contained a high degree of inner consistency and arrived eventually at Marxist conceptions of social development. Thought and language have different roots—thought in its prelinguistic stage being tied to the biological development of man, language in its prerational stage being tied to the social milieu of the child. But these two categories become dialectically involved once the link between them occurs, when the child perceives that every object has a name; from this point onward, one cannot speak of the separateness of thought and language. Internalization of language causes thoughts to be expressed in inner speech; the effect of logic on speech results in coherence and order in oral communication.

Several aspects of Vygotsky's scheme remained unclear. For example, he drew a parallel between the prelinguistic thought of a child and the mental activity of animals, such as chimpanzees. Yet Vygotsky of course granted that, physiologically, there are genuine differences between the brain of a child and that of a chimpanzee. Nonetheless to what extent those differences result in a qualitatively different sort of prelinguistic thought in the child was not clear in his writings. Within his conception the sociohistorical influences conveyed in language surpassed the biological superiorities of the brain in accounting for the distinctions between man and animal. As a materialist and monist, Vygotsky agreed that the very sociohistorical factors that he emphasized also had their material causal sources, back in the biological development of man. He quoted Engels' descriptions of the influence of the use of tools upon the development of man. In the final analysis, then, the different roots of thought and language were only relative, not absolute. In the life of the individual human, however, the roots were distinct, and it was here that Vygotsky put his emphasis.

Vygotsky's opinion that language and thought have different roots and that "prelinguistic thought" exists in the early life of a child directly conflicted with Stalin's teachings on linguistics. Stalin wrote in *Marxism and Linguistics:*

> It is said that thoughts arise without language material, without the language shell, in, so to speak, a naked form. But this is absolutely wrong. Whatever the thoughts that may arise in the mind of man, they can arise and exist only on the basis of language terminology and phrases. Bare thoughts, free of the language material, free of the "natural matter" of language—do not exist. . . . Only idealists can speak of thinking as not connected with the 'natural matter' of language, of thinking without language.[29]

A clearer contradiction by highest authority can hardly be imagined, if one remembers not only Vygotsky's identification of separate sources of thought and language, but also his assertion that "there is no clear-cut and constant correlation between them" (p. 41). Consequently, the rebirth of interest in Vygotsky's writings occurred only after Stalin's death. The ruler of the state had dictated an interpretation of Marxism that the Marxist scientists and intellectuals of the country failed to perceive.

At this point I would like to shift attention to the post-World War II period and, particularly, to the person of S. L. Rubinshtein, a Soviet scholar who in the last forty years has exercised great influence in questions concerning the philosophical interpretation of psychology and physiology. First, however, it is necessary to describe the ideological pressures upon Soviet psychologists and physiologists in the immediate post-1945 period. The physiology session of 1950 was one of the most important events of this sorry epoch in Soviet scholarship. From an intellectual standpoint the 1950 conference is much less interesting than that of 1962, when de-Stalinization had revived Soviet physiology and psychology, and consequently, the later session will receive more attention in this chapter. For those persons more interested in the 1950 meeting and its immediate results, an English version of the proceedings is available, as well as several other accounts.[30]

In the period immediately following 1945 Soviet scientists in many fields initially hoped for a relatively relaxed ideological atmosphere. This hope was not realized; immediately after A. A. Zhdanov's death in 1948 controls in several scientific fields, including physics, genetics, cosmology, structural chemistry, and physiology, were tightened. The causes of this ideology campaign are very difficult to identify; the personal characteristics of Stalin seemed to be the most important factor, although the strained international situation and the availability of levers of control in Soviet society were also important conditions permitting Stalin to exercise extraordinary influence on science and scholarship. During the years 1948–1952 conferences on science and ideology were held in a number of different fields at which political pressure was exerted on scientists; the "Pavlov" session on physiology and psychology occurred in June 28–July 4, 1950, and was sponsored jointly by the Academy of Sciences of the USSR and the Academy of Medical Sciences of USSR. Unfortunately, the English translation of the speeches given at this conference, published in 1951 in Moscow as *Scientific Session on the Physiological Teachings of Academician I. P. Pavlov*, does not contain the speeches of P. K. Anokhin, I. S. Beritov, L. A. Orbeli, and others. These speeches were critical of the official position.

In the inaugural address Sergei Vavilov, president of the Academy of Sciences and brother of the deceased geneticist Nikolai Vavilov, indicated that the function of the congress was to return to established Pavlovian teachings; he thus implied what was already known, that there would be no genuine effort at the congress to seek new understandings of the difficult problems of physiology and psychology on a materialist basis. Coming almost two years after the genetics conference where Lysenko and his Michurinist school were officially established as the representatives of the only correct approach to genetics, the physiologists and psychologists were quite aware that the outcome of their conference was predetermined. Vavilov gave the official diagnosis of the state of Soviet physiology and psychology when he commented in his opening statement:

> There have been attempts—not too frequent, happily—at an erroneous and unwarranted revision of Pavlov's views. But more frequently, the ideas and work of researchers have not kept to the high road, but wandered into byways and field paths. Strange and surprising though it may seem, the broad Pavlov road has become little frequented, comparatively few have followed it consistently and systematically. Not all our physiologists have been able, or have always been able, to measure up to Pavlov's straightforward materialism. . . . The time has come to sound the alarm. . . . Our people and progressive humanity generally, will not forgive us if we do not put the wealth of Pavlov's legacy to proper use. . . . There can be no doubt that it is only by a return to Pavlov's road that physiology can be most effective, most beneficial to our people and most worthy of the Stalin epoch of the building of Communism.[31]

The Soviet physiologists who came under the heaviest criticism at the conference were P. K. Anokhin, L. A. Orbeli, and I. S. Beritov. I. P. Razenkov, vice president of the Academy of Medical Sciences, charged that Anokhin, one of the Soviet Union's most distinguished physiologists, "has been guilty of many a serious deviation from Pavlov's teachings, has had an infatuation for the fashionable, reactionary theories of Coghill, Weiss and other foreign authors. . . ."[32] The attribution of pejorative meaning to the term "foreign authors" was typical of the chauvinistic temper of these Stalinist years. Anokhin's thoroughly materialist and scholarly approach to physiology will be considered in a separate section of this chapter.

In a history of Soviet psychology published in Moscow in 1967, a work described by an American psychologist as "pioneering" despite its faults,[33] A. V. Petrovskii told of the "dogmatism" in Soviet psychology following the 1950 session.[34] Petrovskii observed that in the early 1950s there was a strong tendency toward the "liquidation" of psychology entirely, replacing it with Pavlovian physiology. This "nihilistic attitude" toward psychology, Petrovskii continued, was reminiscent of the reflexological currents of the early twenties, when the legitimacy of psychology had also been doubted, but:

> If in the twenties the negative attitude of the reflexologists and behaviorists toward psychology could be largely explained—though not justified—by the objective need to criticize the vestiges of subjectivism in psychology,

by the beginning of the 1950s the idea of "liquidating" psychology could not be based on any principled considerations whatsoever.[35]

Thus, the major Soviet historian of Soviet psychology condemned Stalinism in his field in strong terms. To be sure, he dodged the issue of the extent to which the events of the fifties were the responsibility, not only of Stalin, but of the system that permitted him to exercise such power.

Despite the political and ideological pressures of these years Soviet physiology and psychology continued to live and to develop. With better conditions after Stalin's death these fields moved forward once again. One of the best illustrations of the survival ability of Soviet scholars and of their continuing intellectual vitality in the face of great obstacles is found in the person of S. L. Rubinshtein.

SERGEI LEONIDOVICH RUBINSHTEIN (1889–1960)

One of the lifelong goals of Sergei Leonidovich Rubinshtein was to give a theoretical analysis of the nature of consciousness and thought on the basis of dialectical materialism. His attempt in this direction was obvious in his writings over a period of many years, from his 1934 article entitled "Problems of Psychology in the Works of Karl Marx" to his 1959 book on the principles of psychology, in which he commented that his interpretation was heavily influenced by the "dialectical materialist understanding of the determination of psychic [mental] phenomena."[36]

Rubinshtein was important in the formation of contemporary Soviet attitudes toward psychology. In 1942 he founded the department of psychology at Moscow University. Around him in the psychology section of the Institute of Philosophy of the Academy of Sciences of the USSR, which he headed from 1945 to 1960, there grew up a whole school of investigators of the relationship of the psychological to the physiological within the theoretical framework of Marxism. His advanced textbook *Foundations of General Psychology*, published in several editions, was the most authoritative voice in the field for Soviet graduate students. The first edition, published in 1940, received a Stalin Prize. His later work, *Being and Consciousness*, is regarded at the present time as a "deeply creative Marxist work" and has been published in many countries and languages, including Chinese; in 1959 it received a Lenin Prize.

From all these official honors one might think that Rubinshtein was an ideological hack, a mere apologist for Marxism. He was not. Possessing a broad-ranging and subtle mind, he produced even in his relatively elementary 1934 article "what is regarded as the first adequate Marxist theory of motivation and ability."[37] During the worst period for scholarship in the Soviet Union, the Stalinist years immediately after World War II, Rubinshtein came under heavy criticism for his "objective, non-Party" approach to scholarship and for certain of his theoretical formulations. He bent under the pressure, but he did not break. Though he sharpened the point of his ideological pen, he was still the sort of person who, at the 1947 discussion of the ideological failings of Aleksandrov's *History of Western European Philosophy*, would make a plea for the study of formal logic.[38] This was at a time when formal logic was being displaced by dialectical logic, a campaign with much political support from Party followers. In the 1960s, Rubinshtein emerged again as the most prominent theoretical voice on the knotty problems of the nature of consciousness.[39] He published three books on the topic in 1957, 1958, and 1959. Upon his death in 1960 the editors of *Problems of Philosophy* honored him with a necrology which observed that his work would long continue to be of value to psychology.[40]

Although certain themes—for example, the definition of "consciousness"—run through almost all of Rubinshtein's works, there was something of an evolution in his views, a slight but perceptible change that does not seem entirely explainable as a result of political pressure. He was a psychologist, not a physiologist, and his first works are deeply psychological in tone. As time went on, however, he moved more and more toward physiology, maintaining that only with a recognition of the material basis of mental activity could one proceed to an analysis of its most difficult problems.

In the 1946 edition of his *Foundations of Psychology* Rubinshtein discussed at length the nature of the human psyche and the degree to which consciousness could be described in terms of chemistry and physics. He refused to reduce the psychic to the physical, yet he wished at the same time to guard against subjectivism or psychophysical parallelism. In attempting to solve this problem he advanced what he called the principle of psychophysical unity:

> The principle of psychophysical unity is the basic principle of Soviet psychology. Within this unity the materialistic bases of the psyche are determining, but the psyche retains its qualitative specificity; it is not

reduced to the physical properties of matter and is not converted into an ineffective epiphenomenon.[41]

Rubinshtein attempted, therefore, to work out a position in which there is between the psychic and the physical a unity that allows each to retain its specific characteristics. Consciousness is neither one nor the other, but both. This unity is one of contradictions, resulting in a sort of complementarity between the psychic and physical properties of consciousness, a complementarity that parallels the wavelike and corpusclelike properties of light particles. (This analogy was not used until later, however, since complementarity was having its own troubles in Soviet physics.)

Rubinshtein's 1946 formulation was not successful, and reading his writings of that time, one thinks that he realized it. It papered over apparently irreconcilable differences. When physics attempted to escape the dilemma of quantum mechanics by simultaneously attributing wavelike and corpusclelike properties to light, it was not quite destroying itself in the process (though it might have seemed that way). Materialists could (and did) adjust to this strange concept of physics by speaking of relativistic "matter-energy" instead of matter alone, and observing that both waves *and* particles, and all combinations thereof, would be matter-energy. But a materialist could hardly say that consciousness is both "psychic" and "physical" and leave it there. He needed an equivalence principle here, too, but he did not have one conveniently at hand. If "psychic" is a category, either one must in some way equate it with matter-energy, or one must abandon the view that only matter-energy exists, thereby destroying a fundamental assumption of dialectical materialism. Rubinshtein knew that the only solution lay in linking the psychic to some form of matter—hence his statement above that "the material bases of the psyche are determining"—but he was extremely vague on this linkage. He recognized his solution as "unfinished," and called for further attacks on this "difficult assignment."[42]

Although Rubinshtein's 1946 position was vulnerable, the criticisms that were made of him by V. Kolbanovskii in the Party journal *Bol'shevik* in September 1947 were lightweight intellectually. Most of the criticism was based on Rubinshtein's alleged insufficient political militancy, his failure to criticize adequately psychological theories advanced in Western Europe and North America, and his lack of Party spirit.[43]

One of the theoretical criticisms advanced against Rubinshtein stuck, however, and in 1952 he revised his position, abandoning in the process his principle of psychophysical unity, which supposedly described the "dual correlation" of the psychical and the physical.[44] As he wrote:

Materialistic monism means not a unity of two sources—the psychical and the physical—but the presence of a single source, a material source in relation to which the psychical is a product.[45]

This was the beginning of Rubinshtein's revision of his theoretical position, the final result of which was his 1957 monograph, *Existence and Consciousness: Concerning the Place of the Psychical in the Universal Inter-Connections of the Material World.* In the latter work he arrived at a stronger materialistic formulation of the psychophysical problem. Thus, Rubinshtein's revisions seemed to have been more a result of his own awareness of the inadequacy of his earlier position than of the superficial criticism he received during Stalin's last years.

Existence and Consciousness was a book in which Rubinshtein attempted a more systematic and complete analysis of psychic activity than in his earlier text. In order to understand this analysis, it is necessary first to see some of the assumptions on which it was based and then proceed to its details, including the extensions of materialism that it contained.

Rubinshtein's approach was based on a rejection of the "classic" argument for cognitive idealism:

> The basic argument of idealism is the following: In the process of cognition there is no way for us to "jump out" of our sensations, perceptions, and thoughts; this means that we can not attain the sphere of real things; therefore, we are obligated to recognize that the very sensations and perceptions themselves are the only possible objects of cognition. At the basis of this classical argument of idealism lies the thought that in order to attain the sphere of real things, it is necessary to "leap out" of the sphere of sensations, perceptions, and thoughts—and that, of course, is impossible.
>
> This line of argument assumes what it is trying to prove. It assumes that sensations and perceptions are only subjective constructs, external to things themselves, to objective reality. But actually objects participate in the very origin of sensations: sensations, arising as a result of the influence of objects on the sense organs, on the brain, are connected with objects in their very origin.[46]

Rubinshtein was correct in stating that this standard argument for idealism assumes what it is trying to prove—that is, it assumes that sensations and perceptions are something other than material reality and therefore must be escaped from in order to approach reality. Since that escape cannot be accomplished, the argument goes, one must accept sensations and perceptions as objects of cognition themselves, and can define them as ideal forms if one wishes. But what Rubinshtein did not explicitly say (although it was implicit in his argument) was that his argument also assumed what it was trying to prove. The person who believes that sensations and perceptions are meaningful only as forms of material reality has also made an unprovable assumption. He has as much right to his assumption as the idealist does to his, but he can not justifiably maintain that he has "proved" his case while the idealist has merely assumed what he pretended to prove. All of this merely restates my earlier opinion that the option between materialism and idealism is a matter of philosophic choice, not a matter of logical proof. As the parallel postulate in geometry is the starting point from which several geometries can be constructed, depending on the assumptions made, the mind-body problem is the point from which several philosophies can be built, depending on the assumptions made. The genuinely difficult problem in the case of epistemology is not what can be proved and what can not, but the dilemma presented by the occasional grounds for choice among philosophic assumptions, recognized as such. If science had to wait at every point for rigorous proofs, it would not proceed far. The best form of materialism could be constructed on a few principles openly recognized as unprovable assumptions for which there are, nonetheless, persuasive arguments. Rubinshtein never stated that he was proceeding on such a basis, but what he did say was perfectly reconcilable with such a position.

To Rubinshtein, then, sensations and perceptions do provide an entree into the real material world. He described an epistemology of interaction, of praxis. In 1946, he had rejected the theory of mutual interaction on the basis that it assumed separate interacting series of psychic and physical events. He still, in 1957, rejected such a theory; his new epistemology of interaction was based on the premise of the interaction of an internal material brain with reflections of external material objects. Two totally separate series of events were not interacting, since both series were based on matter. Thus, what he earlier called experience, or subjectivity, was to be unpeeled in layers, like an onion, and revealed as also based on objective reality, on matter.

The general philosophic framework from which he approached the problem was one in which the universe is an interconnected material whole. It is an age-old concept, one with similarities to many older systems. As Rubinshtein described this universe:

All phenomena in the world are interconnected. Every action is an interaction: every change of one entity is reflected in all the others and is itself an answer to the change of still other phenomena acting upon it. Every external influence is refracted by the internal properties of that body, of that phenomenon to which it is subjected. . . . It was not for nothing that Lenin wrote: . . . it is logical to propose that all matter possesses a property essentially similar to sensation, to the property of reflection. . . .

This property of reflection is expressed in the fact that every thing is affected by those external influences to which it is subjected. External influences condition even the very internal nature of phenomena and are, so to speak, laid up in it, preserved in it. On the strength of this, all incident influences, all influencing objects, are "represented" or reflected in all other objects. Each phenomenon is in a certain degree "a mirror and echo of the universe." At the same time, the result of this or that influence of any entity is conditioned by the very nature of the latter; the internal nature of phenomena is that "prism" through which single objects and phenomena are reflected in others.

This expresses the fundamental property of existence. On this conception is based the dialectical materialist understanding of the determination of phenomena in their interaction and interdependence.[47]

In this interesting and ambitious passage Rubinshtein based himself on concepts already existing within Soviet dialectical materialism, but he presented them in a more complete and speculative form than that in which they are usually found. The statement that every phenomenon is in a certain degree "a mirror and echo of the universe" derives directly from Marx; commenting on the physiological function of eyes and ears, Marx commented that "these are the organs that tear man away from his individuality, converting him into a mirror and an echo of the universe."[48] However, whether Marx would have extended this limited statement concerning man's sense organs to the broader generalizations of Rubinshtein is by no means clear. The concept of "reflection" that runs through the passage is, of course, derived from Lenin, as Rubinshtein quoted to indicate. Here again, a small comment was expanded into broader meaning. Lastly, a principle of determinism, of universal causation, is also obvious in the passage.

This formulation of causation in an interconnected world became important to Soviet psychology, however. To Soviet theorists as well as to others it has a certain speculative persuasiveness. Rubinshtein's "prism," the internal state of an object through which external influences are refracted, was frequently cited. The editors of *Problems of Philosophy* commented in 1960: "The position defended in *Existence and Consciousness*, in which external causes act through internal conditions, has an essential meaning for the whole system of scientific knowledge."[49]

In the section of his book immediately following the quoted passage, Rubinshtein addressed himself to the problem of the prism more directly. Here he tried to assess the relative weight of "internal factors" and "external factors" in the process of reflection, that property inherent in all matter. The higher the level of the evolution of matter, the more weight the internal factors have: "The 'higher' we rise—from living organisms to man—the more complicated is the internal constitution of phenomena and the greater is the share of the internal conditions compared with the external."[50] Consciousness in man is that form of material reflection in which internal factors play a greater role than in any other form of reflection. Rubinshtein's position on the nature of psychic activity now unfolded. Psychic activity, he said, is both an activity of the brain and a reflection of the external world. Therefore, psychic activity has two different aspects—the ontological and the epistemological.[51] The ontological aspect of the brain is its existence as a nervous system, a material object of great complexity currently being studied by physiologists. The epistemological aspect of psychic activity derives from the cognitive relationship of psychic phenomena to objective reality. Rubinshtein believed the distinction between these two aspects to be relative rather than absolute. While the epistemological aspect of psychic activity is dominated by connections with the outside world and the ontological aspect is primarily determined from within, it should always be remembered that the brain itself is also, in the end, a result of the influence of the external world. Thus, there is a difference of causal time scales here. The brain is a product of the external environment acting over the entire period of natural history. It is a material brain of great organizational complexity formed by natural selection from matter of simpler organization. But ontologically, it exists as a completed entity at any given point in time that cognition takes place, and its internal constitution "refracts" the reflection of external reality, which is also material. Thus , the interaction that occurs is material in origin on both sides, and both sides are products of objective reality, but being formed at different times, in different places, and in different ways, they interact.

According to Rubinshtein, internal factors are very important in the formation of perceptual forms of reality, more important than in any other case of the universal phenomenon of reflection, but they are still less important than the external factors, the links to objective reality existing outside the brain. Thus, man's knowledge is still in an important sense a faithful reproduction of external reality. Man confirms the truth about that objective reality in practice when his formulations are either proved or disproved by actual results.

The causal sequence involving consciousness is not, Rubinshtein believed, from consciousness to external reality, but from external reality to consciousness: Therefore the question, How do perceptions make the transition from forms to things? is an incorrectly posed question. "Man does not exist because he thinks, as Descartes put it; he thinks because he exists."[52]

In his assignment of relative weights to internal and external factors Rubinshtein had added another unprovable though fruitful assumption to his system. A strict materialist could accept an explanation of the process of cognition in which the internal factors played more of a role than the external ones without contradicting himself, so long as he added to this explanation the belief that the internal factors were also material and had, in their turn, been caused by external influences during the process of evolution. The verification of truth through practice could still play the same role as in Rubinshtein's scheme. Rubinshtein, as we have seen, accepted this evolutionary understanding of the brain. His addition of a weighting scheme was gratuitous, but reassuring within a tradition that preferred an epistemology in which there occurred as faithful a transmission of information from objective reality to consciousness as possible.

Rubinshtein still believed that the term "subjective" is a legitimate one. "Subjective" was to him a term used to indicate that every aspect of psychic activity displays characteristics unique to the person concerned. Every sensation, every thought, was subjective in this sense. The value of the word "subjective" was not destroyed, in Rubinshtein's opinion, by the fact that these subjective qualities of the individual had, in turn, their objective origins. At any one point in time, every person is influenced by both subjective and objective factors, although the human race over the period of its whole history has been influenced only by objective ones. Out of this evolutionary process are created two causal chains that interact with each other. The product of the interaction is consciousness. Psychology studies this interaction. Physiology studies the brain as an organ of the human body.

To a person who is willing to pay the price of some speculation in order to arrive at a conception of consciousness, Rubinshtein's scheme possessed strong points. It advanced a more sophisticated conception of consciousness than was previously found within the tradition of materialism. To be sure, it possessed weaknesses, the most obvious of which was connected with the oldest problem in philosophy, pushed back into a more remote recess, but still there. The mind-body problem emerged now around Rubinshtein's "forms" (obrazy) of reality. He defined sensations and perceptions as forms of external material reality. Were these forms material themselves? Is psychic activity, consciousness itself, material? Rubinshtein said no; the forms were "reflections" of objects, not objects themselves.[53] In this way, he said in 1959, "psychic activity is ideal as a cognitive activity of man, and the term 'form' of an object (or phenomenon) is an expression resulting from this recognition." Thus, the dialectical materialism of Rubinshtein contained a category of phenomena called "ideal" that was different from "material." Was this not a surrender of his assumption of monistic materialism? Not at all, he maintained: "The key to the solution of the problem is the fact that, to use a phrase of Hegel's that was specially noted by Lenin, one and the same thing is both it itself and something else, since it appears in different systems of connections and relations" (p. 9). Relying on this Hegelian principle, Rubinshtein maintained that in an epistemological sense the psychic is ideal, while in an ontological sense it is material. The ideal element is precisely the "forms" of reality. Rubinshtein stoutly affirmed, "We are convinced that the recognition of the idealness of psychic activity does not convert it into something spiritual, does not withdraw it from the material world" (p.11). Many of his critics remained unconvinced. As Rubinshtein observed shortly before his death, "more and more frequently people are affirming that the psychic is material. The partisans of this point of view, which has recently received a certain currency in our philosophic literature, are shutting themselves up inside the ontological aspects of the problem and do not take the trouble to correlate it with the epistemological aspect" (p. 8). We shall hear more from these "partisans of the materiality of consciousness," who were indeed speaking loudly in the philosophic literature of the late fifties and sixties.

ALEXANDER ROMANOVICH LURIA

Alexander Romanovich Luria (1902–1977) was one of the members of that unique generation of Soviet scientists whose formative years coincided with the first years of the revolutionary regime. At the time of his death he was a world-famous psychologist. While his psychological views may now be familiar to many Western scientists, his philosophical and political opinions are much less well known. Luria was a convinced Marxist who attempted, in several different ways, to tie Marxism and psychology together. As a disciple of Lev Vygotsky, who has already been discussed in detail on pp. 168ff., he shared Vygotsky's belief in the importance of the social environment in the formation of the human psyche. And like Vygotsky, Luria got into political trouble when he tried to extend his Marxist theory of social conditioning to citizens of the Soviet Union. Yet he remained a loyal member of the Communist Party, and shifted the focus of his work in response to political criteria as well as in line with his own intellectual views.

Although Luria from his first publications recognized the importance of Marxism, he followed several different lines in the actual working out of the relationship between psychology and dialectical materialism. At first, before being influenced significantly by Vygotsky, Luria believed that Freudian psychoanalysis was highly compatible with Marxism. Writing in 1925 in a book entitled *Psychology and Marxism*, Luria called for "a radical reworking of psychology in terms of the scientific method of dialectical materialism."[54] Psychoanalysis seemed to him to be the path down which to go because, he believed, it coincided with Marxism in several ways: (1) It was monistic and materialistic, denying a difference between mind and body; (2) It defended the concept of "consciousness" from the attacks of the mechanistic behaviorists; and (3) While defending consciousness it, nonetheless, remained scientific and did not speculate about the essence of "mind in general." We see from these points that Luria's ideas at this stage about what Marxism meant for psychology were still rather primitive.

Even in this most enthusiastic stage of his attitude to psychoanalysis, however, Luria realized that its coincidence with Marxism was not full; Marxism pays a great deal of attention to society as a whole, rather than just to individual experiences. Psychoanalysis seemed to concentrate too much on the single subject. Luria suggested that the followers of Freud and Jung take another step and "integrate the organism into a system of social influences. Only then," he added, "will the theory of psychoneural activity advance from mechanical materialism to dialectical materialism."[55]

Vygotsky helped Luria to turn from psychoanalysis to a more independent psychological path. Vygotsky believed that psychoanalysis made the mistake of trying to deduce human behavior from the biological "depths" of mind, when it would be much better to deduce it from the social "heights." Luria, Vygotsky, and a third young psychologist who would become prominent in the Soviet Union (see pp. 211ff.), A. N. Leont'ev, formed a trio ("*troika*") of young scholars who set about reconstructing psychology by pursuing the view that "the origins of higher forms of conscious behavior were to be found in the individual's social relations with the external world."[56] Vygotsky was, said Luria, "a genius," and also "the leading Marxist theoretician among us."

The three men described the principles of the new psychology as being "instrumental," "cultural," and "historical." By "instrumental" they meant that higher functions in humans are not simple stimulus-response processes as the behaviorists and Pavlovians believed, but instead mediated responses in which the subject provides part of his or her own stimuli. A human being not only responds to the stimuli of the experimenter, but modifies those stimuli. A simple example may be that people sometimes tie a string around a finger in order to remember something. Luria and his colleagues were to show that children from the ages three to ten display many more complex examples of the self-modification of stimuli.

By "cultural" Luria, Vygotsky, and Leont'ev meant that society organizes specific tasks in certain ways which have a strong impact on the behavior of humans. One of the best examples of a cultural influence was language, upon which Vygotsky put so much emphasis as a factor determining human thought.

By "historical" the scholars meant that a purely functional approach to psychology was insufficient; social history must be considered also. Members of different social classes and different ethnic groups think differently. Language and the process of writing are evolutionary products which must be studied in terms of their social histories and their consequent impacts on human thought. The historical element was obviously closely connected with the cultural one; as Luria wrote, "It is through this interiorization of historically determined and culturally organized ways of operation on information that the social nature of people comes to be their psychological nature as well."[57]

Operating on the basis of these principles, Luria in 1929 and 1930 published a series of pathbreaking analyses of the development of speech, thought, and writing in children.[58] In analyzing children's speech, he hypothesized that "it should not be surprising if the speech of children from different social classes were not all similar," and he believed that these differences would, in turn, have effects on their thinking. Several of his publications were based on studies of city, rural, and homeless children. In conducting word association studies on the rural children he found that their responses reflected the "unchanging and monotonous environments" in which they lived. He observed that "the rural child may think that the word association he gives as a response is out of his own head, (but) in actual fact it is merely the environment speaking through him." He found that some words have "completely different meanings" to homeless children and those raised in a normal home environment. And the children from different backgrounds varied greatly in their relationships with other people, including the psychologists. The homeless children were, for example, much more distrustful. Luria concluded that "it is absolutely meaningless to study children divorced from the environmental factors that shape their mental makeup," and he called for changes in Soviet pedagogy and course materials that would reflect social differences.[59]

In an article published in 1929 in the journal *Natural Science and Marxism* Luria attempted to show that a child's thought passes through three chronological stages: primitive thought, formal thought, and dialectical thought.[60] The first stage is highly similar to Vygotsky's "pre-linguistic thought" discussed on pp. 170ff. When the child learns that every object has a name, and begins to speak, his thought gradually changes under the impact of language, which forces a certain logic on his thinking process. Later, the child begins to grow out of this second "formal thought" stage under the impact of being involved in "practical work situations" and "complicated, active social contact." The child becomes aware of "his own concepts," begins to think about his own thoughts, and moves beyond the formal stage to the true "dialectical thought" which distinguishes adult human behavior. And in these last two stages the impact of society, its form of language, its work relationships, and its social organization all have major impacts on the very modes and forms of the thinking of its members. It was obvious to Luria that people living in the different epochs of history as described by Marxism—feudalism, capitalism, socialism, communism—would possess literally different ways of thinking corresponding to their different social forms.

The same emphasis on stages of development which become dialectically intertwined marked Luria's original studies of the "pre-history" of writing. He believed that before a child is able to write he or she goes through some of the same stages that civilization itself did in developing writing, such as pictographic and representational writing. The development of writing, like that of speech, was "dialectical": "the profoundly dialectical uniqueness of this process means that the transition to a new technique initially sets the process of writing back considerably, after which it then develops further at the new and higher level."[61]

In emphasizing the influence of the social environment on child psychology, materialistic determinism, and dialectical development, Luria thought that he was applying dialectical materialism, which he called "the most important philosophy of the age," to psychology. But he did not realize at first that some of the psychological assumptions that he was making could get him into political difficulties in the Soviet Union. If, as Luria believed, the social environment is the most important factor forming the psyche, then different social environments should result in different psyches. This view ran counter to the opinions of some Western scholars (e.g., W. H. R. Rivers; much later, Noam Chomsky) who believed that universal thought patterns and concepts of logic exist in all people in all societies. Luria and his colleagues decided to test that hypothesis by studying people in the Soviet Union living in very different social environments from that of Moscow and Leningrad. Luria and his colleagues were eager to conduct psychological tests and interviews with members of a primitive, preliterate society to see if these people thought differently than people living in modern societies. What better opportunity could present itself than to go to areas of the Soviet Union that the literacy and modernization movements had not yet touched, such as remote areas of Kirghizia and Uzbekistan? Luria thus embarked on an ambitious undertaking which has never, until the present day, been entirely described in the published literature.

Luria and his colleagues went to remote areas of Kirghizia where the conditions were so primitive that the women were still held in *purdah*. These women were not permitted to speak to males, so they were interviewed by female members of the expedition. The Muslim males were more free to move about, but they also were illiterate.

Among the many tests that Luria conducted was one having to do with the forms and categories by which people classify objects. The Kirghiz natives were shown the following forms[62] and asked to describe them and say which ones were similar:

1   2   3   4   5   6   7

Luria found that the typical list of names given by nonliterate women living in remote villages was as follows:

1. a plate
2. a tent
3. a bracelet
4. beads
5. a mirror
6. a clock
7. a kettle stand

In contrast, when Luria asked Muslim women in nearby cities who had attended school to describe the same shapes, the typical answers were geometric forms: circles, triangles, squares.

When Luria asked the primitive women which of the forms were similar, they would group forms together because of their concrete functional likenesses. Numbers 1 and 7 above might be grouped together, for example, because both a plate and a kettle stand are used in cooking, and 3 and 4 because both are jewelry. The women from the cities, however, would group 1 and 3 together because both are variations of circles or 2, 6, and 7 because all three are kinds of triangles.

When the members of the expedition asked the primitive women if numbers 1 and 3 were not similar (the two forms that educated women classified together as circles), the primitive women would answer negatively, seeing no similarity between a plate and a bracelet, or, others would similarly answer, between a coin and the moon.

On the basis of this kind of data Luria and his colleagues concluded that it is doubtful that there are "universal laws of perception," as some Gestalt psychologists believed, but instead that "categorical perception reflects historically developed and transmitted ways of classifying objects in the world around us" (p.66). Primitive subjects do not "single out a common attribute and denote a category that logically subsumes all the objects" in the way that educated subjects do, but instead classify objects in terms of "real life relations among objects" (p. 67).

Luria wished to push this form of analysis further and determine if primitive subjects were capable of thinking in logical terms. Would they understand a question based on a syllogism, such as: 1. In the far north, where there is snow, all bears are white. 2. Novaya Zemlya is in the far north. 3. What color are the bears there? According to Luria, many of his subjects, male and female, would answer with a statement such as "I've never been in the north and never seen bears" or "If you want an answer to that question, you should ask people who have been there and have seen them" (pp. 77–78).

Luria observed, "Although our nonliterate peasant groups could use logical relations objectively if they could rely on their own experience, we can conclude that they had not acquired the syllogism as a device for making logical inferences. . . ." He dubbed these and similar research projects in Muslim Central Asia

"anti-Cartesian experiments" because we found critical self-awareness to be the final product of socially determined psychological development, rather than its primary starting point, as Descartes' ideas would have led us to believe. . . . In all cases we found that changes in practical forms of activity, and especially the reorganization of activity based on formal schooling, produced qualitative changes in the thought processes of the individuals studied. Moreover, we were able to establish that basic changes in the organization of thinking can occur in a relatively short time when there are sufficiently sharp changes in social-historical circumstances, such as those that occurred following the 1917 Revolution. (p.80)

In Luria's opinion these psychological findings were confirmations of the Marxist principle that being determines consciousness, and not the reverse. But to the radical critics becoming predominant in the early thirties, a time of great ideological militance and political passions, Luria's findings were based on ethnocentric elitism and a bourgeois contempt for lower classes and ethnic groups. And if the Muslim natives of Central Asia who were illiterate were intellectually backward not only in terms of knowledge but even in their ways of thought, would not the same be true for Russian peasants and workers still not literate, of whom there were still millions? Luria's reply that the situation could be quickly changed by introducing education and the advantages of a socialist economy did not protect him from the charge that he had been influenced by concepts of Central European and, particularly, German anthropology in which all societies are arranged on a value scale and in which modern industrialized societies are superior not only in terms of their material possessions and technologies, but also in some essential cultural and intellectual sense.[63] This charge was probably partially true, since Luria did, indeed, follow German psychological and anthropological literature closely. The rejoinder that classical Marxism itself, with its scheme of historical succession of socioeconomic formations from slavery to communism, also represents a value scale was also of no help in the passionate debates of the early thirties. Soviet ideologists were emphasizing the appeal of Marxism to primitive, lower-class, and non-Caucasian cultures, and did not want to be reminded of Marxism's inherent European ethnocentrism. So Luria was unable to publish the results of his research, and moved into a different area of research, that of neuropsychology. Although he continued to be a Marxist, he was more cautious about directly linking his research to dialectical materialism, having learned that such claims can backfire during ideologically passionate moments.

THE 1962 CONFERENCE

The most interesting event concerning Soviet Marxist philosophy and psychology in the sixties was a great conference on the subject held in May 1962 in Moscow. This All-Union Conference on Philosophic Questions of Higher Nervous Activity and Psychology was convened jointly by the Academy of Sciences of the USSR, the Academy of Pedagogical Sciences of the Russian Republic (RSFSR), and the Ministries of Higher Education of both the USSR and the RSFSR. More than one thousand physiologists, psychologists, philosophers, and psychiatrists participated, coming from all over the Soviet Union. The reports and debates of this conference were published in a volume of 771 pages.[64] Buried in this report are many sharp differences of opinion. It is the best single source for an understanding of the philosophic issues in Soviet physiology and psychology after the passing of the Stalinist era.

The resolution that was approved at the conclusion of the conference inevitably involved such compromises among various points of view that it reveals much less than the debates themselves, which will be discussed below. Nevertheless, the resolution did reproduce the general tone of the conference. The statement noted that the physiology of the nervous system, like other facets of biology and psychology, was going through a special period of development in which it was coming even closer to the physical and mathematical sciences. New methods of experimental research—electrophysiology of brain structures and nerve formations on the cellular and subcellular levels; use of computers; statistical methods; the theory of information; and cybernetics—all were leading to new understandings of physiology and psychology. Cybernetics in particular seemed promising. The task of Marxist psychologists and physiologists was to find a way of incorporating these new and valuable sources of knowledge into their disciplines without falling prey to crass materialism on the one hand or idealism on the other.

In the conference reports and debates themselves, two issues emerged as those of the greatest importance. The first was: In view of all this remarkable new knowledge about physiology and information systems, is the reflex approach advocated by Pavlov still valid? The second question was the old one: How now must we define the term "consciousness"? On both issues the conference broke into contrasting points of view.

The Validity of the Reflex Approach

The question of the validity of the reflex approach arose in several different forms: there were discussions of the significance of Pavlov, the usefulness of the term "reflex arc," and the meaning of the phrase "higher nervous activity." The most energetic critic of the Pavlovian concept of reflexes was N. A. Bernshtein. Bernshtein's opinion that the Pavlovian teaching had become quite obsolescent in the light of modern science was supported by, among others, N. I. Grashchenkov, L. P. Latash, I. M. Feigenberg, M. M. Bongard, and, more indirectly, P. K. Anokhin. Opposing these speakers, in the most direct fashion, were E. A. Asratian, L. G. Voronin, Iu. P. Frolov, A. I. Dolin, N. A. Shustin, A. A. Zubkov, and V. N. Chernigovskii.

All of these speakers acknowledged Pavlov's immense stature in the history of psychology and physiology. The difference of opinion centered not on his past significance, but on the continuing fruitfulness of his approach. Some of the disagreements were semantic: The defenders of Pavlov tended to describe his views in a very broad, methodological fashion; the new critics looked upon Pavlovianism in a way similar to that of most non-Soviet physiologists and psychologists—that is, as a stimulus-response approach to nervous behavior. Yet underneath the misunderstandings and heated arguments was a real issue: Was the dialectical materialist understanding of physiology to be tied to the name of Pavlov, or would it acquire other means of identification? This was a question of authentic concern. As one of the supporters of the traditional point of view, V. N. Chernigovskii, observed: "We know that there is a whole group of young people who are skeptical about a whole series of principles of [Pavlov's] teaching on higher nervous activity. . . . I call this group the Young Turks" (p. 113). Yet the Young Turks were in many cases not so young.

N. A. Bernshtein thought that a revolution had occurred in physiology since the beginning of the second quarter of the twentieth century, requiring the modification of many traditional physiological concepts but, given the necessary attention, permitting a new and superior interpretation of life within the traditions of dialectical materialism. The most important element of this revolution, he maintained, was cybernetics. He agreed that cybernetics had some dangers, particularly in the form in which its foreign founders expressed it, but he thought that if this new subject was placed on "the correct methodological rails," it could bring invaluable assistance to the study of biology in general and physiology in particular.

The most important contribution of cybernetics to the problems concerning Bernshtein was the possibility that it presented of explaining on a materialist basis the process of goal seeking. An organism, seen from the cybernetic point of view, has a definite goal of action; Bernshtein spoke of a "physiology of activity" to distinguish it from the "simply reactive" physiology portrayed in Pavlovian reflex theory. This goal of action must be analyzed carefully, he said.

> The goal of action—in other words, the result that the organism is striving to attain—is something that must be achieved but that still does not exist. Therefore, the goal of action is a reflection or model of the necessary future, coded in one way or another in the brain . . . We should notice that the concept of the reality of such a coded brain model—the extrapolation of the probable future—creates the possibility of a strictly materialist interpretation of such concepts as purposefulness, advisability, etc.
> . . .
> To speak in a metaphor, we can say that the organism constantly plays a game with nature surrounding it—a game whose rules are not defined and whose course of progress, "conceived" by the opponent, is unknown. (pp. 308–12)

In contrast to Pavlovian theory, which Bernshtein characterized as assuming "an equilibrium between the organism and its surrounding milieu," the new conception of life processes assumed "an overcoming of that milieu," a surmounting of the environment. The activity of organisms was directed, he thought, not at simple self-preservation or homeostasis, but at movement toward "a specific program of development" (p. 314).

Bernshtein was quite aware of the dangers of his formulations, which soon resulted in his being criticized at the conference as a teleologist, but he believed his critics were simply ignorant of modern science. He thought that physiologists had been very slow in adjusting to the full implications of the concepts of probabilistic laws in nature. Many of the physiologists of the Pavlovian school, he implied, still dreamed of explaining the human body as a "reactive automat" with its actions rigidly determined in a way that was thoroughly predictable once sufficient facts had been collected. But these orthodox determinists were actually crippling modern materialism, Bernshtein indicated, by tying it to outdated concepts:

> Of course, the form of behavior of a reactive automat is more obviously deterministic than the behavior of an organism that is constantly forced to make active choices in stochastic conditions. But the discarding of the concept of an organism as a reactive automat, existing 'because' of the stimuli that affect it, is by no means a retreat from scientific determinism in the broad sense; that this is so should be clear from the fact that the shift from describing phenomena by means of single-valued functions to its description by means of the theory of probability does not mean a retreat from a position of strict science. (p. 322)

The possibility of many-valued functions in biological phenomena was also very attractive to Grashchenkov, Latash, and Feigenberg. They, too, believed that the old conception of the structure of the reflex was "incapable of explaining the observed physical facts" (p. 43). But they thought that Pavlov's system contained a great deal more flexibility than some of his critics believed. They key to many-valued functions in physiology was in the past experience of the organism, as they said Pavlov himself had indicated in his writings on reinforcement. This emphasis on the past, on the genetic approach, was a traditional characteristic of Marxism and should be easily accepted.

Grashchenkov and his colleagues were of the opinion that the concept of prediction on the basis of past experience was the premise of many schemes being currently proposed by Soviet physiologists; Anokhin's "acceptor of action," Bernshtein's "physiology of activity," E. N. Sokolov's "nerve model of a stimulus," and several of I. S. Beritov's views on the physiological structure of behavior all stemmed from such a premise. The characteristic feature of all these hypothetical "predictive structures" was the probabilistic nature of prediction: "Of all possible predicted results the one is chosen which has the highest probability." And Grashchenkov and his friends observed, "The fact that in the process of evolution organisms have developed a mechanism for probabilistic prediction should not be surprising." Such an ability was essential to survival. Furthermore, rather than contradicting determinism, it broadens it by showing that "the final result of dynamic reactions is determined by the information flowing into the brain and by the past experience of the organism" (pp. 47–48).

V. S. Merlin, of the Perm Pedagogical Institute, also thought that the new concepts of probability were very fruitful in physiology. He maintained that a given "nervous-physiological process" does not necessarily give rise to a given "psychic process." In the old days, Merlin continued, such a view would have seemed unacceptable for a materialist, but now that the full significance of quantum mechanics has been realized by materialists, it becomes apparent that laws of probability are fully acceptable as "causal," and therefore there is no reason that a similar approach cannot be taken in psychology and physiology (pp. 521–25). This would obviously leave room for a much less strictly determined psychology.

But there was still such a thing as "too much room." Grashchenkov, Latash, and Feigenberg guarded against carrying the new concept of probability all the way to a belief in complete spontaneity in psychic phenomena. The distinguished Australian neurophysiologist J. C. Eccles was frequently criticized at the conference for using the uncertainty of quantum mechanics as a means for postulating a realm of action for "mind" as distinct from matter. In his *The Neurophysiological Basis of Mind* (1952) Eccles had given considerable credence to the view that "mind could control the behavior of matter within the limits imposed by Heisenberg's Principle of Uncertainty."[65] The dialectical materialists rejected such a view as being based on the assumption of mind-body duality.

In sum, then, Graschenkov, Latash, and Feigenberg agreed with Bernshtein in attempting to modify traditional Pavlovian conceptions, but they were more careful in observing the pitfalls of such an approach.

Another issue very much debated was the continuing validity of the term "reflex arc." Bernshtein believed that the concept of a reflex arc was a part of obsolescent "classical" reflex theory of the first quarter of the twentieth century; he suggested the term "reflex circle" (pp. 302–3). Grashchenkov, Latash, and Feigenberg were equally unhappy with the concept of an open-door reflex arc, but suggested instead what they called a "cyclical innervational structure" (p. 44). Still another speaker, V. N. Miasishchev, of the Bekhterev Psychoneurological Institute of Leningrad, proposed that the reflex be considered a "spiral." He maintained that this model "quite obviously follows the Leninist formula of development. It is a concept that is correct both philosophically and scientifically" (p. 535). He was referring here to Lenin's statement that the approach of the human mind to reality is not a "mirroring," but instead an approach that is "split in two, zigzaglike" (see the discussion in ch. 2 of the present volume, p. 45).

Each of these proposed modifications had the same goal: to indicate that nervous activity is based on a continuous flow of feedback (afferent) signals that serves as the source of information for constant corrective signals. This inward flow of information also changes the very structural nature of the corrective mechanism itself by increasing the store of past experience "deposited" in it. In a sense the corrective mechanism "manufactures itself" from this store of information. The Soviet interpreters saw in this approach a way of uniting social history (the past history of the individual) and natural history (the inherited characteristics of the species) in a single materialist explanation of behavior.

These critics of the traditional reflex approach were soon themselves the objects of considerable disapproval. The defenders of Pavlov accused the Young Turks of simplifying Pavlov's views by equating his concept of the reflex with the mechanistic one of Descartes. E. V. Shorokhova and V. M. Kaganov, for example, said that Bernshtein regarded reflexes as purely physiological phenomena, ignoring Pavlov's view that they were both physiological and psychological. Shorokhova and Kaganov continued that Bernshtein's concept of the "physiology of activity" contained a definition of reflex that had not changed since the days of Sechenov and was limited in the same sense as the one current in "modern west European physiology." They wished to discard this "atomistic" view but retain the term "reflex" as a description of a phenomenon that was "internally cybernetic" (pp. 87–88).

L. G. Voronin, Iu. P. Frolov, and E. A. Asratian, old supporters of the Pavlovian school, deprecated the originality of people like Bernshtein, Grashchenkov, and Anokhin. Asratian maintained that these three men put great store in novel terms that actually describe phenomena long ago known. He believed, for example, that feedback was described in physiological terms by such people as Bernard, Pavlov, and Sechenov (pp. 727–28). Frolov, who described himself as the oldest pupil of Pavlov still working, similarly doubted the originality of cybernetics and said it had no philosophy of its own and could be used by people of different schools; much was currently being made of it, he continued, by neopositivists and Gestaltists. Voronin, of Moscow University, maintained that the new criticism of Pavlovianism was not so much based on new scientific facts or proof that Pavlovianism had "aged" as it was simply a revealing of positions that these critics had long wanted to take (pp. 509–15). The Young Turks were actually Old Turks. Grashchenkov and Anokhin, he continued, were insisting on modish terms primarily in order to bring in concepts that they long ago favored but did not have cybernetic vocabularies to back up.

There was a ring of truth in this criticism. Grashchenkov had, indeed, characterized Pavlovianism in the thirties as "mechanistic";[66] Bernshtein had called for a replacement of "reflex arc" with "reflex circle" as early as 1935;[67] Anokhin—a biographer of Pavlov, and usually very respectful of him—had criticized his teaching before World War II rather sharply and had, in turn, been the subject of strictures at the 1950 Pavlov session (see pp. 174ff. of the present volume). But to see the controversy of 1962 over Pavlovianism entirely as a reflection of disputes of the thirties would be quite inaccurate. The new developments in neurophysiology and information theory, as exemplified by the works of such people as W. Ross Ashby and Arturo Rosenbleuth, were by 1962 exercising great influence on Soviet physiologists and psychologists.[68] These developments seemed to promise new successes in the explanation of decision making and goal-directed biological development on the basis of materialist assumptions. Since the materialist tradition in physiology was particularly strong in the Soviet Union, it was only natural that these two streams of thought would come together and had, indeed, been anticipated by certain Soviet scholars of the thirties. These older leaders spoke out in 1962 as the most prestigious members of the "cybernetic school," but they were supported by many younger workers. Although this point of view obviously did not go unopposed at the conference, the emphasis in the final resolution on the importance of cybernetics to physiology and the prominent place given to the reports of the cyberneticists indicate that they had achieved an advantageous position in their discussions with the more traditional members of the Pavlovian school.

The Definition of "Consciousness"

If the debate over the validity of the reflex concept was one in which physiologists were the most active participants, the definition of "consciousness" was the issue on which psychologists and philosophers spoke out most frequently. This debate was carried to incredibly fine degrees of detail.

In order to avoid the trap of dualism that the total separation of physiology from psychology presented, the philosophers around Rubinshtein had devised in the late fifties a formula that said that reflex activity is *both* physiological and psychological. Since at this time reflex activity was considered synonymous with psychic activity, the product of this analysis was the position that psychic (reflex) activity is studied in two different aspects by two different kinds of specialists. The physiologist studies psychic (reflex) activity in its ontological aspect, which is material, and he concerns himself with neurophysiology. The psychologist studies psychic (reflex) activity in its epistemological aspect, which is ideal, being based on the ideal forms (*obrazy*), and he concerns himself with cognition ("the refraction of external reality by internal conditions").

This formulation began to break down in the late fifties and early sixties when certain physiologists (Bernshtein and others) began to say that reflex activity is not synonymous with psychic activity because the reflex concept is too simple to explain psychic activity; if physiologists would go beyond the reflex approach, they could identify physiological mechanisms (the physiology of activity, the acceptor of action, and so on) that would explain many phenomenon earlier thought to be reserved for psychologists. This approach alarmed many psychologists who feared that the more aggressive physiologists were trying to "swallow their field," as one speaker at the 1962 conference phrased it.

Furthermore, the compromise position of the late 1950s was being undermined from a different quarter. Certain philosophers and psychologists (V. V. Orlov and others) were also arguing that psychic activity was not the same as reflex activity. But while the physiologists, like Bernshtein, argued this so that physiology could shed its shackles to reflex theory and then proceed more successfully into the realm of psychology, Orlov had other consequences in mind: he wanted to wed physiology to "reflex activity" in order to leave "psychic activity" free for psychologists. He thought that psychic activity should be defined as the "ideal (spiritual) activity of the material brain" and should be the province of psychologists.[69] The physiologists would study the "material brain" itself, and if they wished to describe its functions as "reflex activity," that seemed perfectly natural to Orlov, who saw the study of reflexes as in the tradition of Sechenov and Pavlov, both physiologists. So the situation in 1962 was paradoxical, and can be sharpened in the following way: Both the aggressive physiologists and the aggressive psychologists denied the premise that reflex activity is the same as psychic activity, but for contrasting reasons. The aggressive physiologists denied it because they thought that reflexes were not a sophisticated enough weapon for their continuing campaign to explain psychic activity on a physiological basis; the aggressive psychologists denied it because they looked upon the field of psychic activity as their own domain and did not wish constantly to have to assure their audiences that ontologically everything they were talking about had a material, reflex base. They were not much cheered that the aggressive physiologists no longer thought all psychic activity had a reflex base since they felt that the intrusion of physiologists belonging to the new cybernetic tradition was no more pleasant a prospect than the intrusion of the physiologists of the old Pavlovian school.

These debates were related to worldwide discussions in physiology and psychology at this time, but they took a different tone and somewhat different path in the Soviet Union because all concerned—physiologists, psychologists, philosophers—could openly call themselves only materialists. Understandably, therefore, the psychologists felt somewhat more insecure than elsewhere. In terms of the theoretical definition of consciousness or of the psyche the biggest difference of opinion was between F. F. Kal'sin and V. V. Orlov. The end of the spectrum toward which Kal'sin's views tended was called by his critics "vulgar materialism." The opposite end, with which Orlov's opinions were associated by those critical of him, was predictably termed "dualism."

The problem of the nature of consciousness was probably the most serious and divisive issue facing Soviet philosophy of science in the 1960s. On other questions—quantum mechanics, relativity physics, genetics, and the rest—coherent and defensible positions had been found, positions that gave viable theoretical statements of the problems at hand, yet allowed room for disagreement and further development of science. The problem over the relative roles of the environment and heredity in human behavior which would become so vexing in the seventies and eighties had not yet clearly emerged. But in the sixties the problem of consciousness seemed intractable. Soviet philosophers could not avoid the problem by calling the question of the definition of consciousness "meaningless" in the fashion of many positivistic non-Soviet scholars; they were committed to the constant improvement of an intellectual scheme that included explanations of the stages of development of all matter, and conscious man was ultimately material in that framework.

A thorough description of the shades of opinion in Soviet writings in the sixties on the nature of the psyche would require a book in itself. Here in broad strokes are some of the more identifiable positions.[70]

A few Soviet authors, such as V. M. Arkhipov and I. G. Eroshkin, continued to affirm that psychic activity itself was material; they identified consciousness with nervous processes.[71] They represented the extreme materialist wing of the authors who published on the subject. Close to them were F. F. Kal'sin, and less outspokenly, N. V. Medvedev, B. M. Kedrov, and A. N. Riakin, who characterized psychic activity and thought as a special form of the movement of matter—a form of movement that is no doubt extremely complex, but nonetheless a movement of matter.[72] The scholars so far named were criticized for leaning toward vulgar materialism by still other Soviet writers, such as M. P. Lebedev.[73] The scholars in Rubinshtein's old circle in the Institute of Philosophy affirmed that psychic activity is both physiological and psychological, and continued to maintain that the term "ideal" is perfectly legitimate when used with reference to epistemology (the "reflected" is ideal; the "reflecting" is material).[74] Still other writers openly denied that the term "material" can be applied to psychic activity at all.[75] And V. V. Orlov, as we have seen, did not hesitate to speak of "the spiritual (dukhovnyi) activity" of the material brain.[76] The position of the professional philosophers closest to the institutional seats of power—particularly those in the Institute of Philosophy—was in the middle. Their earlier compromise was breaking down, but they hesitated to insist on a new formulation in view of the current effort not to intervene in scientific discussions. But for them dialectical materialism continued to be a middle way between, on the one hand, those scholars—particularly the psychologists—who separated psychic activity entirely from its material substratum, and on the other hand, vulgar materialists like the behaviorists and ultracyberneticists, who questioned the very validity of the term "consciousness."

PETER KUZMICH ANOKHIN

One of the most prominent physiologists in the Soviet Union during the past decades was Peter Kuzmich Anokhin (1898–1974). In the 1920s as a student and young lecturer Anokhin worked in the laboratories of Pavlov and Bekhterev and much of his life was devoted to an evaluation and extension of the Pavlovian tradition.[77] He attended physiological congresses abroad and was well known outside the Soviet Union; his biography appeared in such standard references as the *International Who's Who*. After 1955 he was head of the faculty of the First Moscow Medical Institute and after 1966 a full member of the Academy of Sciences of the USSR. His research concerned primarily the central nervous system and embryoneurology.

Anokhin frequently praised dialectical materialism as a philosophy of science. Throughout his career one of his primary motivations, by his own account, was the effort to elaborate a materialist and determinist explanation of nervous activity; he attempted to discover physiological mechanisms underlying forms of human behavior previously described by such indefinite terms as "intention," "choice," "creativity," and "decision making."

In 1962 Anokhin stated:

> The methodology of dialectical materialism is strong precisely because it permits one to rise to a higher level of generalizations and to direct scientific research along more effective routes leading to the most rapid solution of problems.[78]

Anokhin continued that dialectical materialism frequently warns a researcher against falling into interpretations that are ideologically "unacceptable for us." But he also saw a danger in this warning function: It is possible, he observed, to have a science that is philosophically correct but scientifically stagnant. The "enormous motive force hidden in the dialectical materialist methodology" would be fully revealed only if one combined the admonitory function of dialectical materialism with the "logic of scientific progress"—that is, the constant checking, elimination, and confirmation of working hypotheses by experimental facts.[79] Thus, Anokhin hoped for a synthesis of dialectical materialism and rigorous experimental science. There could be no contradiction between the two, he thought, because the principles of dialectical materialism are developed by science. To be sure, dialectical materialism contained the a priori assumptions of materiality and lawfulness, but these were the assumptions of science itself. He commented in 1949, "Nature develops according to the laws of the materialistic dialectic. These laws are an absolutely real phenomenon of the objective world."[80]

In one of his earliest works, published in 1935, Anokhin advanced several of the ideas that were in modified forms to play an important role in his understanding of nervous activity. Future historians of neurophysiology and of cybernetic concepts in physiology will need to turn to this early source to evaluate Anokhin's claims to have anticipated such concepts as "feedback" with his "sanctioning afferentiation." Anokhin of course had no knowledge in 1935 of the mathematical foundation of information theory. Furthermore, discussions of "integrated nervous activity" were common in physiology at this time. Charles Sherrington's seminal *The Integrative Action of the Nervous System* had appeared long before, in 1906. Nonetheless, when a person now reads Anokhin's work of 1935, the vocabulary and the concepts do have a ring similar to that found in the subsequent literature of neurocybernetics. He spoke, for example, of neurophysiology in terms of "functional systems" in which the execution of functions is based largely on the set of incoming signals "that direct and correct" the process.[81]

Throughout his life Anokhin was convinced that a physiologist should be both loyal to the Pavlovian school yet simultaneously critical of it. Always proudly calling himself a student of Pavlov, Anokhin nonetheless questioned some of his teacher's concepts. Even in his most critical moments, however, he stoutly defended the materialist assumptions underlying Pavlovianism. In the period immediately after World War II Anokhin declared that he had made errors in several of his earlier writings in which he had criticized Pavlov's method or pointed to predecessors of Pavlov in certain lines of work. Although it cannot be proved, there is considerable reason to believe that these corrections were in response to the changing political scene after the war, when efforts to establish Russian priority in science and ideological factors became more prominent than earlier. Thus, in 1949 Anokhin commented that in his survey of the history of reflex theory from Descartes to Pavlov, published in 1945, he had given too much attention to eighteenth-century materialists and had thus detracted from Pavlov's eminence.[82] Also in 1949 he corrected a criticism of Pavlov that he had published in 1936; in the 1936 publication he had advanced the opinion that it was not correct to say that Pavlov always studied the "whole organism." This synthetic approach was more true of the early Pavlov, who studied blood circulation and digestive processes, than it was of the later Pavlov examining reflex activity.[83] Anokhin in 1936, therefore, implied that the mature Pavlov was something of a reductionist.

In the late 1940s and early 1950s Anokhin became more orthodox while under the shadow of the criticism advanced against him at the 1950 physiology conference, but in the late fifties and sixties he returned to his earlier innovative, even speculative approach and advanced ideas concerning a new architecture of the reflex arc, the use of cybernetics in neurophysiology, and the reliance on more concepts from psychology (as compared with physiology) than earlier. In this later period he clearly believed that the Pavlovian concept of the reflex arc needed modifying, however much he continued in debt to his teacher. He commented in 1962:

Scientific results and theories should be judged according to whether they correspond with reality. . . . [But] some people completely disregard this elementary critical approach and ask only, 'Does this new thing concur with what Pavlov said?' And if it does not concur, then it is automatically proclaimed to be a 'revision of Pavlov.' On the basis of such comparisons we eliminate all possibility of finding anything new. I am not worrying about whether my interpretation will depart from the interpretation of my teacher Pavlov. This is quite natural; we live in a different epoch.[84]

Despite the slight variations in his viewpoints, Anokhin followed a fairly consistent approach to the Pavlovian tradition throughout his life. This approach can be described as one between two extremes. In his 1949 biography of Pavlov, Anokhin saw dual dangers of opposite nature facing the followers of the great physiologist. On the one hand was the danger that the guiding ideas of Pavlov would be dissipated; on the other was the possibility of turning his teaching into dogma. Anokhin correctly predicted that the greatest danger was that of "canonization."[85]

In 1949, before the physiological congress at which Anokhin was criticized for deviating from Pavlov's principles, Anokhin published a long article surveying what he called "The Main Problems of the Study of Higher Nervous Activity." This article, together with similar surveys published in 1955 and 1963, contains a summary of the work of Anokhin and his school.

Anokhin made it quite clear in 1949 that for twenty years he and his co-workers had attempted to modify the classical method used by Pavlov in studying conditioned reflexes. They had gone beyond Pavlov's reliance on easily observable secretory glands and muscular reflexes to encephalographic investigations of conditioned reactions, to embryophysiological studies of higher nervous activity, and to morphophysiological correlations (studying in a parallel fashion both conditioned reflexes and the architectonic features of the cerebral cortex).[86] On the basis of these new approaches they had concluded that the Pavlovian concept of conditioned reflexes was too simplified, particularly its model of the reflex arc with its three links.

Anokhin believed that the very approach utilized in the classical Pavlovian method blinded researchers to important processes intermediate between the conditioned stimulus and the response. He asked, "Is not the secretory indicator only an organic part of the external expression of the integrated conditioned reaction of the animal, the general form of which took shape long before the stimulation reached the effector mechanisms of the salivary gland?"[87] In other words, Anokhin was turning attention to the internal nervous structure of the conditioned reflex and implying that it was far more complex than Pavlov had indicated.

In the course of his endeavors to explain nervous activity on the basis of material physiological systems Anokhin utilized several terms that have come to be closely linked to his name. These included "return afferentiation"; "sanctioning afferentiation"; "acceptor of action"; and "anticipatory reflection." In the fifties and sixties Anokhin usually dropped the phrase "sanctioning afferentiation," first used by him in 1935, but still retained "return afferentiation" (obratnaia afferentatsiia) and "acceptor of action" (aktseptor deistviia). "Anticipatory reflection" (operezhaiushchee otrazhenie) was a development in the last part of his life. Each of these phrases described a part of conditioned reflex activity, which Anokhin considered to be characteristic of all organisms of the globe, a means of "entering into temporary adaptive relations with the surrounding world."

Those physiologists who followed the views of Descartes, Anokhin continued, believed that reflex activity is adaptive or goal-directed from the very beginning of the process. Consequently, they concentrated on discovering already prepared reflex responses. But with Pavlov's discovery of conditioned reflexes and the phenomenon of "reinforcement," it became clear that a creative, adjusting process lies at the base of reflex activity. The inadequacy of classical reflex theory became even more clear as a result of experiments in which reflex functions were at first eliminated by vivisection, then restored by compensation. It was through such experiments that Anokhin approached these problems for the first time.

Anokhin soon came to the view that the organism could not begin the process of compensation without signals from the periphery telling of the presence of a defect. But the question still arises, How does the organism "know" that compensation is needed? Anokhin maintained that without what he called "return afferentiation" an answer to this question could not be attempted. By this term he meant "the constant correction of the process of compensation from the periphery."[88] Schematically he represented return afferentiation in the following way:[89]

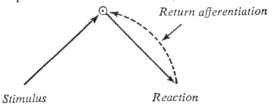

Stimulus   Reaction

Anokhin considered this return link in the reflex arc to be intrinsic to reflex activity: "It is difficult to imagine any kind of reflex act of an intact animal that would end with only the effector link of the 'reflex arc,' as is called for in the traditional Cartesian scheme" (p. 22). Every act is, instead, accompanied by an entire integral of afferentiations, greatly varied in terms of strength, localization, time of origin, and speed of transmission. These afferentiations are visual details; temperature, aural, and olfactory sensations; and kinesthetic sensations. The total variety of combinations is infinite. Together they make up one process: "In the presence of constant return afferentiation accompanying, like an echo, every reflex act, all the natural behavioral acts of an intact animal may arise, cease, and be transformed into other acts, making up as a whole an organized chain of effective adaptations to surrounding conditions" (p. 22).

As a simplified schematic diagram, Anokhin would represent this "organized chain" in the following way (p. 25):

In this chain, return afferentiation serves as an "additional or fourth link of the reflex." (Anokhin was sharply disputed on this point, whether a fourth link is a necessary and legitimate addition to Pavlovian teaching.) In the final step, the desired result has been obtained, so there is no further effector action. If the process is one of compensation for a previously destroyed function (for example, by brainslicing), the desired compensation has occurred in the final step. If the process is a more normal one, such as simply picking a glass off the table, that particular goal has also been attained in the final step.

Anokhin guarded against his conception being understood simply as the belief that "the end of one action is the beginning of the next." Such an incorrect understanding of what Anokhin was describing would result in a different diagram, one that Anokhin rejected (p. 25):

Anokhin meant, instead, that the end of one action is a source of return afferentiation that is transmitted to the nervous center where it is processed before it serves as the cause of a new action. It is in this central point that the "decision" as to whether the desired result has yet been obtained is made. This mechanism was called by Anokhin the "acceptor of action" and deserves a special treatment. It is the acceptor of action that controls the whole process.

In his discussion of the acceptor of action Anokhin made an attempt to study intention and will from a physiological and deterministic standpoint. He initially asked, "How does the organism know when it has reached its goal?" And he replied, "If we stand on a strictly deterministic position, then essentially all the neurophysiological material that we have in our arsenal fails to give us an answer to this question. For the fact of the matter is that for the central nervous system of an animal, all return afferentiations, including sanctioning (that which corresponds to the desired goal) afferentiation, are only complexes of afferent impulses; from the normal point of view of causation there is no obvious reason why one of these stimulates the central nervous system to the further mobilization of reflexive, adaptive acts and another, on the contrary, halts adaptive actions (p. 26).

There is only one way out, thought Anokhin, and that is the view that there exists in the organism some sort of prepared pattern of nervous impulses with which return afferentiation can be compared. This pattern had to exist before the reflex act itself occurred. If the afferent information coincides with the prepared pattern, then the desired goal has been reached. If it does not, then further effector action is necessary. The whole question then becomes, of course, What is the physiological mechanism containing this pattern, and how was the pattern originally produced?

In order to explain the way in which Anokhin attacked this problem, it is necessary to review several features of classical Pavlovian reflex theory, particularly the relationship between a conditioned reflex stimulation and an unconditioned one. It will be remembered that Pavlov believed that every conditioned reflex is formed on the basis of an unconditioned one. Thus, an unconditioned stimulus—such as food in the mouth—will automatically cause the flow of saliva on the first or nearly first occasion, evoking strong activity in the brain. Such an unconditioned stimulus is usually also accompanied by other stimuli that may become conditioned through training—visual or olfactory sensations and so on. A "temporary" connection is formed between these points, and one can, after a little training, henceforth stimulate the secretory or motor centers of the brain merely by the conditioned stimulus.[90] However, this temporary connection will not be maintained unless it is periodically reinforced by stimulation of the unconditioned center. That is, in the classic experiment saliva will not flow on the strength of the bell signal alone unless periodically it is followed by the presence of food in the mouth of the dog and the stimulation of the unconditioned salivary reflex on which the conditioned reflexes are based.

Anokhin now incorporated his return afferentiation into this scheme. He believed that every conditioned stimulation is sent through the sense organs to the center of the brain that *in the past* had been stimulated many times by the unconditioned stimulus, and that *shortly afterward* the center will again be stimulated by the unconditioned stimulus. Therefore, there arises the possibility of a "matching" or "mismatching" of the *representation* of an unconditioned response that the conditioned stimulus evokes and the actual conditioned response itself, following in a short period of time. Schematically this is represented as follows (p. 30):

Three successive stages in the development of a conditioned reflex

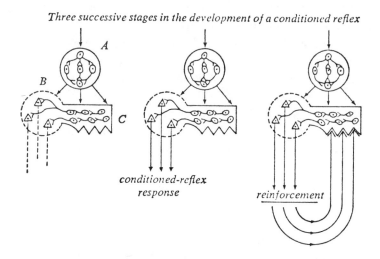

conditioned-reflex
response

reinforcement

In stage one the conditioned stimulus falls upon the appropriate sense organ. In stage two it causes a conditioned reflex response based on a "representation" of an unconditioned reflex, a step that has occurred frequently in the past, but has not yet occurred in this sequence. In stage three, the unconditioned stimulus itself (food in the mouth, for instance) has occurred; the unconditioned response turns out to "match" the conditioned representation of it, and reinforcement occurs.

Anokhin now pushed farther in order to ascertain how powerful the "matching" or "controlling" mechanism was. He found that it was very powerful indeed, as one of his experiments illustrated. He conditioned a dog to go to a feeding box on the left side of a training box in response to the sound "la," and to a feeding box on the right side in response to the sound "fa." In all cases the food was sugared bread. The dog soon became thoroughly conditioned and would immediately go to the correct side. On one day (and only for one time) he introduced a change, however. He placed not bread but meat in the box on the left side and gave the appropriate signal. The dog went to the left box as was its custom, but was obviously surprised to find meat instead of bread there. It demonstrated what animal psychologists call an "orienting research reaction," but after this moment's hesitation, devoured the meat.

From this point onward, and for twenty days thereafter, the dog's actions were governed by this one event. No matter whether the sound "fa" or "la" was sounded the dog would always bound to the left box. The experimenters continued to run the experiment as if the exception had never occurred, using sugared bread for food, and placing it in a box on the left side if the signal "la" was to be used and on the right if "fa" was to follow. Yet the dog long persisted in disregarding its old conditioning and searching only the left box for meat. If it found bread there (which it always did if the signal had been "la"), it refused to eat. Only after a long period of total lack of reinforcement was the old pattern restored, so strong an impression had the one occasion made (p. 32).

Anokhin believed that this experiment provided further evidence for the presence in the nervous system of a mechanism called the acceptor of action, which is based on very strong, inherited unconditioned reflexes that, in turn, can be linked to conditioned stimuli. In the case of the dog, the unconditioned reflex was the food reflex of carnivorous animals. Anokhin observed that "the acceptor of action" was an abbreviated term for the more accurate but cumbersome phrase "the acceptor of the afferent results of a completed reflex act." The word "acceptor" was a key term conveying both the ideas "to receive" and "to approve" that are contained in the Latin *acceptare* (p. 43).

According to this scheme, if the nervous system of an animal is acted upon by a conditioned stimulus that has in the past been reinforced by meat, then the acceptor of action will define to what degree the received information corresponds to the earlier afferent experience of the animal. Anokhin represented schematically two cases: the one in which the match is correct and strong reinforcement occurs; the other in which there is a mismatch between the conditioned and the unconditioned stimuli (p. 43).

Anokhin believed that this approach could help in an understanding of the way in which the nervous system repairs itself after it has been damaged. Let us imagine a form of reflex activity that was schematically

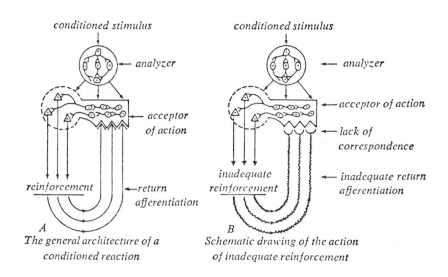

A
The general architecture of a
conditioned reaction

B
Schematic drawing of the action
of inadequate reinforcement

represented by stage A in the drawing, but was destroyed by the existence of some defect caused by surgery or disease. Anokhin would show in the subsequent stages the way in which the components of the appropriate nervous subsystem rearrange themselves until they arrive at an arrangement that yields the proper reinforcement as determined by the afferent signals of the past history of the organism. This reorganization effort is graphically represented by drawing the subsystem in radically different shapes, one after the other, until a proper arrangement is found, shown in the last stage (p. 37):

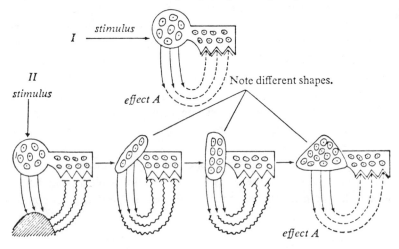

Consecutive stages of compensatory adaptation

Thus, Anokhin with his acceptor of action was trying to arrive at a physiological explanation for the goal-oriented activity of the nervous system. To be sure, he had not solved the problem of teleology, which has plagued biology throughout its history. On a rather speculative basis he had pushed the boundaries of the riddle back a little farther. Furthermore, despite his effort to identify physiological mechanisms, he had made no effort to localize the acceptor of action in the body itself. Accepting his arguments for a moment, however, one could now give something of an answer to the question, How does the organism know when it has reached its goal? He illustrated that the problems of intention and goal-seeking are amenable to physiological investigation, even if many problems remained. Many neurophysiologists of his time were beginning to think in similar terms. His concepts of reinforcement and acceptor of action bore some resemblances to much earlier research, such as Lynn Thorndike's and Lloyd Morgan's law of effect. Thorndike had shown that when he placed animals in labyrinth pens, there occurred a curious causal phenomenon that some people incorrectly described as retroactive. It appeared that when the animal made a correct movement toward its eventual escape, it learned to repeat that movement in a similar situation later even though the success always occurred after the movement. Thorndike believed that the success, as an affect of the movement, "stamped in" the movement that had been the cause of it.[91] Anokhin acknowledged the similarity of Thornkike's law of effect to his own viewpoint, but pointed out that

Thorndike was not so interested as he in the physiological mechanisms behind the phenomenon. Thorndike identified success with pleasure or satisfaction and described the law of effect primarily in psychological or subjective terms. Anokhin attempted to describe reinforcement and goal seeking in terms of physiology: the relationship between conditioned and unconditioned stimuli, and the means by which past experience could provide a pattern contained in the acceptor of action, against which further afferent information could be checked.

ALEKSEI NIKOLAEVICH LEONT'EV (1903–1979)

Aleksei Nikolaevich Leont'ev (Leontiev) was one of the Soviet Union's foremost psychologists, with an enormous influence among educational psychologists. He was born in Moscow in 1903 and educated at Moscow University shortly after the Bolshevik Revolution. At that time he acquired a taste for Marxism that remained one of his most visible characteristics. In 1941 he became a professor of Moscow University and four years later head of the Department of Psychology of the University, succeeding one of his influential mentors, Sergei Leonidovich Rubinshtein, whose views are discussed on pp. 176ff. Leont'ev became a full member of the Academy of Pedagogical Sciences of the Russian Republic in 1950 and of the All-Union Academy of Pedagogical Sciences in 1968. During his long life Leont'ev received many honors, including an honorary degree from the University of Paris in 1968 and a Lenin Prize in 1963 for his book *Problems of the Development of the Psyche*. After the publication in 1978 in the United States of an English translation of his book *Activity, Consciousness, and Personality* Leont'ev's approach to psychology became rather well known in the West.[92]

Of all eminent Soviet psychologists of the post-Stalin period Leont'ev was one of the most ideologically militant. Many of his publications included biting criticisms of Western psychologists, especially behaviorists, supporters of Gestalt psychology, and followers of Freudian psychoanalysis. In American psychology in particular, Leont'ev castigated "factologism and scientism," which, he said, "have become a barrier blocking the road to investigating the principal psychological problems" (p. 1). According to Leont'ev, "Karl Marx laid the foundation for a concrete psychological theory of consciousness that opened completely new perspectives for psychological science" (p. 14). In another spot he continued, "Of particularly great significance is the teaching of

Marx about those changes in consciousness that it undergoes during the development of division of work in society, a separation of the majority of producers from the means of production, and an isolation of theoretical activity from practical activity" (p. 19). And, finally, writing in 1975, at a time when ideological enthusiasm had diminished in many areas of Soviet science, Leont'ev maintained:

> Soviet scientists countered methodological pluralism with a unified Marx-ist-Leninist methodology that allowed a penetration into the real nature of the psyche, the consciousness of man. . . . We all understood that Marxist psychology is not just a different direction or school but a new historical stage presenting in itself the beginnings of an authentically scientific, consistently materialistic psychology. (p. 2)

In order to understand psychology from a Marxist standpoint, Leont'ev believed that the psychologist must emphasize three elements: an historical approach to human psychology that traces out the social context of the subject; a concrete psychological science in which "consciousness" is recognized as a higher form of the Leninist "reflection of reality"; and the study of social activity and its structure. He quoted from Marx's theses on Feuerbach to the effect that "the chief defect of all hitherto existing materialism (that of Feuerbach included) is that the thing, reality, sensuousness, is concerned only in the form of the *object or of contemplation*, but not of *sensous human activity, practice*" (p. 11).

The concept for which Leont'ev is best known is "activity." To him social activity was the mediating influence forming the human personality. In developing this concept he pointed out not only the significance of "labor" in Marxist political literature, but also the importance of any kind of social activity. Labor was the most significant type of social activity, but not the only type. And here Leont'ev drew on the writings of a prerevolutionary Russian psychologist named N. N. Lange. Lange in 1912 had asked the simple question, "Why does a child treat a doll as if it were a living human being?" Many psychologists believed the answer to be based on the fact a doll looks like a human baby. Lange, on the contrary, said that the resemblance of the doll to a baby was secondary, that the important fact was "how the child played with the doll," how the child was "active" with the doll. Lange pointed out that when children are enthusiastically playing, a simple stick can easily become a horse, and a pea can serve well as a man. What really counts is not the appearance of the object perceived by the child, but the social relationship that the child establishes with that object.[93] The child is imitating the activity, the practice, that he or she has seen among adults. Thus, remarked Leont'ev, "behind perception there lies, as if rolled up, practice" (p. 22). Starting out with this concept Leont'ev built his scheme of activity-based social psychology. He had only scorn for behaviorists, who, he said, grounded their views on a simple, mechanical model of "stimulus and response." On the contrary, said Leont'ev, "in order to explain scientifically the appearance and features of a subjective, sensual image, it is not enough to study the structure and work of sensory organs on the one hand, and the physical nature of the effect an object has on them on the other. It is necessary also to penetrate into the activity of the subject that mediates his ties with the objective world" (p. 20).

Leont'ev illustrated the importance of previous "activity" or practice in explaining the results of pseudoscopic experiments in which subjects look through special binoculars which produce a distortion of perception: the closer points of the object seem farther away and vice versa. Psychologists have found that subjects accept the reverse pseudoscopic image only when it is plausible, i.e., when the object being viewed is either unfamiliar or conceivable as a reverse image (i.e., a concave image being seen as a convex one). If the object is familiar, such as the face of person known to the subject, then the subject psychologically reorients the image and sees it correctly despite the distorting effect of the binoculars. Such experiments were to Leont'ev evidence for the necessity of the inclusion of prior knowledge stemming from past social activity as a part of cognition (p. 40).

Because of his emphasis on social activity as a formative influence in human behavior, Leont'ev denied the existence of an "innate human personality." A baby at birth does not yet have a personality, he believed; it was only an "individual," not a "personality." Personalities are not born, he believed, they "become." Even a two-year-old child does not have much of a personality, according to Leont'ev. Only after a long period of social interaction does the child have a true personality.

Leont'ev was critical of psychologists who attempt to explain human behavior in terms of innate human needs, such as sex or hunger. "Personality cannot develop within the framework of need; its development necessarily presupposes a displacement of needs by creation, which alone does not know limits" (p. 137). In the developed human personality, animal needs are "transformed" into something entirely different. And here Leont'ev gave one of his most graphic descriptions, discussing "hunger":

Hunger is hunger, but hunger which is appeased by cooked meat eaten with a knife and fork is a different hunger from that in which raw meat is eaten with the hands, nails, and teeth.

Positivist thought, of course, sees nothing more in this than a superficial difference. After all, a starving man is a sufficient example to disclose "deep" commonality of need of food in man and in animal. But this is nothing more than a sophism. For a starving man, food in reality stops existing in its human form and correspondingly the need for food is "dehumanized"; but if this shows anything, then it is only that man can be reduced by starvation to an animal condition, and it says exactly nothing about the nature of his human needs. (p. 118)

Leont'ev was very critical of intelligence tests, especially the IQ tests that were common in the West. Indeed, Leont'ev's attitude toward these tests is one of the reasons that general intelligence tests are still not used in the Soviet Union, only examinations of disciplinary knowledge. The concept of innate intelligence was as alien to him as that of innate, unchanging human needs. He emphasized the transformational possibilities for human beings in the right environment. It is obvious how well Leont'ev's views fitted with the regime's desire to create a "New Soviet Man." Human beings in a fully developed communist society would have different needs and different and superior capabilities from those in earlier, more primitive societies.

In the seventies and the early eighties Leont'ev's theories came under increasing attack in the Soviet Union. Many of the younger Soviet psychologists associated him with Marxist dogmatism and even Stalinism. As discussed on pp. 224ff., a new school of "differential psychologists" headed by B. M. Teplov and V. D. Nebylitsin began to identify innate differences in personality types, as well as innate abilities in areas like mathematics. Other psychologists began to suspect that certain personality types, such as that of the criminal, may be influenced by genetics, a view that Leont'ev heatedly opposed. Leont'ev's interpretations of psychology became major issues in the new debates over "nature versus nurture" and human biology that raged in Soviet journals in psychology, pedagogy, and philosophy in the late seventies and eighties. These debates are the subject of chapters 6 and 7.

SOVIET FREUDIANISM

Soviet psychologists have seriously underestimated the influence of the subconscious on mental activity. Freudianism, after a period of popularity in the Soviet Union in the twenties, became a prohibited subject. In the sixties Soviet psychologists began to recognize their inadequacies in this area, although they by no means became enthusiastic about psychoanalysis. A concern among many Soviet psychologists, if one judges by the literature, has been the fear that they have surrendered to Freudianism the whole realm of the subconscious; they have wanted to make it clear that this is not so, or at least should not be so. Consequently, there have been a number of efforts in the Soviet literature to show that Freud was by no means the first person to point to the importance of the subconscious realm.[94] This attempt was, no doubt, an attempt to relativize Freud, to make possible a turning of real attention to the phenomena usually associated with the name of Freud without appearing to embrace Freudianism after years of denying its legitimacy. They have criticized the "monopoly" of Freudianism abroad, particularly in the United States (and perhaps with good reason). They have engaged in rather detailed and controversial semantic discussions of the relative validities of the terms "nonconscious" (*neosoznavaemyi*), "unconscious" (*bessoznatel'nyi*), and "subconscious" (*podsoznatel'nyi*), with several scholars preferring "nonconscious" to the other two terms, which they saw as closer to Freudianism.[95] But on the whole, they have been moving more and more toward a recognition of Freud. A. M. Sviadoshch, of the Medical Institute in Karaganda, commented in 1962 to an audience of psychologists, physiologists, and philosophers:

> Without any question S. Freud performed a service for science. He attracted attention to the problem of the "unconscious." He pointed to several concrete manifestations of the "unconscious," such as its influence on slips of the pen or of the tongue. However, he also introduced much that was improbable or fantastic to the subject of the "unconscious," such as his assertion of the sexuality of the small child. He created a mistaken psychoanalytic theory, which we deny.[96]

The work of the Georgian psychologist D. N. Uznadze (1886–1950) was often cited as a Soviet alternative to Freud, although it was also criticized in the Soviet Union as ideologically suspect.[97] After about 1960 it became less sensitive. F. V. Bassin promoted Uznadze's theory of "set" (*ustanovka*) as a basis for building a general theory of nonconscious nervous activity that he considered superior on methodological grounds to that of Freud.

Uznadze worked on his conception from the early twenties, when Freudianism attracted many Soviet thinkers, until his death. His work has been continued, in particular, by the Institute of Psychology of the Georgian Academy of Sciences. Uznadze, in his classical experiments, asked a subject to compare the size of two small balls by the sense of touch, one ball being placed in each of his hands. At first, during a long series of tests, the balls (of equal weight) were always of different volume, and the smaller ball was always placed in the same hand. Then the subject was given balls of the same volume (and weight). In reply to the question "Which ball is the larger?" the subject answered that the larger ball was in the hand that always before received the smaller ball. Uznadze explained this illusion in terms of the "internal state" of the subject. On the basis of simple experiments such as this he built a rather elaborate theory of "set," in which the set is formed by past experience.

Several of Uznadze's defenders in the Soviet Union differed with him on the details of the set theory. Uznadze thought the set remained nonconscious, or at least he was interested in it only when it was. Bassin, on the contrary, thought that much of the merit of Uznadze's approach consisted in the fact that it explained nonconscious factors in terms of a "functional displacement" and thus opened up this realm to objective experiment. Bassin commented, "The nonconscious set fulfills the role, in this way, of an invisible 'bridge' between definite forms of realized experience and objective behavior, a bridge that, according to Freud, must be fulfilled by the subject's 'unconscious.' "[98]

Even in the sixties, however, Uznadze's views met criticisms linked with older Soviet attitudes. I. I. Korotkin, of the Pavlov Physiological Institute, maintained that the set had to be interpreted either as an epiphenomenon—and therefore was unacceptable in science—or as a material phenomenon, which would then differ little, he thought, from the dynamic stereotype of the Pavlovian school.[99] And M. S. Lebedinskii, from the Institute of Psychiatry of the Academy of Medical Sciences, commented that presenting Uznadze as an alternative to Freud was an unsuccessful attempt, since a Freudian analyst would have no trouble accepting Uznadze's views and still remaining a loyal Freudian.[100]

SOVIET SCHOOLS OF PSYCHOLOGY

Soviet psychologists in the seventies and eighties tended to split into three different channels: (1) An old Marxist Vygotsky-Luria-Leont'ev school emphasizing social and environmental influences in human behavior; this school was still dominant, but diminishing in strength as its most prominent leaders died off. One of its most active offshoots recently has been the "engineering psychology" studies promoted by the director of the Institute of Psychology of the Academy of Sciences, B. F. Lomov.[101] These efforts are aimed at the adaptationist goal of improving the productivity of Soviet workers through the use of psychotechnology. Although the old Soviet goal of creating a "new Soviet man" by changing the environment is still central to this school, its leaders have increasingly turned to Western ideas about psychotechnology. (2) A new "hard-headed" behavioral genetics school that revived the whole "nature-nurture" debate and which opposed the traditional Marxist nurturist views of the first school with an emphasis on genetics and innate patterns of behavior. (3) A new set of interests in "fringe sciences" such as biofeedback, EST, human potential, yoga, herbal medicine, and even spiritualism. The last two schools, (2) and (3), were definitely unorthodox to Stalinists and ideological conservatives, but nonetheless had some support in high places.

The first school has been described already in this book on pp. 168–173, 184–191, and 211–214. Although under increasing criticism, it still enjoyed widespread support, as evidenced by a discussion of psychology in 1985 organized by the editor of *Problems of Philosophy*.[102] The second school is described in the following two chapters. In the immediately following pages in the present chapter I will give a brief description of the third school. For appreciation of the significance of this school of thought I am indebted to Sheila Cole, an American writer on Soviet psychology who in the Soviet Union visited several of the "family clubs" that are at the heart of the human potential movement.[103]

In recent years the most surprising development in Soviet psychology has been the growth of "the human potential movement," based in large part on similar trends in the West. At first the established Soviet psychologists opposed the movement, seeing it as "unscientific." Quite a bit of this opposition still exists, but the movement picked up so much strength in the late seventies and early eighties that even some of the established psychologists began to look upon it more charitably. However, the main support for the human potential movement in the Soviet Union continues to be among educated and politically influential people outside the community of professional academic psychologists.

In the Soviet Union the most prominent exponent of the human potential movement has been Boris Pavlovich Nikitin and his wife Lena Alekseevna, whose books on how to raise children have sold over two million copies.[104] Boris Nikitin was educated as an engineer and many of his followers can be found among members of the Soviet technical intelligentsia, people looking for personal and family ties that will make up for their lack of meaningful contacts in official and institutional bureaucracies. Nikitin has encouraged the formation of "family clubs" in which close and nurturing social relations can develop. The members of the clubs concentrate on the tasks of rearing their children in a much less authoritarian environment than official theorists of pedagogy and family relations have recommended. The basic theory underlying Nikitin's recommendations is that every child has a potential which under the right conditions will spontaneously blossom forth. The trick is "to free natural human potential." This potential expresses itself in different forms at different moments in the child's development; if the right conditions for development do not exist at the right moment, the potential may be lost forever.

Members of the family clubs differ greatly in the exact form that their activities take. They meet frequently, build playground equipment according to the Nikitins' specifications, and engage in group play and work. Restoration of old peasant houses in the countryside is a favorite activity. Some of the members are vegetarians, and some abstain from all forms of alcohol, quite unusual in the Soviet Union. The members differ in their interests, but most of these interests have a nonestablishment character: home birth, herbal medicine, bioenergy, biofeedback, yoga, acupuncture, faith healing, T'ai Chi, EST, meditation, massage of various types, rolfing, hypnosis, encounter groups, shamanistic healing, psychodrama, even the building of hot tubs.

A connection exists between the Soviet human potential movement and the American one, specifically through the Esalen Institute in California. A Soviet citizen, Joseph Goldin, became a member of the governing board of the Esalen Institute. The Esalen Institute established a Soviet-American exchange program based on the common interest in the USSR and the United States in the human potential movement. The head of the exchange program was James Hickman, who visited the Soviet Union many times and sponsored sessions there on "biofeedback and human potential," sometimes held in the residence of the American ambassador to the Soviet Union.[105] In return, a number of prominent Soviet officials and intellectuals visited Esalen for conversations on similar subjects. The Soviet embassy in Washington lent its support to the movement, and several Soviet newspapers, especially *Komsomolskaia Pravda*, described it in positive tones.

Sheila Cole asked the question that must occur to every knowledgeable Western observer of Soviet intellectual trends: "Why were the people in charge of the Soviet Union interested in Americans who are known in the United States for the extremes to which they have taken self-involvement?"

From the standpoint of official Soviet ideology, the human potential movement has both positive and negative aspects. The negative features include the following: the movement has no explicit Marxist foundation, and represents an autonomous social and intellectual development, something always regarded suspiciously by Soviet authorities; furthermore, the movement harbors many unscientific and antiauthoritarian attitudes traditionally criticized by the Soviet establishment.

Despite these disadvantages, from the standpoint of Soviet authorities the human potential movement fosters many attitudes valued by the authorities, such as expanded labor productivity, positive feelings about work and play, large families (at a time of declining birth rates), and close family ties (at a time of rising divorce rates).

Expansion of productivity alone might justify the human potential movement in official Soviet eyes. Anyone who reads Soviet newspapers knows that one of the favorite phrases is "hidden reserves," a phrase indicating that labor productivity can be expanded if individuals learn to draw upon hidden capacities at work more efficiently and more contentedly. The human potential movement in the West speaks of "transforming the human personality by a process of self-learning and self-development." This vocabulary is not very far from the traditional Soviet aspiration to create the "new Soviet man" by social transformation. Therefore, the Western human potential movement and the Soviet family clubs share the belief that individual initiative can be released by actions that do not challenge the existing political and economic structure but instead concentrate on personal transformation. This ideology appeals to any power structure.

CHAPTER **6**

THE NATURE-NURTURE DEBATE

Prospero (concerning Caliban)
A devil, a born devil, on whose nature
Nurture can never stick: on whom my pains
Humanely taken, all, all lost, quite lost!

The Tempest 4.1.188–90

In recent years an extensive controversy has been occurring in the
Soviet Union over the relative weight of "nature" and "nurture" in
human development, phrased in terms of "the relationship of the
biological to the social." It is a debate that has raged in a great variety
of publications and on many levels of Soviet society, from the specialized
journals of the biologists, psychologists, jurists, philosophers, medical
specialists and educators, to the popular and literary press, to the political
journals of the Communist Party; furthermore, it has reached from
dissident writers on both the political right and the political left and
their *samizdat* publications on up through much of the academic establishment and in 1983 included even an official pronouncement on
the subject by the head of the Soviet state and party apparatus.

In some respects the Soviet debate parallels and resembles recent
discussions on the same subject in the West—where behavioral genetics,
genetic engineering, sociobiology, IQ and race, and the relationship of
genetics to violence have all also been topics of controversy—but in
the Soviet Union the disputes are seen as fundamentally important to
Marxism, both as an intellectual viewpoint and as the official ideology
of the state. Indeed, at their most strained moments the Soviet dis-
putations over nature and nurture touch closely on the question of the
ruling ideology of society, with the old official views (the supremacy
of nurture, Marxism, ethnic equality, the gradual disappearance of crime)
under attack, and new views (genetic determinism, philosophical idealism, elitism, ethnic superiority) crowding in. The Soviet debates over
nature and nurture have become a part of the current crisis in ideology
in the Soviet Union, with old views waning in strength but new views
too frightening or uncertain to provide an acceptable alternative for the
political leaders.

Western observers do not need to be Marxists to realize that this controversy goes not only to the ideological soul of the Soviet Union but to their concerns as well; Westerners reject the notion that political leaders should be able to determine the outcome of discussions of such subjects, but they usually realize that the conclusions that the scientists draw on these topics have enormous political and social implications for all societies. Indeed, one of the noteworthy aspects of the recent Soviet debate is that Western liberals who study it will often find that while they differ with the ways in which the Soviet dialectical materialists believe that intellectual issues should be resolved, they are likely to sympathize with some of the Soviet Marxist viewpoints because of their own sentiments in favor of an egalitarian and democratic society.

THE BACKGROUND OF THE DEBATES

It is ironic that at the time that most non-Soviet observers assumed that concerns about human beings lay at the heart of Soviet debates about genetics (during the heyday of Lysenkoism, from roughly 1948 to 1965) these concerns were not expressed in Soviet publications; however, in recent years (when Westerners have thought that Soviet worries about genetics have disappeared) a full debate over the relationship of Marxism to human genetics has been occurring.

As discussed in chapter 4, Trofim Lysenko, the autocrat of Soviet genetics in the forties and fifties, did not base his arguments on the relevance of genetics to human beings.[1] Controversies about Lysenkoism in the Soviet Union centered on agricultural crops and animals, not humans. Lysenko emphasized improving agriculture, and concealed his failures in that area behind a great screen of grandiose claims, lack of control groups, inadequate documentation, and support from high political quarters (see pp. 104–150).

The silence of the Lysenkoites on human genetics does not mean, however, that the subject was ideologically unimportant. Indeed, the studied avoidance of the topic was an illustration of its social and political significance; human genetics as a subject of study was banned in the Soviet Union from the early thirties until even after Lysenko's fall in 1965, making a recovery only in the early seventies. The attempt to explain human behavior in terms of innate characteristics or genetics was considered illegitimate from the end of the twenties, when the short-lived Russian eugenics movement, which had included both Marxists and non-Marxists in its membership, ended under heavy pressure from the political authorities.[2] Even before this time, the subject of nature versus nurture was seen by Soviet officials as politically sensitive. Nikolai Semashko, Commissar of Public Health from 1918 to 1930, wrote: "The resolution of the problem of the mutual relationship of biological and social factors in modern medicine is the litmus paper test which defines a Marxist or a bourgeois approach to medical problems."[3] By the 1930s the emphasis that Nazi ideologists were placing on eugenic measures and racial differences meant that no Soviet writer could speak of human genetics without arousing suspicions about his or her political trustworthiness.

The formation of the New Soviet Man was a goal that, during the Stalin and Lysenko periods, was assigned to the psychologists, political leaders, and educators, not to geneticists. The prevailing viewpoint was a "nurture" doctrine, usually combined with Pavlovian teachings about conditioned reflexes. The doctrine was not uniform, since there were Pavlovians and anti-Pavlovians, as well as representatives of other trends, but all the major writers on psychology and education until the late sixties emphasized their ability to mold the personalities and talents of children by constructing a suitable social environment. Pavlovian doctrines were particularly influential in the forties and fifties, but before 1936 and after 1956 the "Vygotsky school" was also strong. L. S. Vygotsky and his renowned pupils A. R. Luria and A. N. Leont'ev (see pp. 184ff.) each had his own research emphases and terminological innovations, but all of them agreed that the social environment is the most important influence on the formation of the human psyche, and all of them connected this principle with Marxism. Vygotsky emphasized that a Marxist approach to psychology centered on the "external" or "social" origins of language and higher thought.[4] Luria wrote that in the study of psychological phenomena "the social and class factors that underlie them must be brought to light."[5] Leont'ev, whose theory of the importance of social "activity" became the dominant psychological viewpoint in the seventies, wrote, "Consciousness from the very beginning is a social product."[6] All believed that the traits and characteristics of the human personality should be explained within a social framework.

By the late sixties this agreement in the Soviet Union on the sources of human conduct was beginning to break up. The reasons for this change are multiple and complex. First of all, Soviet intellectual life was stirring at this time in all areas, after years of Stalinist orthodoxy.

Second, the end of Lysenkoism meant that the general subject of genetics was no longer as ideologically dangerous as it had been earlier; the rebirth of genetics in the study of plants and animals made the question of its significance for human beings seem more and more relevant. Third, in psychology worldwide the significance of physiology, innate structures, and genetics was steadily and impressively growing. By this time, hundreds of human genetic diseases were known, many of them linked to identifiable and specific genetic abnormalities; furthermore, in psychology and linguistics, the theory of the mind as a "blank slate" at birth was losing ground under attack from many directions, including Noam Chomsky's theories about innate readiness for language acquisition in children and findings on the importance of the limbic system for human behavior. The rapidly expanding research evidence in fields such as psychopharmacology and psychoneurology illustrated ever more clearly that mental activity cannot be explained without reference to chemistry, biology, and physiology. The role of inherited brain structure attracted the attention of neurophysiologists. The possibility of artificial intelligence in computers drew attention to mechanistic, inbuilt principles of order and structure, not social environments. And, lastly, many of the social consequences predicted by Soviet Marxist "nurture" theories did not seem to be coming to pass in the Soviet Union. Was there something wrong with the theories? Crime, originally defined by Soviet Marxists as a vestige of capitalism, had not disappeared fifty years after the Revolution, and showed no signs of waning. Alcoholism, prostitution, and social deviance had similarly been scheduled to wither under the influence of proper education and political guidance, but they had turned out to be strikingly persistent, perhaps even growing. (In the absence of Soviet statistics on social deviance, it is impossible for Western observers to determine accurately trends in this area). Faced with all these developments, Soviet psychologists, legal experts, public health specialists, and geneticists began looking around for alternative explanations for the problems that faced them.

The origins of the debate can be found in individual Soviet scholarly dissertations and professional journals. These were places where viewpoints not strictly consistent with orthodox philosophical positions could appear without attracting much attention. Over ten years passed before the scholarly research into previously forbidden questions came to the notice of the public press.

Psychologists were among the first to approach these questions. In 1961 B. M. Teplov published a book entitled *Problems of Individual*

Differences, and, a year later, another entitled *Typological Properties of the Nervous System and Their Significance for Psychology.*[7] These works marked the beginning of a school in Soviet psychology that emphasized different types of mental processes in different people. Teplov's student V. D. Nebylitsin continued this work, becoming the editor of an important series of volumes entitled *Typological Peculiarities of Man's Higher Nervous Activity.* In 1969 Nebylitsin dropped the cumbersome Pavlovian terminology and renamed his series *Problems of Differential Psychophysiology.*[8] One of the members of this school, I. V. Ravich-Shcherbo, concluded that the majority of the individual differences in mental activities that she was studying was genetically determined.[9] At about the same time another researcher, V. A. Krutetskii, concluded that the ability to do well in mathematics is a hereditary gift: "Some people possess inborn characteristics of structure and functional peculiarities of the brain which are extremely favorable (or, to the contrary, very unfavorable) for the development of mathematical abilities."[10]

All this research was considered innovative and mildly subversive by Soviet educational psychologists because it undermined the long-standing commitment of the Soviet educational establishment to its ability to mold talents and personalities without regard to innate differences. But at this stage, the research did not cause much of a stir. Its ability to cause trouble is revealed, however, if we skip ahead for a moment to 1976, when the minister of education of the USSR, M. A. Prokof'ev, finally noticed what some of his researchers were doing, and announced that Soviet education had already illustrated

> the anti-scientific character of ideas about the presence of some kind of inherited limitations to the development of human intelligence—ideas which are seized upon as weapons by bourgeois society in its effort to create support for an educational policy for the benefit of a ruling elite based on class principles. Soviet science has opposed this pseudoscientific assertion with the uniquely correct materialistic principle that man's development in favorable social conditions is one of unlimited possibilities.[11]

In the late sixties and early seventies, however, full battle had not yet been joined, and the psychologists quietly continued their work.

At the beginning of the 1970s several leading Soviet philosophers began to take note of the research of the psychologists and geneticists, and they began discussions of what all this meant for Marxism and dialectical materialism. The editor of the main Soviet philosophy journal at this time was I. T. Frolov, a man who had made his reputation by writing a book on Marxist philosophy of biology in which he opposed Lysenko (see pp. 152ff.).[12] Frolov was eager to get scientists and philosophers to talk together and he wished to avoid the dogmatic tone of earlier Soviet philosophy; as a result, the conversations on "the biological and the social" which he organized were extremely frank— so much so that the complete transcripts have never been published. Nonetheless, several summaries and descriptions of the debates have appeared.[13] In addition, Frolov collected dozens of letters from individual scientists and citizens, the contents of which have also been partially described.

Despite their effort to be tolerant of divisions of opinion, in step with the atmosphere of the early post-Lysenko period, many of the philosophers present were shocked to hear A. A. Neifakh, a biologist, assert that not only were humans dramatically different in their intellectual and artistic abilities, but that Soviet authorities should use these findings of science in order to breed superior individuals.[14] In agriculture, he noted, genetic engineering would permit the most desirable genotypes of plants and animals to be copied, by means of the technique of cloning, with great economic benefit. Why should not the same thing be done with humans, in order to increase human creativity in fields like science and art? Think what could be accomplished, he urged, if genotypes like those of Einstein could be preserved. If we are interested in conserving the most unusual and valuable aspects of nature, he asked, what could be more worthy of our attention than the best examples of the most valuable of all parts of nature—human beings?

In the discussions that followed at these meetings in the early seventies it soon became clear that Neifakh's enthusiasm for human genetic engineering was favored by only a small minority of the scholars present. In fact, not a single person was described as directly supporting his proposal for human cloning. Some, however, agreed that genetic engineering could be applied to man if it were kept under close control. A. A. Malinovskii even observed that there was no reason to "fear" the word "eugenics," since there existed humane as well as inhumane forms of eugenics. N. P. Bochkov, a prominent specialist in medical genetics, said that he disagreed with people who overemphasize the environment when they talk about human behavior. So far as the word "eugenics" was concerned, he thought that "life would show if the term will survive or not."

V. P. Efroimson of the Russian Ministry of Health agreed with Neifakh that different human talents are affected by genes, and he called for the creation of a science of "pedagogical genetics" that would study the genetics of gifted people.[15] Efroimson's views about the influence of genetics on human behavior had not yet appeared in the public press, but they were being circulated in *samizdat*, especially in the underground publication, *Political Diary*.[16] This was a journal edited by the unorthodox Marxist Roy Medvedev, and was a form of criticism of the Soviet leadership "from the left." Efroimson also attempted in Frolov's discussion group to link genetic views to Marxism. It was wrong, Efroimson maintained, to think that Marxism somehow contradicted this view; one of the slogans of Marxism was "from each according to his abilities, to each according to his needs," a statement that, to Efroimson at least, assumed the presence of different innate abilities in different people.

Neifakh came under heavy criticism from some members of the discussion group. The psychologist A. N. Leont'ev (see pp. 211ff.) saw Neifakh's approach as being antithetical to his famous slogan that "personalities are not born, they are formed in the social environment." He said that Neifakh's analysis pointed toward a "false biologism" about human beings. A. F. Shishkin, a philosopher of Marxist ethics, saw Neifakh's major error in his attributing so much attention to the "geniuses" of civilization, an interpretation of the role of the individual in history that he believed contradicted marxism. According to Shishkin, society already has enough geniuses; the "broad masses" are ultimately responsible for the progress of civilization. V. N. Kudriavtsev remarked that efforts to distinguish the "desirable" from the "undesirable" genotypes always lead to prejudices about "chosen" individuals and groups.[17]

Several of the main issues of the later public debate had now been presented, but they were still known to only a few: the participants in the closed sessions at the Institute of Philosophy, subscribers to *Problems of Philosophy* who carefully read between the lines of the summaries of the discussions, or readers of Medvedev's underground *Political Diary*. But in 1971 the nature-nurture issue was featured on the pages of the Soviet Union's best-known literary journal, *Novyi mir* (New World) in three separate articles.

THE BEGINNINGS OF THE PUBLIC DEBATE

The first of the three articles appeared in the September, 1971, issue of *Novyi mir*.[18] Its author, Pavel Simonov, called for a new orientation in Soviet psychology, a turn away from the previous Pavlovian emphasis on the determining role of environmental stimuli to a search for other causes of human behavior, including internal hereditary factors. Simonov emphasized that people are not all the same, that they have different "needs." From a biological and social standpoint it is even a good thing, said Simonov, that people are so heterogeneous, because it is useful for "the species" to possess some individuals who are more adventurous and curious than others. The adventurers will take risks and possibly create something new, while the more conservative people will ensure the continuation of society in case the adventurers fail. Simonov did not believe that emphasizing hereditary factors in human behavior led necessarily to conservative political conclusions. Indeed, he noted that the very desire for freedom itself, so strongly rooted in some individuals, may be hereditarily conditioned or determined.

The author of the second article was V. P. Efroimson, a biologist specializing in human genetics. This article, entitled "The Genealogy of Altruism," became one of the most famous publications in the entire Soviet debate over nature and nurture.[19] Even today it is frequently cited in private conversations in the Soviet Union as the opening salvo in the public controversy.

Just as Simonov had done in his article in the previous issue of *Novyi mir*, Efroimson lamented the fact that in the Soviet Union social influence on human behavior was so exaggerated. In Efroimson's opinion, genes play no less a role than environment in determining intellect.[20] Furthermore, Efroimson, in a burst of exuberant generalizations, wrote that the best ethical instincts of human beings, such as altruism, the sense of fairness, heroism, self-sacrifice, desire to do good, the sense of conscience, respect for old people, parental love (especially maternal love), monogamy, the chivalrous attitude of men toward women, and intellectual curiosity all "were directed and inevitably developed under the influence of natural selection and have entered into the basic stock of man's inherited characteristics."[21] He continued that all these characteristics were adaptive in an evolutionary sense because "a tribe without ethical instincts would be as handicapped as one with people with only one leg, or one arm, or one eye." In defending his belief that altruism is a genetically conditioned human trait, Efroimson referred to the research in the 1960s of William D. Hamilton on "inclusive fitness" and "kin selection" that would, four years later, be so important to Harvard biologist E. O. Wilson in his famous book *Sociobiology*. (But it should be noticed that Efroimson made more ambitious and dubious claims than Wilson in specifying human behavioral traits that he considered to be influenced by genetics.)

So much for Efroimson's view of the positive side of the influence of genetics on human behavior. What about the negative? Here Efroimson's opinions were even more controversial. He asked why crime continued in the Soviet Union when the social environment has so markedly improved. It was his opinion that "with the weakening of the sharpness of indigence and other purely social preconditions of crime the biological preconditions of crime were emerging ever more clearly."[22] Hereditary factors are particularly important, he believed, in chronic, recidivist criminality. He pointed to twin studies that maintained that if one twin is a criminal the other also becomes a criminal twice as often if the twins are identical than if they are not.[23] His citing of these studies revealed the flawed character of some of his evidence; he seemed not to be troubled by the fact that several of the studies he cited were carried out in Germany and Central Europe in the late twenties and in the thirties, a time of many unreliable research projects in human genetics based on prejudiced views about ethnic and genetic superiority. These twin studies have not stood up well under scrutiny, but Efroimson overlooked this fact.[24]

Efroimson thought that recidivist criminals often display observable physical characteristics: "Objective anthropometric measurements of a group of students and young criminals" had shown that "the overwhelming majority of adolescent criminals in the USA are characterized by a uniform physical constitution of so-called mesomorphic-endomorphic types. In simplified terms—this is a stocky, more paunchy, and broad-chested fellow with a predominance of physical over intellectual development."[25]

Does this mean, Efroimson continued, that the nineteenth-century Italian criminologist Cesare Lombroso was correct when he spoke of a "criminal type"? Here Efroimson hedged, saying that it was not inevitable that such humans become criminals; he also made a concession to the Soviet political authorities who would later ban some of his publications by saying that in "the special conditions of the USA" where organized crime, adulation of aggression, racism, and social injustice are rampant this variant of the normal constitution easily leads to criminality. But, despite his disclaimers, it was clear that Efroimson was speaking about the Soviet Union as well as the United States, as his references to continuing Soviet crime despite social improvements indicated.

In the same issue of *Novyi mir* as Efroimson's article there appeared an evaluation of it by the prominent Soviet scientist Boris Astaurov, the president of the All-Union Vavilov Society of Geneticists and Selectionists.[26] Despite a few reservations, Astaurov gave his approval to Efroimson's approach. Calling Efroimson "one of the best experts in the world on human genetics," Astaurov affirmed that

> we must be very grateful to him for the fact that, going along his own independent and original path, he has worked out these ideas that long have been hovering in the air, and has done so in full possession of modern science, combining that knowledge with broad and profound conviction and an optimistic faith in man that is so characteristic of him.

Astaurov acknowledged that critics in the Soviet Union would accuse Efroimson of "an unjustified biologization of social phenomena" and of "Social Darwinism pointing toward racism" (two criticisms often applied by Soviet Marxists to human geneticists), but Astaurov rejected these criticisms: "No, one does not find here an exaggeration of the biological aspects of man or a failure to remember that man is first of all a social being."[27] These were amazingly strong words of support for a clearly controversial and contestable article.

Astaurov's support for Efroimson's article cannot be understood unless we see it against the background of Soviet politics and intellectual life of the late sixties and early seventies. Surprising as it may seem to Western readers who usually associate genetic explanations of human behavior with political conservatism, in the Soviet Union at this time such interpretations were regarded as "liberal" in the sense that they were seen as one more step in the escape from Stalinism, from Lysenkoism, and from Marxist dogmatism. The very fact that all three articles—Simonov's, Efroimson's, and Astaurov's—appeared in a journal normally devoted to literary criticism, not science, but which also had the reputation of being the most liberal journal in all of the Soviet Union, underscores this fact. To anti-Stalinists like Astaurov, this political point was more important than Efroimson's exaggerations, even his depiction of the "physical typology" of criminals.

Anti-establishment and anti-Stalinist intellectuals in the Soviet Union remembered that the suppression of human genetics—and, yes, eugenics—had occurred in the Soviet Union at about the same time as the elevation of Lysenkoism, a pseudoscience that had discredited both Soviet science and the Soviet Union around the world. They held the Party ideologists and their servitors responsible for both events. Furthermore, it was widely known that some of the Soviet Union's most brilliant geneticists in the period before Lysenko had been involved in the eugenics movement, people like N. K. Kol'tsov, Iu. A. Filipchenko, and A. S. Serebrovskii. The American historian of biology Mark Adams has noted that a number of the Soviet "naturists" in the seventies and eighties, including Malinovskii and Efroimson, had been associated with Kol'tsov years earlier, before the rise of Lysenko.[28]

It was only natural for post-Stalin intellectuals to suspect that even after Lysenko's fall in 1965 the Party ideologists had still not allowed the full significance of genetics in human behavior to become known. In a sense, of course, the liberal intellectuals were correct, since the Party's ideological organs *had* remained highly critical of applying behavioral genetics to humans. Furthermore, scientists all over the world *were* granting more and more significance to genetics in human behavior. But at least some of the anti-Stalinist intellectuals tended to overlook how easily theories of genetic determinism can be used in the service of nationalism, elitism, and ethnic prejudice, something that became clear as the debate continued to develop.

The tendency in the Soviet Union for independent-minded intellectuals to associate the "nature" side of the argument with "the good guys" (anti-Stalinists, antidogmatists) and the "nurture" side with "the bad guys" (Party hacks, unreconstructed Lysenkoites) was reinforced when the establishment intellectuals and official Marxists came out in opposition to Efroimson, Neifakh, and Astaurov. The leader of this group was Nikolai Dubinin, a person with a fascinating, complex, and questionable role in the history of Soviet biology.

NIKOLAI PETROVICH DUBININ

Dubinin was a strong supporter of the nurturist interpretation of human behavior and he believed in the unlimited potential of human development. His own biography seemed to be a vindication (and one of the sources?) of his beliefs. Of peasant background, in the years immediately after the Revolution he had been a *besprizornik*, one of the numerous wandering orphans created by the chaos of those times. In his autobiography, written many years later, Dubinin described how as a homeless child he slept in basements, pilfered his food, and associated with all of the wrong social elements.[29] He seemed destined for a life of crime, poverty, and disease. Wandering around Moscow with his hooligan friends he sought excitement wherever he could find it. On one occasion he and his buddies were attracted by street commotion, ran out to investigate, and ended up next to Lenin's motorcade just in time to be photographed by a journalist. It all meant little to Dubinin at the time, but many years later the photo showing him and Lenin not far from each other came to his attention and became one of his proudest possessions. Eventually Dubinin was enrolled in one of the involuntary reeducation camps originally organized by Felix Dzerzhinskii, head of the secret police; in this camp, surrounded by "positive" social influences, Dubinin soon began to excel.

Dubinin finished secondary education and went on to graduate studies in biology. His education coincided with a time when students with lower-class origins were pushed ahead by the political authorities. This type of student was called a *vydvizhenets,* or "person moving up." And move up Dubinin did, becoming an excellent young geneticist. In 1933 N. K. Kol'tsov, director of the Institute of Experimental Biology, made Dubinin the head of a section of the institute studying genetics. Already by this time the institute had been subjected to severe political pressures, including the arrest of its brilliant population geneticist Sergei Chetverikov, who had headed the same section of the institute that Dubinin now led. As Mark Adams has pointed out, Kol'tsov chose Dubinin to take over genetics research not only because he was talented, but also because he had the right political credentials.[30] Chetverikov, like Kol'tsov, came from a distinguished and privileged family, but Dubinin, with his lower-class origins, could help balance out the political profile of the institute. Thus was born the reputation of Dubinin that haunted him thereafter, and which he did little to counteract: the belief that he took advantage of other people on the basis of official Marxist prejudices. At first the accusation was probably unfair, since Dubinin should hardly be blamed for mere ambition; furthermore, his commitment to Marxism was undoubtedly sincere. In later years, however, he chastized his "bourgeois" teachers and parlayed his class origins in his favor in an obvious fashion. His critics later joked behind his back that his autobiography, entitled *Perpetual Motion,* should have been called *"Perpetual Self-Promotion".*

But in the history of Soviet genetics, Dubinin played a positive role for many years. Not only did he do good research, but he opposed the true villain of Soviet genetics, Trofim Lysenko (see, especially, pp. 121ff.). When Lysenko triumphed in 1948, Dubinin spent several years in scientific exile studying birds in Siberia. When Lysenko, in turn, fell from favor, Dubinin was placed in charge of the rebirth of Soviet genetics, becoming head of the Institute of General Genetics.

Dubinin's opponent in the nature-nurture debate of the early seventies, Boris Astaurov, was also a former pupil and associate of Kol'tsov. But unlike Dubinin, Astaurov had never joined the Communist Party and had not involved himself in the political intrigues that attracted Dubinin. Instead of criticizing his teachers for their class origins, he had praised them for their scientific achievements, trying to ensure that the brilliant page in the history of genetics written by Soviet biologists in the twenties would not be forgotten. In the minds of many of the geneticists who suffered through the eclipse of their discipline under Lysenko, Astaurov was a geneticist who did not compromise on questions of principle, while Dubinin was a careerist. Thus, even in terms of the personal rivalry between Dubinin and Astaurov, the "good guys" were seen by most academic geneticists as Astaurov and the defenders of the "nature" side of the debate; similarly, the "bad guys" were Dubinin and his supporters who constantly trumpeted the Marxist theory that human beings are products of their social environments.[31] This confusion of personal and intellectual issues would lead to unfortunate results.

In the early seventies Dubinin wrote article after article in which he opposed genetic explanations of human behavior with an analysis of man's place in nature that was based on a dialectical materialist view that human and social phenomena cannot be reduced to physical and chemical explanations.[32] There have been "dialectical leaps" in the evolution of man, Dubinin maintained, that render impossible and incorrect those explanations of human behavior that give a large role to genetics. The two most important of these leaps have been the origin of life and the origin of consciousness. Human beings are conscious, social organisms who conform to regularities or laws different from those that govern mere molecules; those regularities are the Marxist ones describing the evolution of society toward communism. The social "element" is therefore the determining one in the education and formation of the human psyche. In fact, said Dubinin, young children who do not suffer from disease or deformity are "omni-potential" in their abilities. He found the concept of innate abilities unacceptable.

But while Dubinin continued to produce articles and books of this sort, the tide was still against the nurturists. I. T. Frolov, the innovative editor of *Problems of Philosophy*, continued to attack Lysenkoite and Lamarckist viewpoints in his journal, and this message was often read to be a criticism of the nurture point of view as well. In a 1972 article, Frolov reminded his readers that Darwin had once said, "Heaven save me from the absurd Lamarckian 'striving for progress.' . . .," and Frolov referred to the sad period in the history of Soviet genetics when "false attempts were made to give certain special conceptions and theories a broad ideological and socio-ideological character, which gave birth to the myth about 'two genetics.' "[33]

To scholars like Frolov, Dubinin's effort to make his nurturist views coincide with dialectical materialism seemed another form of Lysenkoism. Dubinin did not help his cause by becoming ever more authoritarian in his personal and bureaucratic relationships with other geneticists. He stopped producing valuable genetic research himself, and even, probably innocently, made several claims later proved to be false.[34] Some of Dubinin's enemies began laughingly to refer to him as "Trofim Denisovich Dubinin," appending Lysenko's first two names to Dubinin's.

During the next few years the debate continued. Astaurov's death in 1974 was a blow to the naturists, but other supporters continued the battles. Some of them took the naturist view no doubt farther than Astaurov himself would have done. Efroimson, for example, pushed the theory of the inheritance of intelligence to the extent that eventually he produced a world history of genius based on genetic assumptions. Soviet publishers would not touch it, but the manuscript circulated in *samizdat*.[35]

In 1976 Dubinin attended a Soviet-American symposium in Dushanbe on "Problems of Mutagenesis and Carcinogenesis of the Environment."[36] Sobering evidence was presented at the symposium on the mutagenic and carcinogenic effects of many pesticides and defoliants used in agriculture, especially in the cultivation and harvesting of cotton, one of the most valuable crops around Dushanbe. Dubinin became very concerned about birth defects caused by chemicals in the environment, and he expressed this anxiety in many of his publications. While Dubinin denied the significance of genetics for the behavior of human beings who are physiologically normal, he stressed that genetics could be extremely important in pathology, and warned that environmental pollution might destroy human genetic reserves. In several of his speeches and articles Dubinin said that 10.5 percent of the children in the world were born with genetic defects, and 3 percent of these were mental defects.[37] Dubinin saw these congenital deficiencies as the result of environmental pollution. Just as Dubinin was deeply offended by proposals to alter the genetic constitution of human beings purposely through genetic engineering, so also he feared its alteration accidentally as a result of environmental degradation. These warnings by Dubinin

were not welcome news to industrial and agricultural managers in the
Soviet Union, whose primary interest was to increase the production
of chemical and agricultural products.

This environmental aspect to Dubinin's writings presented the naturists with a new avenue for criticizing him. One of Dubinin's strengths
had always been that he wrapped himself in the cloak of Marxism,
extolling the traditional emphasis on environmental factors in forming
the human personality. But now that Dubinin had extended his environmental emphasis to include warnings about the effects of current
Soviet agricultural and industrial practices, he no longer seemed quite
so positive an influence from the standpoint of Soviet officialdom. The
naturists soon picked up this theme. The medical biologist N. P. Bochkov, a naturist in the nature-nurture debate, chastized Dubinin on two
counts: not only did he exaggerate the role of the environment in
human behavior, but he also was an unrealistic doom-cryer about the
environment:

> It is possible to demand the immediate prohibition of all kinds of sub-
> stances on the basis of their mutagenic effects, regardless of the fact that
> their significance in terms of overall mutagenic change or mortality is not
> great in comparison with other factors, while at the same time they are
> of great economic or medical effectiveness. Thus, for example, a complete
> refusal to use pesticides, herbicides, and defoliants (several of which have
> mutagenic effects) would immediately decrease agricultural production by
> two or more times, an effect that would be an unjustified calamity for
> the population of the whole earth.[38]

As the debate between the naturists and the nurturists continued to
develop, the two sides began to fragment, with extremists and moderates
on both sides. The extremists on the nature side included a few who
linked crime ever more directly to genetics, and those who began to
worry about the eventual genetic effects on the Soviet population of
the growing proportion of that population that was non-Russian, especially that which was Asiatic. It became clear that the nature argument
might become useful to Russian nationalists and the political right, an
emerging force in Soviet political culture. The extremists on the nurture
side included unreconstructed Lysenkoites, who made several attempts
at a come-back.

In 1975 the Soviet jurist I. S. Noi published the book *Methodological
Problems of Soviet Criminology* in which he underscored the role of
genetics as a source of deviant behavior.[39] The biologist Iu. Ia. Kerkis,
in his article "Do Criminologists Need Genetics?" praised Noi's ap-

proach, and called for Soviet law students to begin the study of biology, which he considered "absolutely necessary for them to have a correct orientation to several complicated problems in their professional activity."[40] Meanwhile, the Ministry of Internal Affairs (MVD), responsible for the police and internal social order, began a series of studies in ten different corrective labor camps on the link between crime and genetics.[41] One cannot help but be struck by the irony that in the twenties it was the police who led in creating corrective labor camps based on nurturist theories, one of which Dubinin as a boy attended, while in the seventies and eighties the police, at a loss to explain the continuance of crime, turned toward genetics as a possible explanation for the phenomenon.

The nature-nurture issue had now become a widely known issue of practical concern. The list of articles and books concerning the topic was rapidly. growing; between 1970 and 1977 in only two Soviet journals, *Problems of Philosophy* and *Philosophical Sciences*, over two hundred fifty articles, reviews and commentaries were published on the topic of "the relationship of the biological to the social." In 1975 and 1977 two scientific conferences were held on the subject.[42]

In 1977 the nurturists launched an influential counterattack on the naturists in the authoritative Party journal *Communist*.[43] The philosopher E. Il'enkov used a particularly successful achievement of Soviet psychologists following the theories of A. N. Leont'ev to try to prove that the human personality is not inborn, that talents can be formed, and that human beings are shaped primarily by their social environments, not by genes. The achievement was based on work with four children who had been deaf and blind from birth. Il'enkov maintained that when the psychologists began to work with these children the term "homo sapiens" could hardly be applied to them. They displayed no characteristics of the human psyche, no personalities, not even "primitive manifestations of goal-directed activity." The brain of each youngster continued to develop, Il'enkov observed, according to the program "coded in the genes, in the molecules of DNA," but this development did not lead to a single sign of "psychic activity." The only way to help these children, Il'enkov continued, was to apply Marxist psychology by "forming the psyche through labor activity." By gradually working with the children, starting with the most elementary feeding activities, they were gradually awakened from their near-vegetable state and converted into human beings. Over a period of many years the psychologists I. A. Sokolianskii and A. I. Meshcheriakov involved the children in "social relations," taught them language, and educated them to the point where they could study at Moscow University in—of all fields—psychology. One of them even, in 1977, became a member of the Communist Party! They now, said Il'enkov, write poetry, lecture to large audiences, and do research. The achievement understandably attracted attention from around the world.

From a rigorous scientific point of view such a heart-warming experience proved little about the role of genetics in human behavior, but to Il'enkov the case of the four blind and deaf children was directly related to the debate. It proves, he said, that talent does not come from genes, but can be formed. "Talent," said Il'enkov, "is not a quantitative difference in the levels of development of people, but a qualitatively new property of the psyche connected with an essential change in principle in the type and character of labor, in the character of the psyche's motivations."[44] Il'enkov added,

> We turn now to the current prejudice according to which only a minority of the population of the earth possess brains from birth capable of "creative work." This is a pseudo-scientific prejudice, surrounded with statistics, decorated with the terms of genetics and higher nervous activity and with "scholarly" discourses about inborn "cerebral structures" allegedly determining in advance the measure of talent of a person, and which simply slanderously shoves on to nature (genes) the responsibility for the extremely unequal distribution of favorable conditions for development in class society.[45]

Il'enkov noted that in 1975 the president of the Academy of Pedagogical Sciences of the USSR, V. N. Stoletov, had called the experiment with the four children "scientific documentation of striking force." Stoletov was well known as an old supporter of Lysenko.[46] Thus, the cause of nurturism was linked in the minds of many Soviet intellectuals with Lysenkoism, a linkage that was not justified by the historical record, since Lysenko never discussed human heredity. Nonetheless, the Lysenkoites had enjoyed a monopoly over Soviet biology at the same time the nurturists had controlled Soviet education and psychology, and both had assigned a predominant influence to the environment in the development of organisms; therefore, the affinity between Lysenkoism and nurturism was no accident.

Dubinin's Dismissal

The high point in the naturists' campaign came in 1981, with the dismissal of N. P. Dubinin as director of the Institute of General Genetics of the Academy of Sciences of the USSR after he was publicly chastised for exaggerating the influence of the environment on human behavior. This "Dubinin Affair" attracted the attention of the entire Soviet genetics community, as well as many other scholars following the nature-nurture controversy. Dubinin's dismissal and reprimand seemed to signal a decisive defeat for the environmentalist camp, whose opinions had been tied to official Soviet Marxism for half a century. However, as we will see, the nurturists did not accept defeat easily, and, in fact, would find new highly placed supporters.

The scholar who assumed the major role in criticizing Dubinin at the 1980 General Meeting of the Academy of Sciences seems, at first glance, to be a strange choice. He was A. D. Aleksandrov, a mathematician. What authority would a mathematician have against a geneticist? Aleksandrov was an internationally known scholar and, more important, he was a person whose ideological commitment to Marxism could not be questioned. Over a period of decades he had written many articles linking Marxism to physics and mathematics in a way that had attracted attention because of their integrity and intellectual rigor (see pp. 363ff.). He had managed to write on Marxism and science even in the Stalinist period without becoming known as a dogmatist. Indeed, his staunch defense of Einsteinian physics within a Marxist framework years earlier had won Aleksandrov credit with both the scientific community and with the more enlightened Marxist philosophers. Only a person with such a reputation might be immune to Dubinin's charge in 1980 in the leading ideological journal *Kommunist* that the naturists were "revising" or even "abolishing" Marxism.[47]

But Aleksandrov also had a personal reason for opposing Dubinin's egalitarian nurturism. Aleksandrov was one of the few full members of the Academy of Sciences of the USSR of noble birth, and he was known to emphasize the importance of good breeding. His grandfather before the Revolution had been captain of the tsar's yacht, the *Standart*. The grandson was a leader of the descendants of the St. Petersburg intelligentsia, many of whom harbored elitist and hereditarian tendencies.[48]

Aleksandrov accused Dubinin of falling prey to "extreme" nurturist views and, in particular, denying that genetics was an important influence on the behavior of physiologically normal people. He quoted Dubinin as saying that "all normal people are capable of practically unlimited mental development," and, further, as maintaining that "giftedness is an efficacious development of the essential human qualities by the normal genotype in combination with favorable conditions for its development (i.e., mainly 'acquired')."[49] If giftedness is so simple a matter, Aleksandrov sarcastically remarked, then any child who does not become a Lomonosov, Marx, Newton, Beethoven, or Raphael has only his parents to blame for not providing the right conditions (all Soviet citizens know that Lomonosov had terrible parents).

To take a position like Dubinin's was not only theoretically incorrect, said Aleksandrov, but was potentially disastrous from a practical standpoint, since society must know how to educate its children and what to expect from them. But rather than allow these questions to be debated in an open way, Dubinin, continued Aleksandrov, was hiding behind the cover of a distorted Marxism and introducing "methods and approaches" which were "alien to science."[50]

In reply, Dubinin insisted that he had not denied that genetics has some influence on human behavior. What he resisted, he said, were growing efforts to link genetics and behavior in a "fatalistic" way. He maintained that some Soviet naturists believed that in the future it would be possible to identify genes that will make their possessors great writers or scientists, and that these genes will be identified in embryos even before birth. Dubinin found such opinions repugnant, and he affirmed:

> I am deeply convinced that my point of view opens up real possibilities for the mental, social, and productive development of every person, but that the point of view of fatalistic genetic predetermination closes off these possibilities.[51]

Dubinin's assertions were not quite to the point. No responsible naturist would say that future distinction in intellectual endeavor is inevitably determined by genes. The question at issue was whether Dubinin left enough room for the role of genetics in interaction with the environment in influencing human behavior. The judgment of the leaders of the All-Union Academy of Sciences was that he did not. Five months after Aleksandrov's sharp criticism of Dubinin was published in the leading journal of the Academy of Sciences, the Presidium announced that Dubinin had been replaced as director of the Institute of General Genetics by A. A. Sozinov, a man who had not participated in the important nurture-nature debates and who was considered to be suitably open to both sides of the argument.[52]

THE NATURE-NURTURE DISPUTE AND THE
CHERNENKO FAMILY

By the early eighties the naturists had won a number of important victories. They had succeeded in having their viewpoints expressed in Soviet publications, marking a reversal of policies of the decades from the late twenties to the early seventies. The most prominent nurturist of all, Academician Dubinin, had been demoted and reprimanded for exaggerating environmental influences. The internationally known nurturist psychologist A. N. Leont'ev had died. The naturist viewpoint enjoyed uneven but surprisingly widespread support across a complex and contradictory spectrum of academic geneticists, literary avant-gardists, dissidents, anti-Marxists, ethnic specialists, conservative nationalists, and police administrators. The top political leaders had refrained from pronouncements on the subject for a number of years, permitting the debate to unroll in a strikingly free fashion. In 1981 and 1982 it appeared possible that Soviet Marxism might abandon its long-standing opposition to attempts to explain, even partially, human behavior in terms of genetics.

However, a new turn in the debate was in embryo even in the seventies. Elena Konstantinovna Chernenko, the daughter of a top official of the Communist Party, became interested in the subject. Like her father, she had studied in a pedagogical institute. Pedagogues have always, understandably, tended to favor the nurture point of view, since they are, by definition, nurturists. In 1974 Elena Chernenko defended a dissertation at the Lenin Moscow State Pedagogical Institute entitled "Methodological Problems of the Social Determination of Human Biology." The title indicated the nurturist position advanced in the dissertation. In 1979 Elena Chernenko published, together with K. E. Tarasov, a book based on her dissertation. Entitled *The Social Determination of Human Biology*, it was a defense of the nurture point of view with heavy reliance on Marxism for substantiation.[53]

Chernenko and Tarasov stated in the introduction of their book that their goal was to show "the social determination of the biology of man and to reveal the significance of the uniquely correct Marxist solution to this problem" (p. 5). The whole book was an attempt to show in dialectical materialist terms, with frequent citation of the laws of the dialectic, that Marxism points to a resolution of the nature-nurture debate in favor of the nurture side. The analysis was carried to incredible details of philosophical and logical analysis, but few empirical or scientific data were introduced. Chernenko and Tarasov drew up graphs indicating no less than sixty different positions on the "biological-social" problem (types, variants, modifications of variants). According to them, of these sixty positions, "the only true point of view from the position of Marxism" is "Type VI, variant 13, modification V" (p. 71). What was this only correct position? They graphed it originally with red and green lines (pp. 64–65) and we have adapted it here in black and white:

This graph shows that "the social," indicated by the lines in the S area, is not only broader than the biological, but also is the determining influence on human behavior, since the S lines go *through* the B circle which denotes "the biological" factor. Chernenko and Tarasov maintained that there was no purely biological influence on human behavior, since even "the biological properties of people are the result of social progress" and do not stand alone as biological properties (p. 84). Thus, they would reject the following model on the ground that while it gives social factors much more influence than biological ones, it still erroneously attributes an autonomous role to biological factors (p. 71):

Despite its approximate and schematic character, Chernenko's and Tarasov's model provides some grounds for discussion of the relationship of biological and social influences on human behavior. Its depiction of the S area (social factors) as being larger than the B area (biological factors) would not be disputed by most Western specialists. However, the really hard question, "What are the relative *sizes* of the B and the S areas?" cannot be answered by philosophical or logical analysis, but only (if it can be answered at all) by scientific research, something to which Chernenko and Tarasov gave scant attention. And by assuming that this very difficult question of the relative weight of biological and social factors can be answered on the basis of dialectical materialism Chernenko and Tarasov were undermining the hard-won relative independence of Soviet scientists. Indeed, they revealed a deep intolerance when they said that the editors of the main Soviet philosophy journal, *Problems of Philosophy*, had erred in stating that dialectical materialism was compatible with a variety of different positions on the nature-nurture problem (p. 75). According to Chernenko and Tarasov, dialectical materialism pointed toward a "uniquely correct" solution, the one they presented.

Even more controversial was Chernenko's and Tarasov's assertion that there is no autonomous area (B in the drawing) denoting biological factors. This thesis that "the biological" is socially influenced can be given two different interpretations, the one rather commonplace and innocent, the other unusual and ominous. The innocent interpretation is that, in agreement with social historians of science all over the world, science is a "social construction" and that even the theories and findings of science are socially influenced. The more ominous interpretation has a peculiar Soviet context: the findings of science are not only socially influenced but should be, in the final analysis, subject to the rulings of political bodies and political leaders.

Elena's father, Konstantin Chernenko, was, at the time his daughter wrote her book, a member of the Politburo of the Communist Party of the USSR with a special interest in ideological matters. We do not know how much attention he paid to his daughter's defense of nurturism, but we do know that the nature-nurture issue began to interest him as well. We can assume fairly confidently that Konstantin Chernenko had some knowledge of his daughter's work on the nature-nurture issue, especially after she had published a book on the topic.

In June, 1983, Konstantin Chernenko gave a speech entitled "Current Problems of the Ideological and Mass-Political Work of the Party" at a plenary session of the Central Committee of the Communist Party. The occasion marked Chernenko's assumption of the position of the late Mikhail Suslov as guardian of the Party's ideological purity. In the speech Chernenko directly raised the nature-nurture issue. Even more important, he revived the Stalinist principle that Party leaders could pronounce on questions of science. Chernenko acknowledged that in science "new facts may bring a necessary addition or correction to established viewpoints," but he stressed that "there are truths that are not subject to re-examination, problems that were simply solved long ago." One of these truths, underscored by "materialist dialectics," he continued, is the supremacy of the social environment in determining the qualities of the human personality. Chernenko observed, "One can scarcely consider those concepts to be scientific which explain the qualities of man like honesty, boldness, and orderliness by the presence of 'positive' genes and which virtually deny that these characteristics are formed by the social environment."[54]

The most important fact about Chernenko's opinion is not what it contained, but who expressed it. Nothing in it directly denied naturist views, since few naturists spoke of actual "positive" genes. However, since he was now the chief ideological spokesman of the Communist Party, Chernenko's speech was required guidance for lower-level Party and intellectual leaders, and it was taken to mean that the Party's official support for nurturism was still alive, even reinforced. After February 1984, when Chernenko succeeded Iurii Andropov as head of the Communist Party, every sentence and pronouncement of his speeches took on an aura of official policy.

Many Westerners no doubt sympathize with the underlying thought in Konstantin Chernenko's speech, since people with egalitarian political beliefs often find hereditarian viewpoints unpalatable. Within the context of Soviet intellectual life with its history of Party interference in academic debates, however, Chernenko's intervention illustrated something entirely separate from Western controversies over nature and nurture. It showed that the leaders of the Communist Party had still not learned fully the lesson of the Lysenko period. The point here is not the truth or falsity of theories of genetic determinism, but the question of who should decide the validity of scientific questions—the Communist Party, or the researchers in the relevant fields? Chernenko showed that he believed that the Party's mandate extended to research findings themselves, since, according to him, "some problems have been solved long ago" on the basis of "materialist dialectics" and should not be reopened.

Following Chernenko's speech Soviet articles on nature and nurture and on science and ideology in general became considerably more militant. A number of authors referred to Chernenko's comment on genetics and human behavior.[55] What is striking to the Western observer is that articles on science and ideology in the Soviet Union in the mid-eighties began to display a more aggressive tone than had appeared in many years. Leading science journals published articles with titles like

"Medicine in the Focus of the Ideological Struggle" and "Ideology and Medicine."[56]

The death of Konstantin Chernenko in 1985 and his succession as head of the Communist Party by Mikhail Gorbachev meant that the views of Konstantin and Elena Chernenko on the nature-nurture issue were no longer as significant as they had been earlier. Nonetheless, the position of the naturists in 1985 was more difficult than it had been in the rather heady days of the seventies when the debate first broke out.

The nature-nurture debate in the Soviet Union is a mirror of changing ideology and politics in that country. If one compares recent Soviet writings on the topic of nature versus nurture to Soviet writings of the 1930s and 1940s, one sees a dramatic loss of conviction in the efficacy of nurturist methods. A person who speaks today in the Soviet Union of the "withering away" of crime and deviance under the influence of socialist society will often receive in reply yawns, or even disbelief, as Dubinin did when he tried to uphold the old views. A generation ago, many people believed in the ultimate victory of nurturist approaches to education; today, only a few do. Instead, there is a yearning for strict discipline and systems of punishment—in other words, negative measures—to correct what earlier was to be eliminated by propitious social conditions and education—in other words, positive measures.

This change is far greater than mere modification of reigning educational and criminological theories; it is a part of the ebbing of the optimism of a revolutionary society. People who are participating in the revolutionary transformation of society believe that they have found the key to the cure of a great many, if not all, social ills. When it becomes clear, a generation or two later, that many of these problems have remained intractable, the children of the revolutionaries begin to look around for alternative explanations. The very fact that genetic explanations were banned for so long makes them all the more attractive as an alternative for people who have become disillusioned with the old ideology.

Academician Dubinin's role in this story was interestingly ambiguous. There was more than a little of the scientific tyrant in him, bred by his being first the victim of administrative arbitrariness and then the beneficiary and producer of it. Should he be seen as a mere unreconstructed dogmatist, or might people feel some sympathy with the lower-class hooligan-made-good who fears that his society is abandoning the principles that saved him and others of his generation? For that matter, is there not some plausibility to Konstantin Chernenko's position on the issue, even if Western observers reject the idea that his opinion should have been so authoritative?

Perhaps the most unfortunate aspect of the whole story is that because of the polarization of the positions of, on the one hand, dogmatic Marxism-nurturism, and, on the other hand, freedom of thought-naturism, the links internal to each of these pairs have never been severed. It appeared in the late seventies that these simplistic intellectual associations might be dissolving. The reentry of the Soviet leadership into the debate in the early eighties, marked by Konstantin Chernenko's speech in favor of his daughter's emphasis on nurturism, recemented the old links. Not enough time has yet passed since Chernenko's death to know whether the Soviet leadership will continue to insist on a dogmatic resolution of the extremely complicated issue of human behavior.

CHAPTER 7

BIOLOGY AND HUMAN BEINGS: SPECIALIZED TOPICS

> You can criticize the socio-biologists all you wish, but they are making an audacious attempt at decisive research investigations. . . . We must carry out similar research projects.
>
> —I. T. Frolov, Soviet philosopher, 1983

In the late seventies and eighties dozens of articles and books concerning biology and human beings appeared in the Soviet press and in academic literature. In this chapter, I have organized some of the more interesting discussions around the specific topics of "Sociobiology," "Crime and Social Deviance," "Lev Gumilev and the Issue of Ethnic Relations," and "Biomedical Ethics."

SOCIOBIOLOGY

The Harvard University entomologist E. O. Wilson published his noted book *Sociobiology* in 1975, at a time when discussions over nature and nurture in the Soviet Union were building to a crescendo. The book attracted considerable attention from Soviet reviewers and authors.

In *Sociobiology* Wilson maintained that some aspects of human behavior, particularly "altruism," have been favored genetically in evolution. The mechanism by which such a characteristic might be "selected for" in human evolution was not straightforward, however, since the individual who altruistically sacrifices himself or herself for another person reduces by that act the contribution of genes that the sacrificing person makes to the next generation. At first glance, selfishness, not altruism, would seem to be the kind of behavior favored by evolution. Wilson pointed to a way out of this dilemma by emphasizing "kin selection" and "inclusive fitness." If, for example, an individual sacrifices himself for his brother, so long as that brother more than doubles his gene contribution to the next generation, the sacrificing brother will have increased *his* gene contribution to the next generation as well, even after his death.

Wilson's interpretation of the effect of evolution on human behavior attracted attention in the Soviet Union for several reasons: first, it seemed different from the normal "Social Darwinist" biological interpretation of society because it used biology to find support for admirable human traits, not the voracious ones usually associated with the "survival of the fittest"; second, its appearance came a few years after Efroimson had made a somewhat similar point in his famous 1971 *Novyi mir* article; and, last, Wilson's sort of social biology had a tradition in Russia, where Peter Kropotkin had in the nineteenth century written an important book entitled *Mutual Aid* in which he maintained that Darwin had exaggerated competition as a characteristic of evolution and underplayed cooperation. The fact that Kropotkin was a socialist (although of the non-Bolshevik, anarchist variety) rendered his form of social biology more attractive to Russian socialists than the writings of apologists for laissez faire capitalism.

For all of these reasons the treatment Soviet writers first gave Wilson's *Sociobiology* seemed surprisingly sympathetic, particularly to a Western observer who knows how roughly Wilson was handled by some radical writers in the West.[1] Undoubtedly the lingering belief that genetic interpretations of human behavior helped break up Stalinist dogmatism smoothed the way. N. Kh. Satdinova gave a surprisingly positive summary of the basic features of sociobiology in the main Soviet philosophy journal.[2] V. T. Efimov wrote that the concrete "sciences of man" such as biology, genetics, physiology, ethology, and psychology were beginning to make genuine contributions to an understanding of human behavior, and he called for more work in this area in the Soviet Union.[3] V. N. Ignat'ev was critical of what he took to be the ideological position of Wilson, but he was obviously fascinated by the theme, and said that sociobiology had some "objective content."[4]

It soon became clear, however, that Wilson's form of sociobiology would be objectionable to the more orthodox Marxist writers. Dubinin and his friends were no more favorably impressed by a biological interpretation of human beings that found support in evolution for humane characteristics than they had been by those that saw nature as "red in tooth and claw." Attempts to find innate "altruism" in human beings were just as mistaken, Dubinin wrote, as those that sought "innate aggression." All such interpretations were repeating the old error of "biologizing" man, regarding him as an animal instead of correctly as a social creature.[5]

The judgment of the Soviet Marxists on Wilson became more obvious when the Harvard scientist published another book with Charles Lumsden (Genes, Mind, and Culture) in which they directly criticized Marxism. According to Wilson and Lumsden, Marxism as an interpretation of human history was similar to Lamarckism as an interpretation of biological evolution, in the sense that both accurately described several features of the processes under study, but both proposed "mistaken mechanisms" for an explanation of those processes. This criticism struck a tender nerve in Soviet writers, for it not only described Marxism as erroneous but linked it to Lamarckism, a doctrine with an exceedingly painful history in the Soviet Union (see p. 131).

Other Soviet scholars now joined Dubinin in castigating sociobiology. A. M. Karimskii linked it to "bourgeois philosophy," along with "social behaviorism," "neo-Malthusianism," and "anti-worker and anti-trade union policies, racism, forced sterilization, and behavior modification." All these evils, Karimskii concluded, were being pursued in the West as a part of international conflict and militarism.[6]

I. T. Frolov, a leading reformer among Soviet philosophers, was more restrained on the subject of sociobiology. He described sociobiology as "weak, even hopeless," but he also said that it contains "interesting observations and conclusions." Its primary flaw, he continued, was that it failed to understand that "the specific characteristic of man as a biosocial being is that his transformation into a 'superbiological' essence basically frees him from the influence of evolutionary mechanisms."[7] But as late as 1985 Frolov continued to display some sympathy for Wilson's views.[8] In a debate with Soviet philosophers who were critical of comparisons of man to other animals, he observed that only about one percent of the genetic information in human beings differs from that in chimpanzees, and he continued that Soviet biologists, just like the sociobiologists in the West, must investigate the significance of this small difference.[9]

THE PROBLEMS OF CRIME AND SOCIAL DEVIANCE

Probably no issue in the Soviet debate about nature and nurture has been more urgent in a practical sense than the one about crime and social deviance. Early Soviet writings had proposed a clear solution to these problems: they were transient phenomena bred by deprivation, exploitation, and injustice under capitalism. The article on "crime" in the first edition of the Large Soviet Encyclopedia (1940) stated that "crime arose only on that stage of development of society when private prop-

erty, classes, and the state appeared, and has a definite class character."
With the elimination by socialism of the environmental causes of social
deviance, crime would disappear.[10]

Yet by the 1970s it had become clear in the Soviet Union that crime
was not on its way to extinction. The increasingly conservative older
Soviet generations were dismayed by the disorderly, sometimes criminal,
patterns of behavior of Soviet youth (and of some of their own cohorts).
The disillusionment led to a search for alternative explanations of social
behavior that began to emerge in novels and popular literature. The
Soviet novelist Iu. Semenov described a militiaman voicing his lost
hopes in conquering crime:

> "I would like to investigate in a theoretical way the thesis that was long
> ago formulated as 'The causes of crime, the bases of crime, have been
> liquidated.' But just what is going on here if this is not the real state of
> affairs? Why do we have burglars? Hooligans? Rapists? What's the matter?
> . . . Was Lombroso really such a reactionary? And must we constantly
> attack Freud? What is the cause of various human anomalies? Can we
> calculate on a computer the genetic code of this or that criminal? Is this
> possible in general to do? Isn't there in all this a violation of our
> morality?"[11]

Soviet jurists, geneticists, and specialists on crime began to demonstrate more interest in genetic interpretations of human behavior. In
the seventies the first Soviet studies of the relationship of criminality
and genetics were published. They even included research on the alleged
link between the XYY chromosome characteristic and violent behavior
in males, an issue that in the United States became so inflamed that
a project studying the relationship in Boston, Massachusetts, had to be
abandoned under community pressure.[12]

If one looks at Soviet sources on criminology one finds a growing,
but still uncertain, tendency to assign a role to innate, as opposed to
environmental, factors in crime. The jurist N. A. Struchkov in 1966
denied that there are biological "causes" of crime but nonetheless noted
that one can speak about the inheritance and transmission of a number
of characteristics of personality.[13] This statement was seen as an undermining of the position of the leading Soviet psychologist of that
time, A. N. Leont'ev, who insisted that "personality" is a product of
environment. S. A. Pastushnyi was in 1973 a bit more outspoken: "A
whole series of facts is known to science which point to definite
preconditions which lie at the basis of such human developments as
imbecility, criminality, etc."[14] In a 1975 text the jurist G. A. Avanesov

did not shy away from the word "cause": "Man . . . possesses definite inborn characteristics. Several of these in facilitating circumstances can, in our opinion, promote criminal behavior and even can be one of the causes of concrete criminally punishable action."[15] In a 1975 text entitled *The Deterministic Nature of Criminal Behavior* the jurist B. S. Volkov maintained that "Biological characteristics exercise a great influence on the formation of the social orientation of a personality."[16] However, the authors of a standard 1979 text on criminology took a more cautious view: "Biological characteristics can affect behavior (including that of a criminal) as conditions, but not as causes."[17] We see, then, continuing disagreement among Soviet writers on the role of biological factors in crime. Those authors who were attuned to dialectical materialist philosophy continued to affirm that crime is not a biological category, but a social one, even though some of these same scholars paid increasing attention to the role of genetics in the formation of the "physiological bases" of the personalities of criminals.[18]

The scholar who was most active in defending the orthodox position that crime is a vestige of capitalism was, not surprisingly, Academician Nikolai Dubinin. In a 1982 book entitled *Genetics, Behavior, Responsibility*, written with two co-authors, Dubinin maintained that if crime is prevalent in the Soviet Union the reason is that communism is still incomplete; he pointed to continuing deprivation in Soviet society.[19] Here we see once again the curious, even paradoxical, position of Dubinin. In order to defend the orthodox Marxist position on crime, an action that ought to have pleased the ideological leaders of the Soviet Union, he had to point repeatedly to the economic inequality that continued to exist there, something that the political leaders did not find altogether pleasant. Just as Dubinin had elicited official displeasure by emphasizing the harmful mutations in human beings resulting from industrially produced carcinogens in the atmosphere, so also he courted displeasure by picturing the inadequacies of Soviet society that might cause crime. Orthodox Marxism had become a two-edged sword in the Soviet Union when it was applied to analyses of continuing social maladies; if Dubinin was to interpret crime in orthodox terms, he had no choice but to emphasize the failures of Soviet society. Thus, the genetic interpretation of crime—however much it flaunted the orthodox Marxist tradition—had some appeal to Soviet authorities, for it provided an escape from the necessity of making deeply critical comments on Soviet society in the eighties.

Dubinin's 1982 book had a tone that varied from the dogmatic, to the pathetic, to the endearing. By this time he had been demoted and officially chastised for exaggerating the role of the environment in human behavior. But he continued to insist on all of the standard Marxist explanations for crime. Do not forget, he entreated his comrades, that we must go a long way before we have created communism; we still have material shortages, wages are unequal, people do not receive "according to their needs," the standard of living is different in urban and rural areas, manual laborers are still too numerous and suffer in comparison with mental laborers, and some ethnic groups are still backward and economically deprived. But do not lose heart, he urged; crime is a "social, historically conditioned phenomenon of class society," and as a "mass phenomenon" will disappear under full communism. Only "interpersonal conflicts" will remain, and even those will be on a much lower level.

Dubinin attempted, through comparisons of different societies and of the Soviet Union at different points in time, to prove his thesis that crime is socially induced. Citizens of East Germany and West Germany have the same genetic heritage, he maintained, but after almost forty years of living in different economic conditions, different patterns of crime have developed in the two countries.[20] Crime was most common in the Soviet Union, he noted, in the early twenties, when the whole atmosphere of Soviet economic life was still heavily under the influence of capitalism and when "exploitation, misery, and homeless children (besprizornost') were rife."[21] (The reference to homeless children was unquestionably autobiographical.)

Despite the appeal of Dubinin's arguments to old-line Marxists and humanitarians, the circumstances of Soviet life in the early eighties made his message a rather unwelcome one, not only to many intellectuals who had tired of Marxist panaceas, but also to Soviet managers and police administrators who were trying to cope with rising crime and disorder.

LEV GUMILEV AND THE ISSUE OF ETHNIC RELATIONS

In the late seventies politically conservative viewpoints in the Soviet Union began to be merged more and more frequently with biological interpretations of history and human behavior. Some of these could not be published in the official Soviet press, and therefore began to circulate in samizdat. The conservative turn was not a surprise, since it was characteristic of Soviet underground political culture at this time.

Western analysts of the "New Soviet Right" have emphasized that underground conservative political writings began to flourish after the original reformist and human rights movements of the sixties and early seventies were suppressed by the police.[23] By the late seventies liberal dissent in the Soviet Union was nearly dead, but conservative dissent won new strength. The police seemed to be more tolerant of the new conservatives than it had been of the older liberals, although from time to time the police cracked down on the conservatives as well.

One of the most famous episodes of the new politically conservative biological thought was the "Borodai-Gumilev" case of 1979–1982. It was a strange story, and many details remain uncertain.

Lev Nikolaevich Gumilev was the son of Nikolai Gumilev and Anna Akhmatova, two of the Soviet Union's most famous poets. L. N. Gumilev's father was executed by Soviet authorities in 1921 for alleged participation in an antigovernment conspiracy. His mother lived on until 1966, and had a special place in the history of the repression of creativity by Stalin; her poetry was banned by decree of the Central Committee of the Communist Party in 1946 and did not reappear until after Stalin's death.

An historian specializing in Oriental civilizations who had spent many years in Stalin's labor camps, L. N. Gumilev was employed as a researcher by the geography department of Leningrad University. He was especially interested in the influence of geography and the natural environment on human behavior. In the early seventies Gumilev published several works on the ethnic history of China in the third century. Gradually, his ambitions became broader, and in the mid- and late seventies he wrote a three-volume analysis of the contacts and conflicts of ethnic groups throughout world history, and the consequences he saw emanating from those contacts. Rejected by Soviet publishers, Gumilev took a step to ensure that his work would still become known to a circle of knowledgeable readers: he "deposited" the three-volume work in the manuscript division of the All-Union Institute of Scientific and Technical Information (VINITI), thereby circumventing the publishers' refusals. He would not have been successful in this effort, of course, unless some fairly influential people—perhaps at VINITI—had supported him. Access to VINITI was restricted to researchers with academic credentials and a special pass, but soon quite a few such people were making the trip to VINITI to read the manuscript. Furthermore, the geography department of Leningrad University circulated the manuscript in a mimeographed form. Since the manuscript had a certain official standing as a result of its presence in VINITI and the support of an academic department at Leningrad University, reading and discussing it was not considered to be as risky as dealing with a more typical *samizdat* document. It was merely unpublished, not outlawed by the police or censors.

Word of Gumilev's interpretation of history began to spread among intellectuals in Moscow and Leningrad. Indeed, the fact that not just anybody could read the massive work gave it an enticing air of "secret knowledge." No one seemed quite sure, and at first few seemed to care, exactly where Gumilev's world view fit into the political spectrum. Raisa Berg, in her memoirs published abroad, emphasized how popular Gumilev's views were in the seventies among young Soviet students. Describing a time when she appeared together with Gumilev at a discussion at the faculty of applied mathematics of Leningrad University, she said that the atmosphere was as if they had found "an oasis in the desert of science by decree." But, as a biologist, Berg was also troubled by the fact that in Gumilev's interpretations of the pulsations of history there was "something astrological, something completely unacceptable for me."[23]

The fact that Gumilev was the son of the famous Anna Akhmatova, who had been denounced by Stalin's ideological henchmen, caused many people to assume that he belonged in the "anti-Stalinist, liberal" camp, but a number of readers soon saw that he also had tremendous appeal to the new defenders of Russian national traditions. Others quickly realized that the manuscript was an issue in the nature-nurture debate; Dubinin, for example, in 1982 chastised Gumilev for his hereditarian views.[24]

Gumilev's work, entitled *Ethnogenesis and the Biosphere of the Earth*,[25] had the paradoxical distinction of being a book that was reviewed in the Soviet Union, but never published. (Many Western works are treated in this fashion by Soviet journals, but not Soviet ones.) Much of what we know about the book is based on two reviews that appeared in the Soviet press, one very positive, the other devastatingly critical.[26] In what follows, then, it is possible that Gumilev's opinions will be somewhat misrepresented, since I have had to learn about them not by reading the manuscript itself, but through the accounts of his advocates and detractors. However, Gumilev has been a prolific author on ethnohistory for twenty-five years, and from these books and articles we can find discussions on most of the concepts that later figured in his unpublished magnum opus.[27]

The man who reported Gumilev's views to the Soviet public, and who obviously was an advocate of Gumilev's views himself, was Iu. M. Borodai, a philosopher from the Institute of Philosophy. As Borodai presented it, Gumilev's scheme of world history depended on a largely biological vocabulary, with terms like "ethnos," "mutation," "xenia," "chimera," "symbiosis," "geobiocenosis," "ecosystem," "cancerous tissue," and "exogamy," utilized to describe the rise and fall of civilizations.

The most important unit in the history of civilization, according to Gumilev, is the "ethnos," which he described as a "closed system of a discrete type," in other words, a pure, or fairly pure, ethnic group.[28] Each ethnos in the world has its own "organic and original disposition" and is capable, if left undefiled, to create significant works of art, culture, and philosophy. However, if ethnic groups begin to intermingle, the "incompatible" dispositions are forced upon each other, and a new, extremely negative phenomenon arises: the "chimera," arising from the "inharmonious combination of two or three elemental ethnoses," a melange that commits "antinatural" acts and produces destructive ideologies. (A "chimera" in botany is a special form of intermixture of plant cells produced by grafting). The chimera not only "hates nature" and destroys the natural environment around it, but also "projects" its "world-destroying psychology" outward in the production of ideologies aimed at the elimination of positive human values, such as "goodness," "trust," and "love for motherland, children, and nature." The ideologies that the chimera produces are "vampire-conceptions," feeding off the healthy ethnos. Indeed, the relationship between an ethnos and a chimera is the same as that between "healthy tissue" and a "cancerous tumor."

It was clear that when Gumilev spoke of "intermingling" of ethnoses, he meant intermarriage, for he described the evil effects of intermingling within a single family; he said that the intermingling causes children in a family to "assimilate the heterogeneous, incompatible behavioral stereotypes and value systems of their parents."

Although Gumilev did not stipulate the exact mechanism in his fanciful system by which he believed the negative ideologies based on ethnic mixture arose, he thought it was something inherent or genetic, not environmental. He commented that "one can not say that worsening living conditions or economic difficulties induce people to accept a negative view of the world. No, the conditions are no worse than before, and sometimes better, for in the zones of contact usually there begins intensive exchange of items (industry and trade), people (exchange of labor) and ideas (exchange of faiths)." To see everything in economic terms, Gumilev thought, was to fall prey to "the delusion of the vulgar sociologists who attempt to see everything in terms of class struggle." No surprise, then, that Marxists would object to Gumilev and his views.

Against the background of such a grim portrayal of world history, one wonders how its author could find anything good left in the world, especially since there are no pure ethnic groups anywhere. The history of civilization is a history of contact between ethnic groups. Why, according to Gumilev, have not the "vampire-conceptions" produced by chimeras taken over? In answer to this challenge, he presented several alternative developmental paths: it was possible for different ethnic groups, or ethnoses, to live in proximity to each other without producing ill effects, if they followed certain rules; and even if the worst happened, producing a monstrous chimera, there was an occasional, rare escape mechanism by which normality was restored. The schemes were as follows.

If two ethnic groups lived in proximity but did not intermingle and each let the other live its own life-style, the relationship could be, according to Gumilev, quite favorable. He compared this situation to "symbiosis" in biology, in which two species live together harmoniously. Or, it was possible for one ethnic group consisting of "foreign specialists" to be invited by another to live there in its own settlement, helping the native population to perform certain tasks, but not intermingling beyond the requirements of those tasks. Gumilev called such a relationship "xenia," which in botany is a description of how one part of a plant, the endosperm, serves as a short-lived "nurse" aiding the nutrition of the rest of the plant.

But what if intermingling occurred, and the destructive chimera arose? Then the only chance was that a rare "mutation" would occur in the suffering ethnos that would produce an individual, or individuals, with "heightened activity," a quality for which Gumilev used the term *"passionarnost'"*, which might be translated as "the quality of great passion." To Gumilev, the arising of such mutations were the great moments of history; therefore, the very mechanism of intermingling which usually produces catastrophes occasionally gives birth to new "life-affirming ethnoses."

Gumilev identified the birth of Christianity as one of the great life-affirming mutations in history. According to him it arose as a reaction to the ill effects of the chimera that was produced by the mixture of

"Greek" and "Israelite" ethnoses. But he did not believe that it was inevitable that such positive mutations will arise out of mixtures, nor that it was inevitable that the positive mutations would be able to maintain themselves. Islam, according to Gumilev, arose as a positive mutation from the dreadful chimera of "gnosticism" but failed to maintain itself as a healthy ethnos because of the "exogamy" (outbreeding) that occurred in its harems. The mixture of "Persians, Georgians, Armenians, Syrians, Greeks, Turks, and Berbers" that entered into Islam produced a new chimera with the negative ideology of "Ismailism." Capitalism and Protestantism, too, were, according to Gumilev, negative ideologies that have not yet been overcome, produced by a chimera in Europe rooted in intermingling based on trade, especially by England and the Netherlands. Gumilev had nothing good to say about the Reformation or about any religious heresies, which he saw as products of chimeras. He considered the Albigensian heresy in France, for example, to be a product of a chimera produced by an intermingling of Arabs and the native Languedoc population.

Why did such a ridiculously speculative and scientifically baseless scheme as Gumilev's cause such a stir among Soviet intellectuals? First of all, most of those who discussed it never read it; they merely heard about it. Second, the ideas within it appealed to a heterogenous group of people. The naturists who were battling the nurturists were sympathetic, at least at first, because they saw it as one more salvo in their favor in that ideologically loaded long battle. Biological explanations of human behavior were seen by many Soviet intellectuals as automatically anti-Stalinist, antiestablishment viewpoints; furthermore, Gumilev's parentage gave him instant cachet among liberal, especially literary, opponents of the establishment. Third, the appeal of Gumilev's doctrines cut across the political spectrum, and was as fascinating to the new dissident conservatives of the seventies and eighties as to the dissident liberals of the sixties. Russian history seemed to be one great illustration of Gumilev's doctrines. Foreign invader after invader had tried to submerge the Russian national identity, its ethnos, but eventually had been repelled.

Most dramatic was the case of the Mongols. Soviet geneticists had noted that as one travels across Eurasia, from East to West, the frequency of the gene accounting for the "B" blood group drops dramatically, reaching very low levels in Western Europe. Even before World War II the hypothesis that this gene was introduced into Europe at the time of the Mongol invasion had been advanced in a Western publication.

The degree of intermingling between Mongol and Slav had been high. There is some evidence that the mixing had been greatest among the Russian nobility, many of whom later boasted of their Mongol heritages. The native Slav peasants provided a genetic reserve for the ethnos. Then, the "mutation" producing a person of "heightened energy"— Dimitrii Donskoi, the victorious Russian leader against the occupiers— had arisen, and the Mongols had been driven out. Gumilev observed in his work that the Mongols had lost their force when they collided with other "dominant" ethnoses.

Anyone who is familiar with Russian dissident conservative thought during the last fifteen years will recognize parts of Gumilev's scheme as standard fare. The great heroes who threw back the foreigners are variously listed in that literature, often including Sergii of Radonezh, Dimitrii Donskoi, Minin and Pozharskii, General Kutuzov, and sometimes even Stalin—showing, once again, the ideological heterogeneity of Russian conservatism. In Gumilev's case, as reported by Borodai, the scheme was sufficiently abstract that each person could fill in the details as seemed appropriate, varying the names and events to fit different varieties of ideologies. Russian Orthodox Christians could find solace in Gumilev's respect for Christianity but disdain for Western heresies and sects; environmentalists were attracted by his thesis that the native ethnos always respects nature, but that foreign intruders despoil it; anti-Americans were beguiled by his depiction of America and its treatment of Indians as one of the best examples of his interpretation of history; and socialists were buoyed by his depiction of capitalism as the product of a monstrous chimera.

But serious Soviet Marxists could not accept Gumilev's interpretation because it undermined or ignored the entire Marxist interpretation of history, which based itself on economic and material explanations, underplayed the significance of individuals, and was critical of religion. Interestingly enough, however, the major attack on Gumilev and Borodai came not from the official Party organs, but from a group of three scholars headed by Academician B. M. Kedrov. Kedrov was a sincere Marxist scholar of high quality. His father was a friend of Lenin's, and until his death in 1985 Kedrov remembered playing as a child at Lenin's knee. His father was tortured and killed by Stalin during the purges, an event described by Khrushchev in the famous "secret speech" of 1956. The son always stood for a nondogmatic but convinced Marxism. Immediately after World War II as editor of the main Soviet philosophy journal he tried to escape the confinement of Stalinist dogma, and was fired as a result (see p. 328).

What bothered Kedrov and his colleagues most was not Gumilev's and Borodai's position on the nature-nurture issue (it would have been typical of Kedrov to consider that an issue for the specialists in human genetics) but their total ignoring of historical materialism as an explanation of history and their prejudices about nationalities. Kedrov and his co-authors noted Gumilev's and Borodai's attitude toward racial mixture and observed: "Such affirmations are untrue and directly contradict the line of our party and socialist government on the universal rapprochement of nationalities in the future (even if the distant future) and their merger into a single socialist humanity." They further noted that Gumilev refused to apply class analysis to the religious heresies of history, even though the Albigensian heresy in France could best be explained in their opinion not in terms of ethnic mixture but instead as a "form of revolutionary struggle of the oppressed masses against feudalism and the feudal church." In conclusion, they stated that "the publication of such material, giving an incorrect and antiscientific treatment of a series of important problems, must be decisively recognized as a mistake.[29]

This was heavy criticism. However, it is striking that Kedrov and his friends did not directly accuse Gumilev and Borodai of "racism," the term that most quickly comes to mind. Academician Kedrov, in an interview shortly after he had written the article, told me that he had not called Gumilev and Borodai "racists" because they had not maintained that some races are superior to others—merely that ethnic groups, each "original" and "positive" in its own right, should not intermarry; furthermore, Kedrov said that he and his colleagues wished to avoid the sort of epithet that had so often been used in earlier times in Soviet philosophical discourse to discredit an opponent without further investigation of the basic issues. It was a reply that was typical of Kedrov's career. Although he was described in some Western publications as a "liberal,"[30] he objected to the label, and in fact was not at all a liberal in the Western sense; he believed that such articles as Borodai's should be refused publication. Freedom of the press in the Western meaning of the term was not a part of his vocabulary. But he was a representative of that brand of Marxism in the Soviet Union whose proponents aim toward authentic discourse within the framework of Marxist assumptions about philosophy and society.

BIOMEDICAL ETHICS

Questions of biomedical ethics have been frequently raised in the Soviet Union in recent years. Although these discussions are not identical with the controversies over nature and nurture, they are a part of the same general discussion of the degree to which human beings should be reduced to biological terms. The rapid progress in many countries in recent years in techniques such as organ transplants, use of life-sustaining devices, and genetic manipulation has provoked debates among philosophers, politicians, ethicists, scientists, and laypeople over what limits, if any, should be imposed on such manipulation. In the Soviet Union, just as in other countries, these debates contain both intellectual and political elements. Some of the debates in the Soviet Union are quite similar to those in the West; others have unusual features or overtones resulting from the special characteristics of the social context of science in the Soviet Union.

The question of the definition of "death" is one where the debates in all countries are rather similar. As physicians have developed the possibility of reanimation, or shock therapy, of a heart that has stopped beating, the old definitions of death based on the cessation of heartbeat have obviously become outdated. "Brain death" gradually has replaced "heart death" in many countries.[31]

Even in debates as technical and factual as these, however, the Soviet literature displays its own characteristics. Soviet Marxists usually define a "person" (lichnost') as an individual who has, or is capable of having, social relations. A person is a being who interacts, or in principle could interact, with other beings. The unique characteristic of a human being, as opposed to an animal, is, according to Soviet Marxism, not that humans possess "souls" or religious significance, but that they are social beings shaped by productive relations and are therefore qualitatively different from animals. In the final analysis the status of a person derives from society and not from an innate characteristic. "The preservation of life" without reference to the social characteristics of that life has little urgency within this framework.

Does this mean that the body of a person without restorable brain activity (a Karen Ann Quinlan) could be used as an "organ bank" for other persons needing transplantable organs? At least one Soviet legal scholar, N. Amosov, maintained that it was "permissible to take the heart from a person with a deceased cerebral cortex for the purposes of experimental transplantation."[32] Other Soviet scholars have sharply rejected this suggestion, although they (just like their Western colleagues) are having difficulties articulating the philosophical assumptions behind their juridical positions. One difference, however, is that in the Soviet literature on biomedical ethics religious reservations are not considered legitimate, at least in academic writing, whether philosophical or scientific.

The possibilities of genetic engineering raise ethical issues even more pointedly. Biologists can now transfer DNA between species, using the techniques of recombinant DNA. It has already been done many times in a limited way. What are the ethical restrictions on such research? Suppose a genetic engineer wanted to learn whether or not it is possible to insert human DNA in the embryo of an ape and to continue its development in an ape's womb, or vice versa? June Goodfield wrote in 1977 that Dr. Geoffrey Bourne of the Yerkes Primate Center in Georgia received two letters from the Darwin Museum in Moscow encouraging him to create a hybrid between gorillas and man.[33] Does one just experiment, and worry about ethical issues later? Or should ethical issues enter into the act itself, perhaps influencing the decision whether the experiment should even be initiated? An American scholar gave a tentative justification for the creation of man-animal combinations by saying they could be used to perform demeaning tasks in society or to act as organ banks for transplantable organs.[34] Soviet philosophers object strenuously to such "inhuman" suggestions in the West, but it is not clear exactly on what philosophical assumptions, nor is it clear that Soviet biologists are any less aggressive in their experimentation than Western ones.[35]

Soviet philosophers of science and Party activists have awakened to these issues, and they are demanding that Marxist analysis be heard. The Soviet philosopher of biology R. S. Karpinskaia wrote:

> The social danger of unregulated "gene-oriented" evolution is so great that both theoretical and experimental knowledge must now be directed by a truly scientific and humanitarian world view.
>
> The sense of social responsibility of scientists cannot be intuitive, it must have a scientific ideological base. The philosophical interpretation of the perspectives of biology is becoming an integral part of scientific research, and the more deeply the creators of the brilliant experiments in genetic engineering realize this fact, the more hopeful is the possibility of turning the invincible development of genetic engineering to the benefit of mankind.[36]

The most interesting phrase in this quotation was Karpinskaia's assertion that philosophical interpretation is an "integral part of scientific research," both in theoretical and practical endeavors. Karpinskaia was making a much stronger claim here than the conventional wisdom that scientists are sometimes confronted in their work with philosophical issues of a *cognitive* sort; she was maintaining that a union between Soviet Marxist philosophers and Soviet scientists is necessary for a consideration of these new problems in a *moral* sense. However, most working Soviet biologists were not eager to accept Karpinskaia's call for a "union" of scientists and philosophers; they remembered and resented the interference of the philosophers during the time of Lysenko's influence, and they feared that the advent of the new bioethical issues of the eighties would give the philosophers an excuse to intrude into research once again. Thus, while the philosophers often maintained that scientific research is itself value-laden and must be ethically judged, the working scientists like Academician A. A. Baev often asserted that science is neutral, and can be used for good or evil equally well.[37] The decision about how to use science was, to the latter researchers, a question of application, "external" to research itself. Therefore, no new "union" of scientists and philosophers was needed.

Soviet philosophers in the eighties began to pay much more attention to biomedical ethics and genetic engineering. The most prominent of them was I. T. Frolov, who devoted most of his research to these issues.[38] His interpretation of genetic engineering was rather interesting, differing from that of Soviet natural scientists. While Frolov predictably agreed with Academician Baev that a major cause for concern about genetic engineering is that it will be used by reactionary forces in the bourgeois West, he sharply differed with Baev's view that genetic engineering is just one more technology that can be used either for good or evil. Molecular biology and its applications raise social and ethical problems that are so intense, observed Frolov, that we can justifiably speak of "a new stage in the development of science."[39] This is a stage in which we must see that "science and scientific-technical progress are not a panacea for all ills. . . . The danger has emerged of the development of certain directions in scientific-technical progress which directly and indirectly threaten man and humanity."[40] Frolov had obviously retreated from the optimistic Promethean scientism that characterized so much earlier Soviet writing on science.

According to Frolov, "Modern biological knowledge has posed a series of questions which concern the innermost foundations of human existence and affect the basis of science." The ideological issues are "intertwined with the very 'body' of science, and are not something external to it." Therefore, human genetics cannot be considered a purely scientific question; it is "inevitably included in a sharp philosophical, ideological struggle."[41] Thus, while Baev was arguing essentially that

Soviet molecular biologists could go about their business as usual, Frolov said that the current situation was novel and required a new approach.

Up to this point in his analysis Frolov agreed with the more orthodox Marxists like Dubinin who also worried about the dangers of genetic engineering. However, Frolov considered Dubinin's view that genetic engineering should never be used to mold man's evolutionary future too simplistic. Frolov recognized that Marxism is based on a relativistic vision of the history of civilization in which moral standards evolve in step with the development of material culture. Therefore, the possibility of the conscious and widespread application of genetic engineering to human beings in the future (even in ways that seem morally offensive now) cannot be excluded. On the other hand, maintained Frolov, it would be a great mistake to make such an effort now. For the time being, all eugenic ideas and all proposals to engineer a better human species should be rejected. The reasons, he said, are twofold: the science of genetics is still too incomplete and, even more important, power in the world is too unequally distributed. Even if the science of genetics were nearly perfected, continued Frolov, so long as some classes of people enjoyed many more privileges than others, the widespread use of genetic engineering would inevitably lead to the strengthening of elites and to the exploitation of the underprivileged. At some far future date, however, the question of improving the human species should be raised again; we should leave it to the people of that time, said Frolov, to decide the question, relying on what is anticipated to be their much better science of genetics within a just communist society.[42]

Frolov's position was intelligent and carefully framed. Its synthesis of both scientific and social elements in the analysis of biomedical ethics distinguished it from the more science-oriented views of Baev, Bochkov, and Englehardt, while the ethical relativism in its sophisticated Marxism set it apart from the rather elementary Soviet Marxism of people like Dubinin and Shishkin. The weakness of Frolov's position, however, was its limited utility in handling pressing practical questions. Frolov postponed the hard bioethical questions to the far future but all over the world physicians and researchers were already making decisions on questions such as *in vitro* fertilization, the cessation of care to newly born deformed infants and terminally ill patients, the freezing of human embryos, recombinant DNA experiments involving human genes, priority among patients in receiving organ transplants, fetal research, and gene therapy. Frolov's highly abstract formulations, while on one level commendable, were not very interesting to working scientists and physicians facing these questions.

Control Over Biomedical Ethics

Underneath the philosophical and medical issues involved in questions of biomedical ethics lay, of course, a practical political issue: Who should make the decisions about what is permissible and what is not permissible in biomedical research? The same sort of question was being asked in the United States, and the answer being reached there was not reassuring to Soviet scientists with memories of the painful history of Soviet biology. In the United States the inclusion of moral philosophers and laypeople on ethics advisory boards overseeing scientific research had become widely accepted. In 1976, when David Mathews, Secretary of Health, Education and Welfare, created the Ethical Advisory Board to help him make decisions about the propriety of scientific research being conducted in the National Institutes of Health, he directed that the board must contain a mixture of scientists and nonscientists.[43] Early members of the board included a Catholic priest and a philanthropic leader. The "President's Commission for the Study of Ethical Problems in Medicine and Biomedical and Behavioral Research" under President Reagan included sociologists, ethicists, lawyers, and economists, as well as natural scientists.[44] In hundreds of American universities, institutional review boards evaluated research on human subjects and made recommendations about the ethical permissibility of this research. Regulations governing these boards usually stated that the membership "should be diverse and include members with nonscientific interests."[45]

The argument was frequently voiced by political leaders that when a review board in any society made ethical decisions about scientific research it should reflect the predominant values of that society. For the United States, religious leaders and moral philosophers were logical choices for lay members. In the Soviet Union the analogous members, at least officially, would be Marxist philosophers and Party activists. And there came the rub: if the Soviet Union created ethical review boards to advise on biological research that included Marxist philosophers, the old question of Marxist ideology and Soviet science would take on a new dimension.[46]

As late as the mid-eighties nonscientists were excluded from the biologists' committees in the Soviet Union. The chairman of the Interdepartmental Commission for the Rules for Work with Recombinant DNA was Academician Baev.[47] I was told in Moscow in January 1983 that the commission was made up entirely of natural scientists. The commission in 1978 drafted rules for recombinant DNA research that were highly similar to those used in the United States at the same time.[48] Academician Baev later became chairman of the Interdepartmental Scientific-Technical Council on Problems of Molecular Biology and Molecular Genetics, a group similar to the earlier one but with broader responsibilities.[49] Its members were also all natural scientists—no professional philosophers or ethicists.

Nonscientists in the Soviet Union called for their inclusion in the established bodies making policy about biomedical ethics, although without success. Frolov spoke repeatedly of the necessity for "socioethical and humanistic regulation of science.[50] Frolov was chairman of a scientific council of the Presidium of the Academy of Sciences on "Philosophical and Social Problems of Science and Technology" which included philosophers and historians, but this council was concerned with philosophical problems and was not directly related to policy, in contrast to Baev's committee.[51]

A few attempts were made in the Soviet Union by groups outside the scientific community—people equivalent to "public representatives" in the United States—to have influence on the debates over biomedical ethics. In the publication *Literary Gazette*, popular among the literary intelligentsia, several authors expressed anxiety about possible infringements on human dignity by molecular biologists.[52] In 1974 the Orthodox Church entered the debate, just as religious groups in other countries had done.[53] In an article entitled "A Christian View on the Ecological Problem," the editors of the *Journal of the Moscow Patriarchate* agreed with Marxist philosophers who had called for ethical controls in science; the priests, however, asked for the inclusion of Christian considerations in the deliberations. The Christian authors were careful to point out that ethical control was not needed over "science itself," but only over its application.[54]

The Marxist philosophers rejected the offer of the priests to participate in the debates, pointing out that the Church maintained that science and technology are neutral (just like the scientists headed by Baev!) and that therefore control over science and technology must be based on nonscientific ethical and religious considerations. The Marxist philosophers maintained, on the contrary, that science is not neutral, but contains inherent values. The philosophers—the experts on "values" and ethics—considered themselves scientists just like the biologists and wanted to be included on the scientific advisory committees. They thought that the priests, however, should be excluded because they are not scientists. But neither the Marxist philosophers nor the priests were included on the important committees, so far as we can tell.

The three-way exchange among scientists, philosophers, and priests on the issue of regulating biological research revealed a great deal about science in the Soviet Union. The apparent paradox that the scientists and the priests agreed that science is neutral, while the philosophers disagreed, is not paradoxical at all upon reflection. Each group was expressing its own interests and traditions. The scientists wanted science to be considered neutral so that the official Soviet experts on "values"— the Marxist philosophers—would not be invited into the committees regulating research. The priests also wanted science to be considered neutral because they followed a traditional religious dualistic approach in which nonscientific Christian values are "guides" to practical action; they also knew that the chances of their being accused of "meddling" where they did not belong would be less if they admitted that their values had nothing to do with the science of biology itself, but only its application. The Marxist philosophers, however, considered Marxism, including its ethical values, to be a "science," and they wanted to be considered equals to the natural scientists; they also quoted Marx to the effect that eventually there would be a "single science of man" uniting normative and factual approaches. Therefore, they could not accept the dualistic interpretation of the Church. These three approaches embody dramatically different viewpoints on the relationship of biology to society, and no way has been found in the Soviet Union either to combine them or for one to vanquish the other.

One of the striking characteristics of the Soviet debates about human biology is the way they have confused and eroded traditional ideological lines. Both "liberal" intellectuals and conservative nationalists enjoyed flirting with hereditarian doctrines—the intellectuals because biological determinism was a view that could be explored only as Stalinist controls diminished, the conservative nationalists because biological determinism seemed to support ethnic consciousness and chauvinism. Furthermore, the old-line Marxist dogmatists who tried to uphold the orthodox nurturist line suddenly found, by the seventies, that they could not count on their old allies, as was illustrated by the demotion of Dubinin.

People in the Soviet Union who try today to explain such phenomena as crime, corruption, and social deviance in their country often choose one of two paths: either they remain loyal to original Marxism and admit that these negative phenomena are products of the Soviet environment which still contains enormous inequalities; or, they abandon Marxism and find explanations for all these phenomena that stand "outside of the socioeconomic order," such as genetics. The temptation of the genetic explanation is strong among the managerial and pragmatic leaders who are eager to defend the Soviet order and their place in it; when one adds to this group the literary and nonestablishment intellectuals who are attracted to genetic explanations precisely because they contradict Stalinist Marxism, as well as the ethnic nationalists who wish to base their own conservative and sometimes racist views on genetics, the political and ideological mixture contained in the hereditarian camp is revealed in all its richness.

Western observers, however, can hardly take consolation from the ideological confusion of Soviet authors on the issue of human biology. A striking characteristic of the debates is that they cause ideological confusion in the West, too, in the sense that they often run counter to our earlier expectations and conclusions about Soviet society. Throughout this debate the Soviet authors who took positions that were closest to those of "humanists" in the West—that is, people who warn against scientism, manipulation of human beings, biological determinism, unrestrained genetic engineering, and racism—were dialectical materialists, official and unofficial Marxists. The association of Soviet ideologists with humanism is not a concept for which many Western Sovietologists are prepared. Also troubling to some Western obeservers is the fact that a number of the brave and admirable dissidents in the Soviet Union, people looking for intellectual deliverance from Stalinist ideology, are attracted by theories of genetic determinism.

In these respects the debates over biology and human beings in the Soviet Union differ from other Soviet controversies, for example, those in literature and politics. Most of the views in literature and politics that were suppressed during Stalinism were views with which Western supporters of democracy and human rights sympathized; the hereditarian views that emerged in the Soviet Union after Stalinist controls ebbed contained some elements that are antithetical to democratic values—racism, ethnic chauvinism, fierce nationalism. For that reason, along with the others already mentioned, the Soviet debates about human biology are healthy antidotes to received Western opinion about the Soviet Union.

CHAPTER **8**

CYBERNETICS AND COMPUTERS

It is obvious that global modeling must become the sphere of sharp ideological struggle, since it is connected with presenting more or less concrete ideas about the future of humanity. Here two opposing conceptions inevitably face each other—the communist and the capitalist.
—D. M. Gvishiani, Deputy Chairman, USSR State
Committee on Science and Technology, 1978

Cybernetics as a field in the Soviet Union has swung in status from one extreme to another.[1] Before the mid-fifties it was condemned in several ideological articles as a "bourgeois science." In the sixties and early seventies cybernetics enjoyed far more prestige in the Soviet Union than in any other country in the world. In the late seventies and eighties its status diminished considerably, although it was still popular.

The most unusual period was the sixties and early seventies. During these years cybernetics was a positive rage in the USSR even though computer production, both quantitatively and qualitatively, lagged far behind that of the United States. How does one explain this phenomenon? How, when Soviet computers were obviously underdeveloped, could Soviet writers constantly speak of the unique roles that they believed cybernetics would play in their society? To try to answer this question, we must begin by analyzing the essential concepts of cybernetics against the background of traditional Soviet social aspirations and the philosophic framework of dialectical materialism. To its Soviet supporters cybernetics was a new chapter in the history of materialistic approaches to nature that promised both better ways to conceptualize the world and also achieve social goals.

THE SOVIET STRIVING FOR RATIONALITY

An original promise of the Russian Revolution, for those who supported it, was the rational direction of society. Marxism as an intellectual scheme was heir to the optimism of the French Enlightenment and the scientism of the nineteenth century; one of its primary characteristics was the belief that the problems of society could be solved by man. Nature was not so complicated but that it could be controlled if only the artificial economic barriers to that control erected by capitalism were removed.

The key to progress, then, according to the Marxists, was social reorganization. The Bolsheviks considered the Revolution of 1917 to be the decisive breakthrough toward that reorganization. They admitted, of course, that progress toward efficient administration would be very difficult to achieve in Russia as a result of its primitive state. Even in the early years of Soviet Russia, however, there were at least a few theorists who hoped to achieve centralized, rational direction. The first attempt toward this goal was made during the period of War Communism (1918–1921). However important the civil war may have been in forcing a command economy, it is quite clear that the ideological urge to create a planned communist society also played an important role. From this standpoint the New Economic Policy (1921–27), with its relaxation of economic controls, was a definite retreat. The rapid industrialization that succeeded the New Economic Policy might have been carried out in accordance with any one of several different variants, but all assumed greater planning and centralization.

After the 1930s, however, the goal of a rationally directed society became more remote. The fact most disheartening to the Soviet planners was that the more early difficulties of industrial underdevelopment were overcome, the more distant seemed the goal of rational, centralized control. By the time of Stalin's death in 1953 the economy had become so complex that it seemed to defy man's ability to master and plan it. It would have been convenient to attribute these troubles to the irrationalities of Stalin himself rather than to the inability of Soviet man to control his affairs. Yet by 1957, four years after Stalin's death, it was clear that the trouble lay not in the aberrations of one man but in the entire concept of centralized planning.

By the late fifties and early sixties even Soviet economists were beginning to question whether a complex modern industrial economy could be centrally directed. Every modification of the quantity of one commodity to be produced called for unending modifications in the quantities of others. Even a relatively decentralized economy seemed to have an insatiable demand for bookkeepers and administrators. Academician Glushkov said that if things continued as they were going, the entire Soviet working population would soon be engaged in the planning and administrative process. To use a cybernetic term, the entropy of the system was multiplying at a horrifying rate.

It was at this time in the history of the Soviet Union that cybernetics appeared. Leaving aside temporarily the initial Soviet hostility toward cybernetics (which has been exaggerated outside the Soviet Union), the promise of cybernetics, as it appeared to Soviet administrators and economists, was twofold: first, it held out the hope of rational control of processes that previously had been reluctantly judged uncontrollable because of their complexity; second, it offered a redefinition of what rationality is, at least as far as the direction of complex processes is concerned.

The new hope for rationality in cybernetics seems obvious enough. The subject matter of cybernetics—the control of dynamic processes and the prevention of increasing disorder within them—was exactly the concern of Soviet administrators. Perhaps through the new science of cybernetics, they thought, genuine control of the immensely complex Soviet economy and government could be achieved.

The second result of cybernetics—the redefinition of rationality in controlling complex mechanisms—arose from the very nature of cybernetics. It is necessary, therefore, to spend a little time in defining the subject.

THE SCIENCE OF RATIONAL CONTROL

The term "cybernetics" is often improperly understood as being synonymous with "automation." It brings to mind discussions of unemployment and impressive statistics about the number of operations a computer can perform in one hundredth of a second. In its original sense, however, cybernetics meant something quite different. The founders of cybernetics—Norbert Wiener, Arturo Rosenblueth, Julian Bigelow, Walter B. Cannon, Warren S. McCulloch, Walter Pitts, W. Ross Ashby, Claude Shannon, and John von Neumann—believed they were advancing a generalized theory of control processes.[2] To them, a control process was the means by which order is maintained in any environment—organic or inorganic. In terms of this view of cybernetics, a computer by itself is not a cybernetic device. It can become a part of a cybernetic system when it is integrated with the other components of that system in accordance with a control theory.

The aspiring scientific discipline of cybernetics did not base itself upon the technological innovations that permit the construction of modern computers. Insted, it rested on the concept of entropy, taken from thermodynamics and broadened to mean the amount of disorder in any dynamic system. According to this approach, all complex organisms are constantly threatened by an increase in disorder, with the end point complete chaos. However, certain organisms are arranged in such a sophisticated and efficacious manner that through a dynamic process they can resist, at least temporarily, the tendency toward disorder. Cybernetics studies the common feature of these organisms, particularly their use of information to counter disorder. The more enthusiastic supporters of cybernetics view human society, which also obviously places a premium on order, as a particular type of cybernetic organism. In sum, cybernetics is the science of control and communication directed toward fending off increasing entropy, or disorder.

Cybernetics fits well with materialistic assumptions. It postulates that the control features of all complex processes can be reduced to certain general principles. Yet its mode of operation differs distinctly from the science of the eighteenth and nineteenth centuries out of which the scientific optimism of Marxism arose. In terms of the Enlightenment, rationality came through the knowledge of quantitative laws that would permit the prediction of the future. Such rationality was perhaps best symbolized by the celestial mechanics of Laplace. Control of a process, according to this early view, was based on knowledge of all physical laws and variables and the ability to change the magnitude of the variables. Even the indeterministic nature of modern physical theory, troublesome as it was, did not destroy the belief that rationality is essentially a theoretical rather than an empirical approach. In economics this concept of rationality led to the belief that if a centralized economy were not running smoothly, the difficulty must be either inadequate authority or insufficient knowledge at the center of local conditions and of the necessary economic laws for the changing of these conditions.

Cybernetics—which is based on analogies among all complex self-perpetuating processes, with living organisms the ultimate examples of success in self-perpetuation—does not emphasize exact prediction of future states or conditions. Nor does it call for strict centralized control. The executive or command organs in all truly sophisticated cybernetic mechanisms are arranged in hierarchies of authority, with semiautonomous areas. Furthermore, rather than trying to predict indefinitely the results of its executive actions, a cybernetic system makes constant empirical checks of these results through feedback, and it adjusts its commands on this basis. As Norbert Wiener said, cybernetics derives from control on the basis of actual performance rather than expected performance. Cybernetics thus places a premium on combining two seemingly contradictory principles: local control based upon empirical evidence, and overriding centralized purposes.

It is a mistake to believe that cybernetics makes it possible to control the most complex processes by collecting in a central location enormous amounts of information. Indeed, cybernetics holds that barriers to information matter as much for control of processes as do free-flowing avenues of information. The best example of this paradox can be found in the human body, in many ways the paragon of a cybernetic mechanism. If we were conscious of everything that goes on in our stomachs, or even just the information that some part of our bodies must be aware of in order for proper digestion to take place, we would be very neurotic indeed. Yet the human body represents the greatest victory of control over a complex process to which cybernetics can point; the features of its organization are basic to an understanding of cybernetic systems.

THE REBIRTH OF HOPE

The lesson of cybernetics for the Soviet Union, and especially for its economy, seemed clear. If Moscow knew everything occurring in its factories in Omsk, it would be "neurotic," as indeed it was when it attempted to do so. Cybernetics taught the lessons of *selectivity* of information and relative *decentralization* of control. By adopting these principles, Soviet followers of cybernetics hoped to direct the Soviet economy toward a few overriding central goals, while, at the same time, granting considerable local autonomy.

Cybernetics revitalized, at least temporarily, the Soviet leaders confidence that the Soviet system could control the economy rationally. This renewal came exactly at the moment when the possibility seemed to be irretrievably vanishing.[3] This rebirth of hope was the explanation of the intoxication with cybernetics in the Soviet Union in the late fifties and early sixties; in the period after 1958 thousands of articles, pamphlets, and books on cybernetics appeared in the Soviet press.[4] In the more popular articles the full utilization of cybernetics was equated with the advent of communism and the fulfillment of the Revolution.[5] If the curious mixture of ideology and politics in the Soviet Union can upon occasion affect certain sciences adversely—as it did at one time with genetics—it can also catapult others to unusual prominence.

One can find no other moment in Soviet history when a particular development in science caught the imagination of Soviet writers to the degree to which cybernetics did. Perhaps the closest parallel occurred in the 1920s, when GOELRO, the State Commission for Electrification, was made the subject of poetry.[6] At that time, too, the industrial time and motion studies of Fredrick Winslow Taylor were applied widely and somewhat indiscriminately, and the general enthusiasm for industrialization expressed itself on occasion in such unusual forms as concerts for the workers in which the instruments were factory whistles.[7] But even the twenties will not serve as a parallel. For cybernetics was held out by its most ardent advocates as a far more universal approach than any of the diverse theories of the twenties.

It was quite common in the Soviet Union in the early sixties to find articles on the application of cybernetics in such surprising fields as musicology and the fisheries industry, although frequently such expositions involved distortions of the meaning of the term "cybernetics." A number of the normally stolid and reserved academicians of the Academy of Sciences were the most exuberant disciples of the new field. The Communist Party itself in 1961 endorsed cybernetics as one of the major tools for the creation of a communist society.[8]

Even before formal endorsement the movement toward cybernetics began to take on the dimensions of a landslide. In April 1958 the Academy of Sciences created the Scientific Council on Cybernetics, headed by Academician A. I. Berg, which included mathematicians, physicists, chemists, biologists, physiologists, linguists, and jurists. The Academy's Institute of Automation and Telemechanics began directing most of its research toward cybernetic applications. The Moscow Power Institute, one of the largest and oldest engineering institutions in the country, with an enrollment of seventeen thousand students, devoted approximately one third of its instruction and research to cybernetics.[9] Soviet students were urged to major in cybernetics; science fiction was filled with descriptions of "cybernetic brain-modeling" and the "cybernetic boarding schools" of the future. The Academy of Pedagogical Sciences of the Russian Republic established such an experimental boarding school in Moscow to prepare children from an early age for careers in cybernetic programming.[10]

In 1961 Academician Berg edited a book entitled *Cybernetics in the Service of Communism*, in which Soviet scientists outlined the potential applications of cybernetics in the national economy.[11] In his introduction he argued that no country would be able to utilize cybernetics so effectively as the Soviet Union; since cybernetics consists largely of the selection of optimum methods of performing operations, only a socialist economy could incorporate these methods universally. "In a socialist planned economy," said Berg, "all conditions are present for the best utilization of the achievements of science and technology on behalf of all members of society rather than for various competing groups and the privileged minority."[12]

The combination in a national economy of centralized purposes with decentralized organization obviously contained contradictions. A number of non-Soviet commentators observed that the degree of success that the Soviet Union obtained in one direction would be accompanied by a corresponding degree of failure in the other. Later developments would show that there was considerable truth in this observation. The slowdown of the Soviet economy in the late seventies illustrated that cybernetics would not fulfill its promise for controlling the Soviet economy, although computers were absolutely essential in any advanced system of industrial production and military power.

PHILOSOPHICAL DISCUSSIONS

Cybernetics coincided with the materialism and optimism of Marxism, but it also raised a number of serious philosophical and sociological problems. Cybernetics had obvious applications in a number of fields— psychology, econometrics, pedagogical theory, logic, physiology, and biology—disciplines subjected to ideological restrictions under Stalin. These connections a priori confirmed the sensitivity of the subject. In the early 1950s Soviet ideologists were definitely hostile to cybernetics, although the total number of articles opposing the field unequivocally seems to have been no more than three or four.[13] This number is far fewer than the number of ideologically militant publications that appeared in the other controversies discussed in this volume, a fact that is largely explained, no doubt, by chronology: by the time cybernetics became widely known, the period of severe ideological interference in Soviet science had passed. On the other hand, Soviet scientists and engineers had for many years worked on the mathematical and physiological foundations of cybernetics. Such Soviet scientists as I. P. Pavlov, A. N. Kolmogorov, N. M. Krylov, and N. N. Bogoliubov must be counted among the men who prepared the way for the development of cybernetics, but they did not advance a generalized theory of control processes. The construction of such a theory, which is the heart of cybernetics, instead fell largely to people in North America.

Until the early 1950s the reception of cybernetics in the Soviet Union was silence; not until 1952, a year before Stalin's death, was cybernetics openly attacked, although a few earlier articles questioning mathematical logic could be seen as implied criticism of cybernetics.[14] A 1953 article in the *Literary Gazette* labeled cybernetics a "science of obscurantists" and ridiculed the view that a machine can think or duplicate organic life. The author particularly criticized the efforts of cyberneticists to extend their generalizations to explicate the collective activities of man. In addition, the critic attributed to cyberneticists in capitalist society the hope that their new machines would perform their society's unpleasant tasks for them: the striking and troublesome proletariat would be replaced by robots, bomber pilots who object to bombing helpless civilians would be replaced by "unthinking metallic monsters."[15]

In October 1953 a very critical article entitled "Whom Does Cybernetics Serve?" appeared in the leading Soviet philosophy journal; in later years this article was often referred to by Soviet defenders of cybernetics as the most typical statement of the opposition to cybernetics in the early 1950s. The author of the article, who identified himself only as "Materialist," advanced a criticism of cybernetics based on the dialectical materialist belief in the qualitative difference in matter at different levels of development; thus, a difference in principle existed between the human brain and even the most sophisticated computer. Such authors as Claude Shannon and Grey Walter, who attempted to construct mechanical devices that would display "social behavior," were falling into the same error as the materialists of the eighteenth century, such as La Mettrie and Holbach.[16] But while the views of the latter men were "progressive" in the eighteenth century, since they were directed primarily against religious beliefs, continued the Soviet critic, in the twentieth century such views were clearly reactionary. And, finally, "Materialist" returned to the earlier-expressed view that cybernetics represented a particularly pernicious effort by Western capitalists to extract more profits from industry by eliminating the necessity to pay wages to the proletariat.

Just as the initial hostility of the Soviet writers toward cybernetics can be related to the intellectual scene characteristic of Stalinism, so can the beginnings of a discussion of its merits be explained by noticing the changes in position of the Communist Party toward the natural sciences after Stalin's death. The influential position of the Party should not obscure the fact, however, that many scientists and engineers in the Soviet Union were skeptical of the claims of cyberneticists in the United States for reasons that were not, in many cases, uniquely Marxist in viewpoint.

In the spring of 1954 the Central Committee promoted a policy of much greater leniency on ideological issues in the sciences; a primary criterion for judgment was to be the empirical results of the utilization of scientific theories.[17] This position, while not totally new, was probably connected with the criticism of Lysenko's theories on genetics; it also allowed a more liberal discussion of cybernetics.

The first person to espouse a positive view toward cybernetics seems to have been the Czech philosopher and mathematician Ernst Kol'man, who lived in Moscow for long periods of time and often wrote on questions of the philosophy of science. Kol'man should by this time be a familiar name; involved in the debates over science for over three decades, as a young man he was a severe ideologue, but in later years he rather frequently took the more liberal side in various controversies. On November 19, 1954, Kol'man gave a very important lecture to the Academy of Social Sciences of the Central Committee of the Communist Party, in which he specifically attacked "Materialist" 's 1953 article.[18] Only later would the full irony of this occasion become clear; Kol'man, who assumed the role of champion of cybernetics, was later outpaced in his enthusiasm for the new field by many Soviet scholars, and in subsequent publications appealed for restraint in evaluations of the potentialities of cybernetics.[19] The major point of Kol'man's talk to the Academy of Social Sciences was his belief that the Soviet Union stood in danger of overlooking a technological revolution by discounting cybernetics. The new computing machines could be compared in significance, he said, to the implementation of the decimal numeral system or the invention of printing. The Soviet Union must master new processes and use them for its own goals, he continued.

Kol'man's speech, later published in *Problems of Philosophy*, was the beginning of a debate in the Soviet Union over the legitimacy of cybernetics, which lasted from 1954 to 1958. The first stage in this discussion was an exploration of the reasons for the initial coolness of Soviet Marxists to cybernetics. A group of authors strove for an explanation in mid-1955:

> Several of our philosophers made a serious mistake: Not understanding the essence of the problem, they began to deny the significance of this

new development in science basically because of the fact that around cybernetics abroad there was raised a sensational clamor, and because several ignorant bourgeois journalists promoted publicity and cheap speculations about cybernetics.[20]

The discussion of cybernetics soon turned to attempts to define the field and the technical terms used in it, such as "information," "quantity of information," "noise," "control," "feedback," "neg-entropy," "homeostasis," "memory," "consciousness," and even "life." Many articles seeking such definitions appeared. The adoption of cybernetic methods could not await the formulation of ideologically correct definitions, however; with the peculiar insistence of modern technology, computers found their way into many areas of the Soviet economy, including the defense and space efforts. Thus the Soviet Union turned toward cybernetics rather rapidly even though the new field contained many new concepts that had not yet received philosophic interpretation. This movement was led by scientists and engineers, accompanied by those philosophers, such as Kol'man, who shared their enthusiasm for the adoption of the most modern methods in the Soviet economy and who also saw, quite correctly, no inherent contradiction between Marxism and cybernetics.

Gradually the support for cybernetics became more impressive. Well-known scientists, such as Academician S. L. Sobolev, presented elementary and positive explanations of cybernetics to the philosophers and social scientists. Other scientists publicly underwent obviously sincere changes in their attitudes toward cybernetics. As late as October 1956, Academician A. N. Kolmogorov, whose work on the theory of automatic control was a genuine contribution to cybernetics, refused to accept its validity as a separate field; by April 1957, however, he declared at a meeting of the Moscow Mathematical Society that his earlier skepticism toward cybernetics had been mistaken, and in 1963 he wrote that it is theoretically possible for a cybernetic automaton to experience all activities of man, including emotion.[21]

The three main questions of philosophical concern that cybernetics raised were: (1) What is cybernetics, and how general is its application? (2) Can life processes be duplicated? (3) What is "information," and what is its connection with thermodynamics? In the early stages of the discussion of cybernetics in the Soviet Union questions one and two, which are related, received the most attention. After a certain degree of sophistication was attained, however, the question concerning information seemed the most pressing. Indeed, the problem of information, which may seem quite narrow at first glance, was basic to the whole debate; the answers given to this question affected the other two in unexpected ways.

WHAT IS CYBERNETICS?

The initial question, which concerns the universality of application of cybernetics, was one of the first aspects of the new field to concern the Soviet Marxists. The spectrum of the debate ranged from those who believed cybernetics to be no more than a loose word for process engineering to those who saw it as a new science providing the key to literally every form of the existence of matter. In the hands of its most enthusiastic proponents, cybernetics became an all-embracing system including even human society. Non-Soviet cyberneticists whose research originated in mathematics and engineering, such as Norbert Wiener and W. Ross Ashby, often spoke of the homeostatic properties of society. A homeostat is a random mechanism capable of adapting itself in such a way that it arrives at equilibrium and appears to be "purposeful."[22] Wiener believed that the controlling mechanism of society is its legal system, and that society constantly adjusts its laws on the basis of feedback information concerning the degree of disorder in society.[23] American political scientists, such as Karl Deutsch, quickly followed with models of political behavior taken from cybernetics.[24] Others began to use the cybernetic approach to sociology, history, and public administration.[25] The range of cybernetics loomed so great that the discipline seemed to some Soviet scholars to be a possible rival to Marxism, which advances a philosophy of both the natural and social sciences; the advent of this new field alarmed the more conservative Soviet philosophers. As one author commented:

> The subject of cybernetics is organic and inorganic nature (and technology), social processes, and phenomena concerned with consciousness. . . . But doesn't this mean that cybernetics opposes [Marxist] dialectics, that it is attempting to take its place as a new ideology? If such is the case . . . then the question would be: either dialectics or cybernetics. . . . The attempts to convert cybernetics into some universal philosophical science are completely baseless. Marxists must reject them out of hand.[26]

But it quickly became clear that rather than choose between cybernetics and Marxism, certain Soviet writers wished to unite them. L. A.

Petrushenko, for example, discussed productive labor as a series of processes performed on the basis of feedback.[27] Two other authors discussed the succeeding stages of history according to Marxism as epochs containing progressively smaller amounts of entropy.[28] V. N. Kolbanovskii criticized such extensions of cybernetics, but even he referred to the Marxist "withering away of the state" as a cybernetic phenomenon, a moment when society becomes self-regulating.[29]

Many Soviet scholars applied themselves, however, to the task of defining cybernetics in such a way that it did not even impinge upon Marxism as a general approach to phenomena. Of those scholars who attempted to define cybernetics (Berg, Kol'man, Novik, Shaliutin, Kolmogorov), most emphasized that cybernetics is the science of control and communication in complex systems, while Marxism is the science of the broadest laws of nature, society, and thought. According to this approach, Marxism is so much more general an intellectual system than cybernetics that the two do not conflict. This solution of the relationship of Marxism and cybernetics by placing them on entirely different levels was achieved in 1961 and 1962, when several important studies of cybernetics appeared.[30] However, the "two-plane" solution was not subscribed to by all authors. A number of contributors to Soviet philosophy journals continued to postulate that cybernetic analysis could be applied literally to all phenomena and that "information" was a property inherent in matter. This attempted expansion of cybernetics included occasionally a criticism of Friedrich Engels' writings on science, sometimes openly stated; others wrote that the works of Karl Marx reveal an understanding of the "cybernetic organization of matter," though the term itself was of course unknown to Marx.

CAN LIFE PROCESSES BE DUPLICATED?

Many persons approaching cybernetics for the first time, both in the Soviet Union and abroad, saw the entire controversy in the questions, Can a machine think? and, Can cybernetic mechanisms be considered alive? To narrow all the controversies of cybernetics to these queries is to impoverish the intellectual content of the discussions; nevertheless, the questions were seriously considered by most cyberneticists, and they played important roles in the debates in the Soviet Union. Wiener himself was properly cautious on these issues, but even he felt that in the light of cybernetics research some new definitions of "life" may be necessary. He noted that living organisms and inorganic cybernetic systems are similar in that they are both islands of decreasing entropy in a world in which disorder always tends to increase. He observed that "the problem as to whether the machine is alive or not is, for our purposes, semantic and we are at liberty to answer it one way or the other as best suits our convenience."[31] The question of whether machines are "alive" is clearly not identical with that of whether they "think," but Wiener's answers were similar; he remarked that whether a machine can think is merely a "question of definition." More exactly phrased, the problem of thinking machines was usually posed as: Do computers perform functions that are merely analogous to thinking, or are these functions structurally identical with thinking? With the question phrased in this way, the English logician A. M. Turing was quite willing to face the possibility of thinking machines. He believed that a machine could be considered to think if a man separated from a machine by an opaque partition could not determine whether he was facing a machine or another man, basing his conclusions on the answers that he received to questions addressed to the machine.[32]

Several of the Soviet scholars who first supported cybernetics, such as Kol'man and Berg, later warned against the concept of thinking machines; they admitted only an analogous relationship between the machines' functions and thought. Thus, Kol'man commented, "Cybernetic machines, even the most perfected, handling complex logic processes, do not think and do not form concepts."[33] Berg was even more unequivocal: "Do electronic machines 'think'? I am sure that they do not. Machines do not think, and they will not think."[34] These views were supported by Todor Pavlov, honorary president of the Bulgarian Academy of Sciences, who wrote, "Even the most complex robot does not assimilate, does not sense, does not remember, does not think, does not dream, does not fictionalize, does not seek."[35]

The theoretical explanation of the inability of computers to have consciousness was the same as that given by "Materialist" in 1953: Matter at different levels of development possesses qualitative differences; to attribute mental powers to a mechanical agglomeration of transistors and circuits would be, the critics said, to make the mechanistic mistake of believing that all complex operations can be reduced to combinations of simple ones, a belief specifically denied by their interpretation of dialectical materialism. They maintained that sophisticated organisms differ qualitatively from less complex ones, and cannot be reduced to the same components.

As in the case of the problem of defining cybernetics (see p. 276), it appeared by 1961 that considerable agreement had been reached, in this instance specifically denying the possibility of thinking machines; after that time, however, cybernetics enthusiasts returned with their most effective statements to date. In a 1964 article prefaced with the slogan "Only an Automaton? No, a Thinking Creature!" Academician Kolmogorov commented, "The exact definition of such concepts as will, thinking, emotion, still have not been formulated. But on a natural-scientific level of strictness such a definition is possible. . . . The fundamental possibility of creating living creatures in the full sense of the term, built completely on discrete (digital) mechanisms for processing information and for control, does not contradict the principles of dialectical materialism."[36] Such articles alarmed a number of nonscientists, one of whom, B. Bialik, wrote an article entitled "Comrades, Are You Serious?" in which he refused to believe that a machine can experience emotion, appreciate art, or possess genuine consciousness. Academician S. L. Sobolev, director of the Institute of Mathematics and Computation Center of the Siberian Branch of the Academy of Sciences, answered Bialik in an article entitled "Yes, This Is Completely Serious!" This was probably the most outspoken favorable article on cybernetics by a responsible author to appear in the Soviet press. Sobolev straightforwardly called man a cybernetic machine and posed the possibility of man's creating other machines that would be alive, capable of emotion, and probably superior to men.[37]

Although the question of the ability of cybernetic devices to duplicate living organisms remained controversial in the Soviet Union, an affirmative answer to this question did not receive much support from philosophers. Dialectical materialism may not specifically deny the possibility of thinking machines, but the anthropocentric or humanistic nature of historical materialism was a genuine obstacle to such an opinion. According to a number of Soviet authors, the main difference between man and machine was not technical, but social. As Kol'man remarked, "Those who maintain that man is a machine and that cybernetic devices think, feel, have a will, etc., forget one 'trifle'—the historical approach. Machines are a product of the social-labor activity of man."[38] This view was expressed even more forcefully by N. P. Antonov and A. N. Kochergin:

> It is necessary to emphasize that man works, and not the machine. One can say that the machine functions, but not that it labors. The machine cannot become the subject of laboring activity because it does not and

cannot be possessed of the necessity of work, and it has no social requirements that it must labor to satisfy. This is the main and principal difference between machine and man.[39]

A question even more important than the ability of machines to duplicate man's functions was that of the moral responsibility of man for the actions of his machines. On the whole, non-Soviet cyberneticists were, at least publicly, more fearful than their Soviet counterparts of the possible results of their employment of computers. In 1960, when Norbert Wiener visited the editorial offices of the leading Soviet journal in philosophy, *Problems of Philosophy* (where he received a very warm reception), he commented:

> If we create a machine . . . that is so "intelligent" that in some degree it surpasses man, we cannot make it altogether "obedient." Control over such machines may be very incomplete. . . . They might even become dangerous, for it would be an illusion to assume that the danger is eliminated simply because we press the button. Human beings, of course, can press the button and stop the machines. But to the extent that we do not control all the processes that occur in the machine, it is quite possible that we will not know when the button should be pressed. Thus, the programming of "thinking" machines presents us with a moral problem.[40]

Wiener's uneasiness was expressed in different terms by other cyberneticists who spoke of the possibility of a dictator controlling society through the use of cybernetic machines, while still others referred to the computer as a demon that turns on its master.[41]

These pessimistic views of authors in Western Europe and North America were by and large rejected by Soviet writers. Like the philosophers, Soviet scientists were, with very few exceptions, optimistic in their statements about science. If any of them, in Oppenheimer's phrase, "came to know sin" as a result of their research, they kept this encounter to themselves. Indeed, several Soviet scholars said that the essential difference between man and machine was the fact than man sets his own goals while the machine strives only toward those for which it has been programmed. If society places a premium on worthwhile goals, said the Soviet authors, the machines of that society will be assigned similarly meritorious functions. These writers suggested that cyberneticists in capitalist societies betrayed a lack of confidence in those societies when they were unsure of the roles their computers would be asked to play.

WHAT IS "INFORMATION"?

Cybernetic systems operate on the basis of the collection, processing, and transmission of information. The development of increasingly sophisticated means of evaluating the measuring of information was one of the important factors determining the progress of cybernetics. Yet, interestingly enough, no one devised a thoroughly satisfactory definition of information. Norbert Wiener once observed, perhaps with no great intent, that "information is neither matter nor energy," it is just "information."[42] W. Ross Ashby also warned of the dangers of trying to treat information as a material or individual "thing": "Any attempt to treat variety or information as a thing that can exist in another thing is likely to lead to difficult 'problems' that should never have arisen."[43]

Dialectical materialism asserts that objective reality consists of matter and energy in various forms. If information is neither matter nor energy, then what is it? In the early sixties the attention of Soviet philosophers shifted, at least relatively, from the broader questions of the nature of cybernetics and life to the more narrow problem of the nature of information. They advanced several reasons for this shift of emphasis. In the first place, the more restricted question of the nature of information can be treated more rigorously than such a question as "Can machines think?" Second, upon investigation the problem of information proves to be the key to many of the broader questions raised earlier.

The problem of the philosophic interpretation of the concept of information was a genuine and troublesome one. If information can be measured, some Soviet scholars reasoned, then it must possess objective reality. As early as 1927 R. V. L. Hartley observed that the amount of information conveyed in any message is related to the number of possibilities that are excluded by the message. Thus, the phrase "Apples are red" carries much more information than the phrases "Fruits are red" or "Apples are colored" because the first phrase eliminates all kinds of fruits other than apples and all colors other than red. This exclusion of other possibilities increases informational content.[44] In later years the basic principle enunciated by Hartley was refined and elaborated on a mathematic basis. In 1949 in the fundamentally important publication *The Mathematical Theory of Communication* Claude Shannon and Warren Weaver presented a formula for the calculation of quantity of information in which information increases as the probability of the particular message decreases. In this method, information is defined as a measure of one's (or a system's) freedom of choice in selecting a message. Thus, in a situation where the number of likely messages from which to choose is large, the amount of information produced by that system is also large. To be more precise, the amount of information is defined (in simple situations) as the logarithm of the available choices. Shannon's and Weaver's 1949 formula was

$$H = -K \sum_{i=1}^{n} P_i \log P_i$$

where H is the amount of information in a system with a choice of messages with probabilities $(P_1, P_2 \ldots P_n)$, and K is a constant depending on the unit of measure.[45] This formula is functionally the same as that for thermodynamic entropy devised by Max Planck as the beginning of the century: $S = K \log W$, where S equals entropy of the system, W equals the thermodynamic probability of the state of the system, and K equals Boltzmann's constant.[46]

Some scientists considered the potential implications of this coincidence to be immense. The possibility of an analogy or even a structural identity between entropy and information generated a heated debate among physicists, philosophers, and engineers in many countries. Weaver commented, "When one meets the concept of entropy in communication theory, he has a right to be rather excited—a right to suspect that one has hold of something that may turn out to be basic and important." Louis de Broglie called the link between entropy and information "the most important and attractive of the ideas advanced by cybernetics."[47] If one could demonstrate that the relation between neg-entropy and information is more than functional similarity, and is instead an identity, the construction of a general theory of matter by which all complex systems—inorganic and organic, including human—could be mathematically described seems at least conceivable. The more venturesome dialectical materialists tended to welcome such a possibility, since it seemed to them a vindication of materialistic monism. A literal rephrasing of the three basic laws of the dialectic in cybernetic terms was attempted by the author of an unpublished doctoral dissertation at Moscow University.[48] The more orthodox majority, however, was unsettled by the difficulties of fitting such an ambitious theory into the principles of dialectical materialism.

An additional problem in interpreting information theory in terms of dialectical materialism concerned the supposed "subjective" nature of quantity of information. The proponents of the subjective approach

(Ashby and L. Brillouin, among others) pointed out that one can hardly speak of the quantity of information in any message in absolute terms since a certain message will carry much more information to one observer than to another, depending on the prior knowledge of the observer. Following this approach, several non-Soviet authors called for the attaching of qualitative coefficients to calculations of quantity of information, based on the value of information, the degree of certitude, and meaningfulness. But if information (variety) is to be quantitatively measured, the Soviet philosophers insisted, it must be part of objective reality, and not conditioned by subjective considerations. A. D. Ursul's comment on this topic was appropriate: "First of all we must notice that in a finite system the quantity of variety inherent to it does not depend on the observer and is always finite. . . ."[49]

Not only in the Soviet Union were scholars cautious about information theory; for every enthusiast who might attempt to identify information with neg-entropy, another sober-minded individual added a cautionary note. Ashby, for example, commented: "Moving in these regions is like moving in a jungle full of pitfalls. Those who know most about the subject are usually the most cautious in speaking about it."[50] And yet, despite the warnings, the general trend among cyberneticists in the early sixties was a greater acceptance of the conception that there exists some essential link between entropy and information.

I. B. Novik was one of the more energetic Soviet philosophers who attempted to define information in terms of dialectical materialism. In his book *Cybernetics: Philosophical and Sociological Problems* Novik tried to present a systematic treatment of cybernetics from the standpoint of enlightened Marxism.[51] From the outset he aligned himself with the partisans of cybernetics; he insisted that there was no conflict beteen this new field and dialectical materialism. Wiener to him was an unconscious dialectician. Novik explained that cybernetic information is a property of matter, a property directly connected with Lenin's copy theory of epistemology. Lenin wrote in *Materialism and Empirio-Criticism* that materialism is based on a recognition of "objects in themselves," and that objects exist "without the mind." According to Lenin, ideas and sensations are reflections of these objects; all matter has this property of "reflection." Novik then postulated that "quantity of information" is a measure of the order of the reflection of matter. Novik then called for the creation of a science of the "physics of reflection," and in order to hasten the development of this new field, he proposed a rudimentary law of the conservation of information patterned on the law of conservation of matter, since information is "inseparably linked" to matter.[52]

Other authors, following the lead of the philosophers who in 1961 and 1962 attempted to separate the realms of applicability of cybernetics and dialectical materialism, denied that the concept of information can be related to entropy or to states of matter outside narrowly defined control systems. Thus N. I. Zhukov commented, "Certain authors consider that information processes are characteristic of all processes in inorganic nature. Such a universal understanding of this concept creates difficulties in the development of the theory of information and cybernetics. . . . Information, in our opinion, may be precisely defined as an adjusted change used for the purposes of control."[53]

Nonethless, the enthusiastic proponents of cybernetics continued to maintain that information is a property of all matter and that the evolution of matter, from the simplest atom to the most complex of all material forms, man, may be seen as a process of the accumulation of information. Thus, these authors tied cosmogonical, geological, and organic evolution together in one process of the tendency of matter, at least in certain loci, to increase its informational content. The result was a sort of great chain of being, a ladder in nature of ascending complexity, although evolutionary instead of static.[54]

In 1968 A. D. Ursul, a Soviet mathematician, published an interesting book entitled *The Nature of Information,* in which he defended very strongly his belief that information is characteristic of all matter, from the simplest inorganic forms to human society.[55] Ursul tied this conception of the unity of nature closely to dialectical materialism, arguing that the dialectical laws help one to understand information processes.[56] But he also thought that information theory had added new content to dialectical materialism; he posed the possibility of making a few changes in Marxist philosophy as a result of the contribution to man's knowledge of information theory. In particular, he believed that there was a good argument for converting the concept of information from a scientific-technical one to a general philosophic category, adding it to the existing list of categories in the Marxist dialectic (p. 285). But he also recognized that in view of the short length of time that Marxist philosophers had studied the concept of information, it might still be premature to call for universal acceptance of it as a Marxist category.

Ursul believed that those writers who refused to accept the application of information theory to inorganic systems, on the grounds that these systems do not "use" information, were overlooking an extremely fruitful approach to nature. Information may be either "used" or not "used" in a functional sense, but, according to him, it still exists. Furthermore, an information approach to molecules can even help us to understand the difference between the inorganic and organic worlds: "If the information content of an object is several dozens of bits on the molecular level, then it probably is an object of inorganic nature. If the object contains 10^{15} bits on this level, then we are dealing with a living object (p. 153).

Ursul recognized, however, that analysis of this sort carried with it the dangers of reductionism—the elimination of qualitative characteristics on different levels of matter. He believed, however, that information cannot be entirely described by one method, such as mathematical probability, but instead must be approached from standpoints that include qualitative characteristics, such as topology (p. 35).[57] He also urged that information theory be supplemented with an understanding of dialectical levels of nature. Not all information is the same; it possesses qualitative characteristics, and two different types of information cannot be compared. According to Ursul, each level of nature possesses "its own" information (p. 150). Ignoring this specificity accounts for the incautious way in which many philosophers and scientists have extended concepts derived from physics, such as entropy, to other realms. Instead, Ursul favored "classifying" information (neg-entropy) into different types, each with its own realm of applicability. The Soviet author V. A. Polushkin had already made such an attempt when he divided information into "elementary," "biological," and "logical" types. In this scheme, elementary information was understood as information in nonliving nature. Ursul thought that Polushkin's effort was in the right direction, but suggested that much further work would have to be done; to him, "human" or "social" information was also a type, and within human information he further distinguished at least two aspects: semantic (content) and pragmatic (value) (pp. 47–48).

Ursul thought that the transition from one realm of information to another was, in evolutionary terms, a qualitative jump. He pointed to the possibility of combining this approach with elements of the biological philosophy of Ludwig von Bertalanffy, the Canadian scholar (p. 98).

INCREASING SOVIET SKEPTICISM ABOUT CYBERNETICS

In the late 1970s and early 1980s Soviet scientists and philosophers became much more cautious than many of them had been a few years earlier about the potentialities of computers. In 1979 B. V. Biriukov, one of the earlier enthusiasts, wrote:

> If ten years ago I often emphasized the possibility in principle of making
> a cybernetic model of any well-described information process, then today
> I must say that my views on this matter have changed. . . . The fact of
> the matter is that in the last decade limitations connected with the
> complexity of the problem have emerged very clearly.[58]

The editors of *Problems of Philosophy* commented that "the time has
passed when philosophers and cyberneticists could make predictions
about the possibility and even necessity of a full formalization and
automatization of human activity."[59] Having shed a large element of
their earlier intoxication with cybernetics, the editors now announced
that "the cybernetic approach is, in the common sense of the term, a
'one-sided' approach that looks at a given object which is being modelled
only from the informational point of view."[60]

The more sober view on cybernetics was accompanied by a careful
downgrading of cybernetics relative to Marxism. No longer did Soviet
philosophers speak, as they had occasionally done in the sixties, of
recasting the Marxist laws of the dialectic in cybernetic terms.[61] Even
the mathematician A. D. Ursul, who had once been one of the extreme
promoters of the universality of cybernetics, wrote in 1981 that cybernetics "can not be a universal basis for attaining the unity of scientific
knowledge and, especially, can not substitute for philosophy. Marxist-
Leninist philosophy studies the universal laws of movement and development of existence and thought, while cybernetics studies only
communicative and control processes in the biological and social
spheres."[62]

The editors of *Problems of Philosophy* gave a revealing explanation
for the intoxication with cybernetics that had hit the Soviet Union
earlier. It flowed, they said, from the fact that in the past (during and
immediately after Stalin's last years) there had been excessive criticism
of cybernetics on an ideological basis. In reaction to the dogmatism of
the Stalinist years, many Soviet intellectuals strongly promoted all those
fields that had earlier been condemned, such as cybernetics and genetics,
and in some cases raised them to an unjustified prominence. When
eminent scientists such as Academicians Kolmogorov and Sobolev asserted that cyberneticists could create thinking creatures on the basis
of their computers, Soviet philosophers were reluctant to criticize them
for fear that the philosophers would be castigated as Marxist dogmatists
once again hobbling science. But now the Marxists were regaining their
critical voices.[63]

In the future, wrote Biriukov, philosophers and scientists discussing
the potentiality of duplicating human activity by cybernetics must "avoid

that absolutization of the biological principle in man which is rejected by dialectical materialism. . . . We must take note of the fact that man's needs are the product not just of biological development; their special characteristics in comparison to the animal world are to be found in the history of society. . . . The form of man's needs, motives and goals are formed in human collectives."[64]

Even the remaining enthusiasts for cybernetics were forced to phrase their arguments in a more modest fashion. Academician Glushkov, director of the Institute of Cybernetics of the Ukrainian Academy of Sciences, wrote that he had been mistaken earlier to think that "thinking" machines could fully duplicate human activity; he still saw, however, almost unlimited possibilities for computers if they were used in conjunction with humans, with human intuition and reasoning supplementing the vast potential of the computers.[65] And G. N. Povarov called for a continuing effort to create with the computers forms of artificial intelligence; whatever the result of these efforts, he maintained, important scientific achievements would be produced. If artificial intelligence is actually created, that obviously would be a great scientific event; what is often not noticed, said Povarov, is that if the opposite were proven—if, in principle, such an artificial intelligence can not be created—that also would be scientifically important, similar to the discovery of the impossibility of perpetual motion machines.[66]

NEW DISCUSSIONS OF THE NATURE OF "INFORMATION"

One of the most controversial philosophical issues of cybernetics in the Soviet Union in the eighties continued to be the nature of "information." For over two decades this problem has been discussed by Soviet scientists and philosophers but the debates show no sign of an end. The same question has also attracted the attention of Western scientists and philosophers, but to Soviet theorists the nature of information has a special significance; they connect it to what they call the "basic question of philosophy," namely, the relationship between matter and cognition. On this essential issue they believe that the position of materialism must be constantly defended against the attacks of idealistic Western philosophers. Academician V. M. Glushkov in a 1981 publication charged Western scholars with promoting "new forms of anti-materialistic interpretations of the achievements of modern science—'cybernetic idealism,' 'system idealism,' 'information idealism' and so forth."[67] The mistake of these philosophers, according to Glushkov, was to consider information to be an abstraction without any connection to experience, reality, or matter. Just as there had long been an idealistic school of mathematics, he continued, so now there was an idealistic school of cybernetics.

A primary goal of the Soviet scholars, then, was to give a satisfactory materialistic interpretation of information. Almost all of them believed that the path toward such an interpretation started with Lenin's concept of "reflection."

A major problem existed, however, regarding the question of whether information was to be viewed as an objective attribute of matter itself. Could all forms of matter be arranged on a scale of increasing informational complexity leading up, eventually, to humans and their brains? Citations from Lenin were ambiguous; on the one hand, he said that it was logical to propose that all matter possesses reflection; on the other hand, he did not speak of information. How tightly should the concept of information be tied to the Leninist property of reflection? If reflection and information were made identical, then it seemed necessary to conclude that all matter, even inorganic, contains information as an attribute. But some Soviet philosophers saw that this path led dangerously close to anthropomorphic, teleological, and even hylozoistic concepts.

The disagreements among the Soviet philosophers were compounded by the fact that there was no unanimity among them even on the question of reflection, not to speak of information. Some believed that reflection existed objectively even in inorganic matter, since a change in one body is usually "reflected" in another in many different ways, even if only in the most rudimentary gravitational or electromagnetic fashion; others believed that reflection in inorganic bodies should be considered only a "potential," not a real or objective phenomenon. To the latter, "influence" was not the same as reflection, since reflection was much closer to sensation.[68]

Different positions on the nature of information were connected with the differences on reflection. Obviously a person who equated information with reflection and who believed that reflection was a characteristic of all matter was logically driven to the conclusion that information is an attribute of all matter, including nonliving matter. Several leading Soviet philosophers tried to escape this conclusion, however, by making a distinction between information and reflection. B. S. Ukraintsev, who in the late seventies and early eighties was the director of the Institute of Philosophy, steadfastly maintained that information arises only in highly organized matter and is connected with the process of control. He wrote that "without control processes there cannot be information."[69] Therefore, inorganic matter does not possess information.

This position that information is not a universal attribute of matter won more support from leading professional philosophers, especially those holding positions of ideological responsibility, than it did from information theory specialists. P. V. Kopnin, the director of the Institute of Philosophy before Ukraintsev, had also denied that information was intrinsic in all matter, and so did a number of other philosophers.[70]

A different view was expressed by a rather large group of scholars consisting mainly of specialists in information theory and a few philosophers closely connected with them. This group relied strongly on mathematical approaches to information. They were not as worried as the leading professional philosophers about what the effects on Marxist philosophy might be of creating a universal theory of information potentially applicable to all aspects of the universe and all levels of matter, including "socially organized matter," i.e., society itself. Leading exponents of this view included Academicians A. I. Berg and V. M. Glushkov, perhaps the two best-known specialists in cybernetics in the Soviet Union.[71]

By the early eighties it became evident that the viewpoint expressed by the leading professional philosophers—that information should be attributed only to control processes, and not to all matter—was beginning to win out. Most of the articles expressing the contrary, more ambitious, viewpoint had been written in the early period of intoxication over cybernetics. As one might expect, in this period the leading information theory specialists made extremely expansive claims about the significance of their new discipline. As the years passed, however, more sober viewpoints began to predominate, for two reasons: specialists in cybernetics all over the world retracted their ambitions as they learned that the early claims that information could be equated with negentropy produced few actual results outside control processes; and, in the Soviet Union, the philosophers and ideologists wished to eliminate the challenge of cybernetics to Marxism as a universal explantory scheme.

SOCIAL INFORMATION

The newest topic of discussion in the Soviet Union connected with cybernetics, potentially the most controversial of all, is "social information." Although no one yet has produced a good definition of just exactly what social information is, it generally is meant to be information that is used by society, both for its direction and for its enlightenment. Several Soviet writers now consider this topic to be the most pressing research theme for philosophers and political ideologists interested in cybernetics.[72] Just as in the United States where many sociologists and political scientists are beginning to speak of the "information society," so also in the Soviet Union philosophers and political analysts have begun to analyze the impact on society of the rapid spread of new communications systems. In what way will the spread of computer systems, data banks, telecommunication networks, and personal computers affect the Soviet Union? The question is far from a casual one, since the control of information is one of the fundamental principles of Soviet society.

We have already seen (p. 267), that one of the reasons that the Party and government leaders originally became interested in cybernetics was its potential for managing an increasingly complex Soviet economy. Computer systems also had obvious military and intelligence capabilities that would enhance the powers of the leadership.

As time went on, however, it became increasingly clear that computerization of a society strengthens local and unofficial tendencies as well as central and official ones. Some Soviet philosophers noticed that in the biological world complex organisms are not highly centralized, and wondered if the lesson for societies was not similar; in a volume entitled *The Synthesis of Knowledge and the Problem of Management*, a group of philosophers from the Institute of Philosophy observed: "For the further optimization of management, as evolution demonstrates, it is important to preserve and even develop in every possible way the relative independence of information processes. This means, specifically, an increase in the quantity and variety of 'degrees of freedom' in the process being managed, the number of paths and variants of reaction available to the process."[73] The implications for Soviet society seemed obvious.

The decentralizing implications of cybernetics accelerated in the eighties as attention shifted more and more from large computers to microcomputers and personal computers. In Western Europe and the United States microcomputers rapidly became objects of personal possession, used by business people and scholars in their own homes and businesses. In this development there emerged an ominous possibility from the standpoint of the Soviet leadership. Every personal computer with an attached printer is a potential printing press, capable of producing *samizdat* documents in unlimited copies. Yet in the Soviet Union the possession of printing presses by private citizens is prohibited by law. How would the Soviet Union control the rapid spread of computers? Would it permit computer networks and "bulletin board" systems of the types rapidly spreading in the West?

Marxist philosophers began to prepare the way for establishing priorities and principles governing the spread of computer information in the Soviet Union different from those in the West. Several of them wrote that "Soviet researchers are unmasking the falseness of the modish bourgeois sociological conceptions of the 'objective means of information,' of the so-called 'purely informational press,' which are opposed to the Marxist conception of the means of mass information, whose function is the formation of social opinion."[74]

Soviet ideologists such s V. G. Afanas'ev began to differentiate "information" into socially "variant" and "invariant" types. Invariant information, presumably information not deemed harmful to the Soviet system, would be the same in all societies. Variant information, which they dubbed "ideal social information," carries the deep mark of class, national, and other relationships, the imprint of the needs, interests, and psychic traits of the social collective. On this basis they called for a class, Party approach to social information (to its collection, analysis, processing, and use) in a class society.[75]

With the decline of detente in the late seventies, Soviet specialists in management and information theory began increasingly to affirm that the information used in computers is not politically neutral. Cooperation with Western management and computer specialists was fraught with ideological difficulties. D. M. Gvishiani, son-in-law of former Premier Aleksei Kosygin and one of the foremost proponents of cooperation with Western scientists at the International Institute of Applied Systems Analysis (IIASA) near Vienna, noted that ideology made the work difficult. One of the projects promoted at IIASA was "global modeling," the effort to predict future world ecological and energy problems by computer prognoses. Concerning these efforts, Gvishiani wrote:

> It is becoming more and more apparent that the results of global modeling are not defined by formal methods in themselves but by significant theoretical—and, first of all—philosophical and sociological assumptions.[76]

Between the 1960s and the 1980s we can see an essential difference in the ways in which Soviet philosophers and ideologists looked upon information. In the early period, a time of exuberance about cybernetics, information was discussed as if it were a neutral entity, possibly applicable to all of nature, even nonliving matter. By the eighties, information was restricted to control processes in living nature, complex computer systems, and human society. Furthermore, information was now differentiated into different types, some politically neutral, and some highly dangerous politically. The implications for Soviet society seemed clear. Personal computers and data banks would be controlled carefully in the Soviet Union in the ways in which all other information media already are.

For all the persuasiveness of cybernetics upon first contact, it is a very incomplete science.[77] Cybernetics seem to be dissolving into less dramatic sub-areas of information theory and computer technology. As a French specialist in cybernetics observed, "As an adjective, 'cybernetic' threatens to go the way of 'atomic' and 'electronic' in becoming just another label for the spectacular."[78] Many scientists find the use of the term embarrassing. Furthermore, it is now clear that there were genuine defects in the writings of several of the founders of cybernetics who, in their enthusiasm, often confused certain technical terms, such as "quantity of information" and "value of information."[79] And finally, cybernetics proceeds on the basis of analogical reasoning, which by itself leads not to logical or scientific proofs, but instead to inferences that may or may not be significant and fruitful.

The strength of such reasoning depends upon the similarities that can be identified between the two entities being compared. Soon after the development of the methodology of cybernetics, the comparison of the human body as a control system to an economic system, a city government, or an automatic pilot seemed to result in the identification of truly striking similarities. The longer one dwells upon such analogies, however, the more clearly emerge the very genuine differences that exist between the entities being compared.

There have been cyberneticists, such as Stafford Beer, who maintain that cybernetics goes far beyond analogy. They argue that if one abstracts the control structure of two dissimilar organisms, the relationship between these structures may be one of identity rather than of analogy.[80] The control structure of a complex industry and that of a living organism may be identical, according to this view, in the same way that the geometrical form of an apple and that of an orange may be identical circles. This approach may be correct on an abstract level, but it has not resulted in as many discoveries of fruitful similarities and avenues of research, beyond those originally identified, as early proponents of cybernetics hoped.

In cybernetics the absence of dramatic theoretical breakthroughs has lessened the persuasiveness of its conceptual scheme as an explanation of all dynamic processes. In the United States, where computers are applied very widely and where their sociological and economic consequences are still topics of vigorous debate, the decline in interest in cybernetics as a conceptual scheme is clearly evident. The postcybernetic epoch involves not a renunciation of cybernetics, but only a more sober appraisal of its potentialities. The original zeal might be renewed by future developments in theory, but one obviously cannot foretell such events.

Pardoxically, the decline worldwide in interest in cybernetics as a conceptual scheme has occurred at a time when computers have become increasingly important in business, industrial, and military activities. The Soviet Union has lagged behind in finding new applications for computers, but a great effort was made in the eighties to catch up. In 1985 the Central Committee of the Communist Party of the Soviet Union passed a resolution calling for even more urgent efforts to adopt computers in industry and education. Meanwhile, Party ideologists called for a computer "literacy campaign" matching in intensity the basic literacy campaign of the twenties and thirties.[81] This new emphasis on computers will inevitably lead to even more discussion of the philosophical and political implications of "social information."

CHAPTER **9**

CHEMISTRY

British interviewer: "If you look at the history of science since the Revolution there have been a number of cases of direct interference of a political kind in fundamental research. . . . Do you think that could happen again?"

Academician V. Koptiug, chairman of the Siberian Division of the Academy of Sciences of the USSR: "You know, this is a very complex question. . . . When, in the past, from philosophical positions criticisms were made of the concept of resonance in chemistry . . . that, in my opinion, was right. But when from general philosophical positions attempts were made to solve general scientific questions: is genetics a science or a pseudoscience? That was a mistake."

—BBC television interview, November 8, 1981

The nature of bonds between atoms is of fundamental importance to chemistry, since that science is to a large degree a study of the alterations of such bonds. Yet the inadequacy of bond diagrams in depicting important chemical compounds has been known from the very beginning of structural chemistry. Succeeding diagrammatic systems were discarded because of the failure of each system to account for certain phenomena. The ancient contest between idealism and materialism entered the discussion when some chemists began using models that seemed physically inconceivable to other chemists.

The formulas and models constructed by chemists must explain not only the composition of chemical compounds, but also their properties. In the first half of the nineteenth century no single convention or method of representing compounds was accepted. J. R. Partington remarked, "It was apparently considered a sign of independence of thought for every chemist to have his own set of formulae."[1] As late as 1861 Fredrich August Kekulé gave nineteen different formulas for acetic acid.[2]

The reason for the fragmentation of theories and the use of multiple formulas lay in the inability of chemists to observe or measure molecules directly. Chemistry in general, and organic chemistry in particular, were frighteningly unknown. In 1835 Wöhler wrote to Berzelius, "organic chemistry appears to me like a primeval forest of the tropics, full of the most remarkable things."[3] During the next thirty years chemists collected an astonishing amount of data and isolated many compounds, but the formulas for compounds were still conjectures based on very incomplete experimental data.[4]

The nineteenth-century chemists soon discovered that many compounds could not be represented by a single formula that would explain all their known reactions. One formula accounted for one particular reaction, and another explained a different reaction. Perhaps by the use of four or five dissimilar models of the molecule of one compound a chemist could account for all of the known reactions of that compound, but his method merely pointed up the dilemma: common sense indicated to the chemists that any substance should have molecules of a particular shape, which could be reproduced by a model (leaving aside for the moment isomers and tautomers, which are a separate topic: see note 7). But there were only a certain number of ways, geometrically speaking, that a particular model of a molecule could be constructed, and no one of these ways explained all of the reactions of that particular substance. This is the case for many compounds at the present time, the most familiar being benzene.

When Kekulé sketched out the simple hexagon still used to represent the starting point for aromatic compounds, he immediately ran into the problem of the location of the bonds.[5] Kekulé believed that carbon atoms were quadrivalent, so each carbon atom had one bond unaccounted for. Kekulé adopted the idea of alternate double and single bonds:

$$
\begin{array}{c}
C \\
C \quad\diagup\hspace{-0.4em}\diagdown\quad C \\
C \quad\diagdown\hspace{-0.4em}\diagup\quad C \\
C
\end{array}
$$

This formula, although still utilized almost universally, is not satisfactory. If benzene actually were so constituted, it would mean the following two isomers would be possible.

$$
\begin{array}{c}
CCl \\
C \qquad CCl \\
C \qquad C \\
C
\end{array}
\qquad\qquad
\begin{array}{c}
C \\
C \qquad CCl \\
C \qquad CCl \\
C
\end{array}
$$

Upon examination of the above diagrams one will see the difference: In the first case, there is a double bond between the two added chlorine atoms, while in the second, there is a single bond. But two such isomers do not exist, not with chlorine or any other added groups; we know that isomers of orthodisubstituted compounds of benzene can not be created.

In 1872 Kekulé introduced the concept that the bonds are constantly "flapping between alternate sections like a pair of swinging barn doors."[6]

Rather than draw such a complicated model for benzene every time, chemists usually draw two formulas, showing the two positions. These two diagrams are usually called the "ideal Kekulé structures."[7]

The explanation that the bonds of benzene are shifting back and forth satisfied the needs of chemists for many years. Abbreviated or out-of-date histories of chemistry sometimes stop with the story of benzene at this point. However, chemists found that a connection between opposite carbon atoms, or a link between the para positions, also must exist:

This formula was originally suggested by Sir James Dewar, who intended it to supplement the two original Kekulé structures.[8] Now there were three formulas for benzene, and a mental picture of "flapping barn doors" was becoming increasingly difficult. Furthermore, other variants were added. And most perplexing, it became apparent that no actual movement between simple bond configurations was occurring in the benzene molecule.

The resonance theory of valency, developed around 1930 by Linus Pauling and further expanded by G. W. Wheland, is an attempt to explain the structure of molecules such as benzene.[9] The significance of the resonance theory according to Wheland is that "it is considered possible for the true state of a molecule to be not identical with that represented by any single classical valence-bond structure, but to be intermediate between those represented by two or more different valence-bond structures."[10] Such an intermediate structure is known as a "resonance hybrid." Structural chemists have described many such hybrids. The two valence-bond structures "contributing" to the carboxylate ion are:[11]

$$R - C \overset{\displaystyle \ddot{O}:}{\underset{:\ddot{O}:^-}{}} \qquad R - C \overset{:\ddot{O}:^-}{\underset{:\ddot{O}:}{}}$$

The resonance hybrid for the carboxylate ion is usually drawn:

In the case of benzene, five different structures, the Kekulé-Dewar ideal forms, are considered to be contributing to the hybrid:[12]

For other compounds, many more models are used. To explain the reactions of anthracene, over four hundred diagrams are utilized.

Wheland repeatedly reminded his readers that resonance should be regarded not as any sort of oscillation between the various structures, but as a word referring to a molecule in a permanent hybrid state.[13] The five structures are merely aids for descriptive purposes and never, in fact, exist.[14] On this point Pauling commented:

We might say . . . that the molecule cannot be satisfactorily represented by any single valence-bond structure and abandon the effort to correlate its structure and properties with those of other molecules. By using valence-bond structures as the basis for discussion, however, with the aid of the concept of resonance, we are able to account for the properties of the molecule in terms of those of other molecules in a straightforward and simple way. It is for this practical reason that we find it convenient to speak of the resonance of molecules among several electronic structures.[15]

According to the theory of resonance, the bonds between the carbon atoms in benzene would be neither single nor double bonds, but a type of bond between the two, roughly described, perhaps, as a 1 ½ or 1 ⅓ bond. Such a description is supported by electron diffraction and infrared spectroscopic examinations, which show that while the distance between carbon atoms connected by single bond is about 1.54 Angstrom units and by double bonds is 1.33 units, the measurement for benzene bonds is 1.40, between that of a double and that of a single bond.[16]

Although, as Pauling emphasized, the theory of resonance does not rest upon quantum mechanics in its conception, a quantum-mechanical method of calculation is utilized in computing certain properties of the molecules, such as stability during reactions. A wave function, or Schrödinger equation, is written for each of the idealized, or resonance, structures, and then the wave functions are combined in a purely linear fashion, that is, by simple addition, with a weighting factor applied to each equation depending on the amount of "influence" each ideal structure exercises.

The theory of resonance and Pauling's elaboration of it were known in the Soviet Union long before World War II; many years passed before the theory of chemical bonds attracted any particular attention. The theory of resonance became popular among chemists in the Soviet Union. Prominent chemists such as A. N. Nesmeianov,[17] R. Kh. Freidlina, D. N. Kursanov,[18] E. N. Prilezhaeva,[19] M. I. Kabachnik,[20] and many others utilized the theory of resonance in their research and in their published works. In 1946 two Soviet chemists about whom we will hear considerably more, Ia. K. Syrkin and M. E. Diatkina, appeared with their own treatment of resonance in the book *The Chemical Bond and the Structure of Molecules*, which Pauling described as an "excellent work."[21] He added that in his opinion Syrkin and Diatkina were "among the most able [chemists] in Russia today."[22] The two authors' book was adopted by the Ministry of Higher Education of the USSR as a study aid for the chemistry faculties of the universities and received widespread distribution. It subsequently was translated into English for use in the United States.[23] The year after they published their own book, Syrkin and Diatkina translated Pauling's *The Nature of the Chemical Bond* into Russian; again, in the following year, they worked together in translating Wheland's *The Theory of Resonance and Its Applications to Organic Chemistry*, this time with Syrkin as editor and Diatkina as translator.

The resonance controversy was initiated by a zealous, ambitious, but undistinguished chemist, Gennadi V. Chelintsev, who was later accused of trying to gain the supreme position in chemistry that Trofim D. Lysenko had won in biology. Although the eventual outcome of the controversy would be considerably different from what Chelintsev called for, he was a central figure throughout the discussion in the following years.

In 1949 Chelintsev, a professor of chemical warfare at the Voroshilov Military Academy, published a book entitled *Essays on the Theory of Organic Chemistry* in which he proposed to explain molecular structure in a way that would not include the approximate methods of quantum mechanics and would not require the use of more than one formula for one compound.[24] In particular, he said the formula for benzene should be drawn, not on the basis of covalent bonds, but on the basis of electrovalent, or ionic, bonds.[25] Chelintsev would represent benzene in the following way:

The dotted line signified, to Chelintsev, "the leveling out" of the electronic charge. According to him, there were no double bonds in benzene at all. He maintained that the theory of resonance not only was sterile methodologically, but also introduced a mechanistic concept into chemistry, filling a gap in man's knowledge with an unrealistic but comforting mechanical description.

The appearance of Chelintsev's book elevated the theory of resonance to the platform of philosophical discussion at a moment of ideological militance in the Soviet Union. Resonance theory's use of multiple ideal structures, which Chelintsev called mechanistic, made the theory appear susceptible to criticism on philosophical grounds.

That the theory of resonance would be considered philosophically untenable to authors other than Chelintsev was made clear by V. M. Tatevskii and M. I. Shakhparanov in an article in the fall of 1949 entitled "On a Machist Theory in Chemistry and Its Propagandists."[26] The two writers selected for particular criticism Wheland's description of resonance as a man-made concept that "does not correspond to an intrinsic property of the molecule itself, but instead is only a mathematical device, deliberately invented by the physicist or chemist for his own convenience."[27] It would have been possible to center the criticism upon the philosophic implications of this statement rather than upon the resonance theory itself; one could easily maintain, according to a realist philosophy, that the resonance structures had some, perhaps quite indirect, relationship to the actual structure of the molecule, but that this relationship remained obscure. Until more information on the actual structure was obtained, the resonance theory could be used without necessarily subscribing to Wheland's philosophic remarks. Instead, Tatevskii and Shakhparanov affirmed that it would be philosophically incorrect to describe molecules in terms of ideal structures that were physically inconceivable. The primary fault of the resonance theory, according to the authors, was that it utilized more than one structure while insisting that no transformation back and forth between forms occurred. Thus, the theory of resonance had become "divorced from reality." Tatevskii and Shakhparanov maintained that Wheland and Pauling had tried to cover up their ignorance of the true nature of molecules with a clever creation containing false philosophic assumptions:

> The theory of resonance may serve as one example of the Machist theoretic-perceptional tendencies of bourgeois scientists, which are hostile to the Marxist world view and which lead them to pseudoscientific conclusions concerning the solution of concrete physical and chemical problems.[28]

The position taken by Tatevskii and Shakhparanov was paralleled closely by unsigned articles that appeared in the *Journal of Physical Chemistry* and in *Pravda* commemorating Stalin's seventieth birthday.[29] The authors of the articles asked that defects in Soviet science, especially in chemistry, be eliminated.

The discussion of resonance theory contained many references to a prominent and able nineteenth-century Russian chemist, Aleksandr M. Butlerov. Butlerov, a professor of chemistry at the universities of Kazan and St. Petersburg, and a member of the Imperial Academy of Sciences from 1874 to 1880, is only very rarely mentioned in non-Russian textbooks or histories of chemistry. There is little doubt that he deserves much more attention.[30] In 1940, before the resonance controversy began in the Soviet Union, a noted American historian of chemistry, Henry W. Leicester, wrote a biographical article lauding Butlerov for his advanced studies in the field of organic chemistry.[31] In 1953 a French chemist, J. Jacques, asserted that the name of Butlerov should have equal prominence with that of Friedrich Kekulé in the development of theories of molecular structure.[32] In the 1960 edition of his *The Nature of the Chemical Bond* Linus Pauling, who had recently been criticized severely by Soviet philosophers of science, gave credit to Butlerov for his work on valency.[33] In earlier editions of the same work, Pauling had not mentioned Butlerov, evidently because he had at that time not known of his work.[34] Although Butlerov's conception of molecular structure has still not been thoroughly evaluated outside the Soviet Union, Professor I. M. Hunsberger gave what may serve as an interim judgment: "There is no doubt whatsoever that Butlerov has not received the credit he richly deserves and that his monumental contributions to organic structural theory have been for the most part virtually overlooked. . . . Butlerov's contributions certainly equal those of Kekulé and Couper, but it is ridiculous to maintain that Butlerov is the sole author of structural theory."[35] In this light, Butlerov began to receive slightly more attention outside the Soviet Union in the 1950s. As late as the 1955 edition, however, the *Encyclopedia Britannica* did not even list Butlerov, although it gave a whole column to Kekulé. The 1963 edition contained a paragraph on Butlerov.

Butlerov's philosophical views differed from those of such chemists as Charles Gerhardt, who did not believe that chemical formulas represented any sort of reality. Kekulé himself never attributed much physical significance to his formulas; he tended to regard them only as symbols for explaining reactions.[36] Butlerov, on the contrary, believed that one substance should have one structural formula with a real, even if indefinite, relationship to the actual structure of the substance. He remarked,

> If we attempt to define the chemical structure of substances and if we have success in expressing it by our formulas, then those formulas will be, although not completely, real rational formulas. . . . For each substance there will be, therefore, one rational formula, and when the general laws of the properties of substances are well known, such a formula will express all of those properties.[37]

Quotations such as this were convenient for authors who wished to use Butlerov to criticize the multiple forms of resonance theory. Many of these authors ignored Butlerov's further statement on the meaning of chemical formulas that "what matters is not the form, but the essence, the conception, the idea. . . . It is not difficult to realize that any method of notation is good as long as it expresses these relationships conveniently."[38]

From February 2 to 7, 1950, the Institute of Organic Chemistry of the Academy of Sciences of the USSR conducted a discussion on modern theories of organic chemistry.[39] Out of this discussion came a report entitled "The Present State of Chemical Structural Theory," written by D. N. Kursanov, chairman, and a committee of seven other chemists.[40] Later, Chelintsev criticized most of these men.

The committee report referred to the Communist Party's interest in the present discussion and the direct connection to the controversy in biology:

> The decisions of the Central Committee of the VKB(b) [All-Union Communist Party (Bolsheviks)] in regard to ideological problems and the sessions of the VASKhNIL [All-Union Lenin Academy of Agricultural Sciences] have mobilized Soviet scientists for the solution of the problem of a critical analysis of the present state of theoretical concepts in all fields of knowledge and the struggle against the alien reactionary ideas of bourgeois science.
>
> The crisis of bourgeois science, connected with the general crisis of the capitalistic system, has been illustrated by the theoretical concepts of organic chemistry now being developed by bourgeois scientists and has led to the appearance of methodologically faulty concepts, which are slowing down the further development of science.[41]

But while the committee criticized resonance theory and even its own members for using the theory, it forthrightly asserted that Chelintsev's views were based on false scientific grounds. Chelintsev was helpful in the sense that he drew "the general attention of Soviet chemists to the necessity for a critical analysis of resonance theory," but he then "incorrectly identified the theory of chemical structure. . . ."[42] By so doing, Chelintsev tried to halt the application of quantum mechanics to chemistry, which was, in the view of the committee, actually "a further development of Butlerov's theory which made it concrete. . . ."

As for Chelintsev's "New Structural Theory," Kursanov and his colleagues had no kind words:

> An understanding of the nature of the chemical bond requires the application and consideration of all the data derived by modern chemistry and physics. G. V. Chelintsev's "New Structural Theory" is an attempt to construct a new theory of the chemical bond without considering these facts. . . . Significantly, even the author himself does not apply his "New Structural Theory" in his works. This theory should be rejected.[43]

In this report and in several other articles that appeared at this time, four main points seem paramount: (1) Butlerov was the true founder of the theory of chemical structure; (2) the theory of resonance is idealistic and, therefore, unacceptable; (3) although resonance must be rejected, quantum mechanics is essential for scientific research, and a clear line can be drawn between the theory of resonance and quantum mechanics; (4) G. V. Chelintsev is not a competent scientist. As time progressed, points three and four became increasingly important. The leading Soviet research chemists were clearly making a major effort during 1950 to discredit Chelintsev and simultaneously rally as many scientists as possible to the defense of quantum mechanical methods of calculation in chemistry.

In an article that appeared in January 1951, O. A. Reutov recognized that too strict an adherence to Chelintsev's views would result in a simple demand for static mechanical models for molecules. He hinted that past discussions of the theory of resonance had emphasized materialism while ignoring the dialectic. Reutov affirmed that "there are two sides to Butlerov's theory. One is related to the unconditional recognition of a definite structure of molecules. The other aspect of this doctrine asserts the presence of interactions between atoms. . . ."[44] Reutov indicated that any description of molecules must not be of a static model, but of constantly changing ones, the result of the interaction of opposing forces, a truly dialectical process.

On the page following Reutov's article in the January 1951 issue of the *Journal of General Chemistry* a notice was printed announcing a forthcoming All-Union conference on the theory of chemical structure. The topic would now be discussed not only by chemists, but also by hundreds of physicists, philosophers, and educators. The Bureau of the Division of Chemical Sciences of the Academy of Sciences organized a commission headed by the president of the Academy, A. N. Nesmeianov, to prepare the major report, which was to concern Butlerov's views of structural chemistry, a critique of resonance, and the future development of the theory of chemical structure. Readers were invited to write in comments or suggestions.

The conference was held in Moscow on June 11–14, 1951, under the chairmanship of M. M. Dubinin.[45] The main report was given by A. N. Terenin, rather than by Nesmeianov, who was ill and did not attend. A total of forty-four delegates gave speeches, many of them similar in content, but there were several heated debates despite the fact that not one person defended the theory of resonance. The previous articles and discussions had already so set the stage for the conference that it seems to have been a foregone conclusion that resonance would be rejected.

The real issue was finding an alternative. Chelintsev, who evidently would have jettisoned the methods of quantum chemistry as a whole, became increasingly pathetic as he continued to make ineffective attacks against his fellow chemists.

Syrkin, Diatkina, Vol'kenshtein, and Kiprianov retracted their earlier defenses of the theory of resonance and said that they had been mistaken. Syrkin said that when he had written his book, he had not been aware of the correct trend of development in chemistry. Diatkina revealed that at an earlier point she had tried to defend resonance chemistry in terms of dialectical materialism, referring to the "qualitative and quantititive aspects of the theory of resonance."[46] Her effort had failed, and she now called it "a confusion of irrelevant matters." Diatkina's attempt to illustrate the philosophical acceptability of the resonance theory by referring to the dialectic was a parallel, perhaps unknown to her, of the British scientist J. B. S. Haldane's opinions in 1939, when he wrote that the theory of resonance was "a brilliant example of dialectical thinking, of the refusal to admit that two alternatives (two contributing structures) which are put before you are necessarily exclusive."[47]

Terenin's report, to which Diatkina referred and which was the basis of discussion for the conference, was very similar to the report that the Institute of Organic Chemistry had given in February 1950. This similarity is not surprising, since several of the same scientists were in charge of both reports. One difference was obvious, however; Terenin's commission was assigned the task not only of criticizing the resonance theory on the basis of Butlerov's writings, but also of planning the future work of Soviet chemists—that is, suggesting a substitute for resonance theory.

Terenin and his co-workers isolated the error of resonance as being specifically the use of ideal, fictitious resonance structures.[48] Therefore, as long as Soviet chemists did not resort to computations derived from fictitious structures, they could use all of the data that they could collect concerning molecules, and also the mathematical expressions that, as represented in physical terms by supporters of the theory of resonance, led to the contradictions of incompatible physical forms. This alternative approach, which avoided the ideal structures, was named the "theory of mutual influences," borrowing a phrase from Butlerov. The explanation that Terenin and his colleagues gave for this apparent contradiction was the inadequacy of man's knowledge of the structure of matter.[49] Eventually structural chemistry will advance to the point where this contradiction will be resolved. Whatever that more complete answer may be, it cannot possibly be the theory of resonance, which is a blind alley postulating that the form of a molecule is physically inconceivable. The theory of resonance leads to agnosticism, said the authors of the report, which they defined as the Kantian belief that man cannot know his surroundings.

The approach to molecular structure that the report writers suggested would permit one to use all of the data leading up to the theory of resonance as long as one stopped short of representing molecules as hybrids of ideal graphic forms. But the chemists could use the equations themselves, which are the essentials for utilizing the resonance theory.

The difference between the forbidden theory of resonance and the permitted theory of mutual influences was exceedingly subtle. Epistemologically, there was a difference; chemists following the theory of mutual influences as described by the authors of the report could not conclude that molecules are merely intellectual forms, nor that molecules can be explained only in terms of intellectual forms, no matter how persuasive the evidence for one of those alternatives might be. The primary practical distinction between the method suggested by the Soviet chemists and the theory of resonance was that scientists following the first approach would be deprived of the use of resonance forms as visual aids in the classroom and the laboratory.

The theory of mutual influences had a parallel in other countries in an approach known as the "molecular orbit" method, which does not postulate the exact location of certain molecular bonds. Consequently, many chemists believe that it does not explain certain reactions as satisfactorily as does the theory of resonance. Wheland commented, however, that in mathematical form the molecular orbit method becomes virtually identical with the resonance theory.[50]

Professor Chelintsev fiercely tore into the report. The whole conference, he maintained, was failing its task; it was supposed to reject the theories of Pauling and C. K. Ingold, but on the contrary, it had been taken over by the partisans of these two foreign scientists. He added that the theory of mutual influences was only a modification in nomenclature of the mesomerism-resonance theory.[51] "The authors of the report," he accused, "were given the assignment of saving the beloved heart of Ingold's and Pauling's mesomerism theory" (pp. 81, 86). Chelintsev said that the leaders of the conference had suppressed his articles and had camouflaged the resonance theory (pp. 86–87). His frustration at the outcome of the conference emerged in his comments:

> This is the first case in the course of the recent scientific-methodological
> discussions when the approved report advances not a criticism of the
> mistakes but a plea of guilty in their behalf, representing, moreover, not
> an isolated person, but the commission that was named by the Department
> of Chemical Sciences of the Academy of Sciences of the USSR, and
> approved, surely, by the Presidium of the Academy. (pp. 79–80)

Chelintsev announced that he considered it his duty to name the
most active propagandists of the resonance theory; he began with the
president of the Academy of Sciences, A. N. Nesmeianov, and named
twenty-six chemists (p. 87),[52] a good number of them the leaders of
their fields. Almost all the authors of articles denouncing resonance
that had appeared in the previous two years were on the list, including
Tatevskii and Shakhparanov, whose article in late 1949 had indicated
that the criticism of resonance would go beyond that of Chelintsev.
Five of the nine members of the commission of the department of
chemical sciences, which had investigated the resonance theory in
February 1950, were named, as were six of eleven scientists designated
to compile the report for the June 1951 All-Union conference.

After his speech Chelintsev faced a series of questions from the floor.
One questioner sarcastically inquired, "You have read off the defenders
of idealism in Soviet chemistry. Who, in your opinion, in all of Soviet
chemistry, are representatives of dialectical materialism? (laughter in
the hall)" (p. 89). Chelintsev replied that it would be impossible to
name all of the defenders of dialectical materialism because there were
only twenty or thirty men—the ones he named—who ignored dialectical
materialism. Applause from the floor met this reply.

A few supporters of Chelintsev spoke at the conference. S. N. Khitrik
defended Chelintsev's views and also pointed out the "irrefutable fact"
that Chelintsev was the first person to unmask "the idealistic essence"
of the theory of mesomerism-resonance (p. 181).

One of the speakers who followed Chelintsev was A. A. Maksimov,
a member of the editorial committee of *Problems of Philosophy*. Maksimov
had been involved in a long series of squabbles concerning dialectical
materialism and science; he played an unfortunate role in the discussion
of relativity physics, where he attacked not only general but special
relativity. Maksimov's presence, along with that of the journalist V. E.
Lvov, was resented by some of the other participants at the conference.
The chemist Vol'kenstein asked, "Why did this journalist drop in here?"
(p. 350). Vol'kenshtein observed that the year before, Lvov had been
expelled from the midst of the Leningrad physicists for stirring up

trouble. This is an indication that some additional scientists may have united against ideological demagogues as early as 1950.

Maksimov, however, had shifted from the offensive to the defensive in the debate over idealism in science. Rather that supporting Chelintsev, he criticized him. He plumbed Chelintsev's motives in his remark: "According to Chelintsev, he is assuming the role in chemistry of T. D. Lysenko, and the 'Pauling-Ingoldites' named by him are playing the role of Weissmann-Morganists." Maskimov also affirmed, "I know the members of the commission and the 'Pauling-Ingoldites.' . . . I consider them honest, devoted Soviet chemists, sparked by desires for Soviet chemistry to flourish" (pp. 255–56).

When the conference prepared to vote on the final resolution, Chelintsev rose to say that although he had been a member of the commission in charge of drafting the resolution, he had been completely outnumbered by the Paulingites and Ingoldites (he did not cease using these terms although members of the conference had asked him to), and consequently his voice had not been influential (p. 365). In the final vote the three or four delegates who had supported Chelintsev in earlier procedural matters deserted him and Chelintsev alone opposed the resolution (p. 370).

The resolution approved the essence of the report of the chemical section of the Academy of Sciences, which Professor Terenin had read at the beginning of the conference, but noted several "serious defects" in that report. First of all, the report had not illustrated that the perversions in chemistry were closely connected with those in biology and physiology and that all these hostile theories "present a united front in the fight of reactionary bourgeois ideology against materialism" (p. 376). Another defect of the report of Terenin and his partners, according to the resolution, was their failure to describe adequately the great progress of Soviet chemistry.[53]

The conference resolution also reprimanded Syrkin, Diatkina, Vol'kenshtein, and Kiprianov for not giving complete criticisms of the theory of resonance and for not detailing their errors. Vol'kenshtein's and Kiprianov's pleas of ignorance were rejected. The resolution noted, however, that all four of the chemists had admitted their mistakes.

Soviet philosophers, chemists, and physicists were all criticized, each group for a slightly different reason. The philosophers had not been active on the chemical front. The resolution pointed out that chemists, not philosophers, had discovered the ideological weaknesses. The chemists were criticized, nonetheless, for not giving adequate attention to the methodology of science. The resonance theory had long been tolerated when it should have been expelled.

Although Chelintsev had not been mentioned in the resolution of the All-Union conference, his theory did not escape what amounted to official condemnation, at the hands of Nesmeianov himself. If Chelintsev had a correct structural theory, Nesmeianov observed in an article, he should be able to predict reactions. Where are these predictions? Nesmeianov hinted that not even Chelintsev could sincerely believe in his naive pronouncements. He concluded with a barb aimed both at partisans of resonance theory and supporters of Chelintsev: "Our chemistry must be thoroughly cleared of all unhealthy influences of corrupt bourgeois philosophy and science. It must be cleared also of vulgarizations of home origin."[54]

Chelintsev's audacity in the face of such criticism from the scientist with the most institutional authority in the Soviet Union seems rather surprising. In the same issue as Nesmeianov's article, Chelintsev repeated his accusations about the monopoly of Paulingites in chemistry, including Nesmeianov. He rejected Nesmeianov's indication that he did not believe in his own theory:

> As far as my conviction of the worthlessness of the New Structural Theory is concerned, is it really possible to suppose that for a number of years I could bear the whole weight of the struggle with the Ingold-Paulingites who were monopolizing Soviet chemical science if I were not deeply convinced of the correctness and usefulness of my idea?[55]

The fact that the irrepressible Chelintsev's article appeared and that he was so bold indicates that he had support somewhere in the Soviet Union. Furthermore, Nesmaianov would not have bothered to criticize Chelintsev at length if the rebellious Soviet chemist had been as isolated as Nesmeanov indicated. Chelintsev still hoped, apparently, that his views would win the favor of the Party officials. In his continuing battle Chelintsev finally exhausted the patience of his fellow chemists. In January 1953 two Soviet chemists, B. A. Kazanskii and G. V. Bykov, lashed out at Chelintsev:

> Who dares to criticize the New Structural Theory? How can there be a battle of views between other chemists and this author? Any opposition to his 'theory' is made to appear a reprehensible heresy. Anybody opposing Chelintsev's theory or ignoring it is readily accused by him of 'mechanism,' 'agnosticism,' 'Machism,' and similar 'isms.' Chelintsev prosecuted the whole campaign for this theory with a vociferous and defamatory slogan: He who is against me is against dialectical materialism.[56]

This scolding seems to have had the desired effect; Chelintsev's articles disappeared from the pages of the journals. Whether Chelintsev voluntarily withdrew or the editors refused to print any more of his polemics is not known, but Kazanskii and Bykov's article marked the end of the running battle. Chelintsev certainly did not change his mind, because four years later he briefly reappeared, sawing away at his old thesis.

But after January 1953 a relative silence fell upon the controversy, punctuated by an occasional article reaffirming the now official position on the theory of resonance, illustrating that the issue was not dead. An article in the October 1953 issue of the *Journal of General Chemistry* honored the one hundred twenty-fifth anniversary of the birth of Butlerov, but only briefly mentioned the familiar alleged contradiction between Butlerov's views and the theory of resonance, and did not mention Chelintsev in the twenty-seven footnotes.[57] It is quite likely that an attempt was being made to smother Chelintsev with silence.

By 1954 the tone of the few articles that touched upon the theory of resonance had changed discernibly, undoubtedly because of a freer atmosphere of discussion following the death of Stalin the previous year. But this change was a subtle one; no one even hinted that the validity of the theory of resonance should be reconsidered. A few of the scientists who had been accused of ideological errors in the period 1949–1951 started striking back at their critics.[58]

In the post-Stalin period the chauvinistic praise of Soviet chemistry greatly decreased. In Soviet histories of chemistry and in chemistry textbooks Butlerov remained the founder of the theory of chemical structure, but the more strident criticism of Western European chemists began to disappear. This decline in national exaggeration was in part a result of a general diminishing of ideological fervor. Some chemists who had opposed the criticism of resonance theory in the period 1949–1951 or were neutral on the issue had at that time used praise of Butlerov as a means of avoiding the necessity of a direct attack on resonance. A. E. Arbuzov, a member of the Academy of Sciences and a dean of Soviet chemistry, who was forty years old at the time of the Revolution, spoke at length at the June 1951 conference without even discussing the theory of resonance. He confined himself to an exposition of Butlerov's significance in the history of chemistry. Since Butlerov was truly a great chemist, according to all Soviet and non-Soviet scholars who have studied his work, Arbuzov preserved his sense of academic integrity and yet loyally supported the dialectical materialists.[59] In the new atmosphere that existed after 1953, the absence of compulsion to speak out on the issue resulted in fewer praises of Butlerov by people of Arbuzov's position.

An article illustrating the new mood was Nesmeianov and Kabachnik's "Dual Reactivity and Tautomerism," published in January 1955.[60] The problems discussed in this article were closely connected with the theory of resonance, but the old issues were not revived. After describing a series of chemical reactions, the two authors admitted their inability to postulate the structure of the molecules of the compounds involved. They remarked, "Many of these problems, which of late seemed to be solved, were solved incorrectly, and new investigations are required. . . ."[61]

The theory of resonance remained prohibited, at least in name. In August 1957 Chelintsev briefly reappeared, repeating all his old charges.[62]

THE SIGNIFICANCE OF THE FIRST PHASE OF THE RESONANCE CONTROVERSY

If the interpretation of the resonance controversy during the Stalinist period presented here is correct, several older interpretations should be modified. For example, one author described the resonance dispute as being ideologically and politically the same phenomenon as the biology discussion, with the same result. He called the outcome "Lysenkoism in chemistry."[63] One can understand this description, but the result of the discussion was a defeat for Lysenkoism, in contrast to its victory in biology. The initial attack on the resonance theory was a manifestation of Lysenkoism, but the significant feature of the resonance controversy was that the chemists successfully defended themselves against the most serious attack. The modifications of theory were primarily terminological.

Gustav Wetter's short discussion of the resonance controversy also did not mention the central position of Chelintsev.[64] Wetter indicated that the real source of the resonance controversy was central direction from above: "One gets the impression that at this period virtually everything was seized upon and correspondingly inflated, which could in any way offer a handle for convicting Western theories of 'idealism,' 'Machism,' etc.; just as the possibility of embracing Butlerov's theory offered a welcome opportunity for display of 'Soviet patriotism.' "[65]

Rather than being a controversy initiated from above, it appears that the resonance issue sprang up from below, nurtured and prompted by zealous, ambitious chemists who hoped to win Party support in discrediting the scientists who utilized the resonance theory. This initiative probably embarrassed rather than pleased Soviet scientific administrators, who did not want to harm the productivity of the chemists.

The majority of these chemists were willing to defend the tools necessary for the practice of their science, and the quantum mechanical approach, condemned by Chelintsev, was one of these esential tools. Therefore, they decided to accept Chelintsev's diagnosis of the methodological disease in chemistry, but to reject his recommended cure. Without using the fictitious resonance structures, they would preserve the mathematical core of the theory, maintaining that such a solution was compatible with the dialectical materialist approach to science and Butlerov's approach to chemistry.

RESONANCE THEORY IN THE POST-STALIN PERIOD

In 1958 a rather complete criticism of the resonance theory appeared in M. I. Shakhparanov's booklet *Dialectical Materialism and Several Problems of Physics and Chemistry.*[66] Shakhparanov was the same chemist who assisted Tatevskii in writing the signal 1949 article in *Problems of Philosophy* near the beginning of the controversy, and who at one time utilized the theory of resonance himself. Shakhparanov's publication was notable for two reasons: He deemphasized philosophical criticism of the theory of resonance, maintaining that it was incorrect also for obvious scientific reasons; and he presented slightly different philosophical objections to the theory.

Shakhparanov noted that the discussion of the theory of resonance in the Soviet Union had been debated abroad, and that some foreign chemists, particularly in England and Japan, had also criticized the theory. An American commentator had noted, "The resonance theory stands in danger of being largely discredited, at least in so far as it has been applied hitherto. . . . It must never be forgotten that the theory ultimately depends upon the use of limiting structures which, by admission, have no existence in reality."[67] Although these non-Soviet critics did not propose superior alternatives to the theory they believed that the use of multiple fictitious structures for explaining the properties of compounds was only a temporary method.

In August 1959 Ia. K. Syrkin, one of the two chemists who were criticized most sharply in the earlier debate, published an article in

Progress of Chemistry entitled "The Current Situation in the Problem of Valency,"[68] Syrkin had ceased working in the area of structural chemistry after the controversy, but in the late fifties returned to the field. Syrkin did not present any new views in the article, but confined himself to a moderately enthusiastic description of the molecular orbit method of describing compounds and did not attempt to define the location of specific bonds.

The specific problem of the nature of atomic bonds in benzene was taken up in November 1958 by M. I. Batuev in a technical article in the *Journal of General Chemistry*. Batuev attempted to disprove the theory of resonance on the basis of physical measurements by electron diffraction and X-rays. Acording to resonance, all six bonds of benzene are equivalent, and therefore should be of equal length. Batuev, however, maintained that the benzene molecule consisted of not six equivalent bonds, but alternating "three slightly elongated double bonds, and three slightly shortened single bonds." The dimensions he produced (1.382 Angstrom units for single bonds, 1.375 for double bonds) were extremely close (.007 units), especially since plus or minus .005 Angstrom units was often given as the experimental error inherent in the measurement process.[69]

Batuev's article was particularly interesting in that the criticism of resonance in benzene was based entirely on empirical data. This data concerned only benzene among the various molecules to which resonance theory has been applied, and it was not unambiguous. Nonetheless, it helped place the issue on a more normal scientific plane.

When I studied at Moscow University during the 1960–61 academic year, I found that Soviet chemists at that time spoke of the controversy as having "blown over," but observed that the term "resonance" was not used in chemistry lectures on valency and that standard textbooks in structural chemistry continued to avoid resonance theory. In many cases these precautions were mere terminological modifications.

In the early sixties attitudes toward resonance theory in the Soviet Union continued to evolve.[70] In November 1961 Linus Pauling lectured on resonance at the Institute of Organic Chemistry in Moscow to an audience of about twelve hundred people.[71] The large audience was due no doubt to attractions of a poignantly opposite nature: Pauling was simultaneously respected in the Soviet Union by many people of an internationalist frame of mind for his opinions on peace and atomic weapons, and, of course, for his stature as a scientist, while he had also been the object of severe criticism in the Soviet Union because of his authorship of the resonance theory. Pauling later observed that his lecture was favorably received.

Of all Soviet discussions of science and philosophy described in this book, the one over the theory of resonance became the most quiescent after the mid-sixties. Nonetheless, it did not entirely disappear. In 1969 a text for Soviet teachers of chemistry in the secondary schools pointedly avoided mention of the theory of resonance, even though the inadequacy of classical structural diagrams was carefully described.[72] The text, a quite sophisticated one for teachers at the secondary level, included a discussion of the molecular orbital method and the "method of superposition of valence schemes," a phrase used to describe the theory of resonance method without using the actual term. The Soviet author, G. I. Shelinskii, criticized the "superposition method," observing quite sensibly that it approached the problem of the delocalization of the electron charge too indirectly. He emphasized that chemists now speak more and more of "electron clouds" rather than "bonds"; he further commented that retention of the old bond diagrams for such compounds as anthracene became almost impossibly complex, since hundreds of diagrams were needed to describe one compound. Thus, the superposition method loses even its advantages as a visual aid, the argument usually given in its favor. Shelinskii preferred abandoning graphic models when working with the more complex molecules, relying entirely on the mathematical descriptions of the molecular orbital method.

The attention of Soviet scholars interested in the philosophic problems of chemistry began to shift in the sixties from the theory of resonance to more general questions.[73] Iurii Zhdanov in his 1960 book entitled *Essays on the Methodology of Organic Chemistry* was still quite critical of the epistemological basis of resonance theory (he accepted, of course, the quantum mechanical calculations of the molecular orbit method), but he began directing his major attention to broader problems of the meaning of chemical formulas, the meaning of homology in chemistry, and the validity of modeling.[74]

This trend continued in subsequent works. N. A. Budreiko, in a 1970 book entitled *Philosophic Problems of Chemistry*, concentrated primarily on issues such as the definition of the terms "chemistry" and "chemical element," the philosophical significance of Mendeleev's periodic table, and the presence in chemistry of dialectical laws of nature.[75] Unfortunately, Budreiko's book was somewhat elementary and mechanistic; his easy perception of the dialectical laws in chemistry reflected some of the more superficial aspects of nature philosophy, putting him clearly in the camp of the "ontologists." Other Soviet books on philosophy of chemistry of more value concerned the significance of certain issues of importance in the history of chemistry, such as the atomistic views of Dalton, Gibbs, and Mendeleev.[76]

A particularly interesting philosophic work by a prominent Soviet chemist was N. N. Semenov's 1968 article entitled "Marxist-Leninist Philosophy and Problems of Natural Science."[77] Semenov, a recipient in 1956 of the Nobel Prize, was probably the best known of all Soviet chemists at the time. His work revealed a deep interest in the philosophy of science; furthermore, he stoutly defended the materialistic dialectic. He remarked in his 1968 article that since the Marxist dialectic is the method of man's cognition, of man's thought, it is "applicable to the development of all the sciences. Dialectical materialism lies at the base of the conscious transformations of society, its production and its culture."[78] Nonetheless, the particular interpretation that Semenov placed upon the relation of dialectical materialism to science was highly controversial in the Soviet Union. While many of the authors previously discussed believed that dialectics are inherent *in* nature (the ontologists' position), Semenov apparently believed that dialectics are characteristic primarily of man's thought (the epistemologists' position), not of nature existing outside of his thoughts. Semenev believed Soviet philosophers should concentrate on problems of logic and the theory of knowledge.

Semenov attempted to answer the criticisms of his view by the dialecticians of nature:

> Some philosophers sometimes express the following fear: How is it possible for us to consider Marxist-Leninist philosophy as Logic, as the theory of knowledge? Won't such a view lead to a loss of meaning of Marxist philosophy as a world view, to a depreciation of its role, and even to a "breakaway of philosophy from natural science"?
> If one understands Logic in a Leninist fashion, one need not fear. Indeed, the reverse is true: Actually, all our sciences, all our culture, develop with the aid of thought, based on human practice, and therefore the science of thought preserves its universal meaning, its primary role in the development of a scientific understanding of the world.[79]

Traditional dialectical materialists considered Semenov's comments an exaggeration of the role of ideas in the development of science. They maintained that man's thoughts are also a part of nature and are ultimately subject to the same regularities as the rest of nature. They would then continue to search for these regularities in both thought and external reality, terming them, as before, "the dialectics of nature."

Semenov's article appeared in both the *Herald of the Academy of Sciences* and the Party journal *Communist*. Soon thereafter there appeared in the latter journal an article favoring the traditional approach, in which the dialectic was seen as a generalization of specialized scientific knowledge and therefore inherent in nature.[80]

Soviet textbooks of chemistry in the 1980s continued to display some signs of the old interest in a dialectical materialist interpretation of nature, with quite a variety of viewpoints represented. Some textbooks did not discuss dialectical materialism at all, and a few used the term "theory of resonance" without hesitation. An example was the widely used textbook on organic chemistry written by Petrov, Bal'ian, and Troshchenko. After one perfunctory reference to Engels' views on vitalism in the introduction, they freely referred to the theory of resonance in the main part of the book.[81]

Somewhat different was the approach of Karapet'iants and Drakin in their text *General and Inorganic Chemistry*. They preferred the term "hybridization" over "resonance," and they still gave a mild slap to the people who were "fascinated" with the theory of resonance in the forties and fifties and whose interpretation of resonance "often led to confusion and misunderstanding."[82] They did not mention that the principal authors of resonance theory, Pauling and Wheland, specifically warned against these misunderstandings.

Yet a third approach was taken in the 1981 text *Course of General Chemistry*, edited by N. V. Korovin. This book contained a number of references to Marx, Engels, and Lenin, and still made the claim that chemistry leads to a dialectical materialist understanding of nature: "The study of chemistry as one of the most important fundamental natural sciences is necessary for the formation of the ideology of dialectical materialism. F. Engels wrote, 'Chemistry can be called the science of the qualitative changes of substances occurring under the influence of changes in quantitative composition' "[83] Korovin's ideological bent was further revealed by the fact that he did not mention the theory of resonance by name, preferring the term "hybridization," but gave a satisfactory description of the mathematical methods that the theory of resonance incorporates.

Iurii Zhdanov, son of Andrei Zhdanov (both father and son are discussed on pp. 123ff.) continued to write occasional articles on the philosophy of chemistry. As rector of the University of Rostov-on-the-Don and a Communist Party official he exercised considerable influence in Soviet higher education in the seventies and eighties. He was a strong advocate of the necessity for scientists to approach their research topics from a Marxist standpoint. One of his main interests was in transition states that occur extremely briefly (in moments of time of about 10^{-13} seconds) during chemical reactions. Zhdanov saw these moments as illustrations of the dialectical process in nature. He wrote in 1981:

> Being a moment of chemical self-movement, the transition state realizes the true dialectic of chemism; matter in this state is tense, restless, active, contradictory. V. I. Lenin emphasized that movement is a contradiction, a unity of contradictions, a unity of continuity and discontinuity of time and space. In the activated complex of the transition state these characteristics of a dialectical process are fully realized. Research into the transition state is a study of the anatomy of the leap from the old to the new in the development of matter, it is the discovery of just how the transition from quantitative changes to qualitative ones occurs in the sphere of chemism.[84]

In this passage Zhdanov was siding with the ontologists in their dispute with the epistemologists in Soviet dialectical materialism. He obviously believed that the workings of the Marxist laws of the dialectic could be observed in nature, especially in chemistry. This viewpoint was rejected by several other Soviet authors writing on the philosophy of chemistry. R. V. Garkovenko published an article in the same year as Zhdanov's in which he noted that views like Zhdanov's were being "disputed by a series of authors who believe that all attention in the philosophy of science must be concentrated on gnosiological, logical and methodological problems" and not on "the objective dialectic of chemism."[85]

Perhaps the most surprising dialectical materialist criticism of resonance theory in the early eighties came from Academician V. Koptiug of Academic City in Novosibirsk. In an interview in 1981 for the British television science program "Horizon," Koptiug asserted that although mistakes were made in Soviet genetics in the forties and fifties, he agreed with the Soviet critique of resonance theory.[86] Koptiug is an internationally known chemist and Soviet science administrator whose opinions have considerable influence within the community of Soviet chemists. It appears that Koptiug also supported the ontologists, although he spoke so briefly on the subject that one cannot be certain of his opinions.

Vestiges of the controversy over resonance theory could be seen in Soviet disussions over reductionism in chemistry. One of the chemists who had been severely criticized in earlier years because of his support of resonance theory, M. V. Vol'kenshtein, continued to defend the view that, in principle, chemistry could be reduced to the laws of physics. This viewpoint was rejected by dialectical materialists who maintained that, according to Marxism, different laws exist on the different levels of being, and that chemistry would never be reduced to physics. Thus, V. I. Kurashov and Iu. I. Solov'ev, writing in 1984, criticized both Vol'kenshtein and Linus Pauling for trying to absorb chemistry into physics.[87]

By the mid-eighties the philosophy of chemistry had fallen into relative neglect in the Soviet Union, but whenever the topic arose, the dispute between the ontologists and the epistemologists that was going on elsewhere in Soviet science was visible here also. It is interesting to notice that philosophers like Frolov, Garkovenko, and Vikhalemm tended to support the nonintrusive epistemological view, while chemists like Korovin, Zhdanov, and apparently Koptiug sided with the ontologists. This tendency indicates that those Western observers are somewhat mistaken who believe that only the Soviet philosophers are responsible for introducing Marxism into science, while the Soviet scientists supposedly ignore Marxism. Quite a few Soviet scientists have defended the position that dialectical laws are visible in nature, a position that at least some of the professional philosophers find embarrassing.

Very little has been said here in defense of the theory of resonance, although the criticisms of it have been described in considerable detail. Actually, the theory of resonance has already proved its usefulness in science. If the theory of resonance were replaced by a new theory tomorrow, the concept of resonance would have served an important and useful purpose. The originators of the theory have warned repeatedly that no physical significance should be assigned to the resonance structures, which are primarily helpful descriptions. Nevertheless, it is true that some chemists mistakenly think of resonance as a mechanical phenomenon.[88] The theory of resonance is a man-made system for organizing and understanding the complex data collected from chemical reactions—a system that can be thought of, if one prefers a realist epistemology, as bearing a certain resemblance to the structure of a molecule, but that is far from being identical with that molecule.

Yet one should add that underneath the debate over resonance theory there is a philosophical issue of considerable interest. As in the case of quantum theory, the interpretation in terms of a model given to a mathematical formalism is sufficiently far from customary descriptions of physical nature to cause uneasiness to some scientists and philosophers. The essential philosophical problem here, then, is that of the use of models in scientific explanation. This is a serious topic on which philosophers of science have written a great deal; the fact that the participants in the Soviet discussion of resonance never brought out fully the underlying issue does not contradict the fact that it was there. One hopes that in the future Soviet authors will discuss resonance from the standpoint of philosophical analysis, with no question of interfering with the work of scientists arising.

Mary Hesse described the intellectual issue involved in the use of models in the following way:

> The main philosophical debate about models concerns the question of whether there is any essential and objective dependence between an explanatory theory and its model that goes beyond a dispensable and possibly subjective method of discovery. The debate is an aspect of an old controversy between the positivist and the realist interpretations of scientific theory. Many episodes in the history of science may be regarded as chapters in this controversy, including the application of Ockham's razor to scientific theories, the Newtonian-Cartesian controversy over the mechanical character of gravitation, nineteenth-century debates over mechanical ether and the existence of atoms, and Machian positivism.[89]

Among the scholars who have described models as merely dispensable aids for the construction of theories are Ernst Mach, Heinrich Hertz, and Pierre Duhem. Among those who have argued that without some form of material analogy there is no valid ground for prediction are N. R. Campbell, E. H. Hutten, and Hesse herself.

In the case of the theory of resonance a realist or materialist need not be disturbed by his or her inability to construct a model that adequately explains all the reactions of certain chemical compounds. Indeed, the scientific theory that stands behind such classical models— the theory of valency in which chemical bonds are highly localized— has long since been abandoned by chemists. The current theories of valency—in which electrons are recognized as micro-objects in terms of quantum theory and hence have both a wavelike and corpusclelike character—do not permit such structural diagrams. But quantum theory has already acquainted us with this problem of visualization. Thus, although there is much of intellectual interest in the interpretation of chemical valency, there is little reason to believe that it presents obstacles of a uniquely difficult character to supporters of philosophic realism or materialism. As Hesse commented, "We ought to be prepared for, rather than surprised at, the inadequacy of familiar models in much of modern physics."[90]

QUANTUM MECHANICS

Having begun, like many physicists, with a formal application of the mathematics of quantum mechanics, I later began to think about questions of principle. . . . I finally came to the conclusion that Bohr's formulation could be completely separated from the positivistic coating that at first glance seemed to be intrinsic to it.
—Academician V. A. Fock, 1963

Of all the philosophic issues posed by modern physical theory, those involving quantum mechanics have been the most pressing and obstinate. Several problems in the philosophy of science of the past two generations—such as the interpretation of special relativity—held the attention of scholars for several decades or more but have now lost much of their allure; other issues—such as the discussions of information theory and artificial intelligence—have gained prominence only recently. But more than fifty years after the publication of the essential mathematical apparatus of quantum mechanics the controversy continues.[1] It is a debate in which the scholars of many nations have participated, including those of the USSR.

The structure of quantum mechanics may be divided into a mathematical formalism and a physical interpretation of that formalism. The mathematical formalism, which is the core of quantum mechanics, is a differential wave equation, the solution of which is usually termed the psi (ψ) function; the wave equation was first developed by Erwin Schrödinger, who pursued Louis de Broglie's extension of the concept of wave-corpuscle duality from light to elementary particles of matter. The advantage of this formalism is that it yields, on a probabilistic basis, numerical values permitting a more complete mathematical description of microphysical states, including the prediction of future states, than has any other formalism so far. The disadvantage of the mathematical apparatus of quantum mechanics is that the only widely accepted (some would say the only possible) physical interpretation for it contradicts several of man's most basic intuitions concerning matter. Specifically, quantum mechanical computations, in contrast to the classical laws of the macrophysical realm, do not yield arbitrarily exact values for position and momentum coordinates of microparticles. According to the well-known uncertainty relation, the more exactly the position of a microparticle is known, the less exactly the momentum, and vice versa.[2]

In view of the success of the mathematics of quantum mechanics for the derivation of useful physical values, the obvious question arises: What is the physical significance of the wave function? Can it be that matter is, indeed, undulatory? It is over this question of the physical interpretation of the mathematics of quantum mechanics that scores of philosophers and scientists have splintered their pens.[3]

The evolution of quantum mechanical theories is a trail littered with unsatisfactory explanations. De Broglie originally proposed that matter *is* wavelike and that the waves described by quantum mechanics do not "represent" the system; they *are* the system.[4] This explanation encounters enormous difficulties, far too complex to enter into here, but the nature of some of them may be indicated by noting that a literal acceptance of the physical reality of the wave function would involve such conceptions as that of physical space with an almost unlimited number of dimensions. And most graphically, such an interpretation cannot explain satisfactorily the fact that a single micro-object upon impact on a sensitive emulsion leaves a spot, not the imprint of a wave front.[5] Max Born originally suggested the alternative: Matter is corpuscular, and the wave function describes not the particles but our knowledge about them. This ingenious theory unfortunately runs into equally disastrous physical facts, which are best illustrated by reference to the now classic two-slit interference experiment. When particles are allowed to pass through two narrow slits in a barrier before striking a sensitive emulsion, the impacts form an interference pattern that can be explained only on the basis of the wavelike characteristics of microbodies.

The Copenhagen Interpretation, developed by Niels Bohr and Werner Heisenberg, resolves the contradictions of previous interpretations by postulating that no observable has a value before a measurement of that observable has been made. As Heisenberg declared, "The path comes into existence only when we know it."[6] Thus, it becomes meaningless to speak of the characteristics of matter at any particular moment without empirical data in hand relating to that moment. It is senseless to speak of the position of a particle ("position" is a property of the corpuscular theory) without a measurement of position; it is equally unjustified to speak of the momentum (a wave property) without a measurement of momentum. This reconciling of classically incompatible properties by granting them existence only at the moment of measurement is usually called "complementarity" and is the heart of the most critical discussions of quantum mechanics.

Physicists and philosophers of science do not agree on a single definition of complementarity, but a satisfactory definition is the one just given—that is, contradictory properties of a microbody are reconciled by granting these individual properties existence only at separate moments of measurement. Another formulation, one that evades the question of "existence" of properties but that nonetheless is commonly given, is to say that the quantum description of phenomena divides into two mutually exclusive classes that complement each other in the sense that one must combine them in order to have a complete description in classical terms. This latter view was the one accepted by Oppenheimer when he stated that the notion of complementarity "recognizes (that) various ways of talking about physical experience may each have validity, and may each be necessary for the adequate description of the physical world, and may yet stand in a mutually exclusive relationship to each other, so that to a situation to which one applies, there may be no consistent possibility of applying the other."[7] It must also be added that even such early leaders in quantum mechanics as Bohr and Wolfgang Pauli did not entirely agree in their definitions of complementarity.[8] The essential problem was the perennial one in the history of science: giving a verbal interpretation to a mathematical relationship.

Before World War II the views of Soviet physicists on quantum mechanics were quite similar to those of advanced scientists elsewhere. Russian physics was in many ways an extension of central and Western European physics. The work of such men as Bohr and Heisenberg influenced scientists in the Soviet Union as it did everywhere. Indeed, Soviet physicists spoke of the "Russian branch" (filial) of the Copenhagen school, composed of a group of highly talented theoretical physicists, including M. P. Bronshtein, L. D. Landau, I. E. Tamm, and V. A. Fock. And yet behind this exterior of agreement with scientists everywhere on quantum mechanics (or, more accurately, disagreements similar to those everywhere), as early as the 1920s certain Soviet physicists were aware that dialectical materialism might some day be interpreted in a way that could influence their research.[9] Lenin had, after all, devoted an entire book, *Materialism and Empirio-Criticism*, to the crisis in interpretations of physics and had particularly criticized the neopositivism of Ernst Mach, out of which much of the philosophy of modern physics grew. Lenin's assertion that a dialectical materialist must recognize the existence of matter separate and independent from the mind, while not inherently contradictory to quantum mechanics, could be regarded as at least uncongenial to the Copenhagen school's disinclination to comment upon matter in the absence of sensible measurement. And the extension of the concept of complementarity beyond physics to other realms, including ethical and cultural problems, by certain members of the Copenhagen school almost guaranteed some conflict with representatives of Marxism.[10] As early as 1929 the leading Soviet philosopher at that time, A. M. Deborin, gave a lecture on "Lenin and the Crisis of Contemporary Physics" to the Academy of Sciences.[11] But the first serious Soviet critique of the customary interpretation of quantum mechanics in a physics journal, rather than a philosophy journal, occurred in 1936, written by K. V. Nikol'skii.[12] In the dispute that developed between Nikol'skii and V. A. Fock, a leading interpreter of quantum mechanics in the Soviet Union for over four decades and originally an adherent of the Copenhagen school, Nikol'skii called the Copenhagen Interpretation "idealistic" and "Machist,"[13] two appellations that were to be frequently utilized after World War II by Soviet Marxist critics. Nikol'skii's own view of quantum mechanics deserves examination for still another reason: It was a purely statistical approach, with only a few differences from D. I. Blokhintsev's postwar "ensemble" interpretation, which will be discussed in greater detail below.

With mention of Nikol'skii's "purely statistical" approach it is appropriate at this point to insert a few remarks on the concept of probability, which is crucial to any interpretation of quantum mechanics. Probability in quantum mechanics has been interpreted by different scholars in both epistemological and statistical senses. The statistical, or frequency, approach, used by Nikol'skii, was an attempted objective interpretation in which probability was seen as inherent in nature. On the other hand, a number of scholars have seen quantum mechanics, particularly through Born's original interpretation, as containing probability because of its epistemological assumptions, and have even discussed such peculiar things as "waves of knowledge." The distinction between these two approaches, often blurred in discussions of quantum mechanics, is absolutely necessary in attempting to decide whether a theory that is irreducibly probabilistic is also necessarily idealistic.

Fock's interpretation in 1936 of the physical significance of the wave function was essentially the same as that of the Copenhagen school, which combined Born's emphasis on the mathematical description of man's knowledge of the microworld with its own emphasis on the role of measurement; Fock stated in an introduction to a Russian translation of the 1935 debate of Einstein, Podolsky, and Rosen versus Bohr:

> In quantum mechanics the conception of state is merged with the conception of 'information about the state obtained as a result of a specific maximally accurate operation.' In quantum mechanics the wave function describes not the state in the usual sense, but rather this 'information about the state.'[14]

The importance of this prewar position of Fock's lies in its subtle difference from his stated views after the war, when he was placed under heavy pressure to desert the Copenhagen school.[15] Nevertheless, Fock's change in position was small compared to the swerves that occurred in the views of several other prominent Soviet philosophers and scientists.

The debate of the 1930s did not, however, leave a permanent imprint on Soviet attitudes toward quantum mechanics. Even many philosophers accepted much of the Copenhagen view. Early in 1947 M. E. Omel'ianovskii, a Ukrainian philosopher who with Fock and Blokhintsev completes the triumvirate whose views will be examined in detail here, argued a position on quantum mechanics close enough to the Copenhagen orientation to cause him intense embarrassment only a few months after its publication. His 1947 book became more interesting later, since it was a view that Omel'ianovskii later returned to and developed further.[16]

In this work, *V. I. Lenin and Twentieth-Century Physics*, Omel'ianovskii accepted much of the common interpretation of quantum mechanics. He recognized and used such terms as "the uncertainty principle" and "Bohr's principle of complementarity." (A year later Omel'ianovskii's terminology became "the so-called 'principle of complementarity.'") He guarded against using these concepts in a way that might deny physical reality, as he said certain people (including Bohr on occasion) had done, but his major thesis in this book was a defense of the surprising but necessary concepts of modern physics against adherents of the determinism of Laplace, by then clearly outdated.[17] Buried within Omel'ianovskii's arguments, however, one may observe, at least in retrospect, the core of his own interpretation of quantum mechanics and of his later criticisms of the Copenhagen school. Although he acquiesced in the vocabulary of Copenhagen, he emphasized that the correct interpretation of quantum mechanics began with a recognition of the peculiar qualities of microparticles, not with problems of cognition: "And so we have come to the conclusion that Heisenberg's uncertainty principle, like Bohr's principle of complementarity, is a generalized expression of the facts of the dual (corpuscular and undulatory) nature of microscopic objects."[18] Thus, the uncertainty principle was not actually an epistemological limitation or a limitation of knowledge, but a direct result of the combined wavelike and corpusclelike nature of micro-objects, which was the *material* reason why classical concepts could not be applied to the microworld. In view of this material source of the phenomenon of canonically conjugate parameters, one could not expect ever to possess simultaneous exact values of position and momentum of elementary particles. For his recognition of the basic position of contemporary views on quantum mechanics, Omel'ianovskii was soon criticized severely, and eventually produced a second edition of his book, in which, most notable, he repudiated the principle of complementarity.[19]

The most important event of the postwar years for Soviet scholarship was A. A. Zhdanov's speech on June 24, 1947, at the discussion of G. F. Aleksandrov's *History of Western European Philosophy*, an event well known to historians of the Soviet Union. Only near the end of the speech did Zhdanov mention specific issues in science, and less than a sentence referred to quantum mechanics: "The Kantian vagaries of modern bourgeois atomic physicists lead them to inferences about the electron's possessing 'free will,' to attempts to describe matter as only a certain conjunction of waves, and to other devilish tricks."[20]

Although Zhdanov's speech is now known as the beginning of the most intense ideological campaign in the history of Soviet scholarship, the *Zhdanovshchina*, the first few issues of the new journal *Problems of Philosophy* that appeared after the speech were surprisingly unorthodox.[21] Evidently taking seriously the slogan of the journal—"to develop and carry further" Marxist-Leninist theory—the editors promoted vital disussions of several philosophic questions. In no field was this vitality more apparent than in the philosophy of physics; the second issue of *Problems of Philosophy* contained an article by the outstanding theoretical physicist M. A. Markov, a specialist in the relativity theory of elementary particles, which may well still be the most outspoken presentation since World War II.[22] Just why Markov chose this moment, after Zhdanov's condemnation of Aleksandrov and during the tightening of ideological controls, to expose himself to criticism so extensively may never be known, but there are several hints available. Markov was a research scientist in the Physics Institute of the USSR Academy of Sciences, the organization that in the past had most stoutly defended international viewpoints in science and that would do so in the future, incurring sharp criticism from political activists.[23] It is probable that the theoretical physicists in the Academy, aware since the 1930s that, given the will, dialectical materialism could be used against prevalent interpretations of quantum mechanics, decided that the nascent ideological campaign meant that an official position on quantum mechanics was very likely to be imposed and felt that an early attempt to make that official position compatible with contemporary quantum theory was necessary. Markov probably knew well just how controversial his article would be, but hoped, first, that it would be vindicated, and second, that even if his point of view was rejected, the final compromise would be more palatable to the physicists as a result of his strong stand. Furthermore, Markov was able to capitalize on a feud among the professional philosophers. As the course of the debate illustrated, the chief editor of the new philosophy journal *Problems of Philosophy* was disliked by the old guard, which had published *Under the Banner of Marxism*, the major Soviet journal of philosophy from 1922 to 1944. The debate over Markov consequently contained many dimensions: it was an effort by the physicists to protect quantum mechanics, it was a volley in a feud among philosophers, and it was a decisive struggle over whether physicists or philosophers would have the ultimate influence on the philosophy of science in the postwar period.

Markov accepted modern quantum theory completely and agreed with Bohr's position in Bohr's debate with Einstein, Podolsky, and Rosen. Thus, Markov considered quantum mechanics to be complete, in the technical sense that no experiment that did not contradict it could yield results not predicted by it; and he consequently rejected all attempts to explain the behavior of microparticles on the basis of "hidden parameter" theories that would later permit restitution of the concepts of classical physics: "It is impossible to regard quantum mechanics as a classical mechanics that has been corrupted by our 'lack of knowledge.' "[24] Such complementary functions as "momentum" and "position" simply did not have simultaneous values; to suggest that they did would mean contradicting quantum theory.[25]

Not only was Markov's view on conjugate parameters typical of the Copenhagen school, but his approach to science bore few traits of dialectical materialism despite his initial quotations from Marxist classics. He asked that no statements be made that could not be empirically verified; he accepted relativity theory, including relativity of spatial and temporal intervals; he used the term "complementarity" without hesitation. To be sure, he affirmed that his view of science was "materialist" and criticized James Jeans and other non-Soviet commentators on science, but nowhere in his article did he make any effort to illustrate the relevance of dialectical materialism to science.

Markov maintained that "truth" is obtained from many sources; when we speak of knowledge of the microworld, which we gain with instruments, we are speaking about knowledge that has come from three sources: nature, the instrument, and man. The language we use to describe our knowledge is perforce always "macroscopic" language, since this is the only language we possess. The measuring instrument performs the role of "translating" the microphenomenon into a macrolanguage accessible to man. "We consider physical reality to be that form of reality in which reality appears in the macroinstrument."[26] Thus, according to Markov, our concept of physical reality is subjective to the extent that it is formed in macroscopic language and is "prepared" by the act of measurement, but it is objective in the sense that physical reality in quantum mechanics is a macroscopic form of the reality of the microworld.

The role of the measuring instrument is one of the thorniest issues in quantum mechanics. Markov's view was essentially in agreement with that of the Copenhagen Interpretation, according to which the wave describing a physical state spreads out over larger and larger values until a measurement is made, when a reduction of this spread (wave packet) to a sharp value occurs. Such an interpretation does indeed imply that complementary microphysical quantities have no inherent sharp values but that such values instead result from, or are "prepared by," the measurement.

Markov's acceptance of the Copenhagen Interpretation exposed him to criticism from a number of quarters, ranging from dogmatic ideologues to ordinary physicists with hopes for the eventual replacement of the views of Bohr and his colleagues by an interpretation more agreeable to common-sense intuition. The Markov article very quickly became the occasion for a full-blown controversy, involving several dozen participants, on the nature of physical reality and the dialectical materialist interpretation of quantum mechanics.[27]

The polemic began with the appearance of an article by A. A. Maksimov in the Literary Gazette, an unusual place for a commentary on the philosophy of science.[28] The article, entitled "Concerning a Philosophic Centaur," contained very serious allegations against Markov.

As the title indicates, Maksimov considered Markov a strange species, a creature combining Western idealistic views on the philosophy of science with professions of loyalty to dialectical materialism.

After the appearance of Maksimov's article, the editors of *Problems of Philosophy* published a discussion of quantum mechanics. A number of authors (D. D. Danin, M. V. Vol'kenshtein, and M. S. Veselov) gave Markov strong support, revealing the numerous errors of Maksimov, and the noted D. I. Blokhintsev also took a fairly positive view of Markov's interpretation of quantum mechanics. Other critics, however, pointed out Markov's "anthropomorphism" in science, a result of his emphasis on the "observer" (L. I. Storchak) and his disregard of Party loyalty, or *partiinost'* (I. K. Krushev, V. A. Mikhailov).[29] But the factor that determined the eventual disapproval of Markov's article was a decision, beyond any doubt promoted by the Party, to replace B. M. Kedrov as editor of *Problems of Philosophy* by D. I. Chesnokov. It is clear that Maksimov's attack on Markov played an important role in Kedrov's downfall.[30] In a note in the third issue of 1948 the reformed editorial board of *Problems of Philosophy* admitted that the journal had not taken the correct position on quantum mechanics and particularly on Markov's article, which had "weakened the position of materialism." The article had contained "serious mistakes of a philosophic character" and was in essence a departure from dialectical materialism "in the direction of idealism and agnosticism."[31]

In terms of personnel, the immediate casualty of the Markov affair was Kedrov, but in terms of the philosophy of science, the casualty was the principle of complementarity. The period from 1948 to roughly 1960 may be called, with respect to discussions of quantum mechanics in the Soviet Union, the age of the banishment of complementarity.[32] Only a few scientists in this period, most notably V. A. Fock, attempted to include complementarity as an integral part of quantum theory.

This critical attitude toward complementarity after 1948 was made clear in an article by Ia. P. Terletskii that immediately preceded the final statement on the Markov controversy by the editors of *Problems of Philosophy*. Terletskii observed that Markov's article was actually an attempt to justify the acceptance of complementarity by maintaining that as a result of the role of measuring instruments as "translators" of reality, statements about microphysics often contradict each other. Such a view, thought Terletskii, was merely a restatement of Mach's opinion that scientists must describe nature in terms of sensations. A true dialectical materialist approach, however, showed, Terletskii continued, that the principle of complementarity was in no way a basic physical principle and that quantum mechanics could very well "get along without it."[33]

The result of the Markov affair, then, was a victory for dogmatic ideologists. Maksimov, an ideologist, had triumphed over Markov, an active theoretical physicist in the Academy of Sciences. But it also became fairly clear that Maksimov was not capable of advancing an interpretation of quantum mechanics that held any chance of official acceptance.[34] His articles on quantum mechanics revealed all too clearly his ignorance of the subject. And it was the same Maksimov who was simultaneously opposing not only Einsteinian relativity but even Galilean relativity, maintaining that every object has an absolute trajectory and that a meteorite inscribes this trajectory on the earth upon collision with it.[35] Maksimov clearly represented pseudoscience, and his role in both quantum mechanics and relativity theory was a purely destructive one, isolating the "Machists" and "idealists" among Soviet scientists and winning a certain support for that service, but presenting no tenable alternatives to current interpretations of physical theory. As in the case of relativity theory, Maksimov soon lost his influence among Soviet interpreters of quantum theory. The period after 1948 was dominated instead by physicists and a small number of philosophers with some knowledge of physics, all of whom, however, were influenced by the atmosphere created by the Markov affair. Until approximately 1958 the major interpreter of quantum mechanics was the philosopher of science Omel'ianovskii, who drew upon the theories of the physicist Blokhintsev, advocate of the "ensemble" interpretation. Also important was Fock, who termed his interpretation a recognition of the "reality of quantum states." And a good many others, including A. D. Aleksandrov, Ia. P. Terletskii, B. G. Kuznetsov, as well as the foreign scholars Louis de Broglie, J. P. Vigier, and David Bohm, influenced the discussions of dialetical materialism and quantum mechanics.

D. I. BLOKHINTSEV

D. I. Blokhintsev, one of the best-known Soviet specialists in quantum mechanics and after 1956 director of the Joint Institute of Nuclear Research at Dubna, as well as winner of the Lenin and Stalin prizes, was a leading writer in the fifties and sixties on the philosophic implications of quantum mechanics.[35] In his statistical interpretation of quantum mechanics Blokhintsev put great emphasis on "ensembles." He noted that the probability yielded by the wave function was derived from a series of repeated measuring operations. Therefore, when one talked about the wave function of one particle, or one system, what was actually being talked about was a large number of such particles or systems. A collection of such particles that were independent of one another and that could serve as material for repeated independent experiments was called an ensemble. The Heisenberg uncertainty relation, which was often discussed in terms of one particle, was actually a result, according to Blokhintsev, of measuring operations carried out on particles belonging to an ensemble. If all the particles in an ensemble could be described by one wave function, it was a "pure ensemble." If, however, an ensemble consisted of subensembles, each of which was described by a wave function, then the total was a "mixed ensemble." The relevance of this breakdown of the ensembles for the question of the nature of the wave function was the following: if a measurement was carried out on a pure ensemble, according to Blokhintsev, that very operation caused the ensemble to become mixed, since the act of measurement placed those few (perhaps one) microparticles affected by the measurement in a different state described by a different wave function.[37]

The most complete statement of Blokhintsev's criticism of the Copenhagen school and the philosophic significance of his alternative ensemble interpretation was a long article that appeared in a leading Soviet physics journal in 1951.[38] Blokhintsev set himself the task of proving that quantum statistics had objective reality and in no way depended on the observer, in contrast to Bohr's early belief that the statistics could be considered a result of the uncontrollable influence of the instrument upon the object. He noted that radioactive atoms decayed according to statistical laws that were independent of observers and instruments. Blokhintsev considered radioactivity a phenomenon of a "certain statistical ensemble of radioactive atoms, existing independently in nature."[39] Cosmic rays were similarly dependent on objective statistical laws. And, he observed, the microlevel of matter was an area where such statistical laws were inherently "objective" (did not derive from underlying causal factors) and therefore commonplace. In contrast,

> the Copenhagen school relegates to secondary importance the fact that quantum mechanics is applicable only to statistical ensembles and concentrates on analysis of the mutual relations of a single phenomenon and

the instrument. This is an essential methodological error: In such an interpretation all quantum mechanics takes on an 'instrumental' character, and the objective aspect of things is extinguished.[40]

Blokhintsev maintained that quantum mechanics was inapplicable to individual micro-objects, since no individual micro-object could be studied in isolation from its environment. By studying large numbers of microparticles, however, knowledge of objective reality could "in principle" be attained: "Quantum mechanics studies the properties of a single microphenomenon by means of the study of the statistical laws of the collective of such phenomena."[41] Blokhintsev readily granted that a measuring operation would change the state of particular particle, placing the particle in a different ensemble, but asserted that all the other particles in the old ensemble would still be in their previous states. Therefore the scientist could conceive of objective reality though the concept of the totality, or ensemble.

Blokhintsev also indicated that a "hidden parameter" theory of quantum mechanics might at some future date permit a numerical description of the individul microparticle, although at the present time he considered such a description impossible. He dismissed John von Neumann's and Hans Reichenbach's well-known attempts to disprove hidden parameter theories by pointing out that both rested their cases on the existing mathematical apparatus of quantum mechanics, which would surely be changed if a new theory were devised.[42] He also dismissed the position of Einstein, Podolsky, and Rosen, noting that these authors based their views on the application of the wave function to individual particles, whereas he believed it should be applied only to groups or ensembles.[43]

The central weakness of Blokhintsev's interpretation was his definition of ensembles. He failed in his goal of separating the quantum description of matter from the process of measurement, as can be seen by analyzing his definition of ensembles: Blokhintsev defined an ensemble as a combination of the microsystem (a collection of particles) and its macroenvironment. But what did the "macroenvironment" include? According to Blokhintsev, the macroenvironment included measuring instruments as "special cases." He then defined the wave function as the "association" of a particle with an ensemble.[44] But his chain of reasoning had led him full circle, since he had started with the desire to separate quantum mechanics from measurement and ended by including measurement in his definition of the ensemble. Thus, the psi function became, as before, a probabilistic statement of the results of measurement.

In the controversy between Blokhintsev and Fock that soon followed, the concept of ensembles became a basic issue. Fock very quickly located the weakness at the bottom of Blokhintsev's discussions of the ensemble. He extracted the fundamentals of quantum mechanics that Blokhintsev had defined in 1949: (a) an ensemble is a collection of particles that independently of one another are in a state such that the ensemble can be characterized by the wave function; (b) it follows that the state of a particle should be understood as the association of that particle with a definite ensemble, so that (c) the wave function does not concern an individual particle. Fock then demonstrated that these propositions contradict each other:

> In assertion (a) the state of an individual particle is defined by means of its wave function, but in assertion (c) it is denied that the wave function concerns the individual particle. This is a contradiction. Furthermore, in assertion (a) the ensemble is defined by means of the wave function, but in assertion (b) the wave function is defined through the ensemble. This is a vicious circle.[45]

Furthermore, continued Fock, Blokhintsev could not treat the ensembles as statistical collectives, as he intended to do, unless they met the standard criteria of such collectives in accordance with established theory of statistics. By this theory, a statistical collective is a collection of elements that may be sorted out in accordance with a certain indicator (priznak). Such an indicator would be the value of a certain physical magnitude, or a group of physical magnitudes simultaneously measured. But according to quantum mechanics, microparticles do not possess definite values that would permit the sorting out of a definite collective. Therefore Blokhintsev, said Fock, had no way of even denoting the members of his much touted ensembles, which were really only "speculative constructions." Instead, he should frankly state that his quantum ensembles concealed a reference to a statistical statement of the results of measurements on a micro-object, conducted with the aid of a classical instrument designed for measuring given magnitude. Fock concluded that Blokhintsev's incorrect position was connected with that of Bohr:

> We see the basic cause of all difficulties in the fact that a purely statistical point of view is incorrect in a philosophic sense. In contrast to what dialectical materialism teaches us, the statistical point of view issues not from the objects of nature but from observations, not from the micro-object and its state but from the statistical collective of the results of observations. This draws it toward the positivist point of view of Bohr,

which also denies that the wave function relates to the micro-object, and attributes to the wave function only a purely symbolic significance.[46]

A reply to this criticism was no easy task for Blokhintsev, who must have felt somewhat uneasy about the definition of his ensembles, to judge from the waverings in his writings on the subject. Much of his answer to Fock was a criticism of the latter's own belief that the wave function is an objective description of individual microbodies. This aspect of their debate will be considered in the following section, which concerns Fock's own interpretation of quantum mechanics. On the question of the definition of the ensembles, Blokhintsev merely affirmed his previous views, defending himself from Fock's criticism by saying that as long as it is possible to conceive of a pure ensemble, it is possible to separate conceptually the quantum description of matter from measurement and therefore from subjectivism or idealism. This hypothetical ensemble would be one on which no measuring operation had been carried out and which, therefore, could in principle be described by one wave function. But since no measurements had in fact been made, almost nothing could be said about such an ensemble other than "it exists," according to Blokhintsev.[47]

In 1966 Blokhintsev published an interesting book entitled *Questions of Principle in Quantum Mechanics*,[48] which was later translated into English and published jointly in Europe and the United States under the title *The Philosophy of Quantum Mechanics*. The book was Blokhintsev's most complete treatment of philosophical issues in quantum mechanics; as the work of a distinguished Soviet professional physicist, it deserves careful examination. Blokhintsev's approach was highly technical, and he warned his readers that "the present monograph is concerned more with theoretical physics than with philosophy" (p. v). Yet it is clear that Blokhintsev recognized fully the interaction of physics and philosophy, and addressed himself to several major aspects of this interaction. Blokhintsev's study was both enlightened and tolerant; if philosophers have found certain unclear points of definition, it should be remembered that scientists and philosophers everywhere agree that the interpretation of quantum mechanics is an exceedingly difficult problem. There is no agreement anywhere on these matters.

Blokhintsev's 1966 book was essentially an attempt to clarify and support the ensemble interpretation of quantum mechanics that he had earlier developed. True, there were certain small changes of emphasis and aspiration, particularly in his opinion on the possibility of finding latent parameters in quantum mechanics. His description of the psi function also changed a bit. But the differences between him and Fock on the validity of the ensemble approach and the applicability of the psi function to the individual particle remained. The real significance of his new book, however, was not its discussion of these issues, since his opinions here remained essentially unchanged, but his fuller description of causality and his criticism of determinism. Even though the 1966 book was written and published at a time when there was little pressure from ideologists upon scientists in the Soviet Union, Blokhintsev's views were still essentially a continuation and further development of the earlier debates. This continuity derived not as much from politics as from the attractiveness to Blokhintsev of the underlying philosophical issues of interpretation of nature.

Blokhintsev began his 1966 book with a criticism of what he called "the illusion of determinism." He thought that the advance of science, and particularly the new understanding of nature issuing from quantum mechanics, illustrated the weakness of a belief in strict determinism. The fallacies of this "worship of ideal determinism" were seen, albeit incompletely, Blokhintsev thought, by even a few nineteenth-century critics of Laplacian mechanism, such as Engels, who said in *Dialectics of Nature* that "necessity of this kind does not take us outside the theological view of nature."[50]

> For a long time humanity believed in divine predestination, and afterwards in rigid causal connection. Engels appreciated the philosophical resemblance and narrowness of these viewpoints, while failure to appreciate this affinity has over the centuries been the cause of tragedy to many outstanding men. (p. 2)

Determinism in the classic sense meant, Blokhintsev observed, that "the state of a system at a preceding instant completely determines the state at a subsequent instant" (p. 34). Even before the development of quantum mechanics, however, there was reason to doubt the validity of such a conception of the universe. Any attempt to rigidly predict the future of a system, Blokhintsev noted, is influenced by the inaccuracy of the initial data, the unpredictability of accidental forces, and the impossibility of keeping any system completely isolated. All of these three limitations on classical physics were usually ignored, Blokhintsev commented, although the philosophic interpretation of the world that sees it as an interconnected whole should have revealed more fully at least the impossibility of isolating any system. This feature is very important, Blokhintsev thought:

The future of a mechanical system may be predicted only if we can be sure that the system is isolated. The guarantee required here is not implied by the equations of motion but is an additional condition, which produces a great reduction in the reliance on determinism. A vast and depressing "if" arises in the way of the prophet who sets out to predict the future of a real mechanical system. (p. 11)

Thus, he commented, "the input data must from time to time be corrected even in a science as precise as celestial mechanics, in order to eliminate cumulative errors" (p. 14). And he implied that this necessity was not a practical one, but a theoretical one, since there exists in the interconnected universe an infinite number of potential influences.

All of these considerations applied to classical mechanics. With the development of quantum mechanics and the emergence of the necessity of probabilistic descriptions of nature for reasons apparently quite intrinsic to microbodies, the erroneousness of the whole classical approach to determinism became quite apparent.

Does the abandonment of rigid determinism mean a surrender of the principle of causality? Blokhintsev answered this question negatively, as did Fock and other Soviet commentators. He agreed that it was necessary to take a new look at definitions of causality, but felt that such a redefinition was fully justified as a part of man's constant effort to find order in nature. And Blokhintsev defined causality in the following way:

Causality is a definite form of order in events in space and time; this ordering imposes restrictions even on the most chaotic events, and it makes itself felt in two ways in statistical theories. Firstly, the statistical laws themselves are fully ordered, and the quantities that characterize an ensemble are themselves strictly determined. Secondly, the individual elementary events are also so ordered that one may influence another only if their relative location in space and time allows this without violating casuality (i.e., the rule ordering the events). (p. 33)

Within the context of this understanding of causality Blokhintsev considered quantum mechanics causal; to him, Schrödinger's equation expresses causality in quantum theory, since it describes the motion of the quantum ensemble "in a causal fashion, i.e., so that the state earlier in time determines the subsequent state of the ensemble" (p. 35). Thus one could save not only a concept of causality, but even a concept of determinism, although on a much different level than previously.

On the question of the validity of the term "complementarity," Blokhintsev in his 1966 book wrote that Bohr had formulated this concept in a way that reflected his philosophical concepts, "which were far from those of materialism" (p. 22). Blokhintsev regretted this aspect of Bohr's philosophy, which "has been the origin of the far-reaching conclusion that the current mechanics of the atom cannot be compatible with materialism" (p. 22). In order to oppose this conclusion, Blokhintsev would have preferred another term for "complementarity," but he felt that it was now too well established to eliminate:

> It would seem generally better to speak of a principle of exclusiveness rather than complementarity: dynamic variables should be divided into mutually exclusive groups, which do not coexist in real ensembles. However, out of respect for Bohr and his tradition we shall retain the usual terminology. (p. 22)

Blokhintsev took up the topic of the future of quantum mechanics in his chapter "Is the Wave Function Avoidable?" And on this issue he noted a change in his own position. He said, "The present author himself once hoped that the striking similarities" between the equations for the density matrix and the equations of classical physics "would allow the formulation of quantum mechanics as the statistical mechanics of quantities not simultaneously measurable" (p. 41). But he had now almost completely abandoned this hope. In fact, he said that it was impossible to point to a single experimental fact to indicate that quantum theory is incomplete within the range of atomic phenomena. Nonetheless, he admitted that it was still at least theoretically possible that quantum mechanics would be substantially revised. He wrote that:

> one possibility to examine is the introduction of latent parameters such as to give meaning to a proportion of the form
>
> $$\frac{x}{\text{quantum mechanics}} = \frac{\text{kinetic theory of matter}}{\text{thermodynamics}} \quad (1)$$
>
> in which x is some unknown (more complete) theory.
>   It cannot be denied that the symbolic equation of (1), or some similar one, might be soluble, at least in this extremely general and purely methodological formulation of the problem. (p. 110)

Yet Blokhintsev was skeptical of all such attempts, comparing the person who made them with "the seeker for unwettable gunpowder." He thought that the present structure of quantum mechanics was admirably adequate for physicists and need not be disquieting to philosophers—indeed, it had enriched man's understanding of causality and objective reality.

V. A. FOCK

Academician V. A. Fock has already been mentioned in the discussion of the views of Blokhintsev. A separate consideration of Fock's own interpretation of quantum mechanics will be the subject of the following section.

Fock, a theoretical physicist of Leningrad University, was elected to the Academy of Sciences of the USSR in 1939, won the Stalin Prize in 1946 and the Lenin Prize in 1960. His research was on problems of mathematical physics, and particularly relativity theory and quantum mechanics. He was also deeply interested in the philosophical impli- cations of modern physics, writing extensively on this subject until his death in 1974. Both his scientific and his philosophical writing attracted attention abroad.

Throughout a number of controversies Fock was noted for his intense sense of independence, defending himself on numerous occasions against both Soviet and non-Soviet critics. In quantum mechanics, Fock may be correctly defined as a follower of Bohr's Copenhagen interpretation if one defines the Copenhagen Interpretation in terms of its minimum rather than its maximum claims. (This "core meaning" of the Copen- hagen Interpretation was once described by N. R. Hanson as "a much smaller and more elusive target to shoot at than the *ex cathedra* utterances of the melancholy Dane.")[51]

Fock wrote that he entered into philosophical discussion of quantum mechanics because he believed it was possible to agree with Bohr's scientific approach without accepting his philosophical conclusions. He decided that he would strip away the "positivistic coating" on Bohr's formulations.[52]

The most accurate evaluation of Fock's position might be to say that with a few temporary waverings, his thinking underwent transitions quite similar to the shifts in Bohr's thinking. In several cases these shifts, all toward deemphasis of the role of measurement and stress on a realist point of view, occurred first in Fock's interpretation, then in Bohr's, and it is possible that Fock may have been one of the influences on Bohr. The two scientists were aware of each other's work, and in February and March 1957 they held a series of conversations on the philosophic significance of quantum mechanics. The discussions took place in Copenhagen, both in Bohr's home and at his Institute of Theoretical Physics. Fock later reported on the conversations in the following way:

From the very beginning Bohr said that he was not a positivist and that he attempted simply to consider nature exactly as it is. I pointed out that several of his expressions gave ground for an interpretation of his views in a positivistic sense that he, apparently, did not wish to support. . . . Our views constantly came closer together; in particular it became clear that Bohr completely recognized the objectivity of atoms and their properties, recognized that it was necessary to give up determinism only in the Laplacian sense, but not causality in general; he further said that the term "uncontrollable mutual influence" was unsuccessful and that actually all physical processes are controllable.[53]

It was after this exchange that Fock commented, "After Bohr's correction of his formulations, I believe that I am in agreement with him on all basic items."[54] This observation followed a period in which Fock had been rather critical of what he considered Bohr's carelessness on philosophic issues.

In the 1930s, however, when Bohr had been even less cautious in his statements, Fock was one of the leaders of the "Copenhagen branch" in the USSR and repeatedly defended its viewpoint in the journals. His agreement with Bohr in the latter's debate with Einstein over the completeness of quantum theory is quite clear. During and shortly after the war Fock retreated a bit in the terminology of his defense of Copenhagen, but never abandoned its position. Indeed, one of the remarkable aspects of Fock's career, and of the history of Soviet philosophy of science, is that he was able to defend the concept of complementarity during a long period when it was officially condemned in the philosophy journals. During this time Fock occupied an anomalous position: his view on quantum mechanics was disapproved, but his interpretation of relativity theory, which did not include the concept of general relativity, became more and more influential. Nothing illustrates better the subtlety of Soviet controversies in the philosophy of science—a subtlety greater than most non-Soviet observers are willing to grant—than Fock's views being simultaneously under ban and approval. After 1958 Fock's interpretation of quantum mechanics gained greater acceptance and was finally adopted by the philosopher Omel'ianovskii, who had previously supported Blokhintsev. Ironically, in this period Fock's interpretation of relativity, although still very influential, was coming under more and more criticism from such people as M. F. Shirokov.[55] If the shifts seem confusing, some consistency may be perceived in the fact that both of these latter changes (away from Fock in relativity, toward him in quantum mechanics) put Soviet science in a closer position to dominant non-Soviet interpretations, which had themselves undergone certain changes.

Most of Fock's effort in interpreting quantum mechanics was directed toward establishing the fact that the Copenhagen Interpretation, including the principle of complementarity, did not violate dialectical materialism. As early as 1938 he maintained that "the thesis that a contradiction exists between quantum mechanics and materialism is an idealistic theory." Bohr's principle of complementarity was, to Fock, "an integral part of quantum mechanics" and a "firmly established objectively existing law of nature."[56] For more than thirty years he defended the essential Copenhagen position, although he carefully dissociated himself from certain of Bohr's views, such as the latter's early attribution of primary importance to the process of measurement. Nevertheless, his interpretation of the physical significance of the psi function was the same as that of Bohr. Before World War II Fock did not consider the wave function to be a description of the state of matter. This was, he noted, the position of Einstein, who then became involved with paradoxes. Fock, along with Bohr, considered the psi function to be a description of "information about the state" (svedeniia o sostoianii).[57] It is not surprising, then, that Fock engaged in two particularly bitter exchanges with Maksimov, which were separated by a period of fifteen years. Maksimov advertised Fock as a conscious partisan of the idealistic, bourgeois Copenhagen School, while Fock observed that Maksimov was a wonderful example of how *not* to defend materialism.[58]

The most difficult period for Fock was immediately after the Markov affair. The new position, advanced by Terletskii and quickly supported by Omel'ianovskii, was that Heisenberg's uncertainty relation was, indeed, an integral part of quantum mechanics and must be retained, but that complementarity in no way followed from uncertainty.

According to Fock, on the contrary, there was no essential difference between the Heisenberg uncertainty relation and complementarity.[59] Both were the result of crossing the dividing line between the macrolevel and the microlevel. It was quite conceivable, Fock indicated, that if one were to give a description of the microlevel of matter in terms appropriate to that level (microlanguage), then there would exist a new kind of "complementarity" that would arise when one attempted to describe the macrolevel in that microlanguage. This new complementarity would be analogous to, but different from, the complementarity of existing quantum mechanics, which was based on description in macrolanguage.[60] In this view the kernel of objective reality that dialectical materialism demands as a minimum in every physical description becomes very elusive indeed.[61]

Fock's identification of uncertainty and complementarity brought him under very heavy criticism. In the famous 1952 "Green Book" on philosophic problems of science, edited by a group headed by the ultraconservative Maksimov, Omel'ianovskii observed: "Unfortunately several of our scientists . . . have not yet drawn the necessary conclusions from the criticism to which Soviet science subjected the Copenhagen School. For example, V. A. Fock in his earlier works did not essentially distinguish the uncertainty relationship from Bohr's principle of complementarity."[62]

It was this kind of criticism that caused Fock to alter his terminology and temporarily to hesitate in his advocacy of complementarity. While previously he had considered the psi function to be a description of "information about the state," he now called the psi function a characterization of the "real state" of the micro-object.[63] In 1951 Fock indicated that as a result of the blurring of the original meaning of complementarity, he might abandon it altogether:

> At first the term complementarity signified the situation that arose directly from the uncertainty relation: Complementarity concerned the uncertainty in coordinate measurement and in the amount of motion . . . and the term "principle of complementarity" was understood as a synonym for the Heisenberg relation. Very soon, however, Bohr began to see in his principle of complementarity a certain universal principle . . . applicable not only in physics but even in biology, psychology, sociology, and in all sciences. . . . To the extent that the term "principle of complementarity" has lost its original meaning . . . it would be better to abandom it.[64]

One of the most complete statements of Fock's interpretation of quantum mechanics appeared in a collection of articles on philosophic problems of science published in Moscow in 1959.[65] Written at a time of relative freedom from ideological restriction, it is a statement of both scientific rigor and philosophic conviction. Fock began his discussion by considering and then dismissing attempts to interpret the wave function according to classical concepts. De Broglie's and Schrödinger's attempts originally to explain the wave function as a field spread in space, similar to electromagnetic and other previously unknown fields, were examples of classical interpretations, as was also de Broglie's later view that a field acts as a carrier of the particle and controls its movement (the pilot-wave theory).[66] Bohm's "quantum potential" was essentially the same type of explanation, since it attempted to preserve the concept of trajectory.[67] Similarly, Vigier's concept of a particle as a point or focus in a field was an attempt to preserve classical ideas in physics.[68] All of these interpretations, according to Fock, were extremely artificial and had no heuristic value; not only did they not permit the solution of problems that were previously unsolvable, but their authors did not even attempt such solutions.

Fock believed that the true significance of the wave function began to emerge in the statistical interpretation of Max Born, especially after Niels Bohr combined this approach with his own view of the importance of the means of observation. This emphasis on measuring instruments was essential for quantum mechanics, Fock agreed, but it was exactly on this point that Bohr also slipped:

> In principle it seems that it is possible to reduce a description to the indications of instruments. However, an excessive emphasis on the role of instruments is reason for reproaching Bohr for underrating the necessity for abstraction and for forgetting that the object of study is the properties of the micro-object, and not the indication of the instruments.[69]

Bohr then compounded the confusion, said Fock, by utilizing inexact terminology—terminology he was forced to invent in order to cover up the discrepancy that arose when he attempted to use classical concepts outside their area of application. One of the most important of these uses of inexact terminology was his opposition of the principle of complementarity to the principle of causality. According to Fock, if one defines terms with the necessary precision, no such opposition exists. The complementarity that does exist in quantum mechanics is a complementarity between classical descriptions and causality. But this does not deny causality in general because classical descriptions of macroparticles are necessarily inappropriate for microparticles. Using classical descriptions (macrolanguage) is merely a necessary method since we do not have a microlanguage. Realizing that a microdescription of microparticles would be different from a classical description of the same particles, we can say that on both levels (micro and macro) the principle of causality holds. Since we always use a macrodescription, however, we should redefine causality in such a way that it fits both levels. Our new approach, said Fock, should be to understand causality as an affirmation of the existence of laws of nature, particularly those connected with the general properties of space and time (finite velocity of action, the impossibility of influencing the past). Causal laws can, therefore, be either statistical or deterministic. The true absence of causality in nature would mean to Fock that not even probabilistic descriptions could be given; all outcomes would be equally probable. Fock concluded his remarks on causality by commenting that in his recent conversations he had found Bohr in agreement with these observations. Thus, a few redefinitions of complementarity and causality would go far toward strengthening the Copenhagen Interpretation.

Fock's opinion of the role of measurement in quantum mechanics was based on a recognition of objective reality. He accepted Heisenberg's uncertainty relation as a factual statement of the exactness of measurements on the microlevel. But this relativity with respect to the means of measurement in no way interfered with objectivity: "In quantum physics the relativity that arises from the means of observation only increases the preciseness of physical concepts. . . . The objects of the microworld are just as real and their properties just as objective as the properties of objects studied by classical physics."[70] The instrument in quantum mechanics plays an important role, Fock observed, but there is no reason to exaggerate that role since the instrument is merely another part of objective reality, obeying physical laws. The importance of the instrument is that it necessarily gives its description in classical terms.

The root of quantum mechanics, according to Fock, is, however, something radically new in science: the potential possibility for a microobject to appear, in dependence on its external conditions, either as a wave, a particle, or in an intermediate form.[71] This new concept, coupled with the statistical characteristics of the state of an object, leads us to a different understanding of causality and of matter. Bohr tried to find his way to this new understanding by way of emphasizing the role of the instrument and by stressing the concept of complementarity. Fock preferred a slightly different way: "I try to bring in new concepts, for example, the concept of potential possibilities inherent in the atomic object, and it seems to me that the mathematical apparatus of quantum mechanics may be correctly understood only on the basis of these new concepts."[72] Fock, then, considered his essential contribution to the interpretation of quantum mechanics to be the idea of "potential possibilities" and the consequent distinction between the potentially possible and the actually realized results in physics. As will be illustrated below, Fock's approach differed sharply from hidden parameter interpretations, since he did not believe it was possible, in principle, to arrive at an exact description of microparticles.

In experiments designed to study the properties of atomic objects, Fock distinguished three different stages: the preparation of the object, the behavior *(povedenie)* of the object in fixed external conditions, and the measurement itself. These stages might be called the "preparatory part" of the experiment, the "working part," and the "registering part." In diffraction experiments through a crystal, the preparatory part would be the source of the monochromatic stream of electrons, as well as the diaphragm in front of the crystal; the working part would be the crystal itself; and the registering part would be a photographic plate. Fock emphasized that in such an experiment it is possible to change the last stage (the measurement) without changing the first two, and he would build his interpretation of quantum mechanics on this recognition. Therefore, by varying the final stage of the experiment, it is possible to make measurements of different values (energy, velocity, position) all of which are derived from the same initial state of the object:

> To each value there corresponds its own series of measurement, the results of which are expressed as a distribution of probabilities for that value. All the indicated probabilities may be expressed parametrically through one and the same wave function, which does not depend on the final stage of the experiment and consequently is an objective characteristic of the state of the object immediately before the final stage.[73]

In the last sentence, then, is the meaning of Fock's often-quoted statement that the wave function is an objective description of quantum states. The wave function is objective, said Fock, in the sense that it requires an objective (independent of the observer) description of the potential possibilities of mutual influences of the object and the instrument. Therefore, the scientist is correct, Fock believed (contrary to Blokhintsev), in saying that the wave function relates to a given single object. But this objective state is not yet actual, he continued, since none of the potential possibilities has yet been realized. The transition from the potentially possible to the existing occurs in the final stage of the experiment. Thus, Fock completed his interpretation of quantum mechanics with an affirmation of a realist (he would say dialectical materialist) position on the philosophy of science. Nevertheless, the extension of a concept of realism to a statement concerning potential situations rather than actual situations was open to a number of logical objections.

M. E. OMEL'IANOVSKII

M. E. Omel'ianovskii, a member of the Ukrainian Academy of Sciences, was one of the most influential Soviet philosophers of science in the sixties and seventies. In the 1940s Omel'ianovskii helped to create a strong school in the philosophy of science in Kiev; after his shift to Moscow in the mid-fifties he was the most important figure in the largely successful effort to repair the damages of Stalinism in the philosophy of science and to create a tighter union between scientists and philosophers.[74] Although Omel'ianovskii yielded to the political pressures of the 1948–1956 period, he understood modern physical theory and fully appreciated its significance for the philosophy of science, as his pre-1948 publications indicated.[75] Soon after the denunciation of Stalinism at the Twentieth Party Congress in 1956 Omel'ianovskii published an important article calling for a new approach to dialectical materialism.[76] In a personal conversation with me he described the article as one of the most important turning points in his professional development. As a leader of the sector on the philosophical problems of science at the Institute of Philosophy of the USSR Academy of Sciences, Omel'ianovskii was instrumental after 1956 in arranging frequent conferences and publishing collections of articles in which both prominent philosophers and well-known natural scientists participated. As an example, in 1970 Omel'ianovskii edited an interesting volume of original articles on the philosophy of science entitled *Lenin and Modern Science*, in which a number of eminent Soviet scientists and several prominent foreign scientists published articles.[77] Omel'ianovskii also succeeded in attracting to the Institute of Philosophy a number of outstanding young specialists with science backgrounds who approached the problems of the philosophy of science with much more open minds than many of the older philosophers. His influence among his students continued after his death in 1980 and is still visible today.

Omel'ianovskii published in 1956 his most significant independent contribution to a Soviet Marxist interpretation of quantum mechanics, his *Philosophic Problems of Quantum Mechanics*.[78] Although this book was later superseded by Omel'ianovskii's modified views, as had also been the case with his 1947 volume, it established him for the remainder of the 1950s as the major Soviet interpreter of quantum mechanics. Omel'ianovskii agreed completely with no major physicist, Soviet or non-Soviet, although his interpretation was closest to that of Blokhintsev. Among physicists, he set himself apart most markedly, of course, from the Copenhagen School (to which he implied Fock primarily belonged), much less strongly but still significantly from "materialist" non-Soviet physicists such as Bohm and Vigier, and least of all but still perceptibly from Blokhintsev.

Omel'ianovskii viewed the controversy in quantum mechanics as one of the latest developments in the ancient struggle between materialism and idealism, a contest directly connected to class interests. He maintained that the "conception of complementarity grew out of the reactionary philosophy of Machism-positivism. This conception is foreign to the scientific content of quantum mechanics. It is not accidental that P. Frank, H. Reichenbach, and other modern reactionary bourgeois philosophers joined with Jordan, who, invoking Bohr and Heisenberg, 'liquidated materialism,' " (pp. 21–22). Having delivered this simplistic analysis of the relationship of philosophy and the economic order, however, Omel'ianovskii proceeded to the theoretical problems of a physical interpretation of quantum mechanics according to dialectical materialism.

Omel'ianovskii believed that such an interpretation must proceed from the following basic points, considered by him to be intrinsic to any dialectical materialist view of the microworld: (1) microphenomena and their regularities (zakonomernosti) exist objectively; (2) macroscopic and microscopic objects are qualitatively different; (3) although they are qualitatively different, there is no impassable gulf between the microworld and the macroworld, and all properties of micro-objects appear in one form or another on the macrolevel; and (4) there are no limits to man's knowledge of microphenomena. Omel'ianovskii attempted to utilize points one and four as his main criticisms of the "physical idealists" of the Copenhagen School, and point two against misguided but good-hearted critics of Copenhagen who hoped for a return to the laws of classical physics.

In 1956 Omel'ianovskii was critical of the concept of complementarity, which he said arose from Bohr's and Heisenberg's exaggeration of the meaning of the uncertainty relation. The first step in this exaggeration was the raising of the uncertainty relation to a higher rank, the "uncertainty principle." Omel'ianovskii accepted the uncertainty relation as a fact of science, but this physical fact in itself said nothing, he maintained, about the "uncontrollable influence" of the instrument, upon which Heisenberg in particular based the "uncertainty principle" (p. 74).[79] Omel'ianovskii believed this view of the role of the instrument to be directly responsible for complementarity. While he used the term "uncertainty relation," he refused to use the phrase "uncertainty principle," substituting the term "Heisenberg relation." Omel'ianovskii's opinion of the "Heisenberg relation" is revealed clearly by his remark that "the relation established by Bohr and Heisenberg by means of the analysis of several thought experiments—we call it the Heisenberg relation—has no physical significance and is a 'principle' changing the content of quantum mechanics in the spirit of the subjective concept of complementarity" (p. 71). The error of complementarity, in turn, was that it does not emphasize the characteristics of atomic objects, which are the proper subject of study of quantum mechanics, as much as it does the role of the measuring instrument. Omel'ianovskii's position, which ignored the tendency of many members of the Copenhagen School, including Bohr, to attribute the uncertainty relation not to the measuring instrument but to the simple nonexistence of physical values of conjugate parameters, was thus primarily a criticism of alleged subjectivism in measurement.

Omel'ianovskii devoted the last section of his book to a discussion of determinism and statistical laws. In his opinion, determinism, a basic principle of nature, was in no way threatened by quantum mechanics. On this issue he agreed with P. Langevin that "what is understood at the present time as the crisis of determinism is really the crisis of mechanism" (p. 32). Determinism is perfectly compatible, according to Omel'ianovskii, with statistical laws. Furthermore, Omel'ianovskii considered the statistical laws of quantum mechanics to be not the result of the uncontrollable influence of measurement (Heisenberg), nor the result of indeterminism governing the individual micro-object (Reichenbach), nor the result of hidden parameters (Bohm), nor the result of the relationship of the microensemble and its macroenvironment (Blokhintsev), but instead the result of what he called the "peculiar wave-corpuscular properties of micro-objects." Such a position, according to Omel'ianovskii, does not preclude the existence of hidden parameters (contrary to von Neumann), although it does not promise them, and does not suppose that their discovery would result in a classical description of micro-objects, as Omel'ianovskii believed Bohm, Vigier, and the latter-day de Broglie hoped. Thus, Omel'ianovskii completed the edifice of his interpretation of quantum mechanics, a structure consisting almost entirely of statements telling what quantum mechanics *is not* but very rarely hinting what it *is*. In answer to the question, What is quantum mechanics? Omel'ianovskii could cite only the first of his original four points, that it is the study of objectively existing micro-objects and their regularities, a point on which all Soviet interpreters of quantum mechanics agreed.

In the last part of his life, Omel'ianovskii shifted from relying primarily on Blokhintsev to relying on Fock. At a 1958 All-Union conference[80] in Moscow on philosophic problems of modern science Omel'ianovskii changed his position on the significance of the wave function. Whereas earlier he had believed that it could be applied only to Blokhintsev's ensembles, he said at the conference that "the wave function characterizes the probability of action of an individual atomic object." This description was very similar to Fock's statements on the significance of the wave function, and in expanding on his interpretation, Omel'ianovskii revealed that he had also accepted Fock's distinction between the "potentially possible" and the "actually existing." Then in 1963 at the Thirteenth World Congress of Philosophy in Mexico City he agreed even further with Fock by accepting complementarity and even maintaining that it is based on a dialectical way of thinking through its assertion that "we have the right to make two opposite mutually exclusive statements concerning a single atomic object."[81]

In a 1968 article on philosophical aspects of measurement in quantum mechanics Omel'ianovskii emphasized in an interesting and helpful way that contrary to much common belief, it is not really proper to speak of the "uncontrollable influence of the measuring instrument on the micro-object."[82] If we think of a crystalline lattice as the measuring instrument for an electron, before passing through the lattice, the electron is located in a state with a definite momentum and an indefinite position; after passing through the lattice, the electron is in a state with a definite position and an indefinite momentum. Measurement therefore changes the state of the micro-object, but this change is not a result of a force acting on the object, such as gravitational or electromagnetic force. The lattice itself did not exert any force on the electron that passed through it. Rather, the influence of measurement arises from the very corpuscle-wave nature of the micro-object. Omel'ianovskii explained his position most graphically through an analogy: "The change of quantum state under the influence of measurement is similar to the change of mechanical state of a body in classical theory when one makes the transition from one system of reference to another moving relative to the first."[83] This clarification by Omel'ianovskii, which is in agreement with Bohr's views shortly before his death,[84] goes a long way toward resolving many debates over the "uncontrollability" of measuring instruments in quantum mechanics.

At the same time that Omel'ianovskii redefined his interpretation of quantum mechanics, a number of other Soviet scholars became interested in the philosophic problems of quantum mechanics. Some of them displayed interest in de Broglie's "theory of double solution," a hidden-

parameter approach replacing his earlier "pilot-wave theory."[85] Others
were seeking a unified theory that would combine the realms of quantum
theory and relativity theory. Such attempts have been made in other
countries as well, where similarly they have not been successful although
they continue to be interesting. Soviet authors discussing new approaches have become accustomed to handling ideas that in the late
forties or early fifties would automatically have been considered suspect,
such as the theory of a finite universe or the hypothesis that in the
"interior" of microparticles future events might influence past events.
In a 1965 article in *Problems of Philosophy* the veteran philosopher E.
Kol'man pleaded that Soviet scientists be granted permanent freedom
to consider such theories; naturally, he observed, these viewpoints

> give idealists cause for seeking arguments in favor of their point of view.
> But this does not mean we should reject these "illogical" conceptions out
> of hand, as several conservative-minded philosophers and scientists did
> with the theory of relativity, cybernetics, and so forth. These conceptions
> are not in themselves guilty of idealistic interpretations. The task of
> philosophers and scientists defending dialectical materialism is to give
> these conceptions a dialectical materialist interpretation.[86]

After the late sixties a number of changes occurred in Soviet views
on quantum mechanics, although no essentially new theoretical positions
were developed. The most heartening change was the improvement in
tone of most Soviet writings on the subject; at the present time, almost
all articles and books published by scholarly presses are truly philosophical in approach, and not ideological.

Yet it should not be thought that as Soviet discussions of quantum
mechanics became more and more free from political influence, all
Soviet interpretations moved closer to the reigning Copenhagen Interpretation. Some Soviet writers renewed their criticism of the Copenhagen
School, although on a much higher intellectual level than in the early
fifties. One of these was the Soviet physicist A. A. Tiapkin, who in
1970 published an interesting chapter in a book based on reports given
several years before at a conference at the well-known United Institute
of Nuclear Research in Dubna.[87] This conference included physicists
from Dubna, philosophers from the Institute of Philosophy of the USSR,
and scholars from various Soviet universities. Like Blokhintsev in his
most reflective moments, Tiapkin believed that it was possible to create
an unknown, more complete theory of quantum mechanics. The advantage of this new theory, however, would be, according to Tiapkin,

largely philosophical; it would not predict a single new effect or result of measurment that existing quantum theory does not already produce (p. 152). Tiapkin's ambitions were at once both great and modest; on the one hand, he wanted to do the seemingly impossible—to give a statistical description of phenomena that he agreed were in principle "unobservable"; on the other hand, he admitted that if he achieved his goal, it would not directly affect present quantum mechanical computations in any way. Its main advantage, he said, was that it would help to eliminate from physics the positivist slogan "If you can't measure it, it doesn't exist" (p. 144). Tiapkin maintained that Marxist philosophers and physicists should seek to explain the unmeasurable interphenomena of quantum physics in objective terms even though Bohr had been quite correct in demonstrating to Einstein that present quantum mechanics is complete in the sense of predicting all data from measurement.[88] But it was still incomplete, said Tiapkin, in another, broader sense: it made no attempt to describe the movement of micro-objects between moments of measurement. Tiapkin remained convinced, like Einstein, that some kind of movement occurred in those intervals and that the task of a physicist would not be complete until he had given a description of that movement.

Tiapkin believed that a broader theory was not only needed but possible. The one criterion that it must meet, he said, was that it must have a single-valued compatibility with the whole structure of predictions of measurement generated by present theory (p. 152). He suggested then a "reverse course" of seeking the function of the unobservable distribution of probabilities by taking the existing apparatus of quantum mechanics and working backward (p. 152). Such attempts had been made several times in the past by scientists such as Wigner, Blokhintsev, and Dirac, but because of mathematical difficulties they had not succeeded. Tiapkin thought such a solution was still possible and might ultimately be given a physical interpretation. One possibility was dividing the micro-object into a discrete particle, on the one hand, and a continuous wave process in a vacuum that has a statistical influence on the microparticle, on the other (p. 178). Such an interpretation should not be confused, said Tiapkin, with de Broglie's pilot-wave hypothesis, since de Broglie's goal was a dynamic, causal, nonstatistical description of the results of measurement (p. 153). Tiapkin remained convinced that von Neumann was correct in considering such attempts impossible. To Tiapkin, the description of both the measurable and the unmeasurable movement of micro-objects was inherently statistical.

Soviet philosophers and physicists throughout the seventies and eighties continued to produce a great many works on the philosophical problems of quantum mechanics, concentrating on such questions as causality, determinism, and the question of whether recent work in subatomic physics gives justification for postulating a form of existence of matter "outside" space and time.[89] The most influential philosophical interpretation of quantum mechanics in the Soviet Union has continued to be the one advanced by V. A. Fock (discussed on pp. 337ff.), even though Fock died in 1974. Soviet philosophers to the present day credit Fock's theory of "real quantum states" with being a further development of the Copenhagen Interpretation in the direction of "freeing it from certain subjective features which, at one time or another, showed up in the general positions or separate statements of its adherents."[90]

There are few signs left in Soviet philosophy and physics of the earlier uneasiness about quantum mechanics. The notorious term "complementarity," so long opposed by the orthodox dialectical materialists, is now widely accepted among Soviet philosophers of science, as is the opinion that quantum mechanics is complete, i.e., that it will not be replaced by a deterministic theory. "Causality" and "determinism" have been saved by redefining them in terms of "probabilistic causality" and "soft determinism." However, a few dissenting voices still existed in the early eighties. Terletskii (see p. 328) hoped that a more complete quantum theory would be found, and Blokhintsev's idea of quantum ensembles (see p. 330) still had a few adherents. Yet another minority view was that of Lomsadze, who was trying to develop a new interpretation of quantum mechanics within the framework of information theory.

The term "uncontrollable influence" (between measuring instrument and micro-object) remains controversial to the present day. Some Soviet philosophers maintain that Bohr in his later life stopped using this term, thereby clearing the way for Soviet acceptance of Bohr's interpretation. Other Soviet philosophers believe that the concept "uncontrollable influence" is acceptable to dialectical materialists if carefully reinterpreted. Thus, I. S. Alekseev wrote in 1984 that what Bohr called "uncontrollable influence" is really best described as "partial uncontrollable influence," since even in the classic instances of measuring micro-objects, control over the experiments always exists either in terms of a particle or a wave interpretation (but not both). True uncontrollability, he continued, would be absence of control in both respects. Therefore, he concluded, Bohr's interpretation does not violate dialectical materialism.[91]

A physicist who took his dialectical materialism quite seriously in the 1980s and who thought that some of the philosophers were becoming too permissive about the meaning of Marxism for science was V. S. Barashenkov, a researcher at the Dubna accelerator outside Moscow.[92] In the dispute between the epistemologists and the ontologists, Barashenkov took his stand with the ontologists. In his opinion, to reduce dialectical materialism to a philosophy concerned with logic and methodology was to deprive Marxism of some of its greatest strengths. Barashenkov thought that the positions of dialectical materialism—such as Lenin's belief that matter was infinite in its complexity, and that therefore the electron was "inexhaustible"—had genuine value to the working scientist. This position was confirmed, in Barashenkov's mind, by the current efforts to find out what electrons are made of, to explore quarks and other more elementary constituents of matter. Barashenkov acknowledged that some ontologists went too far, converting dialectical materialism into a "nature philosophy," but he was convinced that Marxism was relevant not only to society but to nature as well.

Barashenkov was also upset at those scientists and philosophers who had abandoned Lenin's and Engels' principles of insisting on physical descriptions in terms of space and time. Some physicists, he noted, maintained that spatial and temporal descriptions are impossible in quantum mechanics. These people, continued Barashenkov, correctly note that individual particles can not be assigned trajectories, and then incorrectly discard the whole concept of space-time descriptions. This approach, he said, was a mistake, since physicists have to talk about such things as radii of nucleons, the spatial distribution of electronic charges, and magnetic moments.

Western physicists like Wigner and Chew, said Barashenkov, had mistakenly maintained that "space" and "time" are merely properties of things on the macro level of existence. Barashenkov asserted, on the contrary, that even at the levels of the smallest units of length and smallest units of time yet attained by modern physicists by the use of accelerators there is still no adequate reason to abandon space-time conceptions. Therefore, according to Barashenkov, the Leninist conceptions still are valid.[93]

In his effort to continue to find confirmation of dialectical materialism in current research in physics Barashenkov differed sharply with a number of the Soviet Union's most outstanding physicists. As we will see below, one of Barashenkov's critics on this issue was V. L. Ginzburg, a Soviet astrophysicist of international rank.

The question of whether matter can exist "outside" of space and time continued to be a rather vexing question among Soviet philosophers and physicists. The whole tradition of Marxist materialism, founded on Lenin's and Engels' views on this subject, fitted poorly with a concept of matter shorn of spatial or temporal characteristics. Therefore, the predominant position among Soviet philosophers of science was that what some physicists call nonspatial or nontemporal forms of existence of matter only "confirms the qualitative difference of mega-, macro-, and microscopic forms of the existence of matter, and, more accurately, the qualitative difference of theoretical levels of physical theories describing the indicated levels of structure of matter."[94] This formulation nicely balanced the epistemological and ontological viewpoints on the issue, leaving unclear whether dialectical materialism directly relates to nature itself, or only to scientific descriptions of nature.

The interpretation of quantum mechanics is still a very open question, not only in the Soviet Union, but in all countries where there is an active concern with current problems of the philosophy of science. As I have earlier noted, the Soviet discussion of causality, the influence of the observer, and the possibility of hidden parameters were quite similar to the worldwide controversy.[95] In the Soviet Union the main participants in the debate—Fock, Blokhintsev, and Omel'ianovskii—all had disagreements with each other, and outside the Soviet Union the interpreters of quantum mechanics also have had intense disputes.

All scientists in the course of their investigations must proceed beyond physical facts and mathematical methods; such theorization is one of the bases of scientific explanation. Choices among alternative courses that are equally justifiable on the basis of the mathematical formalism and the physical facts must be made. The choice will often be based on philosophic considerations and will often have philosophic implications. Thus, Fock in his interpretation of quantum mechanics defined "complementarity" as a "complementarity between classical descriptions of microparticles and causality" (see p. 339). In his subsequent choice between retaining either a classical description or causality, he chose causality, and thereby lost the possibility of a classical description. He could have gone the other way. This decision inevitably involved philosophy.

The Soviet scientists and philosophers drew attention to a significant and fruitful concept when they observed that as long as even probabilistic descriptions of nature are possible, the principle of causality can be retained. To them, the nonexistence of causality in quantum mechanics would mean that all possible values of position and momentum for a micro-object would have equal probability. In such a world, a science of quantum mechanics would be impossible.

No one knows if quantum mechanics will retain its present mathematical formalism, or gain a new formalism permitting a more deterministic interpretation of quantum mechanics; the present evidence is not very reassuring for those people who want to find a new realm of strict determinism below the one with which we now work.[96] If the present opinion of most scientists is confirmed and it becomes increasingly clear that causality must be interpreted probabilistically if it is to be retained at all, the resulting disussions could lead to refreshing developments in the age-old debates over determinism and free will, particularly in the Marxist framework in which freedom is seen as knowledge of natural laws; Marxists could allow room for a given situation to generate a range of possible outcomes without resorting to any factors outside the natural world. This concept was advanced by several Soviet physiologists and appears in the discussion of physiology and psychology (see especially p. 195). But the full significance of quantum mechanics in its present form has not yet been adequately absorbed by specialists in other fields, Marxists or non-Marxists.

Whether the future of quantum mechanics will reassure the probabilists or the determinists will depend on science. In the meantime, Soviet philosophers and scientists have found an interpretation—or rather, several interpretations—that makes the world seem more intelligible to them and that could handle either eventuality.[97]

RELATIVITY PHYSICS

Teachings of dialectical materialism helped us to approach critically Einstein's point of view concerning the theory created by him and to think it out anew. It helped us to understand correctly, and to interpret, the new results we ourselves obtained.
—Academician V. A. Fock, 1959

I agree with Fock that the general principle of relativity is empty. We know of course that there is no *physical* equivalence between inertial and accelerate observers. . . . I feel confident that given any laws, mathematicians could find a way of writing these laws in a *mathematically* equivalent way.
—Professor Hermann Bondi, King's College, University of London, 1964

The special theory of relativity (STR), as elaborated by Einstein, flows from two postulates: (1) the principle of relativity, which asserts that physical processes occurring in a closed system are unaffected by non-accelerated motion of the system as a whole, and (2) the principle that the velocity of light is independent of the velocity of its source. The first postulate was accepted in classical mechanics long before Einstein, and is perhaps best illustrated by comparing physical phenomena, such as falling objects, in two different inertial systems (systems within which bodies unaffected by outside forces move at constant speed in straight lines). If a given inertial system is moving at a constant velocity in a straight line relative to another given system, then the laws of mechanics must have the same form in both systems. The common illustration of this relationship is the fact that to an observer in a train moving at a constant velocity, a falling object describes a path identical to the one he would see if he and the object were on the ground. To an observer alongside the moving train, however, the falling object in the train describes a parabola. In this case, a transformation from one reference system to another has been made, and in accordance with classical mechanics the Galilean transformation equations would provide the means of plotting the equation of the parabola from data obtained from inside the railroad car.[1]

Einstein in his development of STR extended the principle of relativity to cover electromagnetic phenomena as well as mechanical ones. This extension necessitated the derivation of new transformation equations, since the Galilean equations could not account for the constancy of the velocity of light in all inertial frames, a constancy that had been illustrated prior to Einstein's work by the noted Michelson and Morley experiment. In order to preserve the principle of the constancy of the velocity of light in different reference frames and to maintain the existence of equivalent reference frames, Einstein modified the rules of transformation from one system to another. The new equations, known as the Lorentz transformations, accomplish this accommodation by providing that clocks in different inertial systems run at different speeds, and that spatial distance between points varies in different reference systems.[2]

Until the end of World War II, professional physicists in the Soviet Union were largely unconcerned with dialectical materialism, despite the attention that Lenin devoted to physics in his *Materialism and Empirio-Criticism*. To be sure, there had been a debate over relativity physics among Soviet philosophers in the 1920s and 1930s.[3] Relativity physics was in these years a topic of discussion and occasional polemic among the literate public all over the world. S. Iu. Semkovskii, the first Soviet Marxist writer to give a careful analysis of relativity physics, declared in 1926 that Einstein's new physics not only did not contradict dialectical materialism, but brilliantly confirmed it.[4] Semkovskii emphasized that space and time according to relativity theory were not products of "pure reason" but "forms of the existence of matter."[5] David Joravsky, an American historian of Russia, even commented that "as for active opposition to the new physics, one might even argue that there was less in the Soviet community of physics than elsewhere."[6]

Russian physicists before the war were fully aware of the controversies over the relation between science and philosophy that had occurred as a result of the widespread acceptance of the views of such scientists as Ernst Mach and Henri Poincaré, and they knew that these new conceptual approaches had been important in Einstein's development of relativity theory. Those Soviet physicists who knew that Mach was the object of lengthy criticism by Lenin may have felt reticent about discussing the philosophical background of relativity, but as scientists they could find reassurance in Lenin's careful distinction between science and philosophical interpretations of science. In university lectures, monographs, and textbooks of the prewar years one finds much evidence that Russian physicists and mathematicians were responding to the same scientific and even philosophical currents as scientists in all countries.

Examples of the typically international attitudes of Soviet physicists can be found in the university lectures of the well-known physicist L. I. Mandel'shtam (1879–1944), who from 1932 until 1944 taught theoretical physics at Moscow University, and who deeply influenced a generation of Soviet physicists. Among his students were G. S. Lansberg and I. E. Tamm. Mandel'shtam, educated in Novorossiisk University and the University of Strasbourg, was greatly interested in and attracted to Western philosophical thought, from Mach onward through the whole trend of the Viennese circle and logical positivism. Mandel'shtam taught his students that there was an essential difference between the logical structure of a scientific theory and the empirical data to which it was related, and he believed that links between the two were created on the basis of definitions, which were neither true nor false in themselves, but merely convenient or inconvenient. This approach, one of the cornerstones of the logical empiricists in the philosophy of science, was apparent in Mandel'shtam's discussions of the metric of length and time. He commented that "the physicist must have a recipe (retsept) in order to find out what length is. He must indicate that he does not discover that recipe, but defines it."[7] Similarly, thought Mandel'shtam, time is defined in relation to some kind of periodic physical phemonenon, such as the rotation of the earth or the movement of the hands of a chronometer; this stipulation is also merely a definition without absolute content: "Let us take for sake of simplicity the definition of time by means of a chronometer. In this fashion, time (that is, what I insert in Newtonian formulae in the place of t) is that which is indicated by the hands of my watch." Without such definitions, thought Mandel'shtam, such equations as those of Newton and Maxwell express only mathematical relationships and are not directly relevant to physical experience.

Mandel'shtam's viewpoints, familiar to physicists and philosophers of science everywhere, and yet not without controversial aspects, were not published during his lifetime even though they were well known among his students and fellow physicists. The appearance of the fifth volume of his works in 1950, in which these statements appeared, caused quite a sensation among philosophers of science in the Soviet Union. (See p. 361.) The case of L. I. Mandel'shtam will serve as evidence, which could be easily supplemented, that physicists in the Soviet Union were familiar, although perhaps somewhat incompletely, with the dominant trends before World War II in the interpretation of the philosophical foundations of relativity theory. Indeed, it would have been quite impossible for them not to have been aware of the discarding of Kantian concepts of space and time that was necessary for the development of relativity theory.

In a 1948 physics textbook approved by the Ministry of Higher Education for use in the universities, the following statement left no doubt about the authors' belief in the conventionality of spatial and temporal congruency. Here one found stated clearly what many Soviet philosophers of science and some distinguished scientists (for example, A. D. Aleksandrov) criticized in later years:

> Einstein showed that simultaneity of spatially distant events is a question of *definition:* It is necessary simply *to agree* what distant events *by definition* will be considered simultaneous, just as we agree to understand *length* as a number indicating how many times a definite rigid rod (standard of length) can be laid down between two given points. It is possible to give *other* definitions of length and of an interval of time, based on *other standards and possible uses of these standards.*[8]

Soon after World War II the increasingly restrictive intellectual environment of the Soviet Union permitted the militant ideologists to attempt a direct influence on the physicists. In his speech of June 24, 1947, A. A. Zhdanov did not mention the issue in science that was already becoming the most heated—biology—but he did criticize certain interpretations of physical theories:

> Not understanding the dialectical path of cognition, the mutual relation of absolute and relative truth, many followers of Einstein, transferring the results of research on the laws of movement of a finite, bounded part of the universe to the whole infinite universe, have begun speaking about a finite world, about its temporal and spatial boundaries; the astronomer Milne even "calculated" that the world was created two billion years ago.[9]

Zhdanov's remarks, although directed more against cosmological interpretations of general relativity than against the basic positions of either special or general relativity theory, prefaced a new debate on the philosophic foundations of relativity theory that lasted until 1955, and that in altered and much more sohisticated forms has continued to the present time. The cosmological aspect of the debate will be considered separately in the following chapter.

Most of the Soviet articles on the philosophic aspects of relativity theory that appeared in the next few years were thoroughly hostile to non-Soviet interpretations, and not a few were opposed to the theory itself, referring to it by such terms as "reactionary Einsteinism."[10] Not until 1951 did the major philosophical journal of the Soviet Union carry an article that presented the theory of relativity in a generally positive fashion, and this article was roundly criticized, not only by individual philosophers, but by the editorial board of the journal itself.[11] As late as 1953, an article appeared in *Problems of Philosophy* that termed the theory of relativity "obviously antiscientific."[12] Because of the protracted life of such objections a historical view of Soviet attitudes toward relativity theory must include a description of their content. However, to equate the positions of the early Soviet opponents of relativity theory with the views of such later prominent critics and interpreters of relativity in the Soviet Union as V. A. Fock, A. D. Aleksandrov, and M. F. Shirokov would be a serious error, since the later writers were genuine intellectuals firmly grounded in the field.

Ironically, one of the first articles on the philosophical implications of relativity theory to appear following Zhdanov's speech was by the same G. I. Naan who later came to the defense of relativity and thereby incurred a great deal of criticism. This article appeared in an issue of *Problems of Philosophy* dedicated to the recently deceased Zhdanov. The article was directed against the "physical idealists" of the United States and England, the physicists and philosophers of science who, according to the author, had questioned the materiality of the world and denied the "regularities" (*zakonomernosti*) of nature. Naan included among the physical idealists a heterogeneous group of Western scientists and philosophers, including A. S. Eddington, James Jeans, Pascual Jordan, E. T. Whittaker, E. A. Milne, Bertrand Russell, and Philipp Frank. Frank was particularly criticized for commenting that neopositivism takes its starting point from Mach but so formulates its position that confusion with idealistic or solipsist doctrines is impossible, since the question of the existence of a real world behind our sensations is only a "pseudoquestion." Naan concluded from this that "the basic problem of philosophy has been christened a 'pseudoproblem.' "[13]

The following issue of *Problems of Philosophy* (No. 3, 1948) was an important one for the philosophy of science in the Soviet Union. It contained several articles on modern physics and also one on biology, as well as an editorial calling for ideological militancy in science. The articles on physics, by M. E. Omel'ianovskii, A. A. Maksimov, and R. Ia. Shteinman followed Naan's example by denouncing many of the prominent non-Soviet interpreters of science; Schrödinger, Reichenbach, and Carnap.[14] Omel'ianovskii was particularly exercised over Rudolf Carnap, an "open enemy" of materialism, for his belief that he has "risen above" the conflict of idealism and materialism. Eddington was criticized for maintaining that many of the constants of physics must be introduced a priori, and Frank for trying to build a bridge between dialectical materialism and logical empiricism.[15]

These Soviet critics of non-Soviet views of physics often utilized as sources the popular and philosophical writings of non-Soviet scientists, which, especially in the cases of people such as Jeans and Eddington, often sacrificed scientific rigor for colorful language and lucidity. But a serious error of the Soviet critics was to proceed from this criticism of informal interpretations to a condemnation of relativity theory itself; it was as if one could hold the theory responsible for all statements, professional and nonprofessional, uttered by its adherents. This was done most flagrantly by A. A. Maksimov, who ended up by denying not only Einsteinian relativity but even Galiliean relativity. Maksimov commented:

A. Einstein wrote in his book about the theory of relativity: ". . . trajectories in themselves do not exist, but each trajectory can be related to a definite reference body." This judgment that a body does not have an objective, given trajectory existing independently from the choice of system of coordinates is completely antiscientific.[16]

The dimensions of this malapropism were so great that the editors of the journal could not refrain from adding a footnote to Maksimov's text explaining that although they shared his desire to criticize idealistic views of modern physics, they felt that his discussion of trajectory did not "embrace this problem in all its complexity."[17] Not deterred, Maksimov tried to buttress his position with the observation that the objective characteristics of a meteorite's trajectory are revealed when it plows a path into the earth's surface, from which a cast can be made suitable for research. Maksimov admitted that the mathematical relations of the Lorentz transformations are valid, but maintained that such concepts as length, time, and simultaneity have objective meanings. He did not, however, attempt to give serious definitions of these concepts.

A considerable amount of time passed before Maksimov received the stern lesson in physics that his article made inevitable. Several subsequent authors, such as G. A. Kursanov, tried to find a more defensible middle ground without specifically denying Maksimov's argument; they agreed that motion cannot be related to any absolutely motionless body, system, or ether—as evidently Maskimov would have it—but they pointed out that this relativity did not contradict the movement of bodies independent from the consciousness of man. Such a view of relativity certainly does not permit, said Kursanov, the consideration of concepts such as "space," "time," "volume," and "movement" as "pseudoconcepts," a position that he attributed to Carnap and the Viennese circle. Kursanov realized, nevertheless, that the relativity of times and lengths is not in the process of observation, but is inherent in the characteristics of physical phenomena themselves, as defined by modern science. To this extent he chastened certain Soviet misinterpreters of relativity theory. But he held to a belief in the existence of absolute simultaneity.[18]

An outright rejection of relativity theory was, of course, highly improbable. At this time physicists utilized certain aspects of special relativity as comfortably and frequently as engineers employed Newtonian mechanics. But now that the topic had been raised to the level of ideological discussion, there *were* certain embarrassing facts about relativity theory. Aside from the basic questions concerning materialism and objectivity was the secondary but quite troublesome historical fact that Einstein had been heavily influenced by Mach, had repeatedly acknowledged his debt to Mach; and yet Mach was the object of criticism of Lenin's *Materialism and Empirio-Criticism*.[19] Could relativity be separated from "Machist idealism"? It was a question that troubled Soviet philosophers of science for some time, although by the end of the fifties it was resolved with an affirmative answer. One possible exit from the situation lay in finding important precursors to Einstein's work other than Mach. Frequent attempts were made by Russian authors to emphasize the importance of Nikolai Lobachevskii, the Russian creator of the first non-Euclidean geometry. Thus, L. I. Storchak commented, "The establishment of the priority of Lobachevskii in formulating the principle of relativity debunks the old myth that the invention of this principle belongs to Mach."[20] But this attempt to employ Lobachevskii as a replacement for Mach was not convincing even in the Soviet Union, although the brilliant Lobachevskii stood in no need of additional honors to assure his place in the history of mathematics.[21]

In early 1951 the Estonian scholar G. I. Naan submitted Maksimov's 1948 article to a thorough criticism, scornfully commenting that for Maksimov to maintain simultaneously that the equations of the STR were correct but that absolute trajectories exist was equivalent to commenting that the multiplication tables are correct but denying that 8

$\times$ 11 = 88.[22] Since his 1948 article, which decried many non-Soviet interpretations of relativity physics, Naan's views had evidently changed greatly. True, he did not directly contradict his previous statements, but while the earlier article had been a militant critique of non-Soviet philosophers of science, the later one was a sober course in elementary relativity theory for philosophers. His only criticism of the physical idealists was now restricted to those who had stated that the relativity of trajectory, kinetic energy, mass, space, and time intervals depends on the observer. In the manner of Kursanov, Naan pointed out that relativity is not a subjective phenomenon, but is inherent in the physical processes themselves. His insistence on the absolute nature of acceleration, however, revealed that he had not fully accepted general relativity. Naan's article could be summarized as a critique of the vulgar materialists such as Maksimov combined with an outline of modern relativity theory. The article was tolerant on philosophic questions to a striking degree in Stalinist Russia, considering its place and time of publication.

Shortly before Naan's article the fifth volume of L. I. Mandel'shtam's works, the one containing his views on relativity theory, was published by the Academy of Sciences. This volume was based on notes taken by his students during his lectures and presented for publication after his death. When combined with Maksimov's articles, the total spectrum of viewpoints on philosophic interpretations of relativity theory now available to Soviet readers was surprisingly broad, considering the intensity of the ideological scene in those years. In Mandel'shtam's works, one could find the interpretation of those scientists and philosophers who greeted the revisions in epistemological thought that originated largely in central Europe at the end of the nineteenth and early part of the twentieth century. Naan's view, while not of the same scale of importance as that of Mandel'shtam, represented that of Soviet scientists who wished most of all to get on with the work of physics and who were quite impatient with the intrusions of philosophers.

This spectrum, although rather diverse, presented little choice for a Soviet Union that would emerge from Stalinism and yet retain a commitment to a universal Marxist philosophy. Maksimov's position was contrary to much of modern physics, Naan's was nearly neutral to dialectical materialism, and Mandel'shtam's was even implicitly opposed to Soviet dialectical materialism in the sense that it drew all its inspiration from non-Soviet and non-Marxist sources and disagreed with current Soviet Marxist interpretations.

A genuine improvement in the intellectual quality of Soviet discussions of relativity theory began to occur even before Stalin's death in March 1953. Several eminent Soviet physicists and mathematicians decided to enter the philosophical debate in order to protect relativity theory from attacks by ideologically militant philosophers and mediocre physicists. This decision eventually resulted in a strengthening of both the scientific content of Soviet philosophy and the philosophical perceptivity of Soviet scientists. The danger to relativity has been made clear in 1952 articles by the philosopher I. V. Kuznetsov and the physicist R. Ia. Shteinman;[23] the articles appeared in the same "Green Book" (edited by the ultra-conservative A. A. Maksimov) mentioned in the previous chapter on quantum mechanics. Shteinman and Kuznetsov proceeded from a criticism of Einstein's philosophy to a call for the overthrow of relativity theory itself. Kuznetsov wrote that a truly materialist understanding of the physical laws of bodies moving at rapid velocities would result in a repudiation of Einstein's special theory of relativity (STR) and the development of an essentially different physical theory.[24] The only alternative, however, that Kuznetsov and Shteinman could present was a return to a prerelativity interpretation of the Lorentz contractions within a framework of absolute space and time. In an article published several months before Stalin's death, V. A. Fock called this approach an attempt to deny the most important achievements in physics of the twentieth century.[25] According to Fock, both special relativity and quantum mechanics had been "brilliantly confirmed" by experiment and, in turn, they were confirmations of dialectical materialism.[26]

Fock defended relativity physics from within the intellectual system of dialectical materialism. Even in the thirties he had written on physics and philosophy in the major Soviet Marxist journal of philosophy.[27] In the political atmosphere of Stalinist Russia no other choice than a dialectical materialist approach was available to him if he wished to defend relativity physics. But one should not be too quick to assume that the attempts of Fock and like-minded scientists to develop new dialectical materialist understandings of nature were merely pretense or entirely tactically motivated. A number of them continued to write on philosophy and science long after the passing of the Stalinist period. Twenty years after Stalin's death Fock was still producing sophisticated writings on dialectical materialism and relativity. There seems to be reason to believe that once committed to dialectical materialism, some Soviet scientists such as Fock decided that its most essential principles accorded with their own and that it had serious potential for development.

The Fock-Aleksandrov interpretation of relativity theory has occasionally been presented as a unitary scheme not divisible into the parts for which each author is responsible. This unitary approach is not, however, the most revealing one. Aleksandrov and Fock supported each other, and their views were not contradictory on major points, but each followed a rather different path and emphasized different portions of relativity theory. Aleksandrov focused his attention on interpreting STR, while Fock concentrated on general relativity (GTR). Furthermore, Aleksandrov wrestled more thoroughly with the problem of spatial and temporal congruency definitions and with definitions of simultaneity than did Fock, who, in the manner of many physicists, covered this topic—crucial from the standpoint of the philosophy of science—rather hurriedly.[28] As a result of the different approaches, Aleksandrov was more vulnerable to criticism by those philosophers who refuse to accept the view that space-time has an inherent metric prior to the assumption of conventions than was Fock, who did not express himself so clearly on the questions of metric. Because of these differences, I will consider Fock and Aleksandrov separately.

A. D. ALEKSANDROV

Aleksandr Danilovich Aleksandrov (1912 –   ) is an internationally known and respected Soviet mathematician who was for some years rector of Leningrad University. He has traveled abroad in both the United States and Western Europe. Among mathematicians he is best known for his book *Intrinsic Geometry of Convex Surfaces*, which was translated into English by the American Mathematical Society in 1967.[29] He is considered to be the founder of the Soviet school of geometry in the large and has published many articles on this subject. He has also published articles with titles such as "The Dialectics of Lenin and Mathematics"[30] and "On Idealism in Mathematics."[31] Earlier in this book, we saw that he became involved in the seventies and eighties in the "nature-nurture debate" (see pp. 237ff.). He has stoutly defended dialectical materialism on many occasions. He once wrote:

> My professional activity involves mainly the proof of new theorems. And for me Marxist-Leninist philosophy is an unquestioned guide in comprehending general questions of my science. Dialectical materialism, needless to say, does not offer methods for solving specific problems in mathematical science, but it indicates true reference points for searches for

scientific truth and arms one with methods for elucidating the true import of theories and the content of scientific concepts. I could cite examples showing how philosophy helps one master the mathematical theory of infinite numbers, Einstein's theory of relativity or quantum mechanics, but this would require the introduction of complicated, specialized concepts. I shall say only that as a student studying in a physics department I was able to understand quantum mechanics to a significant degree thanks to the fact that at the same time I was studying philosophy which helped me to comprehend this difficult theory in the spirit of dialectical materialism.[32]

Aleksandrov often began his statements of his position on relativity with a recognition of the great genius of Einstein, a man who Aleksandrov believed was more importantly influenced by his inherent materialist understanding of natural laws and the concept of causality than he was by Mach and the school of neopositivism. Aleksandrov was one of the prominent Soviet scientists who came to the defense of Einstein at a crucial moment in Soviet history. Aleksandrov, Fock, and other Soviet scholars maintained that most of Einstein's views were an illustration of the relevance of materialism, not its irrelevance. The success of the efforts of such scientists as Aleksandrov and Fock can be in part measured by the great esteem in which Einstein is held in the Soviet Union today. The first comprehensive edition of the collected scientific works of Einstein to be published in the world appeared in Russian translation in the Soviet Union in the 1960s.[33] And yet both Aleksandrov and Fock disagreed with Einstein on a number of points, primarily ones of philosophical interpretation.

In fact, Aleksandrov thought that the effects of positivism, coming to Einstein from Mach, were sufficiently strong to lead Einstein into a number of errors. If Einstein had been left to follow his own inclinations, he would have emphasized even more, thought Aleksandrov, the "deep essence" of the theory of relativity, namely that a new conception of absolute space-time (as distinguished from space and time) reveals the objectivity of nature and, even more importantly, establishes the material and "causal-consequential" (prichinno-sledstvenno) structure of the world: "When the theory of relativity presents itself not as a theory of relativity, but as a theory of absolute space-time, determined by matter itself, it is a theory in which relativity clearly and necessarily becomes secondary and subordinate."[34]

The absolute character of the space-time continuum became the cornerstone of Aleksandrov's system. He noted that Einstein had arrived at the concept of absolute space-time after passing through and then ultimately discarding Newtonian space and time. He had, thus, proceeded from the relative to the absolute. But, Aleksandrov asked, would not a better conceptual approach be based on the reverse transition, from the absolute to the relative, now that, thanks to Einstein, the absolute nature of space-time has been established? In this sense, the relative character of, respectively, time and space could be explained as "only aspects of the absolute space-time manifold" (p. 279). Here Aleksandrov was following a terminology very similar to that of Hermann Minkowski many years before.[35]

Aleksandrov's further development of his view on the necessity of proceeding backward from absolute space-time reveals that his goal was no less than an affirmation of the inherent objectivity of reference systems:

> The principle of relativity is formulated not as a physical law, but as a principle of the dependence of the laws of nature on an arbitrary choice of the system of reference. . . . But the system of reference is something objective. It is in essence an objective coordination of phenomena with relation to material bodies and processes, serving as a base for a system of reference, a coordination, determined, in the final analysis, by material interactions. (p. 282)

Aleksandrov's statement that "a system of reference is something objective" can be taken in two different ways. If he is speaking of a system of reference actually utilized in physical space and time, then the "something objective" may carry a meaning in the same sense as that denoted by such non-Soviet philosophers of science as Adolf Grünbaum, who, after a long consideration of whether there is an empirical warrant for ascribing a particular metric geometry to physical space and time, concluded: "Once the physical meaning of congruence has been stipulated by reference to a solid body and to a clock respectively for whose distortions allowance has been made . . . then the geometry and the ascriptions of durations to time intervals is determined uniquely by the totality of relevant empirical facts."[36] In other words, once a definition for metrical simultaneity has been adopted, then the geometry of physical space and the chronometry of science are determined by experiment.

Was this the intended meaning of Aleksandrov? An analysis of his views on the subject reveals that he differed from Grünbaum's approach in the following way: Grünbaum would make an initial arbitrary definition of a congruency standard; on the contrary, Aleksandrov would select as a congruency standard the physical phenomenon that he considered to possess a universal, objective significance—light. He believed that congruency standards may be obtained by empirical means. He granted that no one would maintain that there are "sets of coordinates etched in the universe" (p. 283), but he nevertheless believed that congruency standards may be established without merely "defining" rigid rods and isochronous clocks (p. 284).

How did Aleksandrov establish his congruency standards—that is, how did he know that his rods are truly rigid and his clocks are truly isochronous? He advanced several attempts to establish such standards.

Aleksandrov followed a path familiar to many students of relativity theory, that of constructing a light-geometry.[37] Following a system reminiscent of that of E. A. Milne, Aleksandrov maintained that the "background of radiation," or the "exchange of signals" between bodies, defines their mutual coordination in space and time. These signals should not be thought of as the result of hypothetical experiments conducted by fictitious observers, as Einstein often implied, but as objective results of natural processes. The "background of radiation" was thus a constantly existing objective reality:

> Radio-location is precisely based on this experimental method of defining distance. . . . It is exactly in this way that the famed definition of the simultaneity of spatially distant events given by Einstein is based on the sending, reflection, and return of electromagnetic signals. All these processes take place constantly in a natural way because the smallest perturbation of a given body gives rise to an electromagnetic radiation— however weak—which is dispersed by bodies it encounters, even if part of it returns to its source. In other words, the process responsible for radio-location in the comparison of clocks according to Einstein proceed constantly in a natural way. They establish the mutual coordination of bodies and their phenomena in space and time, and this occurs without any kind of observer. Therefore, the coordination of bodies and processes with regard to a given body is an objective fact, and thus, the system of reference connected with this body is, in the full sense of the word, real. (p. 303)

Aleksandrov believed that such a view of relativity theory eliminated the necessity for descriptions of temporal and spatial congruency standards by means of conventions.[38] The background of radiation played something of the role of the old ether in providing a preferred reference frame, but Aleksandrov insisted that there was no genuine similarity: "The ether was only a medium. . . . Waves expanded *in* the ether. Radiation . . . is the waves themselves" (p. 301).

It was through the concept of the background of radiation that Alekandrov's views were conjoined with Fock's, who placed great emphasis on the equation for the expansion of the front of an electromagnetic wave. Both Aleksandrov and Fock believed that the speed of such a wave front has universal significance since it establishes the existence of a universal bond between spatial distances and time increments. This relationship is established in the homogeneous space of the special theory of relativity, and they thought that therefore the general theory of relativity cannot be an expansion of the special theory, since the general theory denies the homogeneity of space.

The reference to E. A. Milne's system above indicated that Aleksandrov's view was not original with him; many systems of light-geometry have been constructed in the past. One writer who anticipated many of Aleksandrov's views was the Irish physicist Alfred A. Robb, who as early as 1914 developed an optical geometry of motion in which he attempted to prove that congruency relationships were not assigned, but were inherently contained within the system.[39]

Aleksandrov acknowledged the similarity of his system to that of Robb. He was unaware of Robb's work until 1954, when his attention was directed to it by a member of a seminar in the physics faculty at Leningrad University. After studying Robb's work, Aleksandrov maintained that the reason for the obscurity into which it had fallen was the imposition of positivistic viewpoints upon the theory of relativity (p. 274).[40]

V. A. FOCK

In our discussion of quantum mechanics it was mentioned that V. A. Fock was an internationally known theoretical physicist who was honored in many countries of the world. In the late 1950s Fock established himself as the most authoritative interpreter of the dialectical materialist position on relativity physics, and continued to hold this position in the sixties and early seventies despite the existence of other Soviet interpretations. Even though he died in 1974, Fock's interpretation of relativity physics continues to have influence in the Soviet Union today.

On numerous occasions Fock expressed his debt to Marxism as an approach to science. In the preface to the 1955 edition of his *The Theory of Space, Time and Gravitation* Fock commented:

The philosophical side of our views on the theory of space, time and gravitation was formed under the influence of the philosophy of dialectical materialism, in particular, under the influence of Lenin's "Materialism and Empirio-Criticism."[41]

Such statements were not restricted to the fifties nor merely appended to his scientific works. In 1966, in a reply by mail to a request from an American journal for his comments on dialectical materialism and science, Fock wrote:

The essence of dialectical materialism is just the combination of the dialectical approach with the acceptance of the objectivity of the external world. Without a dialectical approach materialism would reduce to mechanical materialism, which was obsolete even at the beginning of the twentieth century and is still more obsolete now. On the contrary, application of the laws of dialectics permits materialistic philosophy to develop with the development of science. Even such statements of classical materialism as complete independence of existence from the possibility of perception can be reconsidered and, if necessary, revised without altering the essence of dialectical materialism. The ability of this form of philosophy to keep pace with science is one of its characteristic features. Dialectical materialism is a living and not a dogmatic philosophy. It helps to give to experience obtained in one of the domains of science a formulation of such generality it may be applied to other domains.[42]

Fock developed an interpretation of relativity theory that retained the mathematical core of Einstein's work but that led him to several novel concepts. Fock discarded the terms "general relativity," "general theory of relativity," and "general principle of relativity." Instead, he called the theory of Galilean space[43] the "theory of relativity" (rather than "special theory of relativity"), and the theory of Einsteinian space-time the "theory of gravitation" (rather than the "general theory of relativity").

Yet it would be a great mistake to emphasize only Fock's criticisms of general relativity. As a matter of fact, he considered general relativity (he would say the theory of gravitation) to be in need primarily of interpretive clarifications and methodological amendments. In other respects he defended Einstein's approach stoutly, and, indeed, it is quite possible that his initial motivation for writing on relativity and philosophy was a defensive one—that is, to prevent the theory of relativity from being discredited in the Soviet Union. But he discussed and defended relativity within the framework of dialectical materialism; there is considerable evidence that in the process he became sincerely interested in philosophical problems of the sciences. His emphasis on the necessity for physical content in scientific explanations—and not just mathematical forms—is clear in many of his writings. This emphasis was clearly linked to his materialism.

Fock distinguished carefully between physical theories as they appeared in their completed forms and the methods by which these theories were developed. Fock thought that there might even be a difference in principle between the initial ideas on the basis of which a theory was created and the essential ideas contained in the theory after it had been completed.[44] Such, he thought, was the case with general relativity. When Einstein created the theory of general relativity, the "principle of relativity" (mathematically expressed by the covariance of the equations of physics in all reference frames) and the "principle of equivalence" (mathematically expressed by the identity of inertial and gravitational mass) played important roles in his thought; but Fock believed that these principles were not at the base of relativity in a physical sense. Indeed, according to Fock, the principle of equivalence was only approximately valid, while the principle of relativity (general covariance) was actually contradicted by the characteristics of the existing field of gravitation. The principles of equivalence and of relativity could be derived from the completed structure of general relativity as Einstein presented it, but, said Fock, they were not essential to it as a theory of gravitation. Let us consider his analysis in more detail.

The key to Fock's view of general relativity (always to be distinguished from special relativity, which Fock fully accepted) was his opinion that Einstein failed to see the importance of space-time "as a whole," concentrating instead on local areas within the space-time continuum. This emphasis caused Einstein to ignore the fact, said Fock, that his GTR is not a generalization of STR at all, but is instead its restriction. Rather than generalizing the concept of relativity, said Fock, Einstein merely generalized certain geometrical concepts and simultaneously violated his original relativization of space and time.

Fock began his discussion of relativity theory by noting that the theory of space and time may be divided into two parts: the theory of homogeneous (Galilean) space and the theory of inhomogeneous (Riemannian, Einsteinian) space. The first half occupied Einstein's attention in his development of STR, and he then attempted (unsuccessfully, said Fock) to generalize his theory into GTR.

The essential characteristic of Galilean space is its homogeneity, which can be illustrated by the equivalency of all points, directions, and inertial systems within it. Both Newtonian physics and special relativity physics were based on an assumption of homogeneous (Galilean) space. Mathematically, the homogeneity of the space of Newtonian physics was expressed in the Galilean transformations; the homogeneity of the space of special relativity was expressed in the Lorentz transformations. It was only in the transition from special relativity to general relativity that the assumption of Galilean space was discarded, and, said Fock, for very good reason.

Einstein correctly demonstrated, Fock continued, that the universal theory of gravitation (GTR) could not be contained within Galilean space. The most essential reason for the inadequacy of Galilean space, said Fock, was the one given by Einstein: Not only the inertial mass of a body but also its gravitational mass depends on its energy. Einstein found a way of describing the new physics by replacing, mathematically, Galilean space with Riemannian space. In so doing he created what is usually known as the general theory of relativity, a new physical theory. But according to Fock, the new theory, though extremely valuable as a theory of gravitation, was not a physical theory of general relativity at all. Fock later summarized his criticism in what he called "two short phrases": (1) *La relativité physique n'est pas générale;* (2) *la relativité générale n'est pas physique.*[45] Fock's view has been considered seriously by many scientists, both Soviet and non-Soviet. The discussion is continuing even today.

What did Fock consider to be Einstein's conceptual error? The root of it may be found in Einstein's understanding and use of the principle of equivalence, which states that in an infinitely small locality, the gravitational field is equivalent to an acceleration. Einstein illustrated this by a famous thought experiment: If a mass m is suspended by a spring from the top of a compartment (visualize an elevator) in the following fashion,

it is then impossible from within the compartment to decide whether an extension of the spring is caused by an upward acceleration of the compartment in the direction b or a downward gravitational field in the direction g.[46] A more ordinary illustration is that an airplane pilot flying in a cloud "by the seat of his pants" may be unable to distinguish a pull toward his seat caused by gravitation and one caused by flying in a loop, a similarity now illustrated algebraically by describing both forces in terms of g.

Einstein thus explained graphically his principle of equivalence, which may be simply stated as the principle of the equivalence of inertial and gravitational mass. Einstein then proceeded to apply this concept to terrestrial gravitation. At first this might seem an impossibility, since any acceleration involving the earth as a whole would have very different effects at different spots on the earth's surface. However, gravitational forces can be "transformed away" if we consider infinitesimal regions only, permitted through the use of differential equations. Thus if we think of a grid of cells surrounding the earth, with each cell representing an infinitesimal region, in the following fashion,

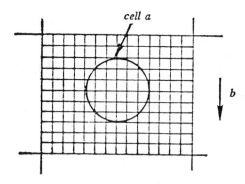

it becomes apparent that the gravitational force at any spot on the earth's surface may be transformed away by imagining an appropriate acceleration of the grid. If we let the above system accelerate at 32 ft/sec² in direction b, the gravitational field at cell a will disappear in the same way in which the force of gravity disappears in a freely falling elevator.[47]

The above examples of the principle of equivalence help one to understand that according to Einstein's theory of gravitation, in any given point of space the gravitational field can be replaced by an appropriate acceleration. The same relationship is conveyed by the observation that even though Einsteinian space as a whole is not homogeneous, in any infinitesimal region it is homogeneous, and the Lorentz transformations are valid.

It is exactly at this point that Fock objected to the Einsteinian view. He maintained that the local equivalence of acceleration and gravitation was not an adequate justification for concluding a complete equivalence of the fields of acceleration and of gravitation in all space. Indeed, Fock considered the principle of equivalence to be valid only in a restricted, local sense. According to Fock, the principle of equivalence in Einstein's completed theory had an "approximate character and was not a general principle."[48]

Fock noted that the physical basis of the principle of equivalence is the law of falling bodies, by which all unobstructed objects fall with equal acceleration. But this law is a general law, said Fock, not a local one, and if it is to be used for the foundation of another general law (of relativity), some way of considering space as a whole must be found:

> In order to construct a theory of gravitation or to apply it to physical problems it is . . . insufficient to study space and time only locally, i.e., in infinitely small regions of space and periods of time. One way or another one must characterize the properties of space as a whole. If one does not do this, it is quite impossible to state any problem uniquely. This is particularly clear in view of the fact that the equations of the gravitational, or any other field, are partial differential equations, the solutions of which are unique only when initial, boundary or other equivalent conditions are given. The field equations and the boundary conditions are inextricably connected and the latter can in no way be considered less important than the former. But in problems relating to the whole of space, the boundary conditions refer to distant regions and their formulation requires knowledge of the properties of space as a whole. One should note that Einstein did not fully appreciate the inadequacy of a local description and the importance of boundary conditions. This is why it is necessary to change substantially Einstein's statement of the basic problems of gravitational theory; this has been done in the author's research. . . .[49]

Fock characterized the boundary conditions in two different ways. In the first case, he assumed space to be homogeneous at infinity in the sense of being characterized by the Lorentz transformations. Masses and their associated gravitational fields were then envisioned as being implanted in homogeneous Galilean space (note, not in finite but unbounded space-time). The second case assumed a space-time that is only partially uniform, with the spatial part of it conforming to Lobachevskiian geometry. Usually termed the space of Friedmann-Lobachevskii, it contains well-defined gravitational fields when the mean density of matter contained within it is not equal to zero.

The important conclusions from these considerations and the ones that reveal most graphically Fock's unorthodox positions concern the question of preferred or privileged systems of coordinates. In each of the types of space considered by Fock—that is, Galilean space, space uniform at infinity, and Friedmann-Lobachevskii space—there "probably" is, according to him, a preferred system of coordinates.[50] The word "probably" here indicated Fock's continuing hesitation in the case of Friedmann-Lobachevskii space; in the case of Galilean space and space uniform at infinity he was confident of the existence of preferred systems of coordinates. The existence of such preferred systems of coordinates in each case would be, of course, contrary to Einstein's concept of the complete relativization of motion. Just as STR is associated with the relativization of inertial motion (and therefore the equivalence of inertial reference frames), so GTR is associated with the relativization of accelerated motion (and therefore the equivalence of accelerated reference frames). But now Fock questioned whether GTR actually was a generalization of STR in this sense.

Fock devoted much of his research to the task of proving that in space uniform at infinity there is a preferred system of coordinates that is well defined apart from a Lorentz transformation. He thought that such a system was formed by harmonic coordinates, which Fock believed reflected "certain intrinsic properties of space-time."[51] Yet it should be noticed that Fock's reliance on harmonic coordinates was one of the most controversial aspects of his approach; a number of physicists who accepted his criticism of the concept of general relativity remained dubious of the preferential status of harmonic coordinates.[52] Fock recognized this criticism in his statement, "The above remarks concerning the privileged character of the harmonic system of coordinates should not be understood, in any case, as some kind of prohibition of the use of other coordinate systems. Nothing is more alien to our point of view than such an interpretation. . . . The existence of harmonic coordinates, defined apart from a Lorentz transformation, though a fact of primary theoretical and practical importance, does not in any way preclude the use of other, non-harmonic coordinate systems."[53]

Fock believed that many physicists had lost sight of the importance of preferred or privileged systems of coordinates as a result of their exaggeration of the significance of the covariance of equations and, particularly, their belief that this covariance reflects some sort of physical law. For example, using the concepts of tensor analysis, physicists may write equations for space-time intervals without presupposing any coordinate system.[54] Such equations are extremely convenient since they permit an enormous economy in the mathematical description of space-time. However, said Fock, the significance of such covariant expressions of physical facts is not that all coordinate systems (in nature) are truly equal. An indication of the essential insignificance (from a physical viewpoint, Fock always emphasized) of covariance is the fact that practically any equation can be stated in covariant form if sufficient auxiliary functions are introduced.[55] In the covariant expression of infinitesimal space-time intervals the auxiliary function that is introduced is the coefficient $G_{\mu\nu}$, a tensor. The important fact is that this introduced function $G_{\mu\nu}$ is the only function used to describe the gravitational field. But one should see, said Fock, that what has happened in the process is that an appropriate theory of gravitation has been introduced into a theory that is then inappropriately dubbed a general theory of relativity, as if the results were a further expression of the relativity of motion. As Fock expressed it,

> When Einstein created his theory of gravitation, he put forward the term "general relativity," which confused everything. This term was adopted in the sense of "general covariance," i.e., in the sense of the covariance of equations with respect to arbitrary transformations of coordinates accompanied by transformations of $G_{\mu\nu}$. But we have seen that this kind of covariance has nothing to do with "relativity as such." At the same time the latter received the name "special" relativity, which purports to indicate that it is a special case of "general" relativity. . . . The term "general" relativity or "the general principle of relativity" is also used, beginning with Einstein, in the sense of "theory of gravitation." Einstein's fundamental paper on the theory of gravitation (1916) is already entitled "Foundations of the General Theory of Relativity." This confuses the issue still further. In the theory of gravitation, space is assumed non-uniform whereas relativity relates to uniformity so that it appears that in the general theory of relativity there is no relativity.[56]

No agreement exists among prominent world physicists on Fock's criticisms of "general relativity." Fock's interpretation has been challenged both in the Soviet Union and abroad. Yet it continues to command respect and attention as a defensible and interesting point of view. In 1964 Fock presented a paper in Florence, Italy, in which he summarized the analysis presented above for the audience of distinguished scholars. In the following discussion certain aspects of Fock's scheme attracted considerable praise, while others proved more controversial. Hermann Bondi, professor of applied mathematics at King's College, University of London, agreed with Fock's criticism of the alleged physical equivalence between inertial and accelerate observers.[57] Professor André Lichnerowicz of the Collège de France also supported Fock's criticism of the principle of equivalence, and Stanley Deser of Brandeis University commented that Fock's analysis of the concept of covariance had been very helpful in his understanding general relativity more fully.[58] But a number of the members of the audience, including both Lichnerowicz and Deser, were less enthusiastic about Fock's use of harmonic coordinates. A considerable number of theoretical physicists have not believed harmonic coordinates to be so appropriate for a description of the gravitational field as Fock has indicated.

By the late 1960s there were many different shadings of interpretation of general relativity in the Soviet Union, of which Fock's was only one, although probably still the most prominent one. P. S. Dyshlevyi wrote in 1969 that Soviet philosophers and scientists could be roughly classified into three different groups in terms of their attitudes toward general relativity.[59] The first group contained those scholars who considered GTR as expressed by Einstein to be essentially complete. They would introduce modifications here and there, but on the whole they fully accepted the Einsteinian interpretation of relativity, believing that it presented neither scientific nor philosophical problems of a serious nature. They considered Fock's criticism (Fock is not in this group) of general relativity too unorthodox in both its terminology and its conceptions. These scholars accepted the use of the term "general theory of relativity" (in contrast to Fock), and they had little criticism of Einstein's use of the principle of equivalence. They were generally skeptical of effects to add a "third stage of relativity," such as a "unified field theory." These scientists were willing to accept the present edifice of relativity theory with its two stories of STR and GTR. Among the Soviet scholars whom Dyshlevyi identified as belonging to this group were: in the past, M. Bronshtein, Ia. Frenkel, A. Friedman (Friedmann), and V. Frederiks; in the late sixties, A. F. Bogorodskii, V. L. Ginzberg, Ia. B. Zel'dovich, Kh. P. Keres, A. S. Kompaneets, and M. F. Shirokov.

The second group of interpreters of general relativity in the Soviet Union was the one to which Fock belonged and of which he was the best-known spokesman. The chief characteristic of this second group was its opinion that the foundations of general relativity needed to be given a thorough reexamination in order to make corrections in the conceptual structure of the theory as presented by Einstein.[60] I have already considered the views of this group in detail in the discussion of Fock. Other scientists whom Dyshlevyi placed in this group were A. Z. Petrov and N. V. Mitskevich.

The third group of Soviet interpreters of relativity theory hoped to achieve a new formulation of general relativity by uniting quantum and relativistic physics in a new quantum theory of gravitation. They approached gravitation from the standpoint of the field theory that had been worked out for the fields in physics other than the gravitational field. Dyshlevyi named as members of this group D. D. Ivanenko, O. S. Ivanitskaia, M. M. Mirianashvili, V. S. Kiriia, A. B. Kereselidze, A. E. Levashev, and V. I. Rodichev.

Of these groups, the second was the only one calling for specific alterations in the interpretations of general relativity. The first group accepted general relativity very nearly in its existing form, especially those customary philosophic interpretations of it that can be accommodated within the tradition of materialism. The third group proposed a program for the future that, if successful, would no doubt have philosophic implications, but that had so far been discussed only in elementary forms. The second group, however, continued to advance the criticisms initially voiced by Fock, and it was this group and its commentators that produced the larger part of the philosophical literature on relativity theory.

Indeed, many of the members of groups one and three avoided philosophical questions of science. With the exceptions of M. F. Shirokov (group one) and D. D. Ivanenko (group three), their names only rarely appeared in bibliographies of articles and books on dialectical materialism.[61] Of these two men, the one whose ideas most directly bore on the discussion of general relativity was M. F. Shirokov.

Shirokov supported the validity of the term "general relativity" against the criticisms of the second group, and he did so—in contrast to some of his colleagues—within an explicit dialectical materialist framework. He maintained that Einstein's interpretation of relativity fully accords with dialectical materialism and is, in fact, a further confirmation of it. In 1964 he wrote of general relativity, "This theory . . . is a great achievement in the materialist understanding of nature, contrary to the numerous idealistic (especially in the spirit of Machism) interpretations of it by several foreign authors."[62] Shirokov thought that Fock and Aleksandrov underrated GTR and greatly simplified its meaning by reducing it to a theory of gravitation. He acknowledged the importance of their work, however, in "confirming" that relativity theory reflects the "objectivity and reality" of nature. Their error was failing to see that when they denied GTR, they also denied the objective reality of fields of inertial forces.[63] Shirokov, like Fock, however, clung to the idea of a preferred reference frame within GTR, relying on his particular view of the concept of "center of inertia." In this sense he agreed with Fock in giving grounds for preferring the Copernican view to the Ptolemaic, but while Fock based his argument on his harmonic coordinates of space uniform at infinity, Shirokov pointed out that the sun represents an appropriate center of inertia of the solar system.[64]

One question connected with general relativity on which there was great disagreement among scientists and philosophers in the Soviet Union was, "What is gravitation?" Answers in many different subtle shades were given.[65] The members of the first group frequently equated the gravitational field with curved space-time. Some of their critics, however, said that this answer comes close to draining gravitation of physical or material content, to identifying nature with geometry, a position that Marxists have traditionally opposed. M. F. Shirokov, a member of the first group, therefore stated his position very carefully. According to him gravitation "reflects the geometric properties of space-time"; the gravitational field does not possess mass or energy; gravitation is not, therefore, matter itself, but is, instead, "a form of existence of matter." D. D. Ivanenko defined gravitation a little differently; it was to him a curvature of space-time caused by matter and the gravitational field itself. Thus, gravitation was to Ivanenko not quite the same as space-time, but instead an independent aspect of the material world. A. Z. Petrov, a member of the second group, described the gravitational field as a "specific form of moving matter." N. V. Mitskevich shared this view and warned against reducing gravitation to geometry. In his opinion, geometry is a manifestation of the gravitational field rather than the reverse. Thus, there was a considerable diversity of views among Soviet scholars. The attempt to define "gravitation" was in the Soviet Union a subject of discussion in a way very similar to attempts to define "information" and "consciousness" in other disciplines. The latter terms were topics of discussion in other chapters.

By the mid-eighties, the philosophical problems of relativity theory seemed less problematic to Soviet philosophers of physics than those of quantum mechanics. Nonetheless, considerable work in this area has been done in the last fifteen years, especially on the heritage of Einstein, now a revered figure among Soviet intellectuals.[66] One problem in relativity theory which did attract considerable attention was the possibility of the existence of particles which travel faster than the velocity of light, called "tachyons" by the American physicist Gerald Feinberg. The center of the Soviet discussion was the question, "Can the mathematics of special relativity serve as a theoretical basis for describing particles with velocity greater than light, and, if so, does this not lead to a denial of causality?" The majority of Soviet physicists and philosophers who wrote on this subject seemed to be willing to answer this question positively, but several expressed concern about the heavy philosophical costs involved in such an admission and therefore counseled caution.[67] Soviet philosophers even in the eighties admitted that this question was both a methodological and an "ideological" issue.[68] Soviet Marxists had managed to make the transition from rigid causality to probabilistic causality in the face of developments in physics, but to be asked to give up causality entirely was a different and more crucial question.

GRAND UNIFICATION THEORIES

A major topic of discussion among physicists all over the world in recent years has been the possibility of the unification of all the laws of physics. This ancient hope was given great new impetus in the seventies by the unification of two of the four fundamental forces of physics, the weak and the electromagnetic, by Steven Weinberg of Harvard University and later by Abdus Salam of the International Center for Theoretical Physics in Trieste. If somehow the remaining two forces— the strong force uniting the atomic nucleus and the gravitational force governing celestial and terrestrial bodies—could be brought together with the other two in a new theory of supergravity, all the forces in nature might be united. Physicists were naturally extremely excited by this possibility; after all, the greatest names in the history of physics were scientists who had created synthetic mathematical descriptions of apparently disparate phenomena in nature: Newton had united terrestrial and celestial gravitation; Maxwell had united electricity and magnetism; Einstein had successfully shown a relationship between an electromagnetic phenomenon—light—and gravitation, and had unsuccessfully further sought a unified field theory of gravitation and electromagnetism. Weinberg and Salam, uniting the weak and the electromagnetic forces, were the newest leaders in this tradition. The scientist who pushed the trend to its logical conclusion and united all forces of nature might well be regarded as the greatest physicist of all time.

Such a momentous scientific achievement would inevitably have enormous philosophical significance. A. A. Logunov (1926–   ), director of the famous Serpukhov Laboratory and later rector of Moscow University, and his physicist-colleague B. A. Arbuzov wrote in 1979 that quantum mechanics and relativity physics were the "foundation of the modern natural-scientific worldview" and that the construction of a new theory uniting the forces of nature would be even more significant. They continued that "knowledge of the structure of the elementary 'bricks' of matter is the foundation of all the natural sciences."[69]

The unification of physical forces had a great appeal to dialectical materialists. One of the distinguishing characteristics of Soviet Marxism is its aspiration to bring all phenomena—natural and social—under the sway of one philosophical system. The appearance of a Grand Unification Theory in physics would be seen by dialectical materialists as a significant step in such a philosophical unification of the natural and social universe. They obviously hoped that the central role assigned to matter in general relativity theory would be carried over into any Grand Theory. Materialism as a philosophical doctrine could then be assigned a new relevance. Yet Soviet philosophers were reluctant to specify just what such a new Grand Theory should look like, or to select a particular candidate for favor. By the eighties most of the physicists, and even many of the philosophers, had learned that great harm can be done to science by trying to buttress a certain physical theory by maintaining that it is supported by Marxism. Nonetheless, Soviet discussions of Grand Unification Theories (GUTS) should be watched carefully by Western scholars interested in the future of the long relationship between Soviet physics and dialectical materialism.

The recent discussions of general relativity in the Soviet Union have been in many ways similar to discussions elsewhere, even if terminological distinctions remained. The reexaminations of general relativity therefore by such non-Soviet scholars as J. Wheeler, R. H. Dicke, J. L. Anderson, and J. L. Synge have attracted much attention in the Soviet Union. The dimensions of debate in the Soviet Union, including the philosophical dimensions, are fully sufficient for consideration of all such views. Indeed, in the person of such scientists as Fock the Soviet scholars made their own important contributions to the discussions of the broader significance of relativity theory and the phenomenon of gravitation.

CHAPTER **12**

COSMOLOGY AND COSMOGONY

We are completely correct in looking upon the singular state ["birth of the universe"—LRG] the way F. Engels looked upon Kant's original dust cloud: ". . . matter before this original dust-cloud passed through an infinite series of other forms."

—V. V. Kaziutinskii, Soviet philosopher, 1979

Questions about the finiteness or infinity of the volume of this Universe, laws of its evolution in time, and all similar considerations are not philosophical questions and must be decided in the light of specific astronomical observations and modern physics.

—V. S. Ginzburg, Soviet astrophysicist, 1980

Clearly, the basic conclusions of cosmology are of major significance for *Weltanschauung* in general.

—I. D. Novikov, Soviet astrophysicist, 1983

The various answers to the basic questions cosmology and cosmogony ask about the origin and structure of the universe have always contained implications for philosophic and religious systems. Usually the connections between empirical investigations of the universe on the one hand and metaphysical systems on the other have been much less direct than the defenders or opponents of the systems have supposed, but intense controversies have arisen nonetheless. It is quite difficult to imagine, for example, any scientific evidence that could "prove" or "disprove" the position of a person asserting the existence of God, given at least a moderate degree of sophistication in that person's arguments. Similarly, it would be difficult to imagine a confirmation or refutation of the position of a knowledgeable materialist asserting an entirely naturalistic origin and evolution of the cosmos. Nonetheless, certain kinds of evidence have, with time, significantly affected the plausibility of versions of these differing arguments, and they have, in turn, evolved in response to the challenges thrown up to them. Here I would like to examine the responses of certain Soviet astronomers and philosophers—those who have actively defended the position of dialectical materialism—to astronomical evidence of recent decades. This attempt will require a very brief review of some of the most important findings of astronomers and of several resulting hypotheses.

Although modern cosmological theories are frequently discussed in popular articles as if there were only two competing models—"big bang" and "steady state"—there have been proposed in the last sixty years a great multitude of models of which more than a dozen have achieved sufficient currency among cosmologists to have common designations. All of the architects of the models have been forced to take into consideration several fundamental theoretical developments and astronomical findings that are totally new to this century. The most important theoretical innovation was the general theory of relativity as advanced by Einstein in 1916. Contrary to the Newtonian concept of an infinite universe situated in Euclidean space, Einstein's theory proposed the determination of the metric of a space-time continuum by the matter existing in the universe. Rather than yielding a unique space-time, however, Einstein's equations opened the door to several types of curvatures of different signs: positive (Riemannian geometry), zero (Euclidean geometry), or negative (Lobachevskiian geometry). The choice among the three types would be made on the basis of undetermined characteristics of matter within the universe, specifically, its average density. Determining the average density of matter within the whole universe was obviously an impossibility, since at any point in time man can see only so far into the universe. Furthermore, in this century many basic measurements affecting density calculations, such as the distances to stars and nebulae, have been highly questionable; they have, in fact, been drastically revised on several occasions. Therefore, the determination of the average density of matter has been a very difficult task.

The most important astronomical finding affecting cosmology so far in this century was the shift of the spectral lines of extragalactic nebulae toward the red end of the spectrum. This phenomenon was first observed by V. M. Slipher in 1912, but it was most thoroughly investigated by Edwin Hubble in the 1920s. Hubble and M. Humason in 1928 formulated a relationship of the red-shift to distance that has become known as Hubble's Law. This well-known but sometimes misunderstood relationship says that the red-shift of a particular nebula is directly proportional to the distance of the nebula from the observer. When interpreted in terms of the Doppler effect, the red-shift yields a large recessional velocity of the distant nebulae; in some cases this velocity is a significant fraction of the velocity of light. Hubble was cautious in applying to his law the interpretation provided by the Doppler effect, but if such application is made, the law can be understood as saying that the recessional velocity of a nebula is directly proportional to its distance from us. This interpretation has gained increasing acceptance among astronomers and cosmologists throughout the world. It is the basis of the various expanding cosmological models. When an expanding model is accompanied by the hypothesis of an original explosion, a moment when the expansion began to occur, the model becomes a "big bang" type.

Immediately after World War II the steady-state model was developed by Hermann Bondi, Thomas Gold, and Fred Hoyle. Originally created as a result of conflict between the time scale of the galaxy and that of the universe according to big-bang models, the steady-state theory soon acquired a rationale of its own that was persuasive to some cosmologists after the original conflict eased. While all relativistic models were based on the cosmological principle (the universe is the same in every direction), the steady-state model was based on what its advocates called the perfect cosmological principle (the universe is the same not only in every direction but at every moment in time). It incorporated the red-shift data by assuming that all galaxies recede from each other in accordance with the Hubble relationship, but that a steady state of the distribution of matter is retained despite this recession as a result of the constant creation of matter in the places of the old galaxies that have moved away. This violation of the law of the conservation of matter had not been detected by scientists, said the steady-state advocates, because it occurs at an extremely low rate, below the level of man's experimental error (as Bondi phrased it, "the steady-state theory predicts the creation of only one hydrogen atom in a space the size of an ordinary living-room once every few million years."[1]

The steady-state model possessed the considerable advantage of being infinite in time; there was no "singular state" when all the matter of the universe was compressed into one compact mass, no "birth" of the universe, as some cosmologists referred to this moment. It possessed the serious disadvantage of violating one of the most fundamental laws of physics: the conservation of matter and energy (because of its hypothesis of the creation of matter). Thus, it became the center of a considerable controversy in many countries. Fortunately from the standpoint of the resolution of the debate, it was a testable hypothesis. Its assumption that the universe was always the same in terms of time could be tested against observations of very distant galaxies, which are "distant in time"; its assumption that all elements could be synthesized at the present time (the heavy ones presented particular problems) was also open to inquiry; and its rejection of a primary catclysm could be tested by a search for evidence of that cataclysm. These efforts have been made in recent decades; the over-all result has been a retreat by the advocates of the steady-state theory, which has become increasingly difficult to support. A version of the "big bang" hypothesis is now supported by the overwhelming majority of cosmologists.

In order not to spend more time on description of cosmological models, I will introduce a schematic representation to which I will refer in subsequent discussion of Soviet views. Because of certain degrees of overlap it is quite difficult to reduce the models to distinct categories, but I have attempted to do so.[2] An indication of the complexity of the problem can be gained by noting that this simplified categorization includes four variants of the big-bang theory (IIa, IIb, IIc, IIIc) and three variants of the steady-state theory (under VI), not to speak of others.[3]

I. Static
   a. Einstein equations of 1915
   b. Einstein (with cosmological term [λ]), 1917

II. Expanding models without cosmological term (λ)[4]
   a. Einstein-de Sitter, 1932 ⎫
   b. Cycloidal   ⎬   based on A. A. Friedmann's
   c. Hyperbolic   ⎭   work, 1922
   d. Oscillating without singular state

III. Expanding models with cosmological term (λ)
   a. Einstein (as modified by Eddington, 1930)
   b. de Sitter, 1917
   c. Eddington (based on Ib)
   d. Lemaître, after 1927
   e. Infinite contraction-infinite expansion

IV. Expanding and rotating
   a. O. Heckmann et al., based in part on Gödel, 1949

V. Kinematic relativity
   a. Milne, 1935

VI. Steady State
   a. Bondi-Gold-Hoyle, 1948 (modification of IIIb)
   b. Electric universe, Lyttleton-Bondi, 1960
   c. Hoyle-Narlikar, 1963

Many discussions of Soviet cosmology that have appeared outside the Soviet Union have concentrated on the most elementary and dogmatic of the sources. Before Stalin's death there was a considerable body of Soviet literature with an extremely simple message: Any interpretation of the universe that could be turned into an argument, however strained, for divine interference was automatically condemned.[5] This condemnation was usually issued without much consideration of the scientific merits of the interpretation or of the possibility that its scientific core could be maintained without the particular theological overtones placed upon it by certain European and American writers. Thus, many prominent non-Soviet astronomers and physicists, such as James Jeans, Arthur Eddington, G. E. Lemaître, F. Hoyle, H. Bondi, T. Gold, O. Struve, C. F. von Weizsäcker, and Bart Bok were accused, at one time or another, of "idealism," "mysticism," or "popism." It is easy to ridicule these Soviet propaganda pieces, and many of them deserved ridicule, but it should be recognized that a number of the above-named authors— but by no means all—did indeed introduce religious elements into their astronomical writings. In some cases, such as James Jeans' discussions of the "finger of God" that started the planets in their orbits, the references were little more than the results of a colorful style; in other cases such as Abbé Lemaître's frequent references to the "birth of the universe" just before the beginning of its expansion, the statements probably did have a connection with religious belief.[6] And in still other instances, the statements were simply too strong to be brushed off; such a remark was E. T. Whittaker's "it is simpler to postulate a creation *ex nihilo,* an operation of the Divine Will to constitute Nature from nothingness."[7] Not only Soviet ideologists were disturbed by some of these references; as the British astronomer William Bonnor wrote:

> One can well understand the enthusiasm with which some theologians accepted the idea that the universe was created 10,000 million years ago. Here was the vacancy for God which they had been seeking. Archbishop Ussher had been a few years wrong with the date, but he had the right idea when he said that God created the world in 4004 B.C.
>
> Unfortunately, some cosmologists have been sympathetic to this attitude. This seems to me quite reprehensible for the following reason. It is the business of science to offer rational explanations for the events in the real world, and any scientist who calls on God to explain something is falling down on his job. This applies as much to the start of the expansion as to any other event. If the explanation is not forthcoming at once, the scientist must suspend judgement: but if he is worth his salt he will always maintain that a rational explanation will eventually be found. . . .

There has been a curious reluctance on the part of the cosmologists I mentioned to do this, and they have preferred to identify the singularity in the equations with God. Now, I argue that scientifically this is unexcusable. . . .[8]

If the use of religious metaphors and even the intentional introduction of religious elements occurred in the writings of some non-Soviet cosmologists, the similar fault of distorting their arguments in the name of militant atheism was even more common in the Soviet Union before the late fifties. When ideologists with little knowledge of mathematics were the authors of these articles, the results were frequently scientifically erroneous. One of the most common arguments was that dialectical materialism required an infinite universe. Historically speaking, the association of spatial infinity with modern science, of course, is a very close one; this association is revealed, for example, in the very title of the eminent historian of science Alexandre Koyré's *From the Closed World to the Infinite Universe*.[9] Religion was a genuine obstacle at certain moments to the theory of an infinite universe (although it should not be forgotten that to Newton an infinite universe with absolute space and time implied God rather than denied him).[10] Because of this association, many recent opponents of religion, in the Soviet Union and abroad, found the relativistic closed models of the universe of this century uncongenial. An important difference, however, is that the closed models of the twentieth century were four-dimensional, while the finite model of medieval scholastic thought was three-dimensional, bounded by the fixed stars. (The "crystalline spheres" were not always taken literally by scholastic thinkers, but the idea of an enclosed space was.) The basis for linking a finite universe to religion was that of historic association—not an entirely trustworthy foundation. One is tempted to say that there was no more logical necessity for dialectical materialists to demand an infinite universe than there was for medieval theologians to demand a finite one (or, for that matter, for many contemporary non-Soviet astronomers to assume a beginning in time). Accordingly, Soviet cosmologists had every reason to be cautious about criticizing finite models on extrascientific grounds. While a few astronomers and mathematicians were very aware of these reasons for caution, the general ideological antipathy toward finite models was very strong. As late as 1955, a Soviet author commented in an astronomy journal:

The Marxist-Leninist doctrine of the infinitude of the universe is the *fundamental axiom* at the basis of Soviet cosmology. . . . The denial or abandonment of this thesis . . . leads inevitably to idealism and fideism, i.e., in effect, to the negation of cosmology, and therefore has nothing in common with science.[11]

The question of the "birth" of the universe is more controversial than its configuration, as indicated above in Bonnor's remarks. While everyone should tread extremely lightly where questions of cosmology are concerned, there are a number of serious reasons for not accepting the concept of a beginning of all time unless absolutely necessary. It is, furthermore, quite difficult to think of circumstances that would make such a concept absolutely necessary. The Soviet critics of "big-bang" theories were usually more aware, at least in their writings, of these considerations than their non-Soviet counterparts; they correctly saw that a hypothesis of the birth of the entire universe (and not merely of one of its phases or parts) was linked to a religious view. These Soviet writers frequently squandered their philosophic advantage on this issue, however, by extending their arguments far beyond what was necessary in order to avoid commitment to a concept of the absolute beginning of the universe.[12]

The most interesting exploration of some of these issues can be found in the writings of several Soviet scientists of recognized distinction; they will be discussed in the following sections.

O. Iu. SCHMIDT

One of the leading early Soviet writers on planetary cosmogony was O. Iu. Schmidt (1891–1956). Schmidt was originally trained as a mathematician and ultimately became a leader of the Moscow school of algebra; his great popularity in the USSR derived largely, however, from his exploits as a polar explorer. He became a very famous man, a hero to a whole generation of Soviet citizens. A member of the Communist Party since 1918, Schmidt held a series of important administrative posts, including director of the State Publishing House, editor of the *Great Soviet Encyclopedia*, and member of the Central Executive Committee of the USSR. After 1935 he was a full member of the Academy of Sciences. A very colorful man, Schmidt was as radical in his personal habits as in his politics, becoming a father to two children by two different women on the same day. No doubt his most famous professional exploit was his command of the ship *Cheliuskin* in 1933 and 1934 in an attempt to repeat his complete transit of the

Northern Sea Route in 1932 (the first complete transit in a single season). During the 1933-34 trip, Schmidt and his men were trapped in the ice of the Arctic Ocean for months; eventually they had to evacuate their sinking ship onto the ice many kilometers from shore. A spectacular rescue followed, and Schmidt became an international hero.[13]

Schmidt gave lectures in the twenties and thirties on the history and philosophy of science; in his scientifc work he spoke proudly of the importance of Marxist philosophy. His private papers now on deposit in the archives of the Academy of Sciences of the USSR show that he was a serious student of the writings of Engels.[14] It is said (and if true, it is matter for congratulation) that when he and his crew were stranded on the Arctic ice, he organized discussions of dialectical materialism in order to cause the men to forget about their plight.[15]

Schmidt is best known to cosmogonists for his theory of the origin of the earth and the planets, published in the form of four lectures in 1949.[16] Since he restricted himself to the solar system, Schmidt did not encounter any of the large-scale problems of theorists of the universe, such as relativity or red-shift, but he nonetheless saw his scheme in terms of a conflict of world views. In his first lecture he wrote: "The history of cosmogony has meaning and is instructive when it is seen as a struggle between idealism and materialism that never ceases at any stage in history."[17] And as we later will explain, Schmidt maintained that his theory of the sun's capture of a gas-dust cloud was supported by a dialectical concept.

Schmidt's views on cosmogony began with a recognition of the continuing importance of the nebular hypotheses of Kant and Laplace. According to these well-known theories (which differ in certain respects), the sun and the planets arose from the gradual condensation of a diffuse mass of material into discrete bodies. Although Kant's and Laplace's hypotheses had enjoyed great popularity in the nineteenth century, by the early twentieth century they were seriously challenged on the grounds that they could not account for angular momentum. One of the very odd characteristics of the solar system is the fact that the major planets, which have less than 1/700 of the total mass of the system, nonetheless possess 98 percent of its angular momentum. On the other hand, the sun, with almost all the mass, has only 2 percent of the angular momentum. The consequent dilemma of astronomers was described in 1935 by H. N. Russell: "No one has ever suggested a way in which almost the whole of the angular momentum could have got into so insignificant a fraction of the mass of an isolated system."[18]

After 1900, various kinds of "tidal" theories were developed to try to explain this phenomenon. The essence of the tidal theories was the hypothesis that the sun had been approached by another star so closely (perhaps even a grazing collision occurred) that solar material was strung out in space. This material later formed the planets. In the Chamberlin and Moulton version, the matter was ejected from opposite sides of both the sun and the star in the form of violent tides; in the variant developed by James Jeans and H. Jeffreys, a cigar-shaped stream of matter was strung out between the star and the sun. The cigar shape (thicker in the middle) would account for the large size of the planets Jupiter and Saturn.

Schmidt believed that the popularity of Jeans' theory of planetary cosmogony in the twenties and thirties was connected with social factors. He commented: "The Jeans hypothesis lasted longer than any of the other 20th century hypotheses. The reason for its popularity was not its scientific value (it had none) and not the undoubted talents of its author but because it was the one most acceptable to the idealist, religious philosophy dominating bourgeois society."[19] The connection between Jeans' explanation of the creation of the planets and bourgeois values was, in Schmidt's mind, the emphasis upon the rarity of the events involved and the consequent miraculous aura of the universe, which Jeans exploited. For a sun and a star to approach each other closely enough for the events described by Jeans and other tidalists to occur would be an exceedingly rare phenomenon. It is obvious that scientists would prefer not to rely upon extremely rare events to explain nature; if the rarity of the event approaches uniqueness, the event tends to pass out of the realm of phenomena explainable by scientific laws, which depend upon repetition. Of course, the grazing of two stars would not be unique, given enough time, but to say only that the creation of the earth was very rare, not unique, would cause some astronomers discomfort.[20] These were the years in which the "age" of the universe was being placed by many astronomers at only a few billion years; therefore, planetary systems would indeed be rare. The issue here is what astronomers call "embarrassment of privilege." If the planetary system is very special, then its inhabitant man is also. Ever since the discrediting of the Ptolemaic system, any variety of anthropocentrism has been considered suspect by most scientists. Schmidt looked upon Jeans' theory as, at least in part, a careless, perhaps even intentional reversion of that tradition.

Schmidt believed that in order to explain the origin of the planetary system it was necessary to disregard the tidalist theories and to build on the inadequate but nonetheless promising nebular hypotheses of Kant and Laplace. The central idea of these systems—the formation of planets from diffuse matter—seemed to him more believable than near-collisions between stars.[21] He postulated that the sun in its orbit had passed through a cloud of dust, gas, and other matter. This cloud possessed a momentum of its own. Out of the interaction of the different momenta Schmidt believed that the peculiar distribution found in the solar system could have evolved. As he wrote:

> If the Sun, passing through a cloud, or near it, could "capture" part of the material and take it with it, the Sun would be surrounded by a cloud out of which the planets could later be formed. If the cloud originated in this way there is no further difficulty with the distribution of the angular momentum. This momentum would result from a redistribution of the angular momentum of the Galaxy; part of the angular momentum possessed originally by the cloud in respect of the passing Sun would be retained by the part of the cloud captured by the Sun.[22]

So far as philosophic considerations are concerned, the superiority that Schmidt claimed for his theory, at least initially, was the greater credibility of the events involved as a result of their greater probability. Interestingly enough, in the passage immediately following the one quoted above, Schmidt did defend his system on philosophic grounds, but not on the issue of the rareness of events. Perhaps he recognized that the events he described would also be considered very unlikely by many astronomers, but that can only be surmised. The specific philosophic grounds that he chose concerned the dialectic concept of the interconnection of all phenomena, which has already been mentioned in the debate over quantum mechanics (see p. 331). Schmidt continued:

> For our explanation of the origin of the solar system we introduce the matter and the forces of the Galaxy. Is this correct? Would it not be more correct to explain the origin of the solar system by the development of the internal forces of the system itself?
>
> The concept of the general interconnection of all phenomena is one of the basic dialectic concepts and is well enough known to all of us. The problem of the relationship existing between the external and internal is solved concretely by materialist dialectics where everything associated

with the given phenomena is taken into consideration. . . . It is this
circumstance that makes the "capture" hypothesis so tempting despite
the fact that there are some difficulties connected with it which we shall
discuss later.[23]

This reliance on the interconnection of phenomena for support of a
particular thesis in planetary cosmogony was a much weaker argument
than Schmidt's original critique of Jeans' theory on the basis of its
improbability. Whether a scientist should study a particular realm of
activity in isolation is usually a result of a consideration of the influence
of the greater outside realm, rather than a simple statement that one
should or should not consider it. It is well understood, for example,
that every problem concerning the influence of gravity on any specific
body in the universe is in actuality an "n-body" problem, and inherently
impossible of solution. The scientist, however, decides to what degree
he can disregard other bodies. Similarly, the support for Schmidt's
argument above, that most scientists would consider telling is not that
he is willing to consider a larger realm, but that such consideration in
this particular instance results in more plausible explanations of the
origin of the planetary system. Whether the last half of the preceding
sentence is true or not has been the subject of much debate.

Before returning to the essential problem of probability of events, it
is necessary to observe that Schmidt's system as described is still
incomplete. A mathematician himself, he clearly realized that the sun
could not capture a dust-gas cloud in the way described so far. In order
for capture to occur, the resultant motion would have to be elliptical;
that is, orbits would have to be formed around the sun. In the case
of two isolated bodies, however, the resultant motion would be hyperbolic and capture could not occur. In order to achieve the necessary
capture, Schmidt introduced the hypothesis that three bodies were
involved; in other words, one could imagine a scenario in which the
sun enters a dust-gas cloud at the same time that a star is also entering
the cloud. Even then the question of the possibility of capture was
problematic; it was an important feature of the famous "three-body
problem," which has occupied mathematicians for several centuries. It
has been demonstrated that no general algebraic solution of the problem
is possible, but in specific cases when initial conditions are known,
numerical solutions are possible, though they were extremely laborious
before the widespread use of computers. In 1947 Schmidt carried out
such a numerical solution that convinced him that capture was possible

in a three-body situation.[24] This conclusion was supported by G. F. Khil'mi.[25]

There remained the problem of the probability of the events, presumably one of the main advantages of Schmidt's system, philosophically speaking, over that of Jeans. Yet most observers would say that Schimidt's scheme demanded very unlikely occurrences as well. Schmidt pointed out, however, that since it was possible for capture to occur in a three-body situation, so was it possible in an approximate arrangement of any number greater than two, given certain ranges of distances and velocities. Furthermore, his supporters introduced other variants of capture, including the influence of collisions and light pressure.[26] Nonetheless, the central question of the rareness of the birth scene of planetary systems remained a major problem to Schmidt. According to his own philosophic beliefs, the system that he had erected was rather awkward, although preferable to the alternatives.

The last part of Schmidt's life was one of interminable illness; confined to his bed with tuberculosis, he struggled to perfect his system. In the last years he turned to the mechanism of capture on the basis of inelastic collisions of particles as the most promising avenue, but the main features of his system remained constant.

V. A. AMBARTSUMIAN

Perhaps no great Soviet scientist has made more outspoken statements in favor of dialectical materialism than the astrophysicist Viktor Amazaspovich Ambartsumian (1908–   ). Ambartsumian studied at Pulkovo Observatory under the Russian astronomer A. A. Belopol'skii, then went on to hold many distinguished positions in Leningrad University, the Armenian Academy of Sciences, and the USSR Academy of Sciences. He supervised the building of the famous Biurakan Astrophysical Observatory near Erevan. For his works on the fundamental importance of stellar astonomy and cosmogony he was honored several times with governmental prizes.[27] He became one of the best-known abroad of all Soviet scientists. His praise of dialectical materialism has been voiced again and again over the years; these affirmations have come when political controls were rather lax as well as when they were tight. We have every reason to believe that they reflect, at root, his own approach to nature. As an example, in 1959 Ambartsumian declared:

The history of the development of human knowledge, each step forward in science and technology, each new scientific discovery, irrefutably attests to the truth and fruitfulness of dialectical materialism, affirms the correctness of the Marxist-Leninist teaching concerning the knowability of the world, the magnitude and transforming power of the human mind, which is penetrating ever deeper into the secrets of nature. At the same time the achievements of science convincingly demonstrate the complete unsoundness of idealism and agnosticism, and the reactionariness of the religious world view.[28]

Two years after the publication of the article in which this statement appeared, Ambartsumian was elected president of the International Astronomical Union in Berkeley, California. Here was an internationally prominent scientist, an honorary or corresponding member of the scientific societies of most of the nations leading in science, an authority in the field of stellar physics, who declared that dialectical materialism was of assistance to his work. Non-Soviet observers usually brushed aside such comments as ornamentation or the result of Party pressures.

At the same time, Ambartsumian was not afraid to reprimand the Communist Party ideologues when they obstructed his research. He observed, "When we boldly posed certain questions and when science came upon something that was still unexplained, several philosophers tried to hold us back—as if our scientists had fallen prey to idealism!"[29]

Ambartsumian confined his most important work to problems of stellar cosmogony rather than planetary, galactic, or universal cosmogony. Each of these problems—the description of the formation of stars, planets, galaxies, or the unvierse—presented its own particular problems. Ambartsumian believed that stellar cosmogony would provide important clues to the other fields and that in the absence of a plausible theory of stellar cosmogony, work in the other areas would have to be based on what he termed an excessive degree of speculation. Nonetheless Ambartsumian's preferences on the larger-scale cosmogony and cosmology can be rather easily discerned by reading his frequent criticisms (particularly before the sixties) of astronomers in Europe and America. His work on stellar cosmogony also contained philosophical elements of general implication; furthermore, despite his reserve, Ambartsumian admitted that the larger cosmological problems were the final and most important problems of astonomy. From these writings we will see that although Ambartsumian considered the construction of a world system premature he generally preferred, like many Soviet astronomers, a model that was relativistic, inhomogeneous, expanding, and infinite in time.

These preferences will be discussed more fully in the following section. They implied a rejection of steady-state models and either a rejection or serious modification of big-bang models.

In the field of stellar cosmogony Ambartsumian was, in his early years, a frequent critic of those "ardent advocates of idealism of the twenties," James Jeans and Arthur Eddington. This criticism extended in several different directions, but one area concerned an argument over the rate of change in the evolution of stars. As a dialectical materialist, Ambartsumian believed that all nature is constantly in evolution; he was suspicious of attempts to postulate even relatively unchanging entities in nature. Jeans and Eddington believed that the mass of stars diminishes over time primarily as a result of the emission of electromagnetic radiation. According to their calculations many hundreds, perhaps thousands, of billions of years would be required before a noticeable change in mass would occur in the average star as a result of this process. But according to the theory of the universe that Eddington and Jeans supported, which was a form of the big-bang class, the age of the universe was only several billion years. Therefore, following Jeans and Eddington, the mass of the stars had changed insignificantly since the birth of the universe; man saw them essentially as they were at the beginning of time.

The Church in the Middle Ages had, of course, favored a view of the universe that went beyond such relatively static celestial bodies to an absolutely unchanging heavenly sphere. One of the more dramatic achievements of Galileo was to show change and irregularity in celestial bodies. Ambartsumian felt that he was continuing that tradition by maintaining that the stars change much more rapidly than Jeans and Eddington believed, and according to a mechanism of which they were supposedly unaware. Speaking of the theories of the two English astronomers, Ambartsumian commented:

> Soviet astrophysics long ago opposed these idealistic views, full of internal contradictions and not corresponding with observational data, with their own materialistic point of view, based on facts. The change of mass in the universe, which existed and will exist infinitely, depends primarily on the direct ejection (*vybrasyaniem*) of matter. [30]

Ambartsumian said that his phenomenon of the ejection of mass by stars leads relatively quickly to significant changes in the physical state of the stars.[31] His colleagues D. A. Martynov, V. A. Krat, and V. G. Fesenkov had all done work in examining the results of the phenomenon; Fesenkov attempted to follow changes in the speed of rotation of the sun on this basis. Thus, said Ambartsumian, "one of the most important results of the work of Soviet astronomers has been the conclusion that the stars themselves change and also change the interstellar environment that surrounds them."[32]

Just as Ambartsumian believed, contrary to some earlier astronomical views, that the stars are perceptibly changing in mass, so he also believed that stars are constantly being born. His theory of the continuous formation of stars at the present stage in the development of the galaxy is now widely known and usually considered a disproof of the belief that all stars in the galaxy were simultaneously formed.[33] This work was also, in Ambartsumian's mind, a confirmation of dialectical materialism. As we will see later, this issue of the evolution of stars bears certain resemblances to the discussions of geology in the early nineteenth century; like Lyell, Ambartsumian believed that the features displayed by nature should be—if at all possible—explained on the basis of processes presently being witnessed in nature.[34]

The exact details of the early life of stars according to Ambartsumian's scheme are necessarily uncertain, as are most such descriptions. The main outlines can, however, be given. Since his description is based on the Hertzsprung-Russell diagram of the relation between the spectral types of the stars and their luminosities, it is necessary briefly to discuss the diagram.

All stars demonstrate dark-line spectra just as the sun does. The absorption lines of these spectra not only tell us the composition of stars, but also allow us to classify them in different groups, with a gradual gradation between types. The standard types are O, B, A, F, G, M, K, R, N, and S.[35] Because of the relative rarity of types O, R, N, and S, we can limit ourselves to a consideration of the six other types. Stars can also be classified in terms of their absolute luminosities, a luminosity of one being equal to that of the sun.

When the stars are placed on a graph in which the abscissa corresponds to spectral type and the ordinate to luminosity, it turns out that they do not fall upon the diagram in a random fashion, but instead form groups, including a diagonal belt known as the main sequence, which includes the great majority of all stars. The resulting Hertzsprung-Russell (H-R) diagram has the following appearance:

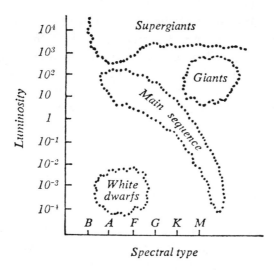

Spectral type

Ambartsumian's description of the life cycle of stars traced their positions on the H-R diagram, and he addressed himself only to the stars in the main sequence. They are formed, he said, in groups ranging from a few dozen to even thousands of members; these loose clusters of young stars are those known to astronomers as "associations." He believed that such associations are being formed out of matter in a prestellar state in our own galaxy at the present time; in other words, the process being described was valid both historically and contemporaneously. These new stars initially appeared on the H-R diagram in positions that on the average are above the center line of the main sequence; later they move toward the center line as a result of changes in their states. The cause of these changes, said Ambartsumian, is a "mighty outflow" of matter from the interior of the stars into surrounding space.[36] Thus, young stars lose mass, decline slightly in luminosity, and enter into the main sequence along its entire front. Once they have entered into the main sequence, the state of the stars begins to stabilize; the outflow of matter continues, but at a much slower rate, and those stars that had a significant rotational moment lose it almost entirely. Ambartsumian believed that the time required for the average star to move into the main sequence was several dozen million years. In view of the several (now frequently about fifteen) *billions* of years given as the "age" of our galaxy, such a shift represented an appreciable rate.

According to this scheme, stars are constantly being born, but not "out of nothing," as Ambartsumian said certain non-Soviet astronomers would have it. The exact details of the birth of stars was one of the most difficult problems; Ambartsumian differed with other Soviet astronomers on the question, and his own views varied somewhat with time. His opinion, already expressed, that stars eject large quantities of matter during their life cycles allowed for a certain amount of available matter for additional star formation. But Ambartsumian admitted that the specific character of the protostars was a weak link in his theory. Rather than believing that the stars were formed from diffused matter, as many Soviet astronomers including Fesenkov did, Ambartsumian believed that the protostars are possibly "globules," or dense, dark clouds of spherical form, and with a diameter of several light-months.[37] But Ambartsumian admitted that work by Fesenkov on star chains supported the view that stars are formed from diffused matter.

The main point, said, Ambartsumian, was that the origin of the stars was not "from nothing," as he described the theory of the West German physicist P. Jordan.[38] Ambartsumian said that not only did Jordan postulate the spontaneous and causeless appearance of stars, but that this view was incorporated into Lemaître's description of the birth of the universe. Ambartsumian considered the terms "birth" or "age" of the universe, used by Jordan, as careless and inaccurate. Nonetheless, he respected highly much of Jordan's work.

Rather than describing the birth of stars, Ambartsumian's theory described their lives during the period immediately after birth. And even within that limitation, it accounted only for stars on the main sequence. It either omitted or was unclear about the evolution of such types as white dwarfs and cold giants. Furthermore, the final phases of the stars of the main sequence were not described. Nevertheless, in the field of cosmogony no theorist can claim completeness for his views. Ambartsumian's theories of star formation have justifiably won him the reputation of one of the leading researchers in the field.[39]

The position that Ambartsumian took on the question of the red-shift provides important clues to much of his thinking on cosmology and cosmogony. Contrary to much opinion outside the USSR, Soviet scientists who at this time interpreted the universe with reference to dialectical materialism did not necessarily question the idea of expansion. In other words, they often accepted the Doppler-effect interpretation of the red-shift, as well as the conclusion that our observable universe is expanding, but they usually had strong reservations about concepts such as the "creation" or "age" of the universe as a whole. There is an obvious connection between the issues of "expansion" and "age."

If astronomers can arrive at a constant speed of expansion, or a variable speed of expansion that can be described mathematically, they can then extrapolate back to a point in time when the universe was concentrated in one infinitesimally small mass: this moment becomes the "birth" of the universe, and the distance in time between that moment and the present, the "age" of the universe. It is such extrapolations that Soviet astonomers such as Ambartsumian warned against.[40] A number of logically legitimate alternatives to "creation theories" existed. One could maintain that there was no overwhelming proof of a long-term calculable velocity of expansion. One could maintain that expansion was only one phase in the history of a universe that alternately expands and contracts. Or one could advance the belief that the calculations of the point in time when the present universe began expansion may be perfectly valid without concluding that this same point was the beginning of all time and of all universes.

Ambartsumian tried to steer a middle course between those people who, on the one hand, rejected the interpretation that the red-shift meant that the universe was expanding and those, on the other, who concluded that this expansion permitted an extrapolation in time back to the birth of the entire universe. When he was asked in 1958 if there were any solution for the red-shift other than the Doppler effect, he replied, "No, it is impossible. At any rate, so far no other plausible interpretation has been proposed. Therefore we must conclude that the system of galaxies and clusters of galaxies surrounding us is expanding. This is one of the most fundamental facts of contemporary science." Similarly, Ambartsumian was asked what his attitude was toward "relativistic cosmology," to which he replied, "Cosmology can only be relativistic."[41] Consequently, any consideration of Ambartsumian's cosmological theories should recognize that the simpler discussions of Soviet views of cosmology stating or implying that Soviet cosmologists rejected both Einsteinian relativity and the concept of an expanding universe were gross reductions of a considerably richer debate.

Ambartsumian criticized both the idealistic and mechanistic schools of cosmology. The idealists, he said, played on lack of knowledge and the frustration involved in trying to answer extremely difficult questions by appealing either to epistemological idealism or religion. The mechanists, on the contrary, simplified nature by trying to explain everything on the basis of principles already known, failing to realize the need for new conceptualizations. Ambartsumian then applied this model of the two erroneous schools of cosmology to the problem of the red-shift phenomenon and its implications for the structure of the universe. A number of physicists and astronomers, he said, assumed that the metagalaxy is ideally homogeneous and then further proposed that this type of system fills the entire universe.[42] Taking the red-shift into consideration, they applied Einstein's interpretation of gravitation to the hypothesis of a homogeneous universe; they then concluded that the universe is finite and expanding. (Such a model would be the Einstein-de Sitter one, IIa above.) At this point, said Ambartsumian, the idealist philosophers and similarly inclined physicists stepped in and drew dramatic conclusions about the creation of the world and about the mysterious force responsible for this creation. This final step was, said Ambartsumian, totally unjustified. It occurred, he said, only because the inadequacy of knowledge about the structure of the metagalaxy left room for "unrestrained extrapolations that led these hypotheses rather far from real science. . . ."[43]

But the opposite extreme, that presented by the mechanists, was no more justified. "Without any kind of experimental evidence they attempted to show that the red-shift is not connected with the Doppler effect but has instead some other cause." Such an attempt was the hypothesis that photons "age" over long periods of time; according to this interpretation, the shift toward the red end of the spectrum would not be a result of a receding velocity, but a change in the nature of light itself. The reason these changes have not previously been witnessed, said the backers of the aging hypothesis, was the insufficient passage of time in laboratory experiments. Ambartsumian believed, as have most other astronomers, that this aging hypothesis was extremely arbitrary; it was an ad hoc explanation developed as a means of avoiding the expansion hypothesis. No evidence for the aging of photons outside of the astronomical red-shift existed. Scientists do not resort to explanations that depend upon unknown and unverifiable phenomena if they have at hand another explanation, verified in at least some instances, that will explain equally well the data in hand. Such an existing explanation was the Doppler effect. Ambartsumian described the efforts of the mechanists and conservatives who would deny the Doppler interpretation as having "suffered a complete failure."[44]

If Ambartsumian's views on the Doppler interpretation were similar to those of the majority of astronomers elsewhere, on what grounds did he criticize many of these same astronomers? The issue on which Ambartsumian concentrated in building his own interpretation, at least until the end of the fifties, was that of the homogeneity of the universe.

At the time that Hubble formulated the red-shift relation, he assumed that extragalactic nebulae populate space with an approximately constant density. On such an assumption, the velocity-distance relationship was linear out to a distance of 250,000,000 light-years. As more complete and refined data were collected, the question of whether the velocity-distance relationship was linear or curved became pressing. The conclusion has obvious implications for cosmology: a curved relationship could indicate that the expansion of our part of the universe is slowing or accelerating, making extrapolations difficult and calling the "age" of the universe into question. As Ambartsumian commented in 1959:

> Twenty years ago one could try to justify the hypothesis of the homogeneous density of the universe by saying that in the absence of sufficient evidence on the distribution of distant galaxies the assumption of the homogeneity of the metagalaxy is a natural but very rough approximation; at that time this view found a certain support in Hubble's calculations; but now the situation has radically changed. New evidence concerning the visible spatial distribution of galaxies turns out to be in complete contradiction with the assumption of homogeneity, even in the roughest approximation. It seems to me that if one tried to characterize in two words that understanding of galactic distribution that has begun to form in the last years on the basis of the latest evidence, then the most successful expression would be extreme inhomogeneity.[45]

In elaborating his view that the universe is inhomogeneous, Ambartsumian acknowledged that the mere fact that clusters and groups of extragalactic nebulae exist is not necessarily evidence that nebulae do not populate space with an approximately constant density. One could maintain that the clusters and groups were only small islands in a broad, general metagalactic field. This general field could be homogeneous, or it could vary according to a continuous gradient. Ambartsumian felt, however, that astronomical research of the early 1950s pointed to the conclusion that the tendency toward the formation of groups and clusters was a basic characteristic of the metagalaxy rather than an exceptional circumstance. Such evidence of inhomogeneity caused a crisis, since the major cosmological models were endangered, a prospect that Ambartsumian found not unpleasant on philosophic grounds.

The question of the homogeneity or inhomogeneity of the universe remained troublesome to Ambartsumian after this date. In the late fifties new evidence led Ambartsumian to believe that his theory of the inhomogeneity of the universe was somewhat more in question. Before

1957, Ambartsumian had based his conclusion on studies showing that up to dimensions of two hundred million parsecs, the universe seemed inhomogeneous.[46] Thus, at a distance of ninety million parsecs from the earth in the constellation Coma Berenices (Berenice's hair) astronomers may observe a cluster of galaxies larger than all other nearer galaxies. If one looks in other directions up to a distance of ninety million parsecs, no other galaxy of such large dimensions can be observed. Therefore, Ambartsumian felt justified in concluding that in order to postulate homogeneity, one would have to speak of volumes with diameters greater than two hundred million parsecs. However, in 1957–58, Ambartsumian received reports from the researches of Zwicky at Palomar that in volumes with diameters in the vicinity of a billion parsecs, it is possible to discern distribution approaching homogeneity. Thus, contrary to Ambartsumian's earlier views, astronomers could speak of an average density of matter at a distance of a billion parsecs approximately equal to the density in the vicinity of our galaxy. Thus, the case for existing cosmological models regained strength. (In the late seventies evidence for homogeneity presented by G. Rainey and other astronomers became even stronger.)

Nonetheless, Ambartsumian was still willing to defend his characterization of the universe as "extremely inhomogeneous." The universe is inhomogeneous in many more ways than in its distribution of matter, he said—for example, in color of galaxies, electromagnetic radiation, and so on. He called the latter "qualitative inhomogeneity."[47] In his opinion this particular type of inhomogeneity was becoming more and more evident. Thus, he concluded:

> Therefore, I venture to add to the observed great inhomogeneity in density and distribution of a number of galaxies the fact of their great qualitative diversity. This diversity is all the more revealed the greater the distances involved. . . .
>
> Thus, one of the bases of contemporary simplified models is undermined. A homogeneous universe such as is described in these models does not exist. But there is also a second consideration: All these models apply as a basic postulate the linear dependence of velocity on distance. Unfortunately, we do not have exact enough knowledge of galactic distances to verify this assumption.[48]

Ambartsumian pointed out that astronomers had often drastically revised their distance scales; in 1952, Hubble's colleague W. Baade reported in Rome to the International Astronomical Union that the previously accepted distance to the Andromeda nebula was probably too small by a factor of two; in 1958, at Brussels, several astronomers proposed enlarging the scale of distance for the more distant galaxies by a factor of five or six over the pre-1952 figure. Each of these revisions obviously affected the distance-velocity relationship. Thus, Ambartsumian concluded that the universe is indeed expanding, as established by the red-shift, but that our data is so rough that we can not conclude very much from it. We certainly had not yet established a linear relationship between distance and velocity. In his mind, discussions of the age of the universe were not only philosophically unjustified, but scientifically premature.

In the sixties and seventies, Ambartsumian wrote more and more on philosophic subjects and on aspects of astronomy with philosophic implications. Although his later views were logical outgrowths of his previous ones, his emphasis changed somewhat. After 1960, for example, he rarely criticized non-Soviet astronomers and philosophers for their idealistic viewpoints. It is quite clear that he evaluated highly the work of such men as Jeans, Eddington, Jordan, and von Weizsäcker, his early criticisms and continuing reservations notwithstanding. In addition, he spoke in the late sixties much less frequently of the problem of homogeneity or inhomogeneity in the universe, recognizing that his position here had become weak. Instead, he concentrated on the problem of the possibility of formulating a single naturalistic picture of the universe and on the problem of astronomical evolution. In a paper given in 1968 at the Fourteenth International Congress of Philosophy in Vienna, Ambartsumian refined and developed his views on these subjects.[49]

Ambartsumian was always opposed to the building of models of the entire universe on the grounds that such efforts are premature. In a lecture in Canberra in 1963 he commented, "The character of these models depends so much on simplifying assumptions that they must be considered far from reality. I personally think that at the current stage it does not even make sense to compare these models with observations in a detailed fashion."[50] He continued to support his view with philosophical arguments. The philosophical principle at the bottom of his interpretation was the antireductionist principle of the transition of quantity into quality; that is, he believed that current physical theory is based on such a limited area of observation that the quantitative transition to truly cosmic scales will reveal qualitatively new physical regularities, laws that are as yet unknown. Like the biologist Oparin and many other Marxist scholars, Ambartsumian believed that objective reality consists of different levels of scale, with each level possessing its own physical principles. When astronomers erected models of the universe based on current physical theory, they were passing from a lower scale to a higher one, and their models thus failed to describe physical reality adequately.[51]

Ambartsumian believed that just as living organisms can not be reduced to the known principles of physics and chemistry, neither can the universe. He maintained that evidence of the inadequacy of contemporary physics to explain the large-scale phenomena of the universe was to be found in the supernovae: at present there are some grounds for thinking that the processes accounting for those explosions can not be explained in terms of existing physical laws, although astronomers disagree on this issue. The same is true of the energy sources in quasars, discovered in 1963.[52] Ambartsumian believed that the peculiarities of nature being found in supernovae, quasars, and pulsars called for a revolution in physics, and that for the first time since the days of Copernicus, Brahe, and Kepler physics would be overturned by data from astronomy. But even after that revolution occurred, Ambartsumian implied that he would remain skeptical of the universal model builders, since the universe was "infinite in the levels of its laws." Nature possessed a double-ended infinite diversity; in the microscopic realm, the subatomic particles are infinitely inexhaustible, as Lenin had emphasized, and on the macroscopic level, the universe itself is infinitely inexhaustible.

Another theme in Ambartsumian's writings after 1960 was his belief in the cardinal importance for astronomy of unstable objects. He had, of course, always emphasized unstable systems and unstable stars as keys to the understanding of the universe; such an approach underlay his early study of the evolution of stars, which has already been described. In 1952, he explained his emphasis on unstable objects in terms that were, again, close to the Marxist philosophical description of evolution as arising from conflicting forces:

> Why is the study of unstable states so interesting for cosmogony? It is well known that the important mover of every developmental process in nature is contradictions. These contradictions are displayed in an especially clear fashion when the system or body is in an unstable state, when there is a struggle of opposing forces, when the bodies are at turning points in their development. . . . This means that objects in unstable states deserve special attention. In recent years important success has been achieved in the study of unstable systems and stars.[53]

In 1969, reflecting on his own work on the evolution of stars, Ambartsumian commented, "Before the middle of the thirties . . . evolutionary ideas did not play an essential role in astrophysics, although the majority of astrophysicists knew very well that they were dealing with changing, developing objects."[54]

In sum, the strongest element of continuity in Ambartsumian's professional life, from his early emphasis on the birth and evolution of stars to his later emphasis on such rapidly changing phenomena in the universe as supernovae and quasars, has been the principle of astronomical evolution.

S. T. MELIUKHIN

In 1958 the Soviet philosopher S. T. Meliukhin published a volume entitled *the Problem of the Finite and the Infinite*, which displayed a greater willingness by Marxist philosophers to accept relativistic models of the universe than had been the case in previous years.[55] Meliukhin's work was a transition, a bridge between the older orthodoxy and a new readiness, even eagerness, on the part of some Soviet philosophers to combine dialectical materialism and factual discussions of recent astronomical evidence. Einstein appeared in Meliukhin's book as a defender, unwittingly, of dialectical materialism. This view of Einstein would in later years gain much strength.[56] Nonetheless, Meliukhin's interpretation of the universe was not a simple recognition of viewpoints previously considered inadmissible, but something of an independent statement.

Meliukhin organized the most interesting part of his discussion around the problems posed by Olbers' and Seelinger's paradoxes. It will be reasonable, therefore, to briefly consider these noted issues in astronomy.

In contrast to the finite universe of the Middle Ages, the Newtonian universe was considered to be made up of an infinitely large number of bodies in infinite Euclidean space. As Newton remarked, if a finite amount of matter were located in infinite space, the force of gravity would result in a tendency for all the matter to concentrate in one mass. By supposing that the number of stars and other celestial bodies was infinite, Newton avoided this problem, since an infinitely large set of bodies has no center. His view of an infinite universe became the standard interpretation of the late eighteenth and nineteenth centuries.

In 1826 H. W. M. Olbers pointed to a problem within the Newtonian universe that has come to be known as Olbers' paradox: If the total number of stars were infinite, then a terrestrial observer should see a sky of blinding brightness, a sheet of solid light. Since intervening stars would block those farther away from the earth, Olbers thought that the level of brightness should be equal to that of the sun in each direction, rather than infinitely bright. Attempts to solve this paradox occupied the efforts of a number of astonomers of the past century; even now it is of some interest, although the assumption of an expanding universe can account for the phenomenon. The point is not that there is no path out of the paradox (it can be avoided by assuming that the brightness of stars diminishes with distance from the earth, or by attributing certain types of relative motion to the stars, or by assuming that the universe changes in certain ways over periods of time), but that any one of the assumptions necessary for eliminating the paradox was, until Hubble's work on the red-shift, of a rather marked ad hoc nature. In other words, the assumption would be introduced for this reason alone without further supporting evidence. Each of the assumptions, furthermore, would have radical cosmological implications. Olbers himself believed that he could solve the puzzle by assuming the existence of dust clouds between the stars and the earth, which would obstruct the passage of light. We now know that Olbers' hypothesis could not provide the answer, since the dust would absorb energy from the stars until it eventually became equally incandescent.

The other paradox to which Meliukhin pointed as a preface to his attempt to provide a coalescence of dialectical materialism and modern cosmology was that of H. Seeliger in 1895. Seelinger maintained that if infinite matter were indeed distributed uniformly through infinite space, as Newton believed, the intensity of the gravitational field resulting from the infinite mass of the universe would also be infinite. Since no such gravitational field exists, the Newtonian assumptions must be incorrect. Seeliger attempted to solve the paradox by introducing to Newton's gravitational law a modification that would have perceptible effects only when very great distances are involved.

Upon reflection, it becomes clear that both Olbers' and Seelinger's paradoxes are merely different expressions of the problem of conceptualizing infinity, as are many of the major problems of cosmology. Yet this does not explain them away, since the infinitude of the universe was considered essential to the Newtonian universe.

Meliukhin realized that since the 1920s an escape from Olbers' paradox was available in the form of theories of the expanding universe (the relative motion away from the earth would result in a weakening effect on the stellar light), but he was reluctant to accept expansion as a phenomenon of the universe as a whole even though he was prepared, as we shall see, to accept it as a phenomenon within limited areas. Furthermore, the expansion theory, even as pure conjecture, did not satisfy him, since he believed it would solve Olbers' paradox only in terms of visibility; the wavelength of the electromagnetic radiation reaching the earth from the stars would be shifted from the band of light to that of radio waves as a result of the outward expansion, but the paradox would, Meliukhin thought, remain. (The problem of the threshold of measurability of radio waves would be relevant to this line of attack, but Meliukhin did not pursue it.)

Instead of explaining the paradoxes on the basis of a postulated expanding universe, Meliukhin posed other possibilities: the Lambert-Charlier model of a hierarchical universe (to be explained below) and the possibility of an interaction of the electromagnetic and gravitational fields with cosmic matter. As we will see the latter view was the one that Meliukhin preferred.

The Lambert-Charlier model, first suggested in the eighteenth century, consists of a universe organized in terms of systems or clusters of the first order, second order, and so on indefinitely, each succeeding system being of larger dimensions than the previous one. Thus, there would be galaxies, supergalaxies, and super-supergalaxies, ad infinitum. The Swedish astronomer C. V. L. Charlier showed how such a hierarchical model could, within the context of classical theory, avoid the problems of the Olbers and Seeliger paradoxes. Meliukhin, however, pointed out that in a hierarchical universe of the Charlier type an extrapolation to infinity would yield an average density of matter in the universe equal to zero, since the average density of matter at each higher level is lower than the preceding one; such "abolition" (uprazdnenie) of matter was to him unacceptable on philosophic grounds: "From this point of view even the very concept of space becomes inconceivable, since space does not have an existence independently of matter, it expresses the extension of matter. . . ." (p. 75). Thus, Meliukhin, like Aristotle and many subsequent thinkers, denied the existence of a void. Furthermore, Meliukhin observed, all those persons who have proposed a hierarchical universe have merely assumed its existence without asking how it came into being. According to dialectical materialism, no state of matter can be maintained indefinitely without change, since no "material system, no matter how great its dimensions, can be eternal. It arose historically from other forms of matter" (p. 178).

Meliukhin had turned away from two possible exits from the Olbers and Seeliger paradoxes: the concept of a universe that, as a whole, expands, and a hierarchical universe. What solution did he propose? He considered the most promising avenue of investigation to be the conversion of quanta of electromagnetic and gravitational fields into "other forms of matter." Accepting the equivalence of matter and energy inherent in relativity theory, Meliukhin believed that in both paradoxes the problem of excesses of electromagnetic or gravitational energy could be solved by the absorption of such energy "accompanying its transition into matter." Modern field theory, he observed, describes both gravitational and electromagnetic fields as specific forms of matter. No violation of the conservation laws is involved in posing the transformation of gravitational energy into matter, Meliukhin noted; such conversions in the reverse direction are evident in the conversion of the mass of stars into radiation. Therefore, Meliukhin believed that he had posed a possible solution to the paradoxes.

This candidate for a solution of the problem has not enjoyed much popularity in the Soviet Union, particularly since the expansion of the metagalaxy, supported by other evidence, solves the same problem. Furthermore, in order to accept Meliukhin's hypothesis one would have to reconsider the Second Law of Thermodynamics, which is usually interpreted as saying that electromagnetic radiations such as heat and light are at the bottom of an irreversible ladder. However, Meliukhin would probably not be dismayed by such a consideration, since "heat death" (*warmetod*) has been criticized by dialectical materialists on other grounds.[57]

Meliukhin criticized those relativistic models of the universe that included reference to the birth of the universe, but in contrast to a number of previous Soviet authors, he spoke positively of certain aspects of some relativistic models:

> In relativistic cosmology there are many rational points and profound propositions that must be utilized and further developed. . . . Even the very idea of a positive curvature of space deserves attention, for the possibility is not excluded that in the infinite universe there exist areas with a density of matter that is in keeping with a positive curvature of space. (p. 189)

Not only did Meliukhin find much that was rational in relativity theory, but he also believed that relativity theory supported dialectical materialism in stating that the characteristics of space-time are determined by the amount of matter within the continuum. Thus, "as incontrovertibly follows from the most important principles of the theory of relativity and dialectical materialism, space and time are forms of the existence of matter and without matter cannot have an independent existence" (p. 194).[58]

In view of his acceptance of general relativity theory, one is tempted to ask why Meliukhin did not rely upon one of the expanding relativistic models (categories II, III, and IV above) to explain the Olbers and Seeliger paradoxes, rather than introduce an otherwise unnecessary hypothesis. The answer to this question seems to be that this would have called for too great an area of expansion; a belief in a universe that expanded as a whole was to him still "antiscientific, contributing to the strengthening of fideism" (p. 195). Nonetheless, Meliukhin did not deny the expansion of the observable portion of the universe: "All the evidence points to the fact that our area of the universe is apparently in a state of expansion—regardless of its causes" (p. 196). Meliukhin was a rather interesting figure; while he was trying to adjust to modern science, he was still clearly an "ontologist," a Marxist philosopher who firmly believed that dialectical materialism reveals truths about nature. Meliukhin in the eighties continued to teach Marxist philosophy at Moscow University, and in 1985 he defended his ontological views at a conference on history and philosophy of science at Boston University.

If many Soviet scholars were willing to accept the concept of the expansion of the part of the universe that we can observe yet were not willing to accept an absolute beginning in time, one type of cosmological model among those being proposed was a logical candidate: a pulsating one. The reluctance of Soviet philosophers and astronomers to embrace such a model has been rather strange, considering the philosophic advantages that it possesses from their point of view; it is infinite in time and does not include a concept of the creation of matter such as the steady-state model supposes. It might, however, contradict the principle of the over-all evolution of matter, contained in dialectical materialism. Even the relatively unphilosophical Soviet astronomer I. S. Shklovskii found a pulsating universe philosophically flawed; he commented in a book written jointly with Carl Sagan, "The simple repetition of cycles in essence excludes the development of the universe as a whole; it therefore seems philosophically inadmissible. Further, if the universe at some time exploded and began to expand, would it not be simpler to believe that this process occurred just once."[59] Much could be said of this statement of Shklovskii's; it is quite possible, for example, to pose a pulsating universe without the absolute reduction of all matter to its most primitive state (type IId), as William Bonner in particular suggested. Some concept of evolution through successive cycles could then be rescued, although at this point such evolution would be conjecture.

With the increasing acceptance of relativistic models in Soviet cosmology after about 1960, the main issues shifted from criticism of those models as a group to a discussion of particular types within the group. In particular, the question of the type of curvature of space-time within the relativistic framework became pressing. The issue was usually seen, as already indicated, in terms of the observable portion of the universe. The problem of a model for the entire universe was, with some exceptions,[60] considered inappropriate for scientists. As A. S. Arsen'ev commented in an issue of *Problems of Philosophy* in 1958, "The natural sciences cannot answer the question, Is the universe infinite or finite? This problem is decided by philosophy. The materialist philosophy comes to the conclusion that the universe is infinite in time and space."[61]

The degree to which discussion of various cosmological theories broadened by 1962 was clearly indicated at a conference held at Kiev in December of that year. Called to inquire into the philosophic aspects of the physics of elementary particles and fields, the conference was attended by approximately three hundred philosophers and scientists.[62] Although cosmology was not the major concern of the meeting, reports by P. S. Dyshlevyi and P. K. Kobushkin on, respectively, the general theory of relativity and relativistic cosmology attracted considerable attention. Kobushkin, who agreed with Dyshlevyi's definition of space and time ("space and time are essentially the totality of definite properties and relations of material objects and their states"),[63] presented the report that was most pertinent to the cosmological issues discussed so far.[64]

Relying on the work of G. I. Naan, V. A. Ambartsumian, V. A. Fock, and Iu. B. Rumer, Kobushkin sketched out an approach according to which it would be possible for him to accept "closed" and expanding relativistic cosmological models, including the much-maligned Lemaître one, without contradicting the principles of dialectical materialism. The operation involved the addition of several interesting amendments, or possible amendments, to the existing models.[65]

In order to arrive at his goal of describing the metagalaxy as a "quasiclosed system immersed in the 'background matter' of an infinite Universe,' Kobushkin pointed out that certain hypothetical stars, those having densities similar to the white dwarfs and masses typical of the super-giants, would have, on the basis of the solution of the general relativity equations obtained by Oppenheimer and Volkoff, the following strange characteristics: material particles and light quanta that were ejected would go out only to a certain boundary, or "horizon," and then would return to the star.[66] The importance of this phenomenon was the following:

> This means that, from within, such a star may be considered a completely closed system with respect to its energetic interaction with the external world by means of such "carriers" of interaction as the usual material particles and light quanta.
>
> Therefore the metric of space-time near such stars is identical to that of spatial closedness. . . . Nevertheless, such a star is not an absolutely closed system; in actuality an interaction with other stars occurs by means of gravitons; this interaction with other stars is formally expressed in the . . . superposition of their gravitational fields. Moreover, such closedness of stars of this type is characteristic only for static fields of spherical symmetry, considered up to that moment of time when the surface of the star, during expansion, touches the "horizon" of (mathematical) solution. As soon as the physical surface of the star touches the "horizon" of solution, the metric of the field is "broken," so to speak, and it then becomes possible for there to be an energetic interaction of the star with the external world by means of normal material particles and light quanta. Henceforth, we will call the solutions of this type of equations in general relativity theory *semiclosed solutions*.[67]

Kobushkin believed that the possibility of such a solution of relativity equations for a star posed the further possibility of a similar solution for the metagalaxy. However, he realized that one of the difficulties with the analogy was that in the case of the hypothetical star cited above, the system would be closed in terms of normal material particles and light quanta, but not in terms of gravitational interaction, while the large cosmological models were considered closed in gravitational terms as well. However, Kobushkin questioned whether the closed cosmological models were, indeed, absolutely "closed." He posed the possibility of the existence of a new kind of particle (called "background particles," or following Rumer, "fundamentons") for which no "world horizon" would exist in the current closed cosmological models, just as there does not exist a "horizon" for the gravitons in the case of the massive super-dense stars already described. The introduction of particles with such strange properties would, Kobushkin thought, be "entirely consistent with the dialectical materialist thesis of the inexhaustibility of the different forms and properties of moving matter."[68] By postulating the existence of these new particles, he could further suppose the interaction of the gravitationally closed models of Einstein, de Sitter, and Lemaître with other parts of the infinite universe.

It might be appropriate to note, at this point, the inaccuracy of the view, expressed from time to time, that Soviet cosmologists could not accept big-bang or expanding cosmological models. Kobushkin in the above passage considered a big-bang and expanding model the most satisfactory of the existing models—with an important amendment about the extent to which the model is identical with the entire universe.[69]

One of the most interesting books on cosmology to appear in the Soviet Union in the sixties was the result of yet another conference of physicists and philosophers held in Kiev, also in 1964, and entitled *Philosophic Problems of the Theory of Gravitation of Einstein and of Relativistic Cosmology*. On first reading, the book seemed to be openly revisionist: its suggestions for changes in cosmological conceptions went beyond anything promoted in the Soviet Union since the end of World War II. Philosophically speaking, however, the book represented something of a return to an older tradition in Soviet Marxism, that of centering on the philosophic "categories" as the area of greatest flexibility within dialectical materialism with respect to the advance of science. An effort to clear the conference of the revisionist label was made by P. V. Kopnin with an opening quotation from Lenin, but the effect, combined with what followed, tended to justify necessary revisionism:

> The revision of the "forms" of materialism of Engels, the revision of his *naturphilosophie* views, not only is not "revisionist" in the accepted sense of the word, but, on the contrary, is necessarily demanded by Marxism.[70]

Kopnin, who was discussed on p. 20 as a reformer in Soviet philosophy, believed that it was time to consider a revision of certain Marxist categories, particularly those of the "finite and infinite," in order to bring Marxism in step with science. He did not doubt the possibility, nor the legitimacy, of making revisions to the categories of dialectical materialism. He pointed out that "contradictions between the content of the philosophic categories and new scientific evidence are connected with great, epochal discoveries," but recognized that the preceding fact does not "in principle exclude the possibility of such contradictions."[71] And the changes of the categories could go beyond "modification" of existing ones:

Since philosophy is a science and not an item of faith, the development of its categories is obviously subject to the general dialectical laws that it itself establishes; this evolution includes both change and clarification of the content of previous concepts and also the birth of new and the death of old concepts.[72]

This effort to modernize dialectical materialism, Kopnin remarked, must go beyond Engels to Lenin himself, who, despite his genius, by no means "did everything" in the direction of bringing dialectical materialism in line with modern science. Each man and each epoch has its own characteristics, and just as Engels and Lenin in their times attempted to incorporate the latest science into the Marxist world view, so must contemporary Marxist-Leninists. Kopnin observed that a revolution had occurred in science since the early twentieth century and in light of this it was only logical, according to Marxism, that such concepts as "finite" and "infinite" must be reexamined:

These categories were formulated a very long time ago, at the dawn of the development of scientific knowledge. Their content was defined in the period when natural science was hardly developed (antiquity, the Renaissance), when the mature concepts of astronomy and physics did not exist, and the only geometry was Euclidean.[73]

Kopnin went on to pose the possibility that the categories "infinite" and "finite" meant nothing other than the affirmation that matter can be neither created nor destroyed, but can, instead, be infinitely transformed into different forms. Such an equation of infinity with the principle of the conservation of matter had a considerable implication for the discussions of cosmological models. Kopnin observed that if dialectical materialists defined "infinity" in such a way that a certain type of metric of the universe was required, they would be repeating the old mistake of "dictating" to science rather than drawing upon it. He believed that dialectical materialists need not bind cosmology to specific geometric characteristics.[74]

Several other authors extended this argument to the point of maintaining, contrary to Soviet cosmology of the period immediately after World War II, that dialectical materialism requires the finitude of man's cosmological models. In the opinion of Sviderskii, this requirement flowed from the dialectical Law of the Transformation of Quantity into Quality. If one grants spatial extension to the limit of infinity, Sviderskii observed, such an enormous accumulation of quantity will surely result in a change in quality, namely a change in space-time structures. To maintain the opposite would be to "absolutize" a specific state of matter (its space-time metric); dialectical materialism is based, he said, on the change of the states of matter in accordance with the dialectical laws.[75] Sviderskii's views on the implications of this dialectical law were by no means accepted by all the other participants at the conference (S. T. Meliukhin and G. I Naan, in particular, objected to them), but his readiness to accept relativistic models, including those with Riemannian space-time, was common to most of the speakers at the conference, philosophers and scientists alike.

This conference was a further development of the ideas expressed at the 1962 meeting; together they marked a new stage in the development of Soviet cosmological discussions. No longer were Soviet cosmologists engaged primarily in polemics (usually unheard by the opposition) with non-Soviet writers. Very little time was spent at these gatherings in the old activity of sparring with the "idealistic views of bourgeois scientists." Instead, the dialectical materialist philosophers and scientists arrived at a point where their primary disagreements were among themselves rather than with scientists and philosophers living in other social systems. At the same time, among their arguments could be found, as before, consistent lines of thought, agreement on certain basic issues beginning, of course, with a commitment to the objective reality and materiality of nature.

In cosmology, the common themes that could be seen in the 1964 conference concerned, in particular, the belief that one should not refer to the metagalaxy as the universe as a whole. All of man's cosmological evidence stems, they said, from only a small part of the universe, and extrapolations from this portion to the entire universe are dubious speculations. The implication of this viewpoint was to cast into doubt the "cosmological principle," the belief in the homogeneity of the universe, an assumption upon which almost all existing models are built. Rejection of these models is not necessary, however, the Soviet authors usually maintained, since they may be perfectly adequate and helpful when applied to the metagalaxy. A further view on which there was agreement was that of the universal "connectedness" of the universe. In other words, one should not postulate the existence of "completely closed finite systems" within the universe—not for the metagalaxy nor for other systems. To do so would deny the integration of nature into a unitary whole. A final agreement—although somewhat less general than those just discussed—was the belief that a pulsating or oscillating metagalaxy would not, by itself, be a satisfactory exit from the cosmological problem since the existing forms of such models are based on endless identical repetition, in which stages are indistinguishable one from another. Such a hypothesis would contradict the principle of the evolution of nature, reverting man's scientific explanation of the universe to an entirely static mold, similar to the Aristotelian model as interpreted by the scholastic philosophers. Presumably a pulsating model that somehow preseved an evolving continuity between stages would be consonant with the dialectical materialist interpretation as expressed at the conference. This latter suggestion was an example of the inner flexibility of Soviet cosmology after the sixties. Almost any model under consideration by scientists anywhere in the world could be, with appropriate adjustments, fitted to the above philosophic requirements, although some more easily than others (the steady-state model would be rather difficult). This inner flexibility did not, however, reduce Soviet philosophy of science to the level of triviality, as some of its critics would maintain: the preferences of dialectical materialists concerning cosmology were still clear, even if they no longer possessed requirements. Furthermore, the same lack of requirements imposed on nature is characteristic of many other philosophic systems. A person might, therefore, be tempted to throw out philosophy and rely on "hard facts." The catch is that then we would almost surely not have something we could call science, and certainly not cosmology.

The degree to which one should rely on facts as opposed to philosophic considerations in constructing cosmological models was a subject of controversy in the Soviet Union, as elsewhere. An example of a person who veered to the side of philosophy at the 1964 conference, relatively speaking, was Sviderskii, while Naan spoke for more attention to science. Sviderskii chose to make statements such as:

> A consideration of the problem of the finite and infinite obviously attests to the fact that these concepts can be clarified only by means of philosophy; the very problem is in the competence first of all of philosophy, and not cosmology, as some people maintain.[76]

Naan looked at things from a different viewpoint:

> The position of dialectical materialism on the infinity of the universe is not a demand, but is a conclusion from the facts of natural science. The content and form of this conclusion constantly change. At first man established that the universe is infinite in the sense of practical infinity. Then it became clear that it is infinite in a deeper sense, in the sense of

unlimited spatial extension. Now we say it is infinite in space-time (but not at all in space and time!) in a still more profound, metrical sense. Topological and still more complex aspects of the problem force us once again to change the very way in which the issue is posed in dialectical materialism.[77]

Naan's emphasis on the determination of philosophy by science might seem to be fundamentally antiphilosophical in intent. Yet Naan, a philosopher himself, further maintained that philosophy can make "very significant contributions" on the issue of cosmological infinity, which was to him a "problem where the boundaries of mathematics, natural science and philosophy meet."[78] Naan clearly stated that his views were influenced by dialectical materialism: his belief in the validity of the "infinity" of the universe, according to a new definition, and his hope to construct "quasi-closed cosmological models" were both results, at least in part, he maintained, of his dialectical materialist viewpoint. With Naan we meet the issue that we have met with Soviet scientists such as Fock, Ambartsumian, Schmidt, Blokhintsev, and others. The degree to which dialectical materialism has been important to them is not something that the outside observer, particularly the observer who comes from a society that scoffs at dialectical materialism, can easily assess. In principle, it is no more difficult to believe that certain Soviet scientists have occasionally been affected in their researches by dialectical materialism than it is to believe that other significant scientists, such as Kepler, Newton, Poincaré, and Heisenberg have been affected in their work by philosophic preferences.

Naan's exposition of the relation of gravitation and infinity at the 1964 conference deserves additional attention. He began by taking note of the criticism of him by Sviderskii. According to the latter, several scientists and philosophers (E. Kol'man, A. L. Zel'manov, Ia. B. Zel'dovich, and Naan) were "attempting to make the conclusions of modern relativistic cosmology, especially the Friedmann model, agree with the requirements of dialectical materialism concerning the infinity of the universe in space and time,"[79] but had "accomplished" this at the cost of "absolutizing gravitation," a price that in Sviderskii's opinion was unacceptable from the standpoint of dialectics. Sviderskii hoped to accomplish the same goal, but by paying a different price: he would demote the gravitational field to the status of the electromagnetic field, to which certain kinds of particles are neutral. Sviderskii's approach, then, was similar to Kobushkin's, and indeed, Kobushkin had referred favorably to Sviderskii's 1956 analysis in his paper at the 1962 conference.

Naan disagreed strongly with this viewpoint. In contrast to the electromagnetic and nuclear fields, the gravitational field was, in his opinion, a universal form of the mutual influence of the forms of matter. This conclusion followed from the following analysis: Physicists had established the equivalence, to extremely exact degrees of measurement, of gravitational mass and inertial mass. Relativity physics had, furthermore, established the equivalence of inertial mass and energy. Therefore, maintaining the existence on nongravitating forms of matter, in the fashion of Sviderskii or Kobushkin, would mean the existence of forms of matter "that are deprived of energy, do not transmit any kind of information, do not take part in any kind of interactions, the existence of which is not evident anywhere or by any means. . . ."[80] To Naan, a postulation of this type violated modern physics "more strongly than the hypotheses of Milne, Jordan, and Bondi." He continued that Sviderskii's statement that science must not make an absolute of gravitation was a vestige of the recent past, when philosophers attempted to state flatly what nature could and could not be like: "The spirit of dialectical materialism is alien to such attempts; it takes nature just as it is."[81]

Naan hoped to achieve a model of a "quasi-closed metagalaxy" just as did Sviderskii, but by means that he considered more consistent with the scientific evidence. This model was based on the researches of Einstein and E. G. Straus on the gravitational fields of point particles, the work of I. D. Novikov on the metagalaxy as an "anticollapsing" system, and the Lambert-Charlier hierarchical model. Einstein and Straus in 1945 had sketched out the beginnings of a "vacuole" model in which point particles in the cosmological substratum are surrounded by expanding spherical vacuums.[82] They showed that the field created by such a point particle does not depend on the field created by the surrounding substratum. I. D. Novikov published in 1962 an article in which he maintained that the metagalaxy could be looked upon as a vacuole in a supermetagalactical expanding substratum. Such a metagalaxy would be an "anticollapsing system."[83]

Naan then combined this possibility with the Lambert-Charlier model, with the exception that it was made up of a hierarchy of relativistic "closed" models, rather than the three-dimensional Euclidean ones of the original Lambert-Charlier model. Naan postulated the existence of a whole series of expanding "bubbles" of vastly different scales. In this way he would combine "great homogeneity" with "extreme inhomogeneity" in a "dialectical unity."[84] The resulting model for our metagalaxy would be that of a vacuole immersed in the substratum that had a "closed" space-time "carcass" whose spatial intersection could be either finite or infinite. The borders of the vacuole would be a Schwarzschild shell,[85] which would not be an "insurmountable barrier" but on the contrary, a unidirectional barrier: it would permit signals to pass inward if the system were collapsing, outward if the system were expanding.

Thus, Naan had constructed a model called, like Kobushkin's, "quasi-closed," but resting on different principles. So far as the metagalaxy is concerned, it could be a relativistic model, finite in Riemannian terms, but nonetheless infinite in the sense that it existed within a larger system, which, in turn, existed within a still larger system. It was "infinite," said Naan, in a space-time sense (but not in terms of space and time taken separately). It was a part of unitary nature in that it could, in principle, transmit or receive signals to or from the "outside" (but not simultaneously). It was also, one might add, exceedingly complicated. It accomplished, however, Naan's goal, which was pre-serving a dialectical materialist interpretation of cosmology in the face of recalcitrant scientific evidence.

A. L. ZEL'MANOV

One of the most interesting recent Soviet writers on cosmogony has been Abram Leonidovich Zel'manov (1913–   ), a theoretical astron-omer at the Shternberg Astronomical Institute of Moscow University. A student of V. G. Fesenkov, who was previously discussed, Zel'manov from an early age has been interested in the application of the general theory of relativity to astronomy. In his attitude toward model building he has an extremely eclectic approach, granting the possibility of many types of cosmogonical models for different areas of the universe.[86] He has stoutly resisted any attempt to rule out a priori either "closed" or "open" models. He believes that outside the Soviet Union theoretical astronomers have been too willing to assume that the universe is homogeneous and closed.

Zel'manov, like many of his contemporaries, has a strong interest in dialectical materialism. He wrote in 1969, "Dialectical materialism has been and remains the only system of philosophical views that is at one and the same time logically consistent in a philosophic sense and harmonious with all of human practice."[87] Similar to Ambartsumian, he speaks of "qualitatively different" areas of the universe, pointing out that different physical forces predominate on different levels of being. Thus, he observed, the most influential kinds of forces on the microscopic level are nongravitational (the so-called "strong," electromagnetic, and "weak" ones) while on the cosmic level gravitational force is predominant. These different levels illustrate, he maintained in 1955, "the dialectical materialist position concerning the inexhaustibility of matter and the infinite multiformity of nature."[88]

One reason for his permissiveness on the question of model building for the metagalaxy was his belief that within the framework of modern physics the question of infinity in traditional terms is "almost trivial."[89] In order to choose a model, he observed in 1959, it is necessary to accept a congruence relation. In other words, in order to construct a model of the universe (or of any surface or volume), it is necessary to accept a convention about what constitutes a unit length in different places, at different times, or in different directions at the same time. By choosing different congruence relations, it would be possible to construct models of an unlimited variety of curvatures.

Zel'manov was critical of both those more orthodox dialectical materialists who resist certain cosmogonical models and also those astronomers, frequently non-Soviet ones, who uncritically accept the cosmological principle, upon which all popular relativistic models rely. In a 1964 article Zel'manov said that rather than assume a homogeneous, isotropic universe, one should notice the possibility of an inhomogeneous, anisotropic one.[90] The cosmological principle dictates, he said, that whatever the curvature of space (positive, negative, zero) it must remain a constant, since the curvature results from the amount, distribution, and movement of matter; if one assumes a universe that is uniform everywhere, the resulting curvature, whatever its sign, would be a constant.

Such an assumption of constant curvature was, to Zel'manov, a gross simplification; it forced the concepts of "closed" and "infinite" to be mutually exclusive. This exclusivity was true even though the Einsteinian theory of gravitation did not, by itself, give a unique answer to the question of the finiteness of the universe. The Einsteinian theory could be retained without forcing commitment on the question of infinity if cosmologists would not insist on unnecessary assumptions: "It is not necessary for cosmologists to supplement Einstein's theory of gravitation with any kind of simplifying assumptions such as those of homogeneity and isotropy."[91]

By posing an inhomogeneous, anisotropic universe, Zel'manov could provide many types of local space-time continuums, including both closed and infinite ones. Furthermore, the fact that the space (considered separately) in a space-time continuum may be infinite does not mean that the continuum as a whole fills the entire universe. As Zel'manov wrote:

> A space-time world, infinite in time and space, possibly does not occupy the whole universe: It may be part of another space-time world, spatially finite or infinite. The space-time world occupying the whole universe, on the other hand, may not be infinite in space and, moreover, may contain spatially infinite world areas. . . . It seems that the question concerning the actual situation, the one interesting us, remains open, and a consideration of homogeneous isotropic models, empty or not, will not give us an answer. But one can hardly expect that the properties of actual space will be simpler than that in simplified models.[92]

Zel'manov envisioned a new stage in physical theory, building upon relativity but going beyond it in the sense that relativity physics went beyond classical physics, introducing necessary corrections in the realm of great distances and velocities.[93] What were the ways in which Zel'manov thought that Einstein's theory of gravitation might be modified to affect cosmology? First, he noted that the cosmological models within the framework of Einsteinian relativity "exclude each other"; in other words, although all these models are relativistic, they describe "different universes." Since there can be, by definition, only one universe, all but one of the models should be false. Yet Zel'manov felt that there were advantages in more than one. He seemed to be hoping for a sort of "complementarity" in cosmology that would allow the possibility of combining mutually exclusive explanations, although he did not use the term. The different models would not be mutually exclusive, Zel'manov maintained, if each of them had its own congruence relation, its own space-time metric. Thus, he returned to the importance of congruence relations, saying that by utilizing various relations, different models could give different descriptions of one and the same universe and its various parts. This would involve giving up the concept of an "ideal standard" of length and time. Such a modification would have other implications:

> This [view] includes not only a change in the understanding of gravitational interaction, but also a change in the very concept of finiteness or infinity in space and time: This [new] finiteness or infinity can not be considered

metric, i.e., as a finiteness or infinity of cubic meters or parsecs or of the number of seconds or years.[94]

Thus, Zel'manov sketched out a model embracing many submodels. Without going further into the details of an exceedingly speculative subject, one can observe that many scientists would consider adopting the complex model that Zel'manov proposed only if there were reasons for that adoption other than the avoidance of a scientifically acceptable, considerably simpler, but philosophically unpleasant alternative. Quite a few scientists would consider existing models of constant curvature preferable in terms of scientific acceptability and structural simplicity, whatever the philosophic implications. Yet this observation does not belittle Zel'manov's major goal; the extrapolations of systems built on the basis of observable evidence to the entire universe (as all existing models are) are, as Zel'manov observed, dubious operations. And the philosophic obstacles involved in accepting a closed universe are troublesome to many scientists in many parts of the world.

In 1969 Zel'manov attempted to integrate his views on cosmology and cosmogony with a conception of all physical knowledge; in his opinion there exists in nature a "structural-evolutionary ladder" extending from the subatomic level to the universe.[95] This material, multiform ladder contains qualitatively distinct levels, but constitutes an interconnected whole. Its most distinguishing characteristic is its incredible variety. Indeed, Zel'manov recommended that scientists accept as a "methodological principle" the view that nature contains the entire multiformity of conditions and phenomena that accepted fundamental physical theories would permit. Hence, Zel'manov would imagine, heuristically, the presence somewhere in nature of all the forms of matter and all the cosmogonical models permitted by existing physical theory.[96] As physical theory changes over time, this hypothesized infinite reservoir of models would change in step, but Zel'manov saw no reason to rule out any model in advance.

In the late 1960s and early 1970s Soviet writing on the philosophic problems of cosmology and cosmogony continued to improve in quality. In 1969 there was published in Moscow an interesting volume of eighteen articles entitled *Infinity and the Universe*.[97] In this volume and in other articles an impressive effort was being made to reach a philosophic understanding of the structure and evolution of the universe. A strong link existed between several leading Soviet astrophysicists and philosophers. Among the scholars doing important work in 1969 and

1970 in this field were A. L. Zel'manov, V. A. Ambartsumian, G. I. Naan, V. V. Kaziutinskii, and E. M. Chudinov.[98] The first two, both of whom have already been mentioned, are distinguished natural scientists; the latter three are able philosophers of science. Ambartsumian and Kaziutinskii have published works jointly in an effort to blend the views of a professional philosopher of science and an astronomer.[99]

These writers all made careful distinctions between science and the philosophic interpretation of science. They maintained that they were ready to accept completely the evidence of science, no matter how upsetting it might be to previous conceptions, but said that they were convinced that this evidence could not only always be accommodated with dialectical materialism, but also was illuminated by it. Furthermore, just as they saw no threat to dialectical materialism in science, they also saw no threat to science in dialectical materialism. Kaziutinskii quoted approvingly the words of the Soviet physicist V. L. Ginzburg that dialectical materialism "does not and cannot place a taboo on any model of the universe."[100] Kaziutinskii believed that even Lemaître's hypothesis of an original exploding atom as the beginning of the universe could be accommodated with dialectical materialism after a few terminological clarifications had been made:

> We should not think that the idea of an explosion of a dense or superdense "primeval atom" is in itself idealistic. If it turns out that the metagalaxy (but not the whole universe!) formed in the way that Lemaître proposed, this would only mean that nature is more "odd" than it seemed earlier, and that it has posed for us still one more difficult question, the answer to which will be found, however, within the framework of natural science.[101]

Dialectical materialists had become so flexible on questions of cosmology and cosmogony that one might suppose that their philosophy had become irrelevant to their approach to nature. This conclusion would not be quite correct, however. They still sought to retain a concept of infinity, often in terms of time for the universe as a whole, but always, as a minimum, in terms of the "inexhaustibility" of matter as man studies it ever more carefully.[102] They differentiated between the words "infinite" and "boundless," pointing out that closed space-time possesses no boundaries "beyond which there must exist something nonspatial."[103] Quite a few of them continued to prefer inhomogeneous, anisotropic models of the universe, finding in them the richness and infinitude that they sought in material reality. And they continued to make a distinction between the observable portion of the universe and the universe as a whole.

Since its discovery in 1965 by A. A. Penzias and R. W. Wilson, cosmic background radiation has caused considerable excitement among cosmologists; increasingly, this radiation has been interpreted as the remnant of the primeval fireball in which the universe began. This development added considerable strength to the arguments of those cosmologists who favored big-bang models of the universe. Coming as it did at a time when the steady-state theorists were retreating on other grounds, most cosmologists, in the Soviet Union and elsewhere, moved toward some version of a big-bang theory. The discoveries of quasars and pulsars have also added valuable information to a field in which new observational evidence is often difficult to obtain. Evidence in astronomy coming from several different directions has recently substantially strengthened the case of those theorists who favor expanding, homogeneous, and isotropic models of the universe. These new findings have complicated the tasks of dialectical materialists like Ambartsumian who in earlier years favored inhomogeneous, anisotropic models. On the other hand, evidence favoring open models rather than closed ones has pleased many Soviet interpreters of cosmology.

V. S. GINZBURG

One of the most trenchant Soviet commentators on the relationship of physics and philosophy in the late seventies and the eighties has been Academician V. S. Ginzburg, an outstanding physicist who heads a department in the famous Lebedev Physics Institute of the Academy of Sciences. Ginzburg comes close to being a universal physicist, having done important research in a variety of fields of physics, including radioastronomy, superconductivity, optics, astrophysics, and cosmology. He is the author of several hundred works, and has received the Lenin Prize and several other awards. He has long been interested in the philosophy of science, and has frequently given popular lectures and appeared on Soviet radio and television.[104]

Ginzburg has been a member of the Communist Party since 1944 and he speaks favorably of the "materialist philosophy" of science. However, he is extremely critical of all attempts directly to link Marxist philosophy with science, making a sharp distinction between "scientific" and "philosophical" questions. In his opinion, any attempt to strengthen or to criticize a given scientific theory by referring to dialectical materialism is a mistake. Ginzburg, then, is an influenctial critic of that group of Soviet scholars called "the ontologists," the people who believe that Marxism bears on concrete topics within the specific sciences, rather than merely providing a mode of analysis of logical and epistemological questions.

Although Ginzburg recognizes that the intellectual atmosphere surrounding Soviet science has improved greatly since the days of Lysenko, he is quite frank in asserting that some dangers are still present. In a 1980 article he noted that the textbook *Foundations of Marxist-Leninist Philosophy* used in Soviet universities continued to contain statements that favored certain scientific hypotheses or theories over others, an intrusion which Ginzburg found inexcusable. As a specialist in astrophysics with a deep interest in cosmological models, Ginzburg's attention was drawn to the following phrases in the 1979 edition of this text, which was printed in 300,000 copies and was required reading for many university students:

> Matter is infinite in its spatial forms of existence.
> All assumptions of the finiteness of time inevitably lead to religious views about the creation of the world and time by God, an assumption that has been completely disproved by all the facts of science and practice.[105]

Ginzburg considered such statements to be a rejection of closed cosmological models "without any kind of scientific argumentation."[106] Ginsburg continued that it was incorrect to blame only Soviet philosophers for employing Marxism to influence scientific questions. He recognized—a rare event among Soviet natural scientists—that part of the blame must be placed on the scientists themselves, who sometimes tried to show that "their theories and activities are supported by dialectical materialism"[107]

In this connection, Ginzburg in the same 1980 article criticized his fellow scientist Ambartsumian (discussed on pp. 391ff.) for surrounding his particular interpretations of astronomy with reference to dialectical materialism and in that way creating the impression that the two are interdependent. He noted that Ambartsumian and his "Biurakan School" (Biurakan Astrophysical Observatory, located 35 kilometers from Erevan in Armenia, has been Ambartsumian's institutional base) tried to show on the basis of dialectical analysis that current astronomical evidence could not be explained within the framewwork of contemporary physics and that therefore a revision of basic physical concepts was necessary.[108] Ginzburg pointed to the dangers of this approach:

> If the Biurakan hypothesis is confirmed, this will be, doubtlessly, an important astronomical event and a great success for V. A. Ambartsumian. The significance which the author gives to philosophy and methodology will permit him in case of success to speak about the triumph of such a methodology. But what will happen if the Biurakan hypothesis is not confirmed and therefore shares the fate of many other astronomical hypotheses? It seems appropriate to emphasize that even in this event the philosophy of dialectical materialism would in no way suffer. We would have one more proof that the connection between philosophical and scientific views is not direct and is very delicate.[109]

Ginzburg here is making the subtle argument that, for the sake of both dialectical materialism and natural science, it is unwise to link dialectical materialism to specific scientific hypotheses. Dialectical materialism should be a metascience, a body of knowledge that stands above physics by generalizing the conclusions that physicists draw autonomously, but it should never contain such strong commitments to specific scientific hypotheses that when a given hypothesis proves incorrect dialectical materialism also suffers.

In a fascinating book in which he tried to identify the "most interesting and important problems of physics" Ginzburg touched upon a great variety of topics that have philosophical and methodological significance. Ginzburg called for tolerance of different viewpoints in scientific discussions and a willingness to allow scientific questions to be decided on scientific grounds.[110] He did not approve of the efforts of some Soviet physicists to try to answer physical questions on the basis of philosophy. Without naming Lenin, he even questioned Lenin's thesis that the "electron is inexhaustible," saying that he did accept the assumption that matter is like a "Russian doll" that can be endlessly opened up. On this question, Ginzburg differed with his fellow physicist Barashenkov. Ginzburg admitted that the case for quarks below the level of electrons was gaining more and more recognition, but said that whether the electron should be described as "consisting" of more basic elements was a physical question, not a philosophical one. Such physical questions, he continued, should be regarded as "open." Ginzburg represents, it is clear, one of the most outspoken opponents of the ontological view among Soviet scientists and philosophers currently writing on the philosophy of physics.

ZEL'DOVICH-NOVIKOV SCHOOL

In the late seventies and early eighties the most influential Soviet school of thought in cosmology was that of Ia. B. Zel'dovich and I. D. Novikov. Their reputation grew markedly in the West as well, especially after the translation into English in 1983 of two of their books, *The Structure and Evolution of the Universe* and *Evolution of the Universe*.

Iakov Borisovich Zel'dovich (1914–) is the leader of an internationally famous research team at the Space Research Institute of the Academy of Sciences of the USSR and is also a professor at Moscow University. For his work on a dazzling array of problems in chemical physics, gas dynamics, fluid dynamics, nuclear physics, astrophysics, and cosmology he has won many honors, both in the Soviet Union and abroad. He has been named a Hero of Socialist Labor three times, and has been awarded two Orders of Lenin. In 1970 he was elected the first chairman of the Cosmological Commission of the International Astronomical Union. He is a member of many international scientific societies.[111]

Zel'dovich's close associate Igor Dmitrievich Novikov was for many years a leading member of Zel'dovich's research group at the Space Research Institute and now heads his own team at the same institute. He also is a professor at the Moscow Physical-Technical Institute.

Zel'dovich and Novikov are representative of the newer breed of Soviet cosmologists in that they do not write about Marxism or dialectical materialism in their technical works. Indeed, they shy away from philosophical and historical questions in general, as if they know such issues can only cause trouble. In their 1983 English-language book they stated rather proudly that their "philosophy is that the history of the Universe is infinitely more interesting than the history of the study of the Universe."[112] This ahistorical and aphilosophical approach allows them to avoid many difficult problems connected with the ideologically fraught history of Soviet cosmology. Indeed, a Western reader of Zel'dovich and Novikov's works might even conclude that they have no connection whatever with ideological controversies, that they are "pure science." Such a conclusion would be incorrect. As Novikov admitted in the introduction to the Russian edition of one of his recent books, "Clearly, the basic conclusions of cosmology are of major significance for *Weltanschauung* in general."[113] But Novikov and Zel'dovich did not themselves draw the ideological conclusions that are inherent in their work, leaving that to others. Nonetheless, ideology is implicit in some of their writings.

One of the first ideological characteristics of Novikov and Zel'dovich's work that the perceptive reader will notice is that—contrary to many Western cosmologists—they do not speak of the "birth of the universe" even though they are ardent defenders of expanding models of that universe. Instead, their favorite phrase is "the beginning of the expansion." The question of the nature of the universe before that moment is left open. Although they occasionally use the term "age of the universe," much more frequently they speak of "expansion time" at points in their writings when a Western astronomer would probably say "age." Thus, they have chosen a vocabulary that is less amenable to religious exploitation than that of many of their Western colleagues, who seem to enjoy the drama inherent in such terms as the "birth" and "age" of the universe. Even in the 1980s, then, terminological differences with ideological antecedents can be found in the published works of leading Soviet and Western astronomers.

A Soviet philosopher of science emphasized in 1979 the importance of using the term "singular state" instead of "birth of the universe":

> The singular state at the beginning of the expansion of the universe fixes the extreme limit in the past to which it is possible to extrapolate the fundamental physical theories and concepts known to us. . . . But this is not the absolute "beginning of everything," but only one of the phases of the infinite self-development of matter. It arose in a way not yet studied by science out of some sort of previously existing state of matter.[114]

Zel'dovich and Novikov no doubt would criticize the above statement as an example of the ontological version of dialectical materialism they avoided, but their vocabulary fitted much better with the Marxist philosopher's viewpoint than that of many of their Western colleagues. In the Soviet tendency to avoid terms like "birth of the universe" and in the Western tendency to embrace such terms, two different sorts of ideological influences are at work.

In most respects, however, Zel'dovich and Novikov are absolutely in step with—or even leading—Western cosmologists. They both enthusiastically greeted the discovery in 1965 of "relict radiation," the leftover radio noise of the initial "big-bang." Novikov and a Soviet colleague A. S. Doroshkevich had even predicted a year earlier the amount by which the intensity of relict radiation should exceed the intensity of microwaves emitted by radio galaxies.[115] Zel'dovich and Novikov wrote in 1983 that "with respect to its overall features, one can consider as known the present state of the universe and that of its recent past."[116] That universe, they continued, is an expanding, homogeneous, isotropic universe in which "every particle (or its predecessor) has emerged from the crucible of the singularity." By "the singularity" they meant the moment at the beginning of expansion when the universe was super-dense and hot. In other words, Novikov and Zel'dovich are supporters of a variation of the big-bang theory of the universe.

Novikov and Zel'dovich's explanation of the universe is a rival to that of Ambartsumian (see pp. 391ff.), and is displacing it. Ambartsumian favored an inhomogeneous universe, while Novikov stated that there is "compelling evidence that the universe is the same in all directions."[117] Ambartsumian also predicted that the known physical laws would prove inadequate for the explanation of the universe, and—relying on the Marxist quality-quantity relationship—called for a "revolution in phys-ics." Novikov and Zel'dovich, on the other hand, believed that the present laws of physics, especially the general theory of relativity (GTR), are adequate for the tasks of modern cosmology, without a "revolution" in concepts:

> We do not agree with the "theories" appearing from time to time with features that violate the fundamental theories of physics. Such theories are, for example, those in which there is constant creation of matter "out of nothing" far from the singularity (the theory of the steady-state universe) or those which involve a decrease of the gravitational constant with time. . . . In short, we adopt the viewpoint that the homogeneous and isotropic universe can be explained within the realm of GTR.[118]

One sees here criticism going in two directions. In step with dialectical materialism, they oppose "matter creation" theories just as does Am-bartsumian and most other Soviet cosmologists. But they criticize Am-bartsumian for assuming, in accord with the Marxist principle of the existence of "different laws on different levels of being," that the explanation of the universe on the largest scale will require a new form of physics beyond GTR.[119]

Soviet cosmologists had demonstrated by the middle of the 1980s a rather striking ability to fit cosmological models into the system of dialectical materialism. These efforts to solve the cosmological problem, to find a model of the metagalaxy that would not violate certain philosophic principles, were not so dissimilar, in essence, from the efforts of many non-Soviet philosophers and scientists. When Michael Scriven, a philosopher in the United States, spoke of the "phases in the universe prior to the present 'expansion,' " or William Bonner, a British theoretical astronomer, spoke of his "preference for the cycloidal model," both were significantly influenced by nonempirical considerations.[120] They both were seeking a model in which a certain concept of infinity could be retained. Soviet cosmologists have experienced similar desires.

CONCLUDING REMARKS

Contemporary Soviet dialectical materialism is an impressive intellectual achievement. The elaboration and refinement of the early suggestions of Engels, Plekhanov, and Lenin into a systematic interpretation of nature is the most original intellectual creation of Soviet Marxism. In the hands of its most able advocates, there is no question but that dialectical materialism is a sincere and legitimate attempt to understand and explain nature. In terms of universality and degree of development, the dialectical materialist explanation of nature has no competitors among modern systems of thought. Indeed, one would have to jump centuries, to the Aristotelian scheme of a natural order or to Cartesian mechanical philosophy, to find a system based on nature that could rival dialectical materialism in the refinement of its development and the wholeness of its fabric.

The most significant function of dialectical materialism in the Soviet Union derives from the comprehensiveness of its conception and the intimacy of its connection with current scientific theory. As a system of thought it is not of immediate utilitarian value to scientists in their work—in fact, converted into dogma it has been a serious hindrance in several cases, although it may have indirectly helped in others—but it does have an important educational or heuristic value. Not only professional Soviet philosophers but many scholars and students in other fields as well have a concept of a unifying principle of human knowledge, the materialist assumption that lies at the base of dialectical materialism. It is not a provable principle, but then neither is it absurd. Soviet scientists as a group have, in fact, faced more openly the implications of their philosophic assumptions than have scientists in those countries—such as the United States and Great Britain—where the fashion is to maintain that philosophy has nothing to do with science. Perhaps out of a meeting of the approaches of Soviet and non-Soviet scholars a way can be found to admit that philosophy does indeed influence science (and vice versa) without allowing that admission to become exaggerated or subject to political manipulation in the way in which it frequently has been in the Soviet Union.

In terms of improving the intellectual position of a materialistic explanation of nature, it is clear that Soviet dialectical materialists have made genuine progress in certain fields, progress that to a degree offsets the damaging effects of their failure in genetics. Thirty or forty years ago the crucial questions that dialectical materialists faced were in the area of physics. The new ideas contained in quantum mechanics and the theory of relativity were upsetting to Soviet materialists, as they were to many other traditional thinkers. The dialectical materialists worried about the effects the new physics would have on assumptions that they had previously considered secure: belief in the existence of objective reality, the principle of causality, and the material foundation of reality. Today it is clear that this phase of anxiety has passed. No one knows what the future of physics will bring—and the nature of science is to bring crises—but at the present moment the philosophical problems in physics are much less difficult for dialectical materialists than they were thirty years ago. It is simply not true, as was frequently maintained several decades ago, that relativity physics and quantum mechanics "destroy materialism at its base." These areas of physics no longer contain unique threats to the assumptions of objective reality, causality, and the primary significance of matter. In terms of the new materialist interpretations of nature, relativity and quantum physics support a more satisfying explanation of natural phenomena than Newtonian physics can yield.

The works of such men as Fock, Blokhintsev, Omel'ianovskii, and Aleksandrov are important in this respect, although somewhat different in content. They pointed out that in the light of modern physics, thinkers should give up determinism in the Laplacian sense, but not causality in general. If there were no causality in nature, all possible outcomes of a given physical state would be equally probable. We know very well that according to quantum mechanics the real situation is far from such absolute indeterminism. A concept of causality, based on probability, can still be maintained. Many thinkers continue to find such a causal concept necessary for an understanding of nature. Once accustomed to it, they usually consider it vastly superior to the rigid Laplacian view.

Other Soviet scholars have turned attention to the fact that in general relativity theory the role of matter is not smaller than in classical (Newtonian) physics, but greater. The density of matter in the universe, according to general relativity, determines the configuration of space-time. Matter therefore acquires a significance of which eighteenth- and nineteenth-century materialists could not have dreamed. It is true that the principle of the interchangeability of matter and energy contained in relativity theory seems to demote matter in status (why, for example, should it be considered more important than energy?), but there is another side to the coin that strengthens the convictions of dialectical materialists. Having accepted this interchangeability, they now consider matter and energy synonymous (matter-energy), and proceeding on the basis of the primacy of matter-energy, they do not encounter the ancient problem of the void faced by classical materialists. All voids apparently contain fields of some kind, at least a gravitational one, and therefore a form of matter-energy. The very concept of the void as something that can exist in the real world is therefore thrown into question.

The originality of Soviet dialectical materialism compared to other areas of Soviet thought is not only a result of the talent of a number of Soviet dialectical materialists; it also derives from the nature of classical Marxism and the breathtaking rapidity of the development of science itself. Marx wrote a great deal about society, but very little on natural science. The brilliance of his original statements on society overshadowed all subsequent efforts by his supporters in political and economic theory. Before 1917, the system of historical materialism was much more developed than the system of dialectical materialism. Engels, of course, wrote extensively on philosophy of nature and in that sense launched dialectical materialism, but his efforts were rather quickly rendered inadequate by the revolutionary development of scientific theory at the turn of the nineteenth and twentieth centuries. After 1917, Soviet dialectical materialists were forced to seek new paths toward an understanding of nature, because scientific theory itself was already flowing along a new path. Deprived of an adequate Marxist explanation of nature and faced by a revolution in science, Soviet dialectical materialists during the past sixty years have made in philosophy of science an innovative effort that stands out in sharp contrast to other Soviet intellectual efforts.

Perhaps even more significant as a reason for the Soviet achievement in philosophy of nature as compared to other areas of thought in the USSR was the system of Communist Party controls over intellectual life, a system that left more room for initiative in scientific subjects than in political ones. The best minds went into scientific subjects, and some of them, naturally enough, were attracted to the philosophic aspects of their work. In the peculiar Soviet environment the esoteric nature of the discussions of dialectical materialism has been something

of a boon to writers, screening away censors. Among those authors
who write on dialectical materialism, the sections of their works of the
highest quality are frequently buried in rather technical discussions.
Those scientists who came to dialectical materialism in the late 1940s
for the purpose of defending their science against Stalinist critics found
that interesting work was possible in the philosophy of science. The
Communist Party officials continued to consider themselves experts on
theories of society, and still crudely intervene today in such discussions.
They learned, after several very injurious experiences, that intervention
in the knotty problems of scientific interpretation is an exceedingly
risky business. Their relative tolerance in this particular field after Stalin's
death had two oddly contrasting effects: some scientists abandoned
conscious consideration of philosophy once they were no longer constantly forced to show the relevance of dialectical materialism to science;
others turned to it with new interest as they saw that there was an
area of wide dimensions, intellectually speaking, in Soviet philosophy
where some innovation is possible.

Of all the issues discussed in this volume, the one that carries with
it the greatest continuing difficulty for dialectical materialists is the one
over human biology discussed in chapters 6 and 7. This issue is still
a critical one for dialectical materialists, and it is impossible at this time
to predict how it will be resolved. It is true that "nurturist" views on
human behavior played a much smaller role in the writings of the
founders of dialectical materialism—Marx, Engels, Plekhanov, Lenin—
than they did in the Stalinist version of that philosophy, but nurturism
remained the favored Soviet view long after Stalin's death. Even today,
it is the preferred (although besieged) explanation of human behavior
in the Soviet Union. Yet nurturism is not best described as a Stalinist
doctrine, since it is favored by liberals and reformers all over the world,
for eminently humane reasons. The debate over nature versus nurture
currently occurring in the Soviet Union is, therefore, both a Soviet and
an international debate, and intellectuals of every political persuasion
have an interest in its outcome. If it turns out that naturism must be
given greater credit than previously thought, as the present evidence
seems to indicate, Soviet dialectical materialism will suffer another
defeat. Nonetheless, materialism as a philosophical doctrine could easily
adjust to naturism. Indeed, it would be a victory for traditional (non-
Soviet) materialism if it turns out that human behavior must be explained
in terms of the material carriers of heredity to a greater degree than
was earlier thought justified. Such a conclusion might have unfortunate

effects for society, but it would not be a threat to philosophical materialism.

In retrospect, it is clear that the controversies discussed in this volume reveal very different, even contradictory, aspects of Soviet society. If one is interested primarily in the way in which the Soviet system of political controls over intellectuals created a situation in which unprincipled careerists could gain extraordinary influence in a few scientific fields, then one should turn to the Lysenko affair. Here one can find abundant evidence of the damage done to science by a centralized political system in which the principle of control was extended to scientific theory itself. The Lysenko affair was one of the most flagrant denials of the right of scientists to judge the validity of scientific theory to occur in modern history. The intensely political character that science assumes in all countries is no justification for the intrusion of controls on the judgment of the adequacies of rival scientific explanations. That decision must belong to scientists.

My major goal in writing this volume was not, however, the recounting of this repressive side of the story of Soviet science; for those readers seeking this aspect, I would recommend the books on Lysenko by David Joravsky and Zhores Medvedev. Instead, I have sought to emphasize the more philosophically interesting, rather than the politically dramatic, aspects of the relation between Soviet philosophy and science. In looking through the literature of the past forty years, I have tried to center my attention on the publications of the best intellectual quality, not the worst. I would do the same if I were studying the relation of Cartesianism to science in the seventeenth and eighteenth centuries, or of Aristotelianism to science in the Middle Ages.

In a commentary on one of my articles on Soviet science the Soviet physicist V. A. Fock wrote ("Comments," pp. 411–13) that Graham paid his "main attention to that part of the discussion which proceeded at a higher scientific level and not to articles and viewpoints rightly described by him [Graham] as 'offensive parodies of intellectual investigations' (particularly numerous in the dark period from 1947 to the early 1950s)." This emphasis meant that I rarely found pertinent items of interest in newspapers, popular political journals, or textbooks of Marxism-Leninism; instead, I looked to the serious monographs and journal articles of Soviet scholars and, wherever possible, to those of natural scientists.

In the eyes of certain of my readers this approach may not seem justified. Those persons who are convinced that all references to dialectical materialism by Soviet scientists have been nothing more than responses to political pressures will doubt that anything worthwhile can be accomplished by studying the work in which these scientists have attempted to illustrate the relevance of Marxist philosophy to their work. I am convinced, however, that quite a few prominent Soviet scientists believe that dialectical materialism is a helpful approach to a study of nature. They have examined many of the same problems of the interpretation of nature that philosophers and scientists in other countries and periods have also examined, and they have slowly developed and refined a philosophy of nature that would almost certainly continue to survive and evolve even if it were no longer propped up by the Communist Party. Only by concentrating on scientific literature, rather than on political or ideological sources, can this independent, unofficial side of dialectical materialism be revealed. By recognizing the intellectual sources of much Soviet writing on dialectical materialism, one can begin to understand why there have been such wide disagreements among Soviet scientists on philosophical interpretations of such issues as the physiology of perception, the nature of the universe, and the uncertainty relation of quantum mechnics.

When in 1972 I published the first edition of this study on the subject of dialectical materialism and Soviet science it appeared that Soviet scientists and philosophers were successfully breaking away from earlier rigid controls and that they were entering a new and much more free period. Unfortunately, these hopes have not been justified. On the contrary, during recent years political controls over Soviet scientists have been tightened again. While dialectical materialism remains an intellectually interesting doctrine, on a political level it has been damaged—probably beyond the point of salvage—by the fact that it is the doctrine of an oppressive, nondemocratic state. In the hands of official ideologists (as opposed to serious scientists and philosophers) it has become, in effect, a state religion. There is little chance that intellectuals in the politically free parts of the world will give dialectical materialism the serious attention it deserves when its strongest exponent is a state that denies its intellectuals elementary civil rights such as the freedoms of expression, political choice, and travel. Sciences such as psychiatry continue to be perverted in the Soviet Union by being made the instruments of political authorities. Dissidents have been declared insane on the grounds that any healthy person would recognize the virtues of the Soviet system. Scientists who defend democracy and human rights, of whom Andrei Sakharov is the best known, have been persecuted.

The authoritarian policies of the USSR have caused many intellectuals there to lose interest in dialectical materialism and in Marxism in general. What was once a liberating and innovative doctrine has become, on the official level, a scholastic and orthodox one.

Most of the controls over Soviet science today touch the political activities of individual scientists, not the internal content of science itself. Thus, so long as a Soviet scientist does not question the Soviet system or argue against Soviet foreign and domestic policy, he or she can write rather freely on science and even on philosophy of science. However, in recent years the danger of increasing dogmatism even on internal intellectual issues has grown, along with the steady accretion of the power of the "epistemologists," as discussed on p. 61. No return to the rigid intellectual controls of Stalinism is indicated, but then neither is the arrival of a period of intellectual freedom in which all issues of dialectical materialism can be explored without fear of Party intervention.

Before turning to a few final observations about the controversies discussed in this volume, it is appropriate to observe that contemporary dialectical materialism possesses several very serious weaknesses. Aside from the political obstacles it still faces in the Soviet Union, the most critical of these, one that seems to be a systemic failing, is the weakness of its defenses against critics standing on the position of philosophic realism. Many scientists and philosophers around the world completely agree with the position of dialectical materialism on the existence of objective reality, but simultaneously decline to consider themselves dialectical materialists. One of the best ways to illustrate their reasons for this refusal is to analyze Lenin's definition of matter:

> Matter is a philosophic category for the designation of objective reality which is presented to man in his sensations, an objective reality which is copied, photographed, or reflected by our sensations but which exists independently from these sensations. (see p. 42)

A philosophic realist can reply to Lenin that he agrees completely that objective reality exists, that there also exist "objects outside the mind," and that there is nothing supernatural in the world. But where, he can continue, did this word "matter" come from? The realist will then observe that he prefers the term "objective reality" to "matter," since it is clear to him that such entities as consciousness and abstractions are real, but it is far from clear to him that they are material.

The criticism of the philosophic realist reveals that the Leninist definition of matter characterizes its relation to the subject and does not contain a definition of matter itself. There is good reason to believe that Lenin realized this very well, but adopted a "relational definition" of matter nonetheless, since all alternatives to it were much more susceptible to attack. The point is that Lenin's definition of matter is both the strength and the weakness of dialectical materialism. The definition is strong because it does not depend on the level of development of natural science and thereby acquires much greater permanence. If dialectical materialists attempted to define matter itself—that is, in terms of the totality of its properties—this would mean that eventually the definition would become obsolescent as our knowledge of those properties changed, just as all definitions of matter given by previous materialists have become obsolescent (for example, those of the Greek atomists, who thought of matter in terms of indivisible units). Lenin considered matter to be inexhaustible in its properties and therefore undefinable in terms of them. This belief is one of the most significant differences between dialectical materialism and mechanistic materialism. The Leninist position avoided the built-in obsolescence of previous definitions of matter, but at the same time opened up dialectical materialists to the criticism that they have no clear way of demonstrating the superiority of the term "matter" to "objective reality."

Strictly speaking, of course, Lenin did not give a definition of matter. The principle of the materiality of the universe does not flow out of the Leninist position on epistemology quoted above. It constitutes, instead, a separate assumption. The assumptive character of materialism is not quite the fatal flaw that its opponents might try to make of it, since all conceptual systems contain some assumptions. Human beings cannot pursue their unique goal of trying to understand without paying the price of making some assumptions. It is a question of choosing one's assumptions carefully and remaining open to other possibilities. One can argue (for example, on the grounds of economy) that some assumptions are more justified than others; furthermore, one can defend materialism against realism on precisely this basis. But the assumptive character of materialism does mean that dialectical materialism does not uniquely flow out of the facts of science, as some of its defenders would maintain.

Turning now to the chapters of this volume and the problems of interpretation of nature described there, we can easily see that they contain many falsely inflated disputes and many examples of attempts at manipulation by political ideologues of issues that belonged to philosophers and scientists. Nonetheless, in all the issues except the

Lysenko controversy over genetics and the resonance chemistry dispute, genuine intellectual questions were contained within the frameworks of the over-all debates. And even in the chemistry discussion—prompted by a crude emulator of Lysenko—there was the very real problem of the significance and meaning of models in nature. The Lysenko affair alone was totally artificial from an intellectual standpoint; the few legitimate scientific and philosophic issues raised there either were outdated or were misunderstood by the supporters of Lysenko. I think that this assessment will stand even if, contrary to current scientific evidence, the inheritance of acquired characters should become accepted in future biology. Lysenko was incapable of understanding the biology of his time. It would be both ahistorical and inaccurate to try to defend him in the name of future biology. Such a defense of the theory of inheritance of acquired characters would be another matter.

In all the disputes discussed in this volume except for the Lysenko controversy we frequently found talented scientists who fully understood modern science making plausible arguments while connecting them with dialectical materialism in ways that do not seem to have been merely the results of political pressure. Some of these opinions were "wrong," as judged by contemporary science, to be sure, but they are frequently still understood by contemporary scientists as legitimate and reasonable points of view in the context of their times. Some of them are quite relevant even now, and more are being developed.

Among the Soviet scholars' viewpoints that have been recognized as valuable, either in their time or at the present time, and in which dialectical materialism may have played a role are: L. S. Vygotsky's opinions on thought and language; A. R. Luria's and A. N. Leont'ev's theories of social psychology; S. L. Rubinshtein's concepts of perception and consciousness; P. K. Anokhin's revision and extension of Pavlovian physiology; V. A. Fock's and A. D. Aleksandrov's criticisms of certain interpretations of quantum mechanics and relativity; D. I. Blokhintsev's philosophical interpretation of quantum mechanics; O. Iu. Schmidt's analysis of planetary cosmogony; V. M. Ambartsumian's views of star formation and criticisms of certain cosmological theories; G. I. Naan's "quasi-closed" cosmogonical models; A. L. Zel'manov's view of a "man-ifold universe"; many Soviet criticisms of the concept of an absolute beginning of the universe or of a nondevelopmental cyclical one; A. I. Oparin's views of the origins of life and his criticism of mechanism in biology; and a number of Soviet philosophers' and scientists' views on cybernetic evolution of matter.

Yet one should be very careful about assuming that the scientific views of any specific one of the above Soviet scientists were, in fact, importantly influenced by dialectical materialism. Above, I said that dialectical materialism "may" have played a role in the intellectual development of these scientists, not that it had in any identifiable case. There is, indeed, no way of demonstrating beyond a doubt that the views of a particular scientist were importantly influenced by intellectual Marxism. Such demonstrations are not in the nature of intellectual history in general, completely aside from the question of Marxism. We can show that a scientist held idea x, as evidenced in his writings, and we often can show that he stated in print that there was a connection between x and concept y in Marxism as he interpreted it. But there is no way that we can prove an actual causal link between x and y. There are, in fact, many possible explanations besides that of true intellectual stimulation. The scientist may have come upon idea x independently and then used y merely as a supporting argument. He may have created such linkages for no other reason than the political pressure being exerted upon him. He may actually have used such linkages merely for the purposes of his career, aware that a scientific interpretation that could be called Marxist would have a better chance of receiving official favor.

What justification do I have, then, for advancing the interpretation that Marxism was important as an intellectual influence in Soviet science? My interpretation derives primarily from the impression given by reading enormous amounts of Soviet literature on philosophy and science written at times of greatly varying political pressures. I have tried to describe the characteristics of that literature in the previous chapters. It is my opinion that when one looks not at any one scientist and his views, but at the total corpus of the writings of the scientists mentioned above, one is justified in observing that their interpretations of science, and even, in some instances, their scientific research itself, demonstrates characteristics that, one can persuasively argue, derive in some degree from dialectical materialism. Furthermore, there is no clear relation between political pressure and the moments when the Soviet scholars wrote on dialectical materialism. Many Soviet scientists continue to write on dialectical materialism today, while many more never do. It is possible in the Soviet Union for a scientist to ignore totally dialectical materialism in his or her publications, a fact that should cause us to take more seriously those who continue to devote attention to it.

In the final analysis, the problem of causation in this study of science and Soviet Marxism is not fundamentally different from that in other areas of intellectual history and in other countries. Philosophy and politics influence scientists in all countries. The filiation of ideas is an extremely difficult process to study, but the attempt is worthwhile. Furthermore, dialectical materialism deserves particular consideration by historians and philosophers of science by virtue of its more intimate interaction with science than any other current in contemporary philosophy.

A sophisticated materialism that is open to criticism and debate, of which dialectical materialism might some day become a true form, is a philosophic point of view that can be helpful to scientists. It is most valuable to the scientist when his research approaches the outermost limit of knowedge, the area where speculation necessarily plays the greatest role—the approach to the cosmic, the infinite, or the origins or essence of forms of being. It is least valuable, and quite capable of being crudely used with harmful results, when applied to the immediate, the next stage of research. Dialectical materialism could not help a scientist with the details of laboratory work. It would never predict the result of a specific experiment. It certainly would never tell him how to raise crops or treat mental illness. But it might warn him not to fall prey to mysticism in the face of the sometimes overwhelming mystery and awe the unknown. Through its nonreductionism it might remind him how contradictory and difficult the explication of nature is and how dangerous it is to reduce the complex phenomena on one level to combinations of simple mechanisms on a lower level. It might warn him that the sudden appearance of anomalies in research is not reason for discarding a realist epistemology or a commitment to the existence of at least some regularities in nature, whether probabilistic or strictly deterministic. It might remind him, through its emphasis on the interconnectedness of nature, of the importance of an ecological approach to the biological world and of the significance of the historical view for an understanding of the development of matter. It might encourage him to erect temporary explanatory schemes larger than any one science, but ones that do not pretend to possess final answers. At the same time, it might also assure him that the retention of commitments to epistemological realism and natural order is by no means a renunciation of art or mystery in nature. Nothing is more baffling than the ingenuity of man and his creations and the beauty of nature, of which man is a part. A sophisticated materialism could handle such considerations equally as well as a sophisticated idealism, and would start from assumptions that are more consonant with the naturalism implicit in most science.

NOTES

1. HISTORICAL OVERVIEW

1. Materialism and atheism are related but not synonymous concepts. Certain materialists, notably in the seventeenth century, combined materialism and theism. Hence I have said here that materialists avoid religious elements in scientific explanations, not that they necessarily deny the existence of God. Materialism in recent times, however, has usually been, explicitly or implicitly, atheistic.

2. One might maintain that the aspect of dialectical materialism that was relevant in the biology controversy was the principle of the unity of theory and practice; according to this interpretation, Lysenko was much more willing than the classical geneticists to apply his theory to the betterment of Soviet agriculture. This point will be discussed in the genetics chapter. In the meantime, one might note that the principle of the unity of theory and practice is based on an unstated concept of time. Any theoretical development in science should be quickly applied, said the dialectical materialists, but how quickly was not specified. Obviously the application of a theory cannot in every case be simultaneous with its development. Premature widespread application would result in great waste. Therefore, the whole question of applying theory becomes subject to discussion. In a rational atmosphere this discussion would revolve around criteria such as completeness of the theory, expenses and risks involved in attempts to apply it, and gains to be obtained from application. From the standpoint of such criteria, the Soviet geneticists of the thirties were not noticeably guilty of divorcing theory from practice. Indeed, Nikolai Vavilov, Lysenko's opponent, was devoted to the union of theory and practice in the best Marxist sense: he wished to combine the highest scientific principles with a commitment to the betterment of society through science. Lysenko, on the contrary, caused great harm to Soviet agriculture.

3. See, for example, Zirkle, *Evolution, Marxian Biology and the Social Scene.*

4. As L. C. Dunn commented, belief in the inheritance of acquired characteristics "solaced most of the biologists of the nineteenth century." *A Short History of Genetics,* p. x.

5. See Joravsky, *The Lysenko Affair,* and Medvedev, *Rise and Fall of Lysenko.*

6. De Broglie would find causality by replacing current quantum theory by a theory (pilot-wave or, later, double-solution) that would restore classical concepts. Ernest Nagel would consider existing quantum theory "causal." See the latter's "The Causal Character of Modern Physical Theory," pp. 244–68; and *The Structure of Science,* pp. 316–24. These issues will be discussed at much greater length in the chapter on quantum mechanics.

7. See ch. 4, note 27.

8. See my *Soviet Academy of Sciences and the Communist Party*, particularly chs. 4 and 5.

9. For Soviet criticism, see Frolov, *Genetika i dialektika*, especially pp. 10–16 and 61–68. See also, for a contrasting view, Paul, "Marxism, Darwinism and the Theory of Two Sciences," pp. 116–43.

10. Egorshin, "Estestvoznanie i klassovaia bor'ba," p. 135.

11. Quoted in Frolov *Genetika i dialektika*, p. 68.

12. *Ibid.*, p. 66.

13. See Bauer, Inkeles, and Kluckhohn, *How the Soviet System Works*, pp. 114, 116–17, and 118–19.

14. See, in particular, the Introduction and chs. 1, 2, 3, and 5 of Bukharin, *Historical Materialism*, pp. 9–83 and 104–29.

15. The literature on the origins of the cold war is enormous, and no attempt can be made to list or summarize it here. For an example of the revisionist literature, see Alperovitz, *Atomic Diplomacy: Hiroshima and Potsdam*. Discussions of the issue, from somewhat different viewpoints, are in Schlesinger, "Origins of the Cold War," pp. 22–52; and Morgenthau, "Arguing About the Cold War," pp. 37–41.

16. See, for example, Thomas Kuhn, *The Copernican Revolution*, pp. 198–99.

17. See, especially, "Lysenko and Zhdanov," in the first (1972) edition of this book, *Science and Philosophy in the Soviet Union*, pp. 443–50. See also, Hahn, *Postwar Soviet Politics*.

18. An example of the cooperation of philosophers with scientists in the defense of science can be found in the second issue of the new journal *Problems of Philosophy*, created in 1947, when the ideological scene was already becoming strained. This issue contained an article by the theoretical physicist M. A. Markov strongly defending quantum mechanics and one by the biologist I. I. Schmalhausen clearly directed against Lysenko. After Zhdanov's death the editorial board of the journal was criticized by Pravda for publishing these articles, and the editor was replaced. See pp. 15 and 325.

19. Maksimov, who received his education as a physicist, might be an exception here, since he was considered by some people to be a philosopher of science. David Joravsky described him as a "physicist to philosophers, a philosopher to physicists." Joravsky, *Soviet Marxism and Natural Science*, p. 185.

20. Ginzburg, *O fizike i astrofizike*; Kapitsa, *Eksperiment, teoriia, praktika*; Markov, *O prirode materii*; and Barashenkov, *Problemy subatomnogo prostranstva i vremeni*. See discussion on pp. 351, 421–423.

21. See Omel'ianovskii, *Dialektika v sovremennoi fizike*; Chudinov, *Teoriia poznaniia i sovremennaia fizika*, *Priroda nauchnoi istiny*, and *Nit' Ariadny: filosofskie orientiry nauki*; Krymskii, *Nauchnoe znanie i printsipy ego transformatsii*; Mamchur, *Problema vybora teorii*; Stepin, *Stanovlenie nauchnoi teorii*; Bazhenov, *Stroenie i funktsii estestvennonauchnoi teorii*; Akhundov, *Problema preryvnosti i nepreryvnosti prostranstva i vremeni*; Gott and Nedzel'skii, *Dialektika preryvnosti i nepreryvnosti v fizicheskoi nauke*; Panchenko, *Kontinuum i fizika*; *Fizicheskaia nauka i filosofiia*; *Teoriia poznaniia i sovremennaia fizika*; *Filosofskie problemy estestvoznaniia*; *Filosofskie voprosy fiziki*; and *Fizicheskaia teoriia (filosofsko-metodologicheskii analiz)*.

22. Akhundov, Molchanov, and Stepanov, "Filosofskie voprosy fiziki," p. 239.

23. For overviews of Soviet philosophy of science and bibliographies of work in this period, see: *Filosofiia, estestvoznanie, sovremennost': itogi i perspektivy issledovanii 1970–1980; Filosofskie voprosy estestvoznaniia: obzor rabot sovetskikh uchenykh; Filosofskie voprosy sovremennogo estestvoznaniia: ukazatel' literatury 1971–1979*.

24. Ukraintsev and Platonov, *Problemy otrazheniia v svete sovremennoi nauki*. Also, see Ukraintsev's "Ob osnovnykh napravleniiakh issledovanii v institute filosofii AN SSSR." For more on Platonov's neo-Lysenkoism, see pp. 153ff.

25. See Graham, "How Valuable are Scientific Exchanges with the Soviet Union?" pp. 383–90, and sources cited therein; and Lubrano, "Caught in the Crossfire," pp. 12–16.

2. DIALECTICAL MATERIALISM IN THE SOVIET UNION: ITS DEVELOPMENT AS A PHILOSOPHY OF SCIENCE

1. "Dialectical materialism" is believed to appear for the first time in the following passage from Plekhanov: "He [Hegel] showed that we are free only to the degree that we know the laws of nature and sociohistorical development and to the degree that we, submitting to them, rely upon them. This was a great gain both in the field of philosophy and in the field of social science—a gain that, however, only modern, dialectical, materialism has exploited in full measure." Plekhanov did not in any way indicate that he was coining a phrase here; it is possible that there was an earlier usage of which Plekhanov was aware. Later in the same article Plekhanov repeated the phrase "dialectical materialism," and without a comma separating the words. Plekhanov, *Izbrannye filosofskie proizvedeniia*, pp. 443, 445.

2. The place where Engels perhaps came closest to saying "dialectical materialism" was in his general introduction to *Anti-Dühring*. There he talked of "modern materialism" in both the organic and inorganic realms. He then said, according to an English translation, "In both cases modern materialism is essentially dialectic. . . ." In the original German, the approach to the term "dialectical materialism" is not quite so close, since in the above sentence a pronoun is used for "modern materialism." After referring to *der moderne Materialismus* in an earlier sentence, Engels said, *"in beiden fällen ist er wesentlich dialektisch. . . ." Anti-Dühring*, p. 24. But the thought is clear enough, and Plekhanov and Lenin were entirely within the spirit of Engels' passage when they used the term "dialectical materialism." For the English translation given here, see *Anti-Dühring* (Moscow, 1959), p. 35.

3. The best single source for Marx's and Engels' writings, and for dates of composition, is Marx and Engels, *Werke*. For Lenin's works see Lenin, *Polnoe sobranie sochinenii*.

4. See Marx, *Matematicheskie rukopisi*, Moscow, 1968, later translated as *Mathematical Manuscripts of Karl Marx*. See also the special edition of *Voprosy istorii estestvoznaniia i tekhniki* (Vypusk 25), 1968, dedicated to the 150th anniversary of Marx's birth; this issue contained a previously unpublished

manuscript on technology and an interesting discussion by Ernst Kol'man of the mathematics manuscripts.

5. This statement is in the preface to the second edition of *Anti-Dühring*, written in 1885. The translation is from *Anti-Dühring* (in English) (Moscow, 1959) pp. 16–17.

6. Engels, *Dialectics of Nature* (New York, 1940), p. 243.

7. Lichtheim, *Marxism: An Historical and Critical Study*, p. 245.

8. Z. A. Jordan, *The Evolution of Dialectical Materialism*, p. 15.

9. Marx, "Razlichie mezhdu naturfilosofiei Demokrita i naturfilosofiei Epikura," in *Marx and Engels, Iz rannikh proizvedenii*, pp. 23–98. See also Marx, *Die Promotion von Karl Marx, Jena, 1841: eine Quellenedition.*

10. Marx, "Razlichie mezhdu . . . ," pp. 46–54.

11. Marx, *Capital*, 1:309.

12. Jordan, *The Evolution of Dialectical Materialism*, p. 26.

13. Engels, *Anti-Dühring* (Moscow, 1959), p. 17.

14. *Ibid.*, pp. 171–72. See also Marx, *Capital*, 1:309.

15. See, for example, the discussion in Nagel, *The Structure of Science*, pp. 29–78. Nagel commented, "We are certainly free to designate as a law of nature any statement we please. There is often little consistency in the way we apply the label, and whether or not a statement is called a law makes little difference in the way in which the statement may be used in scientific inquiry. Nevertheless, members of the scientific community agree fairly well on the applicability of the term for a considerable though vaguely delimited class of universal statements. Accordingly, there is some basis for the conjecture that the predication of the label, at least in those cases where the consensus is unmistakable, is controlled by a felt difference in the 'objective' status and function of that class of statements. It would indeed be futile to attempt an ironclad and rigorously exclusive definition of 'natural law' " (pp. 49–50).

16. Dühring, *Cursus der Philosophie als streng wissenschaftlicher Weltanschauung und Lebensgestaltung.*

17. Engels, *Anti-Dühring* (Moscow, 1969), p. 54.

18. *Ibid.*

19. Engels' positivism in this passage is noted by Joravsky, *Soviet Marxism and Natural Science*, p. 9.

20. His opposition to crude materialism in *Anti-Dühring* would have been clearer if he had printed the original preface to the first edition, which he wrote in May 1878. In this preface Engels diluted the positivistic element with an emphasis on dialectics: "It is precisely dialectics that constitutes the most important form of thinking for present-day natural science, for it alone offers the analogue for, and thereby the method of explaining, the evolutionary processes occurring in nature, interconnections in general, and transitions from one field of investigation to another." Engels later substituted another preface for this one; the original did not appear in print until forty-seven years later as part of *Dialectics of Nature*. See Engels, *Anti-Dühring* (Moscow, 1959), p. 455 and editor's note, p. 451.

21. Engels, *Dialectics of Nature* (Moscow, 1954), pp. 151–227. For an assessment of Engels' views on science, see Cohen, "Engels, Friedrich," pp. 131–47.

22. See Haldane's introduction to *Dialectics of Nature* (New York, 1940), p. xiv.

23. John Keosian, in his *The Origin of Life*, a book used in universities in the United States, wrote, "Engels, in his *Dialectics of Nature*, was among the first to consider the spontaneous generation and the vitalistic theories from a materialist viewpoint. He condemned them both and maintained that life could have resulted only from a continuous evolution of matter, the origin of life being merely a rung in the long ladder of development" (p. 11). See also Bernal, *The Physical Basis of Life*, p. 39 and, as well, his *The Origin of Life*, pp. 4 and 131.

24. Selsam and Martel, *Reader in Marxist Philosophy*, pp. 326–27. Another American philosopher, Paul K. Feyerabend, commented, "There are not many writers in the field today who are as well acquainted with contemporary science as was Lenin with the science of his time, and no one can match the philosophical intuition of that astounding author." To this sentence Feyerabend added the following footnote: "I am here thinking mainly of Lenin's comments on Hegel's *Logik* and *Geschichte der Philosophie*. *Materialism and Empirio-Criticism* is a different story." Lenin's comments on Hegel to which Feyerabend referred are in the *Philosophical Notebooks*. See Feyerabend, "Dialectical Materialism and Quantum Theory," p. 414.

25. This is not the place to give a full discussion of the Soviet Marxist philosophy of science, with all of the varying interpretations of the decades between Marx and Engels' period and the early 1930s. It is necessary to discuss only those aspects of that philosophy that seemed likely to influence scientific interpretations. Those aspects—materialism and epistemology, the laws of the dialectic, the union of theory and practice, and the categories—are discussed below. Engels, especially, wrote a great deal on these subjects. After his death, the center of attention shifts to Russia, where new trends in the philosophy of science centered around Plekhanov, Bogdanov, and Lenin. Then from 1917 to 1931 no less than four "schools" in the philosophy of science successively became influential. These were the antiphilosophical "vulgar materialists," represented by such men as Emmanuel Enchmen and D. Minin; the "mechanists," including I. Stepanov and L. I. Axel'rod; the followers of A. M. Deborin, called "Deborinites" (or, by their opponents, "Menshevik idealists"); and the officially approved "dialectical materialists," headed by M. B. Mitin. Mitin became a member of the editorial board of the chief Soviet philosophy journal, *Under the Banner of Marxism*, in 1931; for many years he was chief editor of the current leading Soviet philosophy journal, *Problems of Philosophy*.

26. Engels, *Anti-Dühring* (Moscow, 1969), p. 76.

27. *Ibid.*, p. 86. Engels' statement here on matter and motion will be relevant in the controversy over the theory of chemical bonds. See p. 300. Engels' view is also very similar to the Aristotelian conception of motion. In Galileo's noted dialogue the role of the Aristotelian was taken by Simplicio, who at one point said that "no motion can either exist or even be imagined except as inhering in its subject." Galileo Galilei, *Dialogue Concerning the Two Chief World Systems*, p. 121. A difference here, of course, is that between "subject" and "matter," a difference a realist (but not a materialist) might find significant.

28. Engels, *Dialectics of Nature* (New York, 1940), pp. 322–23.

29. Engels, *Dialectics of Nature* (Moscow, 1954), p. 328.

30. Engels, *Ludwig Feuerbach*, p. 30.

31. Engels quoted by Wetter, *Dialectical Materialism: A Historical and System-atic Survey of Philosophy in the Soviet Union*, p. 281. The passage is in Engels, *Ludwig Feuerbach*, p. 31.

32. Wetter, p. 281.

33. Engels quoted in *Ibid.*, p. 283.

34. Engels, *Dialectics of Nature*, pp. 310–11.

35. Plekhanov, *Izbrannye filosofskie proizvedeniia*, 1:475.

36. For a helpful and clear discussion of the distinction between "presen-tational" and "representational" theories of perception, see Brennan, *The Mean-ing of Philosophy*, pp. 121–22.

37. Plekhanov, *Protiv filosofskogo revizionizma*, pp. 168–69.

38. Plekhanov, *Izbrannye filosofskie proizvedeniia*, 1:475 and *passim*.

39. Ernst Mach, *The Analysis of Sensations and the Relation of the Physical to the Psychical*, p. 12; originally published as *Beitrage zur Analyse der Empfindungen* (Jena: G. Fischer, 1886).

40. *Ibid.*, p. 8.

41. The principle of economy was not essentially an original idea. From early Greek times the view was rather frequently expressed that simplicity is a desirable characteristic of scientific explanation; this opinion is sometimes sum-marized as the principle of Occam's razor. Despite this rather traditional aspect of Mach's principle of economy, he was unkindly criticized for it. The expression "economy of thought" led to the unfair but clever comment that the best way of economizing thought is not to think. Sir Harold Jeffreys, *Scientific Inference*, p. 15.

42. Mach's opinions helped break the way for such attitudes as the "principle of complementarity" of modern physics, which is considered in some detail in the chapter on quantum mechanics.

43. Bogdanov discussed the two realms of sensations in his *Empirionmonizm*, pp. 15ff.

44. *Ibid.*, p. 25.

45. *Ibid.*, p. 41.

46. Lenin, *Materialism and Empirio-Criticism*, p. 11. The works that particularly irritated Lenin were *Studies in* (Lenin said it would have been more proper to say "against") *the Philosophy of Marxism* (St. Petersburg, 1908), a symposium by Bazarov, Bogdanov, Lunacharskii, Berman, Helfond, Iushkevich, and Suvorov; Iushkevich's *Materialism and Critical Realism*; Berman's *Dialectics in the Light of Modern Theory of Knowledge*; and Valentinov's *The Philosophical Constructions of Marxism*. Lenin attacked these publications in his preface to the first edition of *Materialism and Empirio-Criticism*, pp. 9–11.

47. Even today, in the last years of the century, many intellectuals still believe materialism to be discredited by science, although it is clear that such a conclusion is entirely unwarranted.

48. Cited by Lenin in *Materialism and Empirio-Criticism*, p. 267. See Houll-evigue, *L'Evolution des Sciences*, pp. 87–88.

49. For Lenin on Poincaré, see *Materialism and Empirio-Criticism*, pp. 260–62, 265.

50. *Ibid.*, p. 271.

51. *Ibid.*, p. 130.

52. See the first edition of this volume, *Science and Philosophy in the Soviet Union*, (1972), p. 460.

53. Lenin, *Materialism and Emirio-Criticism*, p. 235.

54. *Ibid.*, p. 271.

55. Selsam and Martel, *Reader in Marxist Philosophy*, p. 331.

56. *Ibid.*, pp. 362–63.

57. Quine, *From a Logical Point of View*, p. 44.

58. *Ibid.*, p. 18.

59. As discussed on p. 282, some Soviet enthusiasts for cybernetics in the early sixties discussed rephrasing the laws of the dialectic in cybernetic terms. See ch. 8, note 48.

60. Hegel, *Science of Logic*, p. 473.

61. *Ibid.*, pp. 477–78.

62. *Ibid.*, p. 475. See also J. M. E. McTaggart, *A Commentary on Hegel's Logic* (Cambridge: Cambridge University Press, 1910), pp. 3–4.

63. Hegel, *Encyclopedia of Philosophy*, p. 77.

64. Engels, *Anti-Dühring* (Moscow, 1959), p. 34.

65. Acton, *The Illusion of the Epoch*, p. 101.

66. *The Logic of Hegel*, p. 205.

67. Engels, *Anti-Dühring* (Moscow, 1959), pp. 175, 176. Since each of these concepts has equal validity in economics and science, according to Soviet dialecticians, the transitions from capitalism to socialism to communism occur according to qualitative leaps resulting from sufficient quantitative changes in modes of production and social organization.

68. Engels then compared this need for a definite, but varying, minimum of cavalry in order to defeat the Mamelukes to Marx's economic principle that a definite, though varying, minimum sum of exchange-values is needed to make possible the transformation of these values into capital. *Ibid.*, pp. 176–77.

69. See, for example, Marx and Engels, *Selected Works*, 2:388–89.

70. The concept of dialectical levels of natural laws was particularly important in the thought of A. I. Oparin, the noted writer on the origin of life (see ch. 3). It was also important in the discussions of physiology and psychology described in ch. 5.

71. Berdyaev, *Wahrheit und Lüge des Kommunismus*, p. 84.

72. *The Logic of Hegel*, p. 22.

73. The principle of the struggle of opposites is ancient in natural philosophy. Fire and water were the most important of the two pairs of Aristotelian elements and were seen as opposites. Some medieval alchemists incorporated parts of Aristotelian philosophy into an essentially materialistic view of nature in which simple forms of matter were changed into superior forms by natural processes that could be, at least potentially, duplicated by man.

74. Engels was drawing here, of course, on early nineteenth-century nature philosophy. For an interesting effort to describe this nature philosophy as of

fundamental importance to the development of field theory, see Williams, *The Origins of Field Theory*. Of particular interest is Williams' discussion of Hans Christian Oersted, many of whose ideas on the polarities of nature were similar to Engels'. *Ibid.*, pp. 51ff.

75. Hegel, *Science of Logic*, 2:66 ff.

76. Engels, *Anti-Dühring* (Moscow, 1959), p. 193.

77. *Ibid.*, pp. 178–96.

78. *Ibid.*, p. 188.

79. Engels admitted the attack, but did not identify the mathematician. *Ibid.*, p. 17.

80. Lenin, *Filosofskie tetradi*, p. 212. Stalin in 1938 omitted the Law of the Negation of the Negation altogether and cast the basic laws of the dialectic in a different mold; see "O dialekticheskom i istoricheskom materializme," in *Istoriia vsesoiuznoi kommunisticheskoi partii (Bol' shevikov): Kratkii kurs*, pp. 101–4.

81. Goncharov, Molchanov, and Manuilov, in a review of *Dialektika otritsaniia otritsaniia* (Moscow, 1983) in *Voprosy filosofii*, p. 163.

82. *Kratkii slovar po filosofii*, p. 119. Subsequent page references in the text refer to this work.

83. Lenin, *Filosofskie tetradi* (Moscow, 1965), p. 229.

84. The *Short Philosophical Dictionary* published in Moscow in 1966 listed the categories as matter, motion, time, space, quality, quantity, reciprocal connection, contradiction, causality, necessity, form and content, essence and appearance, possibility and actuality, etc. See Wetter, *Soviet Ideology Today*, p. 65.

85. This is the eleventh thesis of Marx's *Theses on Feuerbach*, originally printed in 1888 as an appendix to Engels' *Ludwig Feuerbach and the Outcome of Classical Philosophy*. The reference may be found in Dutt, *Ludwig Feuerbach*, p. 75.

86. Engels, *Ludwig Feuerbach*, pp. 32–33.

87. For a Soviet discussion of the importance of practice as a criterion of truth, published near the end of the Stalin period, see Rutkevich, *Praktika-osnova poznaniia i kriterii istiny*.

88. Chudinov, *Priroda nauchnoi istiny*; see also his *Teoriia poznaniia i sovremennaia fizika* and *Nit' Ariadny: filosofskie orientiry nauki*.

89. Kedrov, "Marksistskaia filosofiia," p. 60.

90. Rutkevich, *Dialekticheskii materializm*, especially p. 349.

91. Orlov, "O nekotorykh voprosakh teorii materii, razvitiia, soznaniia," and the responses by S. T. Meliukhin, V. S. Tiukhtin, and L. B. Bazhenov, *Filosofskie nauki* (1974), 5:47–77, especially Bazhenov's "Nekotorye zamechaniia po povodu publikatsii V. V. Orlova," pp. 74–77.

92. *Ibid.*

93. See Suvorov, *Materialisticheskaia dialektika*.

94. Bakshutov and Koriukin, in "Obzor otklikov na stat'iu B. M. Kedrova 'Marksistskaia filosofiia: ee predment i rol' v integratsii sovremennykh nauk,' " p. 131. For further information on the hotly debated issue of the legitimate role of dialectical materialism in science, see *ibid.*, pp. 124–35, and B. M. Kedrov, "Marksistskaia filosofiia," pp. 53–62.

95. See Balabanovich, *A. S. Makarenko: chelovek i pisatel'*.

96. Farrington, *Greek Science*, pp. 94–95.

97. See Koyré, "Galileo and Plato," in his *Metaphysics and Measurement*, pp. 1–43 and his *E'tudes Galileennes*, pp. 277–91. For criticism of Koyré's view, see McTighe, "Galileo's 'Platonism,' " pp. 365–87.

98. Williams, *The Origins of Field Theory*, p. 47.

99. Einstein, *Sobranie nauchnykh trudov*, 4:248.

3. ORIGIN OF LIFE

1. Waddington, "That's Life," p. 19.

2. Fox, ed., *The Origins of Prebiological Systems*, p. 98.

3. Bastian, *The Beginning of Life*.

4. Engels, *Dialectics of Nature* (New York, 1940), p. 189.

5. Quoted in Nicolle, *Louis Pasteur*, p. 67. For a general discussion of the origin of life see Farley, *The Spontaneous Generation Controversy*.

6. See Mark B. Adams, article on Oparin, *Dictionary of Scientific Biography*, Supplementary Volume 2 (New York: Scribner's, forthcoming).

7. Oparin, *Proiskhozhdenie zhizny*.

8. It appeared as Appendix 1 in Bernal, *The Origin of Life*, and was translated by Ann Synge. I was unable to obtain the original Russian edition of 1924 in any library in the United States, although a thorough search was made by the Inter-Library Loan Service. Consequently, I was forced to use the 1967 English translation, which is apparently complete. Subsequent page references in the text refer to this volume.

9. Oparin, *The Origin and Initial Development of Life*.

10. Keosian, *The Origin of Life* (New York, 1968), p. 12.

11. Oparin, "K voprosu o vozniknovenii zhizni," p. 138.

12. Oparin, *The Origin and Initial Development of Life*, p. 4.

13. Haldane, "The Origin of Life," p. 249.

14. *Ibid.*, p. 248.

15. See *Aleksandr Ivanovich Oparin (Materialy k biobibliografii uchenykh SSSR, Seriia biokhimii, vypusk 3)* (Moscow and Leningrad, 1949), p. 5.

16. Haldane, *The Marxist Philosophy and the Sciences*, p. 3.

17. Letter to the author from C. H. Waddington, October 16, 1969.

18. Oparin's discussion, at this early date, of crystals with reference to life was fascinating; it reminds one of Erwin Schrödinger's later discussion in *What Is Life?*, a treatment that was of considerable influence on the early thought of several prominent molecular geneticists, as I mentioned elsewhere (p. 465). Bernal wrote of Oparin: "His consideration of crystals, which also have the capacity of growth and replication of form, came very close to modern ideas of self-reproduction, which has been found to be the key to molecular biology, whose ideas were at that time far below the horizon of research." Bernal, p. 237.

19. Wöhler actually began with organic substances in his "synthesis" of urea. There is a controversy in the history of science over the significance of Wöhler's accomplishment. For reference to that controversy, see *The New York Review of Books*, April 9, 1970, pp. 45–46.

20. Kudriavtseva wrote in 1954, "The carbide theory of Mendeleev, having received a geological foundation, reappears as the most important simple and clear theory of the origin of petroleum, explaining processes of the formation of hydrocarbons in the earth's crust without relying on any kind of mysterious living matter and assuming the development of matter in the usual way, from simpler to more complicated forms." "K voprosu o vozniknovenii zhizni," p. 220.

21. The following exchange took place at a conference at Wakulla Springs, Florida, in October 1963: "Dr. Buchanan [J. M. Buchanan, Department of Biology, MIT]: 'At what point did Dr. Oparin decide that the synthesis of complex organic molecules would come from methane, ammonia, water, and hydrogen, and how did he choose these particular compounds?' Dr. Oparin: 'Almost 40 years ago, in 1924, in the book published at that time, I was led to this view by Mendeleev, who has expressed the hypothesis of inorganic origin of oil, which was then subsequently rejected by geologists. Also, very stimulating to us was the discovery of methane in the atmosphere of the large planets.'" Fox, ed., *The Origins of Prebiological Systems*, p. 97.

22. Quoted in Bernal, p. 21.

23. See the discussion in Fox, ed., *The Origins of Prebiological Systems*, p. 97.

24. See, for example, the discussion in Oparin, *Life: Its Nature, Origin and Development*, pp. 10–13.

25. Oparin, *Life: Its Nature, Origin and Development*, p. 9.

26. Oparin, *The Origin of Life*, p. 162. Subsequent page references in the text refer to this 1936 work.

27. Oparin's hypothesis of coacervates as protocells should not be confused with Olga Lepeshinskaia's later views, which Oparin criticized as a simple belief in spontaneous generation. See pp. 83–84.

28. Medvedev, *The Rise and Fall of T. D. Lysenko*, pp. 137–38.

29. For one of Oparin's strongest defenses of Lysenko, see his *Znachenie trudov tovarishcha I. V. Stalina* . . . , pp. 10–15.

30. Medvedev, p. 214.

31. Lepeshinskaia's views were published as an article in 1950, but appeared in a more complete version in her *Kletka: ee zhizn' i proiskhozhdenie*.

32. Lysenko supported Lepeshinskaia in "Novoe v nauke o biologicheskom vide" (Moscow, 1952).

33. Oparin, *Znachenie trudov tovarishcha I. V. Stalina* . . . , pp. 14–15.

34. A debate over the origin of life occurred in the Soviet Union in the early fifties, much of it of poor intellectual quality. A description of this debate is in Wetter, *Der Dialektische Materialismus und das Problem der Entstehung des Lebens*. The main disputes concerned whether protein was the substance essential to life and whether life was a molecular or supramolecular phenomenon. Z. N. Nudel'man agreed with A. P. Stukov and S. A. Iakushev that the properties of life can be found on the molecular level of protein (and thereby criticized Oparin's view), but Nudel'man explained those properties in terms of the molecular structure of protein, in contrast to Stukov and Iakushev, who held an amorphous and almost vitalistic view of protein. A. E. Braunshtein, who spoke positively of much of Oparin's approach, saw the importance of protein

as the carrier of life, not in its "chemical structure," but in its "special mechanism for the exchange of matter." Nudel'man thought that the qualitative transition from "nonliving" to "living" matter occurred in the transition from the microstructure of the molecule to its macrostructure ("macrostructure" referred to the whole molecule; "microstructure" to its parts). Oparin continued to think that the simplest bit of life was supramolecular. Oparin was criticized both by the simple Lysenkoites, including Lepeshinskaia, who often tended toward vitalism, and also by some of the newer molecular biologists, who thought Oparin failed to recognize the significance of their research. For Lepeshinskaia's recognition of her differences with Oparin, see Ignatov, "Mezhdunarodnyi simpozium po proiskhozhdeniiu zhizni na zemle," p. 154. For an earlier sharp criticism of Oparin from the standpoint of Lepeshinskaia and her supporters, see Skabichevskii, "Problema vozniknoveniia zhizni na zemle i teoriia akad. A. I. Oparina," pp. 150–55. For other articles in the discussion, see: Konikova and Kritsman, "Zhivoi belok v svete sovremennykh issledovanii biokhimii," pp. 143–50; Stukov and Iakushev, "O belke kak nositele zhizni," pp. 139–49; Kudriavtseva, "K voprosu o vozniknovenii zhizni," pp. 218–21; Nudel'man, "O probleme belka," pp. 221–26; Emme, "Neskol'ko zamechanii po voprosu o protsesse vozniknoveniia zhizni," pp. 155–58; Takach, "K voprosu o vozniknovenii zhizni," pp. 147–50; Konikova and Kritsman, "K voprosu o nachal'noi forme proiavleniia zhizni," pp. 210–16; Sysoev, "Samoobnovlenie belka . . . ,"pp. 152–5; and A. V. Kozhevnikov, "O nekotorykh usloviiakh vozniknoveniia zhizni na Zemle," pp. 149–52.

35. Oparin, "K voprosu o vozniknovenii zhizni," pp. 138–42.

36. Russian edition: Oparin and Fesenkov, *Zhizn' vo Vselennoi*; English edition: Oparin and Fesenkov, *Life in the Universe*. Subsequent page references in the text refer to this English edition.

37. Oparin, *The Origin of Life on the Earth*, p. 37. See also Lepeshinskaia, *Kletka: ee zhizn' i proiskhozhdenie*.

38. Oparin, *The Origin of Life on the Earth*, p. 37.

39. *Ibid*, pp. 59–60.

40. *Ibid*, p. 285.

41. *Ibid.*, pp. 95–102.

42. Oparin, *Zhizn', ee priroda, proiskhozhdenie i razvitie*; English edition: *Life: Its Nature, Origin and Development*. For the record of the 1957 conference, see: A. I. Oparin et al., eds., *Proceedings of the First International Symposium on The Origin of Life on the Earth* (London, 1959).

43. H. Fraenkel-Conrat and B. Singer, "The Infective Nucleic Acid from Tobacco Mosaic Virus," in *Proceedings of the First International Symposium on the Origin of Life of the Earth* (New York, 1959), p. 303, and in the same volume, Wendell H. Stanley, "On the Nature of Viruses, Genes and Life," p. 313.

44. Stanley, p. 313.

45. Oparin, *The Origin of Life on the Earth*, pp. 274–75.

46. Stanley, pp. 274–75.

47. Oparin et al., *Proceedings*, p. 368.

48. Oparin, *Life: Its Nature, Origin and Development*, p. 66. Subsequent page references in the text refer to this work.

49. The proceedings of this conference were published as Fox, ed., *The Origins of Prebiological Systems.*

50. Peter T. Mora, "The Folly of Probability," in *Ibid.*, pp. 39–64.

51. Mora maintained that "physiochemical selectivity" could lead only to "a temporary metastable order or function which will cease and tend to disperse more and more as its complexity increases." *Ibid.*, p. 47.

52. *Ibid.*, p. 57.

53. *Ibid.*, p. 48. Mora maintained elsewhere that his approach, like Oparin's, was materialistic. See Mora, "Urge and Molecular Biology," pp. 212–19.

54. J. D. Bernal, communicating by mail, said that it posed the most fundamental questions of the origin of life that had been raised "at this conference or, as far as I know, elsewhere." N. W. Pirie commented, "Dr. Mora, you have started people thinking." Fox, pp. 52, 57.

55. *Ibid.*, pp. 53–55.

56. Oparin, *The Origin and Initial Development of Life.*

57. *Ibid.*, pp. 101–2.

58. Chuvashov, "K voprosu o vozniknovenii zhizni na Zemle," pp. 76–83.

59. See Sullivan, "Moon Soil Indicates Clue to Life Origin."

60. The official reports published by NASA were quite inconclusive. See the special issue of *Science* (January 30, 1970) devoted to the analysis of the lunar materials.

61. For a collection of articles dedicated to Oparin's eightieth birthday and generally praising his views, see *Proiskhozhdenie zhizni i evoliutsionnaia biokhimiia.* Another example of Oparin's continued influence is Burkova, "Razvitie dialektiko-materialisticheskoi teorii zhizni v sovremennoi biologii."

62. Liseev and Fesenkova, "Sushchnost' i proiskhozhdenie zhizni."

63. Engel'gardt, "Integratizm—put' ot prostogo k slozhnomu v poznanii iavlenii zhizni."

64. Chepikov, "Sovremennoe ponimanie sushchnosti zhizni."

65. *Ibid.*, p. 79.

66. Quoted in Chepikov, pp. 80–81. See also Kostiuk, "Mirovozzrencheskie aspekty problemy sushchnosti zhizni."

67. See Veselovskii, *O sushchnosti zhivoi materii.*

68. Chepikov, p. 89.

69. Engel'gardt, "O nekotorykh atributakh zhizni: ierarkhiia, integratsiia, uznavanie."

70. Eigen, "Self-Organization of Matter and the Evolution of Biological Macromolecules."

71. Oparin, "O sushchnosti zhizni," pp. 40, 43.

72. Orlov, "O nekotorykh voprosakh teorii materii, razvitiia, soznaniia."

73. Dubinin, "Dialektika proiskhozhdeniia zhizni i proiskhozhdeniia cheloveka," p. 35.

74. Rudenko, "Evoliutsionnyi kataliz i problema proiskhozhdeniia zhizni," p. 220.

4. GENETICS

1. Both the professional biologists and the professional philosophers had to be ordered to follow Lysenkoism. There was even a "Morganist school" among

Soviet Marxist biologists in the twenties. See Joravsky, *Soviet Marxism and Natural Science,* p. 300. The official pressure exerted upon the Academy of Sciences can be readily seen as early as 1938. In May of that year the Council of People's Commissars (headed by Stalin's assistant V. M. Molotov) refused to approve the Academy's work plan. Lysenko shared the podium with Molotov in criticizing the Academy. See "V akademii nauk SSSR," pp. 72–73. Shortly afterward, the Presidium of the Academy criticized the Institute of Genetics for refusing to recognize Lysenko's work. See "Khronika," *Vestnik akademii nauk SSSR* (1938), 6:75. The philosophers, who as ideologists might be expected by non-Soviet observers to have supported Lysenko, also had to be forced into line. In 1948, after the victory of Lysenko at the session of the Lenin Academy of Agricultural Sciences, the Presidium of the Academy of Sciences criticized the Institute of Philosophy for not giving "the necessary support to the Michurinist, materialist direction in biology." See "Postanovlenie prezidiuma akademii nauk SSSR. . . ."

2. Conway Zirkle maintained that there existed a peculiarly Marxist form of biology from the days of Marx and Engels onward. With the advent of Marxism to Russia this view supposedly gained much strength there. See his *Evolution, Marxian Biology, and the Social Scene.* As I shortly explained above, I disagree with Zirkle's thesis that a peculiarly "Marxist biology" existed.

3. Darwinism attracted much attention among the populists; at first it was accepted with open arms as a symbol of materialism and scientific rationalism. Typical of such reception was that of D.I. Pisarev. Later, however, at the hand of V. A. Zaitsev, a Russian Proudhonist, Darwinism received a racist interpretation that alarmed Zaitsev's fellow radicals. Zaitsev's close friend N. D. Nozhin attempted to reinterpret Darwinism within the spirit of the Proudhonist ideal of *mutualité.* The noted populist N. G. Chernyshevskii was hostile to Darwinism in general and criticized sharply Darwin's comparison of selection of domestic animals with selection in the wild state. Chernyshevskii's superficially brilliant critique was based entirely on the concept of the inheritance of acquired characters. Another criticism of Darwinism from a Russian radical came from Prince Peter Kropotkin, whose identification of cooperation as well as competition in the organic world was valuable in a scientific sense and, contrary to some opinion, could be included within a Darwinist framework. See Pisarev, *Selected Philosophical, Social and Political Essays,* pp. 303–9, 344–452; Zaitsev, *Izbrannye sochineniia,* 1:26, 228–37, 429–37; Nozhin, "Nasha nauka i uchenye" and "Po povodu statei 'Russkago Slova' o nevol'nichestvo" Chernyshevskii, *Polnoe sobranie sochinenii,* 10:737–72, esp. 758–59; Kropotkin, *Mutual Aid, a Factor of Evolution* and Rogers, "Darwinism, Scientism and Nihilism."

4. Here Dunn's comment is appropriate; belief in the inheritance of acquired characteristics, he said, "solaced most of the biologists of the nineteenth century." *A Short History of Genetics,* p. x.

5. See Adams, "The Founding of Population Genetics."

6. On Michurin see Joravsky, "The First Stage of Michurinism." See also Lysenko, ed., *I. V. Michurin: Sochineniia v chetyrekh tomakh,* vols. 1–4.

7. Hudson and Richens commented: "In his firm belief in the importance of the environment in genetic constitution Burbank anticipated the later theories

of Lysenko. Several of his remarks on the power of the environment to modify genetic constitution presaged Lysenko's theory of 'shattering,' while his conclusion that 'heredity is nothing but stored environment' heralds Lysenko's dictum that 'heredity constitution is as it were a concentrate of the environmental conditions assimilated by the plant organism in a number of preceding generations.' His tentative hypothesis of sap hybridization may be the antecedent of Lysenko's theory of graft hybridization. . . ." Hudson and Richens, *The New Genetics in the Soviet Union*, p. 13.

8. A view supported in classical genetics by the belief that wild alleles are usually recessive.

9. An example was Dubinin, "I. V. Michurin i sovremennaia genetika." Michurin's biological views were fully developed before the Revolution; the few changes that did occur in his opinions after 1917 were moves toward Mendelism rather than away from it; see p. 104, and Hudson and Richens, p. 12.

10. Dubinin, p. 64.

11. A useful short biography of Lysenko in English is Mikulak, "Trofim Denisovich Lysenko"; Soviet sources are Voinov, *Akademik T. D. Lysenko* and *T. D. Lysenko*.

12. A bibliography of Lysenko's works from 1923 to 1951 is in Lysenko, *Agrobiologiia*.

13. Lysenko, *Agrobiology*, p. 17.

14. *Ibid.*, p. 18.

15. *Ibid.*, p. 21.

16. Lysenko, "Vliianie termicheskogo faktora na prodolzhitel'nost'faz razvitiia rastenii."

17. Shatskii, "K voprosu o summe temperatur, kak sel'skokhoziaistvenno-klimaticheskom indekse." When the eminent plant physiologist N. A. Maksimov first discussed this formula, he commented that it was of "great interest" but was based on "too few experiments and must be further checked." Maksimov was a critic of Lysenko in later years but was forced to recognize him, as were many others. See Maksimov, "Fiziologicheskie faktory, opredeliaiushchie dlinu vegetatsionnogo perioda," and Maksimov and Krotkina, "Issledovaniia nad posledstviem ponizhennoi temperatury na dlinu vegetatsionnogo perioda." The latter article contains genuine criticism of Lysenko's unclear terms.

18. See Hudson and Richens, *The New Genetics in the Soviet Union*, p. 28, for references to Lysenko's debate over mathematics with the eminent A. N. Kolmogorov. Conway Zirkle suggested that Lysenko was a victim of a frustration complex: "Unable to handle the simplest mathematics, Lysenko resents it violently and denounces any application of mathematics to a biological problem. This puts Mendelism beyond his reach. As he equates all genetics with the 3 to 1 ratio, it is evident that he comprehends practically nothing of the modern developments in this field, and his complex makes him resent the very existence of a science which frustrates him." *Death of a Science in Russia*, p. 96.

19. Lysenko, *Agrobiology*, p. 23.

20. The journal *Agrobiologiia* ceased publication in 1966.

21. *Biulleten'iarovizatsii* (January 1932), 1:63.

22. The most interesting and complete discussion of vernalization I have found is Purvis, "The Physiological Analysis of Vernalization." Interestingly enough, vernalization has been found to have a genetic basis, a fact that Lysenko, if he knew of it, would undoubtedly have found unpleasant: "Up to six genes have been found responsible for the cold requirement of vernalizable plants. In the case of three of these genes, Hh, Ii, and Kk which are found in wheat, barley, rye, and *Arabidopsis*, the cold requirement is caused by the recessive alleles; in the case of the other genes, Ss, Tt, and Uu, found in wheat, barley, *vosoyamus* and *rabidopsis* by the dominant alleles." "Vernalization," *McGraw Hill Encyclopedia of Science and Technology* (New York, 1966), 14:305.

23. Huxley, *Heredity East and West*, p. 17.

24. See Hudson and Richens' discussion of this case, in *The New Genetics of the Soviet Union*, p. 39.

25. See, for example, *ibid.*, pp. 32–51.

26. See Joravsky's discussion in Part 4 of his *Soviet Marxism and Natural Science*, pp. 233–71.

27. Even where Soviet agriculture could have used recent developments in agronomic science, its extreme backwardness made such applications very difficult. The state of development of Soviet agriculture immediately prior to collectivization was a topic of much debate in the Soviet Union immediately after de-Stalinization in 1956. The prevalent interpretation among Soviet historians before 1956 was that the material-technical base of Soviet agriculture had so advanced by 1929 that a "contradiction" between the new productive forces and the old productive relationships had arisen, and this contradiction led to the necessity of collectivization. Post-Stalin interpretations, however, questioned seriously this thesis; the author of the first important study of the problem after 1956 concluded that a new material-technical base had not yet been created by the early thirties. Such a view implied, of course, that an important theoretical justification for rapid collectivization was absent. See Danilov, *Sozdanie material'notekhnicheskikh predposylok kollektivizatsii sel'skogo khoziaistva v SSSR;* and Bogdenko and Zelenin, "Osnovnye problemy istorii kollektivizatsii sel'skogo khoziaistva v sovremennoi sovetskoi istoricheskoi literature," esp. pp. 194–5.

28. Experiments on *Drosophila melanogaster* were conducted in the famous "fly room" at Columbia University from 1910 to 1928; H. J. Muller, one of T. H. Morgan's students, took the first fruit flies to Soviet Russia in 1922. Hybrid corn was available commercially in the United States after 1933, but the greatest expansion came in the forties; by 1949, 77.6 percent of the total United States acreage was in hybrid corn. Dunn, *A Short History of Genetics*, p. 140; Sturtevant, *A History of Genetics*, pp. 45–57; Mangelsdorf, "Hybrid Corn," p. 564. For the impact of Muller's 1922 visit to Russia, see Adams, "The Founding of Population Genetics."

29. A Soviet student discussed the enormous problems in Soviet agriculture after collectivization and the help given by the followers of Michurinist biology in Kuroedov, "Rol'sotsialisticheskoi sel'sko-khoziaistvennoi praktiki v razvitii michurinskoi biologii," esp. pp. 99–105.

30. I am particularly indebted to David Joravsky for an understanding of the importance of Lysenko's nostrums to his ascent in the 1930s.

31. Based on conversations held with Soviet officials in Moscow and Leningrad, May-July 1970.

32. For an article in which Lysenko urged involving "thousands" of collective farm workers in his experiments, see his "Obnovlennye semena: beseda s akademikom T. D. Lysenko." The emphasis here seems to be as much on personal involvement as on technical advantage.

33. There is considerable evidence that vernalization did in fact lead to decreased yields. See, for example, Targul'ian, ed., *Spornye voprosy genetiki i selektsii: raboty IV sessii akademii 19–27 dekabriia 1936 goda*, pp. 189–93, 204–5.

34. Prezent commented, "Genetics gives birth to dialectics." Later he called this "material for the criticism of the path over which I have traveled." *Pod znamenem marksizma* (1939), 11:95, 112.

35. Weiner, *Models of Nature.*

36. Dubinin said at the conference in 1939, "Academician Lysenko is greatly confused about questions of Mendelism. But I think that to a considerable degree this confusion must be attributed, Academician Lysenko, to your helper, Comrade Prezent. (Voice from the floor shouts 'Correct!')" *Pod znamenem marksizma* (1939), 11:186. Hudson and Richens commented, "There is indeed evidence that the full elaboration of the genetical system of Lysenko is principally due to Prezent. . . ." p. 15.

37. Lysenko, *Agrobiology*, p. 65.

38. *Ibid.*, p. 68.

39. Nazi Germany passed a compulsory sterilization law on July 14, 1933. Hudson and Richens commented, "Although still a matter of controversy, there can be no doubt that genetical research has demonstrated the heterogeneity of the human race, and has therefore provided a potential basis for the development of theories of racial and class distinction. It seems clear that Lysenko and Prezent realized these implications and found in them a serious objection to the theory of social equality. The growing political tension between Russia and Germany no doubt served to inflame these suspicions." *New Genetics*, (p. 27). And J. B. S. Haldane, a Communist, bitter foe of fascism, and brilliant geneticist, anticipated the issue in 1932 when he commented, "The test of the devotion of the Union of Socialist Soviet Republics to science will, I think, come when the accumulation of the results of human genetics, demonstrating what I believe to be the fact of innate human inequality, becomes important." *The Inequality of Man*, p. 137.

40. See Filipchenko's numerous articles in *Izvestiia buro po evgenike* and *Izvestiia buro po genetike i evgenike* in the period 1922–26. See also his "Spornye voprosy evgeniki." Corresponding Academician N. P. Dubinin, one of Lysenko's major opponents and director of the Institute of General Genetics of the Academy of Sciences, praised Filipchenko's work of the 1920s and 1930s in an article that appeared after Lysenko's discrediting. "I. V. Michurin i sovermennaia genetika," p. 69.

41. A. S. Serebrovskii, "Antropogenetika," p. 18.

42. His brother, Sergei, eventually became president of the Academy of Sciences of the USSR. See Joravsky, "The Vavilov Brothers."

43. See his statement in Targul'ian, ed., *Spornye voprosy genetiki i selektsii*, p. 462.

44. See also Popovsky, *The Vavilov Affair*, and Roll-Hansen, "A New Perspective on Lysenko." Th. Dobzhansky, the noted geneticist, and also a Russian, commented in 1947: "Vavilov was an ardent Russian patriot. Outside of Russia he was regarded by some as a communist, which he was not. But he did wholeheartedly accept the revolution, because he believed that it opened broader possibilities for the development of the land and of the people of Russia than would have been otherwise. In October, 1930, during a trip to the Sequoia National Park in the company of this writer (and with nobody else present), he said with much emphasis and conviction that, in his opinion, the opportunities for serving mankind which existed in the USSR were so great and so inspiring that for their sake one must learn to overlook the cruelties of the regime. He asserted that nowhere else in the world was the work of scientists more appreciated than in the USSR." Dobzhansky, "N. I. Vavilov, A Martyr of Genetics, 1887–1942."

45. See note 28, above.

46. Sonneborn, "H. J. Muller, Crusader for Human Betterment."

47. See Huxley, *op. cit.*, p. 183.

48. Sonneborn, p. 774.

49. Kol', "Prikladnaia botanika ili leninskoe obnovlenie zemli."

50. See *Ekonomicheskaia zhizn'* March 23, 1931.

51. *Ibid.*

52. Darlington, "The Retreat from Science in Soviet Russia," pp. 72–3. It is useful to compare the corruption of Lysenko by publicity to that of Luther Burbank. See Howard, "Luther Burbank: A Victim of Hero Worship." Of course, the fact that Burbank was lionized, invited to give sermons, pictured on a postage stamp, and honored by placing Arbor Day on his birthday did not interfere with classical genetics in the United States. But his exploitation by shady companies gave an example of the obvious fact that a capitalist society produces its own peculiar forms of corruption.

53. Lysenko, "Iarovizatsiia—eto milliony pudov dobavochnogo urozhaia." As Joravsky has pointed out, Stalin changed his mind frequently; his support of Lysenko at one time is hardly sufficient to explain Lysenko's long period of dominance.

54. After discussing the principle of the transition of quantity into quality, Stalin remarked that Mendeleev's Periodic Table is an illustration of this principle and that "the same thing is shown in biology by the theory of neo-Lamarckism, which is supplanting neo-Darwinism." *Anarkhizm ili sotsializm?, p. 26.*

55. Targul'ian, *Spornye voprosy genetiki i seleksii*, p. 374.

56. Targul'ian.

57. *Ibid.*, p. 72.

58. *Ibid.*, p. 336.

59. Another critic of this sort was A. R. Zhebrak, a well-known Soviet geneticist who lost his teaching job at the Timiriazev Academy in 1948. In 1939 Zhebrak said that classical genetics is a confirmation of the laws of the dialectic, especially of the Law of the Transition of Quantity into Quality. *Pod znamenem marksizma*, (1939), 11:98. N. P. Dubinin also wrote about genetics in Marxist philosophy journals; in 1936 at one point he tried to turn the tables on Prezent by accusing him of following Weismann! Targul'ian, p. 339.

60. Targul'ian, p. 114.

61. The members of the editorial board of *Pod znamenem marksizma* at this time were: V. V. Adoratskii, M. B. Mitin, E. Kol'man, P. F. Iudin, A. A. Maksimov, A. M. Deborin, A. K. Timiriazev, and M. N. Korneev.

62. Vavilov's speech at the 1939 conference has been called "weak" or "ineffective" by non-Soviet commentators, but I find it quite outspoken and carefully grounded on both theoretical and practical arguments. *Pod znamenem marksizma* (1939), 11:127–40.

63. Lysenko on scientific method needs no comment: ". . . in order to obtain a definite result, one must want to obtain namely that result; if you want to obtain a definite result, you will obtain it. . . . I need only those people who obtain what I need.' *Ibid.*, p. 95.

64. V.K. Milovanov quoted in V. Kolbanovskii, "Spornye voprosy genetiki i selektskii (obshchii obzor soveshchaniia)," in *ibid.*, p. 93.

65. Lysenko, "Po povodu stat'i akademika N. I. Vavilova," p. 140.

66. Iu. Polianskii in *Pod znamenem marksizma*, (1939), 11:103.

67. *Ibid.*, p. 125.

68. There is much more information on the arrest, trial, and fate of Vavilov than given here in Popovsky, *The Vavilov Affair*, and in Medvedev, *The Rise and Fall of T. D. Lysenko*, esp. pp. 67–77.

69. Medvedev, p. 110.

70. For evidence on the Zhdanovs' roles, see Appendix 1 of my *Science and Philosophy in the Soviet Union* (1972).

71. *The Situation in Biological Science: Proceedings of the Lenin Academy of Agricultural Sciences of the U.S.S.R., July 31-August 7, 1948, Complete Stenographic Report;* also in Russian, *O polozhenii v biologicheskoi nauke, Stenograficheskii otchet sessii vsesoiuznoi akademii sel'sko-khoziaistvennykh nauk imeni V. I. Lenina, 31 iiulia-7 avgusta 1948 g.*

72. Lysenko, nonetheless, put great emphasis on food, especially at certain points in an organism's growth. This emphasis will be particularly clear in his experiments with increasing the butterfat content of dairy milk. See p. 146. The nutrient theory probably had connections with Darwin's belief that "of all the causes which induce variability, excess of food, whether or not changed in nature, is probably the most powerful." Quoted in Hudson and Richens, *New Genetics*, p. 7.

73. Lysenko, *Agrobiology*, p. 34.

74. See Purvis, "The Physiological Analysis of Vernalization."

75. The connection between vernalization and heredity is clearly revealed in Lysenko's statement: ". . . *during the vernalization of seeds or plants an accumulation of changes takes place.* These changes remain in the cells in which they have taken place and are also transmitted to all the new cells formed by them." *Agrobiology*, p. 50. Emphasis in the original.

76. Lysenko was confident that he could produce new varieties with desirable characteristics in two to three years. In accordance with his theory he eliminated hundreds of varieties without even testing them. He commented, "We have no right, legal or moral, to waste one or two years on phasic analysis in cases where we can dispense with it." *Ibid.*, p. 110.

77. *Ibid.*, p. 83.

78. "Genotype" means the array of genes an individual receives through heredity. "Phenotype" is the totality of the physical and behavioral characters that an individual displays, and is the result of an interaction between the genotype and the environment.

79. Lysenko, *Heredity and its Variability*, p. 10. Emphasis in original. Also notice Lysenko's observation that "a living body qualitatively altered by living conditions always possesses an altered heredity. But it is by no means always the case that the qualitatively changed parts of the body of an organism can establish normal metabolism with many other body parts; hence, the changes do not always become fixed in the sex-cells." *Ibid.*, 24.

80. *Ibid.*, p. 1. Emphasis in original.

81. Lysenko, *Agrobiologiia*, p. 436.

82. Lysenko's writings on the gene were very confused. At one point he said, ". . . we deny that the geneticists and cytologists will see genes under the microscope. . . . The heredity basis is not some kind of self-reproducing substance separate from the body. The heredity basis is the cell. . . ." At another time he said, "Academician Serebrovskii is also wrong when he says Lysenko denied the existence of genes. Neither Lysenko nor Prezent have ever denied the existence of genes. We deny the correctness of your conception of the word 'genes.' " *Agrobiology*, pp. 186, 188. Lysenko did admit the reality of chromosomes.

83. "Desired" conditions in the sense that they were those of a locality in which the Soviet government wished to grow certain plants. Thus, the conditions of northern Russia might be "undesirable" for agriculture in an absolute sense, but the government wished, understandably, to find varieties that could be raised there.

84. Lysenko, *Heredity and Its Variability*, p. 32. Emphasis in original.

85. Erik Nordenskiöld, in his old (1935) but still very valuable *The History of Biology*, commented on Darwin's theory of pangenesis, "Darwin is here, as so often elsewhere, a speculative natural philosopher, not a natural scientist." This remark, typical of those expressed by inductivist historians of science in the period when Darwinism seemed to be yielding to modern genetics, seems excessively critical; a great part of Darwin's genius was his willingness to build a system that was in part speculation, but all the time checking the system against empirical data. Would that Lysenko had been as willing to discipline himself. If he had, his name would probably be known today only to a few specialists in vernalization. For a discussion of inductivist historians of science, unnecessarily combative but generally sound, see Agassi, "Towards an Historiography of Science," pp. 1–31. Agassi has, however, too simple a view of Marxist interpretations of the history of science.

86. Lysenko, *Heredity and Its Variability*, pp. 55–65.

87. *Ibid.*, p. 51. Emphasis in original.

88. Lysenko quoted Michurin's belief that "the farther apart the crossed parental pairs are in respect to place of origin and environmental conditions, the more easily the hybrid seedlings adapt themselves to the environmental conditions of the new locality." *Agrobiology*, p. 85. If applied to man, this view

would be, of course, a strong argument for racial mixing. Lysenko did not extend his system to man, here or elsewhere.

89. Hudson and Richens, *New Genetics*, p. 48.

90. Darwin believed in the possibility of true graft hybrids, as did many nineteenth-century biologists and selectionists. Luther Burbank, who, like Lysenko, kept very poor records, advanced a tentative theory of sap hybridization similar in many ways to graft hybridization. Michurin's "mentor theory" postulated the influence of the stock by the scion.

91. For an elementary discussion of blending inheritance see Sinnott, Dunn, and Dobzhansky, *Principles of Genetics*, pp. 97ff. and 121ff.

92. Hudson and Richens, *New Genetics*, *op. cit.*, pp. 42–43.

93. Lysenko, *Izbrannye sochineniia*, 2:48.

94. Dunn, *A Short History of Genetics*, p. x.

95. Since Darwin ascribed validity to both natural selection and the inheritance of acquired characters, both the neo-Mendelians and Michurinists could call themselves Darwinians.

96. Many writers attribute to Lamarck a vitalistic view of nature. The issue is not nearly that simple; as C. C. Gillispie has commented: "His dichotomy of organic and inorganic nature provides no escape into transcendentalism, and that has always been the door through which vitalists have slipped from science into mystery. Life is a purely physical phenomenon in Lamarck, and it is only because science has (quite rightly) left behind his conception of the physical that he has been systematically misunderstood, and assimilated to a theistic or vitalistic tradition which in fact he held in abhorrence." *The Edge of Objectivity*, p. 276.

97. V. A. Shaumian maintained at the 1948 conference that the influence of the process of milking cows must have an hereditary effect: "Can such a vigorous determining factor of action on an udder applied from generation to generation over an expanse of many years remain without result? We attribute no less importance to the factor of the milking process than to feeding because milking is one of the most important methods and means of exercise for a milch cow." This view is, of course, pure Lamarckism, based on the inheritance of the effects of use, and similar to Lamarck's famous description of the lengthening of a giraffe's neck. Zirkle, ed., *Death of a Science in Russia*, p. 148. Lysenko, on the other hand, commented: ". . . no positive results can be obtained from work conducted from the standpoint of Lamarckism. The very fact that we do succeed in changing the hereditary nature of plants in a definite direction by suitable training shows that we are not Lamarckians." *Agrobiologiia*, p. 221. Prezent was even more outspoken on the issue. But Lysenko in another spot referred to Lamarck more favorably: "Let us note, by the way, that the Morganists are vainly trying to frighten people with Lamarckism. Lamarck was a wise man. The importance of his work cannot of course be compared to Darwinism. There are serious errors in Lamarck's theory. But in his own time there did not exist a more progressive biologist than Lamarck." *Iarovizatsiia* (1936), 5(8):45–68.

98. See, for example, Polianskii and Polianskii, *Sovremennye problemy evoliutsionnoi teorii*, p. 5 and *passim*.

99. Gillispie, "Lamarck and Darwin in the History of Science," pp. 268–69.

100. *Ibid.*, p. 277.

101. See Nordenskiöld, *The History of Biology*, p. 324.

102. Pollen fertilization deserves some comment, since it was one of the most controversial issues in Lysenko's writings. Lysenko believed that the ova of plants would select particular pollen grains (one form of nutrient) at fertilization, those that would result in the best adaptation to local conditions. At one point Lysenko even spoke of "marriage for love" in the plant world. Hudson and Richens, *New Genetics*, p. 38, have tried to show that this belief, although crudely expressed, need not necessarily have been based on anthropomorphic concepts. They say that even when a plant is grown in an environment to which it is not adapted, "it is not inconceivable that natural selection should so refine the selective power that any departure from the norm in the environment should tend to bring about compensating changes in the selection of nutrients at any part of the life cycle." I find the last sentence very dubious; it would, I believe, be improved if "any departure from the norm" were changed to "some departures" (those previously experienced and overcome), and if "any part of the life cycle" were changed to "any part of the life cycle prior to or during the fertile period." Lysenko later abandoned the "marriage for love" phrase and criticized anthropomorphic concepts in biology. The pollen concept has connections with Darwin's ideas on pollen prepotency. For Lysenko's later conservatism, see his statement, "purpose is bound up with consciousness, which is absent in nature." Lysenko, "Teoreticheskie osnovy napravlennogo izmeneniia nasledstvennosti sel'skokhoziaistvennykh rastenii."

103. Dobzhansky, *The Biological Basis of Human Freedom*, p. 10.

104. Dunn, *A Short History of Genetics*, p. 155. Muller's early sympathy for dialectical materialism has already been cited.

105. Sturtevant, *A History of Genetics*, p. 67.

106. Dunn, *A Short History of Genetics*, p. 215.

107. Targul'ian, *Spornye voprosy genetiki i selektsii*, p. 131.

108. *Ibid.*, p. 137.

109. *Istoriia vsesoiuznoi kommunisticheskoi partii (bol'shevikov): kratkii kurs*, p. 101. The same citation was used against physicists who emphasized the distinctness of the boundary between the macrolevel and the microlevel. See p. 331.

110. Lysenko, *Izbrannye sochineniia*, 2:49.

111. As Dobzhansky described it: "Mutations are . . . changes induced ultimately by the environment, but the properties of a mutant are dependent on the nature of the gene that made the change, rather than on the environmental agency which acted as the trigger that set off the change." *The Biological Basis of Human Freedom*, p. 19.

112. Lysenko commented, "It seems to me that what must urgently be found here is not proof of whether Lysenko is right or wrong, but the best and most practical way of achieving the goal the plant breeder has set himself, namely, to breed the best varieties in the shortest time. Every theoretical proposition that helps practical farming will be more useful and, of course, come nearer the truth than all the theoretical propositions that give neither immediate nor

future, neither direct nor indirect, guidance to practical action in our socialist agriculture." *Agrobiology*, p. 111.

113. Lysenko, *Izbrannye sochineniia*, 2:6, quoting from Michurin, *Sochineniia*, 4:72. The opening speech at the 1937 genetics conference, given by the supposedly neutral A. I. Muralov, president of the Lenin Academy of Agricultural Sciences, emphasized the bond between theory and practice: "What must all participants at the conference remember during the discussion of issues in selection and genetics? They must first of all keep in mind the assistance which science must render socialist production, arming it with scientific theory." Targul'ian, *Spornye voprosy genetiki i seleksii*, p. 5. Lysenko forced even his opponents to wish him good luck by such statements as "I think that if the propositions we are advancing, particularizing and developing turn out to be fundamentally wrong, it should be regretted not only by me and my staff, but also by all the opponents of these propositions, for we would be deprived of an effective method of breeding new varieties." *Agrobiology*, p. 112.

114. Schrödinger said that a physicist "would be inclined to call de Vries' mutation theory, figuratively, the quantum theory of biology. We shall see later that this is much more than figurative. The mutations are actually due to quantum jumps in the gene molecule. But quantum theory was but two years old when de Vries first published his discovery, in 1902. Small wonder that it took another generation to discover the intimate connection!" *What Is Life? Other Scientific Essays*, p. 35. This section of Schrödinger's book is based on lectures given in Dublin in February 1943.

115. The same issue was discussed from the standpoint of DNA by a conservative but intelligent philosophy graduate student in the USSR. Pinter, "Aktual'nye voprosy vzaimootnosheniia marksistskoi filosofii i genetiki."

116. Lysenko, *Agrobiology*, pp. 551–52. Emphasis in original.

117. See pp. 334, 335, 352 and *passim*.

118. Several Soviet reviewers observed in 1965: "It is well known that the formula 'Science is the foe of chance' was proclaimed at the end of the 1940s. This formula is incorrect, for it is based on the confusion of two completely different concepts of chance. As is known, it has done no small amount of harm to science and to practice, but nowhere have its authors openly renounced it, and to this day it figures as a component part of the Michurinist teaching, although it has nothing in common with the views of Michurin himself." Knuniants, Kedrov, Bliakher, "A Book that Does Not Deserve High Appraisal." Lysenko's view of chance was criticized in the Soviet Union in 1957 by A. L. Takhtadzhan: "From the point of view of mechanistic materialism, statistical laws are only a temporary stage of our knowledge. In reality statistical laws are just as objective laws of nature as are the laws of the unique." *Botanicheskii zhurnal* (1957), 4:596.

119. The knife cuts both ways. If one accepts the inheritance of acquired characters, building a "new man" may seem more possible, but the same argument would lead to racist positions or even belief in the superiority of aristocracies. As Julian Huxley wrote: ". . . it is very fortunate for the human species that acquired characters are not readily impressed on the hereditary constitution. For if they were, the conditions of dirt, disease, and malnutrition

in which the majority of mankind have lived the thousands of years would have produced a disastrous effect upon the race." Huxley, *Heredity East and West*, p. 138. Of course, any serious discussion of the implications for man of a hypothetical inheritance of acquired characters would have to involve discussions of time: the number of generations required to fix the heredity of a new trait and the number of generations in new conditions to erase it.

120. For a discussion of the issue during the Soviet arguments about eugenics in the twenties, see my *Between Science and Values*, pp. 239–256. As late as 1958, *Pravda* spoke of N. K. Kol'tsov (1872–1940), a prominent Soviet biologist associated with eugenicist views in the twenties, as a "shameless reactionary who is known for his wild theory that preaches 'the improvement of human nature.' " *Pravda*, December 14, 1958. Yet "the improvement of human nature" is precisely the reason given by some writers for the entire Lysenko affair. John Langdon-Davies wrote that the controversy occurred because "a limit was being set to the extent to which environmental change at the hands of the U.S.S.R. planners could be expected to alter human nature permanently for the better." *Russia Puts the Clock Back*, pp. 58–59.

121. A map of the shelter belt scheme was given in *Ogonek* (March 1949), 10:4–5.

122. Bovin, "Na trassakh gosudarstvennykh lesnykh polos."

123. See Lysenko, "Gnezdovaia kul'tura lesa," as well as his "Posev polezashchitnykh lesnykh polos gnezdovym sposobom."

124. See *Pravda*, April 17, 1943, p. 2.

125. Kropotkin devoted his attention primarily to animals, including man, rather than to plants. He wrote, "If we resort to an indirect test, and ask Nature: 'Who are the fittest: those who are continually at war with each other, or those who support one another?' we at once see that those animals which acquire habits of mutual aid are undoubtedly the fittest." Kropotkin did not deny the existence of competition among members of the same species, nor did he actually deny the accuracy of the phrase "survival of the fittest"; he maintained merely that those species that cooperate are "fittest." Kropotkin, *Mutual Aid: A Factor of Evolution*, p. 6.

126. Lysenko commented, "Wild plants, particularly forest trees, possess the extremely useful biological ability of self-thinning. . . . This occurs because a given area of tree crown can support only a certain number of plants. Therefore, some of the trees normally die." "Gnezdovaia kul'tura lesa," p. 7. But Lysenko at another point commented that the example of thousands of tree seedlings crowding each other is actually not a case of intraspecies competition because many seedlings are required to overpower the grass that is trying to crowd them out. See his "Teoreticheskie osnovy napravlennogo izmeneniia nasledstvennosti sel'skokhoziaistvennykh rastenii."

127. *Botanicheskii zhurnal* (1955), 2:213. See also Koldanov, "Nekotorye itogi i vyvody po polezashchitnomu lesorazvedeniiu za istekshie piat' let."

128. In "O vnutrividovykh i mezhvidovykh vzaimootnosheniiakh sredi rastenii," Sukhachev maintained that Darwin was correct, contrary to Lysenko's views, in saying that intraspecific competition exists and that as a general rule, the closer the structure of organisms the more intense the competition. This

phenomenon is important in explaining the progressive separation of characteristics in evolutionary development. Sukhachev observed that one must, however, be careful in talking about "competition" in the plant world, since it can easily be given an anthropomorphic connotation; furthermore, the existence of "competition" does not deny the simultaneous existence of "cooperation." Nonetheless, for lack of a better term, Sukhachev felt that the word "competition" is legitimate. Other authors were less critical of Lysenko's position; the discussion even included an entry by Lysenko himself, a reprint of his article on "species" for the second edition of the Bol'shaia sovetskaia entsikopediia. Lysenko, "Novoe v nauke o biologicheskom vide"; see also Il' in, "Filogenez pokrytosemennykh s pozitsii michurinskoi biologii."

129. See Swanson, "The Bolshevization of Scientific Societies in the Soviet Union."

130. Rukhkian, "Ob opisannom S. K. Karapetianom sluchae porozhdeniia leshchiny grabom."

131. Bibliographies of this debate are given in Botanicheskii zhurnal (1954), 2:221–3 and ibid. (1955), 2:213–14.

132. Rubashevskii was the author of Filosofskoe znachenie teoreticheskogo nasledstva I. V. Michurina (Moscow, 1949). See also the two references above, note 131; and Sukhachev and Ivanov, "K voprosam vzaimootnoshenii organizmov i teorii estestvennogo otbora."

133. "Diskussii: rasshiriat i uglubliat tvorcheskuiu diskussiiu po probleme vida i vidoobrazovaniia," p. 206.

134. Ibid., p. 207, and references at end of article.

135. Ibid.

136. Ibid., p. 208.

137. Ibid.

138. Sokolov, "Ob organizatsii proizvodstva gibridnykh semian kukuruzy."

139. I. Knuniants and L. Zubkov, "Shkoly v nauke," Literaturnaia gazeta (January 11, 1955), p. 1.

140. Sukhachev and Ivanov, "Toward Problems of the Mutual Relationships of Organisms and the Theory of Natural Selection," Current Digest of the Soviet Press (February 16, 1955), 7(1): or see Sukhachev and Ivanov, "K voprosam vzaimootnoshenii organizmov i teorii estestvennogo otbora."

141. "Expand and Intensify Creative Discussion of Species and Species Formation," Current Digest of the Soviet Press (July 27, 1955), 7(24):5, from Botanicheskii zhurnal (1955), 2:206–13.

142. Lysenko and Maltsev had known each other for more than twenty years and spoke well of each other. They were both delegates to the Second All-Union Congress of Collective Farm Shock Workers in 1935. At the Twentieth Congress of the Communist Party in 1956 Maltsev gave a speech that attracted considerable attention.

143. Medvedev, The Rise and Fall of T. D. Lysenko, p. 137.

144. See, for example, his Lysenko's "Shire primeniat'v nechernozemnoi polose organomineral'nye smesy." But Lysenko also took notice of his critics; he accused Sukhachev, the editor of Botanicheskii zhurnal and Biulleten'moskovskogo obshchestva ispytatelei prirody, of "direct denial of the entire concept

of materialist biology" and of launching a "Highly unscientific criticism of my works." T. Lysenko, "Teoreticheskie uspekhi agronomicheskoi biologii."

145. "Rech'tov. N. S. Khrushcheva na soveshchanii rabotnikov sel'skogo khoziaistva Gor'kovskoi, Arzamasskoi, Kirovskoi oblastei, Mariiskoi, Mordovskoi i Chuvashskoi ASSR 8 Aprelia 1957 goda v gorode Gor'kom," *Pravda,* April 10, 1957, p. 2.

146. See Lysenko, "Interesnye raboty po zhivotnovodstvu v Gorkakh Leninskikh," and *Agrobiologiia* (1957), 4:123–27.

147. "Ukaz prezidiuma verkhovnogo soveta SSSR," *Pravda,* September 29, 1958, p. 1.

148. *Pravda* and *Izvestiia* announced on April 10, 1956, that the USSR Council of Ministers had "complied with the request" of Lysenko that he be released as president of the Academy. In June of the same year, however, he was elected a member of the Presidium of the Academy. In August 1961 he was reelected president, but in April 1962 he stepped down again for "reasons of health." The man who replaced him, M. Ol'shanskii, was one of his strong defenders. See, for example, his "Protiv fal'sifikatsii v biologicheskoi nauke."

149. For information on the relationship between cybernetics and genetics in the Soviet Union I am grateful to S. C. McCluskey of Columbia University, who made a short unpublished study of the topic, and also to Mark Adams.

150. Schrödinger, *What Is Life,* p. 71. In his *The Double Helix,* p. 13, James Watson emphasized the importance of Schrödinger's little book to Francis Crick's decision to leave physics and enter biology.

151. Lysenko condemned Schrödinger's essays in his opening address at the 1948 session of the Lenin Academy of Agricultural Sciences. See Lysenko, *The Situation of Biological Science,* p. 23.

152. Many of these articles are available in English, as a result of the translation services of the Joint Publications Research Service (JPRS) of the U.S. Department of Commerce. Serial numbers for the following citations are given in the bibliography. See Berg and Timofeev-Ressovskii, "Paths of Evolution of the Genotype"; Liapunov and Malenkov, "Logical Analysis of Hereditary Information"; Medvedev, "Errors in the Reproduction of Nucleic Acid and Proteins and Their Biological Significance"; Schmalhausen, "Hereditary Information and Its Transformations," and "Fundamentals of the Evolutionary Process in the Light of Cybernetics," "Neutral Selection and Information," and "Evolution in the Light of Cybernetics"; Timofeev-Ressovskii, "Some Problems of Radiation Biogeocenology"; Trincher, *Biology and Information—Elements of Biological Thermodynamics.*

153. At one point he described the Law of the Life of Biological Species as the fact that "everything in the life of each biological species, and consequently of each living body, is directed . . . at preserving and increasing the numbers of the given species. . . ." Lysenko, "Teoreticheskie osnovy napravlennogo izmeneniia nasledstvennosti sel'skokhoziaistvennykh rastenni."

154. Lysenko, "Interesnye raboty po zhivotnovodstvu v Gorkakh Leninskikh."

155. Prikazy po ministerstvu sel'skogo khoziaistva SSSR ot 5 ianvaria 1961 g. No. 3, "Ob opyte raboty eksperimental'nogo khoziaistva 'Gorki Leninskie' po povysehniiu zhirnomolochnosti korov," i ot 26 iiunia 1963 g. No. 131, "Ob

uluchsheniia raboty po sozdaniiu zhirnomolochnogo stada krupnogo rogatogo skota v kolkhozakh i sovkhozakh putem ispol'zovaniia plemennykh zhivotnykh, proiskhodiashchikh s fermy 'Gorki Leninskie,' i ikh potomkov."

156. A very powerful refutation of Lysenko's view, which derived its strength from its illustration of the overwhelming practical utility as well as theoretical beauty of modern genetics, was Medvedev and Kirpichnikov, "Perspektivy sovetskoi genetiki." This article elicited a response from the supporter of Lysenko M. A. Ol'shanskii in "Protiv fal'sifikatsii v biologicheskoi nauke."

157. "O rezul'tatakh proverki deiatel'nosti bazy 'gorki leninskie,'" *Vestnik akademii nauk* (1965), 11:124.

158. Lysenko, of course, never accepted the idea of coexistence of different approaches to biology. For an example of his exclusivity, where he demands that biologists abandon "incorrect" theories, see his *Agrobiology*, p. 135.

159. B. E. Bykhovskii, academic secretary of the Department of General Biology of the Academy of Sciences, commented: "Almost from the very date of the formation of this department we began to receive signals that all was not well in the administration of Lenin Hills farm." *Vestnik akademii nauk* (1965), 11:107. Also see Lysenko's comments on Semenov in *ibid.*, p. 61; Semenov, "Nauke ne terpit sub"ektivizma"; and my chapter on Semenov's reform plans, "Reorganization of the Academy of Sciences," in Juviler and Morton, eds., *Soviet Policy-Making.* Semenov told Walter Sullivan of *The New York Times* in the summer of 1967, "My goal, since 1950, has been to achieve a marriage between biology and chemistry. At first it was slowed by the difficulties of the times—the Lysenko problem. However five years ago I was able to form a new Division of Biophysics, Biochemistry and Physiologically Active Compounds within the Academy. . . . At first it was a mechanical mixture, but now it is nearly a chemical compound." Personal conversation, Walter Sullivan, July 14, 1957.

160. See Medvedev, *The Rise and Fall of T. D. Lysenko,* pp. 215–17.

161. *Ibid.,* pp. 198–99.

162. See, for example, Dudintsev, "Net, istina," for an interesting story of a specialist on polyploidy who was forced out of her job in Vavilov's old institute but who for ten years carried out research in her own garden. Also see Bianki and Stepanov, "Kto napisala oproverzhenie?"

163. Vorontsov, "Zhizn' toropit: nuzhny sovremennye posobiia po biologii."

164. Agranovskii, "Nauka na veru ne prinimaet." The details of this article were later confirmed by the investigating committee of the Academy of Sciences. See "O rezul'tatakh proverki deiatel'nosti bazy 'gorki leninskie.'"

165. *Vestnik akademii nauk* 1965, 11:00.

166. *Ibid.,* p. 93. Notice that there is one exception to the decline in butterfat content, that opposite 9/16 [5/16]. The number 9/16 must be a typographical error in the report. The correct order in sequence would be 5/16; this correction would also explain the comment in the report, "Only in one instance, with a difference of 1/16, was the lower group a little higher."

167. *Ibid.,* p. 108.

168. One of Lysenko's eccentricities may actually have limited the damage he did. He frowned upon artificial insemination. On his own farm it was not

practiced. Therefore, each of his bulls was able to impregnate only forty to forty-five cows a year. Through artificial insemination one bull can service on an average two thousand cows annually, and Lysenko's mixed breed bulls could have spoiled much larger numbers of cows. No doubt artificial insemination was used with some bulls originally from Lysenko's farm, since many Soviet farms employed the practice and Lysenko himself spoke favorably of it on occasion. See *ibid.*, p. 15, for evidence that Lysenko did not permit artificial insemination on his farm; see Lysenko, "Vazhnye rezervy kolkhozov i sovkhozov," for statements showing that he recommended it elsewhere.

169. There is evidence that Lysenko or his assistants tried to conceal important evidence, particularly that pertaining to the reasons for eliminating certain numbers of the herd. *Vestnik akademii nauk* (1965), 11:17, 18.

170. "Raz"iasneniia komissii v sviazi s zamechaniiami akademika T. D. Lysenko," *ibid.*, p. 73.

171. *Ibid.*, pp. 91–92.

172. See p. 144 of this volume.

173. Walter Sullivan, "The Death and Rebirth of a Science," p. 287.

174. Walter Sullivan, personal conversation, July 14, 1967.

175. Dubinin, "Sovremennaia genetika v svete marksistskoleninskoi filosofii." For information about Dubinin's sufferings during Lysenko's period of greatest influence, see Medvedev, *The Rise and Fall of T. D. Lysenko.*

176. As Sewall Wright observed: "I am sure that most geneticists would consider the view that heredity is something that can be sucked out of an egg with a micropipette, or shattered with X-rays, with consequences in later generations that exactly parallel the ones that can be seen in the chromosomes, as less idealistic than such popular relics of sympathetic magic as the inheritance of acquired characters, or the usually associated doctrine of maternal impressions." Sewall Wright, "Dogma or Opportunism?"

177. G. Platonov, "Dogmy starye i dogmy novye." This article, which attempted a sort of "synthesis" of classical genetics and Michurinism, was severely criticized by Efroimson in a letter to *Voprosy filosofii* (1966), 8:175–81.

178. Ferents Pinter, "Aktual'nye voprosy vzaimootnosheniia marksistskoi filosofii i genetiki." Pinter believed that the advent of DNA research and cytoplasmic inheritance proved that in certain aspects the Michurinists were correct in their criticism of Mendelism. This comment ignores the fact that the Michurinists made absolutely no contribution in this direction; on the contrary, this research proceeded directly out of the neo-Mendelian tradition. As Julian Huxley commented, "Even if some new theoretical interpretation proves to be required, it cannot start from far behind the present front of science, as Lysenko does, but must take account of existing knowledge." Huxley, *Heredity East and West*, p. 218.

179. It is, of course, true that Lysenko twisted Michurin's beliefs. This has been pointed out many times, including the 1936 genetics conference. See, for example, Targul'ian, *Spornye voprosy genetiki i selektsii*, pp. 399–400.

180. N. P. Dubinin, "I. V. Michurin i sovremennaia genetika."

181. Frolov, *Genetika i dialektika.* Subsequent page references in the text refer to this work.

182. Platonov, *Zhizn', nasledstvennost', izmenchivost'*.
183. *Ibid.*, pp. 158–159.
184. *Ibid.*, pp. 26–27, 48, 52, 92, 133–34, 152, 177, 181–89, 204.
185. *Ibid.*, pp. 10–48, 181–89. Another Lysenkoite book of the post-Lysenko period was Davitashvili, *Izmenchivost' organizmov v geologicheskom proshlom;* see, especially, p. 45.
186. Ostrianin and Martynenko, "Metodologicheskie voprosy sovremennoi biologii."
187. Pastushnyi, *Genetika ka ob"ekt filosofskogo analiza.*
188. *Ibid.*, pp. 144 ff.
189. *Ibid.*, pp. 55 ff., 98, 108–9, 144, 240 ff.
190. Frolov, *Genetika i dialektika*, p. 13.
191. *Ibid.*, p. 16 and *passim.*
192. Frolov and Pastushnyi, *Mendelizm i filosofskie problemy sovremennoi genetiki.*

5. PHYSIOLOGY AND PSYCHOLOGY

1. Sechenov submitted the manuscript under its original title to the literary and sociopolitical journal *Sovremennik,* where it was stopped by the censor. The very fact that a journal of this nature would attempt publication of a work on physiology reveals the philosophical and political implications seen in Sechenov's interpretation. His treatise eventually appeared in the much more specialized *Meditsinskii vestnik.*

2. E. A. Budilova in 1960 called the main organ of the Moscow Psychological Society, *Voprosy filosofii i psikhologii,* published after 1890, "an organ of reaction in science," a "tribune of militant idealism" for "all twenty-eight years of its existence." E. A. Budilova, *Bor'ba materializma v russkoi psikhologicheskoi nauke: vtoraia polovina XIX—nachalo XX v,* p. 108.

3. David Joravsky is currently working on this topic.

4. Pavlov quoted in Asratian, *I. P. Pavlov, His Life and Work,* p. 60.

5. Pavlov quoted in Babkin, *Pavlov: A Biolgraphy,* pp. 276–7.

6. See my *The Soviet Academy of Sciences and the Communist Party, 1927–1932,* pp. 108, 109, 113, 116–18.

7. Anokhin, *Ivan Petrovich Pavlov: zhizn' deiatel'nost' i nauchnaia shkola,* p. 352.

8. See *Akademik I. P. Pavlov: Izbrannye trudy po fiziologii vysshei nervnoi deiatel'nosti,* p. 167.

9. See, for example, Kupalov, "Uchenie o reflekse i reflektornoi deiatel'nosti i perspektivy ego razvitiia," p. 151.

10. Bassin, "Zakliuchitel'nye slova," p. 720.

11. Petrovskii, *Istoriia sovetskoi psikhologii.* Petrovskii's work, published at a relatively relaxed time, contains interesting discussions of such men as P. P. Blonskii, K. N. Kornilov, and B. M. Bekhterev. These are men whose schools of thought were later criticized by the Communist Party, but Petrovskii gives a fairly sympathetic account of their efforts to reconstruct pre-Revolutionary psychology. Bauer, *The New Man in Soviet Psychology,* is perceptive and scholarly but, surprisingly, does not go very far into the efforts of individual Soviet

writers to link their views with Marxism. The implication is that the efforts were hypocritical. There is considerable truth in his observation that "during the twenties the Marxist ideology appears to have functioned primarily as a screening device whereby certain schools of psychology were rejected as unacceptable" (p. 62), but his approach makes it quite difficult to understand why some psychologists, particularly at later dates, took their Marxism quite seriously.

12. K. Kornilov, "Dialekticheskii metod v psikhologii," p. 108.

13. Struminskii, "Marksizm v sovremennoi psikhologii," p. 213. Struminskii was a militant materialist whose scholarship was careless. See critical reviews of him, and his replies, in *Pod znamenem marksizma* (November–December 1923), pp. 299–304 and March 1924, pp. 250–54, 255–59.

14. See Freud, *Civilization and Its Discontents*, pp. 59–61.

15. B. Bykhovskii, "O metodologicheskikh osnovaniiakh psikhoanaliticheskogo ucheniia Freida," pp. 169, 176–77.

16. Philip Pomper discusses Trotsky's interests in Freud, both in the twenties and the thirties, in his *Trotsky's Notebooks, 1933–35.*

17. There is no space here to discuss important developments in applied psychology, such as the psychology of labor or psychotechnics. These developments do play an important role, however, in the general history of Soviet psychology.

18. See Boring, "Psychology, History of."

19. Bauer, *The New Man in Soviet Psychology*, pp. 93–102.

20. *Ibid.*, p. 124.

21. *Ibid.*

22. Iaroshevskii, *Istoriia psikhologii*, p. 542.

23. Luria quoted in Zangwill, "Psychology: Current Approaches," p. 122.

24. Luria, *Higher Cortical Functions in Man*, p. 2.

25. Brushlinskii, "Kul'turno-istoricheskaia teoriia myshleniia."

26. The translators commented, "Although our more compact rendition would be called an abridged version of the original, we feel that the condensation has increased clarity and readability without any loss of thought content or factual information." Eugenie Hanfmann and Gertrude Vakar, translators' Preface to Vygotsky, *Thought and Language*, p. xii. Subsequent page references in the text refer to this translation.

27. Vygotsky, *Izbrannye psikhologicheskie issledovaniia*, pp. 91–92; also see p. 105.

28. Piaget, quoted in Vygotsky, *Thought and Language*, p. 12.

29. Stalin, *Marxism and Linguistics*, p. 36.

30. See *Scientific Session on the Physiological Teaching of Academician I. P. Pavlov*. For interpretations, see Wetter, *Dialectical Materialism*, pp. 473–87; Tucker, "Stalin and the Uses of Psychology," in *Soviet Political Mind;* pp. 91–121.

31. *Scientific Session on the Physiological Teaching of Academician I. P. Pavlov*, pp. 12–15.

32. *Ibid.*, p. 19.

33. Josef Brozek, "Soviet Contributions to History," p. 433. I am grateful to Professor Brozek for a copy of his review.

34. Petrovskii, *Istoriia sovetskoi psikhologii*, p. 336.

35. *Ibid.*

36. Rubinshtein, *Printsipy i puti razvitiia psikhologii*, p. 3. Rubinshtein wrote in the 1934 article that his major goal was to find solutions to the main problems of modern psychology with the help of Marx's writings and, on the basis of these solutions, to begin the construction of a Marxist-Leninist psychology. See Rubinshtein, "Problemy psikhologii v trudakh Karla Marksa," p. 4. For other important publications of Rubinshtein see: *Osnovy psikhologii; Osnovy obshchei psikhologii;* "Uchenie I. P. Pavlova i nekotorye voprosy perestroiki psikhologii"; *Bytie i soznanie: o meste psikhicheskogo vo vseobshchei vzaimosviazi iavlenii material-nogo mira;* "Filosofiia i psikhologiia"; "Voprosy psikhologii myshleniia i printsip determinizma"; *O myshlenii i putiakh ego issledovaniia;* and *Printsipy i puti razvitiia psikhologii.*

37. Bauer, *The New Man in Soviet Psychology*, p. 118.

38. Rubinshtein, "Rech'."

39. At the 1962 conference on the philosophical problems of physiology and psychology, to be discussed subsequently, E. V. Shorokhova indicated the continuing influence of Rubinshtein: "In our report we are expressing the position of the Psychology Section of the Institute of Philosophy. Our point of view is to a large degree the collective opinion of that group which was created and led, until his death, by S. L. Rubinshtein. We consider it our responsibility to develop Rubinshtien's principles and to defend his views against the mistaken interpretation which they occasionally encounter." See *Filosofskie voprosy fiziologii vysshei nervnoi deiatel'nosti i psikhologii,* pp. 730–31.

40. See "Sergei Leonidovich Rubinshtein."

41. Rubinshtein, *Osnovy obshchei psikhologii*, p. 5.

42. *Ibid.*

43. Kolbanovskii seems to have misunderstood Rubinshtein when he accused him of equating "psychic facts" with material objects, the error for which Lenin once criticized Joseph Dietzgen. Rubinshtein was more vulnerable to the charge that he had removed psychic phenomena from the area of material events than that he had equated them. See Kolbanovskii, "Za marksistskoe osveshchenie voprosov psikhologii," p. 57; and Rubinshtein, *Osnovy obshchei psikhologii,* p. 5.

44. Kolbanovskii much later noted this change. His earlier quite critical tone was now tempered with praise. See Kolbanovskii, "Zekliuchitel'noe slovo."

45. Rubinshtein, "Uchenie I. P. Pavlova i nekotorye voprosy perestroiki psikhologii," p. 201.

46. Rubinshtein, *Bytie i soznanie*, p. 33.

47. *Ibid.*, pp. 10–11.

48. Marx and Engels, *Sochineniia* 1:180.

49. *Voprosy filosofii* (1960), 1:180.

50. Rubinshtein, *Bytie i soznanie*, pp. 11–12.

51. *Ibid.*, pp. 4–5.

52. *Ibid.*, p. 34.

53. Rubinshtein, *Printsipy i puti razvitiia psikhologii,* p. 8. Subsequent page references in the text refer to this work.

54. See Luria, "Psychoanalysis as a System of Monistic Psychology"; this was originally published in K. P. Kornilov, ed. *Psikhologiia i marksizm* (Leningrad; 1925, pp. 476–80.

55. Luria quoted in Cole, ed., *The Selected Writings of A. R. Luria*, pp. 31 and 41.

56. Luria, *The Making of Mind*, p. 43.

57. *Ibid.*, p. 45.

58. The best English-language source is Cole, ed., *The Selected Writings of A. R. Luria*.

59. Luria, "A Child's Speech Responses and the Social Environment," in *ibid.*, pp. 45–77.

60. Luria, "Paths of Development of Thought in the Child," pp. 97–144.

61. Luria, "The Development of Writing in the Child," pp. 145–194.

62. Luria, *The Making of Mind*, p. 65. Subsequent page references to this work will be indicated in the text.

63. Michael Cole in Luria, *The Making of Mind*, p. 214.

64. Fedoseev *et. al.*, eds., *Filosofskie voprosy fiziologii vysshei nervnoi deiatel'- nosti i psikhologii.* Subsequent page references for quotes from various authors at the Conference on Philosophic Questions are from this volume.

65. Eccles, *The Neurophysiological Basis of Mind*, pp. 278–79.

66. Grashchenkov told the conference that after the 1950 Pavlov session he was labeled the Number One Anti-Pavlovian and that as a result he lost his position and could not publish his works for a number of years. See Fedoseev et al., *Ibid.*, p. 736.

67. See *Obshchie osnovy fiziologii truda*, p. 447.

68. See, for example, Rosenblueth, Wiener, and Bigelow, "Behavior, Purpose and Teleology"; and Ashby, *Design for a Brain: The Origin of Adaptive Behaviour.*

69. See *Fedoseev et al.*, pp. 646–47.

70. D. A. Biriukov's similar attempt to classify Soviet authors was very helpful to me; see *ibid.*, pp. 378–79.

71. See Arkhipov, "O material'nosti psikhiki i predmete psikhologii," *Sovetskaia pedagogika;* and Eroshkin, *Psikhologiia i fiziologiia vysshei nervnoi deiatel nosti.*

72. See Kal'sin, *Osnovnye voprosy teorii poznaniia.* Kedrov tried to sketch an over-all classification of moving matter in all nature, from nonliving to living, culminating in human society. See his "O sootnoshenii form dvizheniia materii v prirode," in Fedoseev *et al.*, eds., *Filosofskie problemy sovremennogo estestvoznaniia*, pp. 137–211.

73. Lebedev, "Materiia i soznanie," pp. 70–84.

74. Kolbanovskii, in Fedoseev, et al., *Filosofskie voprosy fiziologii vysshei nervnoi deiatel'nosti i psikhologii*, p. 606.

75. See Georgiev, "Problema chuvstvennogo i ratsional'nogo v poznanii."

76. See Fedoseev et al., *Filosofskie voprosy fiziologii . . .*, pp. 646–47.

77. Several of his important publications are listed in the bibliography.

78. Anokhin, "Metodologicheskii analiz uzlovykh problem uslovnogo refleksa," in Fedoseev et al., eds. *Filosofskie voprosy fiziologii . . .*, p. 158.

79. *Ibid.*

80. Anokhin, *Ivan Petrovich Pavlov*, p. 349.

81. Anokhin, ed., *Problema tsentra i periferii v fiziologii nervnoi deiatel'nosti*, p. 52.

82. Anokhin, "Uzlovye voprosy v izuchenii vysshei nervnoi deiatel'nosti," p. 12.

83. See Anokhin, *Ivan Petrovich Pavlov;* p. 351.

84. See Fedoseev et al., *Filosofskie voprosy fiziologii . . .*, p. 716.

85. Anokhin, *Ivan Petrovich Pavlov*, p. 335.

86. See Anokhin, "Uzlovye voprosy v izuchenii vysshei nervnoi deiatel'nosti," p. 9.

87. *Ibid.*, p. 18.

88. N. A. Bernshtein, whose approach was in many ways similar to Anokhin's, objected to the term "return afferentiation" on the basis of the fact that all afferentiation is "return afferentiation"; a "nonreturn" afferentiation does not exist. Bernshtein, "Novye linii razvitiia v fiziologii i ikh sootnoshenie s kibernetikoi," p. 303.

89. Anokhin, "Osobennosti afferentnogo apparata uslovnogo refleksa i ikh znachenie dlia psikhologii," p. 21. Subsequent page references in the text refer to this article.

90. For a short description in classical Pavlovian terms see Babkin, *Pavlov: A Biography*, p. 311.

91. See Boring, *A History of Experimental Psychology*, pp. 562–63.

92. Leont'ev, *Activity, Consciousness, and Personality*. Subsequent page references in the text refer to this volume which is a translation of Leont'ev's *Deiatel'nost', soznanie, lichnost'* (Moscow, 1975).

93. See Lange, *Teoriia V. Vundta o nachale mifa*, p. 23, and the discussion in Leont'ev, ed., *Vospriiatie i deiatel'nost'*, pp. 9–10.

94. See, for example, Fedoseev, et al., *Filosofskie voprosy fiziologii*, pp. 450–51.

95. *Ibid.*, p. 456.

96. *Ibid.*, p. 685.

97. See Uznadze, *Psikhologicheskie issledovaniia.*

98. See Fedoseev et al., *Filosofskie voprosy*, p. 471.

99. *Ibid.*, pp. 650–53.

100. *Ibid.*, p. 654.

101. See, for example, F. F. Lomov, "Psikhologicheskaia sluzhba strany," *Vestnik akademii nauk SSSR* (1980), 1:20–30; and his "Razvitie tekhniki i problemy psikhologii," *Vestnik akademii nauk SSSR* (1981), 1:30–40.

102. See "Filosofskie problemy deiatel'nosti (Materialy 'Kruglogo stola')."

103. See Sheila Cole, "Soviet Family Clubs and Human Potential."

104. The only one available to me has been: Nikitin, *Stupen'ki tvorchestva.*

105. I attended one of these sessions in Spaso House in Moscow in January, 1983, when Elmer Green, a specialist in biofeedback from the Menninger Clinic, gave a lecture. See Leont'ev, *Activity, Consciousness, and Personality.*

6. THE NATURE-NURTURE DEBATE

1. See p. 138. All of the major scholars studying Lysenkoism agree on this point. See Joravsky, *The Lysenko Affair;* and Medvedev, *The Rise and Fall of T.*

D. *Lysenko;* and the first edition of this book, Graham, *Science and Philosophy in the Soviet Union.* Nonetheless, the myth that Lysenkoism was based on the Soviet desire "to create a New Soviet Man" lives on in much literature on the Soviet Union, proving that no amount of scholarship can kill an attractive idea.

2. See Graham, "Science and Values."

3. Semashko, *Izbrannye proizvedeniia,* p. 312.

4. On Vygotsky's political views, see Kozulin, *Psychology in Utopia,* p. 116.

5. See Cole, ed., *The Selected Writings of A. R. Luria,* p. 6. Cole has pointed out that neither Vygotsky nor Luria opposed genetic studies of human behavior; indeed, both were criticized by Marxists for "dualism" on this issue. Nonetheless, Vygotsky and Luria became known for their heavy emphasis on social influences on the human psyche.

6. Leontiev, *Activity, Consciousness and Personality,* p. 17.

7. Teplov, *Problemy individual'nykh razlichii* and *Tipologicheskie svoistva nervnoi sistemy i ikh znachenie dlia psikhologii.*

8. For Nebylitsyn's description of his reason for the change of title, see *Problemy differentsial'noi psikhofiziologii,* 6:3.

9. See Ravich-Shcherbo, "Otsenka sily nervnoi sistemy po zavisimosti vremeni reaktsii ot intensivnosti stimula"; Ravich-Shcherbo and Shibarovskaia, "Struktura dinamichnosti nervnykh protsessov u detei shkol'nogo vozrasta"; Ravich-Shcherbo, "Vozmozhnyi eksperimental'nyi podkhod k izucheniiu biologicheskogo i sotsial'nogo v cheloveke"; Karpets and Kudriatsev, *Genetika, Povedenie, Otvetstvennost,* p. 23.

10. Krutetskii, *Psikhologiia matematicheskikh sposobnostei shkol'nikov,* p. 399.

11. Prokof'ev, *XXV s"ezd KPSS: stenograficheskii otchet,* 2:179.

12. For an attack on Frolov from a sympathizer with Lysenko, see Shaikin, "S odnostoronnykh pozitsii. O knige 'Genetika i dialektika.' "

13. See Liseev and Sharov, "Kruglyi stol 'Voprosy filosofii': Genetika cheloveka, ee filosofskie i sotsial'no-eticheskie problemy." See also their "Iz redaktsionnoi pochty: po sledam diskussii" and "Nauka, etika, gumanizm: kruglyi stol 'Voprosy filosofii.' "

14. Liseev and Sharov, "Genetika cheloveka," p. 107. See also Frolov, *Perspektivy cheloveka,* pp. 209–14.

15. Liseev and Sharov, "Kruglyi stol . . .," p. 125.

16. Entitled "V. P. Efroimson's Article on the Genesis of Ethics,' the article appeared in *Politicheskii dnevnik* (February, 1969), no. 53.

17. Liseev and Sharov, "Kruglyi stol . . .," p. 126.

18. See Simonov, "Iskriashchie kontakty."

19. See Efroimson, "Rodoslovnaia al'truizma."

20. Efroimson was quoted as making this direct assertion elsewhere: Frolov, *Perspektivy Cheloveka,* p. 209. In later years Efroimson wrote a world history of great intellectuals and political leaders whose activities he interpreted within a genetic framework. He was unable to publish the book in the Soviet Union.

21. Efroimson, p. 204.

22. *Ibid.,* p. 207.

23. *Ibid.,* p. 210.

24. See Gould, *The Mismeasure of Man;* see also R. C. Lewontin, Steven Rose, and Leon J. Kamin, *Not in Our Genes: Biology, Ideology, and Human Nature,* New York, 1984.

25. Efroimson, p. 206.

26. See Astaurov, "HOMO SAPIENS ET HUMANUS."

27. *Ibid.,* p. 20.

28. I am much indebted to Mark Adams for information on this period, both from personal conversations and from his writings. See the bibliography for a listing of Adams' works.

29. Dubinin, *Vechnoe Dvizhenie.*

30. Adams, "Science, Ideology, and Structure," p. 185.

31. *Ibid.* Other Soviet writers besides Dubinin who criticized Efroimson and Astaurov included Fedoseev, "Problema sotsial'nogo i biologicheskogo v filosofii i sotsiologii"; B. G. Anan'ev, *Chelovek kak predmet poznaniia;* and Okonskaia *Dialektika sotsial'nogo i biologicheskogo v istoricheskom protsesse.*

32. See Dubinin, "Filosofskie i sotsiologicheskie aspekty genetiki cheloveka"; "Filosofiia dialekticheskogo materializma i problemy genetiki"; "Integriruiush-chaia rol' genetiki v biologii i evoliutsionnnom uchenii"; "Biologicheskie i sotsial'nye faktory v razvitii cheloveka"; and Dubinin and Gorodetskii, "Geneticheskaia inzheneriia: zadachi sovremennykh issledovanii."

33. Frolov, "Zagadka zhizni, nauchnyi poisk i filosofskaia bor'ba," pp. 90, 92.

34. The most famous of these was the "cucumber affair" of 1972 when Dubinin took seriously a co-worker's joke about improving the flavor of cucumbers by genetic engineering them in a way that allowed them to absorb salt; Dubinin, like many other senior Soviet scientists, was accustomed to taking credit for work performed by his subordinates, and he claimed credit for the marvelous cucumber, thereby making himself the laughingstock of many other geneticists. See the description in Adams, "Science, Ideology, and Structure," p. 192.

35. The manuscript surveyed great figures from Alexander the Great to Einstein. A few women, including Joan of Arc, were featured in the mostly male chronology. A more academic article by Efroimson seeking a biochemical basis for intelligence is Efroimson, "K biokhimicheskoi genetike intellekta."

36. See Kerkis, "Geneticheskie posledstviia zagriaznenii sredy."

37. See, for example, Dubinin's speech at the general assembly of the Academy of Sciences in 1980, as reported in *Vestnik akademii nauk SSSR* (1981), 6:46.

38. Bochkov, *Genetika cheloveka: nasledstvennost' i patologiia,* p. 89, and "Metodologicheskie i sotsial'nye voprosy sovremennoi genetiki cheloveka," pp. 52, 55.

39. See Noi, *Metodologicheskie problemy sovetskoi kriminologii.*

40. Kerkis, "Nuzhna li kriminologam genetika?"

41. Dubinin, Karpets, and Kudriavtsev, *Genetika, Povedenie, Otvetstvennost',* p. 162.

42. See *Sootnoshenie biologicheskogo i sotsial'nogo v cheloveke* and *Biologicheskoe i sotsial'noe v razvitii cheloveka.* See also Tarasov and Chernenko, *Sotsial'naia determinirovannost' biologii cheloveka,* p. 21.

43. See Il'enkov, "Stanovlenie lichnosti: k itogam nauchnogo eksperimenta."
44. Ibid., p. 79.
45. Ibid., p. 77.
46. An example of one of Stoletov's pro-Lysenko articles is his "Nekotorye metodologicheskie voprosy genetiki."
47. See Dubinin, "Nasledovanie biologicheskoe i sotsial'noe."
48. Conversations with Edward Keenan, Cambridge, Massachusetts, Fall, 1984.
49. Vestnik akademii nauk SSSR (1981), 6:44–45.
50. Ibid., p. 46.
51. Ibid., p. 47.
52. See Vestnik akademii nauk SSSR (1981), 12:123.
53. See Tarasov and Chernenko, Sotsial'naia determinirovannost' biologii cheloveka. Subsequent page references in the text refer to this work.
54. Materialy plenuma tsentral'nogo komiteta KPSS, 14–15 iiunia 1983 goda (Moscow: 1983), p. 55. I am grateful to Erich Goldhagen, Divinity School, Harvard University, for originally pointing this reference out to me.
55. For example, see Tsaregorodtsev, "Meditsina v fokuse ideologicheskoi bor'by."
56. Ibid., p. 3; Boshniakov, "Mirovozzrenie i meditsina" and "O nekotorykh metodologicheskikh problemakh sootnosheniia sotsial'nogo i biologicheskogo," Zdravokhranenie rossiiskoi federatsii (1982), 8:9–13; Sapegina and Tsybukh, "Nekotorye problemy vrachebnoi etiki i meditsinskoi deontologii v deiatel'nosti sanitarno-epidemiologicheskoi sluzhby"; and Serdiuk, "Zdorov'e cheloveka, nauchno-tekhnicheskii progress i okruzhaiushchaia sfera."

7. BIOLOGY AND HUMAN BEINGS: SPECIALIZED TOPICS

1. See Caplan, ed., The Sociobiology Debate; Barker, "Racism: The New Inheritors"; Albury, "Politics and Rhetoric in the Sociobiology Debate"; R. C. Lewontin, S. Rose, and L. Kamin, Not in Our Genes: Biology, Ideology and Human Nature (New York: 1984); and Chandler Davis, "La Sociobiologie et son Explication de l'Humanite'."
2. Satdinova, "Sotsiobiologiia—'za' i 'protiv.' "
3. Efimov, "Etika i moralevedenie."
4. Ignat'ev, "Sotsiobiologiia cheloveka: 'Teoriia genno-kul'turnoi koevoliutsii.' "
5. Dubinin, Karpets, Kudriavtsev, Genetika, povedenie, otvetstvennost', p. 196.
6. Karimskii, " 'Sotsial'nyi biologizm' v sovremennoi burzhuaznoi filosofii."
7. Frolov, Perspektivy cheloveka, pp. 58, 69, 74, 84.
8. Conversations with Frolov in Boston, March, 1985. Also, see the review of Western attitudes towards sociobiology in Komarov, "Sotsiobiologiia i problema cheloveka."
9. "Chelovek kak kompleksnaia problema," Voprosy filosofii (1983), 10:44, pp. 37–48.
10. Bol'shaia sovetskaia entsiklopediia (Moscow: 1940), vol. 46, cols. 764–65.
11. In Semenov, quoted in Dubinin, Karpets, Kudriavtsev, Genetika, povedenie, otvetstvennost', p. 59.

12. Literature on the XYY characteristic can be found in: *Zhurnal nevropatologii i psikhiatrii im. S. S. Korsakova* (1976), 3:413–16, "Sindrom XYY (Kratkaia klinikomorfologicheskaia kharakteristika)" G. P. Marinina, T.A. Blagoveshchenskaia, N. I. Oleinikov; *ibid.* (1976), 12: 1839–43, "Shizofrenicheskie i shizofrenodobnie proiavleniia pri sindrome 47, XYY," N. N. Timofeev, L. A. Petrov, R. I. Kulikov; Efroimson, "Khromosomnye anomalii tipa XXY i XYY kak odna iz prichin seksual'nykh narushenii"; *Shestoi vsesoiuznyi s"ezd nevropatologov i psikhiatrov: tezisy dokladov* (Moscow: 1975), 3:505–524; Efroimson and Kalmykova, "Uspekhi nevrologicheskoi i psikhiatricheskoi genetiki"; Kuznetsova, "Kriminologiia i genetika"; and Kuznetsova and Leikina, "Kriminilogicheskii aspekt sootnosheniia sotsial'nogo i biologicheskogo." On the Boston controversy, see Culliton, "XYZ: Harvard Researcher Under Fire Stops Newborn Screening," and Roblin, "The Boston XYY Case."

13. Struchkov, "O mekhanizme vzaimnogo vliianiia obstoiatel'stv, obuslovlivaiushchikh sovershenie prestuplenii," p. 115.

14. Pastushnyi, *Filosofiia i sovremennaia biologiia*, p. 195.

15. Avanesov, *Kriminologiia, prognostika, upravlenie*, p. 91.

16. Volkov, *Deterministicheskaia priroda prestupnogo povedeniia*, pp. 80, 85–86.

17. *Kriminologiia*, p. 108.

18. Bochkov, "Metodologicheskie i sotsial'nye voprosy sovremennoi genetiki cheloveka," p. 53. Despite Bochkov's caution, he was one of the naturists in the debates, and the author of the first Soviet full treatment of human genetics: Bochkov, *Genetika cheloveka: nasledstvennost' i patologiia.*

19. Dubinin, Karpets, and Kudriavtsev, *Genetika, povedenie, otvetstvennost'*, pp. 59–64.

20. *Ibid.*, p. 113.

21. *Ibid.*, p. 109.

22. See Yanov, *The Russian New Right*, and Dunlop, *The Faces of Contemporary Russian Nationalism.*

23. Raisa Berg, *Sukhovei*, pp. 289–291.

24. Dubinin, Karpets and Kudriavtsev, pp. 101–2.

25. Gumilev, *Etnogenez i biosfera zemli.*

26. My analysis here is based on the following two sources and on conversations in Moscow in 1983 and 1984: Borodai, "Etnicheskie kontakty i okruzhaiushchaia sreda," and Kedrov, Grigulevich, and Kryvelev, "Po povodu stat'i Iu. M. Borodaia 'Etnicheskie kontakty i okruzhaiushchaia sreda.'"

27. See the bibliography for a listing of some of Gumilev's works.

28. Other Soviet ethnographers and geographers also used the term "ethnos" without ascribing to it the speculative scheme used by Gumilev. See, for example, Bromlei, *Ocherki teorii etnosa.*

29. See Kedrov, Grigulevich, and Kryvelev.

30. See Werner Hahn, "B. M. Kedrov—A Soviet 'Liberal,'" in his *Postwar Soviet Politics*, pp. 161–81.

31. See Tsaregorodtsev and Ivaniushkin, "Meditsina i etika" and Frolov, "O zhizni, smerti i bessmertii." See also the numerous citations to Soviet literature on death and dying given in the two articles by Frolov.

32. Amosov cited in Malein, "Pravo na meditsinskii eksperiment" and Avdeev, "Pravovoe regulirovanie peresadok organov i tkanei." Also, see Gorelik, "Pra-

vovye aspekty transplantatsii organov i tkanei"; Ioirysh, "Novye vozhmozhnosti biologicheskoi nauki i pravo"; Petrovskii, "Peresadka organov"; Bogomolova, *Donorstvo;* and Gorelik, *Pravovye aspekty peresadki organov i tkanei.*

33. Goodfield, *Playing God,* p. 6.

34. Fletcher, *The Ethics of Genetic Control,* pp. 172–73.

35. O. Desiatchikova wrote, "Soviet genetics conducts an uncompromising struggle for the preservation of the existing genetic constitution of man, and does not try to substitute for it any kind that might today seem better." Desiatchikova, "Sovremennaia genetika i ideologicheskaia bor'ba," p. 71. Frolov criticized Fletcher by name in his "Nauka—tsennosti—gumanizm." pp. 39–40.

36. Karpinskaia, "Mirovozzrencheskoe znachenie sovremennoi biologii," p. 101.

37. Baev, ignoring Marxism's attempted unification of the factual and the normative, followed Hume's separation of the two realms: "The categories of good and evil are not applicable to nature." Baev, "Sotsial'nye aspekty geneticheskoi inzhenerii," p. 145.

38. Frolov, *Chelovek-nauka-tekhnika;* "Chelovek segodnia i zavtra"; *Nauka i nravstvennost';* "O dialektike i etike biologicheskogo poznaniia"; "Perspektivy cheloveka"; *Perspektivy cheloveka; Progress nauki i budushchee cheloveka;* and *Zhizn'i poznanie.*

39. See Frolov and Iudin, "Etika nauki," Frolov, "O dialektike i etike biologicheskogo poznaniia," pp. 39, 41.

40. Frolov, "Aktual'nye filosofskie i sotsial'nye problemy nauki i tekhniki," p. 18.

41. Frolov and Pastushnyi, *Mendelizm i filosofskie problemy sovremennoi genetiki,* p. 4. For additional writings by Frolov touching on genetic engineering, see "Chelovek segodnia i zavtra," especially pp. 16–17 and "Perspektivy cheloveka."

42. Frolov, *Progress nauki i budushchee cheloveka,* pp. 160–175.

43. See "Charter: Ethical Advisory Board," approved December 27, 1976, by David Mathews, Secretary, Department of Health, Education and Welfare.

44. See "In Brief," *Hastings Center Report* (October, 1979), pp. 2–3 (February, 1980), pp. 2–3 and (February, 1981), p. 2. Also see "The Washington Scene: President's Commission One Year Later," *Hastings Center Report* (February, 1981), p. 2.

45. *Federal Register* (January 26, 1981), 46(16):8376.

46. See Graham, "Science, Citizens, and the Policy-Making Process." For Soviet articles where the issue is approached, see Turbin, "Geneticheskaia inzheneriia" and "Genetika i obshchestvo"; Timakov and Bochkov, "Sotsial'nye problemy genetiki cheloveka"; Smirnov, "Metodologiia i mirovozzrenia"; and Grushin, "Dialekticheskii materializm i sovremennaia nauka."

47. See Vel'kov, "Opasny li opyty s rekombinantnymi DNK." Vel'kov was also a member of the Interdepartmental Commission, and he listed Baev as chairman.

48. See *Vremennyi pravila bezopasnosti rabot s rekombinantnymi DNK.* Compare it with "NIH Guidelines for Research Involving Recombinant DNA Molecules," U.S. Department of Health, Education and Welfare, June 23, 1976, and sub-

sequent revisions listed in *The Federal Register* (1979), 44(232), and (1980), 45(20), and 45(22). For Soviet discussions of the risks of recombinant DNA research, see, in addition to the Vel'kov article listed above: Baev, "Sovremennaia biologiia kak sotsial'noe iavlenie"; Uil'iamson, "Budushchee gennoi inzhenerii"; and Shirtsov, "Problema riska pri genno-inzhenernyk issledovaniiakh."

49. *Spravochnik akademii nauk SSSR* (Moscow, 1982).

50. Frolov, "Nauka—tsennosti—gumanizm," p. 30; see also his *Perspektivy cheloveka* and *O dialektiki i etike biologicheskogo poznaniia*, as well as Iudin, "Etika nauchnogo issledovaniia."

51. See Graham, "Reasons for Studying Soviet Science: The Example of Genetic Engineering." See also Frolov, "Nauka—tsennosti—gumanizm."

52. See, for example, Dyban, "Schastlivyi zapret prirody." For a Soviet author who is rather horrified by the whole idea of genetic engineering, see Shishkin, *Chelovecheskaia priroda i nravstvennosti*, who comments on page 223 of his book that "progressive scholars of the whole world are experiencing alarm in connection with the dangers which can be brought by 'gene engineering.' "

53. See "Khristianskii vzgliad na ekologicheskuiu problemu."

54. *Ibid.*, and E. Iu. Solov'ev, in *Voprosy filosofii* (1973), 8:105.

8. CYBERNETICS

1. The first part of this chapter draws heavily from two of my articles that appeared elsewhere: "Cybernetics," and "Cybernetics in the Soviet Union."

2. For a description of the intellectual excitement of the early days of the development of cybernetics, particularly at the time of the Josiah Macy Foundation meeting of 1946 and 1947, see Wiener, *Cybernetics, or Control and Communication in the Animal and the Machine*, pp. 1–29.

3. The first chapter of a Soviet pamphlet on information and control theory was entitled "Ways to Overcome Complexity." See Berg and Cherniak, *Informatsiia i upravlenie*, pp. 6–22. The authors maintained that the complexity of the national economy in the preceding years experienced a qualitative leap, but believed that cybernetics provided ways to cope with these new intricacies.

Glushkov, Dorodnitsyn, and Fedorenko wrote that the application of cybernetics to economic planning would "produce a tremendous national economic effect and at least double the rate of development of the national economy." See their "O nekotorykh problemakh kibernetiki."

4. A surprisingly large number of the important Soviet publications on cybernetics were translated into English by the Joint Publications Research Service of the U.S. Department of Commerce. However, the quality of translation was very poor. Two bibliographies, useful for the earlier debate, are Comey, "Soviet Publications on Cybernetics," and Kerschner, "Western Translations of Soviet Publications on Cybernetics." See also *Programma kommunisticheskoi partii Sovetskogo Soiuza*, pp. 71–73.

5. A simiilar view was also expressed frequently by philosophers. Ernst Kol'man, for example, commented, "The goal of our development—a communist society—is, from the cybernetic point of view, an open, dynamic system with ideal autoregulation." *Voprosy filosofii*, (1965), 10:147.

6. See Nekrasova, *Leninskii plan elektrifikatsii strany i ego osushchestvlenie v 1921–1931 gg.*; see also Dobb, *Soviet Economic Development Since 1917*, p. 339.

7. An interesting person in this sort of activity was Alexei Gastev, a disciple of Taylor, who combined readings of "shock-work poetry" with interests in labor efficiency. Gastev disappeared in the purges; in 1962 he was formally rehabilitated by Aksel I. Berg, chairman of the Scientific Council on Cybernetics of the USSR Academy of Sciences. Iurii. A. Gastev, Alexei's son, became active in cybernetics work in the sixties, especially in education. See Gastev, "O metodologicheskikh voprosakh ratsionalizatsii obucheniia," esp. pp. 466–67. Iurii Gastev eventually emigrated to the United States and in the mid-eighties was writing a biography of his father. Kendall E. Bailes, University of California at Los Angeles, has made several studies of Soviet attitudes toward labor in these years.

8. See *Programma Kommunisticheskoi Partii Sovetskogo Soiuza*, pp. 71–73.

9. My visit to the Moscow Power Institute in May 1963 and the description of cybernetic research by the pro-rector, D. V. Rosewig, is given in Caldwell and Graham, "Moscow in May 1963: Education and Cybernetics," pp. 39–42.

10. Such a school was described to me in Moscow in 1963; see *ibid.*, p. 20.

11. Berg, ed., *Kibernetika na sluzhbu kommunizma*.

12. *Ibid.*, p. 8.

13. These articles were: Tugarinov and Maistrov, "Protiv idealizma v matematicheskoi logike"; Iaroshevskii, "Kibernetika—'nauka' mrakobesov"; and "Materialist" (pseud.), "Komu sluzhit kibernetika?" The first of these three attacked cybernetics only indirectly.

14. Tugarinov and Maistrov was an example.

15. Iaroshevskii, p. 4.

16. To reduce all complex forms of the movement of matter to combinations of simple forms would mean subscribing, many Soviet authors said, to vulgar rather than dialectical materialism. See, for example, Andriushchenko, "Otvet tovarishcham V. B. Borshchevu, V. V. Il'inu, F. Z. Rokhline." It is clear, however, that the basic "laws" underlying this argument—that of the transition of quantity into quality—could be used in favor of the notion of thinking machines as well as against it. A sufficiently sophisticated arrangement of computer components and perhaps even the integration of organic material—as certain Soviet scientists have suggested—could involve a change in "qualitative" relationships.

17. See "Nauka i zhizn.' "

18. Kol'man, "Chto takoe kibernetika."

19. Kol'man, "Chuvstvo mery." Also, in the same spirit, See Kol'man's "Kibernetika stavit voprosy."

20. Sobolev, Kitov, and Liapunov, "Osnovnye cherty kibernetiki," p. 147.

21. Kol'man, "O filosfskikh i sotsial'nykh problemakh kibernetiki," p. 90; Kolmogorov, "Avtomaty i zhizn'," p. 10.

22. See Ashby, *An Introduction to Cybernetics*, pp. 83–5, 270–1; and Kolbanovskii, "O nekotorykh spornykh voprosakh kibernetiki," pp. 257–58.

23. Wiener, *The Human Use of Human Beings*, pp. 105–11.

24. See, for example, Deutsch, *The Nerves of Government*.

25. A general Soviet criticism of the use of cybernetics by sociologists outside the Soviet Union was Arab-Ogly, "Sotsiologiia i kibernetika," Another more

specific criticism of a cybernetic interpretation of history was Aksenov, "O vtorom mezhdunarodnom kongresse po kibernetike," p. 367.

26. Shaliutin, "O kibernetike i sfere ee primeneniia," pp. 25–27.

27. Petrushenko, "Filosofskoe znachenie poniatiia 'obratnaia sviaz' v kibernetike."

28. Akhlibinskii and Khralenko, *Chudo nashego vremeni: kibernetika i problemy razvitiia.*

29. Kolbanovskii, "O nektorykh spornykh voprosakh kibernetiki," p. 248.

30. Berg et al., ed., *Kibernetika, myshlenie, zhizn'* Il'in, Kolbanovskii, and Kol'man, eds., *Filofskie voprosy kibernetiki.*

31. Wiener, *The Human Use of Human Beings*, p. 32.

32. Turing, "Computing Machinery and Intelligence," p. 434.

33. Kol'man, "Kibernetika stavit voprosy," pp. 44–45.

34. Berg, "Nauka velichaishikh vozmozhnostei," p. 21.

35. Todor Pavlov, "Avtomaty, zhizn', soznanie," p. 53.

36. Kolmogorov, "Avtomaty i zhizn'," pp. 22–23.

37. Bialik, "Tovarishchi, vy eto ser'ezno?" and Sobolev, "Da, eto vpolne ser'ezno!"

38. Kol'man, "Chuvstvo mery," p. 53.

39. Antonov and Kochergin, "Priroda myshleniia i problema ego modelirovaniia," p. 42.

40. See "Norbert Viner v redaktsii nashego zhurnala," p. 164.

41. Ashby, like Wiener, at one point said that computers may eventually become so complex that neither the men who constructed them nor the men who operated them would know why they do what they do. See Ashby, "Design for a Brain." This view was sharply criticized by the Soviet author Arab-Ogly in "Sotsiologiia i kibernetika."

42. Wiener, *Cybernetics . . .* , p. 62.

43. Ashby, *An Introduction to Cybernetics*, p. 152.

44. Hartley's ideas were presented at the International Congress of Telegraphy and Telephony at Lake Como in September 1927; see Hartley "Transmission of Information."

45. Shannon and Weaver, *The Mathematical Theory of Communication*, pp. 19, 105.

46. Planck described his formulation of this relationship in his *Scientific Autobiography and Other Papers*, pp. 40–42.

47. Broglie, "La Cybernétique," p. 85.

48. See Novinskii, "Poniatie sviazi v dialekticheskom materializme i voprosy biologii," pp. 324–26. Novik, Biriukov, and Tiukhtin also attempted to apply the vocabulary of cybernetics to the laws of dialectics. Novik, "Kibernetika i razvitie sovremennogo nauchnogo poznaniia"; Biriukov and Tiukhin, "Filosofskie voprosy kibernetiki."

49. Ursul, "O prirode informatsii," p. 134.

50. Ashby, *An Introduction to Cybernetics*, p. 177.

51. Novik, *Kibernetika: filosofskie i sotsiologicheskie problemy.*

52. *Ibid.*, p. 58.

53. Zhukov, "Informatsii v svete leninskoi teorii otrazheniia," pp. 156–57.

54. Sedov, "K voprosu o sootnoshenii entropii informatsionnykh protsessov i fizicheskoi entropii," also Ursul, *Priroda informatsii;* Griaznov, "Kibernetika v svete filosofii"; and Musabaeva, *Kibernetika i kategoriia prichinnosti.*

55. Ursal, *Priroda informatsii.* Subsequent page references in the text refer to this work.

56. He applied, in turn, the Laws of the Unity and Struggle of Opposites, the Transition of Quantity into Quality, and the Negation of the Negation to concepts of information theory. See *ibid.,* pp. 147–56.

57. Ursul credited the work of American scholars such as N. Rashevsky and G. Karreman in providing topological approaches to information.

58. B. V. Biriukov, "O vozmozhnostiakh 'iskusstvennogo intellekta,' " *Voprosy filosofii* (1979), 3:89.

59. "Sotsial'no-filosofskie problemy 'cheloveko-mashinykh' sistem," *Voprosy filosofii* (1979), 2:51.

60. *Ibid.*

61. See Novinskii, "Poniatie sviazi v dialekticheskom materializme i voprosy biologii" and Ursul, *Priroda informatsii.*

62. Ursul, *Filosofiia i integrativno-obshchenauchnye protsessy,* p. 211.

63. "Sotsial'no-filosofskie problemy 'cheloveko-mashinykh' sistem," *Voprosy filosofii* (1979), 2:52. For examples of Kolmogorov's and Sobolev's extreme statements, see: Kolmogorov, "Avtomaty i zhizn'," and Sobolev, "Da, eto vpolne ser'ezno." A book which warned philosophers not to foreclose the possibility of thinking machines on the basis of dialectical materialism was Bazhenov and Gutchin, *Intellekt i mashina.*

64. B. V. Biriukov, "O vozmozhnostiakh 'iskusstvennogo intellekta,' " *Voprosy filosofii* (1979), 3:89.

65. See Glushkov, "Matematizatsiia nauchnogo znaniia i teoriia reshenii," esp. pp. 115–16.

66. Povarov, "Granitsy iskusstvennogo intellekta ustanovit opyt," p. 85.

67. Glushkov and Ursul, "Matematizatsiia nauchnogo znaniia," pp. 176, 216.

68. Among the Soviet writers who believed that reflection is an objective property of all matter were B. S. Ukraintsev, N. I. Zhukov, A. M. Korshunov, and V. V. Mantatov. Among those who believed that reflection exists only "potentially" in nonliving matter was, especially, V. S. Tiukhtin. See Semeniuk, Tiukhtin, and Ursul, "Filosofskie aspekty problemy informatsii"; Ukraintsev, *Otobrazhenie v nezhivoi prirode;* Zhukov, *Informatsiia;* Korshunov and Mantatov, *Teoriia otrazheniia i evristicheskaia rol' znakov;* Tiukhtin, *O prirode obraza,* (Moscow: 1963); Tiukhtin, "Sushchnost' otrazheniia i teoriia informatsii," *Voprosy filosofii* (1967) no. 3; Tiukhtin, "Otrazhenie, sistemy, kibernetika: teoriia otrazheniia v svete kibernetiki i sistemnogo podkhoda.

69. Ukraintsev, "Informatsiia i otrazhenie."

70. Kopnin, *Vvedenie v marksistskuiu gnoseologiiu,* p. 116. Similar positions were taken by: Vdovichenko, *Leninskaia teoriia otrazheniia i informatsiia,* and Zhukov, "Filosofskii analiz poniatiia 'informatsiia.' "

71. See Berg and Cherniak, *Informatsiia i upravlenie;* Glushkov, "Myshlenie i kibernetika" and "Gnoseologicheskaia priroda informatsionnogo modelirovaniia"; Amosov, "Modelirovanie informatsii i programm v slozhnykh sistemakh"

and "Myshlenie i informatsiia"; Zhukov-Berezhnikov, *Teoriia geneticheskoi informatsii*, Siforov, "Nauka ob informatsii" and "Metodologicheskie voprosy nauki ob informatsii"; Biriukov and Geller, *Kibernetika v gumanitarnykh naukakh*; Biriukov, *Kibernetika i metodologiia nauki*; Gushin, "K voprosu o prirode informatsii," "Kategoriia informatsii i nekotorye problemy razvitiia," and "Informatsiia i vzaimodeistvie"; Morozov, "Filosofskie problemy teorii informatsii"; Novik, "Negentropiia i kolichestvo informatsii," *Kibernetika: filosofskie i sotsiologicheskie problemy*, and *Filosofskie voprosy modelirovaniia psikhiki*; Ursul, *Priroda informatsii: filosofskii ocherk, Informatsiia: metodologicheskie aspekty, Otrazhenie i informatsiia*, and *Problema informatsii v sovremennoi nauke*.

72. See Semeniuk, Tiukhtin, and Ursul, "Sotsial'naia informatsiia." For other works on cybernetics and the direction of society, in which social information plays an important role, see: Petrushenko, *Samodvizhenie materii v svete kibernetike*; Setrov, *Organizatsiia biosistem: metodologicheskie printsipy organizatsii zhivykh sistem*; Ukraintsev, *Samoupravliaemyesistemy i prichinost'*; Markarian, *O genezise chelovecheskoi deiatel'nosti i kul'tury*; Abramova, *Tselostnost' i upravlenie*; Afanas'ev, *Sotsial'naia informatsiia i upravlenie obshchestvom* and *Chelovek v upravlenii obshchestvom*; Lebedev, *Ocherki teorii sotsial' nogo upravleniia*; and Kremianskii, "Nekotorye voprosy razvitiia upravleniia."

73. *Sintez znaniia i problema upravleniia*, (Moscow: 1978), p. 178.

74. Semeniuk, Tiukhtin, and Ursul, pp. 268–69.

75. *Ibid.*, and Afanas'ev, *Ob intensifikatsii razvitiia sotsialisticheskogo obshchestva; Nauchno-tekhnicheskaia revoliutsiia, upravlenie, obrazovanie;* and *Nauchnoe upravlenie obshchestvom*.

76. Gvishiani, "Metodologicheskie problemy modelirovaniia global'nogo razvitiia."

77. A brief discussion of some of the more obvious deficiencies is in Tomovic, "Limitations of Cybernetics."

78. Guilbaud, *What Is Cybernetics?*, p. 3.

79. An interesting discussion of the way in which this confusion was transferred from certain European and American texts to Soviet writings is in Bakker, "The Philosophical Debate in the U.S.S.R. on the Nature of 'Information.' "

80. Beer, "The Irrelevance of Automation," p. 288.

81. Soviet newspapers and journals in 1985 were filled with news of the computer literacy campaign. For an example, see Frolov, "K komp'iuteru, pedagogi!"

9. CHEMISTRY

1. Partington, *A Short History of Chemistry*, p. 255.

2. *Ibid.*

3. *Ibid.*, p. 216.

4. Indeed, today chemists still work primarily by gathering data on chemical reactions rather than approaching, as the physicist attempts to do, the submolecular and subatomic levels. The theory of resonance itself, as Linus Pauling pointed out, was derived largely by the chemists' method. This stress upon the empirical approach of chemists at a more gross level does not ignore, of course, the increasing use by chemists of physical methods of investigation such as

spectroscopic, X-ray, and electron diffraction methods, which are valuable supplements to their work. See Pauling, *The Nature of the Chemical Bond,* pp. 219 ff.

5. For Kekulé's exposition of his theory see August Kekulé, "Sur la constitution des substances aromatiques," and "Untersuchungen über aromatische Verbindungen." Alexander Findlay in *A Hundred Years of Chemistry,* p. 147, said, "It is probable that Kekulé regarded his theory mainly as an elegant philosophical system into which all the known facts relating to the aromatic compounds could be neatly and satisfactorily grouped together; and the first to regard the theory capable of experimental proof was Kekulé's pupil, Koerner." Kekulé was a thorough chemist who laboriously checked his theories with empirical tests. Nevertheless, he considered speculation one of the most fruitful methods of investigation; according to his own testimony, he received the inspiration for his two most important scientific theories while dozing. The chain structure of aliphatic compounds is supposed to have come to him while dreaming atop an omnibus on a summer night; the ring structure of aromatic compounds supposedly flashed into his mind while he was dozing in front of the fire.

6. French, *The Drama of Chemistry,* p. 93.

7. Students often think of these structures as being isomers or tautomers, but they are neither, since the Kekulé molecules do not exist. Isomers are compounds composed of the same elements in the same proportions, but different in properties because of differences in structure. Tautomers are isomers that change into one another rapidly and are usually in equilibrium with one another.

8. Armstrong, *Chemistry in the Twentieth Century,* p. 121.

9. The resonance theory was anticipated in the 1920s by several German and English chemists, especially C. K. Ingold in England. Ingold called his particular version of essentially the same phenomenon "mesomerism," a more accurate description than "resonance," since it means literally "between the forms." "Resonance," on the other hand, connotes movement, which does not occur in chemical resonance. The term "resonating system," often used by chemists, is even less precise.

10. Wheland, *Resonance in Organic Chemistry,* p. 3.

11. These configurations for the resonance structure of carboxylate ions are given in Pauling, *The Nature of the Chemical Bond,* p. 275.

12. Here, in particular, the five structures should not be thought of as isomers or tautomers. The latter exist, whereas resonance structures do not.

13. Wheland, pp. 7–8.

14. *Ibid.,* p. 4.

15. Pauling, p. 186.

16. More exactly, the C-C bond (single) length of ethane is 1.536 ± 0.016A, the C-C bond length of benzene is 1.393 ± 0.005A, and the C-C bond (double) length in ethylene is 1.330 ± 0.005A. *Tables of Interatomic Distances and Configuration in Molecules and Ions,* pp. M135, M196, M129. An angstrom unit is equal to one hundred millionths of a centimeter.

17. Use of the theory of resonance is evident in Nesmeianov, Freidlina, and Borisova, "O kvazikompleksnikh metalloorganicheskikh soedineniiakh." In this

article Nesmeianov and his co-workers explained the properties of certain compounds on the basis of the resonance theory, including the concept of superpositioning. They referred to Pauling's 1944 book on resonance.

18. Kursanov and Setkina, "O vzaimodeistvii chetvertichnikh solei ammoniia s prostimi efirami."

19. See Prilezhaeva, Syrkin, and Volkenshtein, "Ramaneffekt galoidoproizvodnikh etilena i elektronni rezonansa."

20. See Kabachnik, "Orientatsiia v benzolnom kol'tse."

21. Syrkin and Diatkina, *Khimicheskaia sviaz' i stroenie molekul.*

22. See "Soviets Blast Pauling, Repudiate Resonance Theory."

23. Syrkin and Diatkina, *The Structure of Molecules and the Chemical Bond.*

24. Chelintsev, *Ocherki po teorii organicheskoi khimii*, p. 2.

25. *Ibid.*, pp. 107–8.

26. Tatevskii and Shakhparanov, "Ob odnoi makhistskoi teorii v khimii i ee propagandistakh."

27. *Ibid.*, p. 177.

28. *Ibid.*

29. See "K 70-letiiu so dnia rozhdeniia I. V. Stalina."

30. A biographical article on Butlerov and additional bibliographical information may be found in *Russkii biograficheskii slovar'* (St. Petersburg; 1908), 3:528–33. For longer but somewhat less reliable articles, see *Bol'shaia sovetskaia entsiklopediia*, (Moscow: 1951), 6:378–83 and 383–9. A valuable article on Butlerov is Potkov, "Teoriia khimicheskogo stroeniia A. M. Butlerova." Butlerov was not unknown to scientists outside of Russia. He traveled extensively in Europe and knew Kekulé well. He spent quite a bit of time among German chemists, worked with Liebig, and delivered papers in German. In 1861 at Speyer, Germany, he developed the concept that the chemical structure of molecules determines the reactions which any particular substance undergoes. In 1876 he was made an honorary member of the fledgling American Chemical Society, which still possesses his appreciative letter of acceptance. See Leicester, "Alexander Mikhailovich Butlerov."

31. See Leicester.

32. See Jacques, "Boutlerov, Couper et la Société chimique de Paris."

33. Pauling, *The Nature of the Chemical Bond*, p. 4.

34. The earlier editions of Pauling's book were published in 1939 and 1944.

35. Hunsberger, "Theoretical Chemistry in Russia," p. 506.

36. See note 5 above.

37. Danilov, "A. M. Butlerov—osnovatel' teorii khimicheskogo stroeniia (1861–1951)," p. 1740.

38. Quoted in Reutov, "O nekotorikh voprosakh teorii organicheskoi khimii," p. 196. Reutov criticized this statement of Butlerov's "if it is erected into a principle."

39. See "Na uchenom sovete instituta organicheskoi khimii AN SSSR."

40. The committee in charge of writing the report consisted of D. N. Kursanov (chairman), M. G. Gonikberg, M. M. Dubinin, M. I. Kabachnik, E. D. Kaverzneva, E. N. Prilezheva, N. D. Sokolov, and R. Kh. Freidlina.

41. Kursanov et al., "K voprosu o sovremennom sostoianii teorii khimicheskogo stroeniia," p. 532.

42. *Ibid.*, pp. 537 ff.

43. *Ibid.*

44. Reutov, "O nekotorikh voprosakh teorii organicheskoi khimii," p. 187.

45. The verbatim record of this conference was published as *Sostoianie teorii khmicheskogo stroeniia; vsesoiuznoe soveshchanie 11–14 iiunia 1951 g.: stenograficheskii otchet.*

46. *Ibid.*, p. 303. Diatkina's defense occurred in a speech at the Institute of Organic Chemistry of the Academy of Sciences of the USSR. I have not been able to find a copy of this speech.

47. Haldane, *The Marxist Philosophy and the Sciences*, p. 101. Haldane's and Diatkina's arguments were based on the dialectic, but the criticism of resonance in the Soviet Union centered on the use of multiple fictitious images.

48. *Sostoianie teorii khimicheskogo stroeniia*, p. 67.

49. *Ibid.*, pp. 47 ff.

50. Wheland, *Resonance in Organic Chemistry*, p. viii.

51. *Sostoianie teorii khimicheskogo stroeniia*, pp. 81, 86. Subsequent page references in the text refer to this volume.

52. Chelintsev named Academicians A. N. Nesmeianov, A. N. Terenin, B. A. Kazanskii; Member of the Ukrainian Academy of Sciences A. I. Kiprianov; corresponding members of the USSR Academy of Sciences Ia. K. Syrkin, V. N. Kondratiev, I. L. Knuniants, A. I. Brodskii; professors and doctors of sciences M. V. Volkenshtein, M. I. Kabachnik, D. N. Kursanov. R. Kh. Freidlina, M. E. Diatkina, D. A. Bochvar, B. M. Berkenheim, A. P. Terentiev, B. A. Ismailskii, B. M. Mikhailov, A. Ia. Iakubovich, A. I. Titov., L. I. Smorgonskii, M. G. Gonikberg; "docents" and "candidates" of sciences V. M. Tatevskii, M. I. Shakhparanov, M. D. Sokolov, and O. A. Reutov. Kabachnik tried to demonstrate that although he had mistakenly supported the resonance theory, he had realized his mistake in 1950 and had published an article correcting himself. At this point there was a shout from the floor, "You were forced to do it." *Ibid.*, p. 270.

53. These defects were "corrected" in a revised (1954) report. See *Sostoianie teorii khimicheskogo stroeniia v organicheskoi khimii.*

54. Nesmeianov, " 'Contact Bonds' and the 'New Structural Theory.' " pp. 215–21.

55. Chelintsev, "O teorii khimicheskogo stroeniia A. M. Butlerova i ee novykh uspekhakh." pp. 350–60.

56. Kazanskii and Bykov, "K voprosu o sostoianii teori khimicheskogo stroeniia v organicheskoi khimii," p. 175.

57. Danilov, "A. M. Butlerov (1828–1886)."

58. See Kalandiia, "Otvet na stat'iu G. V. Tsitsishvili . . . ," Tsitsishvili criticized Kalandiia in his article "Ob oshibakh A. A. Kalandiia . . . ," popytakh utkrepit porognuiu kontseptsiiu rezonansa." The original article of Kalandiia's appeared in *Zhurnal obshchei khimii*, (September 1949), 19:1635.

59. Arbuzov had a bout with the Russian chemist Vladimir Chelintsev in 1913, the curious nature of which raises the possibility that the Chelintsev

family may have been troublemakers in Russian chemistry on more than one occasion. Gennadi Vladimirovich Chelintsev's patronymic indicates that he was the son of Vladimir Chelintsev, but I have not been able to determine whether this Vladimir is the same as the one who debated Arbuzov in 1913. Arbuzov described the debate as "the most important crisis of my career." The exact nature of the issue is unknown, but a full-scale debate between V. Chelintsev and Arbuzov was scheduled in St. Petersburg. Arbuzov many years later said, "The debate for which I prepared myself with great anxiety never did take place since my opponent did not appear. The meeting was held just the same, and I delivered the report in the presence of all the prominent chemists of St. Petersburg. On the question of my controversy with V. V. Chelintsev, all the chemists rallied to my side, and on the next morning I was pleasantly surprised when 100 printed copies of the detailed proceedings of the meeting were handed to me." These comments of Arbuzov's appeared in an article totally unconnected with the resonance dispute. See *Zhurnal obshchei khimii* (August 1955), 25:1387.

60. Nesmeianov and Kabachnik, "Dvoistvennaia reaktsionnaia sposobnost' i tautomeriia."

61. *Ibid.,* p. 71.

62. Chelintsev, "O vtorom izdanii doklada komissii . . . ," *Zhurnal obshchei khimii,* XXVII (August 1957), 2308–10.

63. Quoted in my "A Soviet Marxist View of Structural Chemistry," p. 30.

64. Wetter, *Dialetical Materialism,* pp. 432–36.

65. *Ibid.,* pp. 435–36.

66. Shakhparanov, *Dialekticheskii materializm i nekotorye problemy fiziki i khimii,* p. 86.

67. Note of L. H. Long, translator of Walter Huckel, *Structural Chemistry of Inorganic Compounds,* p. 437.

68. Syrkin, "Sovremennoe sostoianie problemy valentnosti."

69. Batuev, "K voprosu o sopriazhenii v benzole"; See also Pauling, *The Nature of the Chemical Bond,* p. 233.

70. On March 26, 1962, Peter Kapitsa, the outstanding Soviet physicist, criticized the attitude of Soviet philosophers toward resonance theory, as well as their attitudes toward the theory of relativity, Heisenberg's indeterminacy principle, genetics, and cybernetics. See *Ekonomicheskaia gazeta,* March 26, 1962, p. 10.

71. The lecture was later printed in the Soviet Union; see Pauling, "Teoriia rezonansa v khimii." I am grateful to Dr. Pauling for a reprint of this article.

72. Shelinskii, *Khimicheskaia sviaz' i izuchenie ee v srednei shkole.* See esp. pp. 31, 44–46, and 136.

73. In addition to the sources cited below, see: Zhdanov, "Obrashchenie metoda v organicheskoi khimii" Dobrotin, *Khimicheskaia forma dvizheniia materii;* Kuznetsov, *Evoliutsiia predstavlenii ob osnovnykh zakonakh khimii;* the last section of Kuznetsov, *Razvitie ucheniia o katalize;* Kedrov and Trifonov, *Zakon periodichnosti i khimicheskie elementy;* Kucher, "Metodologicheskie problemy razvitii teorii v khimii"; Zak, "Kachestvennye izmeneniia i struktura"; and Zhdanov, "Znachenie leninskikh idei dlia razrabotki metodologicheskikh voprosov khimii."

74. See Zhdanov, *Ocherki metodologii organicheskoi khimii.*

75. See Budreiko, *Filosofskie voprosy khimii.*
76. See Kedrov, *Tri aspekta atomistiki.*
77. See Semenov, "Marksistsko-leninskaia filosofiia i voprosy estestvoznan-iia."
78. *Ibid.*, p. 24.
79. *Ibid.*, p. 25.
80. See Shvyrev, "Materialisticheskaia dialektika i problemy issledovaniia nauchnogo poznaniia."
81. See Petrov, Bal'ian, and Troshchenko, *Organicheskaia khimiia,* pp. 6, 25, 300.
82. Karapet'iants and Drakin, *Obshchaia i neorganicheskaia khimiia,* p. 95.
83. Korovin, ed., *Kurs obshchei khimii: uchebnik dlia vuzov,* pp. 7–8.
84. Zhdanov, "Uzlovoe poniatie sovremennoi teoreticheskoi khimii," p. 89.
85. Garkovenko, "Osnovnye napravleniia issledovanii filosofskikh voprosov khimii," p. 340, citing R. A. Vikhalemm, "O razrabotke filosofskikh voprosov khimii."
86. Post-Production Script, Horizon "Science for the People," November 2, 1981, VT Spool no. L09167. I am grateful to Alan Jehlen of WGBH, Boston, for this reference.
87. V. I. Kurashov and Iu. I. Solov'ev, "O probleme 'svedeniia' khimii k fizike," *Voprosy filosofii* (No. 6, 1984), pp. 89–98; also see Vol'kenshtein, *Fizika i biologiia,* and his "Fizika kak teoreticheskaia osnova estestvoznaniia."
88. For an example of such a misinterpretation of the resonance theory, see "On 'Nonresonance' Between East and West," p. 2474, and the correction sent in by G. W. Wheland printed on p. 3160 of the same volume.
89. Hesse, "Models and Analogy in Science," pp. 356–57.
90. Hesse, "Models in Physics," p. 214.

10. QUANTUM MECHANICS

1. Two valuable collections of articles indicating the diversity of the views expressed are S. Körner, ed., *Observation and Interpretation in the Philosophy of Physics,* and Colodny, ed., *Beyond the Edge of Certainty.*

2. Expressed mathematically as $\Delta\chi\Delta p_x \geqq \hbar/2$, where $\Delta\chi$ and Δp_x are the limits of precision within which the value of a coordinate and of momentum, respectively, can be simultaneously determined and $\hbar$ = Planck's constant divided by 2π.

3. It should perhaps be noted that from the time of classical science to the present there have been many debates over the physical significance of mathematical formalisms. The author of the preface to Copernicus's *De Revolutionibus,* the Lutheran theologian Andreas Osiander, tried (contrary to the astronomer's wishes) to urge Copernicus' readers to regard his system as a useful mathematical fiction not representative of physical truth. One could also cite Newton, who resolutely refused to say that his gravitational theory proved that matter has an innate power of attraction; he insisted that the mathematics were the same as if this were so, but that he could not state that such attraction did in fact exist. The cases of Copernicus and Newton as described are well known; for

easy reference, see Thomas S. Kuhn, *The Copernican Revolution*, p. 187; and Alexandre Koyré, *From the Closed World to the Infinite Universe*, pp. 178–79.

4. See Putnam, "A Philosopher Looks at Quantum Mechanics," p. 78. To say that de Broglie "originally" proposed the undulatory theory means only within the framework of the modern mathematical apparatus; wave interpretations of light extend back to Fresnel and Young in the early nineteenth century and beyond. Similarly, the statement that Born "originally" suggested the corpuscular theory does not deny Newton's (or the early atomists') theories of light. See Ronchi, *Histoire de la lumière*.

5. The explanation for the spot imprint given by de Broglie was that of the "reduction of the wave packet."

6. Quoted in Jammer, *The Conceptual Development of Quantum Mechanics*, p. 329.

7. Oppenheimer, *The Open Mind*, p. 82.

8. The first person to give a precise definition of complementarity was not Bohr but Pauli, and it turned out that Bohr did not quite agree with Pauli's formulation. These differences have continued to plague interpreters of quantum mechanics. See Jammer, pp. 355–56, and particularly the difference between what von Weizsäcker called "parallel complementarity" and "circular complementarity."

9. A summary of the early warnings is in Joravsky, *Soviet Marxism and Natural Science*, *passim*, esp. pp. 285–86. Fock's name will be spelled with a "c," as a result of his preference for this transliterated form, although the transliteration system used elsewhere in this book would dictate "Fok."

10. Bohr indicated that the concept of complementarity might be applied to such areas as physiology, psychology, biology, and sociology in his *Atom theorie and Naturbeschreibung* and "Causality and Complementarity," *Dialectica*. This issue of *Dialectica* was devoted entirely to the concept of complementarity and included one article in which the author advanced the thesis that complementarity is potentially valid in all areas of systematic study: F. Gonseth, "Remarque sur l'ideé de complémentarité."

11. See Deborin, "Lenin and the Crisis of Contemporary Physics."

12. See Nikol'skii, "Printsipy kvantovoi mekhaniki." Nikol'skii later published a book setting forth the same view: *Kvantovye protsessy* (1940). Nikol'skii's 1936 article indicated his agreement with the position of Einstein, Podolsky, and Rosen in their debate with Bohr. See Einstein, Podolsky, and Rosen, "Can Quantum-Mechanical Description of Physical Reality Be Considered Complete?" and Bohr's similarly titled article.

13. Nikol'skii, "Otvet V. A. Foku." In his criticism of Nikol'skii, Fock maintained that quantum mechanics described the action of an individual microobject as well as statistical groups: "K stat'e Nikol'skogo 'Printsipy kvantovoi mekhaniki.' "

14. Fock, "Mozhno li schitat', chto kvantomekhanicheskoe opisanie fizicheskoi real'nosti iavliaetsia polnym?" In his introduction Fock clearly indicated that he considered Bohr the victor in the debate.

15. Fock also engaged in a debate before the war with A. A. Maksimov, another important participant in the later controversy. See Fock, "K diskussii

po voprosam fiziki." In 1937 and 1938 *Pod znamenem marksizma* contained a number of articles on the philosophic interpretation of quantum mechanics, including contributions by Maksimov, E. Kol'man, P. Langevin, and Nikol'skii.

16. See also Omel'ianovskii's defense of relativity theory in this period in his "Lenin o prostranstve i vremeni i teoriia otnositel'nosti Einshteina."

17. Omel'ianovskii, *V. I. Lenin i fizika XX veka, passim*, esp. pp. 77. Omel'ianovskii accepted the relativity of simultaneity and of spatial and temporal intervals, concepts that were to be severely criticized in Soviet philosophical journals in the coming months.

18. *Ibid.*, p. 95.

19. For critical reviews of Omel'ianovskii, see Karasev and Nozdrev, "O knige M. E. Omel'ianovskogo 'V. I. Lenin i fizika XX veka,'" and Perfil'ev's article of the same title. The second edition was published in Ukrainian, *Borot'ba materiializmu proty idealizmu v suchasnii fizytsi* (Kiev, 1947).

20. A. A. Zhdanov, *Vystuplenie na diskussii po knige G. F. Aleksandrova "Istoriia zapadnoevropeiskoi filosofii"*, *24 iiunia 1947 g*, p. 43.

21. The first four issues were under the editorship of B. M. Kedrov, who was replaced by D. I. Chesnokov after Kedrov had sponsored a series of controversial articles. Kedrov obviously supported the Markov article and was held responsible for the criticism it incurred. Five articles in the first issues of *Voprosy filosofii*, including Markov's, were criticized in an article in *Pravda*, "Za boevoi filosofskii zhurnal," September 7, 1949.

22. Markov, "O prirode fizicheskogo znaniia."

23. Maksimov charged that around Fock in the P. N. Lebedev Physics Institute of the Academy of Sciences there was a group of scientists who refused to admit dialectical materialism into science. A. A. Maksimov, "Bor'ba za materializm v sovremennoi fizike," p. 178. When Markov's viewpoint was discussed in this institute, very little substantive criticism was expressed; see L. L. Potkov, "Obsuzhdenie raboty M. A. Markova 'O mikromire,'" *Voprosy filosofii*. The criticism came later.

24. Markov, p. 150. The "hidden parameter" theories were promoted by David Bohm in particular. See his *Causality and Chance in Modern Physics*, esp. pp. 79–81, 106–9, 111–16.

25. Markov, p. 146.

26. *Ibid.*, p. 163.

27. This controversy is described in greater detail in the first edition of this book, *Science and Philosophy in the Soviet Union*, pp. 75–81.

28. Maksimov, "Ob odnoi filosofskom kentavre."

29. See "Diskussiia o prirode fizicheskogo znaniia: Obsuzhdenie stat'i M. A. Markova," *Voprosy filosofii* (1948), 1:203–32. Among the other contributors were B. G. Kuznetsov and S. A. Petrushevskii.

30. Maksimov, "Diskussiia o prirode fizicheskogo znaniia," p. 228.

31. See "Ot redaktsii," *Voprosy filosofii* (1948), pp. 231–32.

32. Soviet philosophers were quite straightforward in recognizing the discrediting of complementarity. Thus, Storchak observed, "In the course of the discussion of M. A. Markov's article it was established that the principle of complementarity was contrived as an idealistic distortion of the foundations of

quantum mechanics." "Za materialisticheskoe osveshchenie osnov kvantovoi mekhaniki."

33. Terletskii, "Obsuzhdenie stat'i M. A. Markova," p. 229.

34. He seems to have played a role in this controversy similar to Chelintsev's in the theory of resonance dispute. See chapter 9.

35. Maksimov, "Marksistskii filosofskii materializm i sovremennaia fizika," p. 114.

36. See Blokhintsev, *Vvedenie v kvantovuiu mekhaniku*, and its revised later form, *Osnovy kvantovoi mekhaniki*. In a laudatory review of Blokhintsev's second edition, Storchak observed that the book would serve well as a dialectical materialist statement of quantum mechanics. See "Za materialisticheskoe osveshchenie osnov kvantovoi mekhaniki," p. 202.

37. Blokhintsev, *Vvedenie v kvantovuiu mekhaniku*, pp. 52, 58.

38. Blokhintsev, "Kritika idealisticheskogo ponimaniia kvantovoi teorii."

39. *Ibid.*, p. 209.

40. *Ibid.*, p. 210.

41. *Ibid.*, p. 213.

42. Many Western analysts of quantum mechanics agreed with Blokhintsev on this point. See, for example, Feyerabend, "Problems of Microphysics," p. 207.

43. This position of Blokhintsev's illustrated that he was not in complete agreement with the interpretation of Nikol'skii before World War II, as has often been said. Nikol'skii agreed with Einstein, Podolsky, and Rosen. See Nikol'skii, "Printsipy kvantovoi mekhaniki."

44. Blokhintsev, "Kritika idealisticheskogo ponimaniia kvantovoi teorii," p. 211.

45. Fock, "O tak nazyvaemykh ansambliakh v kvantovoi mekhanike," p. 170.

46. *Ibid.*, p. 173.

47. See Blokhintsev, "Otvet akademiku V. A. Foku," pp. 172–73. In articles in the sixties Blokhintsev was less concerned with the physical significance of the wave function than with relativistic quantum mechanics, quantum field theory, and attempts to find a system for the rational arrangement of elementary particles. See, for example, his "Problema struktury elementarnykh chastits."

48. Blokhintsev, *Printsipal'nye voprosy kvantovoi mekhaniki.*

49. Subsequent page references for Blokhintsev's *The Philosophy of Quantum Mechanics* will be indicated in the text.

50. Quoted in *ibid.*, p. 1.

51. Hanson, "Five Cautions for the Copenhagen Interpretation's Critics," p. 327.

52. See Fock, "Nil's Bor v moei zhizni," pp. 518–19.

53. *Ibid.*, p. 519.

54. Fock, "Ob interpretatsii kvantovoi mekhaniki," p. 235. In 1965 Fock wrote in the following way of his approving but nonetheless critical approach to Bohr's interpretation: *Le merité d'une nouvelle position du probème de la description*

des phénomènes à l'échelle atomique appartient á Niels Bohr; le point de vue adopté dans le présent article est le résultat de nos recherches et méditations ayant pour but d'approfondir, de préciser—et si nécessaire de critiquer et de corriger—les idées de Bohr. Fock, "La physique quantique et les idéalisations classiques," p. 223.

55. See, for example, Shirokov, "Filosofskie voprosy teorii otnositel'nosti,"

56. Fock, "K diskussii po voprosam fiziki," p. 159.

57. See p. 324 and note 14 above.

58. Fock, "K diskussii po voprosam fiziki"; and "Protiv nevezhestvennoi kritiki sovremennykh fizicheskikh teorii"; Maksimov, "O filosofskikh vozzren-iiakh akad. V. F. Mitkevicha i o putiakh razvitiia sovetskoi fiziki," and "Bor'ba za materializm v sovremennoi fizike."

59. Fock, 'Osnovnye zakony fiziki v svete dialekticheskogo materializma,' p. 39; and Omel'ianovskii, *Filosofskie voprosy kvantovoi mekhaniki,* p. 35.

60. Fock and Migdal, in Krylov, *Raboty po obosnovaniiu statisticheskoi fiziki,* p. 8, "Vzgliadi N. S. Krylova na obosnovanie staticheskoi fiziki."

61. Even if Fock's hypothesis were to be granted, the existence of objective reality would not necessarily be denied, since there is no reason why such reality has to be defined in terms of certain parameters, such as position and momentum. Nevertheless, such an interpretation would require a more so-phisticated view of reality than is often granted it.

62. Omel'ianovskii, "Dialekticheskii materializm i tak nazyvaemyi printsip dopolnitel'nosti Bora," pp. 404–5.

63. Fock, "O tak nazyvaemykh ansambliakh v kvantovoi mekhanike," *op. cit.,* p. 172.

64. Fock, "Kritika vzgliadov Bora na kvantovuiu mekhaniku," p. 13.

65. Fock, "Ob interpretatsii kvantovoi mekhaniki."

66. In 1952 de Broglie, after defending the Copenhagen Interpretation for over twenty years, returned to his earlier belief in its replacement by a theory based on the "instinctive position of a physicist, that of realism. Louis de Broglie, "La Physique quantique restera-t elle indéterministe?" p. 309.

67. See Bohm, *Causality and Chance in Modern Physics.*

68. Vigier remarked, "A particle is thus considered as an average organized excitation of a chaotic subquantum-mechanical level of matter, similar in a sense to a sound wave propagation in the chaos of molecular agitation." In this same article Vigier credited Blokhintsev with providing the essential ideas for his model. J.-P. Vigier, "The Concept of Probability," pp. 75, 76.

69. Fock, *"Ob interpretatsii kvantovoi mekhaniki,"* p. 215.

70. *Ibid.,* p. 218.

71. The intermediate form, said Fock, would be a case when wavelike and corpusclelike properties appear simultaneously (although not sharply), such as when an electron is partially localized (corpusclelike property) and at the same time displays wave properties (wave function has the character of a standing wave with an amplitude rapidly decreasing with increasing distance from the center of the atom).

72. *Ibid.,* p. 219.

73. *Ibid.,* p. 222.

74. See, for example, Omel'ianovskii, "Lenin o prichinnosti i kvantovaia mekhanika"; "Filosofskaia evoliutsiia kopengagenskoi shkoly fizikov"; "Pro-

blema elementarnosti chastits v kvantovoi fizike"; and *Lenin i filosofskie problemy sovremennoi fiziki.*

75. See Omel'ianovskii, "Lenin o prostrantsve i vremeni i teoriia otnositel'nosti Einshteina," and *V. I. Lenin: fizika XX veka.*

76. Omel'ianovskii, "Zadachi razrabotki problemy 'Dialekticheskii materializm i sovremennoe estestvoznanie.' "

77. Omel'ianovskii, ed., *Lenin i sovremennaia nauka.* Omel'ianovskii published an article in the same volume, "Sovremennye filosofskie problemy fiziki i dialekticheskii materializm."

78. Omel'ianovskii, *Filosofskie voprosy kvantovoi mekhaniki.* Subsequent page references in the text refer to this work.

79. See note 2 above.

80. The record of the conference was published in Fedoseev, et al., eds., *Filosofskie problemy sovremennogo estestvoznaniia.* For the Chesnokov reference, see p. 328.

81. Omel'ianovskii, "The Concept of Dialectical Contradiction in Quantum Physics," p. 77.

82. See Omel'ianovskii, "Filosofskie aspekty teorii izmereniia."

83. *Ibid.*, p. 248.

84. See Bohr, "Kvantovaia fizika i filosofiia," p. 39.

85. An interesting discussion of Soviet reactions to the double solution approach is Levy, "Interpretations of Quantum Theory and Soviet Thought." Also see the discussion of quantum mechanics by two men who worked closely with de Broglie in J. Andrade e Silva and G. Lochak, *Quanta* (New York and Toronto: McGraw-Hill, 1969).

86. Kol'man, "Sovremennaia fizika v poiskakh dal'neishei fundamental'noi teorii," p. 122. Kol'man, a Czech who spent long periods of time in Moscow, played a very interesting role in disputes over the philosophy of science. Among Czech scientists he was generally known as an ideologue, but in the Soviet Union after World War II he was often a "liberal" in the various controversies, although before the war he was quite militant and he favored Lysenko in the early genetics controversy. As early as 1938 he was praised by Fock for his views on relativity physics. In cybernetics he was the first person to plead with Party officials for a recognition of the value of the new field. Kol'man, "Chto takoe kibernetika." The article on physics cited above was definitely within this liberal tradition.

87. See Tiapkin, "K razvitiiu statisticheskoi interpretatsii kvantovoi mekhaniki na osnove sovmestnogo koordinatno-impul'snogo predstavleniia." Subsequent page references in the text refer to this article.

88. Tiapkin cited Omel'ianovskii as an example of Soviet philosophers who accepted the Copenhagen School too uncritically. *Ibid.*, pp. 144–45.

89. See Svechnikov, *Prichinnost' i sviaz' sostoianii v fizike;* Sachkov, *Vvedenie v veroiatnostnyi mir;* Seifullaev, *Kontseptsiia prichinnosti i ee funktsii v fizike;* Ivanova, *Determinizm v filosofii i fizike;* Razumovskii, *Sovremennyi determinizm i eksternal'nye printsipy v fizike;* Barashenkov, "O vozmozhnosti 'vneprostranstvennykh' i 'vnevremennykh' form sushchestvovaniia materii"; Kuptsov, *Determinizm i veroiatnost';* Askin, *Filosofskii determinizm i nauchnoe poznanie, Ma-*

terialisticheskaia dialektika i kontseptsiia dopolnitel 'nosti, and *Printsip dopolnitel'nost'
i materialisticheskaia dialektika;* Khiutt, *Kontseptsiia dopolnitel'nosti i problema
ob"ektivnosti fizicheskogo znaniia;* Alekseev, *Kontseptsiia dopolnitel'nosti;* Svechnikov, *Prichinnost' i sviaz' sostoianii v fizike; problemy dialektiko-materialisliches-
kogo istolkovaniia kvantovoi teorii;* Miakishev, *Dinamicheskie i statisticheskie zakonomernosti v fizike;* Antipenko, *Problema fizicheskoi real'nosti;* Bazhan, Dyshlevyi
and Luk'ianets, *Dialekticheskii materializm i problema real'nosti v sovremennoi
fizike;* Kravets, *Priroda veroiatnosti;* Gutner, *Filosofskie aspekty izmerenie v sovremennoi fizike;* and Perminov, *Problema prichinnosti v filosofii estestvoznaniia.*

90. Akhundov, Molchanov, and Stepanov, "Filosofskie voprosy fiziki," p. 249.

91. Alekseev, "O poniatii nekontroliruemogo vzaimodeistviia," pp. 82–88.

92. Barashenkov. *Problema subatomnogo prostranstva i vremeni,* (1979); See
also his *Sushchestvuiut li granitsy nauki.*

93. Barashenkov, *Problema subatomnogo. . .,* pp. 27, 52–53, 185, 197.

94. Akhundov, Molchanov, and Stepanov.

95. See my comments in chapter 1, with comparison of Soviet views on
quantum mechanics to those of Paul Feyerabend, David Bohm, Louis de Broglie,
and Ernest Nagel, p. 5.

96. The Copenhagen Interpretation remained very strong throughout this
period of discussion. Max Jammer said in 1966, "As is well known, this
interpretation is still espoused today by the majority of theoreticians and
practicing physicists. Though not necessarily the only logically possible interpretation of quantum phenomena, it is *de facto* the only existing fully articulated
consistent scheme of conceptions that brings order into an otherwise chaotic
cluster of facts and makes it comprehensible." Jammer, *The Conceptual Development of Quantum Mechanics,* p. vii.

97. Comments by Fock and the American philosopher Paul K. Feyerabend
on an article of mine, as well as my reply, may be found in the *Slavic Review,*
September 1966, pp. 411–20.

11. RELATIVITY THEORY

1. The relationship between x, y, z, t and x', y', z', t' in the two reference
frames S and S' are given by the following equations. The transformation based
on these equations is called a Galilean transformation:

$$x = x' + ut$$
$$y = y'$$
$$z = z'$$
$$t = t'$$

where u is the relative velocity of S and S'.

2. The equations are:

$$x = (x' + ut')\gamma \qquad\qquad t = (t' + \frac{x'u}{c^2})\,/\gamma$$
$$y = y' \qquad\qquad\qquad r = \sqrt{1 - \beta^2}$$
$$z = z' \qquad\qquad\qquad \beta = u/c$$

$$c = \text{velocity of light}$$

3. See the discussions in Mikulak, "Relativity Theory and Soviet Communist Philosophy (1922–1960)," and Joravsky's "The 'Crisis' in Physics," in his *Soviet Marxism and Natural Science, 1917–1932*, pp. 275–95. Dialectical materialist philosophers were aware of the problems of interpretation presented by new developments in physical theory and occasionally in the twenties pointed to the dangers of "Machism" in physics. In 1930 A. M. Deborin gave an official speech in the Academy of Sciences of the USSR entitled "Lenin and the Crisis of Contemporary Physics." The physicists seemed undisturbed, however. See Volgin, ed., *Otchet o deiatel'nosti akademii nauk SSSR za 1929 g.*, vol. 1, Appendix. An established physicist opposing relativity in the name of dialectical materialism was A. K. Timiriazev; some of those scientists who came to its defense in the same name, at least briefly, were A. F. Ioffe, I. E. Tamm, and O. Iu. Schmidt, all men of impressive scientific talent.

4. Semkovskii, *Dialekticheskii materializm i printsip otnositel'nosti*, pp. 9, 11.

5. *Ibid.*, p. 54.

6. Joravsky, "The Crisis in Physics," pp. 275–76.

7. Quoted in Semenov, "Ob itogakh obsuzhdeniia filosofskikh vozrenii akademika Mandel'shtama," p. 200, from L. I. Mandel'shtam, *Polnoe sobranie trudov* (Moscow; 1950), 5:178.

8. Papaleksi, et al., *Kurs fiziki*, 2:539. Aleksandrov criticized this view in his "Teoriia otnositel'nosti kak teoriia absoliutnogo prostranstva-vremeni," p. 284.

9. Zhdanov, *Vystuplenie na diskussii po knige G. F. Aleksandrova 'Istoriia zapadnoevropeiskoi filosofii' 24 iiunia 1947*.

10. For an example of the limits of vulgarity in the criticism of relativity theory, see Maksimov, "Protiv reaktsionnogo einshteiniantsva v fizike." Maksimov had once been considerably more positive about Einstein and relativity theory, although he granted the need to rebuild the philosophic base of relativity. See his "Teoriia otnositel'nosti i materializm." Another example of simplistic opposition was I. V. Kuznetsov's statement, "The unmasking of reactionary Einsteinism in the area of physical science is one of the most pressing tasks of Soviet physicists and philosophers." See "Sovetskaia fizika i dialekticheskii materializm," p. 47.

11. The relatively objective view was Naan, "K voprosu o printsipe otnositel'nosti v fizike," Naan's view was criticized by a host of authors, as will be discussed. The editorial criticism of Naan is in "K itogam diskussii po teorii otnositel'nosti," *Voprosy filosofii* (1955), 1:138.

12. A. A. Maksimov, "Bor'ba za materializm v sovremennoi fizike," p. 194.

13. Naan, "Sovremennyi 'fizicheskii' idealizm v SShA i Anglii na sluzhbe popovshchiny i reaktsii," pp. 290 ff. Naan based his criticism of Frank on the latter's *Foundations of Physics* and articles. Naan criticized Bertrand Russell's *History of Western Philosophy* for its "sensationalism" and James Jeans's comments about the "disappearance" of matter.

14. Omel'ianovskii, "Falsifikatory nauki: ob idealizme v sovremennoi fizike"; A. A. Maksimov, "Marksistskii filosofskii materializm i sovremennaia fizika"; Shteinman, "O reaktsionnoi roli idealizma v fizike," (1948) pp. 105–24, 143–62, 163–73. Omel'ianovskii directed his critique of Carnap at the latter's *The Logical Syntax of Language*. Omel'ianovskii considered Einstein to be a "materialist,"

but not a "dialectical materialist," a view for which he was criticized by M. M. Karpov, who considered Einstein to be a thoroughgoing idealist. See Karpov, "O filosofskikh vzgliadakh A. Einshteina."

15. Omel'ianovskii, "Falsifikatory nauki," pp. 144, 155. Frank included a chapter on "Logical Empiricism and Philosophy in the Soviet Union" in his *Between Physics and Philosophy.*

16. A. A. Maksimov. "Marksistskoi filosofskii materializm i sovremennaia fizika," p. 114.

17. *Ibid.*

18. See Kursanov, "Dialekticheskii materializm o prostranstve i vremeni," *Voprosy filosofii,* p. 186 and *passim.*

19. Einstein commented in his 1916 obituary of Mach: "He (Mach) conceived every science as the task of bringing order into the elementary single observations which he described as 'sensations.' This denotation was probably responsible for the fact that this sober and cautious thinker was called a philosophical idealist or solipsist by people who had not studied his work thoroughly. . . . I can say with certainty that the study of Mach and Hume has been directly and indirectly a great help in my work. . . . Mach recognized the weak spots of classical mechanics and was not very far from requiring a general theory of relativity half a century ago. . . . It is not improbable that Mach would have discovered the theory of relativity, if, at the time when his mind was still young and susceptible, the problem of the constancy of the speed of light had been discussed among physicists." Quoted in Frank, "Einstein, Mach and Logical positivism," p. 85, (1916) 17:101.

20. L. I. Storchak, "Znachenie idei Lobachevskogo v razvitii predstavlenii o prostranstve i vremeni," *Voprosy filosofii* (1951) 1:142–48.

21. Another attempt to avoid Mach by way of Lobachevskii is Markov, "Znachenie geometrii Lobachevskogo dlia fiziki."

22. Naan quoted in Comey, "Soviet Controversies Over Relativity," p. 191. Also, see Shtern, "K voprosu o filosofskoi storone teorii otnositel'nosti"; Blokhintsev, "Za leninskoe uchenie o dvizhenii"; and G. A. Kursanov, "K kriticheskoi otsenke teorii otnositel'nosti' *Voprosy filosofii* (1952), 1:169–74, 175–81, 181–83. Shtern's views were stated in more detail in his *Erkenntnistheoretische Probleme der Modernen Physik.* Shtern's simple view of relativity was later criticized thoroughly by Kard, "O teorii otnositel'nosti," but Kard simultaneously spoke positively of Blokhintsev's effort to preserve a concept of absolute space. See Blokhintsev, "Za leninskoe uchenie o dvizhenii." Blokhintsev believed that each larger and more inertial frame of reference was an improvement over the previous one as a result of its possession of a relative grain of truth. Compare this view with Lenin's statement in *Materialism and Empirio-Criticism* on relative and absolute truth: "Human thought by its very nature is able to give and does give absolute truth, which is accumulated as the sum total of relative truths, but the limits of the truth of each scientific proposition are relative, now expanding, now shrinking with the growth of knowledge." V. I. Lenin, *Sochineniia* (4th ed.) (Moscow; 1947) 14:122.

23. I. V. Kuznetsov, "Sovetskaia fizika i dialekticheskii materializm," and Shteinman, "Za materialisticheskuiu teoriiu bystrykh dvizhenii."

24. Kuznetsov, p. 72.

25. Fock, "Protiv nevezhestvennoi kritiki sovremennykh fizicheskikh teorii," p. 174.

26. *Ibid.*, p. 168.

27. See footnote 15, chapter 10.

28. Thus, Fock briefly mentioned that the statement that the "speeds of light to and fro are equal" is a "natural" assumption. But the attribution to ε of any value between 0 and 1 in the celebrated equation $t_2 = t_1 + \varepsilon(t_3 - t_1)$ is conventional. On the general topic of congruency Fock agreed with Aleksandrov that the precise meaning of x, y, z, and t can be derived from the law of wave-front propagation. They are not given a priori. See Fock, *The Theory of Space, Time and Gravitation.*

29. For Russian and German editions, see A. D. Aleksandrov, *Vnutrennaia geometriia vypuklykh poverkhnostei* and *Die innere Geometrie der konvexen Flächen.*

30. Aleksandrov, "Leninskaia dialektika i matermatika."

31. Aleksandrov, "Ob idealizme v matematike."

32. *Pravda*, October 4, 1966, p. 2. I am grateful to David D. Comey for pointing out this quotation to me and for the translation.

33. Einstein, *Sobranie nauchnykh trudov.* A few small collections of Einstein's scientific works had been published earlier, and in 1922–24 a four-volume collection of his scientific publications through 1922 was published in Japanese; nonetheless, the Soviet editors prepared the first edition covering all of Einstein's lifetime. In preparing this significant publication, the editors corresponded frequently with Einstein's secretary, Miss Helen Dukas. Conversation with Miss Dukas, Princeton, New Jersey, January 16, 1970. Klickstein, "A Cumulative Review of Bibliographies of the Published Writings of Albert Einstein."

34. Aleksandrov, "Teoriia otnositel'nosti kak teoriia absoliutnogo prostranstva-vremeni," pp. 273–4. Subsequent page references in the text refer to this article.

35. In a well-known paper of 1908 on space and time, Minkowski spoke of the "Relativity Postulate," and then commented. "In dem der Sinn des Postulats wird, das durch die Erscheinungen nur die in Raum und Zeit vierdimensionale Welt gegeben ist, aber die Projektion in Raum und in Zeit noch mit einer gewissen Freiheit vorgenommen werden kann, möchte ich dieser Behauptung eher den Namen Postulat der absoluten Welt (oder kurz Welt-postulat) geben." *Gesammelte Abhandlugen von Hermann Minkowski*, p. 437.

36. Adolf Grünbaum, "Geometry, Chronometry, and Empiricism," p. 522.

37. See Aleksandrov and Ovchinnikov, "Zamechaniia k osnovam teorii otnositel'nosti."

38. The difficulties of such an opinion will be discussed later.

39. See Robb, *The Absolute Relations of Time and Space.* For the historically minded, one can point out that cosmologies based on light are very old in the history of science, although considerable differences existed among the various systems. One of the oldest and most extensive cosmologies of light was that of Robert Grosseteste of the late twelfth and early thirteenth century. Grosseteste believed light was the first effective principle of movement by which the operations or "becoming" of natural things were caused. See A. C. Crombie,

Robert Grosseteste and the Origins of Experimental Science, esp. pp. 91–124. In many earlier writings, such as those of the Spanish Jew Avicebron, St. Augustine, Pseudo-Dionysius, and St. Basil, the idea was presented that light is a form that actualizes the potentiality of matter as a universal continuum.

40. Even though Aleksandrov agreed with much of Robb's interpretation, he expressed his wish to dissociate himself from Robb's remark that the Einsteinian relativity of simultaneity converts the universe into a kind of "nightmare." See Robb, p. v.

41. Fock, *The Theory of Space, Time and Gravitation,* p. xviii.

42. Fock, "Comments," p. 412. The above version of Fock's comments is the one approved by Fock. The phrasing is a little awkward in spots, particularly in the sentence beginning "Even such statements. . . ."

43. By the term "Galilean space," Fock meant space of maximum uniformity. As he commented, in such space: "(a) All points in space and instants in time are equivalent. (b) All directions are equivalent, and (c) All inertial systems, moving uniformly and in a straight line relative to one another, are equivalent (Galilean principle of relativity)." Fock, *The Theory of Space, Time and Gravitation,* p. xiii.

44. See the discussion of Fock in P. S. Dyshlevyi, *V. I. Lenin i filosofskie problemy reliativistskoi fiziki* (Kiev, 1969), pp. 148 ff.

45. Fock, "Les principes mecaniques de Galilée et la théorie d'Einstein," p. 12.

46. See Reichenbach, *The Philosophy of Space and Time,* p. 223.

47. *Ibid.,* p. 226.

48. Fock, "O roli printsipov otnositel'nosti i ekvivalentnosti v teorii tiagotenii Einshteina," p. 51.

49. Fock, *The Theory of Space, Time and Gravitation,* p. xv.

50. *Ibid.,* p. xvi.

51. *Ibid.,* p. 351. See also Fock, "Poniatiia odnorodnosti, kovariantnosti i otnositel'nosti," p. 133.

52. See Fock, "Poniatiia odnorodrosti. . .," p. 135.

53. Fock, *The Theory of Space, Time and Gravitation,* pp. 351–52.

54. The most general covariant equation for an interval of space-time is $ds^2 = g_{\mu\nu}dx_{\mu}dx_{\tau}$. Here $g_{\mu\nu}$ is a tensor, that is, a magnitude that transforms according to well-defined rules whenever a transformation to a new coordinate system occurs. In Galilean space-time the coefficient $g_{\mu\nu}$ remains unchanged, but in Riemannian space-time $g_{\mu\nu}$ is a function of the coordinates.

55. Many physicists would emphasize at this point that one of the principles of GTR is that no auxiliary functions are to be introduced.

56. Fock, *The Theory of Time, Space and Gravitation,* p. xviii.

57. Fock, "Les principes . . .," p. 11.

58. *Ibid.,* pp. 9, 11.

59. Dyshlevyi, *V. I. Lenin i filosofskie problemy reliativistskoi fiziki,* p. 143.

60. *Ibid.*

61. See, for example, Bochenski, ed., *Bibliographie der sowjetischen Philosophie.*

62. Shirokov, "Filosofskie voprosy teorii otnositel'nosti," p. 79.

63. Shirokov, "O materialisticheskoi sushchnosti teorii otnositel'nosti," pp. 325 ff.

64. Shirokov, "O preimushchestvennykh sistemakh otscheta v n'iutonovskoi mekhanike i teorii otnositel nosti."

65. See the discussion in Dyshlevyi, "V. I. Lenin . . .," pp. 137–39.

66. Annual editions of *Einshteinovskii sbornik*; Dyshlevyi, *Materialisticheskaia dialektika i fizicheskii reliativizm*; Chudinov, *Teoriia otnositel'nosti i filosofiia*; Gott, Tiukhtin, and Chudinov, *Filosofskie problemy sovremennogo estestvoznaniia*; Delokarov, *Filosofskie problemy teorii otnositel'nosti* and *Einshtein i filosofskie problemy fiziki XX veka*.

67. See Barashenkov, "O vozmozhnosti elementarnykh protsessov so sverkhsvetovymi skorostiami" and *Problema subatomnogo prostransva i vremeni*, p. 149.

68. Akhundov, Molchanov, and Stepanov, "Filosofskie voprosy fiziki."

69. Arbuzov and Logunov, "Chastitsy i sily: poiski edinstva;" p. 153.

12. COSMOLOGY AND COSMOGONY

1. Bondi, "The Steady-State Theory of the Universe," pp. 17–18.

2. Peebles, *Physical Cosmology*; Sciama, *Modern Cosmology*; Silk, *The Big Bang: Creation and Evolution of the Universe*; Weinberg, *The First Three Minutes*, and *Gravitation and Cosmology*; Bonnor, *The Mystery of the Expanding Universe*; Hoyle, *The Nature of the Universe*; McVittie, *Fact and Theory in Cosmology*; Gamow, *The Creation of the Universe*; Struve, *The Universe*; de Vaucouleurs, *Discovery of the Universe*; and Whitrow, *The Structure and Evolution of the Universe*.

3. Categories I–IV are "relativistic" in the sense of accepting both special and general relativity; category V accepts special relativity but rejects general relativity; category VI is a substantial adaptation of relativity involving abandonment of the conservation laws. Models IIa, IIb, IIc, and IIId can be called big-bang models, although IIb might be best described as "multiple big-bang." Models IIIa, IIIb, IIIc, and IIIe are not of the big-bang type; IIIa and IIc start with an infinite length of time in the static Einstein state; IIe contains infinite contraction and expansion phases without a singular state between. IV, in contrast to the other models, is based on a rejection of the cosmological principle.

4. The cosmological term (λ) was originally introduced by Einstein to provide a force of repulsion resisting gravitational collapse in a static model (Ib). He later abandoned it after shifting to expanding models and after seeing, as a result of Friedmann's work, that expanding models could be constructed without it. The cosmological term was retained by other cosmologists (III); its effect, appreciable only when enormous distances are involved, is to speed up the rate of expansion.

5. One should not forget that in the twenties and thirties, before Stalinism deeply affected Soviet intellectual life, there was a more sophisticated body of literature on philosophic aspects of cosmology and cosmogony. Scientists in those years frequently did not have a deep knowledge of dialectical materialism, but even the great A. A. Friedmann made some effort to connect his views of the universe with materialism. See Friedmann (Fridman), *Mir kak prostranstvo i vremia*, esp. p. 32. See Gerasimovich, *Vselennaia pri svete teorii otnositel'nosti*. The work of M. A. Bronshtein is also relevant.

6. Soviet writers were, of course, not the only critics of the later writings of James Jeans. The American physicist Freeman Dyson commented," . . . he went from bad to worse, becoming a successful popular writer and radio broadcaster, accepting a knighthood and ruining his professional reputation with suave and shallow speculations on religion and philosophy." Dyson, "Mathematics in the Physical Sciences," p. 129.

7. Whittaker, *The Beginning and End of the World*, p. 63.

8. Bonnor, *The Mystery of the Expanding Universe*, p. 119.

9. See Koyré, *From the Closed World to the Infinite Universe*.

10. E. J. Dijksterhuis commented, "The strong influence which Newton's religious ideas exercised on his scientific thought is revealed, among other things, in his belief in the existence of absolute space and absolute time. The former to him symbolized God's omnipresence, the latter His eternity." Dijksterhuis, *The Mechanization of the World Picture*, p. 487. In the *Scholium Generale* of his Principia Newton observed, "This most beautiful system of the sun, planets, and comets, could only proceed from the counsel and dominion of an intelligent and powerful Being." *Principia*, 2:544.

11. Quoted in Wetter, *Dialectical Materialism;* p. 436.

12. Kursanov, "Dialekticheskii materializm o prostranstve i vremeni."

13. He returned from the ice escape by way of Alaska and the United States, where he became a member of the New York Explorers' Club.

14. O. Iu. Schmidt, "Dialectics and Natural Science: Examples of the Transition of Quantity into Quality," (in Russian), notes taken in September, 1926; Archives of the Academy of Sciences of the USSR, *fond 496, op.* 1, *ed.* 212.

15. See "Otto Iul'evich Schmidt (1891–1956)," Kuznetsov, *Liudi russkoi nauki;* p. 404.

16. See Schmidt, *Proiskhozhdenie zemli i planet.* Also available in English as *A Theory of Earth's Origin.*

17. Schmidt, *A Theory of Earth's Origin,* p. 11.

18. Russell, *The Solar System and Its Origin,* pp. 95–96.

19. Schmidt, *A Theory of Earth's Origin,* p. 17.

20. The sun is more than four light-years from the closest star; just traveling that distance with a relative velocity of twenty kilometers per second would require approximately 105 years. Struve and Zebergs, *Astronomy of the 20th Century,* p. 173.

21. Another feature of Schmidt's system was his belief that the earth was originally cold and gained heat later as a result of the breakdown of radioactive elements.

22. Schmidt, *A Theory of Earth's Origin,* pp. 83–84.

23. *Ibid.,* pp. 84–85.

24. See Schmidt, "O vozmozhnosti zakhvata v nebesnoi mekhanike" and Schmidt and Khil'mi, "Problema zakhvata v zadache o trekh telakh."

25. Khil'mi, "O vozmozhnosti zakhvata v probleme trekh tel"; see also the bibliography given in Schmidt, *Proiskhozhdenie zemli i planet,* p. 93.

26. See the work of V. V. Radzievskii and T. A. Agekian cited by Schmidt in *A Theory of Earth's Origin,* pp. 92, 132, 137.

27. For a scientific biography of Ambartsumian, see Severnyi and Sobolev, "Viktor Amazaspovich Ambartsumian."

28. Ambartsumian, "Nekotorye voprosy kosmogonicheskoi nauki," p. 86.
29. Ambartsumian, "Nekotorye metodologicheskie voprosy kosmogonii," p. 290.
30. Ambartsumian, "Problema proiskhozhdeniia zvezd," pp. 9–10.
31. See Ambartsumian, "Stars of T Tauri and UV Ceti Types and the Phenomenon of Continuous Emission."
32. Ambartsumian, "Problema proiskhozhdeniia zvezd," p. 10.
33. He was frequently given credit for this achievement in ordinary biographical accounts, outside the Soviet Union as well as within that country. See, for example, John Turkevich, *Soviet Men of Science,* pp. 15–16.
34. Ambartsumian quite sensibly agreed with the uniformitarianism so well expressed by Lyell in the following way: "It may be necessary in the present state of science to supply some part of the assumed course of nature hypothetically; but, if so, this must be done without violation of probability, and always consistently with the analogy of what is known both of the past and the present economy of our system." Lyell, *Principles of Geology,* p. 299.
35. I can not resist giving the mnemonic device for remembering the types: "Oh, Be a Fine Girl, Give Me a Kiss Right Now, Smack!"
36. Ambartsumian, "Problema proiskhozhdeniia zvezd," p. 14.
37. *Ibid.,* p. 18.
38. Jordan was very frequently criticized by Soviet scientists and philosophers. See his *Die Herkunft der Sterne.*
39. See, for example, the article "Interstellar Matter" in the McGraw-Hill Encyclopedia of Science and Technology, 7:222: "V. A. Ambartsumian first pointed out that superluminous stars of high temperature, which cannot be very old because of the tremendous rate at which mass is converted into energy, are always found in clouds of gas and interstellar particles. Such associations are clear proof that stars must form from this material."
40. Just as dialectical materialists did not believe it correct to speak of the "birth" of the universe as a whole, so they also considered it incorrect to speak of its "death." They criticized those non-Soviet writers who spoke of the white-dwarf stage in stellar evolution as the "cemetery of celestial matter," or who used the term "white death of the universe." The Soviet philosophers frequently said that the white-dwarf stage of stellar evolution is simply another "state" of matter, not an end point of the universe. See, for example, G. A. Kursanov, "O mirovozzrencheskom znachenii dostizhenii sovremennoi astronomii," p. 64. A more extended discussion of a similar nature revolved around the Second Law of Thermodynamics and the "heat-death" of the universe. A number of different attempts were made by Soviet authors to refute this theory, most of them based on the belief that it is incorrect to extend the realm of this law from closed systems to infinite ones. Other writers (S. T. Meliukhin and G. I. Naan) believed that there must exist in the universe "anti-entropic" processes counteracting the processes described by the second law. This view also arose in the analysis of cybernetics. Still others (L. D. Landau and E. M. Lifshits) opposed the heat-death interpretation on the basis of relativistic thermodynamics. See "Oproverzhenie 'teorii' teplovoi smerti," in *Filosofiia estestvoznaniia,* pp. 130–36, and references contained therein. See also Sedov, "K voprosu o sootnoshenii entropii informatsionnykh protsessov i fizicheskoi entropii."

41. Ambartsumian, "Zakliuchitel'noe slovo," pp. 575–76.

42. The term "metagalaxy" here refers only to a part of the universe as a whole, that part about which man has direct evidence. The term "metagalaxy" was first used by Harlow Shapley. See, for example, his *The Inner Metagalaxy*. The Soviet philosopher G. I. Naan remarked that although Shapley saw the need for a distinction between "universe" and "metagalaxy," he was not sufficiently careful in using it. See his "Gravitatsiia i beskonechnost'," pp. 275, 278.

43. Ambartsumian, "Nekotorye metodologicheskie voprosy kosmogonii," p. 271.

44. *Ibid.*

45. *Ibid.*, p. 272.

46. The term "parsec" is a contraction of "parallax second"; in terms of distance one parsec equals 19.2 trillion (19.2 $\times$ 10^{12}) miles. When the parallax of a star, as measured from the earth, is one second of arc, the distance to the star is defined as one parsec.

47. Ambartsumian, "Metodologicheskie voprosy kosmogonii," p. 286.

48. *Ibid.*, pp. 287–88.

49. For Ambartsumian's views in the sixties and early seventies, see Ambartsumian, "Vvodnyi doklad na simpoziume po evoliutsii zvezd"; "Nekotorye osobennosti sovremennogo razvitiia astrofiziki"; "Contemporary natural Science and Philosophy," also published in Russian in *Uspekhi fizicheskikh nauk* (September 1968), pp. 1–19; "Ob evoliutsii galaktik," "Mir galaktik," and "Perspektivy razvitiia astronomii," in Ambartsumian, ed., *Problemy evoliutsii Vselennoi*, pp. 85–127, 176–94, and 232–5 respectively; "Kosmos, kosmogoniia, kosmologiia"; "Nestatsionarnye ob"ekty vo Vselennoi i ikh znachenie dlia kosmogonii"; Ambartsumian and Kaziutinskii, "Revoliutsiia v sovremennoi astronomii."

50. Ambartsumian, "Mir galaktik," pp. 188–89.

51. Ambartsumian, "Contemporary Natural Science and Philosophy," pp. 26–29, 60–63.

52. *Ibid.*, p. 62.

53. Ambartsumian, "Vvodnyi doklad na simpoziume po evoliutsii zvezd," pp. 145–46.

54. Ambartsumian, "Nestatsionarnye ob"ekty vo Vselennoi i ikh znachenie dlia kosmogonii," pp. 5–18.

55. Meliukhin, *Problema konechnogo i beskonechnogo*. Page references for this work will be indicated in the text.

56. In 1959, G. A. Kursanov developed the following interpretation: Einstein's world view was a mixture of natural-science materialism and Machist philosophy. Although one could find many points on which Mach and the Viennese group negatively influenced Einstein, in the final analysis, the natural-science materialism of Einstein was the more important influence and was responsible for the greatness of his work. See Kursanov, "K otsenke filosofskikh vzgliadov A. Einshteina na prirodu geometricheskikh poniatii." A similar approach resulting in an even more positive evaluation of Einstein is in B. G. Kuznetsov's biography *Einstein*; Kuznetsov spoke of the "absolute spiritual purity" of Einstein's work

as a "struggle for the sovereignty of the mind against all forms of mystical antiintellectualism." See Kuznetsov, *Einstein,* and my review in *ISIS* (June 1964), pp. 251–52.

57. See note 40 above.

58. Reginald Kapp stated the relationship between space and matter in relativistic conmology in the following way: "Bearing in mind that matter is not so much in space as of space, the most accurate description, and a noncommittal one, of the uttermost elementary constituent of matter may be a bit of differentiated space." Kapp, *Towards a Unified Cosmology,* p. 52.

59. Shklovskii and Sagan, *Intelligent Life in the Universe,* p. 135. By means of an unusual denotation system, it is possible to tell which sentences, and even which phrases, were written by each of the two authors, one a Soviet scientist, the other an American. The two scholars were not, however, in disagreement on basic issues.

60. An example of an exception was I. P. Plotkin, who wrote that the view that physics did not touch upon the problem of systems that are infinitely large "completely denied cosmology as a science." "A refusal to consider such problems," he continued, "would deal a damaging blow to science and philosophy." Among Soviet physicists whom he criticized for avoiding the issue of infinitely large systems were the well-known L. D. Landau and E. M. Lifshits, who in their text *Statistical Physics* commented: ". . . if we try to apply statistics to the universe as a whole, regarding it as a single, closed system, then we immediately run into a sharp contradiction between theory and experimental evidence." See Plotkin, "O fluktuatsionnoi gipoteze Bol'tsmana," and Landau and Lifshits, *Statisticheskaia fizika, klassicheskaia i kvantovaia,* pp. 43–44.

61. Arsen'ev, "O gipoteze rasshireniia metagalaktiki i krasnom smeshchenii," p. 190.

62. An edited report of the conference was published: Shtokalo et al., eds., *Filosofskie voprosy sovremennoi fiziki.*

63. Dyshlevyi, "Prostranstvo-vremennye predstavleniia obshchei teorii otnositel'nosti," pp. 71, 81.

64. Kobushkin, "Nekotorye filosofskie problemy reliativistskoi kosmologii."

65. Kobushkin cited, in particular, Naan as a source for the concept of a "quasiclosed metagalaxy." Naan, *Trudy shestogo soveshchaniia po voprosam kosmogonii,* pp. 247 *passim,* and "O sovremennom sostoianii kosmologicheskoi nauki," *Voprosy kosmogonii.*

66. Such a star would, apparently, violate the mass-radius relation of dwarf stars, which says that the larger the mass, the smaller the radius. According to this relation a dwarf greater than 1.2 solar masses would be reduced to a point. See, for example, W. S. Krogdahl, *The Astronomical Universe* (New York, 1962), p. 371. Also see Oppenheimer and Volkoff, "On Massive Neutron Cores," and the accompanying article by Tolman, "Static Solutions of Einstein's Field Equations for Spheres of Fluid."

67. Kobushkin, p. 125.

68. *Ibid.,* p. 126.

69. Kobushkin was not committed to the Lemaître model, however. He was also very interested in inhomogeneous, anisotropic models such as expanding

and rotating ones (Gödel, Heckmann, et al.; category IV), and spent considerable time discussing them. See Kobushkin, pp. 131–39. He was also fascinated by the possibility of connecting the micro-, macro-, and megaworlds through physical constants, in a fashion similar to that once favored by Arthur Eddington, a person who like Lemaître had once been severely criticized in the Soviet Union. Kobushkin began his work on this topic before World War II, and it is possible that not until the sixties was the ideological scene relaxed enough for him to publish his findings.

70. Kopnin, "Razvitie kategorii dialekticheskogo materializma," p. 5. I consider this essay interesting and unorthodox in terms of its implications for Soviet cosmology, despite the classification by certain non-Soviet authors of Kopnin among the "old guard" for certain works on dialectical logic. See Blakeley, *Soviet Theory of Knowledge*, p. 6.

71. Kopnin, p. 8.

72. *Ibid.*, p. 9. This view, although somewhat controversial in the Soviet context, had been expressed as early as 1931: "In the materialist dialectic there is no closed or complete system of categories, nor can there be such a thing. All that can be spoken of is a systematic account of the laws and categories which truly reflect the dialectic of reality, a further working-out of these, and the exploration of new categories, representing hitherto unknown forms of material motion." Translated and quoted in Wetter, *Dialectical Materialism*, p. 368, from Obichkin, *Osnovnye momenty dialekticheskogo protsessa poznaniia* (Moscow and Leningrad: 1933), p. 80.

73. Kopnin, p. 13.

74. *Ibid.*

75. Sviderskii, "O dialektiko-materialisticheskom ponimanii konechnogo i beskonechnogo," p. 267, *passim*; also see Meliukhin's comments and objections in "O filosofskom ponimanii beskonechnosti prostranstva i vremeni," p. 295.

76. Sviderskii, p. 267.

77. Naan, "Gravitatsiia i beskonechnost'," p. 284.

78. See his "O beskonechnosti vselennoi," *Voprosy filosofii*, No. 6 (1961), pp. 93–105.

79. Naan's description of the debate in "Gravitatsiia i beskonechnost'," p. 269.

80. *Ibid.*, p. 271.

81. *Ibid.*

82. Einstein and Straus, "The Influence of the Expansion of Space. . . ."

83. Novikov, "O povedenii. . . ."

84. He called the combination "dialectical" in a different spot; see Naan, "Gravitatsiia i beskonechnost'," p. 275.

85. A Schwarzschild shell is a stage in the life history of a star; see Bok, *The Astronomer's Universe*, pp. 86–7; and Struve, *Stellar Evolution*, p. 149.

86. See Zel'manov, "Nereliativistskii gravitatsionnyi paradoks i obshchaia teoriia otnositel'nosti"; "K postanovke kosmologicheskoi problemy"; "Metagalaktika i Vselennaia"; "Kosmos, kosmogoniia, kosmologiia"; and "Mnogoobrazie material'nogo mira i problema beskonechnosti Vselennoi."

87. Zel'manov, "Mnogoobrazie material'nogo mira . . .," p. 278.

88. Zel'manov, "K postanovke . . .," pp. 73–74.

89. See "Rech' A. L. Zel'manova," in Fedoseev et al., eds., *Filosofskie problemy sovremennogo estestvoznaniia*, pp. 434–41.

90. Zel'manov, "O beskonechnosti material'nogo mira," p. 260. Beginning in the late forties a number of scientists in various countries had begun to work on anisotropic, inhomogeneous models. See, for example, Gödel, "An Example of a New Type of Cosmological Solutions"; and Raychaudhuri, "Relativistic Cosmology I." For previous work by Zel'manov on the same subject, see Zel'manov, "Khronometricheskie invarianty . . .," and "K reliativistskoi teorii anizotropnoi neodnorodnoi Vselennoi."

91. Zel'manov, "O beskonechnosti . . .," p. 262.

92. *Ibid.*, pp. 263–64.

93. According to the view of the history of science advanced by Thomas Kuhn, relativity physics was, however, not a simple addition, or modification, to classical physics, but a paradigm that inherently contradicted classical physics. See the discussions of this crucial issue in Kuhn, *The Structure of Scientific Revolutions*, pp. 100–1, and the penetrating review of Kuhn's book by Shapere, "The Structure of Scientific Revolutions," especially the discussion of the existence of an inherent contradiction, pp. 389–90.

94. Zel'manov, "O beskonechnosti . . .," p. 268.

95. Zel'manov, "Mnogoobrazie material'nogo mira . . .," p. 280 and *passim*.

96. Zel'manov, "Metagalaktika i Vselennaia," p. 390.

97. See *Beskonechnost' i Vselennaia*. For another interesting book, see Staniukovich, Kolesnikov, and Moskovkin, *Problemy teorii prostranstva, vremeni i materii*.

98. See Chudinov, "Logicheskie aspekty problemy beskonechnosti Vselennoi v reliativistskoi kosmologii," and *Filosofskie problemy sovremennoi fiziki i astronomii*; Kaziutinskii, "Astronomiia i dialektika"; Naan, "Poniatie beskonechnosti v matematike i kosmologii"; and Zel'manov, "Mnogoobrazie material'nogo mira i problema beskonechnosti Vselennoi."

99. Ambartsumian and Kaziutinskii, "Revoliutsiia v sovremennoi astronomii." Ambartsumian also approved of Kaziutinskii's approach in a short foreword he wrote to the latter's *Revoliutsiia v astronomii*.

100. Kaziutinskii, "Astronomiia i dialektika," pp. 140–1, from V. L. Ginzberg, *Kak ustroena Vselennaia i kak ona razvivaetsia vo vremia* (Moscow: 1968), p. 51.

101. Kaziutinskii, *Revoliutsiia v astronomii*, p. 33.

102. See, for example, Chudinov, "Logicheskie aspekty problemy . . .," p. 218. The Estonian philosopher G. I. Naan said in 1969 that the infinitude of the universe is a postulate, rather than something that can be "proved" or "disproved." But, Naan continued, without this postulate in one form or another man can not correctly understand the world as something that exists external to him, his will, and his consciousness. See Naan, "Poniatie beskonechnosti v matematike i kosmologii," pp. 76–77.

103. Bazhenov and Nutsubidze, "K diskussii o probleme beskonechnosti Vselennoi," p. 130.

104. See "Vitalii Lazarevich Ginzburg," *Uspekhi fizicheskikh nauk* (September 1966), 90(1):195–97.

105. See Ginzburg, "Zamechaniia o metodologii i razvitii fiziki i astrofiziki," *Voprosy filosofii* (1980), 12:24–46; for the quotations, see p. 27.

106. *Ibid.*

107. *Ibid.*, p. 31.

108. The articles of Ambartsumian to which Ginzburg referred are ones in which Ambartsumian spoke much of the links between his scientific views and dialectical materialism: see Ambartsumian and Kaziutinskii in the collections *Filosofskie problemy astronomii XX veka*, and *Astronomiia, metodologiia, mirovozzrenie*.

109. Ginzburg, "Zamechaniia o metodologii . . .," pp. 33–34.

110. Ginzburg, *O fizike i astrofizike.*

111. For an English-language summary of Zel'dovich's achievements, see "Personalia: Yakov (sic) Borisovich Zel'dovich (on his sixtieth birthday)," *Soviet Physics Uspekhy* (September-October 1974), 27(2):276–82.

112. Zel'dovich and Novikov, p. xix.

113. Novikov, p. xiii.

114. Kaziutinskii, "Kosmologiia, kartina mira i mirovozzrenie," pp. 249–50.

115. Doroshkevich and Novikov, *Doklady akademii nauk SSSR*, p. 809.

116. Zel'dovich and Novikov, p. xv.

117. Novikov, p. 8.

118. Zel'dovich and Novikov, p. xxi.

119. For the claim that this principle is a Marxist one, see, for example, p. 51.

120. Michael Scriven is quoted in Kapp, *Towards a Unified Cosmology*, p. 49; for Bonnor, see *The Mystery of the Expanding Universe*, p. 204.

BIBLIOGRAPHY

Some of the articles cited below are available in English, as a result of the translation services of the Joint Publications Research Service (JPRS) of the U.S. Department of Commerce. Serial numbers for these publications will be in parentheses following the citation.

Abetti, Giorgio. *The History of Astronomy*. London and New York: Abelart, 1952.

Acton, H. B. *The Illusion of the Epoch: Marxism-Leninism as a Philosophical Creed*. Boston: Beacon Press, 1957.

Abramova, N. T. *Tselostnost' i upravlenie*. Moscow, 1974.

Adams, Frank Dawson. *The Birth and Development of the Geological Sciences*. New York: Dover, 1954.

Adams, Mark B. "Biology After Stalin: A Case Study." *Survey* (Winter 1977–78), 102:53–80.

——"Biology in the Soviet Academy of Sciences, 1953–1965." In J. R. Thomas and U. M. Krause-Vaucienne, eds., *Soviet Science and Technology: Domestic and Foreign Perspectives*. Washington, D.C.: National Science Foundation, 1977).

——"From Gene Fund to Gene Pool: On the Evolution of an Evolutionary Language." *Studies in the History of Biology* (1979), 3:241–85.

——"Science, Ideology and Structure: The Kol'tsov Institute, 1900–1970." In Linda Lubrano and Susan Solomon, eds., *The Social Context of Soviet Science*, pp. 173–204. Boulder: Westview Press, 1980.

——"Sergei Chetverikov: The Kol'tsov Institute and the Evolutionary Synthesis." In Ernst Mayr and William Provine, eds., *The Evolutionary Synthesis: Perspectives on the Unification of Biology*, pp. 242–78. Cambridge, Mass.: Harvard University Press, 1980.

——"Severtsov and Schmalhausen: Russian Morphology and the Evolutionary Synthesis." In Mayr and Provine, *The Evolutionary Synthesis: Perspectives on the Unification of Biology*, pp. 193–225. Cambridge, Mass.: Harvard University Press, 1980.

——"The Founding of Population Genetics: Contributions of the Chetverikov School, 1924–1934." *Journal of the History of Biology* (Spring 1968), pp. 23–29.

——"Towards a Synthesis: Population Concepts in Russian Evolutionary Thought, 1925–1935." *Journal of the History of Biology* (1970), 3(1):107–29.

Afanas'ev, V. G. *Chelovek v upravlenii obshchestvom*. Moscow, 1975.

——*Ob intensifikatsii razvitiia sotsialisticheskogo obshchestva*. Moscow, 1969.

——*Nauchnoe upravlenie obshchestvom*. Moscow, 1972.

——*Nauchno-tekhnicheskaia revolutsiia, upravlenie, obrazovanie.* Moscow, 1972.
——*Sotsial'naia informatsiia i upravlenie obshchestvom.* Moscow, 1975.
Agassi, Joseph. *Towards an Historiography of Science.* History and Theory: Studies in the Philosophy of History series. Beiheft 2. The Hague: Móuton, 1963.
Agranovskii, Anatolii. "Nauka na veru ne prinimaet." *Literaturnaia gazeta* (January 23, 1965), p. 2.
Akademik I. P. Pavlov, Izbrannye trudy po fiziologii vysshei nervnoi deiatel'nosti. Moscow, 1950.
Akhundov, M. D. *Problema preryvnosti i nepreryvnosti prostranstva i vremeni.* Moscow, 1974.
Akhundov, M. D., Iu. B. Molchanov and N. I. Stepanov. "Filosofskie voprosy fiziki." In I. T. Frolov and L. I. Grekov, eds., *Filosofia, estestvoznanie, sovremennost'*, pp. 236–57. Moscow, 1981.
Akhlibinskii, B. V. and N. I. Khralenko. *Chudo nashego vremeni: kibernetika i problemy razvitiia.* Leningrad, 1963.
Aksenov, I. Ia. "O vtorom mezhdunarodnom kongresse po kibernetike." In V. A. Il'in et al., eds., *Filosofskie voprosy kibernetiki*, pp. 359–73. Moscow, 1960.
——"Transportnye problemy kibernetiki." In A. I. Berg, ed., *Kibernetika na sluzhbu kommunizma*, pp. 158–96. Moscow, 1961.
Albury, W. R. "Politics and Rhetoric in the Sociobiology Debate." *Social Studies of Science*, (1980), 10:519–36.
Aleksandr Ivanovich Oparin. Moscow and Leningrad, 1949 (AN ASSR. Materialy k bibliografii uchenykh SSSR. Seriia biokhimii, vyp. 3).
Aleksandrov, A. D. "Dialektika i nauka." *Vestnik akademii nauk SSSR* (1957), no. 6, pp. 3–17.
——*Die innere Geometrie der konvexen Flächen.* Berlin, 1955.
——"Filosofskoe soderzhanie i znachenie teorii otnositel'nosti." *Voprosy filosofii* (1959), no. 1, pp. 67–84.
——"Leninskaia dialektika i matematika." *Priroda* (1951), no. 1, p. 5–15.
——"Ob idealizme v matematike." *Priroda* (1951), no. 7, pp. 36–11; no. 8, pp. 3–9.
——"Po povodu nekotorykh vzgliadov na teoriiu otnositel'nosti." *Voprosy filosofii* (1953), no. 5, pp. 225–45.
——"Teoriia otnositel'nosti kak teoriia absoliutnogo prostranstva-vremeni." In I. V. Kuznetsov and M. E. Omel'ianovskii, eds., *Filosofskie voprosy sovremennoi fiziki*, pp. 269–323. Moscow, 1959.
——*Vnutrennaia geometriia vypuklykh poverkhnostei.* Moscow and Leningrad, 1948.
Aleksandrov, A. D. and V. V. Ovchinnikov. "Zamechaniia k osnovam teorii otnositel'nosti." *Vestnik Leningradskogo universiteta* (1953), no. 11, pp. 95–109.
Alekseev, I. S. *Kontseptsiia dopolnitel'nosti.* Moscow, 1978.
——"O poniatii nekontroliremogo vzaimodeistviia." *Voprosy filosofii* (1984), no. 6, pp. 82–88.
Allilueva, Svetlana. *Only One Year.* New York and Evanston, Ill.: Harper, 1969.
——*Twenty Letters to a Friend.* New York: Harper, 1967.

Alperovitz, Gar. *Atomic Diplomacy: Hiroshima and Potsdam; the Use of the Atomic Bomb and the American Confrontation with Soviet Power.* New York: Simon and Schuster, 1965.

Alpher, R. A., H. Bethe, and G. Gamow. "The Origin of the Chemical Elements." *Physical Review* (April 1, 1948), 73:803–4.

Ambartsumian, V. A. "Contemporary Natural Science and Philosophy." In *Papers for XIV International Wien Philosophical Congress, Section 7*, pp. 41–72. Moscow, 1968.

——"Kosmos, kosmogoniia, kosmologiia." *Nauka i religiia* (1968), no. 12, pp. 2–37.

——"Mir galaktik." In V. A. Ambartsumian, ed., *Problemy evoliutsii Vselennoi*, pp. 176–94. Erevan, 1968.

——"Nekotorye metodologicheskie voprosy kosmogonii." In P. N. Fedoseev et al., eds., *Filosofskie problemy sovremennogo estestvoznaniia*, pp. 268–90. Moscow, 1959.

——"Nekotorye osobennosti sovremennogo razvitiia astrofiziki." In *Oktiabr' i nauchnyi progress*, 1:73–85. Moscow, 1967.

——"Nekotorye voprosy kosmogonicheskoi nauki." *Kommunist* (1959), no. 8, pp. 86–96.

——"Nestatsionarnye ob"ekty vo Vselennoi i ikh znachenie dlia kosmogonii." In V. A. Ambartsumian, ed., *Problemy sovremennoi kosmogonii*, pp. 5–18. Moscow, 1969.

——"Ob evolutsii galaktik." In V. A. Ambartsumian, ed., *Problemy evoliutsii Vselennoi*, pp. 85–127. Erevan, 1968.

——"Perspektivy razvitiia astronomii." In V. A. Ambartsumian, ed., *Problemy evoliutsii Vselennoi*, pp. 232–235. Erevan, 1968.

——"Problema proiskhozhdeniia zvezd." *Priroda* (1952), no. 9, pp. 8–18.

——"Stars of T Tauri and UV Ceti Types and the Phenomenon of Continuous Emission." In George H. Herbig, ed., *Non-Stable Stars*, pp. 177–85. International Astronomical Union Symposium No. 3, Cambridge: Cambridge University Press, 1957.

——"Vvodnyi doklad na simpoziuma po evoliutsii zvezd." In V. A. Ambartsumian, *Nauchnye trudy*, 2:143–63. Erevan, 1960.

——"Zakliuchitel'noe slovo." In P. N. Fedoseev et al., eds., *Filosofskie problemy sovremennogo estestvoznaniia*, pp. 557–64. Moscow, 1959.

Ambartsumian, V. A. and V. V. Kaziutinskii. "Revoliutsiia v sovremennoi astronomii." *Priroda* (1970), no. 4, pp. 16–26.

Ambartsumian, V. A., ed., *Problemy evoliutsii Vselennoi.* Erevan, 1968.

Amosov, N. M. "Modelirovanie informatsii i programm v slozhnykh sistemakh." *Voprosy filosofii*, (1963), no. 12, pp. 26–34.

——"Myshlenie i informatsiia." In *Problemy myshleniia v sovremennoi nauke*, pp. 387–409. Moscow, 1964.

Anan'ev, B. G. *Chelovek kak predmet pozaniia.* Leningrad, 1969.

Andrade e Silva, J. and G. Lochak. *Quanta.* New York and Toronto: McGraw Hill, 1969.

Andreev, N. D. and D. A. Kerimov. "Vozmozhnosti ispol'zovaniia kiberneticheskoi tekhniki pri reshenii nekotorykh pravovykh problem." In A. I. Berg, ed., *Kibernetika na sluzhbu kommunizma*, pp. 234–41. Moscow, 1961.

Andriushchenko, M. N. "Otvet tovarishcham V. C. Borshchevu, V. V. Il'inu, F. Z. Rokhline." *Filosofskie nauki* (1960), 3(4): 108–10.

Anokhin, P. K. *A New Conception of the Physiological Architecture of the Conditioned Reflex.* Moscow, 1959.

——*Biologiia i neirofiziologiia uslovnogo refleksa.* Moscow, 1968.

——*Ivan Petrovich Pavlov: Zhizn', deiatel'nost' i nauchnaia shkola.* Moscow and Leningrad, 1949.

——"Kibernetika i integrativnaia deiatel'nost' mozga." *Voprosy psikhologil* (1966), no. 3, pp. 10–31.

——"Metodologicheskii analiz uzlovykh problem uslovnogo refleksa." In M. E. Omel'ianovskii, ed., *Materialisticheskaia dialektika i metody estestvennykh nauk*, pp. 156–214. Moscow, 1963.

——"Metodologicheskoe znachenie kiberneticheskikh zakonomernostei." In M. E. Omel'ianovskii, ed., *Materialisticheskaia dialektika i metody estestvennykh nauk*, pp. 547–87. Moscow, 1968.

——*Obshchie printsipy kompensatsii narushennykh funktsii i ikh fiziologicheskoe obosnovanie.* Moscow, 1956.

——"Osobennosti afferentnogo apparata uslovnogo refleksa i ikh znachenie dlia psikhologii." *Voprosy psikhologii* (1955), no. 6, pp. 16–38.

——*Ot Dekarta do Pavlova: trista let teorii refleksa.* Moscow, 1945.

——"Problema tsentra i periferii v sovremennoi fiziologii nervnoi deiatel'nosti." In P. K. Anokhin, ed., *Problema tsentra i periferii v fiziologii nervnoi deiatel'nosti*, pp. 9–70. Gor'kii, 1935.

——"Refleks i funktsional'naia sistema kak faktory fiziologicheskoi integratsii." *Biulleten' Moskovskogo obshchestva ispytatelei prirody* (1949), no. 5, pp. 130–46.

——"Uzlovye voprosy v izuchenii vysshei nervnoi deiatel'nosti." In *Problemy vysshei nervnoi deiatel'nosti*, pp. 9–128. Moscow, 1949.

——*Vnutrenee tormozhenie kak problema fiziologii.* Moscow, 1958.

Anokhin, P. K. and E. Strezh. "Izuchenie dinamiki vysshei nervnoi deiatel'nosti. Soobshchenie III. Narushenie aktivnogo vybora v rezul'tate zameny bezuslovnogo stimula." *Fiziologicheskii zhurnal SSSR* (1933), no. 2, pp. 280–98.

Anokhin, P. K., ed. *Problema tsentra i periferii v fiziologii nervnoi deiatel'nosti.* Gor'kii, 1935.

Antipenko, L. G., *Problema fizicheskoi realnosti.* Moscow, 1973.

——"Razvitie poniatiia material'nogo ob'ekta v fizike mikromira." *Voprosy filosofii* (1967), no. 1, pp. 104–13.

Antonov, N. P. and A. N. Kochergin. "Priroda myshleniia i problema ego modelirovaniia." *Filosofskie nauki* (1963), no. 2, pp. 37–47.

Arab-Ogly, E. A. "Sotsiologiia i kibernetika." *Voprosy filosofii* (1958), no. 5, pp. 138–51.

Arbuzov, B. A. and A. A. Logunov. "Chastitsy i sily: poiski edinstva." In *Nauka i chelovechestvo: 1979.* Moscow, 1979.

Arkhipov, V. M. "O material'nosti psikhiki i predmete psikhologii." *Sovetskaia pedagogika* (1954), no. 7, pp. 67–79.

Armstrong, E. F. *Chemistry in the Twentieth Century.* London: Macmillan, 1924.

Arsen'ev, A. S. "Nekotorye metodologicheskie voprosy kosmogonii." *Voprosy filosofii* (1955), no. 3, pp. 32–44.

——"O gipoteze rasshireniia metagalaktiki i 'krasnom smeshchenii.'" *Voprosy filosofii* (1958), no. 8, pp. 187–90.

——"O sub"ektivizme v sovremennoi kosmogonii." *Priroda* (1954), no. 6, pp. 47–56.

Ashby, W. Ross, *An Introduction to Cybernetics.* London: Chapman, 1956.

——"Design for a Brain." *Electronic Engineering* 10(250):382–83.

——*Design for a Brain: The Origin of Adaptive Behaviour.* London: Chapman, 1960.

Askin, Ia. F. *Filosofskii determinizm i nauchnoe poznanie.* Moscow, 1977.

——*Materialisticheskaia dialektika i kontseptsiia dopolnitel'nosti.* Kiev, 1975.

——*Printsip dopolnitel'nosti i materialisticheskaia dialektika.* Moscow, 1976.

Asratian, Ezras A. *I. P. Pavlov, His Life and Work.* Moscow, 1963.

——"Nekotorye aktual'nye voprosy fiziologii vysshei nervnoi deiatel'nosti i ikh filosofskoe znachenie." In S. A. Petrushevskii and V. N. Kolbanovskii et al., eds., *Dialekticheskii materializm i sovremennoe estestvoznanie,* pp. 192–233. Moscow, 1964.

Astaurov, B. "HOMO SAPIENS ET HUMANUS—Chekovek s bol'shoi bukvy i evolutsionnaia genetika chelovechnosti." *Novy Mir* (1971) no. 10, pp. 214–24.

Astronomiia, metodologiia, mirovozzrenie. Moscow, 1979.

Avanesov, G. A. *Kriminologiia, prognostika, upravlenie.* Gor'kii, 1975.

Avdeev, M. I. "Pravovoe regulirovanie peresadkov organov i tkanei." *Sovetskoe gosudarstvo i pravo* (1968) no. 9, pp. 83–88.

Babkin, B. P. *Pavlov: A Biography.* Chicago: University of Chicago Press, 1949.

Baev, A. A. "Sotsial'nye aspekty geneticheskoi inzhenerii," in *Filosofskaia bor'ba idei v sovremennom estestvoznanii.* Moscow, 1977, pp. 144–148.

——"Sovremennaia biologiia kak sotsial'noe iavlenie," *Voprosy filosofii,* (1981) no. 3, pp. 17–26.

Bakker, Donald P. "The Philosophical Debate in the U.S.S.R. on the Nature of 'Information.'" M.A. thesis, Columbia University, 1966.

Bakshutov, V. K. and V. I. Koriukin. "Obzor otklikov na stat'iu B. M. Kedrova 'Marksistkaia filosofia: ee predmet i rol' v integratsii sovremennykh nauk.'" *Voprosy filosofii* (1982), no. 12, pp. 124–32.

Balabanovich, E. N. *A. S. Makarenko: chelovek i pisatel'.* Moscow, 1963.

Barashenkov, V. S. *Problemy subatomnogo prostranstva i vremeni.* Moscow, 1978.

——"O vozmozhnosti elementarynkh protsessov so sverkhsvetovymi skorostiami. *Voprosy filosofii* (1976), no. 5, pp. 90–99.

——"O vozmozhnosti 'vneprostranstvennykh' i 'vnevremennykh' form sushchestvovaniia materii." In *Filosofskie voprosy kvantovoi fiziki,* pp. 248–49. Moscow, 1970.

——*Problema subatomnogo prostranstva i vremeni.* Moscow, 1979.

——*Sushchestvuiut li granitsy nauki: kolichestvennaia i kachestvennaia neischerpaemost' material'nogo mira.* Moscow, 1982.

Barber, Bernard. "Resistance by Scientists to Scientific Discovery." *Science* (1961), 134:596–602.

Barker, Martin. "Racism: The New Inheritors," *Radical Philosophy* (1979), no. 21, pp. 2–17.

Bassin, F. V. "Zakliuchitel'nye slova," in *Filosofskie voprosy fiziologii vysshei nervnoi deiatel'nosti i psikhologii*. Moscow, 1963.

Bastian, H. C. *The Beginning of Life*. New York, 1872.

Batuev, M. I. "K voprosu o sopriazhenii v benzole." *Zhurnal obshchei khimii* (November 1958), 29:3147–54.

Bauer, Raymond A. *The New Man in Soviet Psychology*. Cambridge, Mass.: Harvard University Press, 1952.

Bauer, Raymond A., Alex Inkeles, and Clyde Kluckhohn. *How the Soviet System Works: Cultural, Psychological and Social Themes*. Cambridge, Mass.: Harvard University Press, 1956.

Bazhan, V. V., P. S. Dyshlevyi, and V. S. Luk'ianets. *Dialekticheskii materializm i problema realnosti v sovremennoi fizike*. Kiev, 1974.

Bazhenov, L. V. *Stroenie i funktsii estestvennonauchnoi teorii*. Moscow, 1978.

Bazhenov, L. V. and I. B. Gutchkin. *Intellekt i mashina*. Moscow, 1973.

Bazhenov, L. V. and N. N. Nutsubidze. "K diskussii o probleme beskonechnosti Vselennoi." In *Beskonechnost' i Vselennaia*, pp. 129–36. Moscow, 1969.

Beadle, George and Muriel Beadle. *The Language of Life: An Introduction to the Science of Genetics*. Garden City, N.Y.: Doubleday, 1966.

Beer, Stafford. "The Irrelevance of Automation." *Cybernetica* (1958), 1(4):280–95.

Belkin, V. D. "Kibernetika i ekonomika." In A. I. Berg, ed., *Kibernetika na sluzhbu kommunizma*, 1:185–203. Moscow, 1961.

Berdyaev, N. *Wahrheit und Lüge des Kommunismus*. Lucerne, 1934.

Berg, A. I. "Nauka velichaishikh vozmozhnostei." *Priroda* (1962), no. 7, pp. 16–22.

Berg, A. I. and Iu. I. Cherniak. *Informatsiia i upravlenie*. Moscow, 1966.

Berg, A. I., ed. *Kibernetika na sluzhbu kommunizma*. Moscow, 1961.

Berg, A. I. and E. Kol'man, eds. *Vozmozhnoe i nevozmozhnoe v kibernetike*. Moscow, 1964.

Berg, A. I. et al., eds. *Kibernetika, myshlenie, zhizn'*. Moscow, 1964.

Berg, Raisa. *Sukhovei*. New York: Chalidze Publications, 1983.

Berg, R. L. and N. V. Timofeev-Ressovskii. "Paths of Evolution of the Genotype." *Problems of Cybernetics* (1961) no. 5., pp. 33–59 (JPRS 10, 292, January 1962–1016).

Bernal, J. D. *The Origin of Life*. London: World, 1967.

——*The Physical Basis of Life*. London: Routledge, 1951.

Bernshtein, N. A. "Novye linii razvitiia v fiziologii i ikh sootnoshenie s kibernetikoi." In *Filosofskie voprosy fiziologii vysshei nervnoi deiatel'nosti i psikhologii*, pp. 299–322. Moscow, 1963.

Beskonechnost' i Vselennaia. Moscow, 1969.

Beutner, R. *Life's Beginning on the Earth*. Baltimore: Johns Hopkins University Press, 1938.

Bialik, B. "Tovarishchi, vy eto ser'ezno." In A. I. Berg and E. Kol'man, eds., *Vozmozhnoe i nevozmozhnoe v kibernetike*, pp. 77–88. Moscow, 1964.

Bianki, V. and V. Stepanov. "Kto napisala oproverzhenie?" *Komsomol'skaia pravda* (March 16, 1965), p. 2.

Biologicheskie i sotsial'noe v razvitii cheloveka. Moscow, 1977.

Biriukov, B. V. *Kibernetika i metodologiia nauki*. Moscow, 1974.

Biriukov, B. V., "O vozmozhnostiakh 'iskusstvennogo intellekta,' " *Voprosy filosofii* (1979), no. 3, pp. 88–91.

Biriukov, B. V. and E. S. Geller. *Kibernetika v gumanitarnykh naukakh*. Moscow, 1973.

Biriukov, B. V., D. I. Koshelevskii, and A. E. Furman, eds. *Dialekticheskii materializm i voprosy estestvoznaniia*. Moscow, 1964.

Biriukov, B. V. and V. S. Tiukhin. "Filosofskie voprosy kibernetiki." In A. I. Berg et al., eds., *Kibernetika, myshlenie, zhizn'*, pp. 76–108. Moscow, 1964.

Blakeley, Thomas J. *Soviet Theory of Knowledge*. Dordrecht-Holland: Reidel, 1964.

Blokhintsev, D. I. "Kritika filosofskikh vozzrenii tak nazyvaemoi 'kopengagenskoi shkoly' v fizike." In A. A. Maksimov et al., eds., *Filosofskie voprosy sovremennoi fiziki*, pp. 358–95. Moscow, 1952.

——"Kritika idealisticheskogo ponimaniia kvantovoi teorii." *Uspekhi fizicheskikh nauk* (October 1951), no. 2, pp. 195–228.

——"Obsuzhdenie stat'i M. A. Markova." *Voprosy filosofii* (1948), no. 1, pp. 212–14.

——*Osnovy kvantovoi mekhaniki*. Moscow and Leningrad, 1949.

——"Otvet akademiku V. A. Foku." *Voprosy filosofii* (1952), no. 6, pp. 171–75.

——*Printsipal'nye voprosy kvantovoi mekhaniki*. Moscow, 1966.

——"Problemy struktury elementarnykh chastits." In I. V. Kuznetsov and M. E. Omel'ianovskii, eds., *Filosofskie problemy fiziki elementarnykh chastits*, pp. 47–59. Moscow, 1964.

——*The Philosophy of Quantum Mechanics*. Dordrecht-Holland and New York: Humanities Press, 1968.

——*Vvedenie v kvantovuiu mekhaniku*. Moscow and Leningrad, 1944.

——"Za leninskoe uchenie o dvizhenii." *Voprosy filosofii* (1952), no. 1, pp. 181–83.

Boas, Marie. *The Scientific Renaissance 1450–1630*. New York: Harper, 1962.

Bochenski, J. M., ed. *Bibliographie der sowjetishen Philosophie* vols. 1–5. Dordrecht-Holland: 1959–64.

Bochkov, N. P. *Genetika cheloveka: nasledstvennost' i patologiia*. Moscow, 1978.

——"Metodologicheskie i sotsial'nye voprosy sovremennoi genetiki cheloveka." *Voprosy filosofii* (1981), no. 1, pp. 51–62.

Bogdanov, A. A. *Empiriomonizm; stati po filosofii*, 3 vols. Moscow, 1904–7.

Bogdenko, M. L. and I. E. Zelenin. "Osnovnye problemy istorii kollektivizatsii sel'skogo khoziaistva v sovremennoi sovetskoi istoricheskoi literature." In M. P. Kim et al., eds., *Istoriia sovetskogo krest'ianstva i kolkhoznogo stroitel'stva v SSSR*, pp. 192–222. Moscow, 1963.

Bogomolova, L. G. *Donorstvo*. Leningrad, 1977.

Bohm, D. *Causality and Chance in Modern Physics*. New York: Van Nostrand, 1961.

Bohr, N. *Atom-theorie und Naturbeschreibung*. Berlin, 1931.

——"Can Quantum Mechanical Description of Physical Reality Be Considered Complete?" *Physical Review* (October 15, 1935), 48(8):696–702.

——"Causality and Complementarity." *Dialektika* (1948), 2(3–4):312–19.

——"Kvantovaia fizika i filosofiia." *Uspekhi fizicheskikh nauk* (1959), no. 1, pp. 37–42.

——"On the Notion of Causality and Complementarity." *Dialectica* (1948), no. 3-4, pp. 312-19.

Bok, Bart J. *The Astronomer's Universe.* Cambridge: Cambridge University Press, 1958.

Bokser, O. Ia., D. A. Mishakhin, and S. S. Poltyrev. "Filosofskie voprosy fiziologii retikuliarnoi formatsii." *Voprosy filosofii* (1961), no. 12, pp. 80-91.

Bondi, H. *Cosmology.* Cambridge: Cambridge University Press, 1961.

——"The Steady-State Theory of the Universe." In H. Bondi, W. B. Bonnor, R. A. Lyttleton, and G. J. Whitrow, *Rival Theories of Cosmology.* London: Oxford University Press, 1960, pp. 12-21.

Bonnor, William. *The Mystery of the Expanding Universe.* New York: Macmillan, 1964.

Boring, Edwin G. *A History of Experimental Psychology.* New York: Appleton, 1950, 1957.

——"Psychology, History of." *Encyclopedia Britannica.* Chicago, 1959, 18:713.

Borodai, Iu. M. "Etnicheskie kontakty i okruzhaiushchaia sreda." *Priroda* (1981), no. 9, pp. 82-85.

Boshniakov, D. M. "Mirovozzrenie i meditsina." *Vestnik akademii meditsinskikh nauk* (1983), no. 7, pp. 54-62.

Bovin, A. "Na trassakh gosudarstvennykh lesnykh polos." *Pravda,* May 8, 1950, p. 2.

Brain Mechanisms and Consciousness. Springfield, Ill.: Thomas, 1954.

Braines, S. N. "Nevrokibernetika." In A. I. Berg, ed., *Kibernitika na sluzhbu kommunizma,* pp. 140-52. Moscow, 1961.

Brennan, Joseph G. *The Meaning of Philosophy.* New York: Harper, 1967.

De Broglie, Louis. "La Cybernetique." *La Nouvelle Revue Française* (July 1953), pp. 60-85.

——La Physique quantique restera-t-elle indéterministe?" *Revue de Histoire des Sciences et des leurs applications.* 5 (October-December 1952), 5(4):289-311.

Bromlei, Iu. V. *Ocherki teorii etnosa.* Moscow, 1983.

Brozek, Josef. "Soviet Contributions to History." *Contemporary Psychology* (1969), 14(8):432-34.

Bruner, Jerome. Introduction to L. S. Vygotsky, *Thought and Language,* pp. v-x. Cambridge, Mass.: Harvard University Press, 1962.

Brushlinskii. A. V. "Kul'turno-istoricheskaia teoriia myshleniia." In E. V. Shorokhova, ed., *Issledovania myshleniia v sovetskoi psikhologii,* pp. 123-74. Moscow, 1966.

Buck, R. C. "On the Logic of General Behavior Systems Theory." In H. Feigel and M. Scriven, eds., *Minnesota Studies in the Philosophy of Science.* 1:223-38. Minneapolis, 1956.

Budilova, E. A. *Bor'ba materializma i idealizma v russkoi psikhologicheskoi nauke: vtoraia polovina XIX-nachalo XX v.* Moscow, 1960.

Budreiko, N. A. *Filosofskie voprosi khimii.* Moscow, 1970.

Bukharin, Nikolai. *Historical Materialism.* Ann Arbor: University of Michigan Press, 1969.

Burkova, A. "Razvitie dialektiko-materialisticheskoi teorii zhizni v sovremennoi biologii." In *Metodologiia nauchnogo poznaniia.* pp. 111-19. Moscow, 1976.

Bykhovskii, B. "O metodologicheskikh osnovaniiakh psikhoanaliticheskogo uch- eniia Freida." *Pod znamenem marksizma* (November-December 1923), pp. 158–77.

Caldwell, Oliver J. and Loren R. Graham. "Moscow in May 1963: Education and Cybernetics." Washington, D.C., U.S. Office of Education Bulletin, 1964.

Cannon, Walter F. "The Uniformitarian-Catastrophist Debate." *ISIS* (March 1960), 51:38–55.

Caplan, Arthur L., ed. *The Sociobiology Debate: Readings on the Ethical and Scientific Issues Concerning Sociobiology.* New York: Harper and Row, 1978.

Chargaff, E. "Nucleic Acids as Carriers of Biological Information." In *Proceedings of the First International Symposium on the Origin of Life on the Earth*, pp. 297–302. New York: Pergamon, 1959.

Chelintsev, G. V. *Ocherki po teorii organicheskoi khimii.* Moscow, 1949.

——"O teorii khimicheskogo stroeniia A. M. Butlerova i ee novykh uspekhakh." *Zhurnal obshchei khimii* (February 1952), 22:350–60.

——"O vtorom izdanii doklada komissii OKhN AN SSSR 'Sostoianie teorii khimicheskogo stroeniia v organicheskoi khimii.' " *Zhurnal obshchei khimii* (August 1957), 27:2308–10.

"Chelovek kak kompleksnaia problema," *Voprosy filosofii* (1983), 10:37–48.

Chepikov, M. "Sovremennoe ponimanie sushchnosti zhizni: Filosofskie as- pekty." *Kommunist* (1974), no. 8, pp. 77–90.

Cheremisinov, G. A. "Rech' tovarishcha G. A. Cheremisinova." *Pravda* (February 14, 1964), p. 2.

Chernenko, E. and A. Solopov. "Ispytannyi leninets: k 100-letiu so dnia rozh- deniia M. A. Savel'eva." *Pravda* (February 19, 1984), p. 6.

Chernyshevskii, N. G. *Polnoe sobranie sochinenii.* 16 vols. Moscow, 1939.

Chomsky, Noam. "After Pinkville." *The New York Review of Books*, January 1, 1970.

Chudinov, E. M. *Filosofskie problemy sovremennoi fiziki i astronomii.* Moscow, 1969.

——"Logicheskie aspekty problemy beskonechnosti Vselennoi v reliativistskoi kosmologii." In *Beskonechnost' i Vselennaia*, pp. 181–218. Moscow, 1969.

——*Nit' Ariadny: filosofskie orientiry nauki.* Moscow, 1979.

——*Priroda nauchnoi istiny.* Moscow, 1977.

——*Teoriia otnositel'nosti i filosofiia.* Moscow, 1974.

——*Teoriia poznaniia i sovremennia fizika.* Moscow, 1974.

Chuvashov, B. I. "K voprosu o vozniknovenii zhizni na Zemle." *Voprosy filosofii* (1966), no. 8, pp. 76–83.

Cohen, Robert S. "Engels, Friedrich." *Dictionary of Scientific Biography* (New York, 1978), vol. 15 (supplement), pp. 131–47.

Cole, Michael, ed. *The Selected Writings of A. R. Luria.* White Plains, N.Y.: Sharpe, 1978.

Cole, Sheila. "Soviet Family Clubs and Human Potential." Manuscript, 1984.

Coleman, William. *Georges Cuvier: Zoologist: A Study in the History of Evolutionary Theory.* Cambridge, Mass.: Harvard University Press, 1964.

Colodny, R. G., ed. *Beyond the Edge of Certainty.* Englewood Cliffs, N.J.: Prentice-hall, 1965.

Comey, David Dinsmore. "Soviet Controversies Over Relativity." In *The State of Soviet Science,* pp. 186–99. Cambridge, Mass.: Harvard University Press, 1965.

Comey, David D. and L. R. Kerschner. "Soviet Publications on Cybernetics" and "Western Translations of Soviet Publications on Cybernetics." *Studies in Soviet Thought* (February 1964), 4(2):142–77.

Crombie, A. C. *Robert Grosseteste and the Origins of Experimental Science, 1100–1700.* Oxford: Oxford University Press, 1953.

Culliton, Barbara J. "XYZ: Harvard Researcher under Fire Stops Newborn Screening." *Science* (June 27, 1975), 188:1284–85.

Cuny, Hilaire. *Ivan Pavlov: The Man and His Theories.* New York: Fawcett, 1965.

Danilov, S. N. "A. M. Butlerov—osnovatèl' teorii khimicheskogo stroeniia." *Zhurnal obshchei khimii* (October 1951), 21:1733–48.

——"A. M. Butlerov (1828–1886)." *Zhurnal obshchei khimii* (October 1953), 23:1601–12.

Danilov. V. P. *Sozdanie material'no-tekhnicheskikh predposylok kollektivizatsii sel-skogo khoziaistva v SSSR.* Moscow, 1957.

Darlington, C. D. "The Retreat from Science in Soviet Russia." In Conway Zirkle, ed., *Death of a Science in Russia,* pp. 67–80. Philadelphia: University of Pennsylvania Press, 1949.

Davis, Chandler. "La Sociobiologie et son Explication de l'Humanite." *Annales* (July-August 1981), 36:531–571.

Davitashvili, L. Sh. *Izmenchivost' organizmov v geologicheskom proshlom.* Tbilisi, 1970.

Deborin, A. M. "Lenin and the Crisis of Contemporary Physics." In *Otchet o deiatel'nosti akademii nuak SSSR za 1929 g.,* vol. I, Appendix. Leningrad, 1930.

Delokarov, K. Kh. *Einshtein i filsofskie problemy fiziki XX veka.* Moscow, 1979.

——*Filosofskie problemy teorii otnositel'nosti.* Moscow, 1973.

Desiatchikova, O. "Sovremennaia genetika i ideologicheskaia bor'ba." *Kommunist Uzbekistana* (1974), pp. 67–75.

Deutsch, Karl. *The Nerves of Government: Models of Political Communication and Control.* New York: Macmillan, 1963.

Dijksterhuis, D. J. *The Mechanization of the World Picture.* London: Oxford University Press, 1961.

"Diskussii: rasshiriat' i uglubliat' tvorcheskuiu diskussiiu po probleme vida i vidoobrazovaniia." *Botanicheskii zhurnal* (1955), 40(2):206–13.

Dobb, Maurice. *Soviet Economic Development Since 1917.* New York: International Publishers, 1966.

Dobrotin. R. B. *Khimicheskaia forma dvizheniia materii.* Leningrad, 1967.

Dobzhansky, Theodosius. "N. I. Vavilov, A Martyr of Genetics, 1887–1942." *Journal of Heredity* (August 1947), 38(8):229–30.

——*The Biological Basis of Human Freedom.* New York: Columbia University Press, 1956.

Doroshkevich, A. G. and I. D. Novikov. *Doklady akademii nauk SSSR*. Moscow, 1964.

Dubinin, N. P. "I. V. Michurin i sovremennaia genetika." *Voprosy filosofii* (1966), no. 6, pp. 59–70.

——"Biologicheskie i sotsial'nye faktory v razvitii cheloveka." *Voprosy filosofii* (1978), no. 7, 45–56.

——"Dialektika proiskhozhdeniia zhizni i proiskhozhdeniia cheloveka." *Voprosy filosofii* (1979), no. 11, pp. 32–44.

——"Filosofskie i sotsiologicheskie aspekty genetikii cheloveka." *Voprosy filosofii* (1971), no. 1, pp. 36–45, and no. 2, pp. 55–64.

——"Filosofiia dialekticheskogo materializma i problemy genetiki." *Voprosy filosofii* (1973), no. 4, pp. 94–107.

——"Integrirushchaia rol' genetiki v biologii i evolutsionnom uchenii." *Vestnik akademii nauk* (1977), no. 1, pp. 106–19.

——"Nasledovanie biologicheskoe i sotsial'noe," *Kommunist* (1980), no. 11, 62, 63.

——"Sovremennaia genetika v svete marksistskoleninskoi filosofii." In M. E. Omel'ianovskii, ed., *Lenin i sovremennoe estestvoznanie*, pp. 287–311. Moscow, 1969.

——*Vechnoe dvizhenie*. Moscow, 1973.

Dubinin, N. P. and S. I. Gorodetskii. "Geneticheskaia inzhineriia: zadachi sovremennikh issledovanii." *Vestnik akademii nauk* (1978), no. 3, pp. 67–74.

Dubinin, N. P., I. I. Karpets, and V. N. Kudriatsev. *Genetika, Povedenie, Otvetsvennost'*. Moscow, 1982.

Dudintsev, V. "Net, istina." *Komsomol'skaia pravda*, October 23, 1964.

Dühring, E. *Cursus der Philosophie als streng wissenschaftlicher Weltanschauung und Lebensgestaltung*. Leipzig, 1875.

Dunlop, John B. *The Faces of Contemporary Russian Nationalism*. Princeton: Princeton University Press, 1983.

Dunn, L. C. *A Short History of Genetics*. New York, McGraw-Hill, 1965.

Dutt, C. P., ed. *Ludwig Feuerbach*. New York: International Publishers, 1935.

Dvoriankin, F. A. et al., eds. *Filosofskie voprosy estestvoznaniia: Filosofskoteoreticheskie voprosy michurinskogo ucheniia*. Moscow, 1958.

Dyban, A. "Schastlivyi zapret prirody." *Liternaturnaia gazeta*, August 23, 1978.

Dyshlevyi, P. S. *V. I. Lenin i filosofskie problemy reliativistskoi fiziki*. Kiev, 1969.

——*Materialisticheskaia dialektika i fizicheskii relativitizm*. Kiev, 1972.

——"Prostranstvo-vremennye predstavleniia obshchei teorii otnositel'nosti." In I. Z. Shtokalo et al., eds., *Filosofskie voprosy sovremennoi fiziki*, pp. 57–115. Kiev, 1964.

Dyshlevyi, P S. and A. Z. Petrov, eds. *Filosofskie problemy teorii tiagoteniia Einshteina i relativistskoi kosmologii*. Kiev, 1965.

Dyson, Freeman, J. "Mathematics in the Physical Sciences." *Scientific American* (September 1964), pp. 129–46.

Eccles, John Carew. *The Neurophysiological Basis of Mind*. Oxford: Oxford University Press, 1952.

Efimov, V. T. "Etika i moralevedenie." *Voprosy filosofii* (1982), no. 2, pp. 67–75.

Efroimson, V. P. "K biokhimicheskoi genetike intellekta," *Priroda* (1976), no. 9, pp. 62–72.

——"Khromosomnye anomalii tipa XXY i XYY kak odna iz prichin seksual'nykh narushenii." *Problemy sovremennoi seksopatologii*, p. 67. Moscow, 1972.

——"Rodoslovnaia al'truizma." *Novyi Mir* (1971), no. 10, pp. 193–213.

Efroimson V. P. and L. G. Kalmykova, "Uspekhi nevrologicheskoi i psikhia-tricheskoi genetiki." *Genetika psikhicheskikh boleznei*, p. 250. Moscow, 1970.

Egorshin, V. P. "Estestvoznanie i klassovaia bor'ba." *Pod znamenem marksizma* (1926), no. 6, pp. 108–36.

Eigen, Manfred. "Selforganization of matter and the Evolution of Biological Macromolecules." *Die Naturwissenschaften* (October: 1971), vol. 10.

Einstein, Albert. *Sobranie nauchnykh trudov*, vols. 1–4. Moscow: 1965–67.

Einstein, A., B. Podolsky, and N. Rosen. "Can Quantum Mechanical Description of Physical Reality be Considered Complete?" *Physical Review* (May 15, 1935), 47(10):777–80.

Einstein, A. and E. G. Straus. "The Influence of the Expansion of Space on the Gravitation Fields Surrounding the Individual Stars." *Reviews of Modern Physics* (1945), 17(2–3):120–24.

Emme, A. M. "Neskol'ko zamechanii po voprosu o protsesse vozniknoveniia zhizni." *Voprosy filosofil* (1956), no. 1, pp. 155–58.

Engel'gardt, V. A. "Integratizm—put' ot prostogo k slozhnomu v poznanii iavlenni zhizni." In *Filosofskie problemy biologii*, pp. 7–44. Moscow, 1973.

——"O nekotorykh atributakh zhizni: ierarkhiia, integratsiia, uznavanie." In *Sovremennoe estestvoznanie i materialisticheskaia dialektika*, p. 106. Moscow, 1977.

Engels, Friedrich. *Anti-Dühring.* Berlin, 1962.

——*Anti-Dühring.* Moscow, 1959.

——*Dialectics of Nature.* New York: International Publishers, 1940.

——*Dialectics of nature.* Moscow, 1954.

——*Ludwig Feuerbach.* New York: International Publishers, 1935.

Eroshkin'. I. G. *Psikhologiia i fiziologiie vysshei nervnoi deiatel'nosti.* Leningrad, 1958.

Farley, John. *The Spontaneous Generation Controversy from Descartes to Oparin.* Baltimore: Johns Hopkins University Press, 1977.

Farrington, Benjamin. *Greek Science.* Baltimore: Johns Hopkins University Press, 1961.

Fedoseev, P. N. "Problema sotsial'nogo i biologicheskogo v filosofii i sotsiologii." *Voprosy filosofii* (1976), no. 3, pp. 56–74.

Fedoseev, P. N. et al., eds. *Filosofskie problemy sovremennogo estestvoznaniia.* Moscow, 1959.

——*Filosofskie voprosy fiziologii vysshei nervnoi deiatel'nosti i psikhologii.* Moscow, 1963.

Feigl, Herbert. "The 'Mental' and the 'Physical.'" In Herbert Feigl, Michael Scriven, and Grover Maxwell, eds., *Minnesota Studies in the Philosophy of Science: Concepts, Theories, and the Mind-Body Problem,* 2:370–497. Minneapolis: University of Minnesota Press, 1958.

Fesenkov, V. G. "Evoliutsiia i vozniknovenie zvezd v sovremennoi galaktike." *Voprosy filosofii* (1952), no. 4, pp. 110–24.

——"O kosmogonicheskoi gipoteze akademika O. Iu. Shmidta o sovremennom sostoianii kosmogonicheskoi problemy." *Voprosy filosofii* (1951), no. 4, pp. 134–47.

——"Problema kosmogonii solnechnoi sistemy." *Priroda* (1940), no. 4, pp. 7–15.

Feyerabend, Paul K. "Dialectical Materialism and Quantum Theory." *Slavic Review* (September 1966), 25:414–17.

——"Problems of Microphysics." In R. G. Colodny, ed., *Frontiers of Science and Philosophy*, pp. 189–284. Pittsburgh: University of Pittsburgh Press, 1962.

Filipchenko, Iu. A. "Spornye voprosy evgeniki." *Vestnik kommunisticheskoi akademii* (1927), no. 20, pp. 212–54.

Filosofiia estestvoznaniia. Moscow, 1966.

Filosofiia, estestvoznanie, sovremennost': itogi i perspektivy issledovanii 1970–1980. Moscow, 1981.

Filosofskie problemy astronomii XX veka. Moscow, 1976.

"Filosofskie problemy deiatel'nosti (Materialy 'Kruglogo stola')." *Voprosy filosofii* (1985), no. 2, pp. 29–47; no. 3, pp. 29–38; no. 4, pp. 78–90.

Filosofskie voprosy estestvoznaniia: Geologo-geograficheskie nauki. Moscow, 1960.

Filosofskie voprosy estestvoznaniia: obzor rabot sovetskikh uchenykh, vols. 1 and 2. Moscow, 1976.

Filosofskie voprosy fiziki i khimii. Sverdlovsk, 1959.

Filosofskie voprosy fiziologii vysshei nervnoi deiatel'nosti i psikhologii. Mosow, 1963.

Filosofskie voprosy sovremennogo estestvoznaniia: ukazatel' literatury 1971–1979. Moscow, 1981.

Findlay, Alexander. A Hundred Years of Chemistry. New York: Humanities Press, 1937.

Fischer, George, ed. *Science and Ideology in Soviet Society.* New York: Atherton, 1967.

Fletcher, Joseph. *The Ethics of Genetic Control: Ending Reproductive Roulette.* Garden City, N.Y.: Doubleday, 1974.

Fock, V. A. "Comments." *Slavic Review* (September 1966), pp. 411–13.

——"K diskussii po voprosam fiziki." *Pod znamenem marksizma* (1938), no. 1, 149–59.

——"K stat'e Nikol'skogo 'Printsipy kvantovoi mekhaniki.' " *Uspekhi fizicheskikh nauk* (1937), 17(4):553–54.

——"Kritika vzgliadov Bora na kvantovuiu mekhaniku." *Uspekhi fizicheskikh nauk* (September 1951), 45(1):3–14.

——"La physique quantique et les idealisations classiques." *Dialectica* (1965), no. 3–4, p. 223–45.

——"Les principes mecaniques de Galilee et le theorie d'Einstein." *Atti del convegno sulla relativita generale: problemi dell'energia e onde gravitazionali,* pp. 1–12, Florence, 1965.

——"Mozhno li schitat', chto kvantomekhanicheskoe opisanie fizicheskoi real'nosti iavliaetsia polnym?" *Uspekhi fizicheskikh nauk* (1936) 16(4):437.

———"Nil's Bor v moei zhizni." In *Nauka i chelovechestvo 1963*, 2:518–19. Moscow, 1963.

———"Ob interpretatsii kvantovoi mekhaniki." In P. N. Fedoseev et al., eds. *Filosofskie problemy sovremennogo estestvoznaniia*, pp. 212–36. Moscow, 1959.

———"O roli printsipov otnositel'nosti i ekvivalentnosti v teorii tiagotenii Einshteina." *Voprosy filosofii* (1961), no. 12, pp. 45–52.

———"Osnovnye zakony fiziki v svete dialekticheskogo materializma." *Vestnik Leningradskogo universiteta* (1949), no. 4, pp. 34–47.

———"O tak nazyvaemykh ansambliakh v kvantovoi mekhanike." *Voprosy filosofii* (1952), no. 4, pp. 170–74.

———"Poniatiia odnorodnosti, kovariantnosti i otnositel'nosti v teorii prostranstva i vremeni." *Voprosy filosofii* (1955), no. 4, pp. 131–35.

———"Protiv nevezhestvennoi kritiki sovremennoi fizicheskikh teorii." *Voprosy filosofii* (1953), no. 1, pp. 168–74.

———*The Theory of Space, Time, and Gravitation.* New York: Pergamon, 1959.

Fox, Sidney W. ed. *The Origins of Prebiological Systems and of Their Molecular Matrices.* New York and London: Academic Press, 1965.

Fraenkel-Conrat, H. and B. Singer. "The Infective Nucleic Acid from Tobacco Mosaic Virus." In *Proceedings of the First International Symposium on the Origin of Life on the Earth*, pp. 303–6. New York: Pergamon, 1959.

Frank, Philipp. *Between Physics and Philosophy.* Cambridge: Cambridge University Press, 1941.

———"Einstein, Mach and Logical Positivism." In Edward H. Madden, ed., *The Structure of Scientific Thought*, pp. 84–93. Boston: Houghton Mifflin, 1960.

———*Foundations of Physics.* Chicago: University of Chicago Press, 1946.

French, Sidney J. *The Drama of Chemistry.* New York: Chapman, 1937.

Freud, Sigmund. *Civilization and Its Discontents.* New York: Norton, 1961.

Fridman (Friedmann), A. A. *Mir kak prostranstvo i vremia.* Moscow: 1965.

Frolov, I. T. "Aktual'nye filosofskie i sotsial'nye problemy nauki i tekhniki." *Voprosy filosofii* (1983), no. 6, pp. 16–26.

———*Chelovek—nauka—tekhnika.* Moscow, 1973.

———"Chelovek segodnia i zavtra." *Nauka i zhizn'* (1976), no. 9, pp. 14–17.

———*Genetika i dialektika.* Moscow, 1968.

———"K komp'iuteru, pedagogi!" *Pravda* (August 27, 1985), p. 3.

———*Nauka i nravstvennost'.* Moscow, 1971.

———"Nauka—tsennosti—gumanizm." *Voprosy filosofii* (1981), no. 3, pp. 27–41.

———"O dialektike i etike biologicheskogo poznaniia," *Voprosy filosofii* (1978), no. 7, pp. 31–45.

———"O zhizni, smerti i bessmerti." *Voprosy filosofii* (1983), no. 1, pp. 83–98; no. 2, pp. 52–64.

———*Perspektivy cheloveka.* Moscow, 1979.

———"Perspektivy cheloveka." *Voprosy filosofii* (1975), no. 7, pp. 83–95; no. 8, pp. 127–38.

———*Progress nauki i budushchee cheloveka.* Moscow, 1975.

———"Zagadka zhizni, nauchnyi poisk i filosofskaia bor'ba." *Voprosy filosofii* (1972), no. 3, pp. 88–100.

———*Zhizn' i poznanie.* Moscow, 1981.

Frolov, I. T. and L. I. Grekov. *Filosofiia, estestvoznanie, sovremennost'*, Moscow, 1981.

Frolov, I. T. and B. G. Iudin, "Etika nauki: sfera issledovanii, problemy i diskussii." *Voprosy filosofii* (1985), no. 2, pp. 62–78.

Frolov, I. T. and S. A. Pastushnyi. *Mendelizm i filosofskie problemy sovremennoi genetiki.* Moscow, 1976.

Galileo Galilei. *Dialogue Concerning the Two Chief World Systems—Ptolemaic and Copernican.* Stillman Drake, Berkeley and Los Angeles: University of California Press, 1962.

Gamow, George. *The Creation of the Universe.* New York: Viking Press, 1955.

Garkovenko, R. V. "Osnovnye napravleniia issledovaniia filosofskikh voprosov khimii." In I. T. Frolov and L. I. Grekov, eds., *Filosofiia, estestvoznaniia, sovremennost'*, pp. 336–50. Moscow, 1981.

Gastev, Iu. A. "O metodologicheskikh voprosakh ratsionalizatsii obucheniia." In A. I. Berg et al., eds., *Kibernetika, myshlenie, zhizn'*, pp. 459–72, Moscow, 1964.

Georgiev, F. I. "Problema chuvstvennogo i ratsional'nogo v poznanii." *Voprosy filosofii* (1955), no. 1, pp. 28–41.

Gerasimovich, B. P. *Vselennaia pri svete teorii otnositel'nosti.* Khar'kov, 1925.

Gevorkian, O. S. "Bor'ba osnovnykh filosofskikh napravlenii v sovremennoi kosmogonii." In P. N. Gapochka, B. M. Kedrov, and M. N. Maslina, eds., *Voprosy dialekticheskogo i istoricheskogo materializma*, pp. 244–82. Moscow, 1956.

Gillispie, Charles Coulston. "Lamarck and Darwin in the History of Science." In Bentley Glass, Owsei Temkin, and William L. Straus, Jr., eds., *Forerunners of Darwin: 1745-1859*, pp. 275–91. Baltimore: Johns Hopkins University Press, 1959.

——*The Edge of Objectivity.* Princeton: Princeton University Press, 1960.

Ginzburg, V. L. *Kak ustroena Vselennaia i kak ona razvivaetsia vo vremia.* Moscow, 1968.

Ginzburg, *O fizike i astrofizike.* Moscow, 1980.

——"Zamechaniia o metodologii i razvitii fiziki i astrofiziki." *Voprosy filosofii* (1980), no. 12, pp. 24–46.

Glass, Bentley. "Maupertuis, Pioneer of Genetics and Evolution. In Bentley Glass, Owsei Temkin, and William L. Straus, Jr., eds., *Forerunners of Darwin: 1745-1859*, pp. 51–83. Baltimore: Johns Hopkins University Press, 1959.

Glushchenko, I. E. "Protov idealizma i metafiziki v nauke o nasledstvennosti." *Voprosy filosofii* (1948), no. 2, pp. 133–47.

Glushkov, V. M. "Gnoseologicheskaia priroda informatsionnogo modelirovaniia." *Voprosy filosofii* (1963), no. 10, pp. 13–18.

——"Matematizatsiia nauchnogo znaniia i teoriia reshenii." In I. T. Frolov and L. I. Grekov, eds., *Filosofiia, estestvoznanie, sovremennost'*, pp. 108–17. Moscow, 1981.

——"Myshlenie i kibernetika." *Voprosy filsofii* (1963), no. 1, pp. 36–49.

Glushkov, V. M., A. A. Dorodnitzyn, and N. Fedorenko. "O nekotorykh problemakh kibernetiki." *Izvestiia*, September 6, 1964, p. 4.

Glushkov, V. M. and A. D. Ursul. "Matematizatsiia nauchnogo znaniia." In *Fiilosofiia i mirovozzrencheskie problemy sovremennoi nauki*, pp. 176, 216. Moscow, 1981.

Gödel, K. "An Example of a New Type of Cosmological Solutions of Einstein's Field Equations of Gravitation." *Reviews of Modern Physics* (July 1949), 21:447–50.

Goncharov, S. Z., V. A. Molchanov, and I. M. Manuilov. Review of *Dialektika otritsaniia otritsaniia* (Moscow: 1983), in *Voprosy filosofii* (1985), no. 3, pp. 163.

Gonseth, F. "Remarque sur l'idée de complementarité." *Dialectica* (1948), 2(3–4):413–20.

Goodfield, June. *Playing God: Genetic Engineering and the Manipulation of Life.* New York: Random House, 1977.

Gorelik, I. I. *Pravovye aspekty peresadki organov i tkanei.* Minsk, 1971.

——"Pravovye aspekty transplantatsii organov i tkanei," *Sovetskoe gosudarstvo i pravo* (1968), no. 9, pp. 88–93.

Gott, V. S. and V. F. Nezdel'skii. *Dialektika preryvnosti i nepreryvnosti v fizicheskoi nauke.* Moscow, 1975.

Gott, V. S., V. S. Tiukhtin, and E. M. Chudinov. *Filosofskie problemy sovremennogo estestvoznaniia.* Moscow, 1974.

Gould, Stephen J. *The Mismeasure of Man.* New York: Norton, 1981.

Graham, Loren R. "A Soviet Marxist View of Structural Chemistry." *ISIS* (March 1964), 55:20–31.

——*Between Science and Values.* New York: Columbia University Press, 1981.

——"Cybernetics." In George Fischer, ed., *Science and Ideology in Soviet Society*, pp. 3–18. New York: Atherton, 1965.

——"How Valuable Are Scientific Exchanges with the Soviet Union?" *Science* (October 27, 1978), 202:383–90.

——"Quantum Mechanics and Dialectical Materialism." *Slavic Review* (September 1966), pp. 381–410.

——"Reasons for Studying Soviet Science: The Example of Genetic Engineering." In Linda L. Lubrano and Susan Gross Solomon, eds., *The Social Context of Soviet Science*, pp. 205–40. Boulder, Col.: Westview Press, 1980.

——"Reorganization of the Academy of Sciences." In Peter H. Juviler and Henry W. Morton, eds., *Soviet Policy-Making*, pp. 133–61. New York: Praeger, 1967.

——*Science and Philosophy in the Soviet Union.* New York: Knopf, 1972.

——"Science and Values: The Eugenics Movement in Germany and Russia in the 1920's," *The American Historical Review* (December, 1977), 82(5):1133–1164.

——"Science, Citizens, and the Policy-Making Process: Comparing U.S. and Soviet Experiences." *Environment* (September 1984), 26(7):6–37.

——*The Soviet Academy of Sciences and The Communist Party, 1927–1932.* Princeton: Princeton University Press, 1967.

Gray, Jeffrey A. "Attention, Consciousness and Voluntary Control of Behavior in Soviet Psychology: Philosophical Roots and Research Branches." In Neil O'Connor, ed., *Present-Day Russian Psychology*, pp. 1–38. Oxford: Oxford University Press, 1966.

Greniewski, Henry. *Cybernetics Without Mathematics.* Warsaw, 1960.

Griaznov, B. S. "Kibernetika v svete filosofii." *Voprosy filosofii* (1965), no. 3, pp. 161–65.

Grossman, Sebastian Peter. *A Textbook of Physiological Psychology.* New York: Wiley, 1967.

Grunbaum, Adolf. "Geometry, Chronometry, and Empiricism." In Herbert Feigl and Grover Maxwell, eds., *Minnesota Studies in the Philosophy of Science,* 3:405–526. Minneapolis: University of Minnesota Press, 1962.

Grushin, B. A. "Dialekticheskii materializm i sovremennaia nauka." *Voprosy filosofii* (1978), no. 7, pp. 147–154.

Guilbaud, G. T. *What is Cybernetics?* New York: Criterion, 1960.

Gulyi, M. F. et al., eds. *Filosofskie voprosy sovremennoi biologii.* Kiev, 1962.

Gumilev, L. N. "Biosfera i impul'sy soznaniia. *Priroda* (1978), no. 12, pp. 97–105.

——*Drevnie tiurki.* Moscow, 1967.

——*Etnogenez i biosfera zemli,* vols, 1–3. Manuscript deposited in All-Union Institute of Scientific and Technical Information, Moscow, Deposit numbers 1001–79 and 3736–79.

——"Etnogenez i etnosfera. *Priroda* (1970), no. 1, pp. 46–55; no. 2, pp. 43–50.

——"Etnogenez—prirodnyi protsess." *Priroda* (1971), no. 2, 80–82.

——"Etno-landshaftnye regiony Evrazii za istoricheskii period." In *Doklady na ezhegodnikh chteniiakh pamiati L. S. Berga,* pp. 118–134. Leningrad, 1968.

——"Etnos i landshaft." *Izvestiia vsesoiuznogo geograficheskogo obshchestva* (1968), 100(3):193–202.

——"Etnos kak odna iz obolochek zemli." In *Voprosy fizicheskoi geografii i paleogeografii,* vol. 38 in the series *Uchenye zapiski LGU* (1977).

——"Istoki ritma kochevoi kul'tury Sredinnoi Azii." *Narody Azii i Afriki* (1966), no. 4, pp. 85–94.

——"Izmeneniia klimata i migratsii kochevnikov." *Priroda* (1972), no. 4, pp. 44–52.

——"Khazariia i Kaspii." *Vestnik LGU* (1964), no. 6, pp. 83–95.

——"Khazariia i Terek." *Vestnik LGU* (1964), no. 24, pp. 78–88.

——*Khunnu.* Moscow, 1960.

——*Khunny v Kitae.* Moscow, 1974.

——"Ob antropogennom faktore landshaftoobrazovaniia." *Vestnik LGU* (1967), no. 24, pp. 102–12.

——"O termine 'etnos'," *Doklady otdelenii i komissii geograficheskogo obshchestva SSSR* (1967), no. 3,

——*Otkrytie Khazarii.* Moscow, 1966.

——*Poiski vymsyshlennogo tsarstva.* Moscow, 1970.

——"Po povodu predmeta 'edinoi' geografii." *Vestnik LGU* (1967), no. 6, pp. 120–29.

——"Rol' klimaticheskikh kolebanii v istorii narodov stepnoi zony Evrazii." *Istoriia SSSR* (1967), no. 1, pp. 53–66.

Gur'ev, N. I. "Sovetskaia kosmologiia na sluzhbe ofitsial'nogo mirovozzreniia." *Vestnik instituta po izucheniiu istorii i kul'tury SSSR* (1951), no. 1, pp. 30–37.

Gurgenidze, G. S. and A. P. Ogurtsov. "Aktual'nye problemy dialektiki." *Voprosy filosofii* (1965), no. 10, pp. 130–64.

Gushin, D. A. "Informatsiia i vzaimodeistvie." *Problemy dialektiki* (1972), no. 1, pp. 114–24.

——"Kategoriia informatsii i nekotorye problemy razvitiia." *Vestnik leningradskogo universiteta, seriia ekonomiki, filosofii i prava* (1967), no. 4, pp. 55–63.

——"K voprosu o prirode informatsii." *Voprosy filosofii i psikhologii* (1965), no. 1, pp. 84–93.

Gutner, L. M. *Filosofskie aspekty izmerenie v sovremennoi fizike.* Leningrad, 1978.

Gvishiani, D. M. "Metodologicheskie problemy modelirovaniia global'nogo razvitiia." *Voprosy filosofii* (1978), no. 2, pp. 14–28.

Hahn, Warner. *Postwar Soviet Politics: The Fall of Zhdanov and the Defeat of Moderation, 1946–53.* Ithaca, N.Y.: Cornell University Press, 1982.

Haldane, J. B. S. *The Inequality of Man.* London: Chatto, 1932.

——*The Marxist Philosophy and the Sciences.* New York: Random House, 1939.

——"The Origin of Life." In J. D. Bernal, ed., *The Origin of Life,* pp. 242–49. London, 1967.

Hanson, Norwood Russell. "Contra-Equivalence: A Defense of the Originality of Copernicus." *ISIS* (September 1964), 55:308–25.

——"Five Cautions for the Copenhagen Interpretation's Critics." *Philosophy of Science* (1959), 26:325–37.

Hartlev, R. V. L. "Transmissions of Information." *The Bell System Technical Journal* (1928), 2:535–63.

Hegel, G. W. F. *Encyclopedia of Philosophy.* G. A. Mueller, trans. New York: Philosophical Library, 1959.

——*The Logic of Hegel.* William Wallace, trans. Oxford: Oxford University Press, 1892.

——*Science of Logic.* W. H. Johnson and L. G. Struthers, trans. London: Humanities Press, 1951.

Hempel, Carl G. "General System Theory and the Unity of Science." *Human Biology* (1951), 23:313–27.

Hesse, Mary. "Models in Physics." *The British Journal for the Philosophy of Science* (November 1953), pp. 198–214.

——"Models and Analogy in Science." In *The Encyclopedia of Philosophy,* pp. 354–59. New York: vol. 5, 1967.

Houllevigue, Louis. *L'Evolution des Sciences.* Paris, 1914.

Howard, Walter L. "Luther Burbank: A Victim of Hero Worship." *Chronica Botanica* (1945), 9(5–6):9–11.

Hoyle, Fred. *The Nature of the Universe.* New York: Harper, 1960.

Huckel, Walter L. *Structural Chemistry of Inorganic Compounds.* L. H. Long, trans. New York: Elsevier, 1950.

Hudson, P. S. and R. H. Richens. *The New Genetics in the Soviet Union.* Cambridge: Cambridge University Press, 1946.

Hunsberger, I. M. "Theoretical Chemistry in Russia." *Journal of Chemical Education* (October 1954), 31:504–14.

Huxley, Julian. *Heredity East and West: Lysenko and World Science.* London: Schuman, 1949.

Iaroshevskii, M. G. *Istoriia psikhologii.* Moscow, 1966.

——"Kibernetika—'nauka' mrakobesov." *Literaturnaia gazeta* (April 5, 1952), p. 4.

Ignat'ev, V. N. "Sotsiobiologiia cheloveka: 'Teoriia genno-kul'turnoi koevolut-sii,'" *Voprosy filosofii* (1982), no. 9, pp. 134–41.

Ignatov, A. I. "Mezhdunarodnyi simpozium po proiskhozhdeniiu zhizni na zemli." *Voprosy filosofii* (1958), no. 1, 152–7.

Il'enkov, E. "Stanovlenie lichnosti: k itogam nauchnogo eksperimenta." *Kommunist* (1977), no. 2, pp. 68–79.

Il'in, M. M. "Filogenez pokrytosemennykh s pozitsii michurinskoi biologii." *Botanicheskii zhurnal* (1953), no. 1, pp. 97–118.

Il'in, V. A., V. N. Kolbanovskii, and E. Kol'man, eds., *Filosofskie voprosy kibernetiki*. Mosow, 1960.

Ioirysh, A. I. "Novye vozhmozhnosti biologicheskoi nauki i pravo." *Sovetskoe gosudarstvo i pravo* (1976), no. 12, pp. 64–69.

Istoriia vsesoiuznoi kommunisticheskoi partii (Bol'shevikov): Kratkii kurs. Moscow, 1938, 1945.

Iudin, B. G. "Etika nauchnogo issledovaniia." *Priroda* (1980), no. 10, pp. 97–103.

Ivanova, V. G. *Determinizm v filosofii i fizike*. Leningrad, 1974.

Jacques, J. "Boutlerov, Couper et la Societé chimique de Paris (Notes pour servir a l'histoire des theories de la structure chimique)." *Bulletin de la Societé chimique de France* (1953), pp. 528–30.

Jammer, Max. *The Conceptual Development of Quantum Mechanics*. New York: McGraw-Hill, 1966.

Jeffreys, Sir Harold. *Scientific Inference*. Cambridge: Cambridge University Press, 1957.

Joravsky, David. *Soviet Marxism and Natural Science, 1917–1932*. New York: Columbia University Press, 1961.

——"The First Stage of Michurinism." In J. S. Curtis, ed., *Essays in Russian and Soviet History*, pp. 120–32. New York: Columbia University Press, 1963.

——*The Lysenko Affair*. Cambridge, Mass.: Harvard University Press, 1970.

——"The Vavilov Brothers." *Slavic Review* (September 1965), pp. 381–94.

Jordan, P. *Die Herkunft der Sterne*. Stuttgart, 1947.

——*Physics of the Twentieth Century*. New York: Philosophical Library, 1944.

Jordan, Z. A. *The Evolution of Dialectical Materialism: A Philosophical and Sociological Analysis*. New York: St. Martins Press, 1967.

Juviler, Peter H. and Henry W. Morton, eds. *Soviet Policy-Making*. New York: Praeger, 1967.

"K diskussii po stat'e M. A. Markova." *Voprosy filosofii* (1948), no. 1, pp. 225–32.

"K 70-letiiu so dnia rozhdeniia I. V. Stalina." *Zhurnal fizicheskoi khimii* (1949), no. 12, pp. 1385–86.

Kabachnik, M. I. "Orientatsiia v benzolnom kol'tse." *Uspekhi khimii* (January 1948), 17:96–131.

Kaganov, B. M. and G. V. Platonov, eds., *Problema prichinnosti v sovremennoi biologii*. Moscow, 1961.

Kalandiia, A. A. "Otvet na stat'iu G. V. Tsitsishvili po povodu raboty A. A. Kalandiia 'Raschet molekuliarnykh ob'emov neorganicheskikh soedinenii tipa AnBmOs.'" *Zhurnal obshchei khimii* (January 1955), pp. 193–96.

Kal'sin, F. F. *Osnovnye voprosy teorii poznaniia*. Gor'kii, 1957.

Kapitsa, P. L. *Eksperiment, teoriia, praktika*. Moscow, 1974.

Kapp, Reginald. *Towards a Unified Cosmology.* London: Hutchinson, 1960.

Karapet'iants, M. Kh. and S. I. Drakin. *Obshchaia i neorganicheskaia khimiia.* Moscow, 1981.

Karasev, M. and V. Nozdrev. "O knige M. E. Omel'ianovskogo 'V. I. Lenin i fizika XX veka.' " *Voprosy filosofii* (1949), no. 1, pp. 338–42.

Kard, P. G. "O teorii otnositel'nosti." *Voprosy filosofii* (1951), no. 1, pp. 103–41.

Karimskii, A. M. " 'Sotsial'nyi biologizm' v sovremennoi burzhuaznoi filosofii." *Voprosy filosofii* (1983), no. 9, pp. 74–75.

Karpinskaia, R. S. "Mirovozzrencheskoe znachenie sovremennoi biologii." *Voprosy filosofii* (1978), no. 4, pp. 95–106.

Karpov, M. M. "O filosofskikh vzgliadakh A. Einshteina." *Voprosy filosofii* (1951), no. 1, pp. 130–41.

Kazanskii, B. A. and G. V. Bykov. "K voprosu o sostoianii teorii khimicheskogo stroeniia v organicheskoi khimii. *Zhurnal obshchei khimii* (January 1953), pp. 168–76.

Kaziutinskii, V. V. "Astronomiia i dialektika (k 100-letiiu so dnia rozhdeniia V. I. Lenina)." In *Astronomicheskii kalendar' 1970*, pp. 138–70. Moscow, 1969.

——"Kosmologiia, kartina mira i mirovozzrenie," in *Astronomiia, metodologiia i mirovozzrenie*, pp. 249–50. Moscow, 1979.

——*Revoliutsiia v astronomii.* Moscow, 1968.

Kedrov, B. M. "Marksistskaia filosofiia: ee predmet i rol' v integratsii sovremennykh nauk." *Voprosy filosofii* (1982), no. 1, pp. 53–62.

——"O sootnoshenii form dvizheniia materii v prirode," in P. N. Fedoseev et al., eds., *Filosofskie problemy sovremennogo estestvoznaniia*, pp. 137–211, Moscow, 1959.

——*Tri aspekta atomistiki:* vol. 1, *Paradoks Gibbsa;* vol. 2, *Uchenie Dal'tona;* vol. 3, *Zakon Mendeleeva.* Moscow, 1969.

Kedrov, B. M. and D. N. Trifonov. *Zakon periodichnosti i khimicheskie elementy.* Moscow, 1969.

Kedrov, B. M., I. R. Grigulevich, and I. A. Kryvelev. "Po povodu stat'i Iu. M. Borodaia 'Etnicheskie kontakty i okruzhaushchaia sreda.' " *Priroda* (1982), no. 3, pp. 88–91.

Kekulé, August. "Sur la constitution des substances aromatiques." *Bulletin de la Societé Chimique* (1965), 3:98–110.

——"Untersuchungen über aromatische Verbindungen." *Justus Leibig's Annalen der Chimie* (1966), 137:129–96.

Keosian, John. *The Origin of Life.* New York: Reinhold, 1968.

Kerkis, Iu. Ia. "Geneticheskie posledstviia zagriaznenii sredy." *Priroda* (1976), no. 9, pp. 32–33.

——"Nuzhna li kriminologam genetika?" *Priroda* (1976), no. 7, 148–50.

Khil'mi, G. F. "O vozmozhnosti zakhvata v probleme trekh tel." *Doklady akademii nauk SSSR* (1948), 62:39–42.

Khiutt, V. P. *Kontseptsiia dopolonitel'nosti i problema ob'ektivnosti fizicheskogo znaniia.* Tallin, 1977.

"Khristianskii vzgliad na ekologicheskuiu problemu." *Zhurnal moskovskoi patriarkhii* (1940), no. 4, pp. 35–39.

Khrushchev, N. S. "Rech' tov. N. S. Krushcheva na soveshchanii rabotnikov sel'skogo khoziaistva Gor'kovskoi, Arzamasskoi, Kirovskoi oblastei, Mariiskoi, Mordovskoi i Chuvashskoi ASSR 8 Aprelia 1957 goda v gorode Gor'kom." *Pravda* (April 10, 1957), p. 2.

Khudiakova, E. "Cybernetics and Medical Diagnosis." *The Soviet Review* (February 1961), pp. 58–61.

Kitov, A. I. "Kibernetika i upravleniie narodnym khoziaistvom." In A. I. Berg, ed., *Kibernetiku na sluzhbu kommunizma*, pp. 203–17. Moscow, 1961.

Klickstein, Herbert. "A Cumulative Review of Bibliographies of the Published Writings by Albert Einstein." *Journal of the Albert Einstein Medical Center* (July 1962), pp. 141–49.

Knuniants, I. L., B. M. Kedrov, and L. Ia. Bliakher. "A Book That Does Not Deserve High Appraisal." *Pravda* (January 24, 1965), p. 2. From *Current Digest of the Soviet Press*, XVII, no. 4, (1965), 7.

Knuniants, I. and L. Zubkov. "Shkoly v nauke." *Literaturnaia gazeta* (January 11, 1955), p. 1.

Kobushkin, P. K. "Nekotorye filosofskie problemy reliativistskoi kosmologii." In I. Z. Shtokalo et al., eds., *Filosofskie voprosy sovremennoi fiziki*, pp. 116–48. Kiev, 1964.

Kol', A. "Prikladnaia botanika ili leninskoe obnovlenie zemli." *Ekonomicheskaia zhizn'* (January 29, 1931), p. 2.

Kolbanovskii, V. N. *Dialekticheskii materializm i sovremennoe estestvoznanie.* Moscow, 1964.

——"O nekotorykh spornykh voprosakh kibernetiki." In V. A. Il'in et al., eds., *Filosofskie voprosy kibernetiki*, pp. 227–61. Moscow, 1960.

——"Spornye voprosy genetiki i selektsii (obshchii obzor soveshchaniia)." *Pod znamenem marksizma* (1939), no. 11, pp. 86–126.

——"Zakliuchitel'noe slovo." In his *Dialekticheskii materializm i sovremennoe estestvoznanie*, pp. 399–400. Moscow, 1964.

——"Za marksistskoe osveshchenie voprosov psikhologii (Ob uchebnike S. L. Rubinsteina 'Osnovy obshchei psikhologii')." *Bol'shevik* (1947), no. 17, pp. 50–57.

——et al., eds., *Nekotorye problemy dialekticheskogo i istoricheskogo materializma.* Moscow, 1958.

Koldanov, V. Ia. "Nekotorye itogi i vyvody po polezashchitnomu lesorazvedeniiu za istekshie piat' let." *Lesnoe khoziaistvo* (1954), no. 3, pp. 10–18.

Kol'man, E. "Chto takoe kibernetika," *Voprosy filosofii* (1955), no. 4, pp. 148–59.

——"Chuvstvo mery." In A. I. Berg and E. Kol'man, eds., *Vozmozhnoe i nevozmozhnoe v kibernetike*, pp. 52–64. Moscow, 1964.

——"Kibernetika stavit voprosy," *Nauka i zhizn'* (1961), 28(5):43–45.

——"O filosofskikh i sotsial'nykh problemakh kibernetiki." In V. A. Il'in, V. N. Kolbanovskii, and E. Kol'man, eds., *Filosofski voprosy kibernetiki*, pp. 86–109. Moscow, 1960.

——"Sovremennaia fizika v poiskakh dal'neishei fundamental'noi teorii." *Voprosy filosofii* (1965), no. 2, pp. 111–22.

Kolmogorov, A. "Avtomaty i zhizn'." In A. I. Berg and E. Kol'man, eds., *Vozmozhnoe i nevozmozhnoe v kibernetike*, pp. 10–29. Moscow, 1964.

Komarov, M. S. "Sotsiobiologiia i problema cheloveka." *Voprosy filosofii* (1985), no. 4, pp. 129–41.

Konikova, A. S. and M. G. Kritsman. "K voprosu o nachal'noi forme proiavleniia zhizni." *Voprosy filosofii* (1954), no. 1, pp. 210–16.

——"Zhivoi belok v svete sovremennykh issledovanii biokhimii." *Voprosy filosofii* (1953), no. 1, pp. 143–50.

Kopnin, P. V. "Razvitie kategorii dialekticheskogo materializma—vazhneishee uslovie ukrepleniia soiuza filosofii i estestvoznaniia." In P. S. Dyshlevyi and A. Z. Petrov, eds., *Filosofskie problemy teorii tiagoteniia Einshteina i reliativistskoi kosmologii,* pp. 5–14. Kiev, 1965.

——*Vvedenie v marksistkuiu gnoseologiiu.* Kiev, 1966.

Körner, S., ed. *Observation and Interpretation in the Philosophy of Physics.* New York: Dover, 1957.

Kornilov, K. "Dialekticheskii metod v psikhologii." *Pod znamenem marksizma* (January 1924), pp. 107–13.

Kornilov, K., ed., *Psikhologiia i marksizm.* Leningrad, 1925.

Korovin, N. V., ed. *Kurs obshchei khimii: uchebnik dlia vuzov.* Moscow, 1981.

Korshunov, A. M. and V. V. Mantatov. *Teoriia otrazheniia i evriticheskaia rol' znakov.* Moscow, 1974.

Kostiuk, N. T. "Mirovozzrencheskie aspekty problemy sushchnosti zhizni." In *Dialecticheskii materializm—filosofskaia osnova kommunisticheskogo mirovozzreniia,* pp. 183–93. Kiev, 1977.

Koyré, Alexandre. *Études Galiléennes.* Paris, 1966.

——*From the Closed World to the Infinite Universe.* Baltimore: Johns Hopkins University Press, 1957.

——*Metaphysics and Measurement.* London, 1968.

Kozhevnikov, A. V. "O nekotorykh usloviiakh vozniknoveniia zhizni na Zemle." *Voprosy filosofii* (1956), no. 1, pp. 149–52.

Kozulin, Alex. *Psychology in Utopia.* Cambridge, Mass.: Harvard University Press, 1984.

Kratkii slovar' po filosofii. Moscow, 1966.

Kravets, A. S. *Priroda veroiatnosti.* Moscow, 1976.

Kremianskii, V. I. "Nekotorye voprosy razvitiia upravleniia." In *Sintez znaniia i razvitiia upravleniia.* Moscow, 1978.

Kriminologiia. Moscow, 1979.

Krogdahl, W. S. *The Astronomical Universe.* New York: Macmillan, 1962.

Kropotkin, P. A. *Mutual Aid, a Factor of Evolution.* London: Sargent, 1902.

Krutetskii, V. A. *Psikhologiia matematicheskikh sposobnestei shkolnikov.* Moscow, 1968.

Krylov, N. S. *Raboty po obosnovaniiu statisticheskoi fiziki.* Moscow and Leningrad, 1950.

Krymskii, S. B. *Nauchnoe znaniie i printsipy ego transformatsii.* Kiev, 1974.

Kucher, R. V. "Metodologicheskie problemy razvitii teorii v khimii." *Voprosy filosofii* (1969), no. 6, pp. 78–85.

Kudriavtseva, N. L. "K voprosu o vozniknovenii zhizni." *Voprosy filosofii* (1954), no. 2, pp. 218–21.

Kuhn, Thomas. *The Copernican Revolution: Planetary astronomy in the Development of Western Thought.* Cambridge, Mass.: Harvard University Press, 1957.
——"The Function of Dogma in Scientific Research." In A. C. Crombie, ed., *Scientific Change,* pp. 347–69. New York: Basic Books, 1963.
——*The Structure of Scientific Revolutions.* Chicago and London: University of Chicago Press, 1962.
Kukarkin, B. V. and A. G. Masevich. "Sovetskie astronomy na VIII s"ezde mezhdunarodnogo astronomicheskogo soiuza v Rime." *Voprosy filosofii* (1953), no. 1, pp. 222–30.
Kupalov, P. S. "Uchenie o reflekse i reflektornoi deiatel'nosti i perspektivy ego razvitiia." In *Filosofskie voprosy fiziologii vysshei nervnoi deiatel'nosti i psikhologii,* pp. 106–55. Moscow, 1963.
Kuptsov, V. I. *Determinizm i veroiatnost'.* Moscow, 1976.
Kurashov, V. I., and Solov'ev, Iu. I., "O probleme 'svedeniia' khimii k fizike," *Voprosy filosofii* (1984), no. 6, pp. 89–98.
Kuroedov, Aleksandr S. "Rol' sotsialisticheskoi sel'sko-khoziaistvennoi praktiki v razvitii michurinskoi biologii." Dissertation, Moscow State University, 1952.
Kursanov, D. N. et al. "K voprosu o sovremennom sostoianii teorii khimicheskogo stroeniia." *Uspekhi khimii* (1950), 19(5):529–44.
Kursanov, D. N. and V. N. Setkina. "O vzaimodeistvii chetvertichnikh solei ammoniia s prostimi efirami." *Doklady akademiii nauk SSSR* (April 21, 1949), 65:847–55.
Kursanov, G. A. "Dialekticheskii materializm o prostranstve i vremeni." *Voprosy filosofii* (1950), no. 3, pp. 173–91.
——"K kriticheskoi otsenke teorii otnositel'nosti." *Voprosy filosofii* (1952), no. 1, pp. 169–74.
——"K otsenke filosofskikh vzgliadov A. Einshteina na prirodu geometricheskikh poniatii." In I. V. Kuznetsov and M. E. Omel'ianovskii, eds., *Filosofskie voprosy sovremennoi fiziki,* pp. 393–410. Moscow, 1959.
——"O mirovozzrencheskom znachenii dostizhenii sovremennoi astronomii." *Voprosy filosofii* (1960), no. 3, pp. 61–74.
Kuznetsov, B. G. *Einstein.* Moscow, 1962.
Kuznetsov, I. V. *Liudi russkoi nauki: ocherki o vydaiushchikhsia deiateliakh estestvoznaniia i tekhniki, matematika, mekhanika, astronomiia, fizika, khimiia.* Moscow, 1961.
——"Sovetskaia fizika i dialekticheskii materializm." In A. A. Maksimov, ed., *Filosofskie voprosy sovremennoi fiziki,* pp. 31–86. Moscow, 1952.
Kuznetsov, I. V. and M. E. Omel'ianovskii, eds. *Filosofskie problemy fiziki elementarnykh chastits.* Moscow, 1964.
——*Filosofskie voprosy sovremennoi fiziki.* Moscow, 1958.
——*Filosofskie voprosy sovremennoi fiziki.* Moscow, 1959.
Kuznetsov, V. I. *Evoliutsiia predstavlenii ob osnovnykh zakonakh khimii.* Moscow, 1967.
——*Razvitie ucheniia o katalize.* Moscow, 1964.
Kuznetsova, N. F. "Kriminologiia i genetika." *Sotsialisticheskaia zakonnost'* (1977), no. 7, pp. 57–60.

Kuznetsova, N. F. and N. S. Leikina. "Kriminologicheskii aspekt sootnosheniia sotsial'nogo i biologicheskogo." *Sovetskoe gosudarstvo i pravo*, (1977), no. 9, pp. 102–10.

Landau, L. D. and E. M. Lifshits. *Statisticheskaia fizika, klassicheskaia i kvantovaia.* Moscow, 1951.

Langdon-Davies, John. *Russia Puts the Clock Back.* London: Longmans, 1949.

Lange, N. N. *Teoriia V. Vundta o nachale mifa.* Odessa, 1912.

Lebedev, M. P. "Materiia i soznanie." *Voprosy filosofii* (1956), no. 5, pp. 70–84.

Lebedev, P. N. *Ocherki teorii sotsial'nogo upravleniia.* Leningrad, 1976.

Leicester, Henry M. "Alexander Mikhailovich Butlerov." *Journal of Chemical Education* (May 1940), 17:208–9.

Lenin, V. I. *Filosofskie tetradi.* Moscow, 1938.

——*Filosofskie tetradi.* Moscow, 1965.

——*Materialism and Empirio-Criticism: Critical Comments on a Reactionary Philosophy.* Moscow, 1952.

——*Polnoe sobranie sochinenii.* Moscow, 1958–66, 55 vols. plus index.

Leontiev, A. N. *Activity, Consciousness, and Personality.* Marie J. Hall trans. Englewood Cliffs, N.J.: Prentice-Hall, 1978.

Leontiev, A. N., ed., *Vospriiatie i deiatel'nost.* Moscow, 1976.

Lepeshinskaia, O. B. *Kletka: ee zhizn' i proiskhozhdenie.* Moscow, 1952.

Levy, Edwin Jr. "Interpretations of Quantum Theory and Soviet Thought." Ph.D. dissertation, Indiana University, 1969.

Lewontin, R. C., Steven Rose, and Leon J. Kamin, *Not in Our Genes: Biology, Ideology and Human Nature,* New York: Pantheon Books, 1984.

Liapunov, A. A. and A. G. Malenkov. "Logical Analysis of Hereditary Information." *Problems of Cybernetics* (1982), no. 8. (JPRS 21,048, November 1963–19,390), pp. 293–308.

Lichtheim, George. *Marxism: An Historical and Critical Study.* New York: Praeger, 1961.

Liseev, I. K. and L. V. Fesenkova. "Sushchnost' i proiskhozhdenie zhizni." *Filosofskie voprosy estestvoznaniia: obzor rabot sovetskikh uchenykh,* Part 2. (Moscow, 1976), pp. 25–26.

Liseev, I. K. and A. Ia. Sharov. "Genetika cheloveka." *Voprosy filosofii* (1979), no. 7, p. 107.

——"Iz redaktsionnoi pochti: po sledam diskusii." *Voprosy filosofii* (1971), no. 12, pp. 157–70.

——"Kruglyi stol 'Voprosy filosofii': Genetika cheloveka, ee filosofskie i sotsial'no-eticheskie problemy." *Voprosy filosofii* (1970), no. 7, pp. 106–115; no. 8, pp. 125–134.

——"Nauka, etika, gumanizm: kruglyi stol 'Voprosy filosofii.' " *Voprosy filosofii* (1973), no. 6, pp. 39–82.

Lomov, B. F. "Psikhologicheskaia sluzhba strany." *Vestnik akademii nauk SSSR* (1980), no. 1, pp. 20–30.

——"Razvitie tekhniki i problemy psikhologii." *Vestnik akademii nauk SSSR* (1981), no. 2, pp. 30–40.

Lovejoy, Arthur O. *The Great Chain of Being: A Study of the History of an Idea.* Cambridge, Mass.: Harvard University Press, 1936.

Lubrano, Linda L. "Caught in the Crossfire." *The Sciences* (1981), pp. 12–16.
——*Soviet Sociology of Science.* Columbus: American Association for Advancement of Slavic Studies, 1976.
Lubrano, Linda L. and Susan Gross Solomon, eds. *The Social Context of Soviet Science.* Boulder, Colo.: Westview Press, 1980.
Luria, A. R. *Higher Cortical Functions in Man.* New York: Basic Books, 1966.
——"The Development of Writing in the Child." In Michael Cole, ed., *The Selected Writings of A. R. Luria,* orginially in *Voprosy marksistkoi pedagogiki* (1929), no. 1, pp. 143–76.
——*The Making of Mind: A Personal Account of Soviet Psychology.* Michael Cole and Sheila Cole, eds. Cambridge: Harvard University Press, 1979.
——"Paths of Development of Thought in the Child." In Michael Cole, ed., *The Selected Writings of A. R. Luria,* pp. 97–144; originally in *Estestvoznanie i marksizm* (1929), no. 2, pp. 143–76.
——"Psychoanalysis as a System of Monistic Psychology." In Michael Cole, ed., *The Selected Writings of A. R. Luria,* pp. 3–41, New York: Sharpe, 1978; originally in Kornilov, K. P., ed., *Psikhologiia i marksizm,* pp. 47–80. Leningrad, 1925.
Lyell, Charles. *Principles of Geology.* 12th ed., London, 1875, vol. 1.
Lysenko, T. D. *Agrobiologiia.* Moscow, 1949.
——*Agrobiologiia.* Moscow, 1952.
——*Agrobiology.* Moscow, 1954.
——"Gnezdovaia kul'tura lesa." *Ogonek* (March 1949), no. 10, pp. 6–7.
——*Heredity and Its Variability.* Th. Dobzhansky, trans. New York: Columbia University Press, 1946.
——"Iarovizatsiia—eto milliony pudov dobavochnogo urozhaia." *Izvestiia* (February 15, 1935), p. 4.
——"Interesnye raboty po zhivotnovodstvu v Gorkakh Leninskikh." *Pravda,* July 17, 1957, pp. 5–6.
——*Izbrannye sochineniia.* Moscow, 1958.
——"Novoe v nauke o biologicheskom vide." *Botanicheskii zhurnal* (1953), 38(1):44–56.
——"Novoe v nauke o biologicheskom vide." *Pravda,* November 3, 1950, p. 2.
——*Novoe v nauke o biologicheskom vide—o rabotakh deisvitel'nogo chlena meditsinskikh nauk SSSR O. B. Lepeshinskoi.* Moscow, 1952.
——"Obnovlennye semena: beseda s akademikom T. D. Lysenko." *Sotsialisticheskoe zemledelie* (September 16, 1935), p. 1.
——"On vdokhnovlial nas na bor'bu za dal'neishii rastsvet nauki." *Izvestiia* (September 1, 1948).
——"Po povodu stat'i akademika N. I. Vavilova." *Iarovizatsiia* (1939), no. 1.
——*Posev polezashchitnykh lesnykh polos gnezdovym sposobom.* Moscow, 1950.
——"Rech' tovarishcha T. D. Lysenko." *Pravda* (February 26, 1956), p. 9.
——"Shire primeniat' v nechernozemnoi polose organomineral'nye smesy." *Izvestiia,* (April 27, 1957), p. 2.
——"Teoreticheskie osnovy napravlennogo izmeneniia nasledstvennosti sel'skokhoziaistvennykh rastenii." *Pravda* (January 29, 1963), pp. 3–4.

——"Teoreticheskie uspekhi agronomicheskoi biologii." *Izvestiia* (December 8, 1957), p. 5.
——*The Situation of Biological Science.* New York: International Publishers, 1949.
——"Vazhnye rezervy kolkhozov i sovkhozov." *Pravda* (March 14, 1959), pp. 2–3.
——"Vliianie termicheskogo faktora na prodolzhitel'nost' faz razvitiia rastenii." *Trudy azerbaidzhanskoi tsentral'noi opytno-selektsionnoi stantsii* (1928), no. 3, pp. 1–169.
Lysenko, T. D., ed. *I. V. Michurin: Sochineniia v chetyrekh tomakh,* vols. 1–4. Moscow, 1948.
McCrea, W. H. "Cosmology After Half a Century." *Science* (June 21, 1968), 160:1295–99.
Mach, Ernst. *The Analysis of Sensations and the Relation of the Physical to the Psychical.* New York: Dover, 1959.
McMullin, Ernan, ed. *Galileo: Man of Science.* New York: Basic Books, 1968.
McTaggart, J. M. E. *A Commentary on Hegel's Logic.* Cambridge: Cambridge University Press, 1910.
McTighe, Thomas P. "Galileo's 'Platonism': A reconsideration." In Ernan McMullin, ed., *Galileo: Man of Science,* pp. 365–87. New York: Basic Books, 1968.
McVittie, G. C. *Fact and Theory in Cosmology.* New York: Macmillan, 1961.
Mach, Ernst, *Beitrage zur Analyse der Empfindungen.* Jena: G. Fischer, 1886.
Makarchenko, A. F., P. G. Kostiuk, and A. E. Khil'chenko. "Filosofskoe i estestvenno-nauchnoe znachenie ucheniia I. P. Pavlova o vysshei nervnoi deiatel'nosti v fiziologii." In M. F. Gulyi et al., eds., *Filosofskie voprosy sovremennoi biologii,* pp. 294–325. Kiev, 1962.
Maksimov, A. A. "Bor'ba za materializm v sovremennoi fizike." *Voprosy filosofii* (1953), no. 1, pp. 175–95.
——"Diskussiia o prirode fizicheskogo znaniia." *Voprosy filosofii* (1948), no. 3, p. 222–28.
——"Marksistskii filosofskii materializm i sovremennaia fizika." *Voprosy filosofii* (1948), no. 3, pp. 105–24.
——"Ob odnom filosofskom kentavre." *Literaturnaia gazeta* (April 10, 1948), p. 3.
——"Obsuzhdenie stat'i M. A. Markova (Okonchanie)." *Voprosy filosofii* (1948), no. 3, pp. 222–28.
——"O filosofskikh vozzreniiakh akad. V. F. Mitkevich i putiakh razvitiia sovetskoi fiziki." *Pod znamenem marksizma* (1937), no. 7, pp. 25–55.
——Protiv reaktsionnogo einshteinianstva v fizike." *Krasnyi flot* (June 23, 1952), p. 1.
——"Teoriia otnositel'nosti i materializm." *Pod znamenem marksizma* (1923), no. 4–5, pp. 140–56.
Maksimov, A. A. et al., eds. *Filosofskie voprosy sovremennoi fiziki.* Moscow, 1952.
Maksimov, N. A. "Fiziologicheskie faktory, opredeliaiushchie dlinu vegetatsionnogo perioda." *Trudy po prikladnoi botanike, genetike i selektsii* (1929), 20:169–212.

Maksimov, N. A. and M. A. Krotkina. "Issledovaniia nad posledstviem ponizhennoi temperatury na dlinu vegetatsionnogo perioda." *Trudy po prikladnoi
botanike, genetike i selektsii* (1929–30), no. 2, 23:427–73.

Malein, N. S. "Pravo na meditsinskii eksperiment." *Sovetskoe gosudarstvo i pravo*
(1975), no. 11, pp. 35–41.

Mamchur, E. A. *Problema vybora teorii.* Moscow, 1975.

Mangelsdorf, Paul C. "Hybrid Corn." In L. C. Dunn, ed., *Genetics in the 20th
Century,* pp. 555–71. New York: Macmillan, 1951.

Markarian, E. S. *O genesize chelovecheskoi deiatel'nosti i kul'tury.* Erevan, 1973.

Markov, M. A. "O prirode fizicheskogo znaniia." *Voprosy filosofii* (1947), no. 2,
pp. 140–76.

——*O prirode materii.* Moscow, 1976.

Markov, N. V. "Znachenie geometrii Lobachevskogo dlia fizike." In A. A.
Maksimov et al., eds., *Filosofskie voprosy sovremennoi fiziki,* pp. 186–215.
Moscow, 1952.

Marx, Karl. *Capital,* vol. 1. New York: Random House, 1967.

——*Die Promotion von Karl Marx, Jena, 1841: eine Quellenedition.* Berlin, 1983.

——*Matematicheskie rukopisi.* Moscow, 1968.

——*Mathematical Manuscripts of Karl Marx.* New York, 1983.

Marx, Karl and Friedrich Engels. *Izbrannye pis'ma.* Moscow, 1947.

——*Werke.* Berlin, 1956–67.

——*Iz rannikh proizvedenii.* Moscow, 1956.

——*Selected Works.* 2 vols. Moscow, 1958.

"Materialist" (pseud.). "Komu sluzhit kibernetika." *Voprosy filosofii* (1953), no. 5,
pp. 210–19.

Materialy XXII s"ezda KPSS. Moscow, 1962.

Medvedev, Zhores A. "Errors in the Reproduction of Nucleic Acid and Proteins
and their Biological Significance." *Problems of Cybernetics* (1963), no. 9.
(JPRS 21, 448, November 1963–19,750).

——*The Rise and Fall of T. D. Lysenko.* New York and London: Columbia
University Press, 1969.

Medvedev, Zhores and V. Kirpichnikov. "Perspektivy sovetskoi genetiki." *Neva*
(1963), no. 3, pp. 165–75.

Mehl, Lucien. "Les sciences juridiques devant l'automation." *Cybernetica* (1960),
no. 1, pp. 22–40; no. 2, pp. 142–70.

Meliukhin, S. T. "O filosofskom ponimanii beskonechnosti prostranstva i vremeni." In P. S. Dyshlevyi and A. Z. Petrov, eds., *Filosofskie problemy teorii
tiagoteniia einshteina i reliativistskoi kosmologii,* pp. 292–97. Kiev, 1965.

——*Problema konechnogo i beskonechnogo.* Moscow, 1958.

Miakishev, G. Ia. *Dinamicheskie i staticheskie zakonomernosti v fizike.* Moscow,
1973.

Michurin, I. V. *Sochineniia,* vol. 4. Moscow, 1948.

Mikulak, Maxim W. "Relativity Theory and Soviet Communist Philosophy
(1922–1960)." Ph. D. dissertation, Columbia University, 1965.

——"Trofim Denisovich Lysenko." In George W. Simmonds, ed., *Soviet leaders,*
pp. 248–59. New York, 1967.

Minkowski, Hermann. *Gesammelte Abhandlungen von Hermann Minkowski*. Leipzig and Berlin, 1911.

Molodtsov, V. S. and A. Ia. Il'in. *Metodologicheskie problemy sovremennoi nauki*. Moscow, 1964.

Mora, Peter T. "The Folly of Probability." In Sidney W. Fox, ed., *The Origins of Prebiological Systems and of Their Molecular Matrices*, pp. 39–64. New York and London: Academic Press, 1965.

——"Urge and Molecular Biology." *Nature* (July 20, 1963), pp. 212–19.

Morgenthau, Hans J. "Arguing About the Cold War." *Encounter* (May 1967), pp. 37–41.

Morozov, K. E. "Filosofskie problemy teorii informatsii." In *Filosofiia estestvoznaniia*, pp. 383–404. Moscow, 1966.

Muller, H. J. "Lenin's Doctrines in Relation to Genetics." In *Pamiati V. I. Lenina: sbornik statei k desiatiletiiu so dnia smerti, 1924–1934*, pp. 565–79. Moscow and Leningrad, 1934.

——"Nauka proshlogo i nastoiashchego i chem ona obiazana Marksu." In *Marksizm i estestvoznanie*, pp. 204–7. Moscow, 1933.

——*Out of the Night: A Biologist's View of the Future*. New York: Vanguard, 1935.

Müller-Markus, Siegfried. *Einstein und die Sowjetphilosophie*. Dordrecht-Holland, 1960, 1966. 2 vols.

Musabaeva, N. *Kibernetika i kategoriia prichinnosti*. Alma-Ata, 1965.

Naan, G. I. "Gravitatsiia i beskonechnost'." In P. S. Dyshlevyi and A. Z. Petrov, eds., *Filosofskie problemy teorii tiagoteniia Einshteina i relativistskoi kosmologii*, pp. 268–85. Kiev, 1965.

——"K voprosu o printsipe otnositel'nosti v fizike." *Voprosy filosofii* (1951), no. 2, pp. 57–77.

——"O beskonechnosti vselennoi." *Voprosy filosofii* (1961), no. 6, pp. 93–105.

——"O sovremennom sostoianii kosmologicheskoi nauki." *Voprosy kosmogonii*. Moscow, 1958, 6:277–329.

——"Poniatie beskonechnosti v matematike i kosmologii." in *Beskonechnost' i Vselennaia*, pp. 7–77. Moscow, 1969.

——"Sovremennyi 'fizicheskii' idealizm v SShA i Anglii na sluzhbe popovshchiny i reaktsii." *Voprosy filosofii* (1948), no. 2, pp. 287–308.

——*Trudy shestogo soveshchaniia po voprosam kosmogonii*. Moscow, 1959.

Nagel, Ernest. "The Causal Character of Modern Physical Theory." In S. W. Baron, E. Nagel, and K. S. Pinson, eds., *Freedom and Reason: Studies in Philosophy and Jewish Culture*, pp. 244–68. Glencoe, Ill.: Free Press, 1951.

——*The Structure of Science: Problems in the Logic of Scientific Explanation*. New York: Harcourt Brace, 1961.

"Na uchenom sovete instituta organicheskoi khimii AN SSSR." *Izvestiia akademii nauk: otdelenie khimicheskikh nauk* (1950), no. 4, pp. 438–44.

"Nauka i ideologiia v sovetskom obshchestve." *Posev* (1968), no. 4, pp. 58–59.

"Nauka i zhizn'." *Kommunist* (1954), no. 5, pp. 3–13.

Nekrasova, I. M. *Leninskii plan elektrifikatsii strany i ego osushchestvlenie v 1921–1931 gg*. Moscow, 1960.

Nesmeianov, A. N. " 'Contact Bonds' and the 'New Structural Theory.' " *Bulletin of the Academy of Sciences of the U.S.S.R.: Division of Chemical Sciences (Consultants Bureau)* (1952), no. 1, pp. 215–21.

Nesmeianov, A. N., R. Kh. Freidlina, and A. E. Borisova. "O kvazikompleksnikh metalloorganicheskikh soedineniiakh." *Izvestiia akademii nauk: otdelenie khimicheskikh nauk,* Jubilee Bulletin (1945), pp. 239–50.

Nesmeianov, A. N. and M. I. Kabachnik. "Dvoistvennaia reaktsionnaia sposobnost' i tautomeriia." *Zhurnal obshchei khimii* (January 1955), 25:41–87.

Nett, Roger and Stanley A. Hetzler. *An Introduction to Electronic Data Processing.* New York, 1963.

Newton, Isaac. *Principia.* Florian Cajori, trans. Berkeley and Los Angeles: University of California Press, 1966.

Nicolle, Jacques. *Louis Pasteur: A Master of Scientific Enquiry.* London: Fawcett, 1961.

Nikitin, Boris P. *Stupenki tvorchestva.* Place of publication unspecified, 1976.

Nikol'skii, K. V. *Kvantovye protsessy.* Moscow and Leningrad, 1940.

——"Otvet V. A. Foku." *Uspekhi fizicheskikh nauk* (1937), 17(4):555.

——"Printsipy kvantovoi mekhaniki." *Uspekhi fizicheskikh nauk* (1936), 16(5):537–65.

Noi, I. S. *Metodologicheskie problemy sovetskoi kriminologii.* Saratov, 1975.

"Norbert Viner v redaktsii nashego zhurnala." *Voprosy filosofii* (1960), no. 9, pp. 164–68.

Nordenskiöld, Erik. *The History of Biology.* New York: Knopf, 1935.

Novik, I. B. *Filosofskie voprosy modelirovaniia psikhiki.* Moscow, 1969.

——*Kibernetika: filosofskie i sotsiologicheskie problemy.* Moscow, 1963.

——"Kibernetika i razvitie sovremennogo nauchnogo poznaniia." *Priroda* (1963), 52(10):3–11.

——"Negentropiia i kolichestvo informatsii," *Voprosy filosofii* (1962), no. 6, pp. 118–28.

Novikov, I. D. *Evolution of the Universe.* M. M. Basko, trans. Cambridge: Cambridge University Press, 1983.

Novikov, I. D. "O povedenii sfericheski-simmetrichnykh raspredelenii mass v obshchei teorii otnositel'nosti." *Vestnik MGU,* Seriia 3 (1962), no. 6, pp. 66–72.

Novinskii, I. I. "Poniatie sviazi v dialekticheskom materializme i voprosy biologii." Dissertation, Moscow State University, 1963.

Nozhin, N. D. "Nasha nauki i uchenye." *Knizhnyi vestnik* (April 15, 1866), pp. 175–78.

——"Po povodu statei 'Russkago Slova' o nevol'nichestvo" *Iskra* (1865), no. 8, pp. 115–17.

Nudel'man, Z. N. "O probleme belka." *Voprosy filosofii* (1954), no. 2, pp. 221–26.

"Ob agrobiologicheskoi nauke i lozhnykh positsiiakh 'Botanicheskogo zhurnala.' " *Pravda* (December 14, 1958), pp. 3–4.

Obshchie osnovy fiziologii truda. Moscow, 1935.

Obshchie voprosy kosmogonii: trudy shestogo soveshchaniia po voprosam kosmogonii. Moscow, 1959.

Okonskaia, N. B *Dialektika sotsial'nogo i biologicheskogo v istoricheskom protsesse.* Perm, 1975.

Ol'shanskii, M. "Protiv fal'sifikatsii v biologicheskoi nauke." *Sel'skaia zhizn'* (August 18, 1963), pp. 2–3.

Omel'ianovskii, M. E. *Borot'ba materiializmu proty idealizmu v suchasnii fizytsi.* Kiev, 1947.

——"Dialekticheskii materializm i tak nazyvaemyi printsip dopolnitel'nosti Bora." In A. A. Maksimov et al., eds., *Filosofskie voprosy sovremennoi fiziki,* pp. 396–431. Moscow. 1952.

——*Dialektika v sovremennoi fizike.* Moscow, 1973.

——"Fal'sifikatory nauki: ob idealizme v sovremennoi fizike." *Voprosy filosofii* (1948), no. 3, pp. 143–62.

——"Filosofskaia evoliutsiia kopengagenskoi shkoly fizikov." *Vestnik adademii nauk SSSR* (1962), no. 9, pp. 85–96.

——"Filosofskie aspekty teorii izmereniia." In *Materialisticheskaia dialektika i metody estestvennykh nauk,* pp. 207–55. Moscow, 1968.

——*Filosofskie voprosy kvantovoi mekhaniki.* Moscow, 1956.

——*Lenin i filosofskie problemy sovremennoi fiziki.* Moscow, 1968.

——"Lenin o prichinnosti i kvantovaia mekhanika." *Vestnik akademii nauk SSSR* (1958), no. 4, pp. 3–12.

——"Lenin o prostranstve i vremeni i teoriia otnositel'nosti Einshteina." *Izvestiia akademii nauk SSSR (Seriia istorii i filosofii)* (1946), no. 4, pp. 297–308.

——"Problema elementarnosti chastits v kvantovo i fizike." *Filosofskie problemy fiziki elementarnykh chastits,* pp. 60–73. Moscow, 1963.

——"Sovremennye filosofskie problemy fiziki i dialekticheskii materialzm." In *Lenin i sovremennaia nauka,* pp. 226–52. Moscow, 1970.

——"The Concepts of Dialectical Contradiction in Quantum Physics." In *Philosophy, Science and Man: The Soviet Delegation Reports for the XIII World Congress of Philosophy.* Moscow, 1963.

——*V. I. Lenin i fizika XX veka.* Moscow, 1947.

——"Zadachi razrabotki problemy 'Dialekticheskii materializm i sovremennoe estestvoznanie.'" *Vestnik akademii nauk SSSR* (1956), no. 10, pp. 3–11.

Omel'ianovskii, M. E., ed. *Lenin i sovremennaia nauk.* Moscow, 1970.

——*Materialisticheskaia dialektika i metody estestvennykh nauk.* Moscow, 1968.

Omel'ianovskii, M. E. and I. V. Kuznetsov, eds. *Dialektika v naukakh o nezhivoi prirode.* Moscow, 1964.

Omel'ianovskii, M. E. et al., eds. *Filosofskie voprosy sovremennoi fiziki.* Kiev, 1956.

"On 'Nonresonance' Between East and West." *Chemical and Engineering News* (June 16, 1952), 30:2474.

Oparin, A. I. "K voprosu o vozniknovenii zhizni." *Voposy filosofii* (1953), no. 1, pp. 138–42.

——*Life: Its Nature, Origin, and Development.* Edinburgh and London: Academic Press 1961.

——"O sushchnosti zhizni." *Voprosy filosofii* (1979), no. 4, pp. 35–46.

——*Proiskhozhdenie zhizny.* Moscow, 1924.

——*The Origin of Life.* New York: MacMillan, 1938.

——*The Origin and Initial Development of Life* (NASA TTF-488). Washington, D.C.: GPO, 1968.

——"The Origin of Life." In J. D. Bernal, ed., *The Origin of Life*, pp. 199–234. London: Dover, 1967. Translation by Ann Synge of A. I. Oparin, *Prois-khozhdenie zhizny*.

——*The Origin of Life on the Earth* 3d revised and enlarged ed., Ann Synge, trans. London: Academic Press, 1957.

——*Zhizn', ee priroda, proiskhozhdenie i razvitie.* Moscow, 1960.

——*Znachenie trudov tovarishcha I. V. Stalina po voprosam iazikoznaniia dlia razvitiia sovetskoi biologicheskoi nauki.* Moscow, 1951.

Oparin, A. I. and V. G. Fesenkov. *Life in the Universe.* New York: Twayne, 1961.

——*Zhizn' vo Vselennoi.* Moscow, 1956.

Oparin. A. I. et al., eds. *Proceedings of the First International Symposium on The Origin of Life on the Earth.* London: Pergamon, 1959.

O polozhenii v biologicheskoi nauke. Stenografcheskii otchet sessii vsesoiuznoi akademii sel'sko-khoziastvennykh nauk imeni V. I. Lenina, 31 iiulia–7 avgusta 1948 g. Moscow, 1948.

Oppenheimer, J. Robert. *The Open Mind.* New York: Simon and Schuster, 1955.

Oppenheimer, J. Robert and G. M. Volkoff. "On Massive Neutron Cores." *Physical Review* (February 15, 1939). 55:374–81.

"O rezul'tatakh proverki deiatel'nosti bazy 'gorki leninskie.' " *Vestnik akademii nauk* (1965), no. 11, pp. 1–128.

Orlov, V. V. "O nekotorykh voprosakh teorii materii, razvitiia, soznaniia." *Filosofskie nauki*, no. 5, (1974), p. 50.

——"O nekotorykh voprosakh . . .," and the responses by S. T. Meliukhin, V. S. Tiutkhtin, and L. B. Bazhenov in *Filosofskie nauki* (1974), no. 5, pp. 47–77, especially Bazhenov, "Nekotorye zamechaniia po povodu publikatsii V. V. Orlova," pp. 74–77.

Osnovy obshchei psikhologii, Moscow, 1946.

Ostrianin, D. F. and T. K. Martynenko. "Metodologicheskie voprosy sovremennoi biologii." *Kommunist Ukrainy* (1980), no. 3, pp. 90–93.

Panchenko, A. I. *Filosofskie problemy estestvoznaniia.* Tashkent, 1972.

——*Filosofskie voprosy fiziki.* Leningrad, 1974.

——*Fizicheskaia nauka i filosofiia.* Moscow, 1973.

——*Fizicheskaia teoriia (filosofsko-metodologicheskii analiz).* Moscow, 1980.

——*Kontinuum i fizika.* Moscow, 1975.

——*Teoriia poznaniia i sovremennaia fizika.* Moscow, 1972.

Papaleksi, N. D. et al. *Kurs fiziki.* Moscow and Leningrad, 1948.

Partington, J. R. *A Short History of Chemistry.* New York: Harper, 1948.

Partridge, R. B. "The Primeval Fireball Today." *American Scientist* (1969), 57(1):37–74.

Pastushnyi, S. A. *Filosofiia i sovremennaia biologiia.* Moscow, 1973.

——*Genetika kak ob"ekt filosofskogo analiza.* Moscow, 1981.

Paul, Diane B. "Marxism, Darwinism and the Theory of Two Sciences." *Marxist Perspectives* (Spring 1979), pp. 116–43.

Pauling, Linus. "Teoriia rezonansa v khimii." *Zhurnal vsesoiuznogo khimicheskogo obshchestva im. D. I. Mendeleeva* (1962), no. 4, pp. 462–67.

——*The Nature of the Chemical Bond.* Ithaca: Cornell University Press, 1960.

——*The Structure of Molecules and the Chemical Bond.* New York: Freeman, 1950.

Pavlov, Todor. "Avtomaty, zhizn', soznanie." *Nauchnye doklady vysshei shkoly: filosofskie nauki* (1963), no. 1, pp. 49–57.

Peebles, P. J. E. *Physical Cosmology.* Princeton: Princeton University Press, 1971.

Perfil'ev, V. V. "O knige M. E. Omel'ianovskogo 'V. I. Lenin i fizika XX veka.'" *Voprosy filosofii* (1948), no. 1, pp. 311–12.

Perminov, V. Ia. *Problema prichinnosti v filosofii estestvoznaniia.* Moscow, 1979.

Petrov, A. A., Kh. V. Bal'ian, and A. T. Troshchenko. *Organicheskaia khimiia.* Moscow, 1981.

Petrovskii, A. V. *Istoriia sovetskoi psikhologii.* Moscow, 1967.

Petrovskii, B. "Peresadka organov." *Pravda* (February 1, 1968), p. 3.

Petrushenko, L. A. "Filosofskoe znachenie poniatiia 'obratnaia sviaz' v kibernetike." *Vestnik leningradskogo universiteta: seriia ekonomiki, filosofii, i prava* (1960), 17:76–86.

——*Samodvizhenie materii v svete kibernetiki.* Moscow, 1971.

Petrushevskii, S. A. et al., eds. *Dialekticheskii materializm i sovremennoe estestvoznanie.* Moscow, 1964.

Piaget, Jean. "Comments on Vygotsky's Critical Remarks." Cambridge, Mass.: Harvard University Press, 1962.

Pinter, Ferents. "Aktual'nye voprosy vzaimootnosheniia marksistskoi filosofii i genetiki." Dissertation, Moscow State University, 1965.

Pisarev, D. I. *Selected Philosophical, Social and Political Essays.* Moscow, 1958.

Planck, Max. *Scientific Autobiography and Other Papers.* New York: Williams and Norgate, 1949.

Platonov, G. V. "Dogmy starye i dogmy novye." *Oktiabr'* (1965), no. 8, 149–65.

——*Zhizn', nasledstvennost', izmenchivost'.* Moscow, 1978.

Plekhanov, G. V. *Izbrannye filosofskie proizvedeniia,* vol. 2. Moscow, 1956.

——*Protiv filosofskogo revizionizma.* Moscow, 1935.

Plotkin, I. P. "O fluktuatsionnoi gipoteze Bol'tsmana." *Voprosy filosofii* (1959), no. 4, pp. 138–40.

Polianskii, D. S. "O dal'neishem razvitii sel'skogo khoziaistva: doklad predsedatelia soveta ministrov RSFSR tovarishcha D. S. Polianskogo." *Pravda* (December 23, 1959), pp. 1–2.

Polianskii, V. I. and Iu. I. Polianskii. *Sovremennye problemy evoliutsionnoi teorii.* Leningrad, 1967.

Pomper, Philip. *Trotsky's Notebooks, 1933–35; Writings on Lenin, Dialectics and Evolutionism.* New York: Columbia University Press, 1986.

Popovsky, Mark. *The Vavilov Affair.* Hamden, Conn., 1984.

"Postanovlenie prezidiuma akademii nauk SSSR ot 26 avgusta 1948 g. po voprosu o sostoianii i zadachakh biologicheskoi nauki v institutakh i uchrezhdeniiakh akademii nauk SSSR." *Pravda* (August 27, 1948), p. 1.

Potkov, L. L. "Obsuzhdenie raboty M. A. Markova 'O mikromire.'" *Voprosy filosofii* (1947), no. 2, pp. 381–82.

——"Teoriia khimicheskogo stroeniia A. M. Butlerova." *Zhurnal fizicheskoi khimii* (1962), 36(3):417–28.

Povarov, G. N. "Granitsy isskustvennogo intellekta ustanovit opyt." *Voprosy filosofii* (1979), no. 3, pp. 84–85.

Prilezhaeva, E. N., Ia. K. Syrkin, and M. V. Volkenshtein. "Ramaneffekt galoidoproizvodnikh etilena i elektronni rezonansa." *Zhurnal fizicheskoi khimii* (1962) 36(3):417–28.

"Privetstvi akademiku T. D. Lysenko v sviazi s ego 50-letiem." *Voprosy filosofii* (1948), no. 2, p. 412.

Problemy differentsial'noi psikhofiziologii, vol. 6. Moscow, 1969.

Problemy metodologii sistemnogo issledovaniia. Moscow, 1970.

Programma kommunisticheskoi partii Sovetskogo Soiuza. Moscow, 1961.

Proiskhozhdenie zhizni i evolutsionnaia biokhimiia. Moscow, 1975.

Prokof'ev, M. A. *XXV s"ezd KPSS: stenograficheskii otchet*, vol. 2, Moscow, 1976.

Purvis, O. N. "The Physiological Analysis of Vernalization." In W. H. Ruhland, ed., *Encyclopedia of Plant Physiology*, 16:76–117. Berlin, 1961.

Putnam, H. "A Philosopher Looks at Quantum Mechanics." In R. G. Colodny, ed., *Beyond the Edge of Certainty*, pp. 75–101. Englewood Cliffs, N.J.: Prentice-Hall, 1965.

Quine, Willard Van Orman. *From a Logical Point of View: Logico-Philosophical Essays.* New York: Harper, 1963.

Ravich-Shcherbo, I. V. "Otsenka sily nervnoi sistemy po zavisimosti vremeni reaktsii ot intensivnosti stimula." *Problemy differential'nogo psikhofiziologii*, 6:228–34. Moscow, 1969.

——"Vozmozhnyi eksperimental'nyi podkhod k izucheniiu biologicheskogo i sotsial'nogo v razvitii cheloveka." In *Biologicheskoe i sotsial'noe v cheloveke*, pp. 158–70. Moscow, 1977

Ravich-Shcherbo, I. V. and G. A. Shibarovskaia. "Struktura dinamichnosti nervnykh protsessov u detei shkol'nogo vozrasta." In *Problemy differentsial'noi psikhofiziologii*, 7:95–126. Moscow, 1972.

Raychaudhuri, Amalkumar. "Relativistic Cosmology I." *Physical Review* (May 15, 1955), pp. 1123–26.

Razumovskii, O. S. *Sovremennyi determinizm i ekstemal'nye printsipy v fizike.* Moscow, 1975.

Reichenbach, Hans. "The Principle of Anomaly in Quantum Mechanics." *Dialectica* (1948), 2(3–4):337–50.

——*The Philosophy of Space and Time.* New York: Dover, 1958.

Reutov, O. A. "O nekotorikh voprosakh teorii organicheskoi khimii." *Zhurnal obshchei khimii* (January 1951), 21:186–99.

Robb, Alfred A. *The Absolute Relations of Time and Space.* Cambridge: Cambridge University Press, 1921.

Roblin, Richard. "The Boston XYY Case." *The Hastings Center Report* (August 1975), 5(4):5–8.

Rogers, James Allen. "Charles Darwin and Russian Scientists." *Russian Review* (1960), 19:371–83.

——"Darwinism, Scientism and Nihilism." *Russian Review* (1960), pp. 19:10–23.

Roll-Hanson, Nils. "A New Perspective on Lysenko?" *Annals of Science* (1985), 42:261–78.

Ronchi, Vasco. *Histoire de la lumiere.* Jean Taton, trans. Paris, 1956.

Rosenblith, Walter A. "Postscript." In Ivan M. Sechenov, *Reflexes of the Brain,* pp. 143–45. Cambridge: MIT Press, 1965.

Rosenblueth, A., N. Wiener, and J. Bigelow. "Behavior, purpose and teleology." *Philosophy of Science* (January 1943), pp. 18–24.

Rubashevskii, A. A. *Filosofskoe znachenie teoreticheskogo nasledstva I. V. Michurina.* Moscow, 1949.

Rubinstein, S. L. *Bytie i soznanie: o meste psikhicheskogo vo vseobshchei vzaimosviazi iavlenii material'nogo mira.* Moscow, 1957.

——"Filosofiia i psikhologiia." *Voprosy filosofii* (1957), no. 1, 114–27.

——*O myshlenii i putiakh ego issledovaniia.* Moscow, 1958.

——*Osnovy obshchei psikhologii.* Moscow, 1940, 1946.

——*Osnovy psikhologii.* Moscow, 1935.

——*Printsipy i puti razvitiia psikhologii.* Moscow, 1959.

——"Problemy psikhologii v trudakh Karla Marksa." *Sovetskaia psikhotekhnika* (1934), no. 1, pp. 3–20.

——"Rech'." *Voprosy filosofii* (1947), no. 1, pp. 420–27.

——"Uchenie I. P. Pavlova i nekotory voprosy perestroiki psikhologii." *Voprosy filosofii* (1952), no. 3, pp. 197–210.

——"Voprosy psikhologii myshleniia i printsip determinizma." *Voprosy filosofii* (1957), no. 5, pp. 101–13.

Rudenko, A. P. "Evolutsionnyi kataliz i problema proiskhozhdeniia zhizni." In *Vzaimodeistvie metodov estestvennykh nauk v poznanii zhizni,* pp. 186–235. Moscow, 1976.

Rukhkian, A. A. "Ob opisannom S. K. Karapetianom sluchae porozhdeniia leshchiny grabom." *Botanicheskii zhurnal* (1953), 38(6):885–91.

Russell, H. N. *The Solar System and Its Origin.* New York: Macmillan, 1935.

Rutkevich, M. N. *Dialekticheskii materializm.* Moscow, 1973.

——*Praktika-osnova poznaniia i kriterii istiny.* Moscow, 1952.

Rybnikov, K. A. et al., eds. *Filosofskie voprosy estestvoznaniia: Nekotorye filosofskoteoreticheskie voprosy fiziki, matematiki i khimii.* Moscow, 1959.

Sachkov, Iu. V. *Vvedenie v veroiatnostnyi mir.* Moscow, 1971.

Safronov, V. S. "Problema proiskhozhdeniia zemli i planet: soveshchanie po voprosam kosmogonii solnechnoi sistemy." *Vestnik akademii nauk SSSR* (1951), no. 10, pp. 94–102.

Sakharov, Andrei D. "Thoughts on Progress, Peaceful Coexistence and Intellectual Freedom." *The New York Times* (July 22, 1968).

Sapegina, A. V. and A. T. Tsybukh. "Nekotorye problemy vrachebnoi etiki i meditsinskoi deontologii v deiatel'nosti sanitarno-epidemiologicheskoi sluzhby." *Zhdravokhranenie rossiskoi federatsii* (1983), no. 10, pp. 25–28.

Sartre, Jean-Paul. *Search for a Method.* New York: Knopf, 1963. Satdinova, N. Kh. "Sotsiobiologiia—'za' i 'protiv.'" *Voprosy filosofii* (1982), no. 3, pp. 129–36.

Scanlan, James P. *Marxism in the USSR: A Critical Survey of Current Soviet Thought,* Ithaca: Cornell University Press, 1985.

Schapiro, Leonard. *The Communist Party of the Soviet Union.* New York: Random House, 1959.

Schlesinger, Arthur, J. "Origins of the Cold War." *Foreign Affairs* (October 1967), pp. 22–52.

Schmalhausen, I. I. "Evolution in the Light of Cybernetics." *Problems of Cybernetics* (1965), no. 13. (JPRS 31,567, October 1967—16,376).

——"Fundamentals of the Evolutionary Process in the Light of Cybernetics." *Problems of Cybernetics* (1960), no. 4. (JPRS 7402, March 1961–4686).

——"Hereditary Information and Its Transformations." *Transactions of the Academy of Sciences, USSR, Biological Sciences Section*, 120, 1, (1958), American Institute of Biological Sciences, Washington, D.C.

——"Natural Selection and Information." *News of the Academy of Science, USSR. Biology Series*, vol. 25–1 (1960), (JPRS 2815, September 1960—14,090).

——"Predstavleniia o tselom v sovremennoi biologii." *Voprosy filosofii* (1947), no. 2, pp. 177–83.

Schmidt, O. Iu. *A Theory of Earth's Origin*. Moscow, 1958.

——"O vozmozhnosti zakhvata v nebesnoi mekhanike." *Doklady akademii nauk SSSR* (1947), 57:213–16.

——"Problema proiskhozhdeniia zemli i planet." *Voprosy filosofii* (1951), no. 4, pp. 129–33.

——*Prioskhozhdenie zemli i planet*. Moscow, 1949, 1957, 1962.

Schmidt, O. Iu and G. F. Khil'mi. "Problema zakhvata v zadache o trekh telakh." *Uspekhi matematicheskikh nauk* (1948), no. 26, pp. 157–59.

Schrödinger, Erwin. "Die gegenwartige Situation in der Quantenmechanik." *Die Naturwissenschaften* (November 29, 1935), 23(48):807–12.

——*What Is Life? Other Scientific Essays*. Garden City, N.Y.: Doubleday, 1956.

Scientific Session on the Physiological Teaching of Academician I. P. Pavlov. Moscow, 1951.

Sciama, D. W. *Modern Cosmology*. Cambridge: Cambridge University Press, 1971.

Sedov, E. A. "K voprosu o sootnoshenii entropii informatsionnykh protsessov i fizicheskoi entropii." *Voprosy filosofii* (1965), no. 1, pp. 135–45.

Seifullaev, R. S. *Kontseptsiia prichinnosti i ee funktsii v fizike*. Novosibirsk, 1973.

Selsam, Howard and Harry Martel, eds., *Reader in Marxist Philosophy*. New York: International Publishers, 1963.

Semashko, N. A. *Izbrannye proizvedeniia*. Moscow, 1964.

Semeniuk, E. P., V. S. Tiukhtin, and A. D. Ursul. "Filosofskie aspekty problemy informatsii." In *Filosofskie voprosy estestvoznaniia*. Moscow, 1976. Part 2, pp. 253–54.

——"Sotsial'naia informatsiia." In *ibid.*, pp. 266–70.

Semenov, A. A. "Ob itogakh obsuzhdeniia filosofskikh vozzrenii akademika L. I. Mandel'shtama." *Voprosy filosofii* (1953), no. 3, pp. 199–206.

Semenov, N. N. "Marksistsko-leninskaia filosofiia i voprosy estestvoznaniia." *Vestnik akademii nauk* (1968), no. 8, pp. 24–40.

——"Nauka ne terpit sub'ektivizma." *Nauka i zhizn'* (1965), no. 4, pp. 38–43.

Semkovskii, S. Iu. *Dialekticheskii materializm i printsip otnositel'nosti*. Moscow and Leningrad, 1926.

Serdiuk, A. M. "Zdrov'e cheloveka, nauchno-technicheskii progress i okruzhaiushchaia sfera." *Voprosy filosofii* (1983), no. 6, pp. 107–14.

Serebrovskii, A. S. "Antropogenetika." *Mediko-biologicheskii zhurnal* (1929), no. 5, p. 18.

"Sergei Leonidovich Rubinshtein." *Voprosy filosofii* (1960), no. 2, pp. 179–80.

Setrov, M. I. *Organizatsiia biosistem: metodologicheskie printsipy zhivykh sistem.* Leningrad, 1971.

Severnyi, A. B. and V. V. Sobolev. "Viktor Amazaspovich Ambartsumian (K shestidesiatiletiiu so dnia rozhdeniia)." *Uspekhi fizicheskikh nauk* (September 1968), pp. 181–83.

Shaikin, V. S. "S odnostoronnykh pozitsii. O knige 'Genetika i dialektika,'" *Sel'skaia zhizn'* (May 17, 1969), p. 5.

Shakhparanov, M. I. *Dialekticheskii materializm i nekotorye problemy fiziki i khimii.* Moscow, 1958.

Shaliutin, S. M. "O kibernetike i sfere ee primeneniia." In V. A. Il'in, V. N. Kolbanovskii, and E. Kol'man, eds., *Filosofskie voprosy kibernetiki,* pp. 6–85. Moscow, 1960.

Shannon, Claude, and Warren Weaver. *The Mathematical Theory of Communication.* Urbana: University of Illinois Press, 1949.

Shapere, Dudley. "The Structure of Scientific Revolutions." *The Philosophical Review* (July 1964), 63:383–94.

Shapley, Harlow. *The Inner Metagalaxy.* New Haven: Yale University Press, 1957.

Shatskii, A. L. "K voprosu o summe temperatur, kak sel'skokhoziaistven noklimaticheskom indekse." *Trudy po sel'sko-khoziaistvennoi meteorologii* (1930), 21(6):261–63.

Shelinskii, G. I. *Khimicheskaia sviaz' i izuchenie ee v srednei shkole.* Moscow, 1969.

Sherrington, Charles, S. "Brain." In *Encyclopedia Britannica,* vol. 4. Chicago, 1959.

Shirokov, M. F. "Filosofskie voprosy teorii otnositel'nosti." In V. N. Kolbanovskii et al., eds.,*Dialekticheskii materializm i sovremennoe estestvoznanie,* pp. 58–80. Moscow, 1964.

——"O materialisticheskoi sushchnosti teorii otnositel'nosti." In I. V. Kuznetsov and M. E. Omel'ianovskii, eds. *Filosofskie voprosy sovremennoi fiziki,* pp. 324–69. Moscow, 1959.

——"O preimushchestvennykh sistemakh otscheta v n'iutonovskoi mekhanike i teorii otnositel'nosti." *Voprosy filosofii* (1952), no. 3, pp. 128–39.

Shishkin, A. F. *Chelovecheskaia priroda i nravstvennosti.* Moscow, 1979.

Shivtsov, O. V. "Problema riska pri genno-inzhenernykh issledovaniiakh." *Vestnik akademii meditsinskikh nauk* (1981), no. 2, pp. 77–83.

Shklovskii, I. S. and Carl Sagan. *Intelligent Life in the Universe.* San Francisco: Holden-Day, 1966.

Shorokhova, E. V., ed. *Issledovaniia myshleniia v sovetskoi psikhologii.* Moscow, 1966.

Shteinman, R. Ia. "O reaktsionnoi roli idealizma v fizike." *Voprosy filosofii* (1948), no. 3, pp. 163–73.

——"Za materialisticheskuiu teoriiu bystrykh dvizhenii." In A. S. Maksimov et al., eds., *Filosofskie voprosy sovremennoi fiziki,* pp. 234–98. Moscow, 1952.

Shtern, V. *Erkenntnistheoretische Probleme der Modernen Physik.* Berlin, 1952.
———"K voprosu o filosofskoi storone teorii otnositel'nosti." *Voprosy filosofii* (1952), no. 1, pp. 175–81.
Shtokalo, I. Z. et al., eds. *Filosofskie voprosy sovremennoi fiziki.* Kiev, 1964.
Shvyrev, V. "Materialisticheskaia dialektika i problemy issledovaniia nauchnogo poznaniia." *Kommunist* (November 1968), 17:40–51.
Siforov, V. I. "Metodologicheskie voprosy nauki ob informatsii." *Voprosy filosofii* (1974), no. 7, pp. 105–13.
Siforov, V. I. "Nauka ob informatsii," *Vestnik akademii nauk SSSR* (1974), no. 3, pp. 12–20.
Silk, J. *The Big Bang: Creation and Evolution of the Universe.* San Francisco: Freeman, 1980.
Simonov, Pavel. "Iskrashchie kontakty." *Novyi Mir* (1971), no. 9, pp. 188–205.
Sinnott, E. W., L. C. Dunn, and Th. Dobzhansky. *Principles of Genetics.* New York: McGraw-Hill, 1950.
Skabichevskii, A. P. "Problema vozniknoveniia zhizni na Zemle i teoriia akad. A. I. Oparina." *Voprosy filosofii* (1953), no. 2, pp. 150–55.
Smirnov, I. N. "Metodologiia i mirovozzrenia: nekotorye filosofskie problemy biologicheskogo poznaniia." *Voprosy filosofii* (1978), no. 7, pp. 57–68.
Sobolev, S. "Da, eto vpolne ser'ezno." In A. I. Berg and E. Kol'man, eds., *Vozmozhnoe i nevozmozhnoe v kibernetike,* pp. 77–88. Moscow, 1964.
Sobolev, S. L., A. I. Kitov, and A. A. Liapunov. "Osnovnye cherty kibernetiki." *Voprosy filosofi* (1955), no. 4, pp. 136–48.
Sokolov, B. "Ob organizatsii proizvodstva gibridnykh semian kukuruzy." *Izvestiia* (February 2, 1956), p. 2.
Sonneborn, Tracy M. "H. J. Muller, Crusader for Human Betterment," *Science* (November 15, 1968), p. 772.
———"H. J. Muller: Tribute to a Colleague." *The Review* (Alumni Association, Indiana University), Fall 1968, pp. 19–23.
Sootnoshenie biologicheskogo i sotsial'nogo v cheloveke. Moscow, 1975.
Sostoianie teorii khimicheskogo stroeniia: vesesoiuznoe soveshchanie 11–14 iiunia 1951 g.: stenograficheskii otchet. Moscow, 1952.
Sostoianie teorii khimicheskogo stroeniia v organicheskoi khimii. Moscow, 1954.
"Soveshchanie rabotnikov sel'skogo khoziaistva oblastei iugo-vostoka." *Pravda* (March 19, 1955), p. 2.
"Soviets Blast Pauling, Repudiate Resonance Theory." *Chemical and Engineering News* (September 10, 1951), 29:3713.
Stalin, I. V. *Anarkhizm ili sotsializm?* Mosow, 1950.
———"Ekonomicheskie problemy sotsializma v SSSR." *Bol'shevik* (1952), no. 18, pp. 1–50.
Stalin, Joseph. *Marxism and Linguistics.* New York: Progress, 1951.
Staniukovich, K. P., S. M. Kolesnikov, and V. M. Moskovkin. *Problemy teorii prostranstva, vremeni i materii.* Moscow, 1968.
Stanley, Wendell H. "On the Nature of Viruses, Genes and Life." In *Proceedings of the First International Symposium on the Origin of Life on the Earth,* pp. 313–21. New York: Pergamon, 1959.
Stepin, V. S. *Stanovlenie nauchnoi teorii.* Minsk, 1976.

Stoletov, V. N. "Nekotorye metodologicheskie voprosy genetiki." In *Aktual'nye voprosy sovremennoi genetiki*, pp. 499–539. Moscow, 1966.

——"Printsipy ucheniia I. V. Michurina." *Voprosy filosofi* (1948), no. 2, pp. 148–70.

Storchak, L. I., "Znachenie idei Lobachevskogo v razvitii predstavlenii o prostranstve i vremeni," *Voprosy filosofii* (1951), no. 1, pp. 142–48.

Struchkov, N. A. "O mekhanizme vzaimnogo vliianiia obstoiatel'stv, obuslovlivaiushchikh sovershenie prestuplenii." *Sovetskoe gosudarstvo i pravo* (1966), no. 10, pp. 113–15.

Struminskii, V. "Marksizm v sovremennoi psikhologii." *Pod znamenem marksizma* (March 1926), pp. 207–33.

Struve, Otto. *The Universe*. Cambridge: Harvard University Press, 1962.

——*Stellar Evolution*. Princeton: Princeton University Press, 1950.

Struve, Otto and Velta Zebergs. *Astronomy of the 20th Century*. New York: Macmillan, 1962.

Stukov, A. P. and S. A. Iakushev. "O belke kak nositele zhizni." *Voprosy filosofii* (1953), no. 2, pp. 139–49.

Sturtevant, A. H. *A History of Genetics*. New York: Harper, 1965.

Sukachev, V. N. "O vnutrividovykh i mezhvidovykh vzaimootnosheniiakh sredi rastenii." *Botanicheskii zhurnal* (1953), 38(1):57–96.

Sukachev, V. N. and N. D. Ivanov. "K voprosam vzaimootnoshenii organizmov i teorii estestvennogo otbora." *Zhurnal obshchei biologii* (July–August 1954), 15(4):303–19.

Sullivan, Walter. "Moon Soil Indicates Clue to Life Origin," *New York Times* (January 7, 1970).

——"The Death and Rebirth of a Science." In Harrison E. Salisbury, ed., *The Soviet Union: The Fifty Years*, pp. 276–98. New York: Harcourt, Brace, and World, 1967.

Suvorov, L. N. *Materialisticheskaia dialektika*. Moscow, 1980.

Svechnikov, G. A. *Prichinnost' i sviaz' sostoianii v fizike*. Moscow, 1971.

——*Prichinnost' i sviaz' sostoianii v fizike: problemy dialektiko-materialisticheskogo istolkovaniia kvantovoi teorii*. Uzhgorod, 1972.

Sviderskii, V. I. *Filosofskoe znachenie prostranstvenno-vremennykh predstavlenii v fizike*. Leningrad, 1956.

——"O dialektiko-materialisticheskom ponimanii konechnogo i beskonechnogo." In P. S. Dyshlevyi and A. Z. Petrov. eds., *Filosofskie problemy teorii tiagoteniia Einshteina i relativistskoi kosmologii*, pp. 261–68. Kiev, 1965.

Swanson, James M. "The Bolshevization of Scientific Societies in the Soviet Union; An Historical Analysis of the Character, Function and Legal Position of Scientific and Scientific Technical Societies in the USSR 1929–1936." Dissertation, Indiana University, 1967.

Syrkin, Ia. K. "Sovremennoe sostoianie problemy valentnosti." *Uspekhi khimii* (August 1959), 27:903–20.

Syrkin, Ia. K. and M. E. Diatkina. *Khimicheskaia sviaz' i stroenie molekul*. Moscow, 1946.

——*The Structure of Molecules and the Chemical Bond*. New York: Dover, 1950.

Sysoev, A. F. "Samoobnovlenie belka i svoistvo razdrazhimosti-vazhneishie zakonomernosti zhizennykh iavlenii." *Voprosy filosofii* (1956), no. 1, pp. 152–55.

Tables of Interatomic Distances and Configuration in Molecules and Ions. London, 1958.

Takach, Laslo. "K voprosu o vozniknovenii zhizni." *Voprosy filosofii* (1955), no. 3, pp. 147–50.

Tarasov, K. E. and E. K. Chernenko. *Sotsial'naia determinirovannost' biologii cheloveka.* Moscow, 1979.

Targul'ian, O. M., ed. *Spornye voprosy genetiki i selektsii: raboty IV sessii akademii 19-27 dekabriia 1936 goda.* Moscow and Leningrad, 1937.

Tatevskii, V. M. and M. I. Shakhparonov. "Ob odnoi makhistskoi teorii v khimii i ee propagandistakh." *Voprosy filosofii* (1949), no. 3, pp. 176–92.

Teplov, B. M. *Problemy individual'nykh razlichii.* Moscow, 1961.

——*Tipologicheskie svoistva nervnoi sistemy i ikh znachenie dlia psikhologii.* Moscow, 1962.

Terletskii, Ia. P. "Obsuzhdenie stat'i M. A. Markova." *Voprosy filosofii* (1948), no. 3, pp. 228–31.

The Situation in Biological Science: Proceedings of the Lenin Academy of Agricultural Sciences of the U.S.S.R., July 31–August 7, 1948. Complete Stenographic Report. New York, 1949.

Tiapkin, A. A. "K razvitiiu statisticheskoi interpretatsii kvantovoi mekhaniki na osnove sovmestnogo koordinatno-impul'snogo predstavleniia." In *Filosofskie voprosy kvantovoi fiziki,* pp. 139–80. Moscow, 1970.

Timakov, V. D. and N. P. Bochkov. "Sotsial'nye problemy genetiki cheloveka." *Voprosy filosofii* (1973), no. 6, pp. 50–69.

Timofeev-Ressovskii, N. V. "Some Problems of Radiation Biogeocenology." *Problems of Cybernetics* (1964), no. 12, (JPRS 31, 214, September 1965–14, 503).

Tiukhtin, V. S., *O prirode obraza.* Moscow, 1963.

Tiukhtin, V. S. "Otrazhenie, sistemy, kibernetika: teoriia otrazheniia v svete kibernetiki i sistemnogo podkhoda." Moscow, 1972.

Tiukhtin, V. S. "Sushchnost' otrazheniia i teoriia informatsii," *Voprosy filosofii* (1967), no. 3, pp. 41–52.

——"Otrazheniia i informatsii." *Voprosy filosofii* (1967), no. 3, pp. 41–52.

Tolman, Richard C. "Static Solutions of Einstein's Field Equations for Spheres of Fluid." *Physical Review* (February 15, 1939), 55:364–73.

Tomovic, Rajko. "Limitations of Cybernetics." *Cybernetica* (1959), 2(3):195–58.

"Torzhestvo sovetskoi biologicheskoi nauki." *Voprosy filosofi* (1948), no. 2, pp. 121–32.

Treadgold, Donald W. *Twentieth-Century Russia.* Chicago: Rand McNally, 1964.

Trincher, K. S. *Biology and Information: Elements of Biological Thermodynamics.* Moscow, 1964 (JPRS 28, 969, April 1965–6475).

Tsaregorodtsev, G. I. "Meditsina v fokuse ideologicheskoi bor'by." *Vestnik akademii meditsinskikh nauk* (1984), no. 1, pp. 3–10.

Tsaregorodtsev, G. I. and A. Ia. Ivaniushkin. "Meditsina i etika." *Voprosy filosofii* (1983), no. 9, pp. 147–52.

Tsitsishvilli, G. B. "Ob oshibakh A. A. Kalandiia v stat'e 'Raschet molekuliarnikh ob'emov neorganicheskikh soedinenii tipa AnBmOs' i ego popytakh ukrepit porognuiu kontseptsiiu rezonansa." *Zhurnal obshchei khimii* (December 1952), 22:2240–45.

Tucker, Robert C. *The Soviet Political Mind: Studies in Stalinism and Post-Stalin Change.* New York: Praeger, 1963.

Tugarinov, V. P. "Sootnoshenie kategorii dialekticheskogo materializma." *Voprosy filosofii* (1956), no. 3, pp. 151–60.

Tugarinov, V. P. and L. E. Maistrov. "Protiv idealizma v matematicheskoi logike," *Voprosy filosofii* (1950), no. 3, pp. 331–39.

Turbin, N. V. "Geneticheskaia inzheneriia: realnost', perspektivy i opaseniia." *Voprosy filosofii* (1975), no. 1, pp. 47–56.

——"Genetika i obshchestvo." *Voprosy filosofii* (1974), no. 2, pp. 105–15.

Turing, A. M. "Computing Machinery and Intelligence." *Mind* (October 1950), 59:433–60.

Turkevich, John. *Soviet Men of Science.* Princeton: Princeton University Press, 1963.

Uemov, A. I. *Veshchi, svoistva, otnosheniia.* Moscow, 1963.

"Ukaz prezidiuma verkhovnogo soveta SSSR." *Pravda* (September 29, 1958), p. 1.

Ukraintsev, B. S. "Informatsiia i otrazhenie," *Voprosy filosofii* (1963), no. 2, p. 36.

——*Otobrazhenie v nezhivoi prirode.* Moscow, 1969.

—— "O vozmozhnostiakh kibernetiki v svete svoistva otobrazheniia materii." In V. A. Il'in, V. N. Kolbanovskii, and E. Kol'man, ed., *Filosofskie voprosy kibernetiki,* pp. 110–33. Moscow, 1960.

——*Samoupravliaemye sistemy i prichinost'.* Moscow, 1972.

——"Ob osnovnykh napraleniiakh issledovanii v institut filosofii AN SSSR." *Voprosy filosofii* (1976), 1, pp. 94–104.

Ukraintsev, B. S. and G. V. Platonov. *Problemy otrazheniiav svete sovremennoi nauki.* Moscow, 1964.

Ursul, A. D. *Filosofiia i integrativno-obshchenauchnye protsessy.* Moscow, 1981.

——*Informatsiia: metodologicheskie aspekty.* Moscow, 1971.

——"O prirode informatsii." *Voprosy filosofii* (1965), no. 3 pp. 131–40.

——*Otrazhenie i informatsiia.* Moscow, 1973.

——*Priroda informatsii: filosofskii ocherk.* Moscow, 1968.

——*Problema informatsii v sovremennoi nauke.* Moscow, 1975.

Uznadze, D. N. *Psikhologicheskie issledovaniia.* Moscow, 1966.

"V akademii nauk SSSR." *Vestnik akademii nauk SSSR (1938),* no. 5, pp. 72–73.

Vaucouleurs, Gerard de. *Discovery of the Universe.* New York, 1957.

Vdovichenko, G. G. *Leninskaia teoriia otrazheniia i informatsiia.* Kiev, 1967.

Vel'kov, V. V. "Opasny li opyty s rekombinatnymi DNK." *Priroda* (1982), pp. 18–26.

Venikov, V. A. "Primenenie kibernetiki v elektricheskikh sistemakh." In A. I. Berg, ed., *Kibernetika na sluzhbu kommunizma,* 1:272–91. Moscow, 1961.

"Vernalization." *McGraw-Hill Encyclopedia of Science and Technology.* New York. 1966; vol. 14.

Veselovskii, V. N. *O sushchnosti zhivoi materii.* Moscow, 1976.

Viatkin, Iu. S. and A. S. Mamzin. "Sootnoshenie strukturno-funktsional'nogo i istoricheskogo podkhodov v izuchenii zhivykh sistem." *Voprosy filosofii* (1969), no. 11, pp. 46–56.

Vigier, J. P. "The Concept of Probability in the Frame of the Probabilistic and the Causal Interpretation of Quantum Mechanics." In S. Korner, ed., *Observation and Interpretation in the Philosophy of Physics*, pp. 71–77. New York: Dover, 1957.

Vikhalemm, R. A. "O razrabotke filosofskikh voprosov khimii." In *Voprosy filosofii* (1974), no. 6, pp. 90–95

Voinov, M. S. *Akademik T. D. Lysenko.* Moscow, 1950.

——*T. D. Lysenko.* Moscow, 1953.

Vol'kenshtein, M. V. *Fizika i biologiia.* Moscow. 1980.

——"Fizika kak teoreticheskaia osnova estestvoznaniia." In *Fizicheskaia teoriia filosofsko-metodologicheskii analiz*, pp. 110–117. Moscow, 1980.

Volgin, V. P., ed. *Otchet o deiatel'nosti akademii nauk SSSR za 1929 g.* Leningrad, 1931, vol 1, Appendix.

Volkov, B. S. *Deterministicheskaia priroda prestupnogo povedeniia.* Kazan, 1975.

Vorontsov, N. "Zhizn' toropit: nuzhny sovremennye posobiia po biologii." *Komsomol'skaia pravda* (November 11, 1964), p. 3.

Voskresenskii, A. D. and A. I. Prokhorov. "Problemy kibernetiki v meditsine." In A. I. Berg, ed., *Kibernetika na sluzhbu kommunizma*, pp. 126–39. Moscow, 1961.

Vremennyi pravila bezopasnosti rabot s rekombinantnymi DNK. Pushchino, 1978.

Vygotskv, L. S. *Izbrannye psikhologicheskie issledovaniia.* Moscow, 1956.

——*Thought and Language.* Cambridge, MIT Press, 1962.

Waddington, C. H. "That's Life." *New York Review of Books* (February 29, 1968), p. 19.

Watson, James D. *The Double Helix.* New York: Weidenfeld, 1968.

Weinberg, S. *Gravitation and Cosmology: Principles and Applications of the General Theory of Relativity.* New York: Wiley, 1972.

——*The First Three Minutes: A Modern View of the Origin of the Universe.* New York: Basic Books, 1977.

Weiner, Douglas. *Models of Nature: Conservation and Ecology in the Soviet Union, 1917–1935.* Bloomington: Indiana University Press, 1987.

Weizsacker, C. F. von. "Uber die Entstehung des Planetensystems." *Zeitschrift fur Astrophysik* (1943), 22:319–55.

Wetter, Gustav A. *Der dialektische Materialismus und der Problem der Entstehung des Lebens. Zur theorie von A. I. Oparin.* Munich: 1958.

——*Dialetical Materialism: A Historical and Systematic Survey of Philosophy in the Soviet Union.* Peter Heath, trans. New York: Praeger, 1958.

——*Soviet Ideology Today.* New York: Praeger, 1966.

Wheland, G. W. *Resonance in Organic Chemistry.* New York: Wiley, 1955.

Whitrow, G. J. *The Structure and Evolution of the Universe.* London: Hillary, 1959.

Whittaker, E. T. *The Beginning and End of the World.* London: Oxford University Press, 1943.

Wiener, Norbert. *Cybernetics, or Control and Communication in the Animal and the Machine*. Cambridge. Harvard University Press, 1962.
——*The Human Use of Human Beings: Cybernetics and Society*. New York: Avon, 1954.
Williams, L. Pearce. *The Origins of Field Theory*. New York: Peter Smith, 1966.
Wright, Sewall. "Dogma or Opportunism?" *Bulletin of the Atomic Scientists* (May 1949), pp 141–42.
Yanov, Alexander. *The New Russian Right*. Berkeley: University of California Press, 1978.
"Za boevoi filosofskii zhurnal." *Pravda* (September 7, 1949), p. 1.
"Za bol'shevistskuiu partiinost' v filosofii." *Voprosy filosofii* (1948), no. 3, pp. 3–15.
Zaitsev, V. A. *Izbrannye sochineniia*. Moscow, 1934.
Zak, S. E. "Kachestvennye izmeneniia i struktura." *Voprosy filosofii* (1967), no. 1, pp. 50–58.
"Zakon o dal'neishem sovershenstvovanii organizatsii upravleniia promyshlennost'iu i stroitel'stvom." *Pravda* (May 11, 1957), pp. 1–2.
Zangwill, O. L. "Psychology: Current Approaches." In The Editors of *Survey, The State of Soviet Science*, pp. 119–25. Cambridge: MIT Press, 1965.
Zel'dovich, Ya. B. and I. D. Novikov. In Gary Steigman, ed., *The Structure and Evolution of the Universe*, Leslie Fishbone, trans. Chicago: University of Chicago Press, 1983.
Zel'manov, A. K. "K postanovke kosmologicheskoi problemy." In *Trudy vtorogo s"ezda vsesoiuznogo astronomo-geogezicheskogo obshchestva 25–31 Ianvaria 1955 g.* pp. 72–84. Moscow, 1960.
——"Khronometricheskie invarianty i soputstvuishchie koordinaty v obshchei teorii otnositel'nosti." *Doklady akademii nauk SSSR* (1956), 107(6):815–18.
——"K reliativistskoi teorii anizotropnoi neodnorodnoi vselennoi." In *Trudy shestogo soveshchaniia po voprosam kosmogonii*, pp. 144–73. Moscow, 1959.
——"Kosmos, kosmogoniia, kosmologiia." *Nauka i religiia* (1968), no. 12, pp. 2–37.
——"Metagalaktika i Vselennaia." In *Nauka i chelovechestvo 1962*, pp. 383–405. Moscow, 1963.
——"Mnogoobrazie material'nogo mira i problema beskonechnosti Vselennoi." In *Beskonechnost' i Vselennaia*, pp. 274–324. Moscow, 1969.
——"Nereliativistkii gravitatsionnyi paradoks i obshchaia teoriia otnositel'nosti." *Nauchnye doklady vysshei shkoly: fiziko-matematicheskie nauki* (1958), no. 2, pp. 124–27.
——"O beskonechnosti material'nogo mira." In M. E. Omel'ianovskii and I. V. Kuznetsov, eds., *Dialektika v naukakh o nezhivoi prirode*, pp. 227–69. Moscow, 1964.
Zhdanov, A. A. *Doklad o zhurnalakh 'Zvezda' i 'Leningrad.'* Moscow, 1946.
——*Essays on Literature, Philosophy, and Music*. New York: International Publications, 1950.
——*O mezhdunarodnom polozhenii. Doklad, sdelannyi na informatsionnom soveshchanii predstavitelei nekotorykh kompartii v Pol'she, v kontse sentiabria 1947 goda*. Moscow, 1947.
——*Vystupitel'naia rech' i vystuplenie (na soveshchanii deiatelei sovetskoi muzyki v Tsk VKP (b),) v kn.: Soveshchanie deiatelei sovetskoi muzyki v Tsk VKP (b)*. Moscow, 1948.

——Vystuplenie na diskussii po knige G. F. Aleksandrova 'Istoriia i sovetskoi muzyki v TsK UKP (b),) v kn.: Soveshchanie deiatelei sovetskooevropeiskoi filosofi,' i muzyki v TsK VKP (b). Moscow, 1948.

——Vystuplenie na diskussii po knige G. F. Aleksandrova 'Istoriia zapadnoevropeiskoi filosofii,' 24 iiunia 1947 g. Moscow, 1947, 1951, 1952.

——"29-ia godovshchina velikoi oktiabrskoi sotsialisticheskoi revoliutsii. Doklad na torzhestvennom zasedanii moskovskogo soveta 6 noiabria 1946 goda." Moscow, 1946.

Zhdanov, Iu. A. "Dialektika tozhdestva i razlichiia v khimii." *Filosofskie nauki* (1958), no. 4, pp. 168–75.

——"Entropiia informatsii v reaktsiiakh aromaticheskogo zameshcheniia." *Zhurnal organicheskoi khimii* (1965), no. 9, pp. 1521–25.

——"Entropiia informatsii kak mera spetsifichnosti v reaktsiiakh aromaticheskogo zameshcheniia." *Zhurnal fizicheskoi khimii* (1965), no. 3, pp. 777–79.

——"Estestvoznanie i gumanizm." *Priroda* (1962), no. 5, pp. 7–12.

——"Khimiia i estetika." *Priroda* (1964), no. 10, pp. 8–13.

——*Lenin i estestvoznanie*. Moscow, 1959.

——"Metody sinteza i svoistva uglerodzameshchennykh uglevodov." Dissertation, Moscow State University, 1959.

——"Molekula i stroenie veshchestva." *Priroda* (1962), no. 5, pp. 63–74.

——"Obrashchenie metoda v organicheskoi khimii." Rostov, 1963.

——*Ocherki metodologii organicheskoi khimii*. Moscow, 1960.

——"O kritike i samokritike v nauchnoi rabote." *Bol'shevik* (1951), no. 21, pp. 28–43.

——"O nauchnom tvorchestva molodezhi." *Komsomol'skaia pravda* (May 25, 1948), p. 1.

——"O perekhode kachestvennykh izmenenii v izmeneniia kolichestvennye." *Voprosy filosofii* (1956), no. 6, pp. 206–10.

——"Poniatie gomologii v khimii i ego filosofskoe znachenie." Dissertation, Institute of Philosophy, Academy of Sciences of the USSR, Moscow, 1948.

——"Protiv sub"ektivistskikh izvrashchenii v estestvozanii." *Pravda* (January 16, 1953), p. 3.

——"Tovarishchu I. V. Stalinu," *Pravda* (August 7, 1948), p. 1.

——"V chem zakliuchaetsia ateisticheskoe znachenie ucheniia I. P. Pavlova." *Voprosy filosofii* (1954), no. 5, pp. 234–36.

——"Kriterii praktiki v khimii." In *XXI s"ezd KPSS o teoreticheskikh voprosakh stroitel'stva kommunizma v SSSR*, pp. 181–215. Kharkov, 1959.

——"Uzlovoe poniatie sovremennoi teoreticheskoi khimii." In I. T. Frolov and L. I. Grekov, eds., *Filosofiia, estestvoznaniia, sovremennost'* pp. 76–90. Moscow, 1981.

——"Vzaimootnoshenie chasti i tselogo v khimii." *Filosofskie nauki* (1960), no. 1, pp. 82–89.

——"Znachenie leninskikh idei dlia razrabotki metodologicheskikh voprosov khimii." *Filosofskie nauki* (1970), no. 2, pp. 80–90.

Zhukov, N. I. "Filosofskii analiz poniatiia 'informatsiia.' " *Voprosy filosofii* (1974), no. 12, pp. 90–96.

——*Informatsiia*. Minsk, 1971.

——"Informatsiia v svete leninskoi teorii otrazheniia." *Voprosy filosofii* (1963), no. 11, pp. 153–61.

Zhukov-Berezhnikov, N. N. *Teoriia geneticheskoi informatsii.* Moscow, 1966.

Zirkle, Conway, ed. *Death of a Science in Russia.* Philadelphia: University of Pennsylvania Press, 1949.

——*Evolution, Marxian Biology and the Social Scene.* Philadelphia: University of Pennsylvania Press, 1959.

Index